146. Old St. St Lukes.

1-7-06

IRON CURTAIN

IRON CURTAIN

FROM STAGE TO COLD WAR

PATRICK WRIGHT

OXFORD

UNIVERSITY PRESS

OXFORD

UNIVERSITY PRESS

Great Clarendon Street, Oxford OX2 6DP

Oxford University Press is a department of the University of Oxford.
It furthers the University's objective of excellence in research, scholarship,
and education by publishing worldwide in

Oxford New York

Auckland Cape Town Dar es Salaam Hong Kong Karachi
Kuala Lumpur Madrid Melbourne Mexico City Nairobi
New Delhi Shanghai Taipei Toronto

With offices in

Argentina Austria Brazil Chile Czech Republic France Greece
Guatemala Hungary Italy Japan Poland Portugal Singapore
South Korea Switzerland Thailand Turkey Ukraine Vietnam

Oxford is a registered trade mark of Oxford University Press
in the UK and in certain other countries

Published in the United States
by Oxford University Press Inc., New York

British Library Cataloguing in Publication Data

Data available

Library of Congress Cataloging in Publication Data

Data available

Typeset by SPI Publisher Services, Pondicherry, India
Printed in Great Britain
on acid-free paper by
Clays Ltd, St Ives plc

ISBN 978–0–19–923150–8

1

Praise for Patrick Wright

'Wright is a fantastic, oblique social historian with a real eye for the absurd and humorous'

Will Self

'Wright belongs in a select club of literary sleuths ... a pin-sharp miniaturist who can see the world in a grain of sand'

Boyd Tonkin, *Observer*

'Patrick Wright is a living national treasure of a rather weird variety: a historian who uses the imagistic logic of a fiction-writer in the service of explanation, drawing out the many-sided truth of the past by letting unexpected connections form'

Francis Spufford, *Evening Standard*

Praise for *Tank*

'Wonderful, illuminating, and astute. Not just a military history, Tank is a *tour de force*, a cultural history of our dreams and illusions.'

Simon Schama

'This witty, trenchant and engaging chronicle of the tank is, indeed, something more instructive and astonishing than anything H. G. Wells ever dreamed of.'

Chris Lehman, *Washington Post*

'An excellent military history ... written in a lively prose and with a wealth of unfamiliar detail.'

Gordon A. Craig, *New York Review of Books*

'We should all be deeply grateful that [Wright] has done us the favor of pouring so much into this rich, fascinating, definitive book.'

Bruce McCall, *New York Times Book Review*

'A treasure trove of facts usually eclipsed in conventional military or technical histories'

Publishers Weekly

'Wright is superb in evoking the metal monster we associate with "tank"'

San Francisco Chronicle

'A completely fascinating history; shrewd, wry and fiercely intelligent'

William Boyd

'Hugely enjoyable ... An immensely readable, well researched book, filled with interesting detours, unusual stories and idiosyncratic discussions linking the tank to philosophy, religion, art, politics, and even necromancy'

General Sir Michael Rose, *The Times*

'Richly researched and brilliantly written … compelling'

Richard Overy, *Sunday Telegraph*

'An extraordinary achievement … Patrick Wright transforms what in lesser hands would have been a plodding piece of military history into a text that dances with verve and interest on every page'

James Le Fanu, *The Tablet*

'Not only tells the history of a 'monstrous war machine' … but discusses in elegant and - yes - entertaining prose the symbolism of the tracked and armoured fighting vehicle'

Jan Morris, *Observer Books of the Year*

'A fascinating sideways look at the history of twentieth century warfare and politics through one of the most potent symbols of destruction and power'

Will Self, *The Times*

Praise for *The Village that Died for England*

'I don't think I have read a better book about this country than *The Village that Died for England*. It is a work of Pynchonesque coherence and revelation, the inexhaustible systemic comedy of a Musil, the subversiveness of a Bunuel — a work of genius'

Michael Hofmann

'Arguably the subtlest, most exhaustive rummaging through the overstuffed baggage of twentieth-century Englishness so far attempted'

Jonathan Keates, *Spectator*

'Possibly the best book about the country ever written'

David Hayes, *New Statesman*

'Exhilarating'

Jane Dunn, *Observer*

'Wright is, as ever, a finder, a noticer, a powerful sustainer of argument'

Iain Sinclair

'A beautifully written exploration of Englishness, unpicking a litany of lost causes and passionate eccentrics with the steadiest of hands'

Adam Thorpe, 'top ten books with a sense of place', *Guardian Books* website

'Charts, with a wealth of most peculiar detail, every variety of romantic nostalgia, greed, tolerance and outrage which has contributed to the decline of rural England'

John Mortimer, *Daily Mail*

'An infinitely subtle parable about the politics of landscape … Wright makes a dazzling array of connections to create what is really a masterpiece of English irony'

Richard Bradley

For A.R.D.W. and H.M.W

Pretext

A fire-stopper   An offence against God   A severed Atlantic cable
A challenge to Bach   A divided horizon   A fear of otherness
A psychological deadlock   A guillotine   Armour for a distressed queen
An outcome (and ally) of Censorship   A mirror of newsprint
A maker of peace traps   The health of the State   A Balkan precedent
A begetter of legends   (Ogreland   A Sea-coast for Bohemia   The 'nationalization'
of women)   An electrified fence between Belgium and Holland   A chauvinists'
charter   A deformer of patriotism   A naval blockade   A camouflaged dugout
A Potemkin village   A folding card table in a French Marshal's train   A cigarette
packet discarded in snowy woods   A bowl of sugar in a Finnish log cabin   A sky
full of diamonds   A divided International   Alice's looking-glass   A demilitarized
zone   An occasion for melodrama   A Liberal dilemma   A bridge between
Heaven and Hell   A portrait by Augustus John   A new use for the English
Channel   The promise of Locarno   A temptation for Quakers   A trench dug by
women in Karelia   A proletarian poodle   A theatre on Federal Street, Boston
Tintin's first adventure   A farewell dinner at the Casenave Restaurant, Paris
A wrap for Trotsky   A pilgrim's muddy kiss   A buried Canadian report
A dissenter's claim   A headstuffer's excuse   A test of journalism
A zealot's choice   An overlooked famine   A licence for idiocy
A Nazi prophesy   Churchill's coinage

Acknowledgements

Whatever its remaining frailties, this book is much stronger for the comments of Grace E. Brockington, Heather Glen, David Hayes, Paul Laity, Chris Mitchell, and Sheila Rowbotham who have read early drafts and made various improving suggestions. Many thanks to them all.

The late David Roden Buxton put me onto Vernon Lee's trail, and my indebtedness to him quickly extended to his wife, Mary, and to their children, Ben, James, Richenda, and Francesca, who have given me access to manuscripts and photographs and, in the case of Ben especially, replied to many requests for information about both Charles Roden and Dorothy Frances Buxton. I am also grateful to the following: Selina Cadell and Michael Thomas, who helped me to understand the theatrical dimensions of the story; Dr Margaret Siriol Colley and Nigel Linsan Colley, who informed me about Gareth Jones (see also their website: www.colley.co.uk/garethjones); R. A. Francis and David James Fisher, who helpfully responded to my queries about Romain Rolland; Francis King, who did the same regarding Fedor Il'ich Dan; Alex Vanneste, who kindly sent me a copy of his article about Germany's closure of the border between Belgium and the Netherlands during the First World War; Jan Morris, who gave me some leads in Trieste; Heinrich v. Berenberg, who drew my attention to J. M. Keynes's account of his meetings with Carl Melchior; Ray Monk, Andrew Bone, and Kenneth Blackwell, who helped me differentiate Bertrand Russell and Clifford Allen in photographs of the British Labour Delegation of 1920; Sir Geoffrey Chandler, who was encouraging when the project was threatened; Sukhdev Sandhu, who, having come across a loosely bound draft at about the same time, gave the unpublished book an undeserved 'samizdat' status and cited it in the *New Statesman's* 'Books of the Year' listings for 2006. Meanwhile, Nicholas Kenyon helpfully responded to my enquiry about the controversy surrounding German music at the time of the 1914 Promenade concerts, and Professor Jay Carr invited me into his house in Fulton and talked most informatively about *King's Row* and its author, Henry

Bellamann. For various other ameliorations, I would like to thank Paul Silroy, Patsy Aldana, Lindsay Waters, Michael Leaman, and Phil Pochoda.

In my treatment of Polish matters I am, once again, much indebted to Malgosia Pioro, Andrzej Krauze, Michal Komar, and Tadeusz Pioro. Thanks also to Michal Garapich, who wrote an article on my behalf requesting information about Antoni Klimowicz, published in the London-based *Polish Daily & Soldiers Daily* ('Gdzie jest uciekinier z "Dabrowskiego"?', *Dziennik Polski*, 18 February 2003). Through this, I became further indebted to Julie Hykiel, Mrs Genowefa Kwiekinska of Carnforth, Lancashire, her sister Irene Mizera of Oak Lawn, Illinois, and also Lydia Banek of Vineland, New Jersey. For information about J. H. Cort and Josef Rudinger's peptide research in Prague, I would like to thank Dr Jean W. Dodds, Dr Milan Zaoral, Dr Leon Barstow and Dr John Jones, of Balliol College, Oxford. Dr Claire Lawton's contribution remains quite immeasurable, and I am also most grateful to Tim James and Dr Elizabeth James for permission to quote from Dr Derrick James's diary of his 1954 trip to China.

I am, of course, obliged to my colleagues and students at the Institute for Cultural Analysis, Nottingham Trent University, and also at the London Consortium, where both Steve Connor and Barry Curtis have assisted directly. I thought the book was as good as finished by late September 2006, when I went to Ann Arbor to spend a month at the University of Michigan's Eisenberg Institute for Historical Studies. In the event, I found myself launched into a further set of explorations by various conversations and encounters. I am especially indebted to William G. Rosenberg, who has saved me from diverse embarrassments, and who also remained polite when I expressed the hope that, though my inability to read Russian was plainly a disadvantage, the early history of the Iron Curtain was so closely connected to Western perceptions of Soviet Russia that its development might still usefully be traced largely from one side. My thanks, too, to Kathleen Canning, Geoff Eley, Kali D. Israel, Alex Potts, Lee Schlesinger, John Whittier-Ferguson, Clapperton Mavhungha, Peter Soppelsa, and others who brought so much life to the lecture and seminars in which I presented some of my findings.

My debt to the staff of various libraries and archives should also be acknowledged. I have done much of my research in the University Library at Cambridge, the British Library, and the British Library of Political and Economic Science at the London School of Economics. I would also like to thank the staff at the Churchill Archives Centre at Churchill College, Cambridge; the Labadie Collection for Social Protest at the University of

Michigan; Boston Public Library; the library of Rhodes House in Oxford; and the Winston Churchill Memorial & Library at Fulton. I am grateful to the librarian of Somerville College, Oxford, for permission to quote from the correspondence of Vernon Lee, Romain Rolland, and Charles Roden Buxton, and also to the Vernon Lee Collection at Colby College, Waterville, Maine, for permission to quote from Irene Cooper Willis's correspondence with Vernon Lee.

This book's journey to publication has been vexatious, even by my high standards. It was initially commissioned by Faber and Faber in Britain and by Viking/Penguin in the USA. With impressive unanimity, both repudiated their contracts when they awoke to the direction I was pursuing. After a year in which these increasingly distant powers continued to play fast and loose with my finances, the book was taken up by Oxford University Press. I am especially grateful to my editor, Luciana O'Flaherty, and to her colleague, Matthew Cotton. It has also been a pleasure to work with Celia Dearing, who has raised a remarkable selection of photographs from sources around the world, with Rowena Anketell, who has copy-edited the text, and with Catherine Berry and Kate Hind, who have seen the book through production. I am much obliged to OUP's two anonymous readers, whose helpful suggestions have, I hope, been adequately heeded in the final text. Thanks also to my former agent, Patrick Walsh, for a promising start, to Emma Parry of Fletcher & Parry for more than damage limitation, necessary as that was, and to Kate Pool of the Society of Authors, who helped out a lot towards the end.

P. W.

June 2007   www.patrickwright.net

Contents

List of Plates   xv
List of Cartoons   xvii

Introduction: Paths Cross on the *Jaroslaw Dabrowski*   1

Part I. Carrying On in Missouri

1. Bullet's Big Day   21
2. In the Name of the Common People   34
3. Prophecy and Hindsight   51

Part II. From Drury Lane to the Theatre of the West (1914–1918)

4. First Call   65
5. Dividing Europe's Horizon   76
6. The Belgian Variation   96
7. In Defence of Otherness   109

Part III. Wrapping Red Russia (1917–1920)

8. First Delegation   131
9. Not Just a Frontier   154
10. Relocating the Allied Blockade   162
11. Fact-Finding with Limousines   191

Part IV. The Broken International (1921–1927)

12. The View from Locarno   221

13. Snapshots from a Land of Contrasts   235

14. Comrade Bukharin's Version   262

Part V. Stalin's Ring of Trust (1927–1939)

15. No End to the Potemkin Complex   283

16. Friends against Famine   292

17. Steeled Minds and the God that Failed   321

Part VI. Succession and Afterlife

18. Sliding Back to Churchill   339

19. After the Crossing   354

Afterword: Gone with the Berlin Wall?   375

Appendix I: *Bach's Christmas Music in England and in Germany*   389
            by Vernon Lee

Appendix II: *The Refreshment Room at Narva*   391
            by Charles Roden Buxton

Notes   393

Index   469

List of Plates

1. The *Jaroslaw Dabrowski* on the Thames, 1 August 1954

2. Antoni Klimowicz addresses a press conference at the headquarters of the Polish Ex-combatants' Association, Queensgate Terrace, London, 8 August 1954

3. Drs Joseph and Ruth Cort in the offices of the National Council for Civil Liberties, Paddington, London, 12 June 1954

4. Winston S. Churchill and Harry S. Truman arriving in downtown Fulton, Missouri, 5 March 1946

5. Churchill and Truman on the way to Westminster College, Fulton, Missouri, 5 March 1946

6. 'C-T Day' crowds in Fulton, Missouri, 5 March 1946

7. Churchill and Truman with Phil M. Donnelly, governor of Missouri (left), and Dr Franc 'Bullet' McCluer, president of Westminster College (right), at Westminster College, 5 March 1946

8. Churchill delivering 'The Sinews of Peace' lecture in Westminster College gymnasium, 5 March 1946

9. Thomas Rowlandson, Drury Lane Theatre, London 1808

10. Safety curtain with advertisements, Grand Theatre, Wolverhampton, c.1930

11. Vernon Lee at Sestri, 1914 (Photo: Margery Taylor)

12. Elisabeth, queen of the Belgians, De Panne, Flanders, 1917

13. Elisabeth, queen of the Belgians, taking a snapshot of King George V presenting decorations to Belgian officers, De Panne, 13 August 1916

14. Charles Roden Buxton, Ethel Snowden and Robert Williams at King's Cross Station, London, *Daily Sketch,* 28 April 1920

15. British Labour Delegation in Stockholm, May 1920 (Photo: Th. Skadin, Stockholm)

16. British Labour Delegation arriving at Narva, Estonia, 10 May 1920

17. British Labour delegates, Will Thorne MP, James O'Grady, and William Stephen Sanders, among soldiers near Petrograd, April 1917

18. P. A. Kruskopf, lithograph of the Rajajoki river, between Finland and Russia, 1845

19. Alexander Berkman and Emma Goldman in New York at the time of their trial, July 1917

20. David Roden and Dorothy Francis Buxton, c.1922

21. Interior portrait of the men of the British Labour Delegation, Russia 1920
22. Artistically enhanced version of the above, Russia 1920
23. Zinoviev, Lenin, Serrati, and Balabanova at a political meeting, Russia 1920
24. Augustus John, portrait of Gustav Stresemann, 1925
25. The Kremlin from Moskva River, 1927 (photo: David Roden Buxton)
26. Street market and secularized church, Arbat Square, Moscow, 1927 (photo: David Roden Buxton)
27. Homeless boys (*bezprizorny*), Russia 1927 (photo: David Roden Buxton)
28. Jurievets, upper Volga, Russia 1927 (photo: David Roden Buxton)
29. Dorothy and Charles Roden Buxton arriving at a *kollectiv* en route to Sokolischchi, Russia 1927 (photo: David Roden Buxton)
30. The Buxtons resting beside an alleged 'main road', Lopatishchi, Russia 1927 (photo: David Roden Buxton)
31. Sokolishchi and Lavrovka, Dorothy Buxton far right, Russia 1927 (photo: David Roden Buxton)
32. Carpenter at Sokolishchi, Russia 1927 (photo: David Roden Buxton)
33. Armed workers and soldiers mark the tenth anniversary of the Bolshevik revolution, Red Square, Moscow, 7/8 November 1927
34. Parade in Red Square, Moscow, celebrations on the tenth anniversary of the Bolshevik revolution, 7/8 November 1927
35. Children with flags, tenth anniversary celebrations, 7/8 November 1927
36. Panaït Istraţi and Nikos Kazantzakis (seated), Russia 1928
37. Collectivized farm workers going to work, Moscow Region, 27 May 1931
38. Food queues during famine, Ukraine, 1932
39. Dead on street during famine, Ukraine, 1932
40. George Bernard Shaw talking to peasants at the Lenin Farming Cooperative, August 1931
41. Karl Radek, Anatole Lunacharsky, Lady Astor, George Bernard Shaw, and Artashes Khalatov, Russia, summer 1931
42. George Bernard Shaw visiting the Kremlin, Moscow, 21 July 1931
43. Christian Rakovsky, c.1930–2
44. Nikolai Bukharin, c.1936
45. Andrei Vyshinsky, chief prosecutor, summing up at the trial of Bukharin and others, 1938
46. 1930s show trial proceedings in the Hall of Columns, House of Trade Unions, Moscow
47. Clare Sheridan as member of the Independent Labour Party, 1945
48. Mikhail Gorbachev speaking on 'The River of Time and the Imperative of Action', Fulton, Missouri, 6 May 1992

List of Cartoons

1. David Low, *Evening Standard*, 25 September 1945 — 377
2. Leslie Gilbert Illingworth, *Daily Mail*, 6 March 1946 — 378
3. Leslie Gilbert Illingworth, *Daily Mail*, 28 May 1946 — 379
4. Leslie Gilbert Illingworth, *Daily Mail*, 10 December 1947 — 380
5. David Low, *Manchester Guardian*, 8 June 1955 — 381

Introduction
Paths Cross on the
Jaroslaw Dabrowski

One day in August 1954, the *Boston Daily Globe* informed its readers that 'Leaping Lena' had landed in New York. Flown in by plane from Munich, this red-eyed carrier pigeon received 'the kind of welcome usually reserved for human dignitaries'.[1] Fifteen press photographers clicked away as the incomer was greeted by four 'hero pigeons' from the Second World War, including at least one prospective mate. Carefully primed pigeon fanciers had brought along several hundred other birds, which were ceremoniously released at the chosen moment. One carried a message telling President Eisenhower of the occasion.

'Leaping Lena' owed her celebrity to an exhausted landing she had earlier made in Pilsen, Czechoslovakia, having become disorientated while racing from Munich to her home loft in Klatzenbach, West Germany. A Czech had found the bird and, recognizing the band on her leg, sent her home with a message addressed to Radio Free Europe. This anonymous fellow begged for 'speedy liberation' and urged the West not to waver in the fight against Communism. Radio Free Europe had promptly adopted the pigeon that 'crashed the iron curtain' and brought her to New York as a fund-raising mascot for its '1955 Crusade for Freedom'.

Later that same day readers of the *Boston Evening American* were offered a story headed 'Dog Busts Iron Curtain'.[2] This told of a West German police dog which 'seems to have piloted his dog house right smack through the Iron Curtain'. The dog in question hailed from Passau, and its odyssey had commenced early in July, when it was swept away by a flooded Danube. According to the mayor of Passau, the creature was seen sitting on the gable of its doghouse as it 'bobbed down' the swollen river. It was spotted at the

German–Austrian border a few days later, and again at Linz on 10 July. The floating hound's passage through Vienna and Bratislava apparently went unrecorded but the mayor had now received a postcard from Budapest, some 350 miles downstream from Linz. Reporting that a police dog with a Passau tag on his collar had floated ashore on a doghouse, the Hungarian writer hoped that arrangements might somehow be made to ship the creature back to the other side.

In an atmosphere still pervaded by McCarthyism, these fleeting animal sagas must have had a particular charm. Such were the events of that summer, however, that they could scarcely outshine the human crossings. They were overshadowed by ongoing speculation about Dr Otto John, the West German security chief who had mysteriously vanished some ten days before and then reappeared in East Berlin, vowing to work for the reunification of a Germany that was 'in danger of being perpetually torn in the dispute between east and west'.[3] They were further eclipsed by a drama that had opened even more recently in London.

Antoni Klimowicz Heads West

It was the afternoon of Wednesday, 28 July and Mr Sidney Palmer was unloading a freighter at Mark Brown's Wharf on the south bank of the Thames. Named after a Polish officer who died heroically as commander-in-chief of the Paris Commune in 1871, the *Jaroslaw Dabrowski* had just arrived from Gdynia, a Polish port on the Baltic, and its cargo consisted of wood shavings, exported for use as packaging material. Together with his mate, Palmer had gone into the hold to secure these bales of 'wood wool' to the crane that would hoist them ashore. As they worked their way down through the load, he glimpsed an arm reaching out and, convinced that he had seen a ghost, let out a startled cry.

Removing more bales, the two dockers discovered a young man who was obviously in a bad way—parched, starving, too weak to stand. Though unable to make any sense of their cockney English, this stowaway managed to plead for 'English police' and 'water' in alternating gasps. As Palmer would later recall, 'I gave him a cigarette and my mate went to fetch some water. We laid him on a board and attached the crane chairs to it, and swung him up to the deck. If we had known then what we do now, we could have swung him ashore.'[4]

As it was, the 24-year-old Antoni Klimowicz had no sooner been lifted onto the deck of the *Jaroslaw Dabrowski,* than he was seized by members of the ship's crew and presented to the officers in charge, who ordered that he be marched off and locked up in a stateroom. Over the next day or so Klimowicz was worked on by the ship's political officer and a representative of the Polish consulate in London. Hoping to avoid difficulties with the British authorities, they promised him a scholarship at Poland's Merchant Marine Academy if he signed a statement saying that he wished to return to Poland of his own free will. Klimowicz knew better than to trust this rosy promise, and he proved no more compliant when his interrogators changed tactic and threatened him with dire consequences if he refused. All seemed lost when the British officials who came aboard to interview Klimowicz turned out to be reliant on the ship's Captain Glowacki for a 'translation' of the discussion. Klimowicz had no passport and it was decided that, as an ordinary stowaway, he had no right to land.

That might have been the end of the matter, had the dockers not passed news of Klimowicz's plight to Polish émigré organizations in London. By the evening of Friday, 30 July, one hundred or so Poles had gathered at the quayside, where they marched up and down, chanting anti-Communist slogans and demanding Klimowicz's release. Aware that time was fast running out, one of these émigrés concocted the unlikely claim that Klimowicz had stolen his wallet, and must therefore be arrested before the ship left British jurisdiction. A hasty visit to a magistrate produced the necessary paperwork (the magistrate is said to have raised the sum of money in the wallet to £10 in order to make the alleged theft seem more plausible), but the police inspector at the quayside still rejected the allegation as blatantly fictional. Soon enough, the *Jaroslaw Dabrowski* took on a pilot and, despite rage, tears, and cries of 'Murder' at the quayside, set off down the Thames on its return journey to Gdynia.

While that inadequate story about Klimowicz and the stolen wallet was being cooked up, other British Poles had been pursuing a more effective strategy. They had decided to invoke the Habeas Corpus Act of 1679, which enabled anyone knowing of a person's unlawful detention to oblige the jailer to present the prisoner at the Royal Courts of Justice.

Since it happened to be a bank holiday weekend, it was necessary to chase down senior legal figures in their rustic retreats in order to initiate such a claim. It would appear that at least two attempts were made. The news reached the Union of Polish Journalists, and from here it travelled to

Boleslaw Wierzbianski, chairman of the International Federation of Free Journalists, who set off to raise Britain's Lord Chancellor. Meanwhile, Jan Jaxa, attorney for the Polish Ex-Combatants Association, persuaded the registrar of the High Court to stand by through the holiday, while he tried to raise a judge to authorize the writ. Hastening to the village of Great Missenden, in Buckinghamshire, he found Mr Justice Davies wearing corduroys and tending his rose garden. Davies informed Jaxa that he had come too late, but only because the Lord Chief Justice himself had just granted leave for a writ to be issued.

The departing *Jaroslaw Dabrowski* was stopped by police launches as it passed through Woolwich Reach at 2.20 on Saturday morning. For a time, it seemed likely that the Polish ship might break through the cordon of police launches, and head for the open sea. When informed about the 'communist kidnapping' taking place so close to the heart of London, Britain's Conservative prime minister, the elderly Winston Churchill, is alleged to have asked 'Haven't we any destroyers left?'[5] As a former First Lord of the Admiralty he may well have feared that the British navy was going the same way as the precious empire, much reduced under the Labour government that had come to power in 1945. Soon enough, however, HMS *Obdurate* was on its way. Indeed, a second destroyer was also standing by at Chatham, ready to prevent the *Jaroslaw Dabrowski* escaping.[6]

By Sunday, 1 August, so the *Boston Sunday Herald* announced, the Polish freighter was 'rolling at anchor' in Erith Harbour some 10 miles downstream from London. It was also reported that 'wild Cossack music blared across the water from a gramophone on the deck', while police launches circled the vessel and fifty policemen patrolled the water front.[7] Crowds had gathered to watch the confrontation, and Captain Glowacki was thought to be preparing for a long stand-off: he had sent out for celery, tomatoes, and one hundred 2-lb loaves of bread.

In their first approach to the freighter, British immigration officials had been repelled by the 'menacing attitude' of the crew.[8] So a more considerable force was mustered and, at about 10.45 on the morning of Saturday, 31 July, the *Jaroslaw Dabrowski* was boarded by a bevy of 'husky policemen in their tall cloth helmets', who clambered up with the help of a rope ladder. As the Home Secretary would later explain, eighty police were involved in the operation. Once on board, Sir John Nott-Bower, commissioner of the Metropolitan Police, demanded that the captain deliver Antoni Klimowicz under the Habeas Corpus Act of 1679. Captain Glowacki refused to obey, as advised by the Polish ambassador with whom he had been in contact throughout the day. A search was ordered, and when the stateroom was found to be locked, the door was smashed open with fire axes. Wearing a blue jersey and with his face 'half hidden in a muffler',[9] the man whom the *Boston Sunday Herald* would describe as 'the haggard refugee from Communism', was led ashore through the 'openly hostile' crew 'made of picked communists'.[10]

On Tuesday, 3 August, Klimowicz, who was by now being harboured by free Polish organizations in London, appeared before the Lord Chief Justice at the Royal Courts of Justice and, after a hearing of less than two minutes, was declared a free man. Aware that the Habeas Corpus Act had once been used to free slaves who managed to reach 'sanctuary' in the port of London, the *Boston Daily Globe* reported the event under the heading 'Old Slave Law in Britain Frees Pole from Reds'.[11]

By this time, Klimowicz's rescue had been blown up into a full-scale international incident. Granted permission to sail after midnight on Saturday, the *Jaroslaw Dabrowski* was reported to have passed Gravesend on its way out into the North Sea at 4.40 a.m. on Sunday morning. No sooner had it arrived back at Gdynia, than Warsaw radio was relaying the protests of crew members who claimed to have been viciously beaten by British police. The Polish government delivered a note to the British Embassy in Warsaw, denouncing Klimowicz as a 'criminal and smuggler' who was wanted in Poland and had twice been punished for smuggling by the British authorities. It too condemned the British police for forcing doors and making rough use of their famous truncheons. Insisting that the police raid constituted a breach of international law, they demanded compensation for the injuries two crewmen were said to have suffered at the hands of British police, and for damages caused by the delay.

Klimowicz would admit to having once tried to smuggle a camera into Britain, explaining that Polish sailors commonly did this in exchange for nylons and razor blades. Yet on 7 August, the Home Secretary, Sir David Maxwell Fyfe, rejected these charges together with the associated 'slanders' against the British police. Indeed, he insisted that the British police had faced aggressive actions from the Polish crew, who hurled 'missiles' at them and poured a pail of boiling water over one of their launches. Fyfe had no hesitation in declaring that Klimowicz would be allowed to stay in Britain. The Communist authorities in Poland replied by awarding decorations to the *Jaroslaw Dabrowski*'s crew, commending them 'for behaviour worthy of seamen sailing under the peoples' flag'.[12]

Once safely ashore in Britain, Klimowicz was taken in hand by Mr P. Heciak of the Federation of Free Poles, who found him accommodation with a Polish family at a secret address in London.

By 8 August, indeed, he was dressed in grey flannels and a sports jacket, and giving a press conference at the London headquarters of the Polish Ex-Combatants Association.[13] The event was widely reported in the international press. It was also filmed and broadcast by both the BBC and Radio Free Europe. It emerged that the 24-year-old stowaway was not a student as first reported, but the son of a worker. He had served as a deck hand on the *Jaroslaw Dabrowski* for two years from 1949, but was declared 'politically unreliable' in 1951 when he refused to collaborate with the 'political officer' who wanted him to spy and inform on his shipmates. Conscripted into the army, where his chances of escape would be much fewer, he had spent two years as a private before unsuccessfully applying for work as a seaman, only to be refused on the grounds that he 'did not know how to work in a team'.[14]

Klimowicz explained that he had tried to board the *Jaroslaw Dabrowski* in February 1954, but been turned away by guards. He had better luck on 22 July. Having found onshore work at the docks, he chose a moment when most of the crew were ashore and boarded the ship by showing the guards his old pass. He hid in the hold, where he was soon enclosed in a space 'no bigger than a coffin' as the bales were loaded on top of him. His ordeal is said to have been aggravated by the fact that he was lying on salt—perhaps left over from a previous cargo. It would certainly have been shorter, had the loaded ship not been delayed for two days in Gdynia docks while a mechanical problem was sorted out. As it was, he had gone without food or water from 8 p.m. on 22 July to 4 p.m. on 28 July. When apprehended as the British dockers lifted him out of the hold, he had told the Polish sailors 'I want freedom'. Hustling him off, they replied that he was a 'traitor, swine and dog'. One member of the crew, a Greek Communist, had even tried to stab him when the English police finally took him ashore at Erith. Klimowicz was getting over his ordeal despite the reluctance of Western reporters to let him relinquish the 'haggard and hollow-eyed' look of the stowaway who had broken through the Iron Curtain. Asked about his plans for the future, he hoped that he might be allowed to become a seaman in the British merchant navy.

By Land, Sea, and Air

The Polish expatriates who assembled at Mark Brown's Wharf to clamour for Klimowicz's release might reasonably have been surprised as well as gratified to find a sizeable contingent of reporters converging on the *Jaroslaw Dabrowski*. After all, Polish liberty was not particularly high on the Western political agenda at that time. Many Poles had served valiantly with the Allies in the Second World War, but their more recent anti-Communism did not sit so easily with the British authorities, entrenched as they now were in the realpolitik of the Cold War.

Refugees from Eastern Europe were hardly a novelty either. In April 1954, the Federal Statistics Department of the West German government in Bonn had declared that over ten million 'expelled persons and refugees' were living in West Germany.[15] Since the end of the Second World War there had been a massive westward migration from the Soviet sector of Germany, where the Communist authorities had taken their first steps to prevent the exodus in May 1952, when they closed the demarcation lines between East and West Germany.

A smaller and necessarily more heroic flight had also been under way from Communist Poland. Distinguished musicians and dancers reached the West by leaping out of closely chaperoned concert tours. Diplomats in Western cities turned carefully judged corners and never looked back. Airforce pilots took off in their MIG-15 jets and flew 'over the top of the Iron Curtain' to Bornholm, a Danish island in the Baltic, where Lieutenants Jarecki and Jazwinski climbed out of their planes asking for asylum in January and May 1953 respectively.[16]

Over 62,000 people are estimated to have been arrested trying to leave Poland illegally between 1945 and 1955.[17] For most of that time, people quitting the Russian sector in Germany only had to walk, or take a train into western Berlin. Those who made it through Poland's increasingly guarded frontiers with Czechoslovakia and East Germany faced a more arduous transit. Some reached the West by clinging to the underside of trains, or squeezing themselves into secret compartments built into cars, coaches, and inland barges on the river Oder. As the Baltic sea-routes were cleared of mines, fugitives also set sail in canoes, reconditioned amphibious vehicles, and catamarans improvised out of old cayaks. Some were picked up by foreign vessels, while others made it to Bornholm, where exhausted refugees arrived on resort-style pedal boats and perilous rafts made of inflatable mattresses.

Polish seamen had become well known for jumping ship too. In 1949, the Communist authorities ruled that all Polish fishing boats must be painted bright yellow to increase their visibility. In 1951 it was further decreed that these vessels should sail and work in easily guarded groups. Yet despite these precautions and the increasingly severe penalties imposed on would-be escapers, trawlermen kept emerging from the North Sea to claim asylum in Britain. Some struggled ashore on life-rafts, while others took more drastic action, including the seven seamen who would stick a knife into their intransigent 'political officer', lock up the captain in the lavatory, and hijack their own trawler off the English coast at Whitby in September 1954.[18]

Polish sailors also kept leaping for asylum from freighters such as the *Jaroslaw Dabrowski* or the larger *Praca,* which lost over twenty members of its crew after being detained in Formosa (Taiwan) in October 1953.[19] There had been no immunity, either, for the proudest passenger liner in the Polish fleet. Having been refitted in Antwerp and returned to Poland after serving as an Allied troopship during the Second World War, the 16,000-ton MS *Batory* had gone into post-war service as a hard-currency earner and spy carrier travelling between New York, Southampton, Copenhagen, and Gdynia.

Special care was taken to crew the *Batory* with highly indoctrinated young Communists. Closely observed by the 'cultural officer' and secret police informers in the crew, these sailors had been warned that the superficially attractive ports they would visit in the West were actually deceptive places where things were not at all as they looked. Despite the alluring appearances of prosperity and freedom, they were to understand that murderers lurked in every Western doorway, that anyone who seemed approachable or friendly was actually a spy or an agent provocateur.[20] As for the luxurious goods they might see piled up in shop windows, these were just 'traps for the unwary', since only the very wealthy could actually afford to buy such things. They were assured that the great mass of working people lived behind these brightly exhibited scenes, grindingly poor and viciously exploited by the capitalist system.

Even for the 'strenuously indoctrinated',[21] however, these Stalinist fictions could not bear much contact with reality. Sailors may have stepped down into Western ports apprehensively and in carefully formed pairs, but they soon discovered that nobody was inclined to attack them at all. The MS *Batory* is said to have lost crew members on every voyage. Having found their names on a secret police informer's list, no less than thirty leaped for freedom during the course of one of the ship's last visits to New York.[22] By June 1953, even the captain of this notorious 'Communist liner', Jan Cwiklinski, had been ready to quit. While the *Batory* (now employed on a new route between Europe and India) was being refitted in a dry dock at Hebburn-on-Tyne, near Newcastle, he slipped past the 'cultural officer' who was already building a case against him, and caught a train to London where he walked into a police station and claimed political asylum—a condition he enjoyed for a while, before going off to America to address the Senate and produce his ghosted memoir, *The Captain Leaves His Ship*.

Dr & Dr Cort Go East

Within hours of being lifted out of the hold, Antoni Klimowicz found himself at the centre of the world's attention. Yet the journalists and broadcasters who conveyed him there were by no means all drawn to the *Jaroslaw Dabrowski* by compassionate interest in the story of one more Polish stowaway. A good many, indeed, were far more interested in the embarkation of two young Americans intent on travelling in the opposite direction.

Like Klimowicz, Drs Joseph and Ruth Cort boarded the *Jaroslaw Dabrowski* in search of asylum. The 26-year-old Dr Joseph Henry Cort had grown up in Boston, Massachussetts, and his departure from London was a matter of acute interest to the *Boston Daily Globe,* which hung a mugshot of the bespectacled young doctors just below the masthead of its front page, together with an article announcing their departure for 'Red asylum' in Czechoslovakia and noting that Dr J. H. Cort's parents, Mr and Mrs Boris Cort of Washington Street, Brookline, could not immediately be reached for comment.[23]

Klimowicz was already locked up on board by the time the Corts joined the *Jaroslaw Dabrowski* on Friday, 30 July. Though they may scarcely have set eyes on the mistreated Pole, they must have been surprised by the delay to their departure, and perhaps also discomforted to find their story mixed up with that of a lowly stowaway who only wanted the freedom they themselves were surrendering.

The Western press would find the situation confusing too. In Boston, there may have been palpable disappointment in the articles reporting that the police, who eventually boarded the ship at Erith, 'were not interested in Dr. Cort, but in Klimowicz'.[24] In London, *The Times* declared the liberation of Klimowicz all the more noteworthy since 'on the same ship there sailed the known American scientist Dr. Joseph Cort'. It also remarked that, while Klimowicz would be welcomed with open arms, the British government had refused Dr Cort's request for asylum, even though 'his application was supported by well-known scientists, and representatives of the political world, among them members of the British parliament'.[25]

The *New York Times* had been less concerned about the injustice, or otherwise, of Dr Cort's involuntary departure from England. Instead, it treated the Corts as if they were tourists going to 'sample a way of life'[26] which Klimowicz had taken grave risks to escape. For Alexander T. Jordan, a British journalist writing two years later for the fiercely anti-Communist Foundation for Economic Education, Cort's left-wing illusions were rendered all the more ridiculous by the comparison. 'Did the Klimowicz case give them some food for thought? Here was a simple sailor, the son of workers, risking his life to escape Soviet rule. Here was the government machinery of a great nation set in motion to secure the freedom of one humble human being.'[27] Perhaps the American doctor had been prompted to wonder again about the 'terror and persecution' he anticipated if he returned to the United States, or even about the real condition of the 'Red sanctuary' towards which he and his wife were bound.

In a 'shipboard interview', given while the *Jaroslaw Dabrowski* was anchored at Erith, Cort had repeated his claim that 'political persecution and victimisation' awaited him if he returned to America. He also said of the future, 'I hope to find work in a university in Prague or scientific and research work'.

A graduate of Harvard University and also Yale Medical School, Cort's difficulties had opened shortly after he decided not to take up an internship at Yale. In 1948 he had travelled to England, where he held a fellowship at the University of Cambridge. He had returned in the summer of 1951 with a one-year permit to study kidney physiology. He had encountered no difficulty in extending his residency for a further year when the time came, or again in February 1953, when he was appointed lecturer in physiology at the University of Birmingham, settling there with his wife, Dr Ruth Cort, who had found work as a house physician at the city's Queen Elizabeth

Hospital. In June 1954, however, the 26-year-old doctor had been informed that he must leave the country when his permit expired at the end of the month. The order was made by the British Home Office, but only, so Cort explained, 'after enquiries instituted by the United States Embassy'.[28] He also announced that efforts were being made to intercede with the Home Secretary, and that a question would shortly be asked in Parliament 'whether we can be granted political asylum'.

Some Britons were contemptuous of the suggestion that a decent American citizen would ever need to request political asylum in their country. Others had already come to terms with the fact that, as the Labour writer and MP Michael Foot had told the House of Commons at the beginning of the year, 'there is a new kind of refugee in the world, of whom there are some in this country already, namely, refugees from the United States'.[29] The integrity of Dr Cort had certainly been questioned at home. It was alleged that, having ignored several demands that he surrender his passport and report for a physical examination either in America or at an appropriate facility in Europe, the young doctor had also refused to return to Boston to face his draft board in September 1953. Having conducted what the *New Statesman and Nation* characterized as a 'Kafka correspondence'[30] with him through their London embassy, the American authorities were claiming that he was 'a delinquent' who had moved to Britain in order to evade military service.[31] Cort had rejected the charge when interviewed by the Birmingham police, apparently acting on behalf of the US authorities, in December 1953. He had, so he insisted, been declared physically unfit for service in 1948, due to an attack of polio suffered at the age of 8. He had also been cleared by his local draft board, which he had attended in order to register under the Doctors' Draft Act, shortly before he left the United States in 1951.

In Cort's version, the American demand for his return really had a quite different motivation. In 1953 the House Un-American Activities Committee had been informed that Cort had been part of a 'secret Communist cell' while a medical student at Yale.[32] Though he now claimed 'no political affiliations', Cort admitted that he had joined the American Communist Party between his two visits to Cambridge, and remained a member for two years until 1951. Branded as a 'subversive', he anticipated that he would face 'bankruptcy, loss of citizenship and possible imprisonment'[33] if he returned to America in the existing climate.

Harry Backer, secretary of Birmingham Trades Council, spoke for a good many Britons when he protested that 'The long arm of McCarthyism must not be allowed to stretch out into this country. When people come from Eastern Europe and say they are being persecuted we welcome them, and we should do the same if they come from the west.'[34] There could be little doubt that, indirectly or not, the pressure on Cort was the work of Senator Joseph McCarthy, who remained insistent, despite those who were by now challenging his degradation of political life in the American Senate, that Communists needed 'rough' handling. As the witch-hunting senator would proclaim at the beginning of August 1954: 'you can't go skunk-hunting with top hats and lace handkerchiefs'.[35]

In Britain, meanwhile, Dr Cort's appeal had quickly been turned into a major political cause. His supporters may well have felt personal sympathy for the two young Americans who, as would be claimed in the House of Commons, only wanted to 'settle down quietly' and perhaps also start a family. Yet they were also defending British democracy against the cringing submission to American power that many feared to be the now revealed meaning of the 'special relationship' so dear to Winston Churchill. As the *New Statesman and Nation* declared in an influential editorial on 'The Case of Dr. Cort', it was necessary to defend the principles of the 'free world' against the McCarthyist deformation that had elevated 'the smear' over the 'due process of law', thereby ensuring that 'the distinction between America and Iron Curtain countries grows every day less clearly defined'.[36] American anti-Communists had been 'making a farce of the Bill of Rights' by enacting laws such as the infamous McCarran Act of 1950, which had reintroduced 'the medieval penalty of outlawry' imposed on Cort when he was denied renewal of his passport in 1952. Since Britain was apparently now the 'principal trustee' of the institutions of freedom, the government would be performing a service to America's beleaguered democracy by allowing Cort to stay.[37]

Cort's early champions included the eminent physiologist and former Conservative MP, Professor Archibald Vivian Hill FRS. Having earlier founded the Academic Assistance Council to secure refuge for intellectuals and scientists facing persecution by the Nazis, Hill now mocked America's anti-Communist panic: 'It appears that, while he was a medical student at Yale, Cort got infected with Communism—chiefly because, as he explained to me, he was in favour of a National Health Service! He has now got over that particular children's disease.'[38] The Corts were backed by the vice-chancellor of the University of Birmingham, by 161 members of the teaching staff of Cambridge University, including nineteen professors and no less than eleven Fellows of the Royal Society. The National Council for Civil

Liberties took their side, as did 120,000 British citizens who signed a petition in their favour. American supporters included Dr Brown of Harvard Medical School, who had confirmed that Cort would indeed face 'persecution' if he went home (the fact that Brown's letter was printed in the Communist *Daily Worker* did not necessarily help win mainstream support for the Corts).

Dr Joseph Cort had found his champions in Parliament too, and not just among the seven Labour MPs whose constituencies were in the Birmingham area. In April, Cort had written to Anthony Wedgwood Benn. Sympathetic to his plight, the young Labour MP for Bristol South-East led a larger deputation to see the Conservative Home Secretary Sir David Maxwell Fyfe, who persisted in his view that 'There is nothing in the circumstances of Dr. Cort's case to justify regarding him as a political refugee.'[39] Insisting that the principal of 'returnability' was essential if refuge was to be granted, he added, as British Home Secretaries so often do, that to allow political asylum to the passportless American would therefore open a 'dangerous precedent' and pave the way for Britain's 'inundation by stateless persons'.

A cable on behalf of 150,000 trade unionists was sent to the prime minister, Winston Churchill, and the government's decision was also strongly opposed in the newspaper correspondence columns. One writer insisted on 'the humanitarian principle' that, since before the time of Karl Marx, had 'enhanced Britain's prestige and … contributed richly to her industrial, scientific, and intellectual strength'.[40] Speaking in the House of Commons on 1 July, the leader of the Labour opposition, Clement Attlee, declared himself on the side of the young American doctor, explaining that 'if there happened to be in a country a wave of persecution hysteria it was essential that this country should stand by its own principles'.[41] In the same debate, James Chuter Ede, who had been Home Secretary in Attlee's 1945 government, counted off Cort's numerous medical imperfections—'residual poliomyelitis, residual tuberculosis, a dangerous allergy, and marked myopia'—and asked 'in what army in the world could a man suffering from all that be any use?' Others condemned the Conservative Home Secretary's insistence that Cort was free 'to go to any country he wishes, and need not return to the United States'.[42] Given the cancellation of his passport, this was 'nothing short of hypocrisy'.[43] In support of Cort's request, Horace King (Labour MP for Southampton, Test) reminded the Home Secretary that political asylum was 'one of the precious traditions of British life', without which neither Victor Hugo nor Émile Zola would have been allowed to come to Britain.

Anthony Wedgwood Benn, meanwhile, attacked the government's assumption that Cort was 'a "draft dodger," to use an American expression'.[44] He insisted that Cort had twice registered for service with his draft board, in 1946 as well as in 1948, and that, on leaving the USA, he had also left the authorities his address in England. The attempt to categorize Cort as a draft-evader was, as various objectors pointed out, 'completely bogus'[45] and 'merely a device by the U.S. authorities to get him home'.[46] As for the Home Secretary's refusal to see any 'political' victimization in Cort's case, Benn pointed out that three of Cort's friends in the Communist Party at Yale had been dismissed following the hearings, and that Cort himself had seen four offers of assistant professorships in America withdrawn after his name was mentioned.[47]

Benn was also concerned about an apparent asymmetry in the government's use of political asylum. His earlier enquiries about Cort had been answered by an under-secretary at the Home Office, who had written that 'Except in the case of refugees whose homes are behind the Iron Curtain, the Home Secretary is not prepared to allow foreigners to settle here.'[48] Dismayed by this one-sided argument, Benn had asked the Home Secretary 'why aliens in danger of losing their nationality are only allowed to remain in Britain if they come from countries behind the Iron Curtain'.[49] The question prompted Fyfe to insist that the 'same rules applied to both sides', while acknowledging that, in the years following 1945, Britain had indeed accepted many 'aliens' from behind the Iron Curtain as a contribution to Europe's then pressing problem with displaced people. Unconvinced, the *New Statesman and Nation* condemned 'the panic into which the McCarran Act has thrown the Home Office, which is willing to grant asylum to persons deprived of their nationality from countries behind the Iron Curtain, because it assumes that they will be anti-Communist, while it is needlessly scared that England may be flooded by stateless Communists from other parts of the "free world"'.[50]

The argument continued through the one-month extension granted to Cort, but when this was about to expire at the end of July, the American doctor had revealed an unexpected new twist in a letter to Benn: 'This is to tell you that Ruth and I are going to Czechoslovakia. We are very grateful to the Czech government for granting us asylum and making it possible to carry on our medical research. We leave with feelings of warm gratitude to the British people who treated us so hospitably, and supported us so strongly in our efforts to remain in England.'[51]

Some Britons may have heard this news as proof that Dr Cort really was one of Senator McCarthy's 'skunks'. It is, for example, likely to have been received this way by Captain Kerby, the Conservative MP for Arundel and Shoreham, who had earlier sought reassurance from the government that 'this alien' would indeed be removed from the country.[52]

Anthony Wedgwood Benn, however, thought differently. Having read out Dr Cort's letter, 'with some emotion' in the House of Commons, he condemned the 'utter stupidity' of the Home Secretary's decision, and, in words that would be widely quoted (and colourfully summarized by the *Boston Evening American* on 31 July[53]), hurled the situation in the face of Winston Churchill's government: 'Here is a man whose only offence was that he was a Communist as an undergraduate. Yet the apparatus of two modern States is turned on him to hound him out and hound him behind the Iron Curtain.'

After condemning the 'tide of prejudice' constraining opinion in the USA, Benn expressed regret that the Corts had decided to go to Czecho-slovakia.

> But I cannot find it in my heart to criticise them for going there, because it is one place which is open to them—for all I know the only place—where they can carry on their work and where they can do the job which they are fitted to do. The irony is that Dr. Cort's father is a Russian by birth and that he left the Soviet Union as a result of the Revolution. He went to America for freedom, and his child is now being pushed back again by the hamhandedness, lack of imagination and meanness of the people of the western world.

So the Corts sailed away over North Sea and Baltic. Leaving the *Jaroslaw Dabrowski* in Gdynia, they journeyed overland to Prague, where their progress would be scrutinized from afar. On 28 August, the *New York Times* noted that Cort had presumed to 'score' Western science as it was pursued in his rejected McCarthyite homeland. Writing on 'Science in the United States' for the Czech labour union journal, he had declared that 'Political terror and intimidation makes most Americans afraid of speaking out or thinking of anything except their present jobs'.[54] It was also reported that the man who 'fled to Communist Czechoslovakia rather than face a draft board at home' had indeed found employment as a scientist in his new country. By September, Cort was said to be working at the Prague Institute for the Study of Circulatory Diseases.[55] The following month, Moscow radio announced that his wife Ruth had also found a new position as a paediatric physiologist.[56]

A Longer Cold War

There is more to be said about both Antoni Klimowicz and the Corts, and the way history shaped their lives. This book, however, is primarily concerned with the formidable division through which they passed. To penetrate the Iron Curtain in 1954 was to make a journey that could be charted on a conventional map, yet it was also like falling off the edge of the known world. While it entailed crossing a guarded frontier between antagonistic states, it also meant negotiating a passage through layers of ideologically driven propaganda, official censorship, speculation, and legend. Klimowicz and the Corts travelled in opposite directions yet, in official terms at least, both were transformed from renegades into heroes as they passed between polarized worlds where nothing was necessarily quite as it seemed.

When I began my investigations, I shared the widespread assumption that the story of the Iron Curtain opened in 1946 and then reached forward through four decades of Cold War to the events of 1989, when the Berlin Wall was breached, the wire that had long divided Austria and Czechoslovakia was twisted into a great heart-shaped sculpture, and 'people power' seemed to triumph at last. It wasn't long before I realized that, whilst this was indeed the reality of the Iron Curtain as experienced by many millions, it was also a formulaic conception, and one that remained tightly framed by Cold War attitudes.

My doubts intensified when, in April 2003, I visited Fulton, Missouri. There is, of course, no question that Winston Churchill came here early in March 1946 to deliver the epoch-making speech in which he announced the descent of the Iron Curtain and its threatened division of Europe. Yet it remains a strangely theatrical experience to drive into this small town in the American Midwest and to find at its heart a Churchill memorial consisting of a relocated London church by Sir Christopher Wren, bordered by a little 'English' garden on one side and an artistically adjusted stretch of the Berlin Wall on the other. It was also curious to stay across the road at the Loganberry Inn, a late Victorian timber house with bedrooms named after previous guests, remembered as if they had only just departed: Margaret and Dennis Thatcher, President Lech Walesa … Churchill's speech was a huge event for Fulton, but the enthusiasm with which his brief visit is now commemorated as the opening act of the Cold War left me scratching my head at the breakfast table.

My suspicions were confirmed soon enough. Shortly after returning to England from Missouri, I happened to go to Grantchester, the little village just west of Cambridge, in order to visit a distant cousin. David Roden Buxton was very elderly by then, and we sat by the fireside as he reminisced over some albums of photographs. He had travelled alone in the USSR in the late 1920s and early 1930s, studying and photographing medieval churches, including many marvellous examples of both stone and wood that had been destroyed later in the Stalinist period. Asked how he had come to assemble this evocative record, he explained that he had first gone to Russia with his sister and parents in the summer of 1927. The family had visited Moscow and other cities, and also walked considerable distances through the countryside.

In the course of this conversation, he produced a copy of a book written by his father, a now forgotten Labour politician, humanitarian, and colonial reformer named Charles Roden Buxton. *In a Russian Village* contained a description of the days its author had spent, seven years earlier in 1920, exploring conditions in several villages near Samara on the Volga. It was a work of vivid testimony, rendered all the more poignant by the fact that the settlements Charles Roden Buxton observed in their early encounter with Bolshevism had been overwhelmed by famine in the months between his visit and the completion of his book.

Yet, this was not all. Pasted inside this battered family copy was a newspaper article clipped from an edition of the *New Leader,* the paper of the Independent Labour Party. Headed 'Behind Russia's Curtain' and published in October 1927, this yellowed fragment contained Charles Roden Buxton's reflections on his more recent second visit to Soviet Russia. The title alone caught my attention and I was further surprised by the first paragraph, in which Buxton quoted an earlier condemnation of the 'iron curtain' written by a certain Vernon Lee. At that time, I was vaguely aware that a woman named Violet Paget had lived behind this pen name and that, in the nineteenth century, she had written aesthetic studies and also stories concerned with history and the supernatural. Yet here was Vernon Lee as a political writer, lamenting the isolation, ignorance, and hatred into which the 'iron curtain' had plunged its violently separated peoples, and doing so some three decades before Churchill went to Fulton.

To begin with, I resisted this discovery as a meaningless coincidence of language: a verbal snare that should have had a large sign stating 'Digression' posted beside it. I tried to shake off the idea, returning to the later story of

McCarthyism, rereading spy novels from the post-war period, and flying to Lübeck in northern Germany to walk along the little beach at Priwall where, from 1952, the fence dividing East from West Germany had joined the Baltic Sea. Yet that reference to Vernon Lee persisted in my mind and I eventually decided to track it down. It took me the best part of a year to locate the original article. By then, I had found several other instances of the phrase 'iron curtain' being used in this earlier period. I had also come to the conclusion that these usages could not be dismissed either as trivial accidents or relics of an intriguing but ultimately irrelevant prehistory. It was surely they, and not the Missouri ground supporting Fulton's transported Wren church, that indicated the true foundations of Churchill's famous expression.

While this book is indeed concerned to trace the emergence of a political metaphor, it is also an anticipatory exploration of the division that came to be known as the Iron Curtain after 1946. That barrier was, after all, a powerful political and cultural reality, and certainly not just an armed frontier between East and West Europe. Many of its characteristics, including the pronounced sense of theatricality it would bring to international politics, were inherited from the period before the Second World War.

The historian Eric Hobsbawm has recently introduced us to the idea of 'the short twentieth century'. My investigation is shaped by a connected hypothesis, which might be identified as the long Cold War. It journeys through the back of Winston Churchill's mind, and into an early twentieth-century world where the 'iron curtain' was first described by a largely forgotten collection of internationalists for whom it testified to the resurgence of the European nation state, with its habits of imperial rivalry, secret diplomacy, press-stirred chauvinism, and war. My purpose in excavating this earlier history—a story of lost horizons as well as of new vertical divisions — is not to reclaim the Iron Curtain for Europe, but to assist in the ongoing task of dismantling Cold War perspectives, 'triumphalist' or otherwise, and of creating a differently informed understanding of the problems besetting international relations in the twenty-first century.

PART

I

Carrying On in Missouri

Mr. Churchill, as usual, was unable to resist the dramatic gesture.

George Dangerfield,
The Strange Death of Liberal England (1936)

I

Bullet's Big Day

It was said that the sun 'peeped from behind overcast skies' as the motor-cade entered Fulton, a small town in Missouri where all roads had earl-ier been jammed 'with every form of vehicle including cars, lorries and farm carts'.[1] Having arrived from the state capital, Jefferson City, shortly after noon on Tuesday, 5 March 1946, the vehicles swung into Courthouse Square and, with tyres rumbling on a brick road that is carefully preserved to this day, drove into a restrained explosion of flags, balloons, and welcom-ing banners. Three bands were stationed along the route: at home with the Missouri Waltz but more than willing to launch into 'God Save the King' to mark what that morning's *Fulton Daily Sun-Gazette* had proclaimed as the town's 'Biggest Day in History'.[2]

President Harry Truman and Mr Winston Churchill were perched in half-standing position against the rear seat of their open limousine. Seated between these two raised figures was Dr Franc 'Bullet' McCluer, president and 'peppery mainspring'[3] of Fulton's Westminster College, where Churchill would deliver his lecture. The governor of Missouri, Phil M. Donnelly, sat in the forward row, alongside Truman's chief of staff, Admiral William D. Leahy. Four secret policemen were also in conspicuous attendance. Wearing hats and tightly buttoned civilian suits, they were hanging off the corners of the passenger compartment and scanning the crowd for any indication of trou-ble—aware, no doubt, of the plot to 'blow up Old Churchill', threatened in an anonymous letter sent to McCluer from Kansas City the previous January and duly passed on to the FBI.[4]

It was estimated that 25,000 Missourians turned out to line the streets of Fulton that day. Press photographers found the crowd rich in individual figures. Mr Walter Harrison of Fulton was pictured standing at the kerb: an austere and powerful-looking man dressed in formal hunting costume.

There were family groups with carefully turned-out children clutching balloons. Some of the old-timers had been shown practising for the great
occasion a few weeks earlier—standing about in their long winter coats and
puffing on huge Churchillian cigars rather than 'Mississippi Meerschaums'
of the customary corncob variety that had been tossed as tributes into the
presidential train as it pulled Churchill and Truman through the Missouri
town of Washington earlier that morning.[5]

The people of the Midwest were known for their strongly held isolationist views. Yet few even of the more sceptical observers would have come
close to the deranged fury of the bomb-threatening scribbler, who had told
McCluer that Churchill was to blame for 'our boys' killed in the recent war
in Europe and that the British war leader 'should of been shot and hung up
by his heels same as the Ducho'.

Photographs suggest that the Missourians surveyed the living monument that was 'Winnie' with respectful curiosity: taking in his paunch, his
jowls, and his equally famous rugged jaw, and perhaps seeking to establish
whether journalists were right to claim that the 71-year-old British leader,
who had indeed tried hard to bring America into the Second World War
before the matter was clinched at Pearl Harbor, 'even resembles John Bull in
appearance'. A student from Westminster College's sister institution, William
Woods College, wrote to her grandfather in Blythville, Arkansas, saying
that having surveyed the bulky and stout-hearted visitor from her college's
appointed place on the sidelines, she could understand how the British had
been able to take the 'terrible pounding' they had received early in the war
and still come out victorious.[6] Many are likely to have shared the more
general sense of incredulity expressed by the *Kansas City Times* as it reported
on 'This fantasy in Fulton—the spectacle of two world leaders appearing
together in a small town in America's midlands.'[7]

Onlookers also discovered that on the rare occasions when History visits
a place like Fulton, it does so briskly and without displaying any desire
to hang around. Having anticipated a great visitation, they were surprised
by the modesty of the motorcade, which featured only one state highway
control car, two armoured vehicles, and a closed car preceding the one in
which the distinguished passengers rode. It also passed by much faster than
they had anticipated. People had no sooner seen the limousine than they
were rushing 'pell mell' to take up another position along the route. Necks
were craned as assorted Missourians tried to haul the escaping vehicle back
into view, eager to complete their appraisal of the victorious British war

leader who had returned to civilian life as leader of the Conservative Party, only to be unceremoniously dumped in the 'landslide' general election of July 1945, and replaced by a Labour government that talked of socialism whilst at the same time trying to secure a loan—still being heavily contested in Congress—of well over $3 billion from the United States of America.

Churchill smiled into the crowd as the motorcade wound its way through the swept and smartened town. He waved and raised his hat, exposing the 'single wisp' of hair that had been sighted covering his crown in Miami a few weeks earlier.[8] He displayed his famous Victory sign and brandished the expected cigar even though, according to one report at least, he had some difficulty keeping the thing alight. It was a familiar performance, and the great Briton persisted with it as the cars looped round to drive back along the residential stretch of Court Street.

As he glanced at Fulton's wide-porched timber houses, Churchill may briefly have felt curious about the 'sleepy' little town he was about to turn into the focus of the world's attention. Certainly, the press had been making enquiries ever since the beginning of the year, when his approaching visit first became known. Investigating reporters found Fulton to be located in the foothills of the Ozarks and at the eastern edge of 'Little Dixie', the tier of Missouri counties that had customarily voted the Democrat ticket as regularly as the South. Visiting this 'almost railroadless town of tall trees and Confederate traditions',[9] they noted the new courthouse, and also the attractions of the historic centre: 'The mellowness of age and quaintness is glimpsed in near-by structures, but it is not seedy.' The population had been recorded as 8,297 in the official census of 1940. However, this figure included 1,700 patients in the psychiatric hospital based in Fulton and known as 'State Hospital Number 1'. These unfortunate 'inmates' were quietly subtracted to provide the generally quoted figure of 6,500 true Fultonians.

Local spokesmen were less guarded about their rapidly modernizing agriculture. Many soil conservation schemes were under way, and nearly half the 3,000 or so farms in surrounding Callaway County would soon have electricity thanks to co-operative schemes funded through the Rural Electrification Administration.[10] Fulton also had its manufacturers, producing firebricks, shoes, and a power-driven post-hole digger sold in eighty countries around the world by the Danuser Machine Company. Yet the town's leading inhabitants insisted that theirs was fundamentally 'a community of culture'.

As the St Louis Globe-Democrat reported in late January: 'Irked at being called hillbilly, Fultonians consider their town a small but active cradle of

learning, and base this proud claim on the fact that they have three schools—
Westminster College for men, William Woods College for women, and the
Missouri School for the Deaf.'[11] It was the presence of these institutions that
made Fulton what it was—a small town, as locals freely admitted, but definitely not a hick town. The claim would be confirmed by the *New York Times*'s
famous English-born foreign correspondent Anne O'Hare McCormick:

> Nothing could be more typical of this country than the little college towns
> that dot the Midwestern states as thickly as raisins in a pound cake. Mostly
> denominational in origin, the universities of farmers and rural communities,
> they represent the attachment to religion and the desire for learning that were
> carried across the wide rivers and wide prairies of this continent with the
> waves of westward migration.[12]

Prompted by reporters seeking precedents for the visit in Fulton's past,
many locals recalled the day in 1936 when 20,000 people had gathered
for the triumphant return of the 18-year-old Woods College athlete Helen
Stephens, also known as 'The Fulton Flash', who had won two gold medals in
the Berlin Olympics and established a new world record, running 100 metres
in 11.5 seconds, before coming home to find Missouri's proud cheers mixed
with whispered insinuations that she was really a man.[13] Others raised their
example from an earlier time when Fulton was a 'hotbed of Secessionism'
and its county, originally named after Daniel Boone's son-in-law, came to
be known as 'the Kingdom of Callaway' thanks to the ingenuity with which
its people had contrived to stay out of the Civil War despite their strong
Confederate sympathies. It was concluded that Fulton had seen 'nothing
like'[14] Truman and Churchill's visit since 1875 when the former president
of the Confederate states, Jefferson Davis, had stood by a still-extant tree in
the town and addressed the people of Callaway: 'In the minds of oldtimers,'
it was said, 'nothing ever could take place to top that event.'[15]

Other aspects of Fulton's history were not drawn into the frieze of
improving local detail with which the press decorated the visit. There was
no attempt to identify the place with the small town evoked in *Kings Row*,
a best-selling novel first published in 1940. The notoriety that the author
Henry Bellamann had brought to his former home town was hardly an
occasion for unmixed pride. Having left to become an eminent music edu-
cationalist in New York City, this graduate of Westminster College had used
historical melodrama to cut through the superficially 'attractive picture'
Fulton offered its visitors and to reveal, behind the 'simulated' mellowness
of this stage-managed front, a community that was actually corroded by

'a kind of dry rot'.[16] Though founded by independent and self-respecting pioneers at a time when 'the great names were still echoing—Jefferson, Adams, Franklin', Kings Row had since become a backwater, drained of vitality by the fact that 'the great trunk lines built across the continent in the latter half of the nineteenth century had passed it by'.[17] By the 1890s, in which Bellamann's novel is set, the town was an ossified place where anyone displaying the slightest sign of 'difference' could expect lifelong persecution; and where the rising generation had to struggle constantly against a corrupted atmosphere of bigotry, sadism, racism, inter-generational 'sex jealousy' and incest.

The latter failing had been replaced by a less shocking drama of psychiatric illness by the time *Kings Row* was made into one of the most successful movies of 1942: marketed, at least in its later years, under the slogan 'Behind the picture-postcard façade lies *murder* and *madness*.'[18] Filmed in Hollywood rather than Missouri,[19] MGM's version starred Ronald Reagan as young Drake McHugh, who wakes to find both his legs unnecessarily amputated by a vengeful doctor and, with his voice rising to a wail, asks his loyal girl, '*Randy*—where—where's the rest of me?'

The three-piece suit worn by Reagan is now a treasured possession of Fulton Chamber of Commerce: displayed in a glass case at the Heart of Missouri Tourism Center, just off a busy intersection at nearby Kingdom City. Yet those responsible for preparing Fulton for 'C-T Day' in 1946 did not follow the example of the movie by placing a notice near the city limits declaring their town to be, in words quoted directly from the opening of Bellamann's novel, 'A good, clean town. A good town to live in, and a good place to raise your children.' Many Fultonians had worked hard to ensure that Truman and Churchill received just such an impression, but they evoked it in different words and without the slightest concession to Bellamann's undermining irony.

Shooting at the Moon?

After cruising down West Seventh, the motorcade approached the rising ground of Westminster College: a small liberal arts college which, on this day especially, would be said to have 'an English soul', its name commemorating the founding of Presbyterianism at the Westminster Assembly of July 1643.[20] The campus has developed other attractions since Churchill's visit, but in 1946 its tone was set by 'scores of stately elms'[21] and a prominent row of six Corinthian columns, carefully preserved remnants from the portico of an administration building destroyed by fire in 1909. The plain and 'bare-girdered'[22] gymnasium, in which Churchill would speak, was draped with the flags of the forty-eight states, and also the members of the new United Nations Organization, formed the previous year, after fifty nations signed the charter in San Francisco. Other buildings on the campus had been spared florid ornamentation, thanks to the restraining influence of Dr Franc 'Bullet' McCluer, who had reminded his fellow townsmen that 'this is a serious lecture, not a football game'.

According to the *Washington Post,* Churchill looked 'cherubic, pink-cheeked and very fit' as he stepped out of the car and, once again, displayed his famous V-Sign 'to the delight of the admiring throng'. Dr McCluer also had good reason for smiling as he ushered his guests through the freshly painted porch of his own presidential home, Washington West House, where lunch awaited them. Westminster was a small college which had only enrolled a hundred or so new students in that still demobilizing post-war year, and yet 'Bullet' McCluer had actually managed to pluck 'the choicest plum in the lecture field'.[23] As the *St Louis Globe-Democrat* had declared in late January, 'If there was ever a case of shooting at the moon and hitting it, the instance of Fulton and the British war leader is it.' *Time* magazine agreed: 'Last week the townspeople of Fulton agreed that never had Bullet shot so high, or rung the bell such a bong.'[24] Commending McCluer as 'a whirlwind of energy and salesmanship', its reporter explained that he had 'earned his nickname, as an undergraduate, for the machine-gun force of his debating'.

Dated 3 October 1945, McCluer's letter of invitation had been received by the British war leader when he returned to London after a month painting and resting in Italy. Though Churchill was officially now only leader of the Conservative opposition in the House of Commons, McCluer approached him as a giant, informing him that Westminster College had a lecture series, the Green lectures, named after an eminent St Louis attorney and run by his English-born Canadian widow. Fully aware that he might be overreaching himself, McCluer offered such modest inducements as lay in his power. There would, of course, be a fee (an offer Churchill would shortly reject—his staff were eager that Westminster College issue a press release leaving no doubt that Churchill considered his visit 'a courtesy to President Truman'); and in this case the college would happily allow their speaker to retain publication rights should he so wish. Aware that Churchill might expect a larger venue and audience than Westminster College could provide, he also wrote that the college would be willing to host an additional lecture in St Louis, a hundred or so miles away, where many thousands would certainly attend.

Yet the significant string in McCluer's hand was connected not to Churchill but to President Truman, who had grown up on a Missouri farm and remained closely associated with the state. In his approach to Truman, McCluer was assisted by a Fulton banker, Mr Thomas H. VanSant, who had run two of Truman's senatorial campaigns in Callaway County, and also by Truman's military aide, Brigadier General Harry H. Vaughan, who happened to be a former student of Westminster College. With their assistance, McCluer was able to ensure that Churchill received his letter of invitation from Truman's office, and with a handwritten note from the president scribbled at the bottom of the page: 'This is a wonderful school in my home state. Hope you can do it. I'll introduce you. Best regards Harry Truman.'

From the moment of Churchill's acceptance, Fulton was launched into elaborate preparations. 'C-T Day' confronted the town with what one paper called 'all the problems that go with a super-event in a small setting', and every service in the locality had groaned in anticipation. As superintendent of Fulton's telephone system, Mr J. K. McQuire set about installing extra equipment and hiring an additional sixteen telephone operators to ensure that his apparatus would not be overloaded. No such option was available at Fulton's two hotels, which could muster only twenty-six rooms between them. When asked how he was going to accommodate the anticipated multitude, the 'pleasant white-haired night clerk' in one of these establishments raised his hands into the air 'in a spirit of futility', smiled, and told the reporter 'That's up to "Bullet"'.

In the event, no fewer than ten committees had been put to work, organized through the Chamber of Commerce's 'Special Arrangements Committee', and chaired by the superintendent of the Missouri School for the Deaf, Mr Truman L. Ingle. Restrooms were imported and five hundred patrolmen drafted in to direct the traffic. Every spare room in the town was mobilized, and arrangements were made to stack visiting journalists and reporters on two-tier bunks in the college fraternity houses. Food was a particular problem, since Fulton could squeeze at most 400 people into its ten or so cafés, none of which intended to stay open for 'C-T Day' anyway. The women of the various churches were mobilized ('They'll deal out sandwiches and coffee as fast as they can ladle'), and 'box lunch concerns' from St Louis were invited to consider selling perhaps as many as 32,000 additional sandwiches from the sidewalk.

McCluer was certainly busy enough preparing Westminster College to leave the wider town's preparations to others. He had to fend off at least 30,000 applications for tickets, acknowledging the local hierarchy, while at the same time turning some of its more esteemed members away. Priority and pride of place in the gymnasium was given to the mothers of the fifty-seven former students who had laid down their lives in the war. Then came college graduates, staff, and students. Two hundred members of the press had to be seated, and allowances were also made for parents of students and the heads of nearby colleges. The town was rigged with loudspeakers so the speech could be heard by perhaps another 30,000 gathered variously on the grass outside the gymnasium, in nearby chapels and churches, in the auditorium at William Woods College, or around the Courthouse building in Fulton's main square. McCluer had to make arrangements with radio companies and telecasters, and also with the FBI, which vetted all ticket-holders, reporters, and journalists. He had to turn away diverse over-optimistic requests: an agent offering the Coon Creek Boys as an entertainment feature; members of the Daniel Boone Association hoping President Truman would have time to open their new museum; the Daughters of the American Revolution at Arrow Rock who wondered if Mr Churchill might be able to join them for a tavern meal. After days full of arrangement and negotiation, he could also look forward to receiving phone calls at all hours of the night from officials in London, who didn't seem to grasp the time differences.

Mrs McCluer, meanwhile, was preparing to make culinary sense of the Anglo-American 'special relationship' that would soon be advocated on her doorstep. Since the beginning of the year, the press had been amplifying her deliberations as to how she should feed her two alarmingly distinguished visitors. Should it be 'something grand like lobster', or 'something simple and native American like hot dogs'?[25]

Since Churchill was well known for his devotion to roast beef, a 27-lb, seven-rib joint was acquired for the buffet supper to be served after the speech as Churchill and his retinue prepared to depart on their return journey to Jefferson City. It was to be cooked by Ulysses Threlkeld, a young African American who would work under the close supervision of a dietitian named Mrs Siddie Watson. For the lunch before, however, Mrs McCluer was determined to show 'the Fultonian way', and 'not try to imitate what might be had in London or Washington'.

'There'll be no cateress,' she said, promising to avoid excessive protocol and to aim instead for 'the homely personal air of a family reunion'. Her

Spode and sterling silver would just about cover the main twenty-place banquet table, and other arrangements would be made for the less exalted guests seated on portable tables (like 'rayon-topped card tables') spread out through the sitting room and living room. By late January, the *St Louis Globe-Democrat* announced that she and Mrs Baker Trigg, the chief cook at Fulton Country Club, would be serving country ham.

The decision prompted detailed discussion of the difference between a proper 'Callaway County country ham and a "packing house ham"'. The key was declared to be the method of curing:

> A country ham is smoked in a specially constructed smoke-house where a hickory-log fire is tenderly cared for by the farmer who personally raised and butchered the hog. It is treated with sugar and spices and allowed to hang for eighteen months or more. After a year or so, an ice-pick is thrust into the centre of the ham. If it doesn't hit a soft spot, you know the ham is good—cured to the very center.

It was also reported that 'They say in Fulton that "a ham is not properly cured unless it bounces when dropped on the floor".'[26]

The same Missouri paper joked that such prodigious fare, served in thick slices and swimming in red gravy, would surely leave Churchill both satisfied and 'stirred with desires for imperialism beyond the horizons of the present British Empire'. In the event, Churchill does appear to have been appreciative, pronouncing politely that 'In this ham, the pig has reached its highest form of evolution.'[27] He was surely too courteous to disclose that he had already stowed away another hickory-smoked ham before arriving in Fulton. That example hailed from Cole County rather than Callaway and had been presented to him (together with a box of Havana cigars) by Governor Donnelly in Jefferson City as he and Truman stepped off the special presidential train that had brought them—joking, drinking brandy, and playing poker—from Washington DC.

No Ordinary Tourist

Local papers may have extracted all the human interest they could find in the story of Mrs McCluer's intended menus, but more serious speculation was focused on the likely content of Churchill's speech. The British leader had been in America for some weeks, resting, painting landscapes in Florida, visiting Cuba in a plane laid on by President Truman. Yet despite repeated claims to this effect, Churchill was plainly not just a private citizen on holiday. Historians of the Cold War would later make a point of 'discovering' this fact but, in Fulton, it had been obvious from the start that the British leader would not be coming all that way for nothing. Writing from Miami Beach, Florida, on 30 January 1946, Churchill had told Dr McCluer that he hoped to see Truman in February, 'and I will discuss with him the arrangements for the time and the subject matter of my address. In all the circumstances, it will be a political pronouncement of considerable importance.'

That meeting with President Truman took place in Washington DC on 10 February. As readers of the *Little Rock Gazette* in Arkansas were informed the next day, the two leaders 'talked for an hour and a half last night in the White House, but there was no inkling as to the topic of their conversation'. It was suspected that Churchill's real purpose was to help secure the vast dollar loan requested by his war-bankrupted country. Truman was thought to be already on side, but much depended on how well Churchill went down with the Congressmen of the Midwest, who were opposing the requested loan on the grounds that it would help Britain's new Labour government implement socialist policies. According to the *Weir Spectator* (Kansas), 'Churchill must convince them that all of England must have the loan, not just the Labor Party, and that the Labor Party is behaving very like the Conservative Party. He must subtly convey the idea that instead of promoting socialism the loan will actually strengthen England to oppose the western march of Russian socialism across Europe.'[28] As for the political aspect of his forthcoming pronouncement, on 15 February, the *St Joseph Missouri Gazette* had sensed a different but equally suspect British intention: 'the song he sings is the security of the British Empire, which he once swore he would never liquidate'. Anticipating the Iron Curtain (although getting its main geographical orientation quite wrong), this paper saw Churchill's desire for a 'shield' between the British Empire and Soviet Russia and imagined this protective structure extending East–West: not 'from Stettin in the Baltic to Trieste in the Adriatic', as Churchill would shortly declare, but 'from Hong Kong across Asia to Iran and the Mediterranean sea'.

While some considered Churchill little better than a high-class beggar peddling Britain's imperialist agenda to Truman, it was also widely anticipated that he would enter what the *Kansas City Star* called 'an anti-Red Plea' ('The demand that the English-Speaking nations join hands to resist the spread of Russian influences will be voiced by Winston Churchill in his nation-wide broadcast, at Westminster College, Fulton'). On 4 March the *Omaha Evening World* listed a number of recent developments that inclined the International News Service to expect Churchill's speech would include sharp criticism of the Soviet Union. A Republican Senator from Nebraska, Kenneth Wherry, had recently 'ripped into the Reds' for the 'vicious leadership' of Russian representatives and agents who had aggravated the breakdown of America's industrial reconversion programme. Iran's ambassador to Washington had just called on the United States to join Britain in demanding that Russia explain the continued presence of Red Army troops in Iran despite treaty obligations. A semi-official despatch from China alleged that Russia had seized control of 'all power systems in Manchuria'. And the Canadian prime minister, Mackenzie King, had recently disclosed that members of the Soviet Embassy at Ottawa had, 'under direct instructions from Moscow', formed a spy ring to obtain the secret of the atom bomb.

A similar trawl of wider circumstantial evidence was made by the syndicated political columnist Doris Fleeson, in support of her conjecture that Churchill's speech would reflect 'a stiffened American attitude towards Russia'. On 2 March the *St Joseph Missouri News-Press* carried an article in which Fleeson suggested that 'the new program' had begun to take shape in Churchill's Washington conversation with Truman, and been further shaped in the talks he later held with Secretary of State James Byrnes, who visited him in Florida on 17 February bringing along his long-standing friend the Wall Street banker and presidential adviser Bernard M. Baruch in order to discuss details of the proposed loan.[29] 'It is now known,' so Fleeson wrote, that

> next week in Fulton, MO, Churchill intends to reassert his plea, voiced in 1943, at Harvard, for Anglo-American unity as the only bulwark of democracy in a world threatened with new forms of totalitarianism. He will argue for the British loan as an incident in a relationship which must not be allowed to fail lest the worst should befall the world. The speech will be pointed at Russia.

Fleeson was apparently not yet aware of the 8,000-word 'long telegram' that George Kennan had sent from the American Embassy in Moscow on 22 February, insisting that the implacably hostile Soviet leaders were, as he later put it, 'steeled against'[30] any sort of reasoning that America might try, and recommending that the 'logic of force' now represented the only approach that Stalin respected and understood. Yet she pointed out that the former US ambassador to the Soviet Union, Averell Harriman, had recently returned from Russia in a gloomy frame of mind which has naturally been communicated to Truman. The army and navy are bringing to the White House new reports of the increasing power of the military in Russia. They believe that the red army is pushing the old Bolsheviks hard for power and that internal upheavals may be part of the hidden Russian story. Navy intelligence warns of plans for a Russian fleet to match our own which will be ready in a decade.

These contemporary articles were pretty much on the mark. It was widely and rightly suspected that Churchill's Fulton oration, far from being the detached soliloquy of a superannuated man of history, would be closely harmonized with a fundamental realignment of American foreign policy in response to the perceived Soviet threat. Under Roosevelt, America had taken an accommodating approach to her Soviet Russian war ally, and sought to remain on good terms with Stalin by standing back from Great Britain and its empire. This policy had been vigorously pursued by Vice-President Henry Wallace, and also by Secretary of State Byrnes, who had persisted with it until only a few weeks before. Yet, as Fraser Harbutt has demonstrated, a contrary argument had been growing for some time. It was to be found in *Reader's Digest*, which had been publishing anti-Communist articles on such topics as 'The Soviet Iron Fist in Romania', and in *Harper's Magazine,* which, in September 1945, called for the creation of an Anglo-American strategic alliance, and for the world to be divided into two spheres.[31] The *New York Times* had also countered isolationist suspicion of British intentions, asserting that Anglo-American unity was essential.

The urgency of this discussion was greatly enhanced by the fear that the secret of the atom bomb might soon, as the Canadian spy plot suggested, be betrayed to Stalin's Russia. Churchill's audience at Fulton may not have been aware of the shadows massing over Bikini Atoll, where, in the same month that saw Churchill come to Fulton, 167 residents were evacuated so that nuclear bombs could be detonated over a fleet of redundant American warships. Yet they knew exactly what an atom bomb could do to a city far bigger than theirs, thanks not least to a different British visitor who had given a talk in Fulton only the night before.

Contracted to the London *Daily Sketch* and *Sunday Times,* William Courtenay was a British war correspondent who had recently landed in California after four years attached to US forces in the Pacific, working under General Douglas MacArthur and Admiral Nimitz. While on his way to lecture at the Town Hall in New York City, and also in Washington DC, where he would address the combined chiefs of staff and an audience of

3,600 assembled at the Constitution Hall by the National Geographic Society, this recently declared Honorary Life Member of the 8th US Cavalry Regiment (1st Cavalry Division), had paused in Fulton to tell an audience at William Woods College about the things he had seen and filmed with his colour 16-mm camera after atom bombs had been dropped on Hiroshima and Nagasaki. In words that were printed on the page preceding the text of Churchill's speech in a late edition of the *Fulton Daily Sun-Gazette,* Tuesday, 5 March, Courtenay had given Fulton a terrifying account of the power that Churchill and Truman were now so keen to keep out of the hands of the Soviet Union:

> First there appeared in the sky a great light like the magnesium flare but magnified a thousand fold. Then everyone on the ground felt conscious of a wave of heat passing over them. A deathlike and ominous silence followed—like the awful hushed stillness before a visitation or earthquake.

> There followed a dread noise like that made when the hand is passed rapidly down the slats of a Venetian blind, or the sort of noise made by a small boy running a stick along some railings. It was an orderly noise, a regimentated noise. It was the noise of house after house, street after street, falling before the strange mystic influence of the release of the atomic energy. It was as if a magic wand had been passed over the city dooming it. As each house and street fell it buried the occupants beneath it for every Jap house has a heavy roof and light walls. The houses collapsed and the walls caved in. A hundred thousand fires were started in a hundred thousand homes from the gas fires and kerosene stoves lit at breakfast time. They were the funeral pyres of a hundred thousand people at Nagasaki and Hiroshima and this is the answer to those who say we did not deal harshly enough with Japan.

2

In the Name of the Common People

After lunch, and with the local pleasures of hickory-smoked ham still competing with the looming thought of mushroom clouds, 'Bullet' McCluer and his distinguished guests took their position at the head of an academic procession and advanced up the slope to Westminster College's gymnasium.

President Truman delivered a short introduction with the 'typical simplicity' of a man who had famously once worked as a haberdasher in his Missouri hometown of Independence. According to the *Call Bulletin* the president seemed to maintain 'complete neutrality' as he recalled meeting Churchill and Stalin in Berlin the year before: 'I became very fond of both of them. They are men and they are leaders in this world today, when we need leadership.' Having opened in the spirit of the alliance that had defeated Hitler, Truman then veered much closer to his British guest, hinting at his own complicity in what was about to be said ('I know that Mr Churchill will have something constructive in his speech'), and reminding his audience that the man Fulton knew as 'Winnie' was not only a British John Bull: 'It is one of the great privileges of my lifetime to be able to present to you that great world citizen, Mr. Churchill.'

Churchill opened by joking that 'the name "Westminster" somehow or other seems familiar to me. I feel as if I'd heard of it before.'[1] He thanked his hosts and also President Truman, who had done them all the 'perhaps almost unique' honour of travelling a thousand miles to 'dignify and magnify our meeting today'. He then launched into the serious matter of his lecture: previously announced as 'World Affairs' and then 'World Peace' but now delivered under the tougher title only reported that morning, 'The Sinews of Peace'.

It quickly became apparent that this was to be an 'oration' of the kind that had earlier led Truman to tell his daughter that Churchill was 'as windy as old Langer [a famously verbose Republican senator from North Dakota], but he knew his English language'.[2] There would be pregnant pauses, exaggerated coinages, and much impassioned ebbing and flowing as Churchill delivered his message. A few years later, the editor of the *Washington Post* would describe the great Briton's style as 'orotund' and even 'Corinthian'.[3] For the *Weir KS Spectator,* however, it was enough to anticipate that 'Every word Churchill draws from his magnificent vocabulary will have the treasure of blood of Englishmen hanging on it.'[4] Certainly, there was little prospect of Churchill treating his words as neutral ciphers. He would dramatize them and hurl them forth as if they were great boulders in the stream of history: elements of a withstanding inheritance that belonged to the English-speaking peoples at large.

Churchill was careful to establish that he was speaking as a 'private visitor' with 'no official mission or status of any kind. I speak only for myself. There is nothing here but what you see.' Detached from both the responsibilities of office and the personal ambitions of his youth ('satisfied beyond my wildest dreams'), he would endeavour to fulfil President Truman's wish and use his 'full liberty' to give 'my true and faithful counsel in these anxious and baffling times'. This stance may have reflected the 'Messiah complex' detected in Churchill by America's minister in Cuba (by this time in his life, Churchill had more justification than most for his long-standing habit of confusing the history of the world with his own autobiography). It may also have served to enhance Churchill's status as a representative of the democracy that had allowed him but not, alas, Stalin to be voted out of office.

Recent scholarship suggests that this claim of detachment from the responsibilities of international diplomacy was also 'disingenuous'.[5] Churchill had consulted with Truman, whose policy towards Russia had been hardening for some months, and who knew very well what was coming (his later insistence that he had not read the speech apparently rested on the entirely specious grounds that he had only read 'a mimeographed reproduction'). Churchill's message also suited the British prime minister, Clement Attlee, and his strongly anti-Communist Labour Foreign Secretary, Ernest Bevin, freeing them from responsibility for views they shared but could not themselves publicly state. Attlee may not have read any version of Churchill's text, but he had telegrammed Churchill a week earlier, declaring 'I am sure your Fulton speech will do good'.[6]

Having prepared his audience for the honest reflections of a retired elder looking back over the colossal 'experience of a lifetime', Churchill proceeded to review the present moment in international relations. With the war against Nazism won, America now stood at 'the pinnacle of world power'. This was a 'solemn moment for the American democracy', for with power came an 'awe-inspiring accountability to the future'. The opportunity was there, 'clear and shining for both our countries', but so too was the possibility that the future or 'after-time' would look back and see that it had been rejected, ignored, or 'frittered away'. Churchill hoped that 'constancy of mind, persistence of purpose, and the grand simplicity of decision' would guide the conduct of the English-speaking peoples in peace as they had done in the recent war.

He then set out to paint a picture of the post-war world and its associated challenges. Using a whole series of picturesque and proverbial expressions, he sketched a world of 'awful ruin', in which the very 'frame of civilized society' had collapsed and millions of survivors were now stalked by famine. It was a 'haggard' and insecure world, still brightened by the Allied victory over fascism, but darkly threatened by the 'gaunt marauders, war and tyranny' (echoes here, surely, of the five 'giants'—Want, Disease, Ignorance, Idleness, and Squalor—targeted in the founding document of Britain's post-war welfare state, Lord Beveridge's 1942 report on *Social Insurance and Allied Services*), and by the nuclear apocalypse that threatened to bring back the Stone Age on 'the gleaming wings of science'.

Churchill placed a 'cottage home' at the centre of this damaged and uncertain landscape. Buffeted by the winds of history, this pastoral and characteristically English fixture was by no means unique to the Fulton oration. Indeed, in a Conservative Party political broadcast delivered less than a year previously (4 June 1945), Churchill had offered it as a prize to Britain's homecoming soldiers. Condemning the rapidly advancing Labour Party ('these Socialist dreamers' who would surely have to fall back on 'some form of Gestapo' if they were really to establish their welfare state), he had urged 'let us make sure that the cottage home to which the warrior will return is blessed with modest but solid prosperity, well-fenced and guarded against misfortune, and that Britons remain free to plan their lives for themselves and for those they love'.[7]

That 'cottage home' had been an anachronistic fixture even in this earlier manifestation: suggestive not just of liberty and humbly contented family life but of the idealized village community that remained a strong source of Conservative inspiration even after more than a century of industrial urbanization. Those returning British 'warriors' had roundly rejected their war leader's homely vision in the 1945 election, yet Churchill was not dissuaded from employing it again. Lord Halifax, then British ambassador in Washington, records that he had 'tears almost rolling down his cheeks' as he revised his picture of the 'cottage home of happy humble people' in preparation for the Fulton oration.[8]

In a bid to engage urban American listeners, Churchill paired his English cottage with an 'apartment home', and then multiplied both to produce what he identified, with teasing reference to American military jargon, as the 'overall strategic concept' of that post-war moment. The challenge, he explained, must be to secure 'the safety and welfare, the freedom and progress, of all the homes and families of all the men and women in all the lands'. He then went on to define this inordinate project a little more closely: 'I speak particularly of the myriad cottage or apartment homes where the wage-earner strives amid the accidents and difficulties of life to guard his wife and children from privation and bring the family up in the fear of the Lord, or upon ethical conceptions which often play their potent part.'

Churchill's battered 'cottage home' may have retained an old-fashioned rose at its door, but many of the 'ordinary' or 'common people' to whom it belonged in 1946 were in abject shape. They had survived, more or less, but the war had reduced them to a bare form of life. As 'humble folk', they were 'confronted with difficulties with which they cannot cope. For them all is distorted, all is broken, all is even ground to pulp.'

The people who had lined the streets of Fulton that morning were not so beaten. In Europe, however, Churchill had seen many who were—including the Berliners who had gathered in the ruins of their city to cheer him as he visited the ruins of Hitler's Chancellery in July 1945 ('I was much moved by their demonstrations, and also by their haggard looks and threadbare clothes').[9] Although they formed the foundation of the democracy that was to be revived in their name, the people in Churchill's evocation were damaged, demoralized, and utterly dependent on the initiative of leaders, who must now establish the 'grand simplicity of decision' over their heads and 'guard' them from the 'horrors and miseries of another war'.

This idea of the 'common people'—as traumatized creatures who needed to be herded by superior statesman with little more than their elevation in common—may indeed have reflected the perilous condition of much of the world after the war. Yet it also confirmed the outlook of a war leader who had made many momentous decisions over the heads of the masses: not least in the summit meetings in which he, Roosevelt, and Stalin had met to decide the shape of the post-war world. At the Tehran conference in November and December 1943, where the 'Big Three' discussed the post-war division of Germany and Eastern Europe, Churchill found a special use for three matches, which he moved about on a map in order to show Stalin how the borders of Germany, Poland, and Russia might all be shifted west.

A different method was employed on 9 October 1944, when Churchill and Stalin met in Moscow to consider how the Balkan countries would be distributed between distinct Russian and British 'spheres of influence'. Churchill recalls using 'a half-sheet of paper' to sketch out the proportions of Russian and British power in various countries in the Balkans—splitting Yugoslavia and Hungary fifty-fifty, allocating Russia 90 per cent in Romania, 75 per cent in Bulgaria, and then awarding Britain 90 per cent in Greece. Having drawn up this little scheme, he pushed it across the table to Stalin, who paused a little after hearing the translation, and then used his blue pencil to make a large tick on the sheet before passing it back to Churchill. 'It was', as the British leader recalled, 'all settled in no more time than it takes to set down.'

This process had culminated in 1945, when the 'Big Three' met in the Crimean resort of Yalta to establish the terms of the new United Nations Organization, agree a provisional government for Poland, and divide Germany into Russian, French, British, and American zones of occupation. The encounter was resumed later that year at Potsdam, but it was 'Yalta' that lent its name to a post-war system of world government in which superpowers dominated and the distinct 'spheres of influence' soon solidified into opposed 'blocs'.

As such, Yalta would draw much condemnation over the decades to come, not least in Eastern Europe, where it had been widely believed that Churchill and Roosevelt must have secured at least some guarantee of civil rights in lands ceded to the Soviet sphere. People in the West might say that Churchill, Roosevelt, and later Truman had done what they could to bind Stalin to a respect for civil liberties and democratic elections. However, a more critical analysis would emerge from within that roughly separated sphere.

In the words of two Hungarian critics, the 'Big Three' 'arbitrarily decreed new national borders, ordered—or, at least, promoted—forcible population-transfers, declared certain nations collectively criminal (even if not in so many words but by punishing them substantively), released others from the bonds of responsibility, created spheres of influence over nations that had sacrificed millions in order to make others independent'.[10] The world system that emerged at Yalta may have been based on the indisputable fact that global order had broken down and could not be re-established by any single power.[11] Yet it was also deemed to reflect 'the unassailable conviction shared equally by the "Big Three" that they had the unquestionable right to decide the future of the world among themselves, without even going so far as to discuss the pertinent details with the parties (and sometimes the continents) involved'.[12]

When it came to overcoming the first of his two 'gaunt marauders', namely War, Churchill gave his guarded blessing to the new United Nations Organization, a 'world organization' that had the considerable advantage of American membership—unlike its precursor the League of Nations, which was established after the First World War but proved incapable of stemming the advance of Italian and German fascism or the Japanese invasion of Manchuria and then China. Remembering that failure, Churchill was insistent that the United Nations must be made 'fruitful … a force for action and not just a frothing of words'. Painting in another picturesque edifice alongside his cottage home, he declared that the new international organization must become a 'true temple of peace in which the shields of many nations can some day be hung up, and not merely a cockpit in a Tower of Babel'.

While commending the United Nations, albeit in this reserved fashion, Churchill was resolutely opposed to the idea of giving up 'national armaments' until it was absolutely clear that the new 'temple of peace' was built on rock rather than upon 'shifting sands and quagmires'. Claiming to have urged the same for the League of Nations when he was Britain's Secretary of State for War immediately after the Great War, he proposed that the powers and states should dedicate a number of 'air squadrons' to the service of the United Nations—trained and uniformed by their own countries, but sent into service with special badges identifying them as part of a UN International force.

Though happy to advance this 'definite and practical proposal to make for action', Churchill remained adamant that it would be 'wrong and imprudent'—'criminal madness', indeed—to entrust the UN with the secret knowledge of the atom bomb, then held by the United States, Great Britain, and Canada. Aware of what these 'dread agencies' might mean had they been monopolized by 'some Communist or neo-Fascist State', he argued that this awe-inspiring science should be withheld until the 'ultimate' time when 'the essential brotherhood of man is truly embodied and expressed in a world organization with all the necessary practical safeguards to make it effective'. He was not prepared to put even an approximate date on the coming of this unlikely 'after-time'.

Turning to his second 'marauder', Tyranny, Churchill declared that the 'liberties enjoyed by individual citizens throughout the United States and throughout the British Empire' had been, or were in the process of being, abruptly extinguished elsewhere. In many states, the 'common people' were under the thumb of police governments, their liberties being ignored and extinguished. Churchill had presided over Britain's part in the Allies' futile military intervention against the Bolshevists in the Russian Civil War of 1918–20, but he did not call for a repeat performance. It was not 'our duty at this time when difficulties are so numerous to interfere forcibly in the international affairs of countries which we have not conquered in war'. Yet 'we must never cease to proclaim in fearless tones the great principles of freedom and the rights of man which are the joint inheritance of the English-speaking world and through which Magna Carta, the Bill of Rights, the Habeas Corpus, trial by jury, the English common law find their most famous expression in the American Declaration of Independence'.

These democratic principles had not been incorporated into the wartime agreements of the 'Big Three', despite Churchill's own insistence, at Potsdam, on the importance of free elections in Poland.[13] At Fulton, however, Churchill asserted them strongly, using words that would resound through the decades to come:

> that the people of any country have the right, and should have the power by constitutional action, by free unfettered elections, with secret ballot, to choose or change the character or form of government under which they dwell; that freedom of speech and thought should reign; that courts of justice, independent of the executive, unbiased by any party, should administer laws which have received the broad assent of large majorities or are consecrated by time and custom. Here are the title deeds of freedom which should lie in every cottage home. Here is the message of the British and American peoples to mankind.

Insisting that this message was to be practised as well as preached, Churchill then raised his lights, suggesting that the prospects were generally bright. The world was still 'plunged in the hunger and distress which are the aftermath of our stupendous struggle', but this suffering would pass quickly if the moment were seized. Science and cooperation could deliver 'an expansion of material well-being beyond anything that has yet occurred in human experience'. Only 'human folly or sub-human crime' could 'deny all nations the inauguration and enjoyment of an age of plenty'.

This caution brought Churchill to 'the crux of what I have travelled here to say'. The main assertion of his speech, and the point over which he was most concerned to win American agreement, was that neither the prevention of war nor the 'continuous rise of the world organization' would be possible 'without what I have called the fraternal association of the English-speaking peoples'. This in turn would mean 'a special relationship' between the British Commonwealth and Empire and the United States of America.

The 'special relationship' has been claimed as the truly original coinage of the Fulton oration.[14] Churchill advocated 'not only the growing friend-ship and mutual understanding between our two vast but kindred systems of society, but the continuance of the intimate relation between our military advisers, leading to common study of potential dangers, the similarity of weapons and manuals of instruction, and to the interchange of officers and cadets at technical colleges'. Besides leading to important cost savings, joint use of 'all Naval and Air Force bases in the possession of either country all over the world' would 'perhaps double the mobility of the American Navy and Air Force' and 'greatly expand' that of British Empire Forces too. 'Already we use together a large number of islands; more may well be entrusted to our joint care in the near future.'

Churchill would later insist that he was advocating a 'fraternal association' rather than a military alliance between the United States of America and the British Empire. Yet he certainly had more in mind than 'the usual hands across the water stuff' that Truman had reassured some suspicious enquirers would be the British leader's message. Gazing ahead on that quiet Missouri afternoon, while transcripts were being prepared and beamed out by frantic technicians hidden in the basement of Westminster College's gymnasium, Churchill saw the 'outstretched arm' of destiny, reaching in from a future in which 'common citizenship' between Britain and America might also one day become established.

Its strong military aspect notwithstanding, this 'special relationship' would certainly not be inconsistent with Britain and the USA's 'overriding' loyalties to the United Nations Organization. Returning to his idea of the emerging UN as a 'temple of peace', Churchill likened America and Britain to two old friends who might be found working together in its construction. The 'special relationship' would be a formidable nuclear alliance, with capability greater than anything on earth, and yet, as he suggested, it would also enable the new international organization to 'achieve its full stature and strength'. The USA already had such an undertaking in its Permanent Defence Agreement with Canada, and other relations with the South American republics. Britain had its undertakings too, including its twenty-year 'Treaty of Collaboration and Mutual Assistance with Soviet Russia'. In Churchill's view, 'Special associations between members of the United Nations which have no aggressive point against any other country, which harbour no design incompatible with the Charter of the United Nations, far from being harmful, are beneficial and, as I believe, indispensable.'

Drawing the Line

'Your palette is keyed too high', so Mrs Dean Acheson would tell Churchill at a British Embassy dinner when he got back to Washington on 7 March.[15] She was criticizing the paintings he had made while staying in Florida during the weeks before his Fulton visit. The same tendency was surely also evident in the Fulton oration.

Churchill portrayed the post-war world as if it were a landscape in thrall to a dramatic and unpredictable weather system. Great beams of sunlight broke in to promise a future in which 'the essential brotherhood of man' would be established. Yet, Churchill had no sooner sketched the radiant prospect of a coming age of peace and benignly harnessed science, than he raised the dismal 'shadow' that had 'fallen upon the scenes so lately lighted by the Allied victory'. The atom bomb certainly provoked anxiety, but it was a different development that threatened to take the shine off Churchill's 'temple of peace', and to pull the emerging world back into a darkly realized study of wire, bunkers, and grinding war machines.

The starting point was that 'Nobody knows what Soviet Russia and its Communist international organization intends to do in the immediate future, or what are the limits, if any, to their expansive and proselytising tendencies.' Churchill hedged his point with diplomatic utterances, paying tribute to the bravery of the Russian people and hailing Stalin over the air waves as 'my wartime comrade'. Yet while welcoming Russia to 'her rightful place among the leading nations of the world' and recognizing her need for security on her western frontiers, it remained Churchill's 'duty' to declare that Stalin's Soviet Union was now a cause for alarm.

It was at this point that Churchill launched into the epoch-making passage that had not appeared in advance copies of his text, and seems likely to have been added on the train from Washington:[16]

> From Stettin in the Baltic to Trieste in the Adriatic, an iron curtain has descended across the Continent. Behind that line lie all the capitals of the ancient states of Central and Eastern Europe. Warsaw, Berlin, Prague, Vienna, Budapest, Belgrade, Bucharest and Sofia, all these famous cities and the populations around them lie in what I must call the Soviet sphere, and all are subject in one form or another, not only to Soviet influence but to a very high and, in some cases, increasing measure of control from Moscow. Athens alone— Greece with its immortal glories—is free to decide its future at an election under British, American and French observation.

Stettin (Szczecin), on the river Oder, was indeed just inside Poland's new western border, as decided at Yalta and Potsdam. Yet as it loomed in the opening sentence of this famous declaration, the iron curtain was still largely a poetic structure, which owed the route of its descent as much to rhyme as to any precise consideration of geography. Secured by a clatter of 'T's to the north and a gentler association of 'R's to the south, it had yet to approach the beach at Priwall, some 250 kilometres west of Stettin, where the fences and 'control strip' would actually touch the Baltic once the East German authorities decided to seal their frontier with the West in May 1952.

It was, by this account, Stalin who had lowered the 'iron curtain' across Europe and yet it was Churchill who now drew the line, insisting that this antithetical new 'fact' must be faced ('our difficulties and dangers will not be removed by closing our eyes to them'). On the other side, peoples were being isolated, previously 'very small' Communist parties were being elevated into power and, in Poland particularly, 'millions of Germans on a scale grievous and undreamed-of' were suffering mass expulsions from their homes. Police governments were being consolidated in every East European state, except in Czechoslovakia, which at that time still clung to its threatened democracy. A year previously, Churchill had warned the British House of Commons that the people in these lands were ruled by fear of the 'knock on the door'; and there had been further alarms during the course of his American visit. In conquered Germany, the American and British armies had withdrawn, sometimes to a depth of 150 miles, along a front 400 miles long, to allow their Russian allies to occupy areas as previously agreed. And the Soviet government was now trying to 'build up a pro-Communist Germany in their areas'. This, as Churchill remarked, was certainly not 'the Liberated Europe we fought to build up. Nor is it one which contains the essentials of permanent peace.'

Churchill identified 'further causes for anxiety' in events taking place 'in front of the iron curtain which lies across Europe'. The Communist Party loomed in Italy, even though hampered by having to support Tito's Yugoslavian claims to former Italian territory in the Adriatic. France remained weak, and, like other countries both in Europe and the Far East, was threatened by 'Communist fifth columns', which 'work in complete unity and absolute obedience to the directions they receive from the Communist centre' and 'constitute a growing challenge and peril to Christian civilization'. These were, as Churchill pronounced, 'sombre facts for anyone to have to recite on the morrow of a victory gained by so much splendid comradeship in arms and in the cause of freedom and democracy; but we should be most unwise not to face them squarely while time remains'.

Having completed his survey of the 'haggard' world, and compared the prevailing sense of beaten gloom to the 'high hopes' that had prevailed at the time of the Treaty of Versailles (1919), Churchill went on to 'repulse the idea that a new war is inevitable; still more that it is imminent'. The Soviet leaders wanted 'the fruits of war and the indefinite expansion of their power and doctrines', but they did not crave war itself. Like George Kennan in his 'Long Telegram' of two weeks earlier, Churchill concluded that 'our Russian friends and allies' admire nothing so much as strength.

It only remained for Churchill to reassure his American listeners about the 'abiding power of the British Empire and Commonwealth'. It was true that Britain was then sadly reduced, growing only half its own food supply and experiencing considerable difficulty in 'restarting our industries and export trade after six years of passionate war effort'. Churchill avoided any mention of Britain's requested loan from America, or of the 'socialism' of Attlee's new Labour government, the thought of which had prevented a significant section of American opinion from supporting Britain's request. But he insisted that the British Empire would survive 'these dark years of privation', and become a major force in defence of the 'causes which you and we espouse'. 'If the population of the English-speaking Commonwealths be added to that of the United States, with all that such co-operation implies in the air, on the sea, all over the globe, and in science and in industry, and in moral force, there will be no quivering, precarious balance of power to offer its temptation to ambition or adventure.' This 'overwhelming assurance of security' was what Churchill meant by 'The Sinews of Peace'.

Reception: from Shaw to Shenandoah

After the speech, honorary degrees were gratefully conferred on Truman and Churchill. The latter also received a gold watch, presented by Westminster College's Presbyterian professor of philosophy. Described as a 'kindly, bewhiskered old gentleman who walks with a jaunty step over Fulton streets', 'Danny' Gage had been at the college for sixty-five years, first as a student and then as a teacher of Bible theology. 'I don't believe in any of this so-called liberalism,' he had earlier told the *Fulton Daily Sun-Gazette*: 'You may have your own theories of life, but there can be no divergence from the moral code.' He now commended Churchill as the man who had done more than any other to prevent 'the world-wide crash of Democracies, the break-up of liberal institutions' and to stop mankind from sinking into 'the deep mire of fathomless moral depravity'. As for the watch, 'in many ways it reminds me of you. In the first place, it is pure gold. Its smooth success in its movements is due to the fact that there are within it some precious jewels. It keeps abreast with the times. It is full of good works and its hands are ever busy.'

There was more along those lines, but Fulton was by now shrinking back into itself. The wireless transmitters had been switched off, and nobody in the wider world was listening. The man whom the Missouri School for the Deaf had honoured with the title 'Signmaker of the Century' on account of his famous V-sign, was preparing to quit too: satisfied, as he would declare on the train back to Washington DC, that he had delivered 'the most important speech of my career'.[17]

Brigadier General Harry H. Vaughan estimated that 'Our town of Fulton will not be back to normal before mid-summer'[18] but the world's press was hardly willing to wait. A habitual scourge of the Midwest, the *Baltimore Sun* printed a mocking cartoon of Fulton on the morning after Churchill launched the 'Iron Curtain'. Captioned 'The Captains and the Kings Depart', it showed a scruffy old hick standing among discarded newspapers in an empty street, corncob pipe stuffed firmly back in his mouth as he watches a car escape from a small town that has already reverted to dismal obscurity.

On the wider stage, meanwhile, Churchill's speech went on to make the huge 'stir' he and Truman had anticipated.[19] His advocacy of a 'special relationship' between Britain and America drew some support in the United States, especially on the East Coast. It was also denounced as a barely disguised act of aggression. Critics feared that the proposed military alliance would exacerbate difficulties with the Soviet Union and compromise America's democracy by, in the words of the *Boston Globe,* making it 'heir to the evils of a collapsing colonialism'.[20] The *Chicago Sun* rejected Churchill's 'poisonous doctrines';[21] and a similar line was taken by the eminent columnist and former war correspondent Walter Lippmann, who insisted that America's interests were not the same as those of the British Empire. The Nobel Prize-winning left-wing novelist Pearl Buck described Churchill's intervention as a 'catastrophe' that only brought war nearer.

In Britain, the elderly Irish dramatist George Bernard Shaw, also a seasoned pacifist and 'friend' of the Soviet Union, declared it 'nothing short of a declaration of war on Russia' and a return to 'the old balance of power policy'.[22] In France, the prospect of the English-speaking peoples achieving a 'common nationality'[23] was dryly noted, along with the fact that it appeared to be 'the fate of France to be dragged mercilessly at the heels of Great Power policy'. In South Africa, Churchill was strongly supported by the leader of the Re-United National Party, Dr Daniel Francois Malan: while he wasted no time in identifying Russia as the main enemy, this rising Afrikaner champion of apartheid foresaw 'grave internal troubles' in the event of a war, since, as he added in an opportunistic phrase that identified Churchill's iron curtain with the colour-line, 'Communism was spreading among non-Europeans'.[24] In London, *The Times* was respectfully worried by Churchill's presentation of Western democracy and Soviet Communism as 'irreconcilable opposites dividing or attempting to divide, the world between them to-day'.[25] Insisting that 'it would be an assumption of despair to hold that they are doomed to a fatal contest', it declared that 'intermediate' forms of government were surely possible, and that the two systems had much to learn from one another (Russia could learn about individual liberty from the West, while itself providing useful lessons on the subject of 'economic and social planning').

In Britain as elsewhere in the emerging Western bloc, many on the left were outraged. The *New Statesman,* edited by Kingsley Martin, condemned 'Mr. Churchill's Defeatism', insisting that Britain and America should open the military bases they proposed to share around the world to Russia, thereby creating a 'real International force'.[26] Over one hundred predominantly Labour MPs united to censure the speech in the House of Commons. Such was the strength of feeling that, within a few days, both Prime Minister Attlee and President Truman had tactfully dissociated themselves from Churchill's views.

As the storm reverberated around the world, the people at Westminster College tried to maintain their connection with the man who had unleashed it from their gymnasium. Dr McCluer wrote to Churchill, care of the British Embassy in Washington, thanking him profusely and telling him that Westminster, which had once been described as 'a great small college', was certainly 'the greater because of your visit'. Churchill replied that 'the ceremony and the warm welcome I received in your midst will ever be a living and happy memory for me'. McCluer then procured yet another home-cured ham and shipped it to Churchill at the Waldorf-Astoria Hotel in New York, together with detailed instructions on its preparation, carefully written out by Mrs McCluer. He also arranged for a lithograph to be sent, asking Colonel Frank Clarke at the British Embassy to get Churchill to sign and return it so that it could be displayed as 'a permanent reminder' of his visit. The ham was duly acknowledged on Churchill's behalf, but the lithograph was reported lost in the avalanche of mail that arrived at the embassy after the speech (it was suggested that replacement copies should be sent to Churchill at his private address in London).

Churchill's secretary, Miss Nina Sturdee, appears to have managed rather better with the letters and telegrams that poured into the Waldorf-Astoria Hotel. She fended off impossible invitations, politely declining influential Wall Street bankers who wanted to take Churchill to dinner at the Knickerbocker Club (and could hardly believe his failure to answer their first letter of invitation).[27] She was gentle in declining the British war correspondent, William Courtenay, whom she had earlier met at Fulton ('It was such a pleasure to sit next to an Englishman at the Ceremony the other day, amid so many strangers'), and who now wished to come over to the Waldorf-Astoria to show Churchill his films of the war in the Pacific.[28] A simple acknowledgement would suffice for Mr Frank A. Bueno from Brooklyn who only wanted details of 'those famous, long Havanas we all associate with you',[29] and also for the many others who wrote to praise Churchill, or to remind him, with the help of old newspaper cuttings, of the dark days in 1940, when 'All civilization trembled—but Churchill did not.'[30] More elaborate letters of thanks were despatched to a respectful wine merchant who had presented Churchill with a magnum of Hine brandy from 1870, and also to the Celanese Corporation of America, which declared itself honoured to deliver three dozen sets of underwear to Churchill's hotel as ordered and, perhaps aware that Churchill's spending power was constrained by Britain's then very tight currency restrictions, absolutely refused to accept any payment at all.[31]

Back in Fulton, 'Bullet' McCluer had many envelopes to open too. Congratulations poured in from former students, local businessmen, and colleagues in charge of other colleges in the region. Those who had not been able to attend the event in Fulton commended the broadcast version ('one of the greatest thrills I've had since the invention of radio'), declaring the quality of reception 'perfect' or 'smooth as silk' as if that too had been McCluer's brilliant doing.[32] Churchill's words of warning had sounded just 'perfect' in the Central Shenandoah Valley in Virginia and also in Osceoloa, Arkansas, but reception had been more difficult in the Dominican Republic. Writing from the Hotel Jaragua, a former student declared 'Couldn't get much of the first half because of Spanish interpellation, but the rest was clear and your ringing presentation fully equal to the great occasion.'

Some correspondents remained stiffly isolationist, suspecting that the American republic would be deformed and its democratic principles betrayed if it entered Churchill's proposed 'special relationship' with the decadent and dying British Empire. A few days before the speech, L. Stahlbehl, a Missouri resident of Bavarian extraction, had warned McCluer that 'The British government has lived on world exploitation for centuries. They are in greatest measure responsible for many wars and misery from which the whole world suffers today.' A different objection was expressed by Mrs Ernest L Ohle, who wrote from University City in Missouri declaring 'distinct shock' at the fact that 'a Christian College' should have given a platform to a manoeuvre designed to make the British loan more palatable to the American people, 'and thus prepare the way for further loans. … I fear Westminster College will lose far more that it will gain by its use for propaganda purposes, and regret it exceedingly.'

There were ruder communications too, which Dr McCluer's secretary stuffed into a file labelled 'crank letters'.[33] One proposed that 'Any "drunk" could have done as well as he': 'I never saw a more disgusting personality to think the American people are so gullible to swallow anything English & "whitewash" such a piece of humanity'. Another fierce teetotaller set his sights on Truman rather than Churchill, denouncing the president as a 'boozer' who set a bad example to the young people of the nation and should never have been indulged by a Christian Church. Drink was one issue, to be sure, yet it should not be allowed to eclipse 'the murderous, destructive record of European Christians and their corporate allies in America'. It was, so McCluer was informed, 'in poor grace' that the outstanding leader of the western European 'life-liners' presumed to condemn the New Russia as 'a growing challenge and peril to Christian civilization'. The American 'life-line' must be withdrawn, and the underlying problem that was Europe should be solved by 'migrating their overcrowded number, westwardly, or to self-sufficient continental areas of the world'. Writing from Walnut Creek, California, S. Christensen was blunter still: 'Tell ol' England and her big business men to blow their damn heads off. ... Loan them no moneys and force them to return all lend-lease materials.' From this point of view, Churchill was no more than a representative of British greed: come here with 'super sales' talk aimed at extracting the 'Gift loan' out of America. They want 'more and more and more'.

In general, however, McCluer's letters appear to confirm the *New York Times*'s judgement that 'Fulton liked Churchill and Churchill liked Fulton'.[34] Mr E. J. Mudd, vice-president of the Mercantile-Commerce Bank and Trust Company in Saint Louis, had come home 'with the definite impression we had heard a most memorable speech by one of the world's great men'. Ray Nolte from the Nolte Brokerage Company, told McCluer that 'your old title of Bullet is worn out and I would say that you are now a "Rocket", when you can reach over to London and pick one of the best men out of Parliament. You certainly are a whiz.'

The critical reaction to Churchill's speech remained a matter of concern even to those inclined to count it as further tribute to the nerve of McCluer and his little college. As a lawyer from Kansas City wrote, 'It seemed to me that some of the newspapers misconstrued, to some extent anyway, some of Mr. Churchill's language and that they used headlines that were not borne out by the words he used.' H. Spencer Edmunds, of the First Presbyterian Church, wrote on 16 March remarking that 'I enjoyed Churchill's speech, albeit I did not agree with a part of his thesis. It sounded better than it looked in print.'

Edmunds went on to say 'I was in New York day before yesterday, and several men on Broadway were handing out the enclosed leaflets. I got a kick out of this. "The show" in Fulton, Missouri, reverberates on Broadway in New York!' Headed 'Do you want another war?', the leaflet, issued by the National Council of American-Soviet Friendship, invited those who wanted 'PEACE' to attend a protest meeting to be held on Monday, 18 March in Madison Square Park. It derided Churchill as a 'bankrupt statesman' who, having been 'discarded by the British people', had come here 'to sell a program he dared not propose at home. He comes here as a guest of the United States to threaten war against our Soviet ally.'

That argument was made in more detail by another leaflet that found its way to Westminster College from the West Coast. Printed by the American Communist Party in San Francisco and entitled 'Alarm: World War III in the making!', the tract accused Churchill of peddling 'outright lies' about the Soviet Union in order to create a hostile Anglo-American alliance. Britain and America had been made safe by immense Soviet sacrifices at the battle of Stalingrad in 1942, but now here was Churchill proving that 'the old plot is back'. Churchill's appeal for a 'special relationship' was really 'a joint American-British imperialism, racial in its appeal, for what he says in effect is that the English-speaking peoples must dominate the world'.

As far as the authors of this tight little Stalinist pamphlet were concerned, a resurgent anti-Communist 'plot' could clearly be detected in the series of revelations that had recently filled the capitalist press. Canada's prime minister, Mr MacKenzie King, announced a spy plot intended to gain the secret of the atomic bomb for Soviet Russia.[35] Herbert Hoover had been asked by Truman to guide food distribution in Europe: since he had done the same after the Great War, this request proved that food was once again to be used as a weapon (It had been 'Apples for the unemployed in 1931, and apples for the starving people of Europe in 1919 IF they let him mark their ballots for them'). The Vatican had made thirty-two new cardinals in ceremonies described as 'a worldwide mobilization against Communism'. On 26 February the financier and presidential adviser Bernard Baruch visited Churchill in Florida, and then attacked Communism in a speech. On 27 February Senator Vandenberg delivered an anti-Communist blast in the Senate, and the day after that Secretary of State Byrnes made a similar pitch in a speech before the Overseas Press Club. On 1 March, John Foster Dulles, who, like Vandenberg, had been an American representative to the United Nations Organization, pitched the same line in Philadelphia. On 3 March, the former US ambassador Joseph Kennedy, derided as 'the American Firster', called for a loan to Britain as a 'bulwark against communism'. Add Churchill's speech to this stiffening list, and you had incontrovertible proof of a 'Holy crusade against communism—exactly the cover behind which Hitler built World War II'.

3

Prophecy and Hindsight

Seven months after the day that would be remembered as 'Fulton's finest hour', 'Bullet' McCluer was to be found in his house playing a tape of the oration to Churchill's son Randolph, who declared his father's wisdom and, indeed, moderation, to be already proven by subsequent events.[1] Winston Churchill himself would never return to Missouri. Yet, as the Cold War hardened, Fulton would exploit the memory of his fleeting visit as the rock on which to refound itself as a site of world history.

Over the years to come many world leaders visited Westminster College to lecture in Churchill's wake, joining a steady procession of distinguished visiting speakers that would include former colleagues of Churchill, his doctor and literary assistant, and the many, often British, historians who would be invited to pay tribute at the great chronicler and statesman's American shrine. Harry S. Truman returned, by then a former president, to give the Green Lecture in 1954. He was followed by Vice-President Hubert Humphrey (1967), former president Gerald Ford (1977), and the former British prime minister Edward Heath, who passed through in 1982. In 1988 George Bush Senior came here to inform the people of Fulton that the Iron Curtain was 'rusting' and that 'shafts of light from the western side, our side, the free and prosperous side, are piercing the gloom of failure and despair on the other side'. Margaret Thatcher spoke on the fiftieth anniversary of Churchill's speech in March 1996 (it is rumoured that President Clinton declined the invitation to join her in Fulton for a second double-act), and Lech Walesa made the pilgrimage from Poland in 1998.

The first physical memorials to Churchill's visit consisted of a lost litho-graph and the modest little plaque still fastened to Westminster College's gymnasium, but greater monuments were to come. Since the late 1960s, indeed, the Corinthian columns preserved from Westminster College's burned administration building have had to compete with a much grander

classical structure. Built by Sir Christopher Wren to replace an earlier church
destroyed by the Great Fire of 1666, the church of St Mary the Virgin,
started its life at Aldermanbury in the City of London. Gutted by a Nazi
incendiary bomb during the Blitz of 1940, it lingered on for twenty years
as a gaunt ruin—deprived of its parish and unwanted by London planners
preparing to unleash their new traffic and development schemes. In 1961,
the year in which the Berlin Wall was built by the East German authorities,
the then president of Westminster College, Dr Robert L. D. Davidson, conceived the apparently impossible idea that one of London's bombed and
redundant Wren churches—recently featured in *Life* magazine—would suit
Fulton's desire for a grander tribute to Churchill's prophetic Iron Curtain
speech.[2] Appropriate enquiries were made and, by the end of the year, the
remains of St Mary the Virgin had been presented to Westminster College
by the Diocese of London. Cleansed of soot and carefully numbered, its
stones were then crated up and transported to Fulton, 4,500 miles away.
British newspapers may have scoffed at this example of America's 'senti-
mental extravagance' but not Churchill, who was informed of the project in
1962 and declared himself 'honoured' by the 'imaginative concept'.[3]

The migrant church that now towers over the Westminster College campus is by no means exactly the one that stood for nearly three hundred years
in the City of London. It has been reinforced to withstand Missouri's storms,
refloored with Indiana limestone, and completed with carved wood salvaged
from other redundant London churches. Its twelve Wren columns stand on
new foundations and are no longer expected to bear the weight of the roof
above them. The crypt has given way to a considerable 'undercroft' housing the Winston Churchill Memorial and Library: complete with museum,
galleries, offices, and the Lady Clementine Spencer-Churchill Reading
Room—a peculiar cross between a wood-panelled country house library,
a Cabinet room, and a windowless command bunker. Despite these varia-
tions, Fulton's has been hailed as the purest Wren church in existence, largely
thanks to the fact that later Victorian wall tablets and other additions were
not reinstated when it was rebuilt in Missouri. At the rehallowing ceremony
on 7 May 1969, Churchill's daughter, Lady Mary Soames, even traced the
'special relationship' into the surrounding Missouri landscape: it reminded
her 'of our Cotswold region in England with its lovely, rolling green hills'.

Bordered on one side by a narrow 'English' memorial garden, the church
of St Mary the Virgin is attended on the other by a bronze statue of Winston
Churchill walking with a stick and perhaps missing the mid-century London

fog a little. Installed in 1971, this addition to Fulton's Churchill memorial was created by Franta Belsky, a Czech sculptor who became a British citizen after serving as a gunner with the Allies in the Second World War. Beyond it stands another transported fragment of Europe: a length of the Berlin Wall, placed here in its new manifestation as a sculpture by Winston Churchill's granddaughter, Edwina Sandys. Conceived during the great events of 1989, the work consists of eight 4-foot-wide sections which had once stood near the Brandenburg Gate. Bright and colourful graffiti adorns one side (the west) while the other is merely drab and grey, revealing East Germany as, in the words of the artist, 'the prison it was … It's almost like you're in a black-and-white world, then you're in glorious technicolour.'[4] That magical one-way transit is suggested by two human-shaped holes in the wall, one male, the other female. Cut through the concrete, these heroic Popeye-like breaches convert Fulton's relic of totalitarian confinement (kindly donated by the outgoing East German authorities) into a work of art entitled 'Breakthrough'.

Further explanation of Edwina Sandys's sculpture was provided by former president Ronald Reagan, who came here to dedicate the work on 9 November 1990: 'Here, on a grassy slope between the Church of St. Mary the Virgin and Champ Auditorium, a man and a woman break through the wall and symbolically demolish whatever remaining barriers stand in the way of international peace and the brotherhood of nations.'[5] Recalling how, in June 1987, he had stood in West Berlin and called on President Gorbachev to 'Tear down this wall', Reagan now offered a generously non-partisan interpretation of its fall at the hands of the people, who had turned out not to be so abject or sheeplike after all.

Avoiding reference to the 'evil empire' he had himself denounced so vehemently, Reagan honoured the sacrifices made by 'brave men and women on both sides of the iron curtain' so that 'we might inhabit a world without barriers'. In dedicating 'this magnificent sculpture', he commended the future to the young Americans of Westminster College: 'may we dedicate ourselves to hastening the day when all God's children live in a world without walls. That would be the greatest empire of all.' Mockers might deride him for his 'mysticism', but Reagan sensed some 'divine plan' in the fact that America was placed 'between the two great oceans to be found by people from any corner of the earth—people who had an extra ounce of desire for freedom and some extra courage to rise up and leave their families, their relatives, their friends, their nation and come here to eventually make this country.'

For Reagan, Churchill's Fulton oration had been 'a firebell in the night, a Paul Revere warning that tyranny was once more on the march'. He was, however, reluctant to follow Churchill by conceding 'the brotherhood of man' to the United Nations. He preferred America as 'the one spot on earth where we have the brotherhood of man' and concluded, under a huge blue Missouri sky, that 'maybe one day boundaries all over the world will disappear as people cross boundaries and find out that, yes, there is a brotherhood of man and this world can become that brotherhood of man in every corner'.

As far as Fulton was concerned, the circle of history that Churchill had opened in 1946 was formally closed on 6 May 1992, when Mikhail Gorbachev, former president of the dissolved USSR, delivered a speech entitled 'The River of Time and the Imperative of Action'. Having started the fourth day of his thirteen-day American tour with a speedy visit to a veggieburger plant in Illinois, the former president of the now dissolved USSR flew to Missouri in a borrowed Boeing 727 emblazoned with the words 'FORBES Capitalist Tool'. The architect of perestroika arrived at Westminster College to find an estimated 15,000 people assembled by the grassy slope to hear him address the world from the podium used by Churchill, this time placed directly in front of the 'Breakthrough' sculpture.

Gorbachev started by commending Edwina Sandys's 'remarkably expressive' work for conveying 'the drama of the "Cold War"' and the 'irrepressible human striving to penetrate the barriers of alienation and confrontation'. He then insisted that the post-war opportunity to establish a new basis for relations between the USSR and the West had been lost in the 1940s, due to errors on both sides. The Stalinist leadership of the USSR had 'committed a major error in equating the victory of democracy over fascism with the victory of socialism and aiming to spread socialism throughout the world'. The USA, meanwhile, had been quite mistaken about 'the probability of open Soviet military aggression', and wrong, therefore, to have unleashed a nuclear arms race. Both sides had failed to produce a strategic response to the challenges of the moment, and had instead taken refuge in a spurious rhetoric of 'love for peace'.

Addressing Westminster College on the fiftieth anniversary of Churchill's speech in March 1996, Margaret Thatcher would insist that the end of the Cold War marked 'complete victory for the west'. Gorbachev, however, repudiated partisan polemics, and not just because he wanted to place his own policies of 'Perestroika and the New Thinking' at the root of the changes in the Soviet bloc. He attributed the lifting of the Iron Curtain to the triumph of common sense, reason, and democracy over a bipolar scheme that was 'becoming slowly congealed and leading us to destruction. It was a shattering of the vicious circle into which we had driven ourselves.'

Ghosts at the Table

Revered as a founding charter in Fulton, Churchill's renamed Iron Curtain speech would be proclaimed as the start of things in the wider world too. In 1986, the historian Fraser Harbutt confirmed that Churchill's Fulton oration had been the carefully prepared 'first step'[6] on a path that led to the Truman doctrine, the Marshall Plan, the policy of 'containment', and the formation of NATO.

It would be recognized as an inaugural moment on both sides of its division. In the West, it would be celebrated as the brilliant diagnosis of an unflinching 'man of the century' who, having refused to appease Nazism, was now prepared to look another evil empire in the eye.[7] In the Soviet bloc, as Gorbachev confirmed when he spoke at Fulton in 1992, Churchill's speech was also singled out as 'the formal declaration of the "Cold War"'. That was Stalin's argument initially, but it persisted up to and beyond the fall of the Berlin Wall in 1989. Revealing his own understanding to be still strongly shaped by that Soviet ideology, Gorbachev proclaimed, emphatically, that 'This was indeed the first time the words, "Iron Curtain," were pronounced.'

There can be no doubt either that Churchill launched the phrase into wide circulation, or that it would quickly become established as a political metaphor all over the world. The Iron Curtain was a widely recognized European reality long before the East German government started closing their border with the West in 1952. Twinned with the 'bamboo curtain' established around China after Mao's victory in 1949, it soon found its American equivalents too. These would include the 'little iron curtain' which Louis Budenz lowered around the offices of the American Communist Party at 50 East Thirteenth Street in New York City when, as a former member, he unmasked the CPUSA as a Soviet 'fifth column', a conspiracy and a threat to American democracy.[8] The 'gold curtain' was named by Katharine Bruce Glasier, the so-called 'grandmother of British Socialism', who saw this wall of gleaming dollars raised up around the USA as she looked west from her

flowery garden in the English Pennines in June 1948.[9] Soon enough, there
would also be the 'cactus curtain': placed around the Mexican imagination,
so the artist José Luis Cuevas insisted, by the isolationist tactics of Diego
Rivera and other exponents of the left-wing muralist movement.[10]

And yet, as the polarized perspectives of the Cold War themselves recede
into history, it becomes increasingly apparent that, while the post-war Iron
Curtain may have seemed alarmingly novel as it came sliding down in 1946,
it was actually made of familiar historical materials. Churchill had gazed
into the future at Fulton, but he did so with an eye swollen with hindsight.
The Fulton oration was effective as 'a brilliant exercise in political prophecy',[11] yet it could only be so because it also reflected an abiding preoccupation with the recent past. As Churchill said of the rise of Hitler, 'Last
time I saw it all coming and I cried aloud to my own fellow countrymen
and to the world, but no one paid any attention.' In grandiose moments,
Churchill was certainly inclined to cast himself as the hero of history, but
he also knew how heavily the past and its responsibilities weighed on that
post-war moment.

Stalin too looked back in his furious reaction to the Fulton oration. Not
content with driving his tanks further into Iran (thereby sharpening Western
fears that he was heading for Turkey and Iraq as well as Tehran), he accused
Churchill of issuing a 'call to war' and, in the same interview published in
Pravda on 14 March 1946, denounced his proposed Anglo-American 'special
relationship' as a race theory like those espoused by Hitler.[12]

It was Churchill, Stalin recalled, who had 'raised the alarm and organised' the Allied Intervention against Russia after the Bolshevik revolution
of October 1917. On 11 March 1946, *Pravda* had advanced the same criticism, condemning Churchill as 'the sharpshooter and standard bearer' of
the anti-Soviet campaign of 1919–20, who was now trying to destroy the
United Nations Organization by restoring 'the formula of a "cordon sanitaire" against Russia'.[13]

The same historical reference point was invoked by the English-speaking
left: the American *People's Daily World* accused Churchill of promoting 'the
new encirclement' being used to isolate the Soviet Union by the assembled
forces of 'world imperialism'.[14] In an article entitled 'Churchill's Speech
Divides Britain', Harold Laski, chairman of the British Labour Party and
a charismatic socialist professor of political science at the London School
of Economics, also declared that the Churchill who spoke at Fulton 'has
become very like the Churchill who in 1919-20 was hag-ridden by the

spectre of advancing communism. He hates it so much that, man of action as he is, he begins to think at once in terms of the strategy necessary to its defeat.' Laski was in no doubt that 'Such urging of an Anglo-American military alliance, together with the retention of the secret of the atomic bomb, would exacerbate every nervous tension in the Russian mind.'[15]

The memory of the failed Allied intervention on the side of White anti-Bolshevik forces in the Russian Civil War of 1918–20 may silently have informed Churchill's insistence that Britain and America should not interfere forcibly (at least not 'at this time'). Yet the Fulton oration also contains explicit references to that earlier moment of post-war crisis. Churchill recalled his close friendship with David Lloyd George, the British Liberal prime minister at the time, and also his own concern, as a government minister in Lloyd George's War Cabinet, about the harsh reparations policy imposed on Germany and the defeated Central Powers under the Treaty of Versailles. His memory of the League of Nations, founded by the victors at the end of the Great War, directly informed his cautious commendation of its replacement, the United Nations, favoured to the extent that this international body might replace the 'quivering, precarious balance of power' against which Churchill warned at Fulton.

Against this background, it is not surprising that the speeches Churchill gave in the two post-war intervals of 1918–20 and 1945–6 should bear such a striking resemblance. The 'title deeds of freedom' that should be placed in every cottage home, as declared in Fulton, were surely direct descendants of those invoked in November 1919. Speaking just three days before Prime Minister Lloyd George revealed that Britain's Coalition government was abandoning its failed military intervention against Red Russia, Churchill had given the contrary message, insisting of the Bolsheviks that 'I cannot believe that the title deeds of national Russia will ever rest durably or recognisedly in those hands'.[16]

Churchill's advocacy in Fulton of an armed Anglo-American alliance recalls the arguments he advanced at a dinner hosted in January 1919 by the American Society in London to mark the changeover of American ambassadors in London. Churchill may not have used the phrase 'special relationship' when he addressed that earlier gathering at the Savoy Hotel, but he did speak of the urgent task facing the 'English Speaking nations'. He also commended President Woodrow Wilson, saying that, by bringing America into the recently finished war, he had 'begun again the common history of all the great branches of the English speaking family which had been interrupted but must now always flow forward together'.[17] Just as he would later do at Fulton, the younger Churchill had insisted that the looming threat of Bolshevism necessitated the continuation, rather than the peaceable dissolution, of the Anglo-American alliance: 'Indeed, the circumstances of the present time should excite constant anxiety and vigilance. It would be vain and idle to cry "peace", leaving unsettled all the causes which might light up again and spread conflagration.'

As in 1946, he had gone on to pay his respects to the new international body (the League of Nations) that promised peace and global security, while also carefully hedging his tribute with the insistence that 'the victorious nations had the responsibility for the guidance of the world', and that the countries whose leaders were then in Paris thrashing out the Treaty of Versailles should 'hold themselves with all their forces, solid, military, naval, political, and economic, braced in every country ready to enforce the decisions which would be reached in Paris, and make them effective for prolonged period for the benefit of the great mass of the human race'. He had reiterated his point a month later, in February 1919, when, in the course of chairing a dinner of the English-Speaking Union, he warned of a sagging of political will in the post-war world—a 'great relaxation',[18] as he called it—and then proceeded, just as he would at Fulton in 1946, to emphasize both the opportunity and the dangers of that post-war moment: 'This is the moment: if we lose it or abuse it, all the prodigies that have been achieved in the field will avail us very little.'

The memory of these early twentieth-century struggles hovered over Churchill during his days in New York. It was a history he had in common with many of his American friends, including the financier and statesman Bernard M. Baruch, with whom he met several times during his visit, and who hosted a party for him in New York on 18 March. They talked about the American loan to Britain, which they had discussed the previous year, when Baruch visited Britain and spent weekends with Churchill at Chequers. Yet their friendship, and also the shape of their deliberations, went back much further.

Baruch had first come into contact with Churchill during the Great War: as chairman of America's War Industries Board, he had exchanged many cables with Britain's then minister of munitions. The two men had met in Paris, during the negotiations for the Treaty of Versailles. In France as an assistant to President Wilson, and also an American representative on the Economics and Reparations Commission, Baruch had good reason to remember an occasion when he and Churchill were walking in the Bois de Boulogne. Being concerned to ease the punitive spirit in which France and Britain were then approaching the question of reparations from Germany, he was pleased when, at a salient moment in their conversation, Churchill indicated a greater threat than the defeated Central Powers. Pointing his walking stick to the east, 'where the Red revolution had erupted', the Briton had remarked: 'Russia. Russia. That's where the weather is coming from.'[19] Churchill was still gesturing towards those eastern stormclouds as he conversed with Baruch in March 1946: using the fear of Soviet aggression to break through his friend's reservations about the huge loan Britain was now hoping to secure from America.

Various American correspondents also evoked the memory of that earlier age in their attempts to tug at the visiting British leader's sleeve. Among the letters that arrived at the Waldorf-Astoria Hotel, was one from John Brown, an Americanized Briton who had worked on the British leader's election campaign when he won Dundee for the Liberal Party in 1908, and who now wrote to remind him of the great 'hullaballoo' put up by protesting suffragettes when his victory was announced.[20] Earlier in the year, Churchill had received repeated supplications from the elderly American Charles Henry Davis, who wanted him to stay on his estate on Cape Cod (he boasted that his mansion had no fewer than twenty-one external doors, and guaranteed that Churchill would be free to wander the grounds undisturbed). Identifying himself as a founder trustee of the World Government Foundation, established at the time of the Paris Peace Conference of 1919, Davis hoped that the visiting Briton would consent to be the guest of honour at a large hotel dinner where Davis would reveal the 'know-how' necessary to tame the threat of the atomic bomb.[21] His invitation failed, as did his rumoured plan to raise $2 million for an enormous statue to be mounted on the white cliffs of Dover (the proposed monstrosity would apparently have shown Churchill holding his cigar in a confident manner intended to echo that in which the Statue of Liberty brandishes her torch).[22]

Churchill steered clear of Davis and his embarrassing projects. He also disappointed the New York architect Edwin H. Denby, who had written in the hope of showing Churchill the place near the Manhattan Club where his American mother had been brought up, and also of talking with him about Victor Hugo, the French writer and republican who, in the years after the revolution of 1848, had dreamed of a peaceable future in which the 'United States of America' would cooperate with the 'United States of

Europe' to form the 'United States of the World'.[23] Advocated repeatedly by Hugo and rejected as 'erroneous' by Lenin in 1915,[24] the vision of a 'United States of Europe' had been espoused in Europe during the inter-war years,[25] and also by President Roosevelt as he prepared to depart for Yalta, where he would meet with Stalin and Churchill in 1945.[26] Churchill, who politely declined Denby's invitation, would make his own use of Hugo's phrase a few months later. In Zurich, on 19 September 1946, he would call for Germany and France to take the lead in creating a 'United States of Europe' in a speech that is sometimes claimed as anticipating the inauguration of the European Community.

Similar precedents can be found for the 'temple of peace', a phrase Churchill used at Fulton to name, and lightly mock, the newly established United Nations Organization. Consciously or not, he shared the expression with the late Frank B. Kellogg, the lawyer and Republican who had served both as an ambassador to Great Britain and as Secretary of State under President Coolidge. Together with the French foreign minister, Aristide Briand, Kellogg had been a leading exponent of the Pact of Paris, first signed in August 1928, in which eleven states undertook to forbid war as an instrument of national policy and to stipulate that international conflicts must be settled by peaceable means. In November 1929, Kellogg had visited England to collect an honorary degree from the University of Oxford. During his stay, he also spoke as guest of honour at a widely reported dinner of the Anglo-American Pilgrims Society, hailing the Pact of Paris (by this time proclaimed by more than sixty nations and recognized as a major initiative in international law), as 'the foundation on which will be erected the permanent temple of peace'.[27]

Historical memory would soon enough be stalking the 'iron curtain' too. The idea that Churchill had coined this phrase from scratch was quickly established on both sides of the global division, and further enforced by the undeniably new fact of nuclear weaponry. Within a couple of years of the Fulton oration, however, earlier usages were being listed by correspondents who used the pages of the London journal *Notes and Queries*[28] to tug at the coat-tails of a post-war Zeitgeist that was plainly determined to ignore them. More recently, historians have acknowledged this prehistory, quoting, and in some cases confidently (and also erroneously) ranking the earlier citations that can now be found in most dictionaries of quotations and picturesque expressions. Since the years of détente, it has become customary to suggest that Churchill 'popularized' the phrase, and gave it a new and more systematic meaning, even if he didn't exactly originate it. Yet there is a significant history here, and certainly not just a disconnected accumulation of utterances of a 'well-worn phrase'[29] that had yet to be applied to the field of international relations. If there was, as an increasing number of historians now suggest, a 'first Cold War' in the wake of the Bolshevik revolution of 1917,[30] there was certainly also a 'first iron curtain': a cultural and geopolitical reality that shaped and provided much of the material used in the version that would divide the world after 1946.

Churchill's Fulton oration may indeed have heralded a new era in international relations. However, it also signalled the resumption of an older one, in which Western leaders had not felt obliged to respect Soviet Russia as the ally it had become in the Grand Alliance of 1941. In this respect, Stalin and the loyal pamphleteers of the American Communist Party were right to suggest that something resembling 'the old plot' was back in play. With the polemical constraints of the Cold War now receding into history, the Fulton oration can be understood differently: not just as an inaugural moment around which a church and many statues, speeches, and other tributes have since been arrayed, but as the pivot of a longer history that was interrupted when Stalin joined the Allies in the war against Nazi Germany.

That said, Churchill, who was in the habit of writing history as well as playing a leading part in it,[31] was happy to take credit for the phrase. Just as his friend Bernard M. Baruch would wrongly claim to have 'introduced' the expression 'Cold War',[32] Churchill was by no means opposed to the idea that he had been the first to name the 'iron curtain'. In May 1951, he received a parcel containing a complimentary copy of Random House's new *American College Dictionary*. In an accompanying letter, the editor-in-chief, Mr Jess Stein, acknowledged that 'it has usually been suggested that the phrase "iron curtain" was originated by you'. However, there were, as Stein continued tactfully, 'a number of other theories about the origin of the phrase and I wonder, therefore, whether you recall having met the phrase prior to your first use of it'. When his private secretary asked for an answer, Churchill said 'No. I didn't hear of the phrase before—though everyone has heard of the "iron curtain" which descends in a theatre.'[33]

PART II

From Drury Lane to the Theatre of the West (1914–1918)

The iron curtain is at best a clumsy device. Its brief career is probably ended by the successful working of the light, elegant asbestos of Terry's Theatre, which would certainly check the progress of fire long enough to allow of the theatre being emptied.

'Terry's Theatre', *The Times,* 18 October 1887

Many people still refuse to believe that there are only two sides, that the only choice lies between absolute conformity to the one system or absolute conformity to the other. Call such people impractical if you will; but it would be wrong to treat their hopes as a matter for contempt.

Czeslaw Milosz, *The Captive Mind* (1953)

'No, the book
Which noticed how the wall-growths wave,'
said she,
'Was not by Ruskin.'
I said. 'Vernon Lee?'

Robert Browning, *Asolando* (1889)

4

First Call

On the evening of Friday, 24 February 1809, the principal actors and officers of the Theatre Royal, in London's Drury Lane, were dining in nearby Lincoln's Inn Fields. According to their music director, Michael Kelly, 'all was mirth and glee' when, at about eleven o'clock, their host stood up to propose 'Prosperity and Success to Drury Lane Theatre'. The guests were just raising their glasses when an actress burst in screaming that the theatre was ablaze. Rushing out into the square, they saw a fire so ferocious that it 'perfectly illuminated Lincoln's Inn Fields with the brightness of day'.[1]

Richard Brinsley Sheridan, the Irish dramatist and radical Whig politician who was also the Drury Lane Theatre's controlling shareholder, was not drinking with his theatrical colleagues that night. He was in the House of Commons, in Westminster, listening sceptically as the Conservative Foreign Secretary, Mr George Canning, defended his government against opposition demands for an inquiry into the shattering retreat of the British army recently sent, under Sir John Moore, to fight the French in Spain.

Canning managed to complete his justification of the government's conduct of war, but not without a growing sense of distraction. *Hansard* records that 'A cry of Fire! Fire! frequently interrupted the latter part of the hon. Secretary's speech,' and also that 'Mr. Sheridan in a low tone, stated across the table that Drury-lane theatre was on fire.'[2] Describing the interruption in a letter to George III, the Chancellor, Spencer Perceval, wrote that 'the immense blaze of light from the conflagration shone in at the windows of the House, as strongly as if it had been in the speaker's garden'.[3] Overwhelmed by curiosity, some members rushed out onto Westminster Bridge to look at this 'most tremendous and splendid sight'. The leader of the opposition proposed an adjournment but Sheridan declined, observing that 'whatever might be the extent of the individual calamity, he did not consider it of a nature worthy to interrupt their proceedings on so great a national question'.[4]

Theatrical engineering

Fire was an all too familiar hazard of the Georgian theatre. And not surprisingly of a stage that was lit by candles and oil lamp chandeliers, and which achieved its special effects with the help of volatile lightning machines, trays full of burning spirits, and considerable fireworks too.[5] As one contemporary witness pointed out, the London theatre seemed recently to have taken over a scourge that had previously fallen most heavily on sugar-bakers, linen-drapers, and printing offices.[6] The Pantheon, in Oxford Street, had burned in 1772, followed by the Haymarket opera house in 1789. Astley's Ampitheatre was twice gutted—first in August 1794, when it was still known as the Royal Saloon, and then again in 1803. The Royal Circus followed in 1805. Just five months before disaster struck at the Theatre Royal in Drury Lane, its only large-scale rival in London, the Covent Garden Theatre, had been engulfed with the loss of several lives, allegedly due to the negligence of a sleeping watchman.[7]

Sheridan had been well aware of the threat, and also of the justified nervousness of the London theatregoer. Indeed, his son's tutor recalls his quick-witted reaction on an earlier occasion when the scenery at the Drury Lane theatre caught fire. The audience was alarmed and 'in an instant the confusion would have been dreadful'. This time, however, the blaze had been suppressed, and an actor named Suett immediately rushed up to ask Sheridan whether he should tell the audience it had been successfully extinguished. Sheridan retaliated, 'You fool, don't mention the word "fire"; run and tell them that we have water enough to drown them all, and make a face.' The actor did as instructed and, instead of a fatal stampede for the doors, 'the house was calm in an instant, and was in a tumult of laughter only, at the strange grimaces of which Suett was such a master'.[8]

The Irish dramatist certainly had a lot to lose. In 1791, he had closed the dilapidated Drury Lane Theatre, built to a design by Sir Christopher Wren more than a century before, and set about replacing it with a new theatre by the architect Henry Holland—a 'perfect and magnificent' structure, as he promised would-be subscribers, in a development that would also include new taverns, coffee houses, shops, and residences.[9] The plans were approved by George III but the cost of the building turned out to be vastly in excess of the architect's initial estimate, and the new theatre had landed Sheridan with horrifying debts. Opened with considerable ceremony on 12 March

1794, it boasted the largest stage of any theatre in Europe, and a semicircular auditorium that could accommodate over 3,600 people.

The fact that Sheridan had taken precautions to fireproof his new theatre was advertised in an 'epilogue' written especially for the inaugural performance and recited 'in a fascinating manner' by the popular actress Miss Elizabeth Farren:

> Our pile is rock, more durable than brass,
> Our decorations gossamer and gas;
> The very ravages of fire we scout,
> For we have wherewithal to put it out,
> In ample reservoirs, our firm reliance,
> Whose streams set conflagration at defiance;
> Consume the scenes, your safety still is certain,
> Presto—for proof, let down the iron curtain.[10]

According to Michael Kelly, Miss Farren was emphasizing 'the utility of an iron curtain and a reservoir of water, in case of accidents by fire'. As *The Times* would explain the following day, the roof of the new building actually housed 'four very large reservoirs, from which water is distributed over every part of the house, for the purpose of instantly extinguishing fire, in any part where such an accident is possible'.[11] The iron curtain, meanwhile, was intended to 'completely prevent all communication between the audience and the stage, where alone accidents by fire have been known to commence'.

Similarly optimistic contraptions would be fitted into theatres elsewhere, and launched into the public eye with comparable poetic effusions. Four years later, indeed, Miss Farren's epilogue found its American equivalent in the Dedicatory address written by Robert Treat Paine Jr. (the wayward literary son of a founding father) and recited on 29 October 1798, at the opening of the new Federal Street Theatre in Boston. The original theatre on Federal Street had been destroyed by fire the previous February, and Paine's oration—generously praised by both George Washington and John Adams—invited the audience to imagine the 'Phoenix stage' engulfed by another terrible inferno, with actors 'raving' and the scenery, which featured Mont Blanc and even the ocean itself, bursting into flames. He then issued his version of the formulaic reassurance: 'But let no belle in sweet hystericks fall; | Our Iron Curtain will protect you all.'[12]

Boston's new Federal Street Theatre may have got away with its unlikely promise, but not so the Theatre Royal in London's Drury Lane. Shortly after it had been reduced to a pile of ashes, those boastful lines from Miss

Farren's epilogue would be quoted with a very different meaning in mind. To the evangelical Englishwoman, Ann Alexander, whose pamphlet *Remarks on the Theatre* was published anonymously in 1812, there was good reason why the modern theatre had proved so liable to catastrophic blazes—and she was not referring to the conspiracies of rogues seeking to cash in on new style insurance policies, as had been suggested in London.[13] Prompted by news of the dreadful inferno that obliterated a theatre in Richmond, Virginia, during a packed Christmas pantomime on 26 December 1811, Alexander asserted that incinerating theatres and their audiences was God's way of punishing those who preferred sinful entertainment to worshipping the Lord and studying the Scriptures. For Alexander, who enjoyed the easy satisfactions of hindsight, the Drury Lane Theatre's proudly exhibited safety features had been 'almost impious' because they sought to defy 'the means Providence makes use of for the humiliation of his creatures'. Futile, so this zealot gloated, to try to place an iron curtain, or any other prophylactic barrier, between God and the deserving objects of his wrath.

Providential or not, there can be no questioning the power of the inferno that gutted the Drury Lane Theatre fifteen years after its safety curtain had first been lowered on a stage containing nothing more alarming than 'a well-turned compliment to Shakespeare, whose statue was discovered under a mulberry tree'.[14] As was customary on Fridays during the Lent season, the theatre had been empty on the night of destruction. The flames, which were first seen flickering behind a window on the second floor, caused no alarm for about twenty minutes. But then, with 'electric rapidity', the upper part of the theatre suddenly burst into a massive sheet of flame that covered the entire 450-foot front of the building. The valuable patent licensing Sheridan and others to run the theatre was saved by firemen who managed to recover an iron chest full of documents from the theatre's 'Treasury'. Everything else was lost to a huge nocturnal conflagration that quite upstaged every previous performance. It was watched by as many as a hundred thousand souls: not just the surrounding streets but 'the tops of all the houses in all directions were covered with people'.

Speculating that the Drury Lane fire was 'perhaps the grandest spectacle of the kind' since the Great Fire of London (1666), *The Times* reviewed the calamity for its special effects. As they stretched along the full width of the theatre, the flames cast the upper windows and balustrade into such strong relief that they 'resembled the ancient aqueducts which are still remaining in the south of Europe'.[15] The cupola and the surmounting statue of Apollo—a 17-foot-high figure carved in wood (and 'strongly fort-ified with iron')—fell magnificently at about midnight. Thomas de Quincey would remember the lyre-bearing figure's dive into the inferno as a 'mimic suicide',[16] an apparently voluntary act that prompted 'a sustained uproar of admiration and sympathy' from the enraptured crowd.

There had been more such gasps as the walls came crashing down soon afterwards. Viewed from Blackfriars Bridge, the conflagration

> far surpassed in magnificence any of the mimic representations which were ever viewed within its walls ... From the frame of the edifice arose a broad sheet of flame: no wind stirred to break the symmetry of its ascent, so that it terminated in a 'fiery pyramid'. This vast splendid body threw an interesting light on the surrounding objects. The Thames and St. Pauls were rendered unusually beautiful. Thus the effect was rather that of an elaborate work of art than of a fatal casualty; to be lamented by all the Arts.[17]

That dramatic impression, or one very like it, was captured by the artist Pether Abraham, whose oil painting *Old Drury Lane Theatre on Fire, February 24 1809*, shows the conflagration from a downstream bridge over the Thames: a huge and tumultuous red glow illuminating the entire city and reconstel-lating the night sky with burning debris.

Sheridan's young friend, Lord Byron, would hail the burning theatre as a 'new Volcano' and liken it to a biblical pillar of fire chasing 'the night from heaven'.[18] Yet the tenor and music director Michael Kelly found neither poetry nor pleasure in the spectacle: 'I had not only the poignant grief of beholding the magnificent structure burning with merciless fury, but of knowing that all the scores of the operas which I had composed for the theatre, the labour of years, were then consuming: it was an appalling sight; and, with a heavy heart, I walked home to Pall Mall.'

Sheridan himself is said to have lingered in Parliament, eventually com-ing over to watch the destruction from the leaded roof of the Hummums, a piazza hotel and former Turkish bath (now named Tuttons and holding its own against a modest branch of Starbucks next door) on the eastern side of Covent Garden. Legend has it that, when asked about the 'philosophical calmness' with which he faced ruin, he remarked that 'A man may surely take a glass of wine by his own fireside'.[19]

The theatre's proudly exhibited safety equipment seems to have made no difference at all. 'The reservoir of water on the top ... was like a mere bucket-full to the volume of fire on which it fell, and it had no visible effect in damping it.'[20] Indeed, it only gave the show an extra crowd-pleasing turn. Landing with 'a violent concussion' it produced 'a shock like an earth-quake'[21] and forced burning debris up into the air in a dramatic stream that 'resembled a shower of rockets'.

Neither was there anything to be said for the iron curtain. The device that had promised to bring a life-saving separation of space into an institution which, as has recently been noted, everyone knew to be 'drilled full of apertures, trapdoors and back-passages',[22] had previously, so *The Times* reported, been 'found so rotten, the machinery so impracticable, that it had been removed'.[23]

Victorian Improvement

Chances were still being taken in the 1870s, when the head of the London Fire Brigade, Captain Eyre Massey Shaw, set out finally to break through the wilful ignorance—he actually spoke of 'cowardice and folly'—of the theatre managers who 'would rather not be made acquainted with the dangers that surround them'.[24] Shaw attacked the persistent problem with the modernizing zeal that other Victorian reformers would apply to public education, waste-disposal, and the social question. As he wrote in his pamphlet *Fires in Theatres*, 'I am strongly convinced that with proper construction, judicious management, and sound precautions, there would be no danger for the audience, and very little for the building, and this is my reason for writing on the subject.'[25]

The aim of fire prevention was to reduce the possibility of a fire spreading by dividing the building in question into 'the greatest possible number of distinct and separate risks'.[26] In a theatre, as Captain Shaw admitted, such precautions could only be taken so far: 'there are some parts, which cannot be divided, as, for instance, the stage, and again the auditorium; and this it is which makes the danger of such places inseparable from their existence'.[27] This regrettable fact may have licensed an attitude of resigned fatalism in the minds of theatre managers. Since Victorian London was a place of strange and artificial pleasures, it may also have encouraged some theatregoers to enjoy the frisson of danger: venturing into the theatre 'as they go into the hunting field, or onto the sea, or, as sometimes still happens, even into battle, for amusement'.[28]

For Captain Shaw, it was intolerable that such incendiary institutions should remain scattered through the close-built capital—a danger to people

and surrounding property alike. He drew up a list of bristling recommendations that would soon be consolidated into a seventeen-point code by the
Metropolitan Board of Works.[29]

Richard Brinsley Sheridan had squeezed a potentially lucrative collection
of taverns, coffee houses, and trinket shops into the Drury Lane Theatre in
his perpetual struggle to make the place pay (the fire of 1809 was eventually
blamed on varnishers finishing off a new 'Chinese lobby').[30] In Shaw's strict
judgement, however, shops around theatres were 'always more or less objec-
tionable'. Workshops should be taken out of the spaces above and beneath the
stage. Lobbies must be spacious, exits sufficient to allow hasty evacuation, and
aisles must under no circumstances be blocked by people standing or sitting
on camp-stools. Hand pumps and buckets should be easily available, together
with portable hoses. As for the 'fireman' who was meant to be in attendance
during performances, it was time to say farewell to the 'theatrically got-up' but
wholly untrained 'sham' so often to be found standing about in the aisles.

It was plainly impossible, as Captain Shaw admitted, to separate the stage
from the auditorium in full accordance with the doctrine of divided 'risks',
but the point 'at which the curtain falls' still demanded special vigilance.
This dangerous opening could be much reduced by the introduction of a
proscenium wall built of solid brick to specified dimensions, and extending
from the basement to a height of some 4 or 5 feet above the roof. It should
be 'perforated at the sides at each landing', but the communicating doors
must be made of wrought iron and certainly not framed with wood.

Captain Shaw also specified that the main opening in this wall should be
protected by a metal curtain, supported by steel or iron chains that could be
dropped at a moment's notice. He understood that 'such curtains, it is true,
have before now been tried and have not found favour with managers of
theatres'. However, this was no excuse for continued negligence: 'They may
have been badly made, badly fitted, or badly worked; but even so, it must be
obvious that, in the event of a fire happening, they would have done *some*
good.' Given the 'present condition of mechanical skill and knowledge', it
would be 'simply monstrous to say that the thing is impossible'.

One of the most dramatic theatre fires of this period broke out in Dublin.
On 9 February 1880, the Theatre Royal on Hawkins Street ignited shortly
before a matinee performance of *Ali Baba and the Forty Thieves*. Setting off
to light the lamps, a boy with a burning taper walked into a cloud of gas
leaking from a badly repaired bracket. The place was soon ablaze, despite

the frantic efforts of the manager, Mr Francis Egerton, who tried to fight the conflagration with the stage fire-hose, which was not in working order, and then refused to leave as urged by the withdrawing stagehands. The fire took hold, aided by a series of massive gas explosions, and the building was wholly destroyed along with Mr Egerton and five others.

The Dublin fire will have provided Captain Shaw with yet more proof of the low priority given to safety in theatres. It also impressed one 5-year-old boy sufficiently to remain among his earliest memories. For a period in the late 1870s, Winston Churchill lived at the Viceregal Lodge in Dublin, where his father, Lord Randolph, worked as private secretary to the Lord Lieutenant. He had been looking forward to seeing *Ali Baba*. 'Then', as he later recalled, 'we were told we could not go to the pantomime because the theatre had been burned down. All that was found of the manager was the keys that had been in his pocket. We were promised as a consolation for not going to the pantomime to go next day and see the ruins of the building. I wanted very much to see the keys, but this request does not seem to have been well received.'[31]

Theatres kept blazing elsewhere too. In 1881 the Nice Opera House went up, killing sixty-two people. In December that year, more than 500 were lost in the Ring Theatre in Vienna when scenery caught fire as the audience were taking their seats for a performance of Offenbach. By 1882, *The Times* could insist that, whilst Captain Shaw's axioms were now more or less 'universally accepted', London's theatres still remained 'a formidable front to reform'.[32]

The case for systematic regulation of British theatres was not decisively clinched until September 1887, when the recently built Theatre Royal in Exeter was suddenly engulfed during a performance of *Romany Rye*. A safety curtain had in fact been lowered when fire broke out behind the stage. Due to the negligent design of the building, however, the fire could not escape upwards through the flies and had quickly built up such pressure that the inadequate curtain had billowed outwards, releasing great gouts of flame and smoke into the auditorium. Sent to investigate by the Home Secretary, Captain Eyre Shaw heaped the blame on the architect, proprietor, and the local licensing authority: together they had ignored the relevant safety codes (his own) and conspired in the creation of a death-trap in which well over a hundred people had died.[33] After Shaw's findings were published, cost-conscious theatre managers in London were no longer able to shrug their shoulders and settle for merely symbolic safety measures.

In the wake of the Exeter fire, the case for thoroughgoing reform was forcefully advanced in *The Times*. It was pointed out that in continental Europe theatres were under government supervision, and that the 'Inspector-General of Theatres' ensured that they were built in open squares, whereas in London proprietors had for too long been able to erect them 'just where they please'.[34]

Correspondents included Clark, Bennett & Co., a manufacturer of iron curtains based in London's Oxford Street.[35] This company's model consisted of two screens of wrought iron plate, with 6 inches of air between them. Securely framed at the sides, it could be raised or lowered in thirty seconds. It was, so the manufacturer claimed, far more effective than the gauze curtains tried in Vienna, or the 'practically useless' single plate curtains that were compulsory in Germany and, since Paris's Opéra-Comique burned down (with 200 fatalities) on 25 May 1887, in France too.

Their claim would be supported by the proprietor of the Prince of Wales Theatre in London. On 11 January 1888, he wrote to *The Times* protesting that the iron curtain in his theatre (one that Clark, Bennett and Co. had earlier cited as an example of their recent work) was a highly effective piece of equipment maintained in good working order, and certainly not just a 'ponderous piece of mechanism'[36] rusting above the stage. Impressive claims were also made for the asbestos safety curtain installed in Walter Emden's new Terry's Theatre, which had opened on the Strand a few months earlier.[37]

Such was the efficiency of these late Victorian devices, which descended like slow guillotines and really did seem to promise an absolute and impenetrable separation between stage and auditorium, that another contributor to *The Times*'s ongoing discussion of 'Fires in Theatres' felt obliged to sound a new note of caution. This correspondent, who was prepared only to sign himself 'X', spoke out on behalf of the increasingly forgotten people who worked on 'the other side'.[38] Once the iron curtain was lowered and the iron doors in Captain Shaw's solid proscenium wall were locked, the actors and others employed on or around the stage would be left, so 'X' claimed, with no choice but to struggle up a narrow staircase, battling their way through smoke and flames to escape through a narrow stage door at the level of the flies. Perhaps himself an actor, this anonymous letter-writer was spooked by the one-sided thinking displayed by advocates of the by now alarmingly effective iron curtain: 'Simultaneously with the safety of the public that of those on the other side of the curtain must be provided, or there will be none for either.'

Blazing for Young Winston

No longer just a primitive, audience-calming prop dressed in poetic promises, the iron curtain was ready to be adopted as a metaphor of wider divisions. It had become an awe-inspiringly capable barrier, at once reassuring
and menacing in its powers of separation, and it had done so in the same
years that saw Europe divided into a bipolar system of allied states in which
France, Russia, and Britain were squared off against Germany in its alliances
with Turkey.[39]

There was, however, one kind of theatre that quite escaped the zealous Captain Shaw's safety regulations, and the young Winston Churchill
was among its enthusiasts. By the mid-1880s, he was absorbed in his toy
theatre, guiding pasteboard puppets through the melodramatic scripts and
brightly painted scenes that he bought from the combined tobacconist and
toy theatre shop run by Mr W. Webb in Old Street, London. Webb remembered the young Winston as a 'jolly and impulsive lad', who had his own
enthusiastic way of 'vaulting' over the shop counter; and who sometimes
ordered dramatic scenes and other toy theatre equipment to be sent to him
at preparatory school in Brighton:[40] As Churchill later confirmed, 'For three
or four years of my life a model theatre was a great amusement to me.'[41]
Of the plays he bought from Mr Webb's shop, the one he best remembered
was *The Miller and his Men*. A popular classic of the genre, this 'cardboard
thriller' was a Gothic drama, set in a florid Bohemia of dark forests, ravines,
and craggy cliffs. Its central character, the miller Grindoff, is actually the vil-
lainous leader of a band of robbers; and he is pursued to his richly deserved
end by noble Count Friberg and his soldiers.

In 1946, some thirty years after Churchill wrote to A. E. Wilson confirming
his childhood enthusiasm, another amateur historian would review the panto-
mime-like world of the nineteenth-century toy theatre. For George Speaight,
the legacy of this dying art form consisted of 'bright "twopence coloured"
images in the fog, exaggerated shadows like caricatures, a touch of drama, a
brave and boyish romance, the breath of poetry'.[42] With its highly keyed colours, its melodramatic gestures, its simplified philosophy built around a 'clear
division between the good and the bad', the toy theatre had fired the imagin-
ations of Charles Dickens, Robert Louis Stevenson, and G. K. Chesterton.

As Speaight suggested, the memory of its 'high bombastic speeches,
mouthed with relish to shake the gallery rafters' had surely also lingered

in Churchill's mind to echo in the great speeches of 1940. When Speaight heard Churchill declaring 'We shall fight on the beaches, we shall fight in the hills: we shall never surrender!' (a far from accurate recollection of the galvanizing words spoken by Churchill in the House of Commons on 4 June 1940), he was instantly transported back to the gaudy, polarized world of the toy theatre and, more particularly, to the closing scenes of *The Miller and his Men*. Chased back into his mill by Count Friberg, Miller Grindoff climbs up into the gallery and, with a 'proud defiant boast', refuses to accept defeat: '"Surrender," cries the Count. "Surrender?" answers Grindoff with a terrible snarl. "Surrender? Never! I have sworn never to descend from this spot alive."'[43]

At that point, the forces of justice ignite the windmill's powder magazine to produce the prodigious 'blow-up' towards which the play has been manoeuvring since its opening scene. Mill-stones, spars, and dismembered bodies are seen flying out of the exploding mill, while smoke billows upwards and blazing vermilion flames ignite the buildings nearby. It was the most lurid climax in the entire repertoire of the Victorian toy theatre and there was no safety curtain, whether of iron or asbestos, to contain it.

5

Dividing Europe's Horizon

The frontier lines of Europe wavered under one's eyes.

Irene Cooper Willis[1]

Though named 'No Place, Nowhere', the setting is immediately recognizable as a European town square, across which stands a prominent building inscribed 'The World; a Theatre of Varieties, Lessee and Manager, SATAN'.[2] The houses of the SLEEPY VIRTUES stretch out to form a crescent on either side. TRUTHFULNESS, JUSTICE, TEMPERANCE, EQUANIMITY, and others can be seen yawning behind their windows or wearily stepping out into the square to gaze on as the orchestra's players arrive.

Dressed in 'appropriate allegorical garments' these HUMAN PASSIONS are identified by silver badges around their necks: GREED, LOYALTY, DISCIPLINE, COMRADESHIP, JEALOUSY, EGOTISM, BULLYING, ENNUI … Alarmingly energetic by comparison with the SLEEPY VIRTUES, they arrive with hand-carts containing diverse musical instruments, which they carry into the theatre through a stage door to the rear. They also unload the balustrade that will separate them from the audience in the stalls. This suggestive device is inscribed: 'Patriotism; reserved for members of the Orchestra'.

A small earthquake suddenly interrupts the preparations and then, as the rumbling subsides, SATAN arises from a chasm opened at the foot of the theatre steps. Infusing the abruptly darkened world with his own dingy luminosity, he raises his attendants out of the depths—first the MUSE OF HISTORY, and then 'the classic and unsubstantial chorus of AGES-TO-COME'.

A 'long, lank figure' in a black evening coat, BALLET MASTER DEATH now turns for the first time, revealing himself to be a grinning skeleton lifted from a sixteenth-century woodcut by Hans Holbein the Younger. Greeting

SATAN, with whom he has collaborated on so many 'joint shows' in the past, he regrets that Mankind has 'coddled its Passions up of late years', feeding them on 'humanitarian water-gruel' that has left them lackadaisical and anaemic. Satan declares this situation 'quite easily mended'.[3] 'It is time', he pronounces, 'to reopen the Theatre of the West. The Politicians and Armament Shareholders have long got all the stage-property in readiness, and the Scene-Shifters of the Press are only waiting for the signal.'[4]

Such are the opening scenes of *The Ballet of the Nations*, an allegorical (as well as heavily capitalized) work written by Vernon Lee during the Great War. Lee was in her late fifties when the fighting began. Born as Violet Paget she had been raised in continental Europe, the child of expatriate British parents whose habit of moving every six months is said to have been motivated at least partly by her father's passion for shooting and fishing.[5]

Twenty-four years old when she made her first visit to Britain in 1881, Lee was, as an obituarist would eventually declare, 'cosmopolitan from her birth, without any single national tie or sympathy'.[6] She had lived in Germany, France, Switzerland, and also Italy, where she had grown up alongside the American artist-to-be John Singer Sargent. She had made her home in Florence for many years before 1914, when she found herself stranded in England by the war that broke out during her annual summer visit. Financially independent (her maternal grandfather had accumulated a since dwindled fortune in the West Indies), multilingual, and privately educated to a high if also eccentric degree, she had been a prominent exemplar of the 'New Woman' since the late nineteenth century: a cosmopolitan author, aesthete, and literary intellectual, whose circle of acquaintance had included Walter Pater, Oscar Wilde, Robert Browning, Henry James, and Edith Wharton; and who appeared, as George Bernard Shaw observed in one of the few reviews of this unusual work, to have 'the whole European situation in the hollow of her hand'.[7]

Inspired by the example of medieval masques, Lee's ballet started out as, in her own words, 'an extemporised shadow play'. It was the 'grotesque embodiment' of a war that seemed to be 'about nothing at all; gigantically cruel, but at the same time needless and senseless like some ghastly "Grand Guignol" performance'.[8] She wrote the first version while staying with radical suffragist friends (Bessie and Isabella Ford) at Adel Grange, near Leeds, over Whitsuntide in 1915: a time when Britain was convulsed with patriotic hatred of all things German following the torpedoing of the *Lusitania* off the Irish coast. A slim twenty-page volume with a deceptively attractive

'pictorial commentary' by the Quaker-educated artist Maxwell Armfield, it was published, to very little effect, in time for Christmas 1915. As
representatives of Lee's morbidly curious AGES-TO-COME, we might suspect
that every aspect of the Great War has since been dramatized, re-enacted, or
otherwise worked over. Yet despite ongoing attempts to project Lee into the
pantheon of lesbian writers,[9] *The Ballet of the Nations* has hardly detained
the historians: a faint rumour, if anything at all, echoing in an off-road
oubliette labelled 'Pacifism'.

Christmas Eve, 1914

Vernon Lee's emblematic 'theatre of varieties' betrays no sign of an iron
curtain of the kind earlier demanded by Captain Eyre Wallis Shaw of the
London Fire Brigade. Yet there is good reason for this omission. By spring
1915, when *The Ballet of the Nations* was first drafted, she had already removed
the device and installed it in the warring European world—Satan's 'theatre
of the West'—her allegorical playhouse could only inadequately represent.

At about noon on what might now be called 'Day Three' of the war,
6 August 1914, Vernon Lee was to be found sitting with her back against
a corn-stook in a freshly harvested field somewhere beneath the English
South Downs. It was the day after a British ship had cut the communication
cables between Germany and the United States, but Lee can have known
nothing of that first strike in the coming propaganda war.[10] Surveying the
millions of uncut heads still awaiting the reaping-machine parked nearby,
she thought instead of the armies gathering in Europe and feared that an
even larger acreage would be required to symbolize 'the human beings
whom war is going to plunge into death and starvation and mourning'.[11]

Lee would later come to imagine that radiant landscape turned into a
'lurid chasm' as the ongoing war fired its distant farms and blotted out its
charms with rockets and clouds of 'flame-lit smoke and poisonous vapours'.[12]
Even at the beginning, however, she did not confine her reflections to a pastoral moment on the southern English chalk downs. A few days after the
outbreak, she would write a strongly argued letter to H. W. Massingham at
the leading Liberal weekly, *The Nation*. Citing her various contributions
advocating the cause of 'Anglo-German *rapprochement*' over the previous
five years, she berated the editor of this previously sympathetic publication
for backsliding now that war had been declared. Deploring the new reflex

of placing all the blame on Germany, suddenly derided as 'the spiritless and immoral instrument of a mere brutal militarist caste', she declared Britain's Liberal Secretary of Foreign Affairs, Sir Edward Grey, to be guilty of inheriting the worst of Tory habits, and of helping to cast Europe into 'a war of diplomatists, not of peoples'.[13]

Her response to the war would deepen soon enough. December 1914 is now remembered for the informal 'Christmas truce' that broke out along the western front, when British and German soldiers agreed to set aside their weapons and play football in no man's land. Lee, who was living in London at the time, asserted a different idea of common humanity in a fine but now long-forgotten article entitled 'Bach's Christmas Music in England and Germany', first published in *Jus Suffragii,* the journal of the Woman International Suffrage Alliance, on 1 January 1915 (see Appendix I).

She opens this meditation by describing how, on Christmas Eve, 1914, she had gone to the Inns of Court, between Fleet Street and the Thames, to hear Bach's music performed in the Temple church. She had found the 'shimmering double church' (the building combines a thirteenth-century chancel with a round church built by the Knights Templar in the twelfth century) filled with 'old and elderly men, [and] women of all ages'. She also noticed 'a sprinkling of soldier-lads, brought along, on what may be their last Christmas in this world, by their mothers and sisters and sweethearts. Everyone—but it was perhaps that my own eyes and heart were opened— everyone seemed so altered from other perfunctory times, grave, sincere, aware of all it meant.'

As the 'first rasping notes of the organ' tore into 'the veil of silent prayer', Lee was struck by the realization that '*There* also, *There* beyond the sea and the war chasm, in hundreds of churches of Bach's own country (I can see the Thomas-Kirche at Leipzig, where he was Cantor, and the church of his birthplace, Eisenach), *There*, at this very moment, were crowds like this one at the Temple, listening to this self-same Christmas Music.'[14]

Lee had been raised in an atmosphere of anti-religious Victorian rationalism, yet the mystery and enchantment of long past German Christmases—their resin-scented fir trees adorned with glass beads, gilded nuts, and innumerable delicately tinted tapers—nevertheless still featured among her most binding memories.[15] She had spent her earliest years in Germany (residing variously at Frankfurt, Baden, Wiesbaden, and Kissingen) and the imaginative continuities of her childhood were at stake as she envisaged those congregations praying alike for peace 'both on this side and on yonder, of the shallow seas and the unfathomable ocean of horror and hatred', and seeking identical consolation in the thought of the Christ Child that 'lies in every cradle, the incarnate, unblemished hope of every land and every generation'.

Four months earlier, the *Daily Mail* had been pleased to report that German and Austrian music had been removed from Britain's Promenade Concerts.[16] *The Times* had also justified the decision, declaring that 'These are days when neither Strauss nor Don Juan can mean very much to us.'[17] For Vernon Lee, however, Bach's Christmas Oratorio testified to shared European aspirations, which she hoped would persist against such hateful manifestations as Horatio Bottomley's rabble-rousing paper *John Bull,* the violently chauvinistic Anti-German Union, or the advertisements that now urged British newspaper readers to drink French Perrier as opposed to German mineral waters.

Yet Lee went further than this, declaring that, despite the rising flood of patriotic hatred[18] on both sides, the war actually made the opposed peoples more rather than less alike in their threatened humanity. They had been 'played into unanimity' not just by Bach, with his 'tunes and counterpoints', but by the 'ruthless hands' of a calamity that was actually held in common: 'Never have we and they been closer together, more alike and akin, than at this moment when War's cruelties and recriminations, War's monstrous iron curtain, cut us off so utterly from one another.'

Cosmopolitanism and the Warring Nation State

Other writers had made metaphorical use of the iron curtain before Christmas 1914, including H. G. Wells who, in his novel *The Food of the Gods* (1904), imagined 'an iron curtain' falling between a scientist and 'the outer world' disrupted by his dramatic discoveries.[19] This theatrical device would play a leading role in popular romance too, lending steam as well as fire and a fateful sense of separation ('I was born—on the wrong side—of the safety curtain,' gasps a compromised dancing girl) to Ethel M. Dell's torrid story 'The Safety-Curtain' (1917).[20] It was, however, Vernon Lee who took the 'iron curtain' from the theatre—in which it had by now become an effective and often hydraulically powered screen of asbestos rather than just iron—and found it a new application in early twentieth-century international relations.

Though the phrase may not recur in Lee's writing, the polarization she here names, together with the fatal symmetry imposed on its divided peoples, would define her analysis of the war and its consequences over the five years to come. Indeed, that suddenly lowered 'iron curtain' would virtually *become* the war as Lee experienced it in England. It would take some of its metal from the industrial mobilization, the wired trenches, the guns, warships, and submarines. Yet it would be more strongly registered as a 'psychological deadlock'[21] that bent people on both sides to the cause of their belligerent states, while at the same time encouraging young men to enlist in a spirit of ignorant self-sacrifice that Lee considered all too similar to the fit of momentary enthusiasm in which young women had long been entering the life-consuming contract of marriage.[22]

Lee had looked on in dismay as the war was raised to the status of a 'crusade'[23] on both sides of its 'monstrous' curtain. In happier times she had travelled Europe writing about its variegated culture and 'genius of place' ('Out of Venice at Last', 'Switzerland Again', 'Asphodels', 'Tuscan Churches in Summer', etc.). She now saw that marvellous late nineteenth-century world reduced to 'a mere homogenous mass of systematic and automatic imitations of enemy by enemy: conscription, trenches, poison gases, submarines, air-raids, propaganda of hatred, atrocity mongering, coalition government and postal censure having given Britain and Germany and France, Austria and Italy, a most conspicuous and lamentable family-likeness'.[24]

Lee had once believed that the 'ever-stable impersonalities called Principles and Ideals' provided mankind with 'an unshakable anchor against the tides and storms of passion and delusion'.[25] Now, however, she saw these 'Principles and Ideals' dragged into the service of the passions and delusions, leaving that once taken-for-granted mechanism of 'moral and intellectual moorage' as 'a mere hulk' floating on 'the dominant currents'. Some would cling to their belief in unchangeable virtues, but Lee could accept no such consolation. As she studied its progress, the war proved all too capable of making vices out of such virtues as discipline, abnegation, endurance. This satanic reversal of values proved so overwhelming that even pity and mourning for the dead would end up swelling the bloody tide.

Though a singular and in some respects isolated figure in Britain, Lee was far from disconnected in her thinking about the war. If her 'iron curtain' had a future, indeed, this was because it expressed the ideas and anxieties of a wide movement of progressive opinion with which she had been associated before August 1914. Lee was among the objectors who experienced the war as, in the words of another contemporary observer, 'a decline in civilized ways, a recoil from progressive aims, a rolling backwards'.[26] She used her 'monstrous iron curtain' to identify the conflict as a collision between the violently resurgent 'passion of nationalism' and the political and cultural ideals that she and many other internationalists had espoused in a now violently cancelled past that had seemed to promise 'the growing interdependence of all nations'.[27]

Lee would surely have recognized the luxurious cosmopolitanism of the pre-war London capitalist, as later described by the Liberal economist John Maynard Keynes. During the golden age that had been so abruptly cancelled in August 1914, Keynes's uniquely privileged gentleman only had to lift the telephone, while still 'sipping tea in bed', to order up anything he wanted from almost anywhere in the world and look forward to its 'early delivery' on his doorstep.[28] He could 'adventure his wealth in the natural resources and new enterprises of any quarter of the world, and share, without exertion or even trouble, in their prospective fruits and advantages'. His ability to travel had been pretty unlimited too. Having sent out his servant to collect a convenient supply of gold or 'coined wealth' from a nearby bank, he might 'proceed abroad to foreign quarters', where he would be 'greatly aggrieved and much surprised' to encounter 'the least interference' in his movements. Lee had herself drifted about in that passport-free world, but her internationalism was by no means merely a memory of wealth and its bearer's now lost freedom to cruise, unimpeded, through Europe and its various colonies.

Lee's 'iron curtain' may have been an impenetrable barrier lowered between the warring imperial states of Britain and Germany, but it was also a guillotine brought down on the improving aspirations that had inspired many during more than four decades of 'peaceable progression'[29] experienced in Europe since the Franco-Prussian War of 1870–1.

It has recently been argued that the nation 'is always conceived as a deep, horizontal comradeship'.[30] Yet by 1914 many who followed the perspective of the European nation state, taken as the basis for a 'new order' established in 1871,[31] actually subscribed to a vertical conception of the world divided by patriotism, standing armies, imperial rivalries, and balance of power diplomacy. Lee was among the internationalists who had long opposed this way of thinking, placing their hopes for the future in various horizontally conceived projects that promised to lessen, if not wholly overthrow, the vertical divisions between nations: free trade, democratic reform,

Christian humanitarianism, social revolution, racial emancipation, reasoned and disciplined knowledge of the kind represented by the magnificent eleventh edition of the *Encyclopaedia Britannica* (1910).[32] Such were the spatial coordinates of the abruptly reopened 'Theatre of the West' in which 'war's monstrous iron curtain' had made its fatal descent.

In its British version, the horizontally aligned 'peace movement' (a phrase that has been in use since the 1840s) had long been driven by Christian pacifism, including that of the Quakers, who had helped found Britain's first 'Peace Society'—'The Society for the Promotion of Permanent and Universal Peace'—after the Napoleonic Wars in 1816.[33] The Quakers opposed all war as a matter of religious principle, but there were others who hoped to achieve a peaceable international order by realizing political conceptions derived from the eighteenth-century enlightenment. From that perspective, defensive wars might sometimes be considered necessary, especially if carried out to protect small states or political reforms considered vital to international harmony.

The exponents of this internationalist approach found inspiration in various sources: from Voltaire's secular cosmopolitanism to Victor Hugo's repeated advocacy (after the revolutionary upheavals of 1848) of a 'United States of Europe', and the great French historian Jules Michelet's insistence, derived from the banquets associated with revolutionary mobilization in France, on 'the universal banquet of the human race'.[34] For many, the route to peace lay in republican principles stated in the philosopher Immanuel Kant's *Perpetual Peace; a Philosophical Sketch* (1795). By the early twentieth century, this 'idealistic' view of international relations itself combined multiple threads.[35] The Liberal version appealed to free trade and international law. Exponents of the British radical tradition looked forward to a foreign policy truly expressive of the popular will rather than of vested interests and corrupt or incompetent elites. For the socialists of the First and Second Internationals, the way forward entailed class struggle and the revolutionary overthrow of capitalism.

By 1901, when the first Nobel Peace Prize was awarded in Stockholm, other aspects of the 'international mind'[36] were emerging in the United States of America. In Atlanta, W. E. B. Du Bois would soon be using a horizontalist language to attack the 'color-line'—a murderous division that, thanks largely to the colonial expansion of the European empires, was not just an American phenomenon and could be said to form a 'belt' around the entire world.[37] From 1907 to 1910, Du Bois edited and published *The*

Horizon; a Journal of the Color Line, in which the cause of racial emancipation was explicitly aligned with the wider struggle for human equality, universal suffrage, the abolition of war, and socialism.[38]

For the prominent American political scientist Professor Paul S. Reinsch, Europe also provided a negative example. As Reinsch explained in 1913, Europeans lived 'crowded together in a small continent. They have the memory of antipathies of centuries to overcome. Their struggle for exist-ence is grim.'[39] Americans, meanwhile, had enjoyed a very different history since their Civil War. Far from being locked in a hostile rivalry of 'warring nationalities', their republic had never suffered a foreign war in which 'the people really felt their national life threatened', and their experience of successful federal government predisposed them towards the idea of 'inter-national peace secured by respect for law'.[40]

Writing under the auspices of the World Peace Foundation in 1911, Reinsch acknowledged, perhaps not just with Europe in mind, that the 'historical experience of generations' still encouraged people to think in terms of national sovereignty, and to see the varied experience of national life as 'the final form of human civilisation'.[41] He also granted that 'the old cosmopolitan ideal',[42] which had inspired many previous critics of the nation state, had been merely negative in its objectives, and marred by an excessively abstract concept of humanity inherited from eighteenth-century rationalism. Yet he was convinced that this 'barren ideal of no war, no patri-otism, no local interest' had recently given way to a more practical kind of internationalism, which made nonsense of the suggestion that nation states could exist in isolation from one another.

Many proponents of this new and future-oriented internationalism would cite the two Hague Peace Conferences of 1899 and 1907, at which the rep-resentatives of various governments (twenty-six and forty-four respectively) had gathered in the Netherlands to agree measures that would limit arms, curb the excesses of war, and establish systems of judicial arbitration that would eventually be taken over by the International Court of Justice. Others would celebrate the International Red Cross or the 'cosmopolitan clubs' that had emerged at leading American universities in the early years of the twentieth century: the latter were said to work like 'miniature Hague Con-ferences', and their national association also took the message abroad under the slogan 'Above all nations is Humanity'.[43]

Determined to avoid the accusation of lofty 'idealism', Professor Reinsch pointed out that, by 1911, there were more than forty-five public international unions in which many nations cooperated to maintain internationally bind-ing procedures and laws. The first of these seeds of a future 'world-law',[44] the Telegraphic Union, had been launched in 1869. It was followed by the Universal Postal Union in 1879, and the years since had seen the initiation of international unions concerned with such varied activities as railway transportation, agriculture, patents and copyrights, prison reform, and the protection of labour (the International Labour Office was established in Basel in 1901). On both sides of the division between labour and capital, 'the organization of interests is taking on an international aspect'[45] and the advocates of 'national sovereignty' surely had no choice but to adjust their thinking to this fact.

Reinsch's insistence that cosmopolitanism was 'no longer a castle in the air'[46] was matched by voices in Europe. From 1912, the cause had been proclaimed in *La Vie internationale,* the monthly journal of the Brussels-based Office Central des Associations Internationales. Here, too, it was announced that international cooperation was the proven shape of a bet-ter world order to come.[47] Its medium was the international conference or congress, and its advance could be traced not just in the work of the 'international peace movement' or the International Red Cross, but also in the standardization of weights and measures (the Metric Union), police cooperation (Interpol), and in further initiatives connected to maritime law, medical technology, and assurance. Inspired by such developments, the internationalists of the pre-war years had looked forward to the intro-duction of a new world currency,[48] the spread of Esperanto (the universal language invented by the Russian Dr Zamenhoff and launched into the world in 1887),[49] and, even as the Great War broke out around them, the creation of a long-imagined Channel Tunnel between Britain and France.[50]

The Heights of Romain Rolland

As a participant in this movement, Vernon Lee was by no means the only internationalist who thought of music as an embodiment of the cosmopolitan spirit: a 'world-language', in the phrase of the American composer Daniel Gregory Mason, which could seem especially important at a time when more conventional speech was distorted by hatred and war propaganda.[51] With its insistence on a cultural tradition that transcends national enmities, Lee's article about Bach's Christmas music was particularly indebted to the thinking of Romain Rolland, the French author, socialist, and fellow European 'cosmopolitan' to whom she would soon dedicate *The Ballet of the Nations*.[52] Written between 1903 and 1912, at a time when the idea of an impermeable vertical barrier was still more naturally expressed through the metaphor of the Great Wall of China,[53] Rolland's ten-volume novel *Jean-Christophe* traced the arduous life of a German-born composer who journeys through Europe in his struggle to create a new music in which French, German, and Italian influences are triumphantly united.[54] As Rolland had told an admiring Vernon Lee in a letter of August 1908, 'I have a passionate love for our dear Europe of the Occident. I would like to be able to unite in one soul the five powerful souls of her old nations, without sacrificing anything of their individuality.'[55]

Such was Rolland's dream and yet, as he had warned in *The New Dawn* (published as the closing volume of *Jean-Christophe* in 1912), Europe appeared to be rushing in the opposite direction—to such an extent that it already resembled 'a vast armed vigil'.[56] Overtaken by the 'great plague of national pride', the younger generation was apparently bent on reviving a 'monster' that had only recently been vanquished in the name of Liberty and 'the religious aspiration towards the brotherhood of nations and races'.[57] Once the anticipated war broke out, Rolland opposed it in the spirit of Goethe, repudiating 'all national hatreds' and insisting on staying 'above the battle' on those moral heights 'where we feel the happiness and misfortunes of other peoples as our own'.[58]

Where Vernon Lee wrote of a 'war chasm' or 'iron curtain', Rolland would condemn the 'Abyss of hatred and misunderstanding' that had been created between Britain and Germany.[59] He also deplored the 'thick wall of certitude by which Germany is barricaded against the light of day'[60] and excoriated the writers and intellectuals—he named Thomas Mann as well as the dramatist Gerhart Hauptmann—who lent their names to the 'absurd' idea of Germany's cultural and racial superiority. Against the polarizing war propagandists who identified their own nation as wholly good and their enemy's as entirely evil, Rolland advanced the now heretical internationalist view that 'the worst enemy of each nation is not without, but within its frontiers'.[61] In a characteristic letter of July 1917, he would explain his refusal of the vertical 'barriers' that war had lowered between Europe's belligerent nations:

I think that in the present war there is an enormous power of idealism on one hand, and on the other, a monstrous power of materialism, wickedness, ambition, mean and murderous interests (and folly, of course). You think so too.

The great difference between us is that for me, these two forces confronting each other, do not correspond to a division of Europe (and of the world) in two camps, and I see the Enemy everywhere, here more brutal perhaps, but there more hypocritical, and no less menacing, on one side as on the other.

I do not see Europe (the world) divided like this, by barriers:

$$| \quad | \quad | \quad | \quad |$$

I see it divided like this, by superimposed layers:

$$\begin{array}{c} \rule{10cm}{0.4pt} \\ \rule{10cm}{0.4pt} \\ \rule{10cm}{0.4pt} \\ \rule{10cm}{0.4pt} \end{array}$$

Everywhere there are men of good will,—and there are others. Instead of playing the game of the latter, by pitting the former against each other, I aspire to make a union of all men of good will. They are in all nations and, in all of them equally oppressed.[62]

Rolland's opposition to those state-drawn vertical barriers set him against all the institutions of war patriotism and its coercive Sacred Union: 'the death-like submission of the churches, the stifling intolerance of the nations, the stupid unitarianism of socialists'.[63] He deplored patriotism as 'the only instinct under present conditions which escapes the withering touch of every-day life'.[64] Every other human drive might be forced 'to pass under the yoke of denial and compromise' but the war revealed patriotism to be horrifyingly free from such constraints. Even the middle-aged soul 'embraces and lavishes on it the ardour of all the ambitions, the loves, and the longings, that life has disappointed. A half century of suppressed fire bursts forth, millions of little cages in the social prison open their doors.'

With his appeal to the cultural solidarity of Europe, Rolland remained a primary inspiration for Lee (it was allegedly she who proposed him for the Nobel Prize for Literature, which he received in 1915).[65] Yet her opposition to the war also reflects her alignment with the feminist horizontalism of the Women's International League for Peace and Freedom, an anti-war alliance founded at an international congress held in The Hague (with considerable difficulty since some national delegations, including most members of the British, were unable to reach the neutral Netherlands) in April 1915, and variously savaged by the hounds of Fleet Street as 'Folly in Petticoats' (*Sunday Pictorial*), 'This shipload of hysterical women' (*The Globe*), and 'pro-Hun Peacettes' (*Daily Express*).[66]

The Women's International League drew much of its direction from its first president, Jane Addams, the American suffragist and social reformer who, in the 1880s, had founded a settlement named Hull-House (partly modelled on East London's Toynbee Hall) in an industrial immigrant district of Chicago. In her *Newer Ideals of Peace* (1907), Addams had argued that 'pacifism' was not enough if it amounted merely to 'Passivism' and 'the old dove-like ideal'.[67] Writing out of a close involvement with the 'International Peace Movement' of her time, she noted the limitations of Tolstoy's merely dogmatic appeal to 'higher imaginative pity', which need amount to no more than a well-intended 'command to cease from evil'.[68] She also rejected the idea that lasting peace was best achieved by appealing to 'Prudence', a claim that rapidly led to the conclusion that the best way to secure peace was to prepare for war.[69] Instead, Addams advocated a 'dynamic', 'more aggressive', and, to anticipate Churchill's later expression, more sinewy idea of peace: one that would embody 'the later humanism' with its concern for 'social amelioration' and also build on recent attempts (following the first international Hague Peace Conference called by the tsar of Russia, Nicholas II, in 1899) to establish generally accepted forms of international law and arbitration.

As a representative of what George Bernard Shaw described as 'the old guard of Victorian cosmopolitan intellectualism',[70] Vernon Lee would join Romain Rolland in rallying European culture, exemplified by Bach and Goethe, against the barriers of hatred dividing the warring nations. Yet Jane Addams had already found a more social and everyday cosmopolitanism in the poor immigrant areas of American cities such as her own district on the Near West Side of Chicago. Though often derided as mere 'slums', she insisted that these zones of transition actually showed another way of dissolving the 'tribal bond' that had been the cause of so much bloodshed in Europe: with their cross-cultural diversity, their 'new compassion', and their 'gravitation towards the universal', these districts exemplified 'the only sort of patriotism consistent with the intermingling of nations'.[71] Indeed, Addams believed the inhabitants of these mixed urban quarters were 'laying the simple and inevitable foundations for an international order' just as 'the foundations of tribal and national morality had already been laid' in a previous military and war-dominated epoch.[72]

Liberal Memories and the League
for Peace and Freedom

The feminist organizations within the international anti-war movement also had their own understanding of the manipulated theatricality of modern warfare. The US Women's Peace Party (over which Addams presided) made a leaflet of a letter from the English campaigner Emily Hobhouse, who, during the Boer War in 1901, had gone behind the official scenes to reveal the true conditions at Bloemfontein and other concentration camps where the British were starving Afrikaner women and children. Writing her missive to 'American women, Friends of Humanity and Peace,' on 20 December 1914, Hobhouse called for a 'union of neutral women' to investigate suffering among non-combatants, reminding her readers that five civilians had died for every deceased combatant in the Boer War. She also quoted the words of Mrs St Clair Stobart, who had founded the Women's Convoy Corps to assist at field hospitals in Bulgaria during the Balkan war of 1912. Having seen the miseries that the fighting between Bulgaria and Turkey had brought to women and children in Thrace, Mrs Stobart had declared 'It is an evil thing that men only should witness the results of war. Wars will never cease till women—at whatever cost to themselves—are admitted behind the drop-curtain, and discover amongst the cardboard scenery and the grease paints which glorify for the public the tragedy of war, the brutal realities which are the secrets of those behind the footlights.'[73]

It was, surely, with a similar purpose in mind that the London organization of the Women's International League for Peace and Freedom would republish Lee's piece on 'Bach's Christmas Music in England and Germany' as a Christmas leaflet in 1917. Yet that article and her grotesquely theatrical *Ballet of the Nations* were by no means Lee's only contribution to the non-'passivist' anti-war effort in Britain. She had been working for the preservation of peace between Britain and Germany since long before August 1914. As she knew, the tensions that would eventually bring down her 'monstrous iron curtain' had been building since the beginning of the century, when Joseph Chamberlain, then Britain's Secretary of State for the Colonies, had offered an alliance between Britain, Germany, and America. Chamberlain was by then a Conservative and a notorious Imperialist too, but he had been more widely supported in this initiative: by harmonizing the nations with the biggest navy and the biggest land army respectively, his proposed alliance appeared to promise an 'unparalleled bulwark' against war.[74] In the event, however, the initiative was rejected by Germany, and Britain subsequently entered the *entente cordiale* with France in 1904—a development that fuelled a naval rivalry between Britain and Germany, which would soon enough see Europe divided into two 'armed camps'.[75]

For Lee, just as for the dissenters who, in 1911 (the year of the Agadir crisis), joined the Liberal MP Noel Buxton's 'Foreign Affairs Group' in Parliament, this increasingly perilous situation had demanded that the British Radical must give up his habitual indifference 'towards everything that happens outside his islands'.[76] In 1910, she had urged that the Liberal government, which was proving genuinely radical in its domestic programmes, must develop its own foreign policy rather than just continuing along the aggressively anti-German lines established by its Conservative predecessor. The time had come to tear down what she would later describe as 'the wall of Chauvinistic self-complacency'.[77]

It was a plea that might well have evoked a sympathetic response from at least one member of Asquith's Cabinet. Lee's preferred foreign policy was partly rooted in the old Liberal advocacy of free trade against the protection and tariffs espoused by Chamberlain and other Tories. One of the leading and most articulate opponents of Protection in the early years of the century had been Winston Churchill, who crossed the floor of the House of Commons over this issue in 1904. Having joined the Liberals, he applied his fiercest rhetoric to the policy of the Tory party he had just abandoned—declaiming, as he did in the House of Commons on 5 March 1905, 'we do not want to see the British Empire degenerate into a sullen confederacy, walled off, like a mediaeval town, from the surrounding country, victualled for a siege, and containing within the circle of its own battlements all that is necessary for war. We want this country and the States associated with it to take their parts freely and fairly in the general intercourse of commercial nations.'[78]

Yet free trade and the British Empire were by no means the only constituents of the young Churchill's internationalism during his years as a socially minded Liberal. In August 1908, the 33-year-old politician, who had, some three months earlier, been appointed president of the Board of Trade, visited Swansea in South Wales to address a festive 'demonstration of miners'. If the assembled men gave him a 'specially cordial' reception, this was only partly on account of his engagement to Miss Clementine Hozier, which had been announced that same morning. They were also abundantly grateful for the Miners Eight Hours Bill, a 'measure of relief and, as I hold, of justice', which Churchill had just steered through its second reading in the House of Commons.[79] Besides restricting the working day for miners, Churchill was, at that time of severe industrial distress, also seeking to erect various other 'bulwarks of safety' for the British working class. He was involved in the creation of a network of labour exchanges, promoting state-owned industries, regulating the use of 'sweated labour' in the garment trade and pushing, with the assistance of the young William Beveridge among others, for the introduction of a system of unemployment insurance that would bring 'the miracle of averages to the rescue of the masses'.[80]

At Swansea, this inspiring representative of the 'New Liberalism' that would find its most famous embodiment in Lloyd George's 'People's Budget' of 1909, paid tribute to the trade unions: 'let me say if I were a manual labourer the first thing I would do would be to join a trade union (cheers)'. He also urged the Welsh miners to maintain an internationalist outlook and, by implication, not to leave foreign policy to the ruling classes: 'Every man who is a British citizen has interests all over the world, and he must be concerned with the affairs of other countries beside his own.' No doubt Churchill had the British Empire in mind, but he was also acutely concerned about the 'unreal and nonsensical antagonism which is being artificially vamped up' between Britain and Germany.

Warning that a 'collision' between the two nations was likely to result in 'destruction of a most appalling and idiotic character', Churchill condemned those responsible for stirring up the tension. Naming both the crusted Tory imperialist Lord Cromer and also Robert Blatchford, the socialist super-patriot whose *Clarion* magazine was already filled with vicious assaults on Germany, he remarked: 'I think it is greatly to be deprecated that persons should try to spread the belief in this country that war between Great Britain and Germany is inevitable. It is nonsense.' The press, like certain London clubs, might be full of such 'snapping and snarling' but Churchill, gazing out over those appreciative coalminers in Swansea, declared himself confident in the power of the majority to prevent war if only its members awoke to the issues at hand. 'Are we all such sheep?' he asked, before falling back on the melodramatic toy theatre of his childhood: 'Is democracy in the 20th century so powerless to effect its will? Are we all become such puppets and marionettes to be wire-pulled against our interest into such hideous convulsions?'

If the young Winston Churchill was able to answer these rhetorical questions with a resounding 'no', this was because he professed a 'high and prevailing faith in the essential goodness of great people'. In particular, 'I believe that working classes all over the world are recognizing they have common interests and not divergent interests. I believe that what is called the international solidarity of labour has an immense boon to confer upon all the peoples of the world.' He used an improving illustration to bolster this remarkable statement of faith in the horizontally extended humanity of the common people:

> I was reading the other day of a story in the war between Germany and France in 1870. The Germans were occupying part of the French territory, and a visitor saw German soldiers, who were of the hostile garrison, when not on duty, working in the fields by the side of French peasants helping them to get in their crops. One of the German soldiers was asked 'Why do you do that to your enemy?' Said the German, 'War is all very well for the swells, but poor people have to help one another.'

It was an exceptional moment, and one that would be remembered and quoted on the Soviet side of the post-1946 Iron Curtain in Europe,[81] perhaps for the same reasons that it would fail to register in Randolph S. Churchill's official biography of his father.[82] Whether or not Winston Churchill briefly approved not just the comparatively moderate programmes of the International Labour Office in Basel but also the full-blooded socialism of the Second International, neither his optimism nor the smiles of those enraptured Welsh miners would survive for long.

Within two years of that speech Churchill had become Home Secretary in Asquith's Liberal Cabinet, harried by militant suffragettes and sending out troops to subdue rioting strikers in various parts of the country—including, most famously, Tonypandy in the South Wales coalfield.[83] As for his more or less pacifist attitude towards Germany, this died during the Agadir crisis of July 1911, when France occupied Morocco, Germany sent the destroyer 'Panther' to Agadir in response, and the prospect of war loomed as the British government sided with France. Previously known for his strong anti-war convictions, Churchill was now convinced that the British Empire must be prepared for war with Germany. Appointed First Lord of the Admiralty in October 1911, he set about increasing the size of the British fleet. Indeed, he joined the 'Dreadnought contests' of that time with a fervour that betrayed little trace of his earlier confidence in the 'essential goodness' of working people on both sides of the division or, for that matter, of his scorn for anti-German scaremongers. Writing two decades later, George Dangerfield would remember Churchill's new attitude as follows: 'Fleet and squadron, and flotilla, the guns, the tubes, the "murderous queens" of steel, all these were his to play with, to polish, to perfect; the administration of these precise and sanguinary toys touched some rich, secret place in his imagination, so that, lost in a drama as solitary as that of a child which plays by itself, he yet contrived to bring the whole Navy into a state of efficiency which would have been altogether beyond the powers of an ordinary First Lord.'[84]

Against Optical Illusion

Vernon Lee was among the disappointed. When, in August 1914, the long-anticipated war finally interposed its 'monstrous iron curtain' between Britain and Germany, it also severed the possible 'Lines of Anglo-German Agreement' that she had been advocating right up to the brink of war. In a supplement to *The Nation,* published in September 1910, she had reproduced arguments that the eminent German economist Lujo Brentano had advanced at the Antwerp Free Trade Congress in the hope of persuading his Radical friends in England that they 'had it in their hands to diminish the reciprocal distrust of the two great powers'.[85] Writing in May of that year, at a time when the death of Edward VII (the son of Prince Albert and therefore a member of the German House of Saxe-Coburg-Gotha) had momentarily 'brought English and German hearts into sympathy', Brentano, who would also be associated with the Carnegie Endowment for International Peace (established by the Scottish-born American steel magnate and philanthropist Andrew Carnegie in 1910), set out to answer those British fellow Liberals who had asked him why Germany was building warships if she did not intend war against Britain.

Brentano claimed that the problem was actually rooted in 'the traditional doctrine of England's supremacy on sea'—a supremacy that had enabled Britain to dominate the world's commerce ever since the Napoleonic Wars. Richard Cobden and other Liberal advocates of free trade had tried to dislodge this doctrine in the nineteenth century. Further attempts were made at an international conference concerned with maritime warfare, which met in London between 4 December 1908 and 26 February 1909. Initiated by Britain's Liberal Foreign Secretary, Sir Edward Grey, who hoped to see the emergence of 'generally recognized principles of international law',[86] the deliberations yielded a code defining contraband and the legality of naval blockade. The 'Declaration of London' failed when it was not ratified by the British House of Lords, yet Brentano surely had it in mind when he urged British Liberals to accept 'the inviolability of private property at sea' and to relinquish the piratical 'old-world rights of Blockade, Inspection, Search and Prize Money', which obliged even the most Anglophile of German Liberals to approve their own government's increase of arms in the name of self-defence.[87]

Lee's agreement with Brentano's proposed neutralization of the seas had soon brought her into direct conflict with the policies pursued by Winston Churchill as First Lord of the Admiralty. In November 1913, when Churchill announced that estimates for admiralty expenditure were once again to be substantially increased,[88] she had written to *The Nation*, recalling Brentano's unheeded appeal of 1910 and voicing her own support for his more recent advocacy of a state monopoly of arms manufacture: a measure, she suggested, that would create 'a possible saving of wars, and if not of actual wars, most certainly of such war-scares and armament-competition as it is in the obvious interest of the great international armament providers to encourage'.[89]

In support of Brentano, and with important consequences for her idea of the war's 'monstrous iron curtain', Lee had also invoked the arguments of Norman Angell, who, in a 'most remarkable little book' published in 1909, had claimed that the escalating 'rivalry in armaments' between Germany and Britain (epitomized by naval 'Dreadnought contests') was sustained by primitive ideas with no real purchase on modern reality.[90] It was, Angell asserted, only 'Europe's Optical Illusion' that suggested war between 'fully civilized rival nations'[91] could have financial benefits for the victor. Acts of conquest may indeed once have paid off: colonial wars might be followed by enslavement of populations, and medieval conquerors had gained fortunes in removable booty and land. However, such 'gains' or 'fruits' of war were no longer possible under modern conditions—thanks, not least, to the 'complex financial interdependence of the capitals of the world',[92] which meant that a German raid on the vaults of the Bank of England would create almost as much chaos in Germany as in England. Angell declared 'Europe's optical illusion' to be 'a gross and desperately dangerous misconception',[93] which locked nation states into anachronistic rivalry at the very moment when both capital and labour were becoming international and cosmopolitan, thereby dissolving the 'territoriality' that formed the *raison d'être* of the arms race in the first place.[94] Detected and named several years later, Lee's 'iron curtain' would possess exactly the self-perpetuating logic that Norman Angell had attributed to the arms rivalry between Britain and Germany: 'no Government dare reduce its military force while other Governments are dominated by the idea that the military breakdown of their neighbour is their opportunity'.[95]

Vernon Lee may have plucked it out of the theatre in a moment of appalled inspiration but the 'iron curtain' would not remain a disconnected phrase for long. As it descended in its new location between Britain and Germany, this recycled theatrical device described the now justified fears of the pre-war peace movement and, at the same time, represented a devastating setback for the new internationalism that so many political optimists—Lee, Rolland, and briefly also Winston Churchill—had espoused since the beginning of the twentieth century. Yet, as a vivid and suggestive image, the 'iron curtain' would find another expression before Lee and her colleagues in the anti-war movement had finished defining its new geopolitical role in Europe.

6

The Belgian Variation

The border between Belgium and the Netherlands has recently been proposed as the site of the first 'iron curtain' to be built with more conventional materials than the 'psychological deadlock' Vernon Lee had in mind.[1] The fence in question was made of wooden posts and wire, rather than official censorship, propaganda, and patriotic chauvinism. Like the 'iron curtain' that would divide Europe after the Second World War, it was erected with the purpose of keeping people in at least as much as out.

Having invaded neutral Belgium in August 1914, the Germans certainly had good reason to be concerned about the country's north-eastern border. The earliest wartime accounts tell of floods of refugees spilling across the unfortified line to escape the German advance. It remained highly permeable even after most of Belgium had been conquered and annexed. Young men continued to escape through the Netherlands (which remained neutral) to England, where they regrouped before returning to fight the Germans in Flanders. Allied espionage was run across the frontier, and there was even a remarkably efficient illicit postal system, which enabled parents in occupied Belgium to exchange letters with their sons at the front. Faced with these problems, together with persistent commercial smuggling and the flight of German deserters too, the German authorities decided to take steps.

Early in 1915, Germany had sealed up a stretch of the frontier between Alsace and Switzerland, and it was decided in the same year to close the Belgo-Dutch frontier with a fence of high tension electricity wires. As the historian of this 'first Iron Curtain' has written, 'by enclosing the country in a kind of cage, the occupier thought it would be able to put an end to clandestine cross-frontier circulation'.[2] So, between April and August of that year, large tracts of the frontier were wired off with a triple-layered fence consisting of two outer rows of a non-electrified nature and a central one made of 2-metre-high wooden posts, each bearing five or six strands of wire on porcelain isolators, and carrying a current of up to 2,000 volts provided by generators. With guardhouses placed at every 2 kilometres along its length, the fence extended over a distance of some 300 kilometres and passed through many different communes.

For the people living nearby, this solidified frontier was attended by the usual 'separation' problems. Villages were bisected and dismembered. Children could no longer reach their schools or, in some cases, go home for Christmas. Houses near the fence were requisitioned, and farmers found themselves barred from their own orchards and fields.

Those who died at the fence included German deserters, smugglers, and would-be volunteers escaping to serve with the Allies. Yet there were also victims of a more innocent kind, including the Veryheijen sisters, Toke (aged 32) and Joke (37), who found themselves separated by the fence. Toke lived with her parents at Castelré in Holland, while her elder sister lived nearby on the Belgian side at Minderhout. The German guards, in particular a well-disposed fellow remembered only as 'Karl', allowed them to meet by the fence from time to time, turning a blind eye as they exchanged little parcels. On 9 October 1916, Toke approached the fence from the Dutch side and tried to throw a packet over to her sister. Unfortunately, it fell short, landing between the wires. Joke tried to recover it, but she inadvertently brushed the fence with her hair or apron and was immediately electrocuted. Toke attempted to reach her stricken sister but, in her agitation, suffered the same fate. When the bodies were retrieved, it was found that their faces, hands, and wrists had been carbonized by the current. As for the parcel, some would later speculate that it may have contained a bottle of oil or medicine for the sisters' ailing mother. Others suggested a pair of shoes, since there was no shoe shop at Castelré.

The 'death fence' is estimated to have killed some 500 people during the course of the war, but it failed to prevent espionage, or the way of volunteers escaping to fight on the Allied side. Smugglers used ingenious folding frames of wood or open-ended barrels to create a way through the electrified wire. The passage of letters continued too. At the end of the war, the hated fence disappeared with extraordinary speed. In some communes, indeed, it was destroyed several weeks before the armistice was signed. Sold off at public auctions, its materials were returned to the countryside where, for decades to come, old isolators and bullet marks could be found adorning recycled fence posts at the edges of otherwise peaceful fields.

Cladding for a Compromised Queen

It is, of course, only in late twentieth-century retrospect that this electrified Belgo-Dutch frontier appears as a candidate for the title of Europe's first 'iron curtain'. That theatrical expression was definitely employed in Belgium during the first year of the war. However, it was used very differently: not to identify a closed frontier, but to assert an altogether more personal Belgian loyalty against a Prussian aggressor that had left a 'black track of ruin'[3] through that small and neutral land.

In Allied states as well as in America and other neutral countries, Germany's 'rape of Belgium' was recognized, with the help of the war's first exaggerated 'atrocity' stories, as an act of shocking barbarism, quite unprecedented in recent European history. Writing in London, the displaced Belgian poet Émile Cammaerts spoke for millions when he declared, 'Never has the choice between right and wrong been made plainer in the whole history of the world.'[4] It was in this violently polarized circumstance, some three months after Vernon Lee had mobilized the phrase in London's Temple church, that the 'iron curtain' would be invoked by a Belgian for whom Cammaerts's stark choice proved uniquely challenging.

The man who recorded this usage, Louis-Marie-Julian Viaud, was 64 years old when war broke out in August 1914. A retired captain in France's naval reserve, Viaud had sailed the world and then returned to live at Rochefort by the Bay of Biscay. Yet he was also 'Pierre Loti', the famous author of many romantic travel books set in remote and exotic places: Brittany, Turkey, Siam, Tahiti, Egypt, Palestine, China, India, and also Japan, the location of *Madame Chrysanthème* (1888), his partly autobiographical story of a French naval officer's love affair with a geisha (which was to become the source of Puccini's *Madama Butterfly* and thence also of the 1989 musical *Miss Saigon*).

As a celebrated escapist whose love of 'elsewhere' had long reflected his contempt for the 'imbecile materialism' of the West,[5] Loti had turned his house in Rochefort into a fabulous orientalist den, equipped with Arab and Turkish rooms and furnished with exotic fabrics and souvenirs. And yet the German assault on France through Belgium revealed Loti to be a patriot who was not prepared to linger in nineteenth-century dreams of otherness. He contributed a stirring piece to *King Albert's Book*, the *Daily Telegraph's* collection of 'civilised' tributes to the Belgian monarch and his barbarously assaulted people: in his article, Loti measured Germany's brutality with the help of a boy of about 5, reported to have stepped off a train packed with Belgian refugees, exhausted, clutching his 3-year-old brother, and able only to ask 'Madame, is anyone going to put us to bed?'[6] Eager to make a more practical contribution to the war effort, Loti was soon being driven around the front by his chauffeur: an elderly figure dressed in a bafflingly out-of-place naval uniform and carrying out vague missions on behalf of higher authorities.

As a fiercely patriotic Frenchman, Pierre Loti made no attempt to stand 'above' the battle, in Romain Rolland's already notorious phrase, or even to remain 'outside' it in the less elevated stance adopted by Vernon Lee. He was tempted neither to resist the interpretation construing the violated frontier between Belgium and Germany as an absolute division between good and evil, nor to acquit the German people by blaming the war on the folly of statesmen and diplomats. In articles collected in two books of this time, *La Hyèna enragé* (1916) and *L'Horreur allemande* (1918), he portrays the Germans as utter monsters—fit, like their entire Prussianized culture, to be hated without exception. As one of Europe's best-known friends of 'primitive' or anthropological paradises, Loti knew the Germans to be far worse than any authentic savage. Quoting from an old sailor with whom he had once sailed the far seas, he loathed them all as 'barbarians with pink skin like boiled pig'.[7]

Loti paid special attention to the mutilation of neutral Belgium, noting how, in the opening weeks of the war, the Germans had made a rubbish heap of that 'tranquil country', murdering civilians and wrecking the cities and towns that had made Belgium an 'incomparable museum'. In March 1915, he visited Ypres, finding its cathedral mutilated and its famous Cloth Hall burned out by the benzene bombs and 'scrap metal' that the Germans seemed to reserve for historic buildings, and would soon enough unleash, with even more infamous consequences, against Reims cathedral.

Despatched on a mission by the President of the French Republic, Loti also sought out Albert, the 'sublimely heroic'[8] king of the Belgians. Albert had faced the immense challenge of 1914, rallying his outraged people as neutral Belgium became 'the first rampart against barbarism'.[9] As Germany's vastly superior military machine prevailed, Albert and his forces had been obliged to withdraw from Brussels and then, along with hundreds of thousands of terrified civilians, to retreat from Antwerp to Ostend on the coast of Flanders. His troubles had not ended here, as Pierre Loti discovered when he reached the shattered town of Veurne (Furnes), after driving through icy wind, snow, and hail. It too had been 'wantonly and savagely' bombarded after King Albert established himself there, and Loti and his chauffeur were obliged to drive on to the remote village that was by then serving as general headquarters of the Belgian army.

Finding Albert in a modest house among the trees and tombs of an ancient Flemish abbey, Loti is filled with reverence and respect for this man who had distinguished himself as commander-in-chief of the Belgian armed forces even though, having been born only third in line to the throne, he had neither expected nor much wanted to become king. On the death of his uncle Leopold II (who had already lost his son and his older nephew), Albert had taken the crown in the reasonable expectation of 'an era of profound peace, in the midst of the most peaceful of all nations'. Far from fleeing for safety when the German invasion came, Albert became commander-in-chief of his armed forces and led his soldiers in their desperate attempt to stem the German advance for long enough to give France time to muster its resources. Dispensing with unnecessary ceremony, he had, so Loti wrote, 'stood erect in the way of the Monster's onrush, a great warrior king in the midst of an army of heroes'.[10]

Loti didn't hesitate when it came to dividing Good from Evil in the nationally defined way that so dismayed Vernon Lee. He measured the difference between Belgium and Germany in the contrast between Albert and the Kaiser:

> I compare these two monarchs, situated, as it were, at opposite poles of humanity, the one at the pole of light, the other at the pole of darkness; the one yonder, swollen with hypocrisy and arrogance, a monster among monsters, his hands full of blood, his nails full of torn flesh, who still dares to surround himself with insolent pomp; the other here, banished without a murmur to a little house in a village, standing on a last strip of his martyred kingdom, but in whose honour rises from the whole civilised earth a concert of sympathy, enthusiasm, magnificent appreciation, and for whom are stored up crowns of most pure and immortal glory.[11]

Exceptional bravery would also be attributed to Albert's Queen Elisabeth. To reach her refuge, Loti had to drive 'far away and out of the world' into the westernmost corner of Flanders.[12] His destination lay on the western edge of De Panne (La Panne), then a small fishing resort commanding a vast beach on the southern shore of the North Sea.

Arriving at nightfall, he stepped out into driving wind and rain. He heard the sea roaring and, peering out over the dunes, saw the grey outlines of the three unlit seaside villas now occupied by Albert and Elisabeth and their much-reduced court. Having been received at the first of these dwellings, which accommodated officers and ladies-in-waiting, he was escorted across the sand towards the villa in which the queen was living—reputedly the last house before France. De Panne's famous sands were pale in the darkness, swept by cold wind and 'white butterflies' that turn out to be flakes of snow. 'Would you not imagine it a sight in the Sahara?' asked the lantern-bearing aide-de-camp, mindful of Loti's travels in North Africa, and adding that the illusion had seemed complete when France's Arab cavalry were recently in the area.[13] Loti, however, declared that the gloomy overcast sky of the northern night made Flanders' 'transported' Sahara far too deeply melancholic.

They then entered the red brick Villa Maskens, in which Albert and Elisabeth had initially expected to spend only a few nights, and certainly not the four long years to come. Some visitors to this makeshift royal home found the place damp and all but overwhelmed by freezing winds beating in off the North Sea. A British colonel, who noted that the building stood open to attack from both air and sea, commended the patriotic determination with which the queen ignored the passing aeroplanes as she took tea.[14] Raymond Poincaré, president of France, had declared the villa 'furnished with extreme simplicity', when he visited Elisabeth in November 1914.[15] Four months later, Loti found it brightly lit and warmed against the 'wintry squalls' by a blazing fire. Noting the fine and unusually white carpentry of a packing-case resting on two chairs, the author of *Madame Chrysanthème* was pleased to be informed that it contained a 'magnificent ancient sabre' recently presented to King Albert by the Japanese, much moved by the plight of their invaded Belgian ally.

Soon enough Elisabeth, queen of the Belgians, appeared in the room. When President Poincaré of France visited she had been dressed in white, composing a figure of 'exquisite charm': 'frail and delicate, one would think a breath of wind would blow her away and that anyhow she would be broken by the storm which is raging around her, but she has nerves of steel and a soul which no Kaiser will conquer'. Emerging from behind a screen of red silk, she impressed Loti as 'a dazzling little vision of blue—the blue of her gown, but more especially the blue of her eyes, which shine like two luminous stars'.[16] Though in her mid-forties, the queen of the Belgians retained a remarkable 'air of youth; she seems this evening twenty-four, and scarcely that'.

Elisabeth may have been physically slight, but she had already become a vast figure in Allied legend. Her husband was revered as 'Albert the Brave', the reluctant 'warrior-king' who, though without any previous military distinction, had led his troops through three months of courageous if also impossible defence of his little country. As his inspiring consort, Elisabeth was feted as a war hero too—adored and celebrated as Belgium's 'nurse-queen'. Rather than staying in England, where she had taken her three children to find refuge at the home of Lord Curzon, she had returned to share the trials of her people. Drawing on skills she had learned while helping her late father, Karl-Theodor (who had been an ophthalmologist as well as a Bavarian duke), she was said to have set up field hospitals and worked as a nurse with wounded soldiers. During the withdrawal from Antwerp, in the second week of October 1914, she was to be found handing out encouragement and cigarettes to exhausted soldiers. At De Panne, she had worked with Dr Antoine Depage and the International Red Cross, creating a large hospital for wounded soldiers in a former hotel named 'L'Océan', and equipping it through orders placed with Harrods and other London stores. She secured Christmas trees, clothes, and other presents for the patients, and was reported even to have made individual floral arrangements for the wounded.

In reality Elisabeth may only have assisted Dr Depage in a small number of surgical operations, just as she only attended the wounded under exceptional circumstances. Yet her reputation as the virtuous 'nurse-queen'[17] was confirmed by widely distributed photographs portraying her in white nursing garb. Together with her ongoing efforts on behalf of children, her hospital work was sufficient to establish her as a saintly figure: an embodiment of the soul of little Belgium, and even the 'mother' of the nation's struggling armed forces. At Christmas 1914, some characteristic tributes had been published in *King Albert's Book*. In a poem by the American actor Edward H. Sothern, 'Elisabeth of Belgium' became a saviour among the wounded and dying: 'Laving the bleeding feet and making whole | The battle-broken' and, even in her country's darkest night, embodying the bright dawn to come.[18] Remembering the French conscripts who had named themselves 'Marie-Louises' in 1813, the French dramatist Maurice Donnay suggested that Belgian soldiers might aptly call themselves 'The Elisabeths' after their queen.[19] The Belgian poet Émile Verhaeren contributed to the transformation, turning Elisabeth, in her customary white clothing, into a symbol of purity and delicate refinement confronted by the blackest barbarism. Her small physical stature suggested courage and dignity as well as the defencelessness of a small neutral nation faced by an overwhelming bully.[20] The legend of the 'nurse-queen' was put to good use in America where it prompted sympathy for Belgium, the Allied cause, and also for Herbert Hoover's Commission for Relief in Belgium.

No doubt there were some for whom this boosted imagery only went to show that, in the words of the radical British journalist H. N. Brailsford, 'Propaganda in the modern world weaves the mind of the mass, much as a mill weaves cotton.'[21] Pierre Loti, however, was not among the doubters. He presents himself as all but overwhelmed by his regard for the Belgian queen and her 'devotion to duty, the superlative dignity of her actions, her serene resignation, her admirable, simple charity'. And yet their conversation in that villa on the dunes circulated around a delicate and initially unspoken fact. The queen opened by talking about books and the Far East, where both had travelled. Once confidence was established, they moved on to discuss Germany's destruction of Belgian towns such as Ypres and Vuerne. Loti volunteered that enough remained standing to allow for accurate reconstruction in the better times that were surely to come. But Elisabeth found limited consolation in this prospect. It would indeed be possible to rebuild, 'but it will never be more than an imitation, and for me something essential will always be lacking. I shall miss the soul which has passed away.'

Throughout this exchange Loti was searching Elisabeth's face for indications of 'what stirs in the depths of her heart when she contemplates the drama of her destiny'. The inconvenient fact was that Elisabeth had been a Bavarian princess when she married Albert in 1900. The legend of the 'nurse-queen' had been used partly to forestall the awkward realization that the queen of the Belgians was herself a child of the monstrous enemy. By her selfless actions and her agony over the ruin of Belgian cities, Elisabeth had, in Maurice Donnay's words, 'become a Belgian by her crown and heart'.[22] Yet good works could not entirely obscure her German origins.

To begin with, Elisabeth had tried to rescue something of her cosmopolitan past. A few weeks into the war, speaking with 'much emotion' to France's minister to Belgium, she had lamented 'the acts of cruelty committed by the German armies on a quiet and inoffensive population', adding that 'Those who planned this war and are carrying it on are mad; nothing but madness can explain such a horror.'[23] As Loti closed in on the same question six months later, she persisted with the idea that 'There has been some change in them ... They used not to be like this. The Crown Prince, whom I knew very well in childhood, was gentle, and nothing in him led one to expect—Think of it as I may, day and night, I cannot understand— No, in the old days they were not like this, of that I am sure.'

As an uncompromising Hun-hater, Loti was not inclined to grant any such concession: nor, for that matter, was he much interested in differentiating Bavarian Huns from Prussian ones. Though maintaining a respectful silence as the queen of the Belgians agonized, he reassured his readers that the Germans had, as he well knew, been 'the same from the beginning under their inscrutable hypocrisy', their souls always 'steeped in lies, murders, and rapine' as their appalling literature and philosophy testified. Yet he could not bring himself 'to contradict this Queen, born among them, like a beautiful, rare flower among stinging nettles and brambles'. Loti recognized that 'one of the most dreaded duties that falls almost invariably to the lot of queens is having to reign over adopted countries while exiled from their own'. For Elisabeth this fate had been unusually agonizing: 'In the special case of this young martyred queen, this doom of exile which has befallen her, and many other queens, must be a far more exquisite torture, added to all the other evils endured, for a crushing fatality has come and separated her for ever from all who were once her own people, even from that noble woman, all devotion and charity, who was her mother.'[24]

Loti made some show of revering Elisabeth as the well-loved queen who had suppressed her own agonies in order to serve as a companion to her husband, to the wounded and bereaved among her adopted people, to the poor who had lost everything to fire and pillage. Yet those German roots lay there, undeniable and exposed to examination among the red furnishings of that room in the Villa Maskens.

Elisabeth was not the only European monarch who would become embarrassed by her German origins in the Great War; but she was in no position to pursue the solution eventually adopted by George V in 1917 when he changed the name of the British royal family, creating the House of Windsor and casting the name of Saxe-Coburg-Gotha firmly into the past. After a moment of silence, broken only by the beating wind outside, Loti made a conciliatory move, reporting that Bavarian soldiers in the German army had apparently been troubled by the persecutions inflicted on their former princess by a Prussian kaiser who had gone so far as to target her children with his artillery fire. Elisabeth, however, would allow no concessions to her personal agony, which had certainly been intensi-fied, as Émile Cammaerts would later point out, by 'the fact that some of her kinsman were among the leaders of the German invasion'.[25] No sooner had Loti opened the question than she headed him off, raising her hand in 'a gesture which signifies something inexorably final' and uttering 'this phrase which falls upon the silenced with the solemnity of a sentence whence there is no appeal:"It is at an end. Between *them* and me has fallen a curtain of iron which will never again be lifted."'[26]

No Easy Succession

Elisabeth's iron curtain was a personal fate as well as a calculated promise: an absolute and final separation to be born stoically because the alternative was not just to yield to a monster, but to become one in the eyes of her own adopted people. Her submission to nationality was also a requirement of the propaganda war, without which it would have been impossible for Belgian patriots and their Allied sympathizers to revere the queen while at the same time hating the Germans as, in Loti's expression, 'barbarians with pink skin like boiled pig'.

Elisabeth's invocation of the iron curtain has since been much cited. In one biography she is alleged to have made the remark during the first days of the war, in August 1914. The translation varies too. One writer quotes the queen as saying, 'it is finished. Between her and me there is an iron curtain which has descended for ever.'[27] Others refer to a 'bloody iron curtain', while also dating the remark to 1914. It has been said that Elisabeth 'coined' the phrase that would later be 'immortalised' by Churchill.[28] However, the original source for this quotation appears to be Loti, who dated his own account of 'Some Words Uttered by Her Majesty, the Queen of the Belgians', to March 1915.

It is impossible to establish whether or not Elisabeth had read Lee's article about 'Bach's Christmas Music in England and Germany' when it first appeared in *Jus Suffragi* on 1 January 1915. Yet the worlds of these two women may conceivably have touched. Long known for her commitment to social improvement as well as her strong musical interests, Elisabeth may have felt, behind the cover of her defensive iron curtain, considerable empathy with those who opposed the causes of war rather than just the loathed and demonised Prussian enemy. As a woman of pronounced cosmopolitan interests, she may also have known about the International Woman Suffrage Alliance (the publisher of *Jus Suffragi*): not just through the work of its International Women's Relief Committee, which set up a special fund for Belgian Refugees in Holland, but also through the Belgian Woman's Patriotic Union, a 'bureau for the centralisation of feminine energy',[29] established at the beginning of the German invasion by the Belgian suffragist Madame Jane Brigode.

Elisabeth would not establish the still flourishing Queen Elisabeth International Music Competition until 1937 (two years after the death of Vernon Lee); and it would be even longer before she emerged as the so-called 'Red Queen' who made controversial visits to Communist Poland (1955), Russia (1957), and China (1961), often using invitations to music festivals as her justification for breaking through the politicized frontiers she found increasingly intolerable.[30] She would also develop a high regard for Romain Rolland, the French humanitarian and internationalist. Their paths may not have crossed by March 1915, but in those years Rolland already represented much that Elisabeth valued: a strong dedication to music conceived as witness to the European soul; a devotion to the International Red Cross; and, in the early weeks of the war, outrage at the kaiser's onslaught, which Rolland had denounced for burning paintings by Rubens and destroying the great library of Louvain: 'Kill men if you like, but respect masterpieces. They are the patrimony of the human race.'[31]

Although strongly opposed to the war, Rolland had consented to appear alongside Norman Angell, Lloyd George, Winston Churchill, Edward Carpenter, and scores of other more or less 'representative' figures in the pages of *King Albert's Book*. In this volume of tributes raised by the *Daily Telegraph,* he commended 'the miracle of Belgian resistance'. Claiming that Belgium's heroic stand had actually secured 'the liberation of the oppressed idealism of the West', he went on to praise neutral Belgian's soil as 'the most fertile in Europe in the harvests of the soul. From it sprang the art of modern painting, which the school of the Van Eycks spread throughout the world at the time of the Renaissance, and the art of modern music, of that polyphony which thrilled through France, Germany, and Italy for two centuries.'[32]

Elisabeth and Rolland would become acquainted in the 1930s, when she visited him at his home in Vézelay. Yet, at the beginning of 1915, the socialist author of *Jean-Christophe* had his doubts about the emerging cult of Elisabeth the 'nurse-queen'. Shortly after his copy of *King Albert's Book* arrived, he wrote to his mother lamenting the 'inept' quality of the heroism there exhibited, wondering about the absence of H. G. Wells and George Bernard Shaw from the list of contributors, and singling out the French composer Camille Saint-Saëns for his description, at once fawning and self-important, of how Elisabeth, the increasingly propagandized queen of the Belgians, had once taken *his* photograph.[33]

Whatever its derivation, Elisabeth's 'iron curtain' was more like a defensive garment than the propaganda-fired 'psychological deadlock' that Vernon Lee had seen planted in the minds of the belligerent peoples. First described by Loti, it would later be brandished by other defenders of the queen, including Maurice des Ombiaux, a Belgian poet whose highly patriotic portrait of Elisabeth was published by the French royalist journal *L'Action française* in 1915.[34]

Like the more socialist Flemish-born poet Émile Verhaeren, des Ombiaux was enraptured by the thought of Elisabeth, and happy to disseminate her legend as a woman of rare sensibility and conscience. He hailed her as a musician who had intervened personally to save the sight of a despairing artist, Eugène Laermans, and also as a social activist who, long before the war, was known for her work against tuberculosis, and for taking, each year, three hundred children from poor working-class districts for a holiday by the sea.[35] So impressive had she been in her commitment to the health and welfare of the common people, that she is said even to have tamed 'the tigers of Belgian socialism', who conceded that Albert might be retained as president of their promised republic.[36]

Des Ombiaux burnishes the legend of the 'nurse-queen', telling how, shortly after retreating to De Panne on October 1914, Elisabeth had taken over a shop near her villa, and filled it with gifts, driven over from London in thirty-five cars, which she would present to wounded soldiers at Christmas.[37] There was, he emphasized, no need to ask Elisabeth what she thought of 'Belgium's executioners', because she had already told Pierre Loti about the iron curtain that now formed a permanent barrier between Germany and herself.[38]

Elisabeth's 'iron curtain' would serve this purpose repeatedly. Writing about her parents more than fifty years later, Elisabeth's daughter, Marie José, recalled that Georges Clemenceau, who became France's prime minister in November 1917, had initially hesitated to pay his respects to Elisabeth, obsessed as he was by her German origins. She condemned this response on the grounds that Clemenceau must surely have known very well what

Elisabeth had earlier said to Loti.[39] President Raymond Poincaré, who was always respectful of Elisabeth, would recall how 'German calumnies against the King and Queen of Belgium' had penetrated into the British, Belgian, and French armies, and were even to be heard in the streets of Paris.[40] These whispers, which went so far as to insinuate that Elisabeth was a German spy feeding information back through agents in Switzerland,[41] impressed Poincaré as an 'abominable campaign' of slanders. They help to explain why, in its Belgian variation, the iron curtain became a suit of armour that a still-fondly remembered queen had to wear to preserve her status as a personification of the soul of her savaged little country, and not stand condemned as another bloody Hun.

7

In Defence of Otherness

War fever is an infectious mental disease. When infection is rife it is the moral duty of the healthy to avoid contamination.

Douglas Goldring[1]

By the time Elisabeth of Bavaria sat gathering the 'iron curtain' around herself on the windswept dunes of De Panne, Vernon Lee was developing her less personal version into a far-reaching analysis of the war as it came to dominate the public mind in Britain. Elisabeth had been alone as she fended off the suspicions of Pierre Loti but Lee was by no means so isolated in her endeavours. Her views were strongly opposed by many, and yet her stand against the war and its 'monstrous iron curtain' would be pursued as a shared objection.

Speaking at a public meeting in Manchester on 17 December 1914, the campaigner E. D. Morel had condemned the war as a 'wall of fire and steel'[2] that separated soldiers on the opposed sides while at the same time linking them by 'a catholicity of suffering'. It was exactly this doubled and contradictory impact, registered with the same sense of outraged humanitarianism, that Lee attributed to her 'iron curtain' when she described listening to Bach's Christmas music at the Temple church a week later. As this coincidence may suggest, Lee continued to think and write as a member of a wider anti-war movement: an internationally minded circle that helped prepare the ground on which the League of Nations would be established five years later.

'During the fatal opening days of last August, when the hopes of a generation withered before our eyes and civilisation plunged back into barbarism, a small group of men met together in the house of one of them.'[3]

That, as E. D. Morel recalled, was how the Union of Democratic Control
(UDC) came to be launched in September 1914. Having long feared that
Europe's statesmen were leading their nations towards a catastrophe, thanks
largely to the secret diplomacy with which they manoeuvred for advantage
within an inherently unstable balance of power, Vernon Lee was among the
women who joined Morel's 'small group of men', many of whom she had
already encountered in the pre-war peace movement. Other supporters of
the, at first, tiny campaign included Ramsay MacDonald, Fred Jowett, and
Philip Snowden (all of the Independent Labour Party), the philosopher and
later conscientious objector Bertrand Russell, and the Quaker chocolate
magnates George Cadbury and Arnold Rowntree. Norman Angell attended
the early meetings, as did the veteran anti-imperialist John A. Hobson, the
journalist and Balkan expert H. N. Brailsford, and also the radical Liberal
MPs Charles Trevelyan and Arthur Ponsonby.

E. D. Morel became the UDC's secretary. The son of Anglo-French
Quakers, he had looked 'behind the veil' of secret diplomacy before the
war, when he spent eleven years contesting the 'atrocious system of slavery' perpetrated in the 'Congo Free State' under Leopold II of Belgium
(a murderous regime maintained, as Morel had insisted on behalf of the
Congo Reform Association, with the knowledge of 'every Chancellery
in Europe').[4] In August 1917, Morel would be jailed for trying to send a
couple of pamphlets to Romain Rolland, then working for the International
Committee of the Red Cross in neutral Switzerland.[5] By that time, the
UDC had branches all over the country, a hugely expanded membership
(650,000 people are said to have been affiliated by October 1918), and links
with like-minded bodies in many other countries, including the United
States of America where a Committee for Democratic Control was set up
to campaign along the same lines. The latter organization's founders, who
included the literary radical Randolph S. Bourne, and also Max Eastman and
Winthrop D. Lane,[6] shared the young Walter Lippmann's optimistic if not
frankly naïve designs on 'the future of patriotism',[7] hoping to see allegiances
steadily transferred from Europe's warring nations to the international world
government of their desired scenario.

In the wake of international feminist agitation in Europe, the cause had
also been joined by the prodigiously wealthy car-manufacturer Henry Ford.
In November 1915, Ford issued an appeal from his temporary headquarters
in New York's Hotel Biltmore, inviting diverse 'representatives of American
democracy' to join himself and a large posse of journalists on a 'peace

pilgrimage' intended to save the peoples of Europe from their warring governments, which were plainly prepared to slog on with the slaughter until one side won or both were bled white.

Aiming to appeal to the belligerent nations by organizing representatives of Europe's six remaining neutral countries into a 'conference for continuous mediation', Ford's delegation would board the Scandinavian-American steamship *Oscar II* and sail from New York on 4 December. Fuelled by optimistic slogans promising to 'get the boys out of the trenches by Christmas', this 'peace ship' would visit Christiana (Oslo), Stockholm, Copenhagen, and then The Hague where its passengers looked forward to meeting Spanish and Swiss delegations. By that time, so Ford anticipated, 'the moral power of the peace movement will be irresistible'.[8] He had not anticipated the internal disputation that would break out shortly after the peace ship had left New York, and only get worse when his 'crusade', in which idealistic principles had been at loggerheads with pragmatic questions of diplomacy, presentation, and management from the start, arrived in Europe.

Henry Ford abandoned his fractious and widely mocked pilgrimage quickly enough, quitting the mission's hotel in Christiana on Christmas Eve, and sailing for home as speedily as he could. The UDC, however, would prove more durable. Some sense of its founding premiss can be gleaned from the writings of Goldsworthy Lowes Dickinson, an influential member who was also a fellow of King's College, Cambridge. Shortly after the outbreak, Dickinson wrote that the war had been started, against the wishes of the people on both sides, because 'certain men' in positions of power had fallen captive to 'the governmental theory'. In this dangerously deficient outlook, 'the world is divided, politically, into States. These States are a kind of abstract Beings, distinct from the men, women and children who are, have been, or will be their members. They are in perpetual and inevitable antagonism to one another.'[9] It was an argument that would be reprised elsewhere, including in the USA, where Randolph S. Bourne famously declared that 'war is the health of the State'.[10]

Wary of just striking dogmatic pacifist positions, the Union of Democratic Control sought to settle the war by replacing the scheming of powerful imperialist states with a new 'International Council'[11]—or 'League of Nations', as the UDC would also call it, following Lowes Dickinson who had started promoting this idea in the opening weeks of the war[12]—capable of guaranteeing the security of small nations and of overseeing a common programme of disarmament. The publications in which the UDC spelt out its 'Cardinal Points' also reveal a strong commitment to the liberal principle of 'publicity'. This entailed a thoroughgoing rejection of secret diplomacy of the kind that had bound Britain, without the knowledge of Parliament or even some members of the Cabinet, to enter the war on the side of France. Convinced that Sir Edward Grey's secret treaties had, as one objector put it, enabled 'a handful of diplomats to plunge the world into war on an August Bank Holiday',[13] the UDC was determined to democratize the Foreign Office and, in the words of E. D. Morel, to make it impossible ever again for a Foreign Secretary 'to pledge the country's honour without the country's knowledge'.[14]

The members of this circle would also come to be much concerned with the cultural dimensions of the conflict as it dragged on over four years. They opposed the war not just as a series of military engagements on foreign fronts but as a manipulated 'state of mind' that gripped each nation at home. It was easy enough for *The Times* to print letters attributing this problem to the enemy side: quoting Professor Otfried Nippold's account (written in Berne, Switzerland) of the 'flood of chauvinism' that had 'debauched the national mind' in Germany,[15] or unmasking Goethe as the prophet of 'self-culture' who had inspired so many 'smaller men' in their Hunnish megalomania.[16]

The UDC, however, addressed the problem as it existed in Britain. In the first issue of its bulletin (later renamed *Foreign Affairs*), the radical Liberal campaigner and philanthropist Charles Roden Buxton pointed out that serving soldiers did not generally hold extreme pro-war views: 'It is the civilians at home who treat war as a game, and who demand that it shall continue until some kind of dramatic triumph has been achieved which will make a striking headline in their daily paper and will give them a glow of satisfaction.'[17] The UDC would make that point repeatedly, although its writers and lecturers usually blamed the press rather than the civilian readers who were so deliberately orchestrated in their patriotism.

Alongside the Union

Vernon Lee was not among the UDC members who were jailed, personally assaulted as Hun-loving traitors at the behest of the *Daily Express*, or, in Charles Roden Buxton's phrase, 'shouted down' for their allegedly unpatriotic views.[18] She did, however, write leaflets, pamphlets, and articles for

the cause, insisting on the importance of 'the democratic principle' in international relations and outlining the UDC's route to 'Peace with Honour'.[19]
In personal encounters she revealed herself to be a 'white-heater' sufficiently
fierce against Allied war policy to repel other objectors: the novelist Frank
Swinnerton judged her 'very pro-German'[20] and Goldsworthy Lowes
Dickinson, who met Lee at the house of Arthur Ponsonby, listened to her
'fantastic diatribes' and concluded that, like Rupert Brooke, she had simply
'abandoned the pursuit of reason'.[21]

As part of her contribution to this wider struggle against the war, Lee
kept reworking her *Ballet of the Nations*: expanding and equipping it with
both a Prologue and an Epilogue in which Satan uses a cinematic projector
to display a sequence of distinctly UDC-shaped preliminary scenes—'bare
caricatures'[22] as he admits—from the years building up to the outbreak.
Diplomats are shown scheming within the paranoia-inducing alliances that,
in mockery of all Liberal principles, had placed Britain on the side of the
tsar's brutally repressive Russian empire. Capitalist manufacturers are shown
demanding that politicians take ruthless measures to assist their exploitation
of Africa. Complacent fathers, who had championed 'Liberty' and the Paris
Commune in their youth, now refuse to stir themselves except in defence of
'order and property'. Newspapermen and propagandists rail against 'Aliens'
and drive the masses into war with the help of carefully planted poems,
invocations of 'heritage', and cooked-up atrocity stories.[23] Assorted statesmen reject peace overtures as among 'the most dangerous things in the
world',[24] thereby pleasing both the international armament manufacturers,
who proclaim war as a chance to imprison pacifists and make 'first class
patriots' out of 'Socialist ruffians', and also the generals who yearn to put an
end to 'all this unmanly and dangerous democratic twaddle'.[25]

Recognizing how little of the truth about this protracted modern war
could be captured in a pseudo-medieval allegory, Lee also enlarged on the
themes of her *Ballet of the Nations* in a remarkable series of 'psychological
essays'[26] written between 1917 and August 1919. In 1920, the work that had
started out as a 'crude emblematic improvisation' of some twenty pages in
length was republished as the much-enlarged centre of a 300-page treatise
on the war and its consequences. Still dedicated to Romain Rolland, it now
appeared as *Satan the Waster: A Philosophic War Trilogy with Notes & Introduction*. The work was largely ignored once again—'boycotted' so Lee would
claim in 1930, when she somehow persuaded her publisher to reissue rather
than pulp the unsold copies.[27]

It was a demanding project, to be sure. Lee's most recent biographer fears that the 'modern-day reader' will find *Satan the Waster* 'a pompous bombastic exercise in futility'.[28] Certainly, the book is exasperating, yet this should not be attributed only to Lee's 'wordiness, shrillness, illogical thinking'. *Satan the Waster* is the work of a writer who found her views on the war unwanted even by once favourably disposed editors. Driven into what another UDC member would remember as 'internal exile'[29] she was left firing tirades at her desk, and her book became a disorderly refuge for unwanted ideas that, having no other outlet, could only fight their own war inside her head. Remembering how, in 1904, she had published a collection of 'moral essays' under the title of *Hortus Vitae*, or 'the Garden of Life', Lee confessed that her more recent 'war thoughts', being raised in a ruinous 'Garden of Death',[30] were 'extraordinarily unattractive' even to her own taste.[31] Yet these relentless pages offer a fiercely intelligent analysis of the conflict—one in which the vertical division Lee had earlier named war's 'monstrous iron curtain' remains a dominant and much elaborated feature.

Admitting that many of her friends had been deeply offended by her *Ballet of the Nations* when it was first published at the end of 1915, Lee defended herself against the charge of 'aloofness', while at the same time conceding that she had indeed been engaged in 'looking on at the War' and 'trying to understand its spiritual phenomena'[32] from outside—although not, in her friend Romain Rolland's derided formulation, from 'above'—the mêlée.[33] In personal terms her outlook was that of a well-appointed 'dweller in several lands':[34] a distressed cosmopolitan who refused, absolutely, to align herself with any exclusive national identity.

Long before the war divided the European empires, Lee had, so she explained, already parted with 'the natural habit' of detecting 'a portrait of the Nation in the works of its painters and poets' or of 'crediting the inhabitants of any country with the sublimity or charm of that country's landscape'.[35] If her alleged 'aloofness' consisted of rejecting the blinding partiality of state-fostered nationalism, it also reflected an intellectual refusal of 'temporary perspectives' and the one-sided passions of 'the here and now'. This vantage point may have been uncomfortable for Lee as well as for her outraged friends and acquaintances, but it had at least enabled her to observe not just 'my country's danger at the enemy's hands', but the extent to which the war represented both 'a common catastrophe' for the belligerent nations and a general 'danger to civilization'.[36]

Unlike those of her 'pacifist friends' who remained 'judicious and unperturbed' in their moral certainty,[37] Lee felt corroded by a 'war atmosphere' in which her own self and convictions, rather than the engulfing conflict, came to seem 'incomprehensible'. Her inherited idea of authorship was among the first casualties. Before the war, she had imagined that 'it was in the power, as among the duties, of a writer to teach new ways of wisdom and train the docile generations to pursue them'.[38] Writers were still inclined to wear 'the cast-off vestments of priests, prophets and augurs', yet the war had caused Lee to question their 'always excessive individual presentation' of ideas that actually belonged to the ongoing flow of thought in mankind. The writer's job, she now realized, was not to 'furnish' the public 'with ready-made conclusions' of the kind that so often came to grief when 'hustled into action' prematurely. Indeed, the views and prescriptions of this or that writer would not alter anything, except to the extent that they tallied with the already established 'tendencies of thought' of the reader: 'This comes to saying that we really are, rather than teachers, expressers, making our readers' latent thoughts manifest to themselves, sometimes even with the effect of their starting away from them in terror or laughter.'

Perhaps the thought of peace and decency did lurk in the national unconscious during those years of slaughter. Yet it was with small chance of gaining wide purchase as an 'expresser' of 'latent thoughts' that Lee went on to condemn the war's division of the nations as 'an outrage on the Reality of Things'.[39] Reality, she insisted, is always characterized by *otherness,* by the knowledge that 'It always has *other* sides; the sides you do not happen to see or think of; the sides which don't interest you at this present; the sides which happen not to be in any manner, yourself.'[40] War 'cuts that Reality in two, hiding one half thereof; and so abolishes in our thoughts Reality's most essential characteristic, which is that it has no sides, has no divisions, is but one ceaselessly moving, inextricably interacting mass, in whose perpetual inner and outer change every portion impinges on another portion, but never on quite the same'.[41]

With its 'monstrous iron curtain', the war separated nation from nation, cancelling all empathy and exchange, and placing impenetrable barriers, distorting mirrors, and an infantile division of Good and Evil between its opposed peoples. As a vicious outcome of the 'balance of power' that had separated Europe into secretive and scheming camps, it established a barbarous identity within each nation, overriding natural incompatibilities and uniting 'honesty with knavery, wisdom with folly'.[42] With the help of a satanic repertoire of 'intellectual deteriorations'[43] it encouraged people on both sides of the division to project all guilt onto their adversaries beyond the 'barrier of otherness',[44] while seeing themselves and the combatants of their own side as perfectly innocent. As another dissenting Englishwoman would write, in the course of deploring the war's 'fullscale repudiation' of reason, moral effort, and the critical faculty: 'The English soldier in particular has taken on wings. He partakes of the being of Archangels.'[45] Germany, meanwhile, had become the utterly evil place that Lee named 'Ogreland'.[46]

In the revised version of *The Ballet of the Nations*, the degeneration that follows this lethal severance of 'reality' is summarized by Satan as he prepares the assembled Nations for Death's closing dance. He promises to extinguish the light of judgement, and submerge their 'clean volitions' in 'hot and turbid lusts' welling up from the 'dark unconscious' of their souls.[47] He will arrest goodness, commerce, and the marriage of true minds and cancel their previous extension across national boundaries. The 'lucid eye of the spirit' will become bloodshot, and the mouths through which men once 'understood each other's truth and goodness' will foam with lies, boasts, and insults. Hearts, which once went out to others, will instead melt with self-pity or 'blaze in vindictiveness'. As a final touch, he promises that none of the Nations would even be slightly aware of the utter degradation imposed on them.[48]

For Lee, as for others in the UDC circle, nationalism was the devil's creed, and its resurgence had put a brutal end to 'forty-three years of peaceable progression'.[49] Having opposed the rising 'sense of nationalism'[50] before the war, she now participated in a wider analysis of the outbreak. According to Caroline E. Playne, a friend and fellow pacifist campaigner whom Lee would later encourage to produce a multi-volume study 'sounding the psychological undertones of the war-years',[51] the decades following the resolution of the Franco-Prussian War of 1870–1 had made possible huge improvements in the economic, scientific and political dimensions of life. They also promised the creation of an 'international organism' or 'world parliament' that would regulate international affairs 'on a basis of justice and understanding between peoples who resembled one another in all essentials of civilized existence'.[52] Yet a shocking 'recrudescence of barbarism'[53] had swept through Europe instead. The force that had lured the European peoples away from this improving historical script, had been anticipated by John A. Hobson in his book *The Psychology of Jingoism,* published in 1901. Writing about the Boer War (which he had observed as a reporter for the *Manchester Guardian*), Hobson identified jingoism as an 'inverted patriotism' in which 'love of one's own nation is transformed into the hatred of another nation'.[54]

Like a latter-day theorist of globalization, Caroline E. Playne would attribute the 'Neuroses of the Nations' to the fact that people were 'rattled'[55] in the early twentieth century: shaken out of their customary worlds, and disconcerted by a changing experience that was full of promise but also 'disjointed, uncertain and superficial'. It was 'a restless, capricious, nervous age'[56] in which the pace of life had been dramatically speeded up. Playne suggested that the 'mental calibre' of the cultural elite had undergone an inevitable 'deterioration'[57] as it encountered the rising 'group mind' of mass culture. Religious certainties had been eroded by science and a theory of evolution which, with its account of the descent of man, encouraged a widespread exaltation of 'the animal side of man's nature'.[58] Further instability followed from social agitation, including the campaign for women's rights and working-class demands for 'freedom and economic opportunity'. The result was a 'mental excitation', which the politicians and press of the competing European states only had to stir with a chosen mixture of imperialism, jingoism, and nationalism to set their peoples marching into the shambles with a terrible gleam in their eyes.

It was not just the tub-thumping demagogues and national chauvinists who were responsible for converting the war into a crusade. According to the barrister and writer Irene Cooper Willis, a close and abiding friend of Vernon Lee's ('I saw her almost daily in the War'[59]), Britain's war against Germany owed much of its symbolic character to the manoeuvres of embarrassed Liberal commentators. Since the outbreak actually represented a defeat of everything their party had stood for over the previous decade, Liberals could hardly sail into the maelstrom as blithely as the Conservatives, who 'greeted the war with a cheer; they had seen it coming and met it like an old friend'.[60]

Yet when Britain took up arms against Germany, the Liberal *Daily News*, which had previously been a strong advocate of British neutrality, quickly resigned its critical stance with the words 'Being in, we must win.'[61] Even some who would become prominent members of the UDC followed this line at first ('We are in the War and we must win', as Charles Roden Buxton repeated, a couple of weeks later, in a letter to *The Nation*[62]). This way of 'falling in' with the war would prove a challenging stance to maintain. As Willis wrote, 'the acceptance of a war for no other reason than that of "being in" it is a state of mind which is intolerable to reasoning men'. Torn 'between abhorrence and acceptance',[63] Liberal commentators in both the *Daily News* and *The Nation* had to make 'a truce with their consciences'.[64]

They did so, Willis would argue, by elevating the catastrophe into 'England's Holy War': investing it with 'higher than material aims'[65] that enabled them to embrace it with full-blooded yet still idealistic zeal.

So it was that former pacifists suddenly started arguing that the war had been inevitable all along: the 'natural consequence'[66] of the balance of power and the paranoid diplomacy that had yielded what *The Nation* described as 'the system of two armed camps'.[67] Far from being a lapse into savagery, the war was hailed as a struggle 'on behalf of civilisation'. According to A. G. Gardiner of the Liberal *Daily News,* it was a battle for the 'liberties of Europe', waged against not the German people but 'the tyranny of personal government armed with a mailed fist'.[68] H. G. Wells, whose immediate conversion seemed especially shocking to Vernon Lee (she attacked her former friend's arguments in a letter to *The Nation* in New York[69]), welcomed the conflict as 'The War to end War' and insisted that 'Every sword that is drawn against Germany is a sword drawn for peace'.[70] He proposed that the Allies were engaged not in slaughter but in a necessary 'War of the Mind': a 'conflict of cultures' in which the 'real task' lay 'beyond the business of the fighting line'.[71] The real job, as he wrote, 'is to kill ideas. The ultimate purpose of this war is propaganda, the destruction of certain beliefs and the creation of others.'

It was Liberal commentators, far more than Conservatives or rank chauvinists such as Horatio Bottomley or the super-patriotic socialist Robert Blatchford, who needed such virtues to cling on to. The Conservative press might indeed make use of this improving imagery, but it was the Liberals who sanctified the war and converted it into a choice between 'two mental conditions': one corresponding to hell and the other to the utopia in which, after the enemy had been properly crushed, Europe would be remade as a harmonious and equable 'concert' of nations.[72]

Living Off Odes

Vernon Lee's 'iron curtain' drew symbolic potency from this wider analysis. The war was condemned as a 'monstrous' outcome of the failure of the pre-war balance of power, which, as Lee wrote, 'is for ever turning into the "isolation" or the "encircling" of one power by the others'.[73] It was a product as well as a reflection of the chauvinistic nationalism pressing on it from either side. Yet it was also reinforced by every idealization that Liberal apologists applied to the Allied war effort—including the redemptive promise that, when the war was won, the barrier dividing the warring empires would be lifted and the world demilitarized by an international League of Nations. As Willis ventured provocatively, 'Probably, if the war had gone on longer, the Liberals, while continuing to support it, would have become completely engrossed in the discussion of a League of Nations.'[74]

Lee shared the UDC's repudiation of the secret diplomacy and nationalism that had combined to cause the outbreak of war, but she also set out to explain why the conflict had dragged on for years beyond any expectation of human endurance. She acknowledges the capabilities of 'hitherto undreamed of military machinery' yet, as the war extended through its third and fourth years, she would place far more emphasis on the psychological constituents of her 'monstrous iron curtain'. As a 'spiritual mechanism of errors and myths', this polarizing apparatus interposed 'the same veil of passionate or expedient delusion' between 'all the warring peoples'.[75] In doing so, it surrendered public opinion to the warmongers who dismissed successive peace overtures as 'peace traps' and rejected any notion of a negotiated or compromise settlement in favour of pressing on for the 'knock-out blow' (Lloyd George) that would leave the German enemy utterly vanquished. It also blocked all routes to a settlement by sanctioning the imperialist chimeras governing the minds of the belligerent statesmen. Lee would mockingly show these men insisting that 'We statesman don't live off odes'[76] and yet demanding, in their various council chambers, that the war must continue until they had been granted dominion over such poetical kingdoms as Brobdingnag, Lilliput, and even the Shakespearian (and non-existent) 'seaboard of Bohemia'.[77]

Alert to systematic deceptions of the kind Norman Angell had named 'optical illusions', Lee described how this new psychological 'orientation' blinded those who were 'in' the war from seeing the 'realities of the case'. Taking up the phrase that Irene Cooper Willis would quote from the *Daily News* ('Being in, we must win'), she described 'being in war' as a condition curiously similar to being in love. In both, 'you have jumped into a sea, whose depth and whose extent is incalculable in your experience, in which your soul will sink or swim according as it possesses capacities which you have never tested'.[78]

The war mind could be sustained by various means. Lee blamed the intellectuals of her age for their willingness to sacrifice the imperfect stabilities of the present for the sake of a future all too easily imagined as preferable.

There had, she said, been far too much fantastic disengagement and tawdry utopianism from H. G. Wells and other 'minor prophets of the press',[79] who treated the future as a 'reversed present' or 'a dumping-ground for our own pre-occupation, the "sphere of influence" of our own passionate preoccupation and imaginative exploitation'. Lee had opposed Wells's scientific utopianism in 1907, arguing that 'what small amount of civilisation mankind has hitherto achieved' was due 'not to the thought of the future but to the care of the present'.[80] The war now convinced her of the utter perversity of thinking that the present should ever be sacrificed for the future: 'Why should we kill, starve, ruin ourselves and others to-day, in order to avoid killing, starving, and ruining tomorrow?'[81]

Lee's iron curtain had shiny surfaces in which people on both sides could see themselves reflected as creatures of their warring states, yet it was largely made of paper and printer's ink. This, she wrote, was a war 'wherein words have played their part alongside high-explosives and poison-gases'.[82] Lee ranked the press among the most culpable sustainers of the slaughter: 'flogging up bellicosity',[83] as E. D. Morel put it; filling its pages with propaganda while mocking, distorting, and at the same time, as many associated with the UDC would find out, refusing to print dissenting arguments. Like other objectors, she recoiled from the spouting politicians, the fiercely patriotic former suffragettes and the churchmen who fed the dragooned masses on 'mysteries and hocus pocus, on long words and sonorous phrases'.[84]

She indicts 'catchwords' and 'myths' which she saw usurping accurate perception, and blamed partly on the governmental habit of appealing to patriotic emotion while 'avoiding committal to any definable programme'[85] for bringing the war to a close. Among her British examples, she cites talk of 'conspiracy', of Britain's role as (in Bernard Shaw's phrase) the 'Policeman of the World', and she mentions H. G. Wells's contributions too—dismissing his idea of 'redrawing the map of Europe' as signally useless since 'any betterment for the future must come not from mere "re-drawing" of frontiers, but from the efforts and compromises by which those human wills constituting Europe can adjust themselves for their mutual, their common advantage'.[86] The conflict had a literary momentum in a wider sense too, proving, so Lee wrote, that 'the really dangerous part of literature is that, besides awakening passion, it justifies it'.[87]

Members of the UDC circle were horrified to see 'the reasoning process' rendered more or less criminal[88] and the idea of truth replaced with an appeal to plausibility ('The story reads like the truth'[89] as *The Nation* observed in a phrase that Irene Cooper Willis later deplored as symptomatic of the new attitude). They condemned both the rise of official censorship, which cancelled the information necessary for independent judgement, and also the lies and exaggerated stories with which the state then set out to bind its subjects to the slaughter. 'Delusion bursts in',[90] as Lee wrote, encouraged by a propaganda machine bent on an 'unprecedented wholesale fabrication of public opinion'.

Arthur Ponsonby, the Liberal (later Labour) MP and UDC member to whom Lee dedicated the new Epilogue to her *Ballet of the Nations*, shared her dismay at the state's deliberate use of the 'weapon of falsehood'—a measure that proved all the more necessary in countries without military conscription where the public had to be 'worked up emotionally by sham ideals'.[91] 'Duping the people'[92] was achieved with the help of false arguments including 'the myth of Germany's *sole* responsibility for the war', and the official pretence that the war only started with the German invasion of Belgium (which, as Morel, Ponsonby, and other members of the UDC circle would insist, was actually neither unexpected nor genuinely shocking to the British and French governments).

Yet 'the main staple'[93] of the propaganda effort consisted of faked or grossly exaggerated atrocity stories. Vernon Lee mentions the Belgian child whose hands were said to have been hacked off by the Huns.[94] As Ponsonby noted, the press also exhibited a Canadian soldier crucified with bayonets, and an equally fictional Scottish nurse whose breasts had allegedly been cut off by the same barbaric enemy. The repertoire included violated nuns and 'corpse utilisation' factories in which Germany was supposedly rendering bundled war-corpses into soap, pig-food, lubricants, and gelatine.[95] The 'rape' of Belgium's historic cities was also greatly exaggerated—including the alleged destruction of Louvain, which had so horrified Romain Rolland.[96] As the Conservative leader Andrew Bonar Law was said to have remarked of British war patriotism, 'it is well to have it properly stirred by German frightfulness'.[97]

Patriotism and the Muse of History

Looking back on the 'fog of falsehood' brewed up by the belligerent states on both sides, Arthur Ponsonby would later write that 'The amount of rubbish and humbug that pass under the name of patriotism in war-time in all countries is sufficient to make decent people blush when they are subsequently disillusioned.'[98] Whilst opposing chauvinistic war nationalism may indeed have seemed a simple imperative, a much more difficult quandary had awaited those who campaigned for new methods of international government that would make war preventable in future. In 1915, while trying to give practical shape to such a vision on behalf of the Fabian Society, Leonard Woolf had expressed vigorous opposition to the 'extraordinarily crude conceptions of "States" and "nations"', which persisted despite the fact that 'the most vital interests of human beings are hardly ever national, almost always international'.[99]

Woolf was convinced that 'all arguments against International Government based on assertions that it would endanger vital national interests should be regarded with the greatest suspicion'.[100] Yet he also warned that there could be no simple choice between internationalism and the nation state. Both 'the passion for independence' and 'consciousness of nationality and patriotism' were facts of modern life, and anyone who tried to ignore or deny them must be 'very blind or stupid'.[101] Using the familiar metaphor of horizontal (international) and vertical (national and territorialized) perspectives,[102] he insisted that a good system of international governance must combine both.

Many of the UDC's thinkers were also at pains to acknowledge that patriotism was not necessarily limited to the 'baser' varieties that supported 'wars of aggression' and refused the thought of any concession to another country as a national humiliation.[103] Philip Snowden allowed that patriotism could be 'a noble sentiment' when confined within 'the limits of morality',[104] and Caroline Playne would later declare patriotism to be very different from 'nationalistic absorption' of the infatuating kind that had proved 'the bane of the new century'.[105] Before the war Lee had herself insisted on the same distinction, declaring that a 'true sense of nationality' was actually a vital constituent of the new cosmopolitanism: informed by awareness of other nations besides one's own, it was no chauvinistic cult, but would, on the contrary, prove useful in 'making us critical and ironical towards ourselves'.[106]

Once war had broken out, however, she would yield no ground at all on this subject. To the question whether patriotism could ever be a virtue, she answers emphatically, '*not in our modern times*'. Declaring herself to be entirely against this 'bristling and spouting against other countries', she remarks that 'Patriotism, under the present conditions which I see, absorbs the combativeness and endurance and self-renunciation needed for putting one's own house in decent order; and spends it in devastating the house on the other side of the road.' Since escalating war expenditure meant 'a lack of food and rolling-stock and clothes and schools', the result was that both houses are left in 'an excessively ruinous and disorderly condition'.[107]

Lee's absolute rejection of patriotism isolated her from many even in the UDC circle. It also placed her among the 'independent spirits', whom Romain Rolland would praise for having the strength of character to refuse, or to peel off, the 'greasy fleece' of state-imposed patriotism ('warm, silky and beautiful, and at the same time stinking and bloody, made of the lowest instincts, and the highest illusions').[108] As Rolland wrote in his novel *Clerambault:* 'There are now only two sorts of minds: those shut up behind bars, and those open to all that is alive, to the entire race of man, even our enemies.'[109] In his account, it was the few who had been prepared to 'stand alone' against the 'herd-spirit', and certainly not those socialists who had so quickly fallen in with the patriotic perspectives of their warring states, who were to be commended as representatives of the 'true "International"'.[110]

Henry Ford may have been thinking of his 'Peace Ship' and its failed mission to a Europe of bloody and belligerent old nations when, in May 1916, he famously dismissed History as 'more or less bunk'.[111] As a volatile theorist of the iron curtain, Vernon Lee was inclined to pose the problem differently. In one of the most arresting sections of *Satan the Waster* she extends her opposition to patriotism with the help of a figure identified as the 'Muse of History'. In earlier times, Lee had loved the haunting presence of the past as it lingered in her chosen European places. She had once described the past as 'a sheltering spacious church, built by unpractical, imperious longings for everything which reality denies'.[112] But the war now revealed the Muse of History to be 'a sycophantish partisan; a pretentious, often ignorant, humbug'.[113]

Introduced as a drama critic 'by preference and true vocation', Vernon Lee's version of Clio loves the sound and the fury of Satan's 'shows' and recounts the ongoing Ballet of the Nations in lurid and melodramatic terms for the benefit of the Ages-to-Come. She has been 'the nurse of all the artificially incubated Nationalisms and Irredentisms'. She is a desecrator, who takes a decent saint such as Joan of Arc and turns her into a 'tinselled wax doll'. By calling herself History, the Muse has converted 'the recorder of Events into a purveyor of ideal emotions, largely for the pastime of the Ages-to-Come and other bored and futile persons'.[114]

This 'pandering of so-called History to our dramatic instincts'[115] entails a relentless 'witch-hunt' for simple causes and 'Responsibilities'.[116] It also reduces the past to a toy of the present, thereby 'cheating us of History's fundamental lesson, which is that nothing which happens is ever entirely alike'.[117] Hearing the kaiser being likened to Napoleon (even to the extent that some recommended his eventual banishment to St Helena), Lee condemns such 'imperfect analogies' for reducing history to the 'expectancy of repetition', which is really 'the egoistic intrusion of our own motives into the motives of other folks and other times'.[118]

Manipulated and simplistic invocations such as these produce a disorientating loss of the 'one constant of history namely Change, and our recognition of Otherness'. Lee even suggests that 'the notion of Evolution' might have been introduced through the study of human history rather than biology and geology, were it not for the Muse of History who 'has no use for flints and potsherds ... What *she* wants are human personages to gape on at a puppet show or ferret out in the places where we keep rags and dirty linen.'[119]

Militarists on both sides were prepared to stake everything on the prospect of decisive victory on the battlefield, but for Lee there could be no end to the war without removal of the 'monstrous iron curtain' deforming the hearts and minds of the belligerent peoples at home. Having seen how apparently noble Ideals gripped their followers with a religious kind of fervour, and drove them blindly into the slaughter, she calls for making 'Idealists less spectacular and decorative; and Ideals less gimcrack and gaudy; more akin, these latter, to the manly, homespun, wearable things called *standards* and *obligations*.'[120] Citing John Ruskin and William Morris in their condemnation of the modern city and the industrial factory system,[121] she imagines a less pinched and 'arid' society in which people would no longer have to make a habit of settling for what is 'abhorrent to one's instincts', and in which working-class men would be less tempted to join the fatal 'adventure of war' proclaimed, so scandalously to some of his fellow Liberals, by Prime Minister Lloyd George in the early recruitment drives.[122]

Mustering resources against a war that could be embraced as 'a licensed break-up of detestable lives',[123] Lee talks of duties and decency, and calls for the principle of 'public spiritedness' to be won back from a war patriotism that had turned 'the idea of "National Service" into the process whereby schoolmasters and men of science go out to kill and be killed by other schoolmasters and men of science'.[124] She hoped, vaguely as well as furiously, for a renewed 'Altruism' based less on suppression of one's own yearnings than on recognition of the other (*alter*): 'If we thought habitually of what I have thus called the *other* (*other* people, *other* places, *other* moments, *other* qualities, *other* relations, *other* everything and anything)'.

A Dance of Death and the Relocation to Come

Such were the remedies of the 60-year-old woman who had witnessed the 'iron curtain' being dragged out of the theatre and converted, like so much else, into an instrument of war between imperial States. Yet these unheeded aspirations did little to calm her swelling *Ballet of the Nations* or, for that matter, to restrain the ORCHESTRA OF PATRIOTISM, slewed as its members were by intoxicating drinks supplied by the 'well-trained lackeys of the Press and Pulpit'.[125]

So HATRED fingers a double bass; SELF-RIGHTEOUSNESS a harmonium. HERO-ISM (who is both blind and 'a real Cosmopolitan, although his chief business is international extermination'[126]) is ready to beat the war drum, an instrument that Satan declares 'most to my liking'.[127] WIDOW FEAR eventually steps out of her rag-and-bottle shop accompanied by her 'shabby, restless twins', SUSPICION and PANIC. They bring penny whistles, fog-horns, and 'a cracked storm-and-massacre bell, genuinely mediaeval, but wrapped in yesterday's *Daily Mail* and *Globe*'.[128] SCIENCE and ORGANIZATION step up with a gramophone and a 'braying' pianola: 'wonderful mechanical' instruments which, as Satan promises, will sustain the ballet long after 'our classic band have neither strings nor wind left'.[129] The dreadful din makes a mockery of the harmonious 'concert of nations' the UDC hoped to see established in a democratic post-war future, and which Lee had herself distinguished from a bogus 'concert of Foreign Secretaries'.[130]

Arriving on stage, the various DANCING NATIONS are handed over to BALLET MASTER DEATH who whips them into 'the vastest and most new-fashioned spectacle of Slaughter and Ruin I have so far had the honour of putting on to the World's Stage'.[131] Soon they are slashing and trampling each other, unable to resist Death's baton even when their limbs are reduced to bloody stumps. The 'rules of the Dance' allow no pause, so the 'hideous farandole' goes on until there is hardly room to move on a stage piled with blood and mud and entrails:

Yet dance they did, chopping and slashing, blinding each other with squirts of blood and pellets of human flesh. And as they appeared and disappeared in the moving wreaths of fiery smoke, they lost more and more of their original shape, becoming, in that fitful light, terrible uncertain forms, armless, legless, recognizable for human only by their irreproachable Heads, which they carried stiff and high even while crawling and staggering along, lying in wait, and leaping and rearing and butting as do fighting animals; until they became, with those decorous, well-groomed Heads, mere unspeakable hybrids between man and beast: they who had come on to that stage so erect and beautiful.[132]

So the ballet goes until the end, except that there is no end: only the chorus of AGES-TO-COME, in which we are apparently expected to find ourselves, staring at our more recently invented television screens, and frantically yelling 'Encore, Encore' as the 'great and heroic' war grinds on—perpetually rerun as a reminder of 'Man's higher possibilities'.[133]

That conclusion might be taken to confirm Lee's own doubts about the 'shallowness'[134] of her emblematic allegory. The pseudo-medieval form in which she had cast her ballet would not easily accommodate such an unheroic modern innovation as the UDC's proposed answer to the war, namely a democratically conducted League of Nations. It would betray no hint of the coming transformation of patriotism: a 'composite passion' that would in future, so Lee predicted in her 'Notes to the Ballet', be less strongly defined by geographical segregation, religion, and the bogus myth of racial continuity. Nor would it give any representation to Lee's fleeting suggestion that the 'segregating power of class' might soon produce 'a new collective allegiance':[135] one that would oppose the bellicose nationalism of the warring states in the name of a horizontally aligned internationalism that spurned the liberalism she had once shared with Lujo Brentano, and was perhaps only slightly more respectful of the high European spirit of Goethe and Bach that she had advocated alongside Romain Rolland.

Vernon Lee did not explicitly identify her 'new collective allegiance' with the socialism of the Russian Revolution that opened in February 1917. Though not inclined to join those of her friends who blamed all the world's ills on 'the entirely wicked and marvellously simple monster'[136] named Capitalism, Lee had defended Russia's great upheaval against the internal enemies who could be expected to plot with hostile outsiders. Shortly before the Bolshevik coup of October 1917, she wrote that 'Every revolution implies a nation within the nation, a nation of irreconcilable malcontents.'[137]

Later, in the Epilogue to her revised *Ballet of the Nations*, she ridiculed the Allied rejection of the Bolsheviks' attempt to end the war by proposing a peace based on 'No annexations and no indemnities'.[138] She was also aware that, despite the divisions and diversions of its recent history, the advance of this fiery internationalist movement may soon cause the vertical 'iron curtain' with which her Satan had wasted the nations of Europe to be raised from its original position between Britain and Germany and brought down in a different location. As she anticipated, 'The Orchestra will no longer be inscribed Patriotism; but the same Passions will sit and play within its segregating barriers.'[139]

PART III

Wrapping Red Russia (1917–1920)

In reality, a wonderful mental chaos comes from the action of Bolshevism in the world.

Georges Bataille, *The Accursed Share* (1967)

Oh, the great, divinely bounding wisdom of walls and barriers! They may just be the greatest of all inventions. Mankind ceased to be a wild beast when it built its first wall.

Yevgeny Zamyatin, *We* (1920–1)

It was as though we, the ones still here, had been installed in an enormous thick-walled building girded round by rows of blind 'false windows'.

Sigizmund Krzhizhanovsky, *Autobiography of a Corpse* (1925)

8

First Delegation

It is a bewildering place, which, of course, cannot be described in detail—a land on the other side of the looking-glass, where bushes are men and things dissolve when you look at them and the earth collapses, where visions are about and you walk among snares and pitfalls and lose all faith in your dearest friend. It is the grown-up home of make-believe.

special correspondent for *The Times*, after visiting a
British camouflage workshop on the western front in Belgium, July 1917.[1]

Late in the afternoon of 27 April 1920, a well-known English suffragist and anti-war campaigner boarded a ship at Newcastle-upon-Tyne and, after an alarming moment when the departing vessel lurched and nearly tossed her into the water,[2] steamed out into the North Sea. Ethel Snowden, who customarily went under her husband's name as Mrs Philip Snowden, was no admirer of Lenin's Bolshevik regime. Yet earlier that day, when gathering with other members of her party at King's Cross Station in London, she had told the *Daily Herald* that the Russian Revolution was 'the most important experiment of the time',[3] and that she felt honoured to be among those chosen to investigate it at close hand.

Mrs Snowden embarked as a member of what would be proclaimed as the first official delegation to visit Russia since the Bolshevik Revolution of October 1917.[4] Proposed at a special Trades Union Congress the previous December and jointly sponsored by the TUC and the Labour Party, the mission was intended to 'break through the "information blockade"'[5] maintained by the Allies as part of their 'intervention' on the side of now largely defeated anti-Bolshevik White forces in the Civil War, and to carry out an 'independent and impartial inquiry into the industrial, political and economic conditions in Russia'.[6] After consulting with the Allied leaders Lloyd George, Georges Clemenceau, and Woodrow Wilson (then meeting as 'The

Council of Three' at San Remo), the British Foreign Office had issued the delegates with passports that made no mention of Russia, but permitted them to visit Finland and the newly extracted Baltic state of Estonia.

The Bolshevik authorities had been less circumspect. Maxim Litvinoff extended a 'cordial acceptance' of the proposed visit and Lenin himself would predict that, even though few of the delegates could possibly be called friends of the Bolshevik revolution, they would become its 'best propagandists' when they saw what hostile Allied policy was doing to the Russian people.[7]

Though all determined 'horizontalists', in Romain Rolland's terms, the nine delegates represented various positions in the British labour and trade union movement. They were accompanied by two men, R. C. Wallhead and Clifford Allen, who joined them as a separate delegation of the 45,000-strong Independent Labour Party (an older organization, which had persisted within the Labour Party after it was founded in 1906). Also present was the philosopher Bertrand Russell, who travelled with the group in order to conduct an independent investigation of his own. The party included long-standing friends who had campaigned together in opposition to the Great War. Clifford Allen and Bertrand Russell had both been jailed for their stand. Mrs Snowden had addressed hundreds of meetings in both Britain and America, speaking (and also meeting Woodrow Wilson) as a member of the Women's Peace Crusade: a cause she had shared with the only other woman on the Labour delegation, Margaret Bondfield. Tom Shaw was a Labour MP, long associated with the Lancashire textile unions. Dr Leslie Haden Guest, physician and joint secretary to the delegation, was a member of the Fabian Society and a former theosophist who had pioneered health and hygiene clinics as a school doctor with the London County Council. He was also a writer engaged in extensive post-war travel, tracking the emergence of 'new forces' in central and south-eastern Europe as well as Russia.[8]

A considerable number of the delegates had been associated with the Union of Democratic Control, including Russell, Mrs Snowden, and the chairman of the delegation, Ben Turner, a portly Yorkshireman who was mayor of Batley and leader of the General Union of Textile Workers. Charles Roden Buxton was also among this number. In 1917, he had left the Anglican Church and the Liberal Party, judging both to be compromised by their pro-war stance, to join the Quakers and the Independent Labour Party, and he now boarded ship as the second 'joint secretary' to the delegation. He shared Mrs Snowden's view that the shattered post-war world was crying out for 'a new conception',[9] and yet he too felt cautious about Bolshevism: 'I went, I think I may fairly say, with an open mind. I had read everything to which I had access, both in England and on the Continent, on the subject of Russia. I was steeped both in "Bolshevist" and in "Anti-Bolshevist" literature.'[10]

At the beginning of the Russian Revolution, the British Labour Party, TUC and Independent Labour Party had backed the Provisional Government, which took power under Prince George Lvov in February 1917. Despite the continuing war, this administration had initiated a stream of democratic reforms and prepared for the election of a Constituent Assembly in which the Bolsheviks would, had they not seized power in the October Revolution, have formed a minority alongside Mensheviks, Social Revolutionaries, and others convinced that Russia must go through a period of liberal democracy—a 'bourgeois revolution'—before its eventual transition to socialism. At least six of those now travelling to Russia (Snowden, Allen, Williams, Russell, Wallhead, and Buxton) had spoken at the famous Leeds conference of June 1917, in which 1,150 members of various British 'democratic bodies' had met to urge their government to support the Russian Revolution, and to resolve that a network of soviets, or 'Workers' and Soldiers' Councils', should immediately be set up in Britain too.[11]

By 1920, when the delegation undertook its mission to Russia, the long-standing argument between 'constitutional' and 'revolutionary' tendencies within the British labour movement had further intensified over a conflict Mrs Snowden named 'the Battle of the two Internationals'.[12] In Britain as elsewhere, socialists and their parties were locked in heated dispute as to whether the time had come to revive the Second International, which had held its first thinly attended post-war conference in Berne on 3 February 1919, or to accept its wartime disintegration as final and to join the Third International, or 'Comintern', established by the Bolsheviks at a hastily convened congress in Moscow on 2 March 1919 and committed to the worldwide extension of Lenin's 'dictatorship of the proletariat' through illegal and sometimes also armed struggle rather than just the ballot box. As Snowden would later recall, 'Every Socialist movement in Europe was split from top to bottom. America copied.' And while their members squabbled, 'capitalist Europe rocked with laughter'.[13]

On 5 April 1920, a motion advocating conversion to the Third International had been introduced at the Independent Labour Party's annual conference in Glasgow. Mrs Snowden opposed secession from the Second International on the grounds that 'they did not possess full knowledge of the third'. The Labour leader Ramsay MacDonald had spoken contemptuously of the 'nursery politics' of the motion's hot-headed proposers: 'You know perfectly well that when you talk about revolution today you are merely playing with words.' However, he too conceded that 'more information' was needed before a final decision could be made.[14]

The members of the British Labour Delegation took the 'battle of the two Internationals' with them: a feud that smoulders on in their various memoirs. Some, including Dr Haden Guest and Mrs Snowden, would strive to maintain their standing as 'independent' investigators who nevertheless had serious, and at times overwhelming, doubts about Bolshevism. Others were far from 'impartial' admirers of Lenin and his Communist International, including the leader of the Furnishing Trades Federation, A.A. Purcell, and also Robert Williams of the Transport Workers' Federation, who travelled 'frankly and avowedly as a supporter of the Proletarian Dictatorship'.[15] Though sharply divided in their assessment of the Bolshevik government, the delegates would remain united in opposition to the policies of Britain's Secretary of State for War, Winston Churchill, who had from the first seen Bolshevism as a diabolical plague to be purged or, failing that, isolated from the rest of the world. They unanimously deplored Britain's part in the failed Allied military 'intervention', dubbed 'Mr. Churchill's private war'[16] by the British press thanks to the ardour with which he had pursued it.

A Cage Reopened

Perhaps a few apprehensive glances were exchanged at the quayside in Newcastle. Yet these political travellers were committed internationalists whose overseas contacts had been severely curtailed throughout the recent war. As such, they are more likely to have embarked with a sense of liberation of the kind that Ethel Snowden had shared with Margaret Bondfield in January 1919, when the two women shipped out of Folkestone on the way to Berne for the first post-war attempt to reconvene the Second International. The war had caused awful devastation in Europe—Mrs Snowden would see much evidence of a shockingly swift 'rattling back to the beginning of things'—but it had still felt exhilarating to break through the 'cruel cage' that had confined these socialists and feminists behind national borders over the four years of war.[17]

That cage had been real enough. Mrs Snowden, whose renewed international commitments had required no less than four journeys to Berne in the first seven months of 1919,[18] was well aware of the frustration imposed on the British suffragists who, in the autumn of 1914, had hoped to travel to The Hague in neutral Holland to attend a 'meeting of conciliation' involving women from all the warring nations. The initiative had been led by executive committee members of the National Union of Women's Suffrage Societies who refused to follow Mrs Fawcett's insistence that women should now commit themselves to war service.[19] The Home Office had reluctantly issued a few passports at the last minute, although not to any woman judged 'militant'. There had been further obstruction in April 1915, when 100 or so British women attempted to repeat the journey in order to attend the first Congress of the Women's International League for Peace and Freedom (it was this event that, through the advocacy of its Hungarian-born activist Rosika Schwimmer, had helped to spur Henry Ford into commissioning his ill-fated 'Peace Ship' at the end of the year). Though they too eventually received passports, they arrived at Tilbury docks to find their passage cancelled and the English Channel closed, allegedly on account of looming naval engagements.[20]

Members of the labour movement had felt similarly confined. The socialist parties of the Allied countries had managed to maintain their argumentative collaboration at 'Inter-Allied' meetings held in London on several occasions through the war, but insurmountable barriers were placed in the way of attempts to maintain or relaunch the wider socialist International. In September 1915 passports had been denied to British members of the Independent Labour Party wanting to attend the conference for anti-war socialists at Zimmerwald, in neutral Switzerland—an international meeting at which Lenin and other future leaders of Bolshevik Russia had tried (unsuccessfully) to kill off the Second International and to launch a third one dedicated to converting the war between nations into a horizontally aligned class war ('Above the frontiers, above the battlefields, and devastated countries, Proletarians of the world unite!' as the Zimmerwald manifesto proclaimed).[21] In June 1917, it had proved impossible for Ramsay MacDonald and two other members of the British Labour Party to travel to Russia as invited by the Soviets: passports were granted, but passage was obligingly barred by the Seamen's and Firemen's Union.

Further barriers had been brought down later that year, when the Petrograd Soviet proposed that socialists from Allied, neutral, and Central

Power countries should meet in Stockholm to discuss the 'international situation'.[22] An early example of the Bolshevik method of appealing to foreign workers over the heads of their national governments, this gesture had impressed Ethel Snowden's husband, Philip Snowden of the Independent Labour Party, who described the proposed conference as 'the embryo of the parliament of man'.[23] Predictably, however, it alarmed the Allied governments, threatening as it did an elevation of class conflict within each of their states and also a disconcerting new connection between foreign policy and internal politics. In America, it was said that the Stockholm conference was 'merely a German plot'.[24]

A more sophisticated objection was raised in the British House of Commons by the Conservative (Unionist) MP Halford J. Mackinder. A former director of the London School of Economics, Mackinder was the author of a geopolitical theory (which would later influence both the Nazi idea of *Lebensraum* and, after 1946, the geopolitics of the Cold War) in which the vast Eurasian 'Heartland' was conceived as the 'geographical pivot' of history. Though declaring himself in favour of 'movement towards democracy' and against secret diplomacy, Mackinder warned the Commons against 'an international Socialist conference which shall cut at the roots of nationality in Europe, and which shall give us in Europe a distinction, a horizontal distinction, instead of the distinction which we have between the nations'.[25] A source of enormous hope among combatants on both sides, the Stockholm conference was much postponed and finally killed off when the American, Italian, French, and British governments refused to issue would-be delegates with passports.

Shaking Hands with Murder?

The crossing to Bergen was unusually rough, and almost all the British delegates were violently seasick. As they sailed south along the Norwegian coast, the air was also troubled by a sense of war and flaring revolution. They reached Oslo (then known as Christiana) on 30 April, just after news broke that Marshal Pilsudski's Poland had launched a new onslaught against Bolshevik Russia in the Ukraine. They stayed in the Norwegian capital for the May Day celebrations, in which 30,000 people (out of a total population of 250,000) are said to have marched behind the socialist banner. The British delegates were placed at the front of the demonstration, and some of them, including Ethel Snowden, addressed the crowd, conveying 'fraternal greetings' from the British labour movement. Robert Williams and Clifford Allen, who would later be judged among the most pro-Bolshevik of the delegates, reported approvingly in the *Daily Herald* that 'The Norwegian Labour Party unhesitatingly adheres to Soviet principles and the dictatorship of the proletariat.'[26]

The class war had taken another dramatic turn in England by the time these British internationalists left Stockholm, sailing around rather than directly across the still mine-strewn Baltic to reach Estonia. Despite the denials of Britain's Secretary of State for War, Mr Winston Churchill,[27] it had emerged that ships in the London docks were being loaded with planes, guns, and munitions for Poland, where they would be used in the new assault against Soviet Russia. The departure of one vessel had been delayed in Gravesend, thanks to the protest of two firemen and a fortuitous collision that left the delayed ship in a sinking condition. But the trade unionists in the London 'Hands Off Russia' Committee (of which the delegate A. A. Purcell was a leading member) were able to make more of the *Jolly George*, found to be receiving a cargo of munitions in London's East India Docks. Led by Ernest Bevin and encouraged by others including Sylvia Pankhurst and the future British Communist leader Harry Pollitt, dock workers refused to load the ship. The stand-off provided the nervous British authorities with further indication that the Bolshevik revolution, versions of which had recently been crushed in Germany, Austria, Hungary, and Finland if not in Russia, had its adherents in Britain too.

The anxiety generated by these events ensured that, as they approached Russia, the British Labour delegates were sailing through a storm of press speculation. The socialist *Daily Herald,* known to have been receiving funds from the Russian Bolsheviks as the Conservative press alleged,[28] maintained a zealously optimistic view. Its editor, George Lansbury, had visited Soviet Russia in February 1920. Having previously declared himself convinced that Bolshevism, when 'stripped of all the flummery that was round it ... simply stood for government by the people who worked',[29] this big-hearted Christian socialist broke through the Allied 'news blockade' with a series of highly enthusiastic wireless messages from Moscow ('True religion is untouched; true marriage is as sacred as ever. The churches are being restored at public expense. There is nothing here worse than in other capitals; there is much, very much, that is better').[30] He had then returned to give an enthralled account of the Bolshevik revolution to the ten thousand supporters said to have filled London's Royal Albert Hall to welcome the return of their adored East End figurehead.

Lansbury had noticed the large slogan on a wall by the Kremlin (and provocatively close to the Orthodox shrine of the Iberian Virgin), denouncing religion as 'the opium of the people'. Yet even Lenin himself had been unable to convince this future leader of Britain's Labour Party that he and his Bolshevik comrades were atheists and certainly not 'doing what Christians call the Lord's work' as Lansbury nevertheless insisted.[31] Lansbury's meetings with leading Bolsheviks had been furiously denounced by the Conservative press in Britain and his claims for the Christian nature of their revolution were fiercely resisted by Athelstan Riley's hastily mustered Christian Counter Bolshevist Crusade.[32] Yet he blithely turned these accusations around as he gave the Labour delegation his blessing: 'Chief of all they will, in the historic words of the Jingo Press, "shake hands with 'murder'" and discover they are meeting some of the best men and women the world has produced.'[33]

The press war raged despite the fact that, by the time the British Labour Delegation embarked on its tour of inspection, the Allied governments were actually adjusting their policy towards Red Russia. Six months previously, and in an abrupt reversal that horrified Winston Churchill, Britain's Coalition prime minister, Lloyd George, had publicly announced the failure of the inter-Allied military intervention on the side of anti-Bolshevik White forces: 'Our troops are out of Russia. Frankly I am glad. Russia is a quicksand.'[34]

With that embarrassing failure behind it, the British government was now moving towards a re-establishment of trade relations. At the end of May 1920, Leonid Krasin, the People's Commissar for Foreign Trade, would arrive in London with his Russian Trade Delegation (formally from the 'Central Co-operative Society' rather than the Bolshevik state), and start discussing the urgent purchase of locomotives, railway wagons, and other goods. Having lost his 'private' war against Bolshevism, Winston Churchill warned Lloyd George that Krasin's trade delegation was merely a front under which these 'ruffianly conspirators', as he called Krasin and Lev Kamenev, would try to 'foment a revolutionary movement in Britain'.[35] The bulk of the British press, which had turned its eye for lurid 'atrocities' from Germany to Bolshevik Russia after the Armistice of 11 November 1918, also remained intensely suspicious of the new conciliatory initiatives. In its report of the Soviet delegation's first meeting with the British government, the *Manchester Guardian* would mock these widespread Conservative anxie-ties about the monstrous and inhuman aliens now being invited to visit the government from the other side of the barrier isolating Bolshevik Russia: 'A being … erect upon two legs and bearing the outward form and semblance of a man was seen to approach 10, Downing Street, yesterday, to ring at the door and gain admission. … Mr. Lloyd George has seen him and lives.'[36]

The Russian Trade Delegation may not actually have been staffed by monsters, but the most intense suspicion of Bolshevism still circulated in the Allied countries. British and French fears of infiltration were reinforced by news of extraordinary alarms in America, where, in mid-April, the Attorney General Mr Mitchell Palmer, announced that Trotsky and Lenin had pre-pared a 'World-Wide May Day Plot' and would try, on 1 May 1920, to 'seize the reins' of the entire world by a coordinated 'anarchist uprising' involv-ing 'practically all the extreme Radical organisations of the world'.[37] When this vigorously proclaimed conspiracy failed to materialize, Palmer revised his allegation, declaring, more modestly, that the International Workers of the World—the already much-assaulted 'Wobblies'—were plotting the syn-chronized murder of twenty leading Americans.[38]

In Britain, even the *Morning Post*'s literary critic succumbed to the fever-ish atmosphere. Railing against the destruction of the English language threatened by the revolutionary 'free verse' of 'certain American poets', including Carl Sandburg, William Carlos Williams, Ezra Pound, and T. S. Eliot, E. B. Osborn was in no doubt that these 'Bolsheviks of literature' should be confined to the pages of Lansbury's *Daily Herald*.[39]

British justice buckled under the same pressure, and it did so to the particular advantage of Frank Robert Lark, a 66-year-old machinist who was sentenced at the Old Bailey on 12 May. After a political street meet-ing in Hammersmith one month earlier, Lark had assaulted an anar-chist and Communist orator named Sidney Albert Hanson, driving an ice pick into the back of this provocative fellow's neck as he walked home with his wife and child. Lark pleaded not guilty, claiming that he was only doing 'what the Government ought to have done long ago'.[40] Found guilty, he nevertheless got away with only a month in jail and the scarcely disguised commendation of Mr Justice Lawrence, who condemned the victim as a 'pestilential knave' while reluctantly also admitting that 'it did not do to use ice picks for the purpose of opposing doctrines you did not like'.

'Blue Mist': Camouflage and the Potemkin Village

As it sailed east, the British Labour Delegation was buffeted by the con-
jectures of an anti-Bolshevik press that was already preparing its readers
to discount everything these political investigators might conclude from
their mission. Catching up with the delegation in Stockholm, a correspondent for *The Times* noted drily that its members were being 'piloted about'
by the independent socialist leader, 'who styles himself the Soviet Russian
Consul'.[41] In a leading article, *The Times* had earlier pointed to the fact that
no members of the delegation appeared to have any knowledge of Russian,
alleging that they were all 'notoriously strong partisans' and that their report
could 'not possibly command general confidence'.[42] In order to prevent the
delegation's visit from becoming a 'capitulation to Bolshevism', it would, so
The Times suggested, be necessary, at the very least, to include non-Bolshevik
technical advisers, and also to extract a promise from the Bolshevists that
neither the delegates nor any of the witnesses with whom they talked would
be imprisoned or otherwise punished.

Another sceptical correspondent at the meeting in Stockholm remarked
that the delegation's month in the 'immense country' that was Russia would
no doubt give its members 'quite time enough to see all the "Potemkin"
villages ... which the Soviet government would doubtless put up for them
wherever they passed'.[43]

This was not the first time questions had been raised about the peculiar distortions that might influence the perceptions of Westerners who
crossed over into the chaotic and largely unknown world of revolutionary
Russia. Keen to maintain their troubled ally's commitment to the war against
Germany, the French and British had sent three-man delegations of socialists
to Russia a few weeks after the initial revolution of February 1917. They were
careful to select pro-war social patriots from the majority socialist parties,
hoping that such apparently reliable delegates would be heeded as 'more
mature comrades',[44] thereby helping to stiffen the Russians' commitment
to the Allied war effort. In the event, however, these ambassadors of moderation were soon disorientated. Renounced by the Bolshevik-sympathizing
minority socialist parties in their own countries, they were hardly welcomed as avuncular advisers on arrival. Instead, as was recalled by the leader
of the French delegation, Marcel Cachin, they were 'put through a regular
cross-examination and in such a tone that I could see the moment coming

when we should be obliged to retire'.[45] Within a few days, Cachin was making concessions to the Petrograd Soviet's peace proposals, and speaking out with unexpectedly revolutionary ardour. The Irish leader of the British delegation, James O'Grady, also went native, declaring that the international working class would, for generations, be thanking God for the 'great work' of the Russian Revolution.[46]

There had been further concern about false perceptions in June 1917, when the House of Commons discussed the passports issued to Ramsay MacDonald and other members of the Independent Labour Party (ILP), so that they might visit revolutionary Russia as invited guests. In the words of one objector, the pacifist ILP was numerically an 'absolutely insignificant party in this country'; and it was all too likely that the Russians would receive a 'false impression' from the visit, mistaking the ILP's anti-war stance for wider British opinion.[47] Halford J. Mackinder, the eminent geographer and Conservative (Unionist) MP, expressed the same anxiety. He pointed out that the Russian view of Britain had been shaped by recently returned Russian émigrés—revolutionaries who had escaped tsarist persecution by fleeing to Britain where they came into contact with only 'a particular element of this country, not with fair samples of society of the country as a whole'.[48] While not arguing against the two passports already granted, Mackinder had recommended that more should be issued to enable the Russians to meet 'different shades of opinion' and to understand that 'our democracies as a whole should be thought of in Russia as loving freedom and as having pursued it for centuries'.[49] Without this expanded delegation of 'the free parties of our free country', the Russians might easily be persuaded that 'Only those are in sympathy with our revolution who believe as we believe, in the extreme.'[50]

Yet this was only part of the charge that the anti-Bolshevik press now levelled at the British Labour Delegation. The 'Potemkin villages' anticipated by The Times's correspondent in Stockholm in May 1920, extended the accusation in a more theatrical direction, and they did so as part of an attempt to undermine any claims to 'reality' that the fact-finding delegation might make on its return to the West.

Russia's was by no means the first European revolution to be accompanied by charges of theatrical manipulation. In the 1790s, the anti-revolutionary parliamentarian and political philosopher Edmund Burke was accused by Thomas Paine of having dramatized the French Revolution as a tragedy; and he himself condemned the French Jacobins for replacing the Roman

Catholic Church with 'impious, blasphemous, indecent theatric rites, in honour of their vitiated, perverted reason'.[51] The suggestion now, however, evoked a wider application of stagecraft.

It was anticipated that the Bolsheviks would systematically rig the appearances to which the visiting British delegates were exposed: just as, in 1787, Catherine the Great's first minister and lover, Prince Potemkin, was alleged to have erected theatrically constructed pasteboard 'villages' and employed actors to play the part of festive villagers along the banks of the river Dnieper. Potemkin's purpose, so the story went, had been to convince Catherine, together with the various European potentates in whose company she would sail past these artfully constructed scenes, that he was indeed using her money to resettle and, in accordance with her commitment to Enlightenment ideas, improve Ukrainian territories recently annexed into 'New Russia'.[52]

Though disputed by more recent historians, the legend of Potemkin's theatrically constructed façades (which in some versions of the myth were said to have been erected along roadsides in the sure knowledge that Catherine would not stop to get out of her passing carriage and see through Potemkin's 'special effects')[53] would be remembered through the nineteenth century, and identified with later acts of scene-rigging. In the 1850s, for example, it was reported that a row of primitive and unsightly huts in Odessa had been pulled down and replaced, in Potemkin-like anticipation of a later emperor's visit, with a row of painted façades showing superior mansions that actually remained unbuilt.[54]

The charge of Potemkinism would be made many times through the history of the iron curtain, and it would prove spectacularly justified both of Stalin's Russia and of Maoist China. One of the more 'Aesopian'[55] versions of this accusation would eventually be provided by the doomed Bolshevik leader Nikolai Bukharin. In the months before the rigged show trial of March 1938 (in which Stalin would have him maligned and condemned to death as a traitor), Bukharin would remember this sort of stage management as it had been employed by the tsarist authorities in pre-revolutionary times. In his unfinished prison novel, How It All Began, he describes the scene-rigging applied in August 1902, when Tsar Nicholas and Kaiser Wilhelm of Prussia met aboard their warships at Reval (Tallinn) harbour. Not content with dressing up in the uniforms of each other's empire, the kaiser and tsar boarded the Russian flagship Minin to watch a gunnery display laid on by the warships of the Russian fleet. 'The shooting turned out to be very

1. The *Jaroslaw Dabrowski* on the Thames, 1 August 1954.

2. (*left*) Antoni Klimowicz addresses a press conference at the headquarters of the Polish Ex-combatants' Association, Queensgate Terrace, London, 8 August 1954.

3. (*below*) Drs Joseph and Ruth Cort at the offices of the National Council for Civil Liberties, Paddington, London, 12 June 1954.

4. Winston S. Churchill and Harry S. Truman arriving in downtown Fulton, Missouri, 5 March 1946.

5. Churchill and Truman on the way to Westminster College, Fulton, Missouri, 5 March 1946.

6. 'C–T Day' crowds in Fulton, Missouri, 5 March 1946.

7. Churchill and Truman with Phil M. Donnelly, governor of Missouri (*far left*), and Dr Franc 'Bullet' McCluer, president of Westminster College (*far right*), at Westminster College, 5 March 1946.

8. Churchill delivering 'The Sinews of Peace' lecture in Westminster College gymnasium, 5 March 1946.

9. Drury Lane Theatre, by Thomas Rowlandson. Aquatint. London, 1808.

10. Safety curtain with advertisements, Grand Theatre, Wolverhampton, c.1930.

11. Vernon Lee at Sestri, 1914 (photo: Margery Taylor).

12. Elisabeth, queen of the Belgians, De Panne, Flanders, 1917.

13. Elisabeth, queen of the Belgians, taking a snapshot of King George V presenting decorations to Belgian officers, De Panne, 13 August 1916.

14. Charles Roden Buxton, Ethel Snowden and Robert Williams at King's Cross Station, London, *Daily Sketch*, 28 April 1920.

15. British Labour Delegation in Stockholm, May 1920. Front row (left to right): H. Skinner, Leslie Haden Guest, Ben Turner, A. A. Purcell. Second row: R. C. Wallhead, Robert Williams, Clifford Allen, Charles Roden Buxton. Back row: Ethel Snowden, Tom Shaw (with moustache) (photo: Th. Skadin, Stockholm).

16. British Labour Delegation arriving at Narva, Estonia, 10 May 1920.

17. Pro-war British Labour delegates, Will Thorne MP, James O'Grady, and William Stephen Sanders, visit a barracks outside Petrograd to meet the Russian soldier (with fixed bayonet) who first declared for the revolution by persuading his regiment not to fire on the people as ordered, April 1917.

18. Before the division: P. A. Kruskopf, lithograph of the Rajajoki river, between Finland and Russia, 1845.

19. Alexander Berkman and Emma Goldman in New York at the time of their trial, July 1917.

20. David Roden and Dorothy Francis Buxton, c.1922.

21. Interior portrait of the men of the British Labour Delegation, Russia 1920. Left to right Clifford Allen (Independent Labour Party), A. A. Purcell, Ben Turner, Dr Leslie Haden Guest, Robert Williams (with cigarette) Tom Shaw, Charles Roden Buxton, R. C. Wallhead (ILP), H. Skinner. This image and the next (22), both presumably made in Soviet Russia, were preserved in Buxton's scrapbook.

22. Artistically enhanced version of the above, Russia 1920.

23. G. E. Zinoviev, V. I. Lenin, G. M. Serrati (head of the Italian Socialist delegation) and Angelica Balabanova at a political meeting, Russia 1920.

24. Augustus John, portrait of Gustav Stresemann, oil on canvas, 1925.

successful,' as the soon-to-be-shot Bukharin noted, and not surprisingly since, as suspicious sailors later discovered, 'the targets were set up in such a way that "the slightest" breeze would have knocked them over'.[56]

In the early years of the revolution, however, Western suspicion that the Bolsheviks might use screens, masks, and dramatic tableaux to dupe their credulous and linguistically incompetent visitors was less an act of prophecy than a strategic redeployment of a theme long familiar from Russian literature. In Leo Tolstoy's *War and Peace* (1869), the reform-minded landowner Pierre Bezuhov visits his far-flung estates only to be tricked by stewards who have mocked up evidence of improvements: the still wretchedly exploited serfs have been dragooned into smiling demonstrations of gratitude, and the stewards guide their master past hastily contrived building sites that would, so they promised, soon become schools, hospitals, and almshouses.[57] Writing in the 1830s, Nikolai Gogol had already portrayed Russia as a land of chaotic misrecognitions, where plausible stories, outright lies, and vodka-induced hallucinations seemed perpetually to triumph over actuality. For Gogol, the provincial countryside was so remote from the cities that a cunning newcomer could achieve great influence and prestige by buying up non-existent serfs ('dead souls' who had died since being registered in the last census), and a lowly clerk who had just gambled away his final penny could enter a remote village and find himself suddenly mistaken for a visiting government inspector, who must be indulged and bribed at every turn.

Gogol's Russia had possessed a 'civilised veneer', which only sometimes covered its violent and brutish nature; and its most extravagant shopping street, St Petersburg's 'all-powerful Nevsky Prospect', was a place of glassy surfaces, where 'everything, not only the street lamp, exudes deceit'.[58] In May 1920, however, the suggestion that the Bolsheviks would trick their visitors with especially prepared 'Potemkin villages' was also informed by theatrical manipulations of a more recently applied variety. No doubt, it reflected an awareness of the recently war-proven techniques of 'public relations', which had served, just as an American objector had warned in 1914, to convert the world into 'a vast amphitheatre' in which the public would be dragooned as propagandized 'spectators'.[59] However, it was also directly influenced by knowledge of a military 'rigging' of appearances that had been carried out on both sides of the front in the Great War. Thanks to a senior Anglo-Jewish artist named Solomon J. Solomon, these recently developed techniques of 'camouflage' were the object of public controversy at the time of the British Labour Delegation's visit to Russia.

Deception has been an enduring element of warfare. There was, for example, little new in the Allied suspicion that Germany, in the last months of the Great War, was concentrating available food supplies in border towns in an attempt to convince Allied agents that their naval blockade had failed.[60] Yet the word 'camouflage' had, so the *Oxford English Dictionary* claims, only entered English usage in 1917 and Solomon was among the British pioneers who had applied this novel art to the battlefields of the western front. In his book *Strategic Camouflage,* published in May 1920 and noisily reviewed over the following weeks, he attributed the rise of camouflage to a technologically induced mutation in the geography of warfare. With the coming of aerial photography, so he declared on his opening page, '"The Other Side of the Hill" no longer exists.'[61]

Following this sudden discovery, numerous artists and theatre designers on both sides had found themselves searching out new ways of exploiting the fact that, in a phrase Solomon would quote from the eighteenth-century British portrait artist Sir Joshua Reynolds, 'the eye only sees what it knows'.[62] The first 'dummy tree' observation post is said to have been produced by the French artist-camoufleur Guirand de Scévola, and used in the battle of Artois in May 1915.[63] Following this example, Solomon produced his own 'modelled fudge'[64] with the help of a carefully selected band of theatrical scene painters—including, as it happens, the 'head property man'[65] from London's Drury Lane Theatre. He contrived a grass-garnished fishing net, to be draped over tanks and big guns to remove their shadows, and steel-cored observation posts that resembled very slender willow trees. Other effects were created with wire-netting, dyed raffia, papier-mâché, and plaster of Paris, the latter proving especially useful in the construction of dummy heads that could be pushed up over the parapet of a trench to tempt enemy snipers into revealing their positions.

By the beginning of 1918, Solomon was also using his perspectival expertise to see through the deceptive ruses of his counterparts on the other side of the front. Thanks, as Winston Churchill never tired of pointing out, to the Bolsheviks' decision to disengage Russia from the Allied war effort in November 1917, Germany was no longer so committed on the eastern front and had begun secretly massing troops in preparation for a major offensive to the west.

It was during this build-up that Solomon claimed to have made his proudest breakthrough. Studying brightly lit aerial photographs of German-held areas, including the Flanders village of St Pierre Capelle ('the last resting place'[66] of German troops on the way to the front), he saw the world behind the enemy lines melt into an expertly realised '*mise-en-scène*'.[67] Peering through his magnifying glass, he detected shadows that seemed to be cast by fields while a nearby house made none. Strange 'blisters' appeared in apparently empty roads, revealing them to be sham structures raised up to cover real roads that were probably teeming with invisible military traffic beneath. Other 'surprising abnormalities'[68] included hedges that were actually cables stitching together illusory stook-dotted fields—components, he was sure, of a 'colossal' system of concealment capable of accommodating two divisions while still resembling 'the normal incidents of the landscape'. As he scrutinized this prodigiously rigged world behind the front, Solomon had become convinced that Germany was practising a form of camouflage that went far beyond the merely 'tactical' techniques used by the Allies to conceal troops, trenches, and guns.

Seeking to awaken the authorities to his findings, Solomon claimed to have found some interest in the British Cabinet—Winston Churchill was among those who took camouflage seriously—but he found it quite impossible to convince the Allied military command about the 'vast strategic system' that Germany had, he was convinced, built up undetected during the winter before the huge spring offensive of March 1918. Defeated, he had been left shaking his head at the 'fatal and complacent stupidity' of the men who rejected his revelations only weeks before Allied forces were suddenly confronted with 'literally hundreds of thousands of men, coming as it were out of the ground'.[69]

Solomon's claims about German camouflage would remain under discussion through the spring and summer of 1920. Writing in the April edition of the periodical *World's Work*, he declared that his discovery of 'The Secret of German Camouflage' had since been confirmed in the German General Eric Ludendorff's war memoirs (published in English in 1919).[70] Noting that vast areas of 'openwork cover' had been found after the German retreat, he also visited France and Belgium to hunt up evidence of his own.[71]

By publishing his findings in *Strategic Camouflage,* Solomon hoped finally to convince the authorities that 'the Science of the Interpretation of Aerial Photography' would be 'the eye of Command' in all future wars. He was rewarded with hostile mockery. The *Times Literary Supplement* gave the book to a military reviewer who ridiculed Solomon's artistic claims as 'quite fallacious', and concluded: 'its illustrations are beautiful, but will provoke the mirth of expert air photograph readers'.[72] The *Morning Post* quoted a former major with the Royal Engineers camouflage school, Dr A. Mackenzie, who had reassured a meeting of the International College of Chromatics that Solomon's 'fantastic ideas' about German camouflage were fictional and worse than useless.[73] Some months later, a more appreciative review would appear in *Das Technische Blatt* (a supplement of the *Frankfurter Zeitung*).[74] This German consideration of the 'blue mist' of camouflage may actually have offered little more than a summary of Solomon's assertions. Yet it served Solomon's allies as proof that their man had been right all along. In October, news of this German vindication would be communicated to the *Irish Times* by a British officer in Dublin: 'I take the liberty of putting this matter before you, as I feel that, had Solomon's views been considered favourably when first put forward, many lives might have been saved.'[75]

George Lansbury's Example

Accusations of 'camouflage' would fly in both directions as the British argued over the Soviet revolution. Visiting Russia in September 1920, H. G. Wells was repeatedly warned that he would be 'hoodwinked' by the Bolsheviks, and that 'the most elaborate camouflage of realities would go on'.[76] By that time Churchill himself had become engaged in a ferocious correspondence with James H. Baum, the socialist secretary of Leicester and District Trades Council, who had written to denounce the British government's 'war policy against Soviet Russia'. Baum insisted that 'the great mass of the people' had been deliberately kept in the dark, as Churchill must have known 'perfectly well', and that the policy had been 'deliberately camouflaged by you, your colleagues and the vast press that keeps you in power'.[77]

H. G. Wells replied to the charge that he would inevitably be deceived by insisting that 'the harsh and terrible realities of the situation in Russia cannot be camouflaged', since it was 'hardly possible to dress up two large cities for the benefit of two stray visitors'. A similar rebuttal would be made by the French convert Marcel Cachin. Speaking in December 1920 at the Congress of Tours (at which the communist faction won control of the French Socialist Party), Cachin repudiated the accusation that he had been duped by 'Potemkin villages' during his visits to Russia, insisting that 'in reality it is impossible to camouflage an entire country'.[78]

In Britain, the Tory press had allowed no such doubts as it accused George Lansbury of having yielded to systematic stage management when he returned from Bolshevik Russia, brimming with the defiant enthusiasm of a believer who had seen the coming of the Lord, a few weeks before the British Labour Delegation set off on their mission. The *Morning Post* opened the attack by printing a letter by a correspondent who could not, so the paper claimed, safely be identified except as a 'prominent Russian in Moscow'.[79] Dated 16 March 1920, this missive described how the utterly miserable conditions in Moscow had been aggravated by an almost complete absence of electricity. The Kremlin may have glowed all night like a beacon, but ordinary people were reduced to spending 'their last roubles in buying seats for the theatres, not to see or enjoy the plays, but simply because they are the only public buildings in Moscow which are accessible to all and are warm (from the heat of hundreds of spectators) and lighted'. Yet a few weeks previously, so this anonymous witness testified, things had suddenly got better for a few days:

> Quite unexpectedly one evening the current was switched on all over the town, the principal streets were lit up. You can't imagine what a treat it was. The trams were started again ... We didn't know why this transformation took place so suddenly till we heard that a famous English statesman—a certain Lord Lansbury (do you know him?)—had arrived from London to negotiate peace, and our rulers wanted to show off Moscow at her best—aren't they childish—as if any intelligent Englishman, even if he was so carefully 'conducted' over the place and shown only 'Potiemkin [*sic*] villages,' like this Lord Lansbury, could not perfectly well realise what a state Russia is in, and that all the things he was shown were only 'stage-settings'.

Genuine or not, this letter had triggered a heated correspondence. Responding to his own 'accidental' elevation to the peerage, Lansbury named the Western journalists with whom he had shared his visit to Moscow: he dubbed them variously Viscount, Count, Senator, and Judge, and then went on to mock, without specifically denying, the *Morning Post*'s allegations that he had been served with 'sumptuous food' and 'splendid entertainment'.[80] Other anti-Bolshevik witnesses quickly responded to this further provocation, including a number of recently returned Britons who described how they too had seen 'Lord Lansbury' in Moscow, whirling past in a car full of commissars bent on preventing him from 'having intercourse with any but specially chosen people'. As Albert V. Frank wrote of the steps that were taken to control and improve the view from Lansbury's limousine, 'I confirm that not only were the places visited by Mr. Lansbury specially prepared for his visits but also that the streets and boulevards were better lighted for his special benefit than they had been hitherto or have been since his departure'.[81]

When Lansbury tried to see off these additional allegations, Frank claimed the authority of twenty years spent in Moscow and provided a detailed list of the streets and squares that had been specially illuminated for the British socialist's benefit.[82] Frank later teamed up with another Briton who had also been roughly treated in Bolshevik Russia, and challenged Lansbury to a public debate: announcing that he had booked a hall in Westminster, and specifying terms as if he was arranging a duel.[83] That second 'British Refugee', a certain M. Simes, wrote to explain that he had been one of the seventy-four Britishers locked up in the Andronoffsky Monastery Prison Camp. One day, he and his fellow prisoners had heard that Lansbury was coming to visit them. In the event, neither Lansbury nor his ever-present 'Jew Commissar' had showed up, but on the appointed day 'our rations were special and really fit to eat'.[84]

The 'debate' demanded by Messrs Frank and Sime never took place in its expected form. Lansbury specified an acceptable order of proceedings and demanded that the event be staged at the Royal Albert Hall, which he had packed with enraptured admirers on his recent return from Russia. Frank and Sime declined the latter suggestion, claiming that, in stripping them of their wealth, the Bolsheviks had left them without the means to book such a large venue, and also protesting that they had still not recovered sufficiently from the 'privations and ill-treatment' they had suffered in Russia to 'undergo the physical and nervous strain of addressing an audience of 10,000 people in a hall like the Albert Hall'.[85] The meeting was eventually arranged for 12 June, the day Lansbury had suggested, but it was convened in the much smaller Essex Hall by the Strand. There was contemptuous laughter as extracts from Lansbury's glowing *Daily Herald* articles about Bolshevik Russia were read out. But Lansbury himself had failed to show up, and the speakers and chairman (the recently returned British vicar of Moscow, the Revd F. W. North), could only fire their denunciations at an empty chair on the platform, prominently marked 'Reserved for Mr Lansbury'.[86]

Few who anticipated that the British Labour Delegation would be treated to another round of systematic scene-shifting will have been hugely reassured when the chairman, Ben Turner, 'expressed the conviction that there would be no attempt to deceive them, and that the delegates could not fail to get at the bottom of things and ascertain the truth'.[87] It was less an answer than a repudiation of the question, and one that Turner would

repeat when he returned to Britain, dismissing 'all the stories of organised camouflage'.[88] Mrs Snowden also tried to fend off suspicions that the
delegation would see nothing but Potemkin villages: 'We shall demand an
independent investigation … If that is denied us it will answer all our questions.'[89] She, however, would later concede that the circumstances had been
challenging. Acknowledging that 'even educated and cultured people find it
difficult in any given set of circumstances not to exhibit their predilections',
she felt, nevertheless, that all the delegates had made 'a serious and honest
attempt to prepare his, or her, mind for straight looking at, and hard thinking about, the great experiment'.[90] No such claim would have appeased the
Morning Post's special correspondent, who sat in Estonia awaiting the British
Labour Delegation. His articles about their passage through Russia would
be printed under a heading borrowed from Mark Twain's famous account of
Americans touring Europe and the Holy Land: 'The Innocents Abroad'.[91]

Train to Petrograd

Arriving at Tallinn (Reval) in the evening, the delegation was welcomed
by a mixed party of Estonian socialists: bitterly divided in their attitudes
towards the Russian Bolsheviks but united in the fervent welcomes they
extended to their British visitors. Dined by various factions of both right
and left, the delegation also attended a concert by the Russian bass Feodor
Chaliapin, a celebrated 'artist of the people' who shared a smoke with some
of the delegates backstage, and gave no indication of the fact that he would
soon quit his homeland for the West.[92] In the Hotel Petrograd the Bolshevik
representative, Gowkovsky, laid on an immense banquet in their honour,
thereby embarrassing these visitors to 'starving Russia', who had worried, as
they sailed along the coast of Finland, how they could possibly retain their
status as independent 'social investigators' if the Bolsheviks tried to indulge
them as 'a sort of Cook's tourist party or the Royal Family'.[93] Ethel Snowden,
who counted temperance among her most long-standing causes, was especially
horrified to find the delegation supplied with vodka, and bidden to 'drink to
the social revolution in a beverage which the Revolutionary Government, following the wartime example of the Tsar, has had the wisdom to forbid'.[94]

The transformation from 'Cook's tourist party' to visiting royal family
occurred on 10 May, when the delegation entered Soviet Russia at Narva. Met by

Melnitchansky, president of the Moscow Labour Council, they were delighted
by the first expressions of 'intense interest and real pleasure' on the faces
of soldiers and workers who witnessed their arrival.[95] After long delays,
they were then ushered onto a special train complete with dining car and
kitchen[96]—its Pullman carriages 'decorated with red bunting, fervent mottoes,
and the green branches of trees'[97]—which hauled them across war-gouged
terrain to Petrograd (St Petersburg). On the train they were accompanied
by 'many important officials, anxious beyond all words to prove their good
intentions and international solidarity with the representatives of the British
working class'.[98] The sense of ceremony was increased by the escort of Red
Guards and Bashkir cavalrymen from the Urals, the latter clad 'in gorgeous
purple uniforms, with wonderful cloaks and long swords'.[99] For Dr Haden
Guest, the 'flowing blue silk pelisses' covering the backs of those cavalrymen also conveyed a more serious message: one that was hammered home
again when, at their first stop in Russia, the delegates, who included some of
Britain's best-known pacifists and conscientious objectors, found themselves
inspecting a guard of honour, which stood to attention while the 'Internationale' was played by a military band. As he noted, 'One of our strongest
first impressions of Russia was that it is a military power.'[100]

They reached Petrograd in the small hours of 11 May. Transferred into
cars which had previously carried the tsar (and were now among the
Bolsheviks' proudest trophies), they were driven noisily, as Bertrand Russell
remembers, through 'sleeping streets' to a palace on the banks of the Neva,
where they were served a simple meal and welcomed by the trade unionists who would host their stay in the city.[101] A. Losovsky, a member of the
Central Executive of the Russian Trade Unions, shook them by the hand
and said, in French, 'We have seen English shells and guns; we are now very
pleased to see, for the first time, representatives of the great British Labour
Movement.'[102] Russell, who had previously defended the October Revolution but would now rapidly become highly critical of Bolshevism and its
threat to 'the heritage of civilisation',[103] recalls standing at a window in the
early dawn, looking out across the gleaming river to the fortress of Peter and
Paul, long infamous as the prison in which the tsars had tormented their
political enemies. The view was, he thought, 'beautiful beyond all words,
magical, eternal, suggestive of ancient wisdom. "It is wonderful," I said to
the Bolshevik who stood beside me. "Yes," he replied, "Peter and Paul is
now not a prison, but the Army Headquarters".'

Ethel Snowden also looked out at that fortress from the balcony, but the
cruelly tortured victims of the tsars were not the only 'ghosts' to worry her

in that well-appointed palace. Taken to her sleeping quarters, she found herself surrounded by thick velvety carpets, ornately carved and gilded furniture, silk hangings, and a bed with fine linen sheets and eiderdown covers. Until recently 'a beautiful *salon*',[104] the chamber was now divided in two by a flimsy curtain so that Mrs Snowden could share it with Angelica Balabanova, the widely travelled Communist activist responsible for receiving the delegation in Petrograd.

Balabanova would soon enough prove to be no subordinate creature of Bolshevik policy.[105] However, in the outlook shaping many perceptions of the British Labour Delegation's progress through Russia she and Ethel Snowden represented two irreconcilable strands of European socialism as they lay down to sleep on either side of that flimsy curtain. Democracy, reform, and Christian humanitarianism lay tossing and turning on one side while atheism, the revolutionary vanguard party, and the armed dictatorship of the proletariat slumbered, apparently untroubled, on the other.

In Britain, these two factions merely quarrelled. Their dispute had been altogether more violent in Russia where, after the October Revolution, the Bolsheviks had assaulted and persecuted the Menshevik and Social Revolutionary majority in the abolished Constituent Assembly; and also in Germany where, in January 1919, the majority socialists (Ebert, Schiedemann, and Noske) had collaborated with nationalist Freikorps officers in their battle with the revolutionary internationalists in the Spartacus League, thereby becoming complicit in the murder of Karl Liebnecht, Rosa Luxemburg, and others.

Yet these were hardly the ghosts that kept Mrs Snowden awake during her first night in Petrograd. After the 'intense fatigue and excitement' of their journey, Snowden felt grateful for the 'exaggerated kindness' of the Bolshevik hosts who had evidently given their British visitors 'the very best they possessed'. However, doubts still gnawed at her mind through the remnants of that first night, as she tried vainly to sleep while servants tramped through the room as if it were a corridor and Petrograd's 'everlasting light' poured in through uncovered windows. Was all this luxury really 'theirs to give or ours to receive,' she wondered, and 'where is the owner of this beautiful house?'[106] Angelica Balabanova, whom delegate Robert Williams would later hail (mistakenly) as 'the incarnation of Working-Class Dictatorship',[107] was disappointed to find Mrs Snowden 'more distressed over the fate of the upper classes than over the suffering of the masses'.[108] The British feminist would even insist on imagining the recently dispossessed Princess Naryshkin not as a parasitic exploiter who richly deserved her own roughly imposed taste of class justice but as an abused woman 'whose house had been entered by intruders she was powerless to put outside'. 'I felt like a guilty thing, lying uninvited by its owner in that soft white bed, whilst the poor creature who once occupied it might be sleeping on straw.'[109]

A Sequel's Descent

It was as she described arriving at this expropriated palace—fascinated, flattered and yet painfully unable to divide her sympathies in the harsh Bolshevik manner—that Mrs Snowden would write the sentence for which her book of memoirs, *Through Bolshevik Russia*, is sometimes still remembered: 'We were behind the "iron curtain" at last.'[110]

Another meaningless coincidence of language? Surely not. The metaphor of the curtain was indeed fairly commonplace among those who had objected to the recent war and the terms of settlement imposed under the Treaty of Versailles. In that same year of 1920, Douglas Goldring, an English pacifist and friend of E. D. Morel, published a novel in which the 1914–18 war was imagined as a 'black curtain' falling on the hopes of a circle of Bohemians, revolutionary internationalists, and other representatives of 'Young Democracy' in London.[111]

The British Liberal economist John Maynard Keynes would also invoke the idea of a curtain when he looked back on his first meetings with the representatives of defeated Germany in January 1919. In a memoir written some years later, Keynes would recall travelling to the German town of Triers (Trèves) on Marshal Foch's train, together with various British, French, and American officials. Their mission was 'to make preliminary arrangements for the supply of food to Germany, and to explore with German civilian representatives their available means of payment'.[112]

The nine Allied representatives had conducted their business in a train carriage, with an emblematic 'folding bridge table' erected between themselves and the six Germans opposite. The first encounter had been awkward, with neither side knowing whether to bow or shake hands, and the German representatives appearing only to confirm 'the popular conception of Huns'. Yet at various subsequent meetings, Keynes had managed to cultivate one member of the German party, the Hamburg banker Carl Melchior. It was a difficult manoeuvre that demanded considerably more than just reaching out over a flimsy card table. Keynes had to negotiate a passage through both 'the three-barred gate of triple interpretations' and also the 'barriers of permitted intercourse' which at that time still discouraged all informal communication with Germans and, in some French eyes especially, saw treachery in the very attempt.[113] When he encountered Melchior again in October 1919, i.e. some months after those intensely polarized negotiations, Keynes found it 'extraordinary to meet without barriers, we two who had faced one another so often in opposition and etiquette and constraint'. As they looked back on those negotiations, the 'magnificent wickedness' that both sides had been inclined to see on 'the other side of the curtain' was replaced by nothing more systematic than 'the ignorant weakness and vanity and egotism of individual men'.[114]

And the curtain that was of 'iron' rather than cloth? Ethel Snowden may have been the first western visitor to name this divisive apparatus in its new position between Bolshevik Russia and the Allied world, but she had good reason to print the phrase in quotation marks. She can hardly have been aware of Vasily Vasilievich Rozanov, the Russian writer who, a few months before dying of starvation in January 1919, had imagined an 'iron curtain' coming down, 'with a clang, thud and bang', at the end of Russian history ('The performance is over', as Rozanov writes, and the members of the audience, who have stood up saying '"It's time to put on our overcoats and go home"', look round to find that neither their overcoats nor their homes exist any more[115]). She did, however, share the expression with the Labour delegation's joint secretary, her friend and fellow peace campaigner Charles Roden Buxton.[116] He would carry the phrase in mind for years and, as one who had opposed the Great War alongside Vernon Lee in the Union of Democratic Control, he was in no doubt as to its origins.

On 28 December 1922, Buxton would write to Lee saying 'I should like you to know that I always read, every Xmas, the little leaflet you wrote in 1917 for the League of Peace and Freedom. It is a wonderful piece of writing and has always made a deep impression on me.'[117] Such was his regard for her article on 'Bach's Christmas Music in England and in Germany' (which had actually made its first appearance in *Jus Suffragii* in January 1915) that, at some point not long after the Armistice of November 1918, he and his wife Dorothy reprinted it again, identifying it as 'A Leaflet Written during the Great War' and using it for their own private and presumably also seasonal circulation.[118]

9

Not Just a Frontier

He who says 'frontier' says 'bandage.' Cut the bandage, wipe out the frontier,
close down the custom-house, dismiss the soldier; in other words, be free,
and peace will follow.

Victor Hugo, letter to the Lausanne Peace Congress, 4 September 1869.[1]

Historians who looked back on this chaotic period from the perspectives of the post-Fulton Cold War, would be inclined to project the
phrase 'iron curtain' back into the very first fortifications applied by the
Bolsheviks to Russia's frontier with the West. In his *A New History of the
Cold War,* published in 1966, the Hungarian-born American John Lukacs,
would write that 'the rulers of Russia, by 1921, had separated their large
Empire from Europe by an iron curtain'.[2] Eight years earlier, the same con-
nection had been made by George F. Kennan, who, as deputy to Averell
Harriman, the American ambassador to Russia, had done so much to stiffen
American policy against Stalin's Russia with his famous 'Long Telegram' of
February 1946.

In his Pulitzer Prize-winning study of Soviet–American relations between
1917 and 1920, this distinguished veteran of the American Foreign Service
describes the flight of the American diplomats in Russia, whose situation
had deteriorated so rapidly after 4 September 1918, when American forces
landed in Archangel to join the Allied military intervention against the
Bolsheviks. Instructed to quit Russia by any means possible, the American
consul, DeWitt C. Poole, left his besieged Consulate building in Moscow
and, escorted by two members of Norway's diplomatic mission, travelled
by train to the Finnish frontier at Beloostrov. On 20 September 1918 (and
allegedly only ten minutes before the Russian guards received orders to
arrest him), Poole walked over a small railway bridge spanning the creek that

marked the separation of the two countries. A month later, on 17 October, the remaining members of the American group in Russia arrived at the same crossing point. By this time, as Kennan notes, the railway tracks had been removed and iron gates had been added to both ends of the bridge connecting 'the two strife-torn worlds of thought and feeling which no one had been able to hold together'.[3] Evoking the clanking sound of the Finnish gate closing behind the withdrawing Americans, Kennan described these reinforcements as 'one more link in that iron curtain that was to constitute through coming decades the greatest and saddest of the world's political realities'.

That creek at Beloostrov may already have become one of the sites 'where the two worlds divide',[4] yet in 1920, Ethel Snowden used Vernon Lee's 'iron curtain' to name a division that was by no means so closely identified with Soviet Russia's western frontier. Treaties were under way between Bolshevik Russia and the recovered Baltic states—agreements with Estonia and Finland were finally signed at Tartu on 2 February and 14 October 1920 respectively. At the House of Arts in Petrograd, the Russian writer Yevgeny Zamyatin may already have been at work on *We,* a dystopic novel of the achieved Communist future, in which he imagines the scientifically programmed society of the One State sequestered behind a 'Green Wall' of shatterproof glass through which no one has passed since a Two-Hundred-Year War between the city and the countryside.[5] In reality, however, Soviet Russia had yet to convert its frontier into the 'impregnable' barrier of later years, and there was still precious little in the way of fixed border architecture to reassure even the most optimistic Western visitors as they crossed the recently stabilized battlefront and celebrated, as if they had passed into the walled enclosure of paradise itself.

The first party of political deportees to arrive from America entered Bolshevik Russia from Finland on 20 January 1920. Among them was Alexander Berkman, a Lithuanian-born Jewish anarchist who had spent many years in American jails, the first fourteen of them after trying to murder the strike-breaking industrialist Henry Clay Frick in 1892. As he approached Russia, Berkman, who had gone on to edit the anarchist journal *Mother Earth* with Emma Goldman and also his own fiery San Francisco-based organ *The Blast,* found a 'destroyed' railway bridge and a 'frozen creek'. The latter was attended, on the Beloostrov side, by cheering 'red-capped soldiers' as well as by a government reception committee and a 'military Red Band' which played the Internationale as the deportees stepped into a snowstorm to complete what one sympathetic journalist described as 'a 200-yard walk between the old world and the new'.[6] These were 'the visible symbols of the Revolution Triumphant', and they filled Berkman, who, three years earlier, had hailed the Russian Revolution as 'unquestionably the greatest event of modern times',[7] with an urgent desire to kneel and kiss the ground.[8]

Emma Goldman (another Lithuanian-born émigré) was also in that party of 249 alien anarchists and members of the proscribed Union of Russian Workers, who had been rounded up in a series of raids ordered by Attorney General A. Mitchell Palmer and his young special assistant, J. Edgar Hoover, and transported across the Atlantic on the USS *Buford* (also dubbed the 'Red Ark').[9] Having shared so much with Berkman, including a two-year jail term imposed in July 1917 for jointly 'conspiring' against conscription in America,[10] she wrote that 'spring was in our hearts' even though the earth was a frozen 'sheet of white': 'I preferred to be alone when I touched the sacred soil: my exaltation was too great, and I feared I might not be able to control my emotion.'[11] Her face wet with tears, Goldman hailed Bolshevik Russia as the land of freedom and declared 'I feel the same emotion entering Russia as my Jewish people felt thousands of years ago upon entering the Inner Temple. Liberty changes habitation, but it is eternal.'[12]

Feelings also ran high for the 18-year-old deportee Ethel Bernstein. Just before crossing, she received a telegram from the USA announcing that her 'sweetheart' and fellow member of the Harlem-based 'Frayhayt' Group', Samuel Lipman, had been sentenced to twenty years' imprisonment for his part in their shared offence (publishing two leaflets opposing America's joining of the Allied Intervention of 1918). Lipman would himself be deported to Russia in December 1921, but he knew nothing of that as he sat in Atlanta penitentiary composing the words that Bernstein would carry across the frozen river: 'Love goes forth over the years.'[13]

As the group passed through Finland on the way to the frontier, Emma Goldman had gone out of her way to tell every available journalist that the deportees of the 'Red Ark' were 'the first political exiles from American imperialism'.[14] They were also among the first of many pilgrims who would perform such soil-kissing rituals on arrival: confirming that, years before Stalin committed Soviet Russia to the idea of 'Socialism in one country', the spirit of 'international' revolution was already fervently identified with the ground on one side of this new division between states. At a party conference in Leipzig, the German Communist and feminist Clara Zetkin drew 'thunderous applause' when she described how a party of foreign Communists had felt on crossing the frontier into Russia: 'Draw off your shoes! You are standing on holy ground, made sacred by the revolutionary struggle and the revolutionary sacrifice of the Russian workers.'[15] Such was the Communist International's version of vertically aligned patriotism: a 'new collective allegiance' of the kind Vernon Lee imagined replacing the rivalrous loyalties of the nation states, and one that would be intensified in its adoration of the Soviet homeland by the many defeats suffered by the Communist movement in Europe after the Armistice of November 1918.

Making his own way into Russia from Finland in February 1920, George Lansbury had found himself comparing the still modestly armed frontier between the two worlds with more familiar examples closer to home. The sea made a geographical fact of the borders between England and France or Ireland, but the line between England and Scotland had always seemed unreal. He remembered once taking the train from London to Edinburgh with some radical Scottish friends. As they crossed the river Tweed at Berwick, one of his comrades had called out 'Throw open the windows, Lansbury, and let in the pure free air of Scotland.' Lansbury had done as instructed, but could detect no difference in the air or, for that matter, between the people, who seemed to wander about just as aimlessly on either side:

> I was reminded of these incidents when standing on the Finnish side of the little river, the middle of which forms the imaginary border line between Russia and Finland. The men and women on both sides looked exactly alike: most of them spoke the same language. And yet each side of the river is an armed camp. People on the Finnish side are armed to defend a capitalist republic, on the Russian side to defend a social revolution. Only on one side, and that the Russian, did the fighters understand that frontiers are not real dividing lines these days—that only systems really divide, all else being makebelief.[16]

Entering Soviet Russia from Estonia at the end of May, the British Labour Delegation found that 'imaginary' frontier to be only a little more substantial: it was marked by 'a big red flag', the sight of which proved, as Mrs Snowden would dryly recall, 'altogether too much for some of our more ardent spirits'. Inspired to find themselves in what Bertrand Russell noted was actually 'a desolate region of marsh, pine wood, and barbed wire entanglements',[17] these delegates 'burst rapturously into song, first "The Internationalé" and then "The Red Flag," the favourite song of Socialists in Great Britain.'[18] There is no record of how these devotional antics impressed the people Ben Turner saw waiting silently to pass the other way: a party of German prisoners being piloted home and 'a body of peasantry, with all their goods and chattels on the ground, making their way out of Russia'.[19]

On some occasions, the Western pilgrims entering Soviet Russia would come close to clashing with people fleeing in the other direction. That is how it would be for Morris Gordin, who crossed from Latvia, while returning to the revolutionary land of his birth with other members of the Red Star Commune he had formed in the USA. He and his comrades found themselves all but overwhelmed by thousands of refugees leaving Russia, who were 'shocked and bewildered to come upon a crowd of people migrating from America to Russia, as if entirely reversing their concepts of the location of Hell and Paradise'.[20] Gordin recalls violent arguments that raged between the two camps before their train crossed over in the moonlight. Where others had hastened to kiss the soil, Gordin gazed out at the starry sky: 'it seemed to me that never before had I seen such splendid harmony above and below, as if both Sky and Earth were saluting us, restless wanderers on our pilgrimage to the Land of Promise. The Sky and Earth symbolizing to me the future harmony when both hand and mind, labor and intellect, should join together and build society anew on a basis of freedom.'[21]

New Russia's western border was an emotional front attended by violent oscillations between Love and Hate, and not just for those entering the traumatized land George Lansbury had identified as 'New Jerusalem' in the making.[22] Sympathizers used the frontier to embrace Soviet Russia as an island utopia encircled by hostile forces, yet by 1920 diverse witnesses had come tumbling out in the opposite direction, carrying blood-curdling stories of dispossession, murder, starvation, even cannibalism,[23] and desperate to find an unambiguous line that marked the beginning of safety and freedom. Meriel Buchanan, daughter of the British ambassador in Petrograd, left in January 1918—her family's departure hastened by the note issued by Trotsky in December 1917, in which he outlined the Bolsheviks' intention of entering into peace negotiations not with the Allied governments but with socialist parties in all countries. She left by train from Petrograd's Finland Station, sharing a carriage with seven English officers. They arrived at the Finnish frontier town of Torneo too late for the train into Sweden. After a freezing night, they entered Sweden at Happaranda—crossing a frozen river on low open sledges. The extreme weather was hardly the fault of Bolshevism, yet it had an allegorical quality all the same: 'I do not think I shall ever forget the cold of that drive, the wind seems to cut through one's furs as if they were absolutely non-existent.'[24]

A later flight was recorded by Rhoda Power, a young woman from Cambridge who had arrived in Rostov, on the river Don in the south, a month before Tsar

Nicholas was overthrown by the revolution of February 1917. She had planned to spend a year there, learning Russian and working as a governess with a wealthy landowning family. Shortly after her arrival, Power wrote to the *Cambridge Magazine*, describing the fetching appearance of the beggars who followed her down the street: 'delightfully picturesque, brown as berries and wonderfully dressed in coloured rags'.[25] Yet she also had to report that she found herself in a chaotic situation: 'Everything is higgledy-piggledy. You can't put a finger on a steady spot.' Prices were soaring and the servants were playing up too—including the coachman, who chose to sleep rather than prepare the carriage as ordered and only smirked about his newly won 'freedom' when reprimanded. Power was in no doubt that 'By hook or by crook these people's notion of freedom will have to be knocked out of their heads and a very carefully prepared definition hammered in instead.'

This work of mental reconstruction proved beyond the powers of the new Provisional Government under Prince Lvov and Kerensky. Black-mailing letters soon started to arrive from a 'Committee of Adventurers and Apaches', which threatened to bomb houses and kidnap women and children.[26] Not long afterwards a stolen boy was found 'buried in a sitting position, starved and part strangled'. Rhoda Power fled north as the alarms escalated, driving across the steppe in a dangerously conspicuous car and then taking trains through embattled country to arrive eventually at Murmansk, on the Barents Sea, then still in the hands of the White Army and the Allied expeditionary force to Northern Russia.

For Power, the frontier was a gladly forsaken shoreline glimpsed from the stern as she sailed for home, feeling much safer at sea despite the threat of German submarines. Other fugitives broke out closer to Petrograd than Murmansk, including Paul Dukes, who had gone to Petrograd as a musician and stayed on through the revolution to become agent 'ST-25', reputedly the British Secret Intelligence Service's top man in Red Russia.[27] He made his final escape by struggling at night through miles of marshy bog, stealing a fisherman's leaky old boat, and crossing Lake Luban (he and his fellow escapers had to bail constantly whilst using tree-boughs as oars) to arrive in Latvia.[28] Before that, however, Dukes had smuggled various White Russians into Finland, itself engaged, through the first five months of 1918, in a fierce struggle that was both a civil war against internal revolution and a war of independence against Soviet Russia.

On one occasion Dukes made the crossing in Karelia, not far from Lake Ladoga, accompanied by the wife of a British businessman and also the two young daughters of the Grand Duke Paul Alexandrovitch, himself imprisoned and soon to be shot in Petrograd. To reach Finland, they passed through a land of forest and frozen snow crossed by a series of ditches. At one of these snow-filled obstacles, Dukes nobly laid himself down to enable the women in his party to step across along his back. The Grand Duke's daughters may not have kissed the soil when they arrived in Finland but, once they had traversed what seemed to be the final river with the help of a 'rickety plank, ice-covered and slippery',[29] they did fall to their knees and cross themselves devoutly.

For H. V. Keeling, a British printer who fled Russia some months later in January 1919, the ditches began at a greater distance from the border. Keeling had been sent to Russia in February 1914, to help establish a patent photolithography process that his London employer had supplied to a company in Petrograd. He walked out of the city the day after the old Russian Christmas. On his approach to Finland, he had to pass through three rows of defensive trenches, still being dug, as he noticed, by labouring women: 'These trenches were in all parts except where the main road passed through them; they were flanked on both sides by barbed wire entanglements and were supposed to extend right across the country to Lake Ladoga.'[30] Having sneaked or lied his way through the checkpoints, sparsely attended due to Christmas celebrations (which persisted despite Bolshevik disapproval), he negotiated his way past sleighs full of Red Guards, and out along forest paths. Surprised to find neither trenches nor barbed wire nor, indeed, anything distinguishable as an actual frontier, Keeling only became convinced that he had arrived in Finland, when he noticed a discarded cigarette packet by the side of the path: 'As there was practically no tobacco in Russia and certainly no packets of cigarettes, I began to feel reasonably sure that I was really in Finland at last.'[31]

Keeling was not a reliable witness, as is proven by his later allegation that the members of the British Labour Delegation were obliged, before leaving Russia, 'to sign an agreement not to attack the Bolshevist Government in any way in England'.[32] Yet that same contrast between desperate Russian austerity and relative western plenty would later serve to reassure Mrs Emma Cochran Ponafidine, the daughter of an American missionary, who had married a Russian diplomat in 1885. Smuggled to freedom on a horse-drawn sleigh across the frozen and searchlight-swept Gulf of Finland, she eventually found herself in a warm log cabin and was only convinced that she was safely in Finland by the sight of a saucer full of sugar, such as would never exist in starving Russia.[33] The 'iron curtain' that surrounded Bolshevik Russia in those early years certainly had the power to shape reality, but it was not just a frontier—or an iron-gated bridge over a creek—and neither, as Mrs Snowden and her fellow delegates knew very well, was it created from the Russian side.

10

Relocating the Allied Blockade

For two and a half years Russia has been practically *terra-incognita*. We have been shut in by an impenetrable wall. You are the first delegation from another country [which has] succeeded in making a break in that wall, and we are very naturally overjoyed at your presence here amongst us.

Russian speaker at a reception for the British Labour Delegation.[1]

On 21 May 1920, Charles Roden Buxton used a pause in the British Labour Delegation's 'somewhat exhausting' programme to write to his wife and fellow Quaker campaigner Dorothy Frances Buxton in London. Sitting in a Moscow hotel still known as, Delovoy Dvor ('Businessman's Court') despite its recent conversion into 'Soviet House No. 2', he mentioned neither the rudely encouraging slogan displayed opposite the entrance ('We started the Revolution, comrades—we started it alone; let us finish it together'[2]), nor the potted plants that one of the delegation's 'unofficial' interpreters, the already disillusioned ex-American anarchist Alexander Berkman, saw lending 'warmth and colour'[3] to the newly decorated rooms inside. Yet Buxton, who had always chosen to live modestly while devoting much of his considerable private income to progressive causes, was sincerely worried about the luxurious food. 'We can't stop it,' he wrote to his wife: 'they look on our visit as a very great event, and say "we can afford to do this once in 3 years". It is the first contact with the authorised representatives of the working class of another great country.'

Luxury amid terror and starvation: it was the experience of many of Soviet Russia's foreign visitors in 1920. That same May, the German revolutionary and Comintern activist Franz Jung noted a variation on the theme in Moscow's Hotel Lux, also filled with international guests of the Bolshevik government. The samovars in the dining room produced a steady stream of tea, but the food supply had broken down. Neither bread nor kasha were available, and all that remained for the revolutionary visitors was dish after dish of unmixed caviar and smoked salmon. Upset stomachs followed, and the dining room soon resounded with lectures in which indignant foreigners, not content with having eaten their way through the Kremlin's food reserves in a few weeks, complained that much better care would be taken of guests such as themselves if they were running the revolution.[4]

Two months later at the Delovoy Dvor, the Belgian-born Communist Victor Serge would see another wave of international delegates gather for the Second Congress of the Communist International: as he recalled years afterwards, they too were 'sumptuously fed amidst universal misery' and showed disturbingly little interest in 'the real, living Moscow, with its starvation-rations, its arrests, its sordid prison-episodes, its backstage racketeering'. As Serge concluded, 'I discovered a novel variety of insensitivity: Marxist insensitivity.'[5]

As a Christian socialist, Buxton was not guilty of that charge. In years to come his political opponents in Britain would be pleased to remind working class voters that Buxton was a 'millionaire' despite his personal modesty, his ascetic way of life, and his insistence on being known as 'Charlie'. Buxton owned shares in the family brewery in Brick Lane, East London, but he was also conscious of a moral inheritance as the great-grandson of Sir Thomas Fowell Buxton, the prison reformer (in cooperation with his Quaker sister-in-law, Elizabeth Fry) and abolitionist who had seen Wilberforce's Bill for the Abolition of the Status of Slavery through the House of Commons in 1833. Inclined to seek out useful lessons even in the most unpromising circumstances, Charles Roden Buxton used the Bolsheviks' embarrassing indulgence of the British Labour Delegation to identify what he took to be the more fundamental problem: 'I never realized before how keenly they felt the *barrier* between them and the outside world which *we,* from our side, have been denouncing for 2 years past.'[6]

War of Words

The 'iron curtain' that the Allies tried to wrap around the flaming spectacle that was Bolshevik Russia had many features in common with the Anglo-German predecessor from which it was directly descended. Both were shaped by a cancellation of free exchange that enabled 'distorted pictures'[7] to take the place of reliable information. Both elevated the logic of war and propaganda over the rational values essential to what the British Labour Delegation professed as 'independent and impartial inquiry'. Both implied a forceful submission of the individual citizen to the purposes of the modern state. Yet the 'iron curtains' condemned by Vernon Lee and Ethel Snowden were connected in their differences too.

Unlike the symmetrizing version that had fallen between Germany and Britain during the Great War, the 'iron curtain' that now separated Soviet Russia from the surrounding Allied world was a barrier between implacably opposed political systems, each one threatened by the mere existence of the other. Though attended by a comparable range of 'optical illusions' on both sides, the schism between capitalism and Bolshevism was not just a polarization between warring nation states. It was also a front within an aggressively mobile international class war.

Charles and Dorothy Buxton were among those for whom socialist internationalism remained a redemptive project. That was hardly how Lenin's creed appeared to the Allied leaders who, having failed to suppress Bolshevism by military 'Intervention' in the civil war, now tried to check its horizontal extension with blood-curdling denunciation.

Throughout 1919, when the threat of revolution seemed to loom all around the world, Winston Churchill, who was then Britain's Secretary of State for War, had served as his country's most reliable source of lurid anti-Bolshevik rhetoric. In February (a month in which, at Churchill's urging, the British War Cabinet sent tanks and machine guns to overawe an allegedly 'Bolshevist uprising' in Glasgow) he had declaimed that Russia 'now lies prostrate in the bloody clutches of the Bolshevik baboon',[8] as he tried to stiffen the members of the English-Speaking Union against the rampant beast. 'Of all tyrannies in history', so he pronounced at the Aldwych Club in London on 11 April, 'the Bolshevik tyranny is the worst, the most destructive, the most degrading.'[9] On 21 May, he wrote to the prime minister, David Lloyd George, dismissing a proposal that the two sides in the Russian Civil War should be invited to cease fighting, and insisting that all attempts to conciliate between Communism and the West were as useless as trying to reconcile 'fire and water'.[10] On 6 November, he told the House of Commons how, in 1917, a malevolent Germany had used a sealed train to ship Lenin and other leading Bolsheviks to Finland on their way to join the revolution in Russia: they were despatched like 'a phial containing a culture of typhoid or of cholera to be poured into the water supply of a great city, and it worked with amazing accuracy'. It was this speech that prompted the Tory leader, A. J. Balfour, to tell Churchill, 'I admire the exaggerated way you tell the truth'.[11]

The Allied military intervention against the 'diabolical'[12] creed of Bolshevism was as good as lost by the end of 1919, but Churchill was not about to modify his judgement of the 'Red Fever'.[13] He persisted in the belief that Bolshevism promised only a vile future resembling the 'absolute communism' of the shit-eating white ants that would be described by the Belgian poet Maurice Maeterlinck in 1926[14] and remembered by Churchill twenty years later, when he recommended the termitary as a suitable object of study for the American demonstrators who gathered to protest against his Fulton oration as he received an honorary degree from Columbia University in New York on 28 March 1946.[15]

Churchill heaped up this lurid imagery between Russia and the West, and the Bolsheviks responded by putting it to their own roughly dialectical uses. The day after the Third International was formed at an improvised conference in Moscow in March 1919, Lenin had told the visiting British journalist and intelligence agent Arthur Ransome how futile it was for the capitalist governments to try to save themselves by forming a barrier against Russia:

> Tell them to build a Chinese wall round each of their countries. They have their customs-officers, their frontiers, their coast-guards. They can expel any Bolsheviks they wish. Revolution does not depend on propaganda. If the conditions of revolution are not there no sort of propaganda will either hasten or impede it. The war has brought about those conditions in all countries, and I am convinced that if Russia today were to be swallowed up by the sea, were to cease to exist altogether, the revolution in the rest of Europe would go on.[16]

Turning back the anti-Communist rhetoric of Churchill and other Allied leaders, he described Bolshevism as a contagious infection the Allies were too late to prevent: 'We have a saying that a man may have typhoid while still on his legs … Well, England and France and Italy have caught the disease already. England may seem to you to be untouched, but the microbe is already there.'[17]

Lenin kept hammering at this point in his interviews with receptive Western visitors. He assured Robert Minor, the correspondent of the radical and Democratic New York publication *World,* that 'Future society will be organised along Soviet lines. There will be Soviet rather than geographical boundaries for nations. Industrial unionism is the basic state.'[18] Colonel

Raymond Robins, an enraptured Red Cross man associated with America's Progressive Party, heard that, even though the Bolshevik revolution may indeed fail in Russia,

> they would keep the flame burning there until the world blazed up … 'You think America is immune,' he told me. 'But your government lacks integrity. Your representatives are really elected for hidden economic reasons. … We will put in the real producers, not the parasites, and we are going to challenge the world with a producers' republic. We may be overwhelmed, but not before we have destroyed all such governments'.[19]

Convinced that the Allied policy of blockade and military intervention had merely strengthened the Bolsheviks' hand, not least by rallying Russian nationalism behind them, Lenin had mockingly arranged, in April 1920, for Soviet Russia's highest honour, the Order of the Red Flag, to be bestowed on Churchill and Clemenceau 'in recognition of their great work for the international revolution'.[20]

The Balkan Connection

Had Charles Roden Buxton found a moment in the British Labour Delegation's demanding schedule to reflect on the rhetorical salvoes passing between Lenin and Churchill, he might have done so with a sense of personal disappointment as well as political irritation.

The 'barrier' to which Buxton and his wife had objected over the previous two years lay between Russia and the capitalist world, yet it also divided a past that he and Winston Churchill had once held in common. The two had not been close when they overlapped as boys at Harrow School between 1889 and 1892. Yet in the pre-war decade, during which Buxton was helping to establish the activities of the Workers' Education Association and also serving as honorary principal of Morley College in South London, they had shared the Liberal Party's commitment to free trade as opposed to Tory protectionism and also, for a time at least, the 'New Liberal' conviction that freedom of competition did not represent 'the last word'[21] in human progress. Churchill had been Home Secretary during 1910, the year of Buxton's first short-lived spell in the House of Commons as Liberal MP for Mid Devon. At that time he was still close to the radical wing of his party: promoting social reforms of the kind Buxton had advocated as editor of the Liberal *Albany Review* (1906–8), and insisting, like Buxton, that the true political course lay 'midway between individualism and collectivism'.[22] The two men's paths had diverged by the time war broke out in August 1914 but, in the early months of the conflict, they retained at least one interest in common.

Thanks partly to Gladstone's insistence on the principle of 'public right' in European foreign policy,[23] the British Liberal Party had entered the twentieth century with a concern for the security of small nations in a world dominated by powerful empires. Buxton and his more prominent brother, the Liberal MP for North Norfolk, Noel Buxton, had taken a close interest in this theme as it was being played out in south-eastern Europe. Long recognized as 'the danger-point of Europe',[24] the Balkans were, as Buxton and his wife would later describe them, a region of 'small states with no mutual agreements'. These states were inherently 'pugnacious' because 'their frontiers did not correspond to the boundaries of nationality, and each regarded itself as the mere nucleus of some future national state, whose limits must ultimately be decided by war'.[25]

The strategic importance of the Balkans had brought Churchill and the Buxton brothers together in the early weeks of the Great War. Faced with the prospect of Turkey joining forces with Germany, the British government became much concerned to maintain the neutrality of Bulgaria, the country that lay between them, or, better still, to win her over to the side of the Triple Entente. The diplomats in the area could not be trusted with this mission, and the Cabinet thought instead of sending Noel Buxton, who was regarded with great affection in Bulgaria, thanks to his activities as chairman of the Balkan Committee—a group that had been founded by the Buxton brothers in 1902 (the journalist H. N. Brailsford was also closely involved), and which had campaigned, from its office in George Bernard Shaw's house in London's Adelphi Terrace, on behalf of the Christian populations then living under harsh Turkish rule.

So it was that, in September 1914, while E. D. Morel and others were forming the Union of Democratic Control, Noel and Charles Roden Buxton had left London for the Balkans. Their mission might have been official, were it not for the British Foreign Secretary, Sir Edward Grey, who still hoped to keep Turkey neutral and therefore insisted that the Buxtons should travel in a private capacity. The brothers were, however, strongly supported both by the Chancellor, Lloyd George, and also by Winston Churchill. As First Lord of the Admiralty, Churchill wrote to

Noel Buxton on 31 August 1914, advocating not just an agreement with Bulgaria, but also the creation of a 'Balkan Confederation comprising Bulgaria, Serbia, Romania, Montenegro and Greece'. This, he declared, was the time when 'the metal can be cast in the mould'.[26] The Buxton brothers were to communicate how much the Balkan states stood to gain from a post-war redistribution of territory in the Southern Provinces of Austria. Having affirmed the policies of the Balkan Committee as his own, Churchill took steps to ease the passage of these emissaries, despatching a cruiser, HMS *Hussar*, to collect them at Brindisi and take them on to Salonica.

The Buxtons travelled the region, meeting monarchs and political leaders in order to establish exactly which territorial trade-offs might persuade Bulgaria, Greece, Serbia, and Romania to recreate the Balkan alliance that had successfully driven back the Turkish empire in the Balkan war of 1912. Though hailed by the strongly anti-Turkish Bulgarian people and opposition parties, the brothers had been lucky to get out of Romania alive. While seated in a car with the British consul in Bucharest on 15 October (a day when the streets were immobilized by the funeral ceremonies for the late King Charles), both were shot and wounded by a Turkish assassin. Noel Buxton was hit in the jaw, prompting the *Berliner Tageblatt* to celebrate the closing of 'a mouth full of guile and arrogance to everything that was not English', while the Turkish press smirked at the fate of the man judged to be 'Turkey's and Islam's greatest enemy'.[27] Charles Roden Buxton was more seriously shot in the lung.

Having spent over a month in hospital, the Buxtons characteristically insisted on visiting their assailant, Hassan Taxim, in prison. They discussed philosophy, poetry, and the ethics of political assassination with this Young Turk (who turned out to have studied philosophy at the Sorbonne and who claimed a special admiration for the poetry of William Blake). They also conducted a brief experiment in the psychology of political hatred. Noel Buxton placed his (unloaded) revolver on the table and invited the wholly unrepentant Taxim to shoot him again. The assassin declined, leading Noel Buxton to express a faith in direct human contact similar to that his brother Charles would later apply to Soviet Russia: 'Our sense of one another had become too vivid; we were no longer abstractions to each other—the assassin on one side, the anti-Turk on the other. If every man's imagination penetrated the murky barriers of emotion, killing in war as in crime would become impossible.'[28]

Turkey had joined the German side by the time the Buxton brothers had recovered sufficiently to continue their travels. They were celebrated as heroes on their return to Sofia (at the end of the Great War, Charles Roden Buxton was allegedly even offered the crown of Bulgaria; and in 1926 a street near Sofia—formerly the 'Old Boyana Road'—would be formally renamed 'Buxton Brothers Boulevard' in their honour [29]). In Serbia, they found both the king and Prime Minister Pashich willing to accept their proposed territorial settlement in exchange for the Dalmatian coast. In Greece, Prime Minister Venizelos declared himself prepared, in the event of a wider settlement, to restore the recently annexed port of Kavalla to Bulgaria. Pausing in Paris on their way home, they were encouraged by discussions both with France's foreign minister, Théophile Delcassé, and with the Russian ambassador; indeed, they returned to Britain convinced that a workable scheme could be agreed and then successfully 'dictated' to the region by the Allies.

The response to their proposals in London turned out to be disappointing. Arriving home in January 1915, they had found the Foreign Secretary, Sir Edward Grey, quite uninterested in pursuing their recommendations. Indeed, it emerged that, in their absence, Grey had been pursuing a contradictory scheme designed to tempt Italy into the war on the Allied side by means of a secret treaty which promised them 'large slices' of Dalmatia.[30] Churchill was more respectful of the Buxton brothers' efforts. He gave them lunch at the Admiralty, after which Noel Buxton wrote in his diary, 'Churchill most cordial, repeating, "You've shed your blood for your country".'[31] Churchill also declared that 'we can break through', leaving the Buxtons to catch up with the fact that British policy over the Balkans was no longer at the front of his mind, and that he was now committed to the ill-fated Dardanelles expeditionary force.

Churchill and Charles Roden Buxton may have entered the Great War more or less on the same side, but that was not how they emerged from the conflict. By 1920, Churchill was being denounced in the Liberal as well as the socialist press. Writing in the *Daily News,* a book reviewer noted George Lansbury's description of visiting a school in Bolshevik Russia and, in a fit of international solidarity, leading the children into a performance of 'Ring a ring of roses'. Acknowledging that some Britons would be horrified to read of these partisan antics, he himself admitted 'not the slightest doubt' that it represented a better contribution to the welfare of Russia than Churchill's insistence on 'denouncing Lenin as "a monster on a pile of grinning skulls"'.[32]

The same paper's former editor and weekly columnist, A. G. Gardiner, would be far more vitriolic when he found occasion to dub Churchill 'the real red terror'.[33] That moment came towards the end of June 1920, when the Army Estimates presented to the House of Commons revealed that Churchill, as Secretary of State for War, anticipated spending an estimated £3 million creating scarlet dress uniforms for the post-war British army. Churchill was strongly of the view that the 'volunteer' army he was now trying to build needed inducements that had not been necessary for the recent war's khaki army of conscripts, and he was certainly not at his most convincing as he tried to fend off the hostile suggestion that his proposed 'red army'[34] represented an extravagant attempt to 'buy recruits with uniforms'[35]—or with 'gewgaws and millinery'[36] as one sceptical MP would later suggest.

Widely derided around the country, 'Mr. Churchill's scarlet folly' provided Gardiner with the opportunity to condemn this Liberal renegade as an 'ungovernable incendiary' whose aim was to 'thwart the whole current of world pacification' and 'restore a militarised world'. Like his post-war Russian policy, Churchill's 'pink trousers folly' reflected his desire to build up 'great military systems' in France and Poland and, with the help of these 'bastions', to divide Europe into 'the armed and the unarmed' camps. 'This is the concept of the future which Mr. Churchill and Marshal Foch have in mind. It is a conception of Bedlam. It ignores the trifling matter of general economic destruction. It assumes a static relationship between States which is contrary to history and commonsense. ... It is the fevered vision of the fanatics of blood.' The time had come for the British people to discover 'whether Mr. Churchill is to control our destinies or we are to control Mr. Churchill'.

Gardiner's assessment of Churchill as a frankly 'evil influence' was shared by E. D. Morel, leader of the Union of Democratic Control. While preparing for the general election of November 1922, in which he would triumph over the incumbent Churchill to become one of two Labour MPs for Dundee, Morel later remarked: 'I look upon Churchill as such a personal force for evil that I would take up the fight against him with a whole heart'.[37] Buxton may never have gone quite so far but he too was dismayed both by Winston Churchill's fervent anti-Bolshevism, and also by his associated claim, made at a meeting in Sunderland in January 1920, that the British Labour Party, for which Buxton had finally left the Liberal Party in 1917, was 'quite unfitted for the responsibility of Government'.[38]

The Blockade Maintained

It was largely thanks to Allied fear of infection that the 'iron wall of partition'[39] raised against Bolshevik Russia took the form not just of exaggerated political rhetoric, but of an economic blockade enforced by naval power. And here too, Winston Churchill is to be found standing by the foundations, trowel in hand. Though not formally declared, the Allied blockade was first imposed against Germany (and rapidly extended to neutral countries involved in provisioning the Central Empires)[40] at the beginning of the war in 1914. The aim, as an overconfident Allied press reported, had been to starve the enemy into surrender within six months.

By 3 February 1915, Churchill was able to boast that 'For the first time in her history Great Britain can say "The seas are free." Even after Trafalgar we knew nothing like it.'[41] On 15 February 1915, during a discussion of the naval estimates for that year, Churchill told the House of Commons that there were 'good reasons for believing that the economic pressure which the Navy exerts is beginning to be felt in Germany'.[42] Explaining that the blockade had so far been limited to preventing the enemy from importing petrol, rubber, copper, and other raw materials needed for the production of 'war materials', he looked forward to stopping imports of food in the future, and also preventing neutral states from trading directly with German ports. Justifying this development by declaring that Germany had, 'by deliberate policy', placed herself outside all international obligations, he promised that the Allied governments would soon produce a declaration for 'applying the full force of naval pressure to the enemy'.[43]

Vernon Lee may have incorporated some of the Allied blockade's metal into her 'monstrous iron curtain' over Christmas 1914, but the British government had soon faced an altogether more challenging objection from a neutral and strongly anti-imperialist America, which found its mail being intercepted by the British in apparent defiance of the Postal Union Convention (1906)[44] and its exports severely curtailed.[45] The US government repeatedly questioned the legality of the 'Reprisals Order' introduced by the British in March 1915 to justify extending the blockade to shipping bound for neutral Holland, Sweden, Norway, and Denmark.[46] The objections were renewed after the Armistice. Having generated a huge food surplus during the war, the USA now found its exports doubly threatened as the Allies sought cheaper food from the southern hemisphere for their own markets, while at the same time upholding the blockade with the combined purpose of forcing Germany and the defeated Central Powers into compliance with the post-war peace terms and of starving Russian Bolshevism into extinction.

Following protracted negotiations at the Paris Peace Conference, the blockade against the remnants of defeated Austria and Germany had been formally lifted four and eight months after the Armistice respectively. But Russia, which had been blockaded since the Bolsheviks pulled out of the Allied war effort after the coup of October 1917, would experience what the French prime minister, Georges Clemenceau, described as 'economic encirclement'[47] for considerably longer. In January 1920, Lloyd George had persuaded the Allied Supreme Council to pass a motion resuming trade with Russia. Permission was granted on the condition that the exchange was organized through the Russian Co-operative Societies rather than the Bolshevik-controlled Committee of Foreign Trade. The Bolsheviks manoeuvred in order to meet these conditions but, in practice, the blockade stayed in place for many weeks.

At the beginning of May, when the British Labour Delegation entered Russia, the political writer and *Daily Herald* columnist H. N. Brailsford claimed that only one 'small consignment' of medical drugs had got through. The sea-way to Petrograd was still mined. In the Black Sea, allied warships were still bombarding Russian ports, and the French navy was forbidding passage to trading vessels.[48] Four months later Harold Grenfell, who described himself as a retired naval captain, would return to the theme, contesting British government claims that the blockade 'does not exist'.[49] Though technically true, since a blockade is an act of war and Britain had not declared war against Bolshevik Russia, this claim actually marked a return to the principle of 'Nelson's blind eye'. There was, so Grenfell charged, still a 'hidden blockade', which could be enforced quite effectively by warning ships of uncleared mines.

The Times and other Conservative British newspapers would insist that Bolshevism itself was the main reason why Russia starved. But the otherwise fractious Labour delegation was entirely unanimous in blaming the blockade as 'a policy as foolish as it is inhuman'.[50] Insisting that 'hostile pressure from abroad' only served to rally all parties behind the Bolsheviks in the cause of national defence, the delegation rushed out an interim report urging the British labour movement to demand 'the complete destruction of the barrier which Imperialist statesmen have erected between our own people and our brothers and sisters of Russia'. As Buxton put it, 'We have made the grass grow in the streets of Moscow, and for us Englishmen it is not a pleasant sight.'[51] Bertrand Russell alone sounded a note of caution on this point. He accepted that the 'harshness on the ground'[52] in Russia may have been partly caused by having to fight the Allies and their White Russian 'mercenaries'. However, he warned against those among the 'revolution's tourists' who treated the Allied intervention and blockade as an excuse to suppress the crueller features of the regime: 'By this lack of courage they have exposed Western socialism to the danger of becoming Bolshevik through ignorance of the price that has to be paid and of the uncertainty as to whether the desired goal will be reached in the end.'[53]

'From the Baltic to the Adriatic'

The most influential early critic of the blockade and its continuation under post-war Allied policy was surely John Maynard Keynes, the British Liberal economist associated with both Bloomsbury and Kings College, Cambridge. Keynes had attended the Paris Peace Conference as senior representative of the British Treasury, and his scathing account of the settlement, presented in his book *The Economic Consequences of the Peace,* had electrified the world when first published in December 1919 (perhaps especially in America, where the *New Republic* reported an unprecedented response to pre-publication extracts printed in January 1920).[54] Hailed and reviled in many countries, it would shape perceptions of the Paris Peace Conference for decades to come and, to its admirers, seem wholly confirmed in its direst predictions when Hitler emerged to lead a truncated and still aggrieved Germany into the Second World War.

Keynes certainly lampooned the Allied leaders but it was not just his pronounced Bloomsbury hauteur that led him to condemn their 'disastrous' and unenforceable[55] Treaty of Versailles. He faulted the settlement for perpetuating the hatreds of the war and elevating political antagonisms while abjectly failing to establish a proper economic basis for the rehabilitation of Europe.

> If we oppose in detail every means by which Germany or Russia can recover their material well-being, because we feel a national, racial, or political hatred for their populations or their Governments, we must be prepared to face the consequences of such feelings. Even if there is no moral solidarity between the nearly-related races of Europe, there is an economic solidarity which we cannot disregard. Even now, the world markets are one.[56]

It was on the basis of these same economic 'theories of universal interdependence'[57]—to use the dismissive phrase with which Clemenceau struck
back at the British economist who had contemptuously declared him 'dry
in soul and empty of hope'[58]—that Keynes would keep his distance from
Winston Churchill. At the end of a largely, and perhaps uncharacteristically,
respectful review, he admitted to 'a little envy, perhaps, for his [Churchill's]
undoubting conviction that frontiers, races, patriotisms, even wars if need
be, are ultimate verities for mankind, which lends for him a kind of dignity
and even nobility to events, which for others are only a nightmare interlude,
something to be permanently avoided'.[59]

Charles Roden Buxton could scarcely compete with Keynes in economics or, for that matter, in inside knowledge of the Paris Peace Conference.
Yet, as he recalled in his letter from Moscow on 21 May 1920, he and his
wife Dorothy had indeed 'denounced' the Allied blockade many times since
the Armistice of 11 November 1918. In the months following the Armistice,
the Buxtons had made it their business to know as much as possible about
conditions on 'the other side' of the blockade that divided the Allied world
from the defeated Central Powers.

In their book, *The World After the War,* written and published shortly before
the British Labour Delegation departed for Russia in April 1920, they traced
the impact of post-war Allied policy over a vast tract of central and Eastern
Europe.[60] Promising their readers a 'bird's eye view of the results of the war',
they followed a route foreshadowing the one that Churchill would attribute
to his 'Iron Curtain' in Fulton in 1946. 'From the Baltic to the Adriatic',[61]
as the Buxtons declared in a phrase that Churchill would utter to so much
greater effect at Fulton: 'We shall begin on the shores of the Baltic, traverse
the central heights and plateaux which form the geographical backbone of
Europe, and descend to the Adriatic on the South, and the Caucasus on the
South-East.'[62]

It was a faultline that was already being closely examined by others,
including Halford J. Mackinder, the Conservative MP and geographer who
would later be recognized as the man who 'enlisted geography as an aid
to statecraft and strategy'.[63] In a book published in 1919, Mackinder had
divided Europe into East and West by means of a line extending from the
Adriatic to the North Sea. Travelling in the opposite direction to the Buxtons,
he placed Venice and the Netherlands to the west, but split Germany in
two, pushing both Berlin and Vienna into the east. For Mackinder, this line
enabled one to 'think through' the history of four generations, and it was

also assuming a 'new coherency' in the post-war years.[64] It described both a fundamental opposition between East and West Europe, and also a strategic separation between the two geopolitical zones he named the Heartland and the Coastland.[65] As Mackinder concluded in his review of the 'rivalry of empires', 'West Europe must necessarily be opposed to whatever power attempts to organise the resources of East Europe and the Heartland.'[66] It was an argument he would be able to put into practice when, also in 1919, he was appointed high commissioner for South Russia: a position in which he organized support for the White General Deniken in his unsuccessful war against the Red Army.[67]

The Buxtons started their imaginary tour not at Stettin, as Churchill would do in his Fulton oration, but at Riga, the Latvian city on the Baltic which had suffered so much as White terror followed Red under the 'grinding backward and forward of the steam-roller of war'.[68] From there, they flew down over the coalfields of central Europe, where formerly German land was being handed over to create a Baltic 'corridor' for the revived state of Poland, and then on via East Galicia to Hungary, Yugoslavia, and Bulgaria. As they surveyed the ruins of three collapsed empires—Russian, Prussian, and Austrian—they evoked a world racked by small wars, strikes, revolutions, and violent counter-revolutions; where countless masses of people were being displaced, or handed over from one state to another without the barest pretence of consultation; where vital trade routes were being cancelled and transportation systems interrupted; where already broken and defeated states were being separated from the raw materials and foodstuffs that had long been essential to their survival, and reordered within new borders that did not correspond with 'the frontiers of nationality'.[69]

In Austria and Germany, people were so desperate for clothing that they were ripping the cloth seats out of railway trains. Without wood for coffins, starved infants were being buried in cardboard boxes or bundles of newspaper. In Poland, inquests revealed that, in those same post-war months, many had died of hunger with sand and wood in their stomachs. Veering east to glance at the Caucasus, where Armenians were subsisting on 'grass and leaves', the Buxtons quoted reports that recently buried corpses had been dug up and 'the flesh torn off and eaten by starving people'. These desperate conditions were aggravated by rampant disease—typhus, tuberculosis, rickets—and by a shortage of drugs and medical equipment so acute that the most painful surgical operations were being performed without anaesthetics. Beyond this immediate scarcity, they asserted that Allied policy threatened a wider 'Balkanization' of East and central Europe, which would have dire consequences for 'the men, women and children of this vast area'.[70]

The Buxtons drew much of their evidence of the crisis in central and Eastern Europe from an initiative they had earlier launched in direct opposition to the 'iron curtain' named by Vernon Lee over Christmas in 1914. In order to counter that war-sustaining closure of sympathy and understanding between Britain and Germany, Dorothy Frances Buxton had initiated 'Notes from the Foreign Press', a weekly leaflet that aimed to 'supplement what may be found in English papers' by reminding readers of what her husband called 'other people's point of view'.

Produced with the help of volunteers, who gathered at the Buxtons' house in Golders Green to translate selections from foreign papers (many of them acquired through a book-dealer in Stockholm), her extracts and commentary were intended to demonstrate that, say what the 'Get On with the War' propagandists might, there were moderate, peace-seeking voices in Austria, Germany, Hungary, Bulgaria, Holland, America, and elsewhere. Started in the summer of 1915, Mrs Buxton's initiative quickly became established. Renamed 'Foreign Opinion: a Weekly Survey of the Foreign Press' it was soon incorporated into the *Cambridge Magazine* (edited by C. K. Ogden), helping to convert this university weekly into a leading anti-war publication: fiercely opposed by the British state and popular press, but capable of selling hundreds of copies in Glasgow alone. On the British left, the initiative would be remembered for many years as an attempt to 'keep an "International Mind" alive',[71] despite the Defence of the Realm Act, official censorship, and the polarizing propaganda of the time.

In the months following the Armistice, Dorothy Buxton had refocused her survey of 'Foreign Opinion' on the problems of the emerging peace settlement. Still determined to remind readers that, in the description of her husband, 'there is another side to the shield',[72] she used her weekly pages to show Vernon Lee's 'monstrous iron curtain' being refashioned and extended rather than removed from the European theatre. The 'psychological deadlock' identified by Lee persisted in unyielding calls for vengeance and a widespread refusal on the Allied side to recognize the humanity of the zealously 'crushed' enemy. It was there in the implacable refusal of the National Council of Frenchwomen to heed the appeal of German and Austrian women suffering famine and disease (Romain Rolland, who admired the 'freedom of spirit' and 'rich information' of Mrs Buxton's pages in the *Cambridge Magazine,* wrote that the French press even managed to dismiss dying German babies as 'bluffers'[73]). It was there, as Lee also registered in *Satan the Waster,* in the reduction of the idea of 'Justice' to a combined call for punishment of the defeated enemy and apparently limitless reparations: a demand that the Danish paper *Politiken* likened to 'stripping a man of all his clothes and then telling him to turn out his pockets'.[74] Thanks to the Allies' pursuit of these vengeful policies, the peace settlement was, so a great many of Mrs Buxton's foreign journalists warned, all too likely to provoke future wars. 'We are afraid that the opportunity will come only too soon', as the Dutch Liberal paper *Algemeen Handelsblad* remarked on 8 May 1919.[75] 'The reverse of a peace of understanding', judged the Swedish socialist publication *Social Demokraten* on 9 May, while the Oslo paper of the same name declared that '"The war to end war" has closed with a "peace" which signifies the continuation of war.'[76] Blaming this outcome on the fiercely anti-German stance of Clemenceau's France, the Italian Conservative paper *Corriere della sera* declared that 'the French peace … is absolutely lacking in creative power. Inexorable barriers deny the beaten enemy all chance of re-establishing their life, and an infernal machine is enclosed in its structure set to explode at its appointed time'.[77]

By the beginning of 1919, the Iron Curtain was most starkly represented by the unlifted Allied blockade: characterized in Mrs Buxton's pages as a shameful 'Hunger-blockade'[78] or 'The starvation weapon'.[79] News of the hardship caused by the blockade reached Paris throughout the six months of post-war negotiation yet, so Keynes judged, the atmosphere surrounding the peace conference remained largely 'frivolous'. 'Dissociated from events' and characterized by 'levity, blindness, insolence',[80] the proceedings seemed to him shockingly inadequate to the demands of the time. Keynes identified the 'bureaucratic' reason why British administrators were inclined to keep the blockade in place:

> The blockade had become by that time a very perfect instrument. It had taken four years to create and was Whitehall's finest achievement; it had evoked the qualities of the English at their subtlest. Its authors had grown to love it for its own sake; it included some recent improvements, which would be wasted if it came to an end; it was very complicated and a vast organisation had established a vested interest. The experts reported, therefore, that it was our one instrument for imposing our Peace Terms on Germany, and that once suspended it could hardly be reimposed.[81]

Keynes was also withering about the intransigence of the French, who seemed determine to strip starving Germany bare of everything, from milch cows to pension funds. He was gratified when the British prime minister, Lloyd George (whom he mocked as a vacillating Welsh wizard), at last gathered himself up to launch a vicious personal attack on France's finance minister, M. Klotz, at a meeting of the Supreme War Council, on 8 March 1919. Klotz had refused, once again, to countenance the thought of Germany paying for desperately needed food with gold reserves that would otherwise pass to the Allies as reparation; and Lloyd George mobilized vicious anti-Semitic stereotypes to condemn him as an avaricious monster who would let women and children starve before loosening his grip on the money bag he was clutching.[82]

The Buxtons were not privy to these wranglings. However, they knew a moral disgrace when they saw one and Dorothy had been involved with the 'Fight the Famine' Council since it went into action on 1 January 1919.[83] Writing in May that year, Dorothy Buxton had deplored the blockade as an indiscriminate noose that tended to 'strangle friend and foe alike' (measures intended to starve Austria into submission had, as she pointed out, quickly produced dire consequences in Serbia, Bohemia, and Poland).[84] She quoted Winston Churchill, by now a familiar opponent of much that the Buxtons stood for, who had nevertheless recently admitted in *The Times* that the blockade against Germany was 'repugnant to the British nation'.[85] The Berlin paper *Deutsche Allgemeine Zeitung* had recently condemned the blockade as 'the most murderous of all modes of warfare, worse than hand-grenades and poison-gas ... because it does not affect the soldier, but thousands upon thousands of innocent persons, women and children'.[86] And Churchill himself conceded that, with the death toll in Germany alone estimated at 800 per day, the blockade was indeed, as Mrs Buxton put it, 'dreadfully suggestive of the practice of placing women and children in front of the firing line'. Dorothy Buxton's judgement was severe: 'Our spurious patriotism, our moral indolence, all that tissue of pretences which we call "civilisation," has passed the death sentence on the child, but the child in its feebleness and its pain has passed sentence on our "civilisation".'

The Food Weapon

Within weeks of writing those words, Mrs Buxton would be using the resources of the Friends' Emergency Committee as well as her own personal means to press railway trucks loaded with cod-liver oil, condensed milk, rice, and other essential foods through all but impossible bureaucratic barriers between starving Vienna and Switzerland, where a voluntary relief movement was already operating in Berne and Geneva.[87] In May 1919 she and her sister Eglantyne Jebb had also launched the 'Save the Children Fund' with the combined purpose of raising funds to help the innocent victims of the blockade, and encouraging a moral revival that would embarrass governments in donor countries. Their initiative, which Ethel Snowden joined as a member of the executive committee, helped to establish the child as a humanitarian motif that could be understood on both sides of the iron curtain—one that would be much used over the years to come, not least in the stage-managed imagery that Communist regimes offered to potential supporters in the West.

In 'Foreign Opinion', meanwhile, Mrs Buxton and her translators documented the starvation spreading through the haggard remnants of Germany and Austria. In December 1918, two journalists, one English and the other American, who had managed to slip past the French authorities isolating Vienna, reported that the people were hollow-eyed, emaciated skeletons while the city itself felt like 'a churchyard.' Writing from 'shut in' Vienna that same month, the Dutch novelist Karin Michaelis described winter descending upon a city without coal or adequate food, and warned simply that 'Famine is at the door'.[88] The Dutch Liberal paper *Politiken* emphasized that 'The same grievous picture meets us in Germany. The hunger war has lasted for fifty months. But now for the first time the iron ring is closed inexorably round the Central Powers ... they are completely shut out from the world.'

That 'ring' would stay in place throughout much of 1919, its effects aggravated by economic collapse and then generalized by the reparations clauses of the Treaty of Versailles (which came into force in January 1920) after the blockade was eventually lifted. Having lost its Austro-Hungarian empire in a few days, Vienna found itself the centre of what a French correspondent described as 'a small hydrocephalous state, the monstrous capital of which included a third of the entire population'.[89] Filled with refugees withdrawing from formerly Austrian territories granted to other states, this now severely Alpine country was also deprived of its former sources of food and fuel. The Czechs were refusing to ship vital coal and also holding up food sent from Berlin to starving Vienna. Newly separated Hungary would neither allow the passage of food nor return trains and rolling stock arriving in Budapest from Vienna. Even the Argentine ambassador in Vienna was laying

down conditions. In a note that the Italian Socialist paper *Avanti* characterized as 'blackmailing by famine', he declared that the delivery of foodstuffs
from his country would be suspended 'at the least indication of the Bolshevist
movement or Socialist-Communist disturbances'.[90]

The starvation in Austria, Germany, and Hungary was a source of immediate humanitarian concern, but Mrs Buxton and her translators also used
their pages in the *Cambridge Magazine* to trace the emergence of the new
institutions through which the Allies—even in their own official relief
efforts—had converted food into a 'starvation weapon'. According to the
Journal de Genève on 11 June 1918, this infrastructure had been initiated in
August 1917, when the Allies, who between them were estimated to control
about 60 per cent of all human requirements, agreed to establish an inter-
Allied Ministry of Food Supply in London. The first international organization of its kind, and 'clearly a great event in economic history', this agency
would seek to control raw materials and foodstuffs throughout the world,
and to determine the share received by each member.

It was anticipated that 'interest, stronger than theories' would soon oblige
all countries, including neutrals, to deal with the London committees:

> It is an immense peril for the independence of nations. But, if individualism is
> finished with, as it appears, it may well be that the idea of independence will
> transform itself at the same time. What the Allies have created at London, at
> the present moment, is an embryo League of Nations, the genesis of a world
> organisation … It has been done. The League of Nations is in existence in
> the economic field. The site is ready, upon which the new world will be
> constructed.[91]

Similar things would be claimed of the Allied blockade some years later.
It was, as one author would claim, 'a triumph of international over national
government'; and the mechanism it had established would become one of
the principal disciplinary instruments of the 'World Government' that was
surely to come.[92]

Further measures intended to establish food as an instrument of foreign
policy were reported in the American press, and duly extracted under the
heading 'World Food Dictatorship'. On 26 January 1919, the *New York World*
reported that a bill had been sent to the Senate Committee on Agriculture,
requesting permission for the immense sum of $1,250 million to establish a
revolving fund that would enable President Wilson to buy wheat and other
food stuffs at guaranteed prices from American farmers, and then to sell the
same goods, either at home or abroad, at whatever profit or loss he may

deem fit.[93] There were apparently to be no limits on the powers this adjust-ment of the August 1917 Food Control Act would confer on the president. He sought what the *Christian Science Monitor* described as 'absolute con-trol, amounting to a dictatorship of all U.S. food products'. Henceforth, he would be allowed to sell wheat to Serbia or Russia at $1 per bushel, having paid the American farmer a politically guaranteed price of more than twice that. With measures such as these, the provision of food became a way of countering revolutionary unrest and securing 'the maintenance of order' as it was described by Herbert Hoover, the 'food Napoleon' who was by then head of the American Relief Administration.[94]

As they extended their efforts into famine-stricken Russia in the early 1920s, Hoover's relief workers would be both hailed as saviours by the starv-ing people, and condemned as self-interested looters who, so the Bolsheviks alleged with the help of a few well-timed arrests around Christmas, used their immunity from search to smuggle prodigiously valuable jewels and artworks out of Russia, having bought them for a few dollars.[95] This was, perhaps, a predictable perception, and yet Hoover himself would insist that it was not for altruistic or humanitarian reasons alone that America had been shipping food into post-war Europe and Russia. In a hard-nosed art-icle written for American farmers, he reported that American policy had been shaped by the need 'to safeguard the continuous flow' of America's surplus food products—thereby delivering on a 'primary duty' to American producers (whose prices had been guaranteed by the food administration) and avoiding 'a panic in prices through the creation of a glut which our storage could not handle'.[96] Having managed to secure the flow of exports through the difficult post-war months, Hoover recognized that the provi-sion of food could be harnessed to wider political ends.

Cordon Sanitaire

The blockade may have started out as a 'starvation weapon' against Germany but, after being reconceived at the Paris Peace Conference in 1919, it would be re-established as a 'cordon sanitaire' built into the geopolitical structure of post-war Europe. This phrase had traditionally described measures taken to isolate sites of disease and infection, but the prime minister of France, Georges Clemenceau, now used it to recommend the containment not just of Germany but also of the 'germs of Bolshevism in the East'. He may have spoken, especially while the Allied Intervention was continuing, of confining this vivid contagion within a 'barbed-wire ring' or 'entanglement'[97] but Clemenceau's cordon sanitaire was to become a far more ambitious barrier. Not just a fence, electrified or otherwise, nor even an 'advancing ring of fire', as Lloyd George described it on 10 February 1920 (while also opposing it with his preferred vision of renewed trade with Russia[98]), it would be composed of a band of adjusted or newly formed states, pulled out of the wreckage of the recent war and lined up as a buffer zone between barbarism and civilization. Also described as a 'White Ring',[99] Clemenceau's 'sanitary zone' would include Finland and the new Baltic states of Estonia, Latvia, and Lithuania. It would incorporate a restored and Conservative Poland (organized around the 'Curzon line', dividing East from West, and conceived as, in the words of Le Temps, an 'illustrious barrier'[100] against both Germany and Russia), and also Romania, which had laid claim to Russian Bessarabia on the Black Sea. In the judgement of H. N. Brailsford, the cordon sanitaire was a 'ring of little states' that would, no doubt, 'receive their marching orders from Paris'.[101]

The policy of the cordon sanitaire alarmed Lloyd George, but it found strong support in his Coalition Cabinet. Winston Churchill may have followed British army officers in shrinking from a policy of starving mothers and babies in Germany and Austria. However, he needed no convincing that Bolshevism, which had betrayed the Allies by abruptly pulling out of the war in November 1917, was an aggressively advancing plague that promised only 'the worst, the most destructive, the most degrading' of tyrannies.[102] According to Roy Jenkins, it was his abiding hatred of Bolshevism, and the evils brewing up in 'the Russian cauldron',[103] that finally dislodged Churchill from his position on the centre-left of the political spectrum and set him on the rightward course that would cause him to rejoin the Conservative Party in 1924.

The cordon sanitaire was also broadly in line with the geopolitical vision of Halford J. Mackinder. In a 'study in the politics of reconstruction', published in 1919, he had argued that the division of East Europe into 'self-contained nations' would create the preconditions for a proper League of Nations, rather than merely a 'League of Allies'.[104] Convinced that the key to stabilizing East Europe was to have three rather than just two 'State-systems' in the region, he advocated the creation of a tier of independent states between Germany and Russia. The Russians seemed doomed to autocracy by their long stand against Germany, but Mackinder was confident that the non-German 'peoples of the Middle Tier' were capable of sustaining their own independent states. In MacKinder's vision, the Polish and Bohemian nations would stand as 'the apex of a broad wedge of independence, extending from the Adriatic and Black Seas to the Baltic'. Linked by new railways and populated by over 60 million people in all, they would have access to the oceans via the Adriatic, Black, and Baltic seas, and serve to balance the power of the Germans in Prussia and Austria. The great enemy, as he made clear, was horizontal 'class organisation'. In order to resist it, the new independent nations would have to recover an 'organic ideal' and establish themselves as 'provinces of complete life'.

Dorothy Buxton used her survey of 'Foreign Opinion' to track both the 'Bolshevik Wave'[105] and the measures that were taken to stem it. The advance would be violently beaten back in the Baltic states, but Germany and Austria seethed with revolutionary unrest from the moment the fighting ended in November 1918. For a while, Mrs Buxton included a 'Diary of Social Revolution in Germany' reporting the ferment in many cities of that country and duly noting the murder of the leaders of the Spartacus League, Rosa Luxemburg and Karl Liebknecht, in January 1919.

Her pages recorded further upheavals in Hungary, where Count Mihaly Karolyi formed an independent republic at the end of the war, but resigned six months later when the French decreed unacceptable borders for his state. The demise of Karolyi's moderate regime paved the way for Bela Kun's Communist government, which took over in March 1919, prompting the *Frankfurter Zeitung* to observe that 'the power of infection and the explosive force of Bolshevism are immense'.[106] The Viennese *Arbeiter Zeitung* delighted in the prospect, asserting that 'the wave of social revolution sweeps on irresistibly from the East to the West. The hour will come when the working classes of England, America, France and Italy will also burst their chains.'[107]

Bela Kun's revolution threatened 'a hybrid marriage between Nationalism and Bolshevism',[108] but it was extinguished six months later: starved and then bloodily suppressed by Czech and Romanian forces with the encouragement of the Allies. Other outbreaks loomed. In Czecho-Slovakia, Comrade Vorel pronounced that 'The Bolshevik sun which lights all Russia will soon shine in Bohemia.'[109] In Poland, the ground was said to be so 'undermined with Bolshevism' that 'one day the mine will explode there with the same violence as at Budapest'.[110]

Meanwhile, the Bolshevist penetration of the Middle East and Asia was promised: 'fiery proclamations' issuing from Moscow called upon the peoples of Asia to free themselves from 'the foreign yoke'[111] and denouncing the perfidy of the British for the benefit of representatives of Persia, Afghanistan, and the Congress of Indian Nationalists, already bent on 'the expulsion of the British from Asia'.[112] A visiting Japanese Deputy, R. Nagashmia, warned that 40 million Chinese seemed likely to join the Bolshevik cause. Were this to happen, he estimated that similar numbers of 'Hindoos' would be 'naturally precipitated into the same abyss'.[113] Alarms were sounding all over the world yet, as the American *Springfield Republican* noted, 'revolutionary ideas' represented a 'special menace' for Great Britain and its empire:

> Bolshevism as the creed of the exploited has taken a considerable hold on the Asiatic races, as the number of Chinese soldiers in the Russian army shows. The first sweep of any such movement of revolt would menace British holdings at countless points, and this is why for England, perhaps even more than for any other nation, it is imperative to find the right way to head off the further spread of Bolshevism. If the case of Russia is for the time being hopeless, it is the more vital to prevent a like catastrophe in central Europe.[114]

Moving to Russia

In the early post-war months, Clemenceau's cordon sanitaire seemed to be raised against Germany and Soviet Russia alike—a combined 'anti-Boche and Bolshevik Barrier', as Mrs Buxton named it.[115] The blockade had helped suppress Bela Kun's government in Hungary yet, as this tireless scanner of 'Foreign Opinion' also noted, Allied policy would be adjusted once it became apparent how swiftly Bolshevism travelled 'in the steps of famine'.

On 8 December 1918, the Swiss independent paper *Neue Zürcher Zeitung* reviewed the 'catastrophic' situation in Austria and declared that 'if help is not forthcoming the extreme parties may get the upper hand and open the door to Bolshevism, which is on the watch at the frontiers'.[116] The same argument was made repeatedly in Germany and Austria. The pacifist economist Professor Lujo Brentano pronounced that 'so long as the blockade shall continue, no real armistice can exist', and predicted that, unless Woodrow Wilson's Fourteen Points were accepted as the necessary conditions of lasting peace, Germany would face a future of huge emigration, industrial decay, and 'probably Bolshevism'.[117] Theodor Wolff, an editor and journalist whose books would later be burned by the Nazis (he himself would eventually be arrested in Nice and marched off to be murdered in a concentration camp), wrote that 'The men and women who join the Bolshevik procession are led away, not by the new Gospel which to them is incomprehensible, but by malnutrition, and when they call for the Soviet Republic, they mean bread.'[118] The leader of Germany's Catholic democrats, Matthias Erzberger (who had signed the Armistice on Germany's behalf) denounced the blockade as a highly effective encourager of exactly the 'all-devouring hydra of Bolshevism'[119] it was intended to repress.

The persistent Bolshevist threat enabled commentators in Germany, Austria, and other states formerly belonging to the Central Powers to insist that, the recent war notwithstanding, they actually occupied common ground with the victorious Allies. On 24 January 1919, *Frankfurter Zeitung* declared 'We need not emphasis the fact that all the Western Nations have an equal interest in opposing Bolshevist attacks.'[120] Writing from Königsberg in March 1919, Victor Schiff proclaimed that the Allies should stop starving the remnants of Germany into desperate accord with Bolshevik purposes, but instead take positive steps to establish the country as 'the last dam against Bolshevism'.[121] Three months earlier, the new role had been positively embraced by the Conservative burgomaster of starving Vienna, Dr Weiskirchner, who remarked: 'We must all hold together in order to form a bulwark against Bolshevism within the limit of a really free democratic Republic. If the Eastern wave of Bolshevism is allowed to break any further over the West, it will mean the grave of culture and civilisation for decades, perhaps for centuries.'[122] Trotsky agreed with this estimation of the threat to the West. At a meeting held in Petrograd to honour the memory of the murdered Spartacist leaders Karl Liebknecht and Rosa Luxemburg, he declared 'If the German proletariat should not be strong or willing enough to proclaim the permanent rule of Bolshevism in Germany, it will be forced to do so by London and Paris ... Foch and Clemenceau and Lloyd George are our best agents in Germany.'[123]

The suggestion that severe peace conditions would only feed Bolshevism was at first strongly resisted in France, not least by the royalist and Catholic French paper *Action française* which objected that 'By playing the card of Bolshevism, Germany has succeeded in getting herself fed.'[124] Similar suspicions were aired by Clemenceau and his colleagues when the spectre of Bolshevism was raised at the Paris Peace Conference by Lloyd George, who urged that if order was maintained in disintegrating Germany, she would serve as a 'breakwater' between the Allies and 'the waters of revolution beyond.'

Clemenceau, Klotz, and others came over most reluctantly, as did France's Conservative paper *Le Temps*: 'the Allies cannot sacrifice States which are counting on them in Central Europe: they should, on the contrary, make them agree, reinforce them, make of them ramparts of civilisation and pillars of the new order'.[125]

This reorientation was registered in Dorothy Buxton's pages as a step in the direction of American policy. In January 1919, the director of the American Relief Agency, Herbert Hoover, had warned that 'Bolshevism spreads like a disease. It must run its course of destruction, and is no respecter of national borders.'[126] And yet the cure was conveniently at hand—a remedy that would put an end to the shaming stories involving dead 'enemy' babies whilst at the same time helping to confine the Bolshevist plague to its Russian heartland, where it might still be subdued later. That same month Woodrow Wilson had told Congress that the westward progress of Bolshevism could only be checked by food,[127] rather than by deliberately imposed famine and unemployment. As the Philadelphia *Public Ledger* reported under the heading 'Unfix bayonets! Pass the Bread!', 'there can be no barrier to Bolshevism like a bread barrage … The only sure and secure cure is economic content.'

Winston Churchill might have doubted Wilson's idea, reported in December 1918, of setting up an economic commission that would 'help Russia to her feet'.[128] Yet he would accept the argument as it applied to Germany, Austria, and the former enemy states. On 11 April 1919, he told a luncheon at the Aldwych Club that Germany might begin to atone for the recent war by forming itself into 'the bulwark' that would protect 'the civilised world' from Bolshevism. He had been arguing for this policy, which he once summarized as 'Kill the Bolshie, Kiss the Hun',[129] since the last days of the war. The argument was renewed in March 1920, after General Ludendorff signalled his desire to meet Churchill to form an 'Anglo-German' drive against Bolshevik Russia. Rejected by the British Cabinet, the approach nevertheless prompted Churchill to restate his advocacy of 'a strong but peaceful Germany which will not attack our French allies, but will at the same time act as a moral bulwark against the Bolshevism of Russia'.[130]

New Diplomacy and the League of Nations

Like Keynes, the Buxtons attributed responsibility for the chaos prevailing 'from the Baltic to the Adriatic' to the Paris Peace Conference and its outcome, the Treaty of Versailles. To begin with, and like so many war-sickened idealists, they had been immensely heartened by President Woodrow Wilson and the Fourteen Points he first presented to Congress on 8 January 1918 (i.e. before America complicated its virtuous peacemaking image by joining the Allied Intervention against Bolshevik Russia). That 'initial burst of idealism' had seemed to promise a lasting and principled settlement that would break the mould of imperial and national rivalries and establish a 'League of Nations' of the kind that had been proposed by the Union of Democratic Control throughout the war. Yet the settlement that actually emerged would do little to bring about a 'Brotherhood of Nations' of the ethical—if not also impossible—kind Charles Roden Buxton had called for as long ago as 1915: 'a new system of international relations, based upon love and trust, instead of upon (to quote Mr. Asquith's apt and accurate wording) "the clash of competing ambitions, upon groupings and alliances and a precarious equipoise."'[131]

Flowers had been tossed at President Wilson when he arrived in Paris at the head of the American delegation, but the Peace Conference soon became, so the *Gazette de Lausanne* claimed, a contest between opposed conceptions of peace. Some welcomed Wilson's Fourteen Points, finding in them the basis of a horizontally conceived and non-imperialist 'new diplomacy',[132] that promised the removal of trade barriers, disarmament, open rather than secret diplomacy, and an international form of government in which self-determination would replace the European empires' habits of expansion and annexation. Yet there were others among the European Allies who were far from reassured by Wilson's proposals for a peace founded on the principle of 'justice to all peoples and nationalities'. The kinship between the principles of the new diplomacy and the conciliatory wartime utterances of the Pope may have been more or less tolerable, but the Fourteen Points had an airiness about them, and they were also embraced by people, including Mr and Mrs Philip Snowden, who associated them with the outlook of the Socialist International.[133]

Wilson had urged a 'peace without victory'[134] in January 1917, shortly after suggesting that neutral America might mediate between the warring European nations. Yet, as the historian Arno J. Mayer demonstrated, the internationalist principles of the 'New Diplomacy' were initially articulated by the Petrograd Soviet, which, on 27 March 1917, issued its first Proclamation informing the 'Peoples of the World' that the Russian people would now take their stand against the 'policy of conquest' pursued by the overthrown

ruling class.[135] Pressured by the Petrograd Soviet, the Provisional Government soon also spoke out against the tsar's diplomacy of annexations,
secret pacts, and scheming within an inherently unstable balance of power
and, in a statement issued on 9 April 1917, committed 'free Russia' to 'the
establishment of a permanent peace on the basis of the self-determination
of peoples'.[136] On 25 April the call had been renewed by the All-Russian
Conference of the Soviet of Workers' and Soldiers' Deputies, which invited
Allied peoples to pressure their own governments to abandon their plans of
conquest, and renounce both annexation and indemnity.[137]

It was one thing, perhaps, for imprisoned American socialists and conscientious objectors to imagine that Bolshevist internationalism was founded on
the same principles as American democracy.[138] Yet the excitement appears to
have been shared by President Wilson himself. In his preamble to the Fourteen Points, Wilson had described the newly articulated 'voice of the Russian
people' as 'more thrilling and more compelling than any of the many moving
voices with which the troubled air of the world is filled'. He had gone on to
declare 'Their conception of what is right, of what is humane and honourable for them to accept, has been stated with a frankness, a largeness of view,
a generosity of spirit, and a universal human sympathy which must challenge
the admiration of every friend of mankind.'

Wilson's Fourteen Points were endorsed by the British Union of Democratic
Control, whose leading members had helped to shape them. They were also
commended by Lenin, who described them as 'A great step ahead towards
the peace of the world'.[139] Millions of copies of Wilson's speech before
Congress were printed and circulated in Soviet Russia. With Soviet assistance, copies were also distributed in Germany, where Wilson's words had the
intended divisive effect, aggravating tensions between those who were for
and against democratization, and spurring revolutionary protest against the
government. This lineage, in which American democracy seemed closely
intertwined with Russian Revolution, was a source of alarm to tradition-
alists, including those who became convinced that the idea of open rather
than secret diplomacy was a Bolshevik plot designed to make government
impossible. It was vehemently opposed in France, where Le Temps warned
that the nations had arrived at a crossroads, and must choose between 'the
way of the nationalities' and 'the way of the classes'.[140]

Whether or not he wholly 'collapsed' as Keynes claimed, there can be no
doubt that Wilson was outdone at the Paris Peace Conference. Though supported by many neutral countries and also by moderate socialists (includ-

ing Count Karolyi of Hungary), his redeeming creed of open diplomacy, self-determination, and removal of 'all economic barriers' was rivalled and eventually overwhelmed by an 'imperialist' settlement that, so its opponents believed, turned the peace into little better than a 'division of the booty'.[141]

The League of Nations had been promised as a 'general association of nations'—an organization that would provide 'mutual guarantees of political independence and territorial integrity to great and small states alike'. There were people in all countries, including Germany, for whom the idea was sourced not in Woodrow Wilson's vaporous slogans, but in the Enlightenment proposals of Immanuel Kant's 'Perpetual Peace: a Philosophical Sketch' (1795). In February 1918, Dorothy Buxton's 'Foreign Opinion' summarized an article from the Berlin socialist paper *Vorwärts*:

> Kant and Fichte may be read with profit as exponents of the ideas of the League of Nations. Fichte discovered the intimate connection between what is now termed 'internal' and 'external' policy. No people can demand that its adherence to the League of Nations should be taken seriously, unless internally it shows a disposition to turn itself into the true State, knowing no oppression, and no privileged ruling class. Everywhere the path to the League of Nations goes via Democracy and Socialism.[142]

But not, it must be said, at the Paris Peace Conference in 1919.

For H. N. Brailsford, Buxton's friend and erstwhile collaborator on the Balkan Committee, the League of Nations that was eventually squeezed into existence was the 'pathetic survival' of Wilson's 'defeated idealism'.[143] For the Liberal journalist A. G. Gardiner it was merely a 'sham',[144] disguising the true intentions of Churchill and Marshal Foch. The Buxtons agreed: far from being 'some genuine form of supernational Government, representing the interest of all the states, and capable of being called to account by the humblest of them', the League of Nations turned out to be 'the Allied and Associated Powers under a new name'.[145] Former or anticipated future enemies—Germany, Austria, Hungary, Bulgaria, Turkey, and also Russia—had not been admitted to the League, and power was retained by America, Japan, and the Western Powers.[146] As these critics saw it, the horizontally aligned new diplomacy was cut down at the Paris Peace Conference, and replaced with another system of national alliances: a weighted balance of power which promised not so much 'peace' but a new sequence of wars to come. The same point was made by Vernon Lee, who noted in March 1919 that the 'present starving and ruining' imposed on Germany by the Allied leaders at Versailles, only served, within Germany, to justify having gone to war in the first place: indeed, it served to show 'how wise Germany was in trying to break the iron circle of foes bent on her destruction'.[147]

Far from being a genuinely international body, capable of overcoming the secret diplomacy of the old balance of power, the League of Nations had turned out to be a barely pacified instrument of war. This outcome had been anticipated in earlier editions of Dorothy Buxton's survey of 'Foreign Opinion'. It had been simply put by the Viennese daily *Neue Freie Press* on 7 January 1919: 'The inhabitants of the earth are divided into two classes, those who order and those who obey. He who rebels is condemned to starvation; the group of the victors disposes of the raw material which is necessary for work.'[148] The same verdict was reached by Francesco Nitti, the former Italian Chancellor of the Exchequer and prime minister, who wrote of the Treaty of Versailles: 'History has not on record a more colossal diplomatic defeat than this treaty, by which Europe has been neatly divided into two sections: victors and vanquished; the former being authorized to exercise on the latter complete control until the fulfilment of terms which, even at an optimistic point valuation, would require at least thirty years to materialize.'[149]

Far from being dissolved by the new machinery of international relations with which Wilson had once promised to bring about disarmament under international guarantee, freedom of the seas and 'the removal, so far as possible, of all economic barriers', the iron curtain that Vernon Lee had first detected between Britain and Germany over Christmas 1914, had been reinstated. Having stepped through it as they entered Russia in April 1920, Buxton, Ethel Snowden, and the other British Labour delegates had to conduct their investigations on a violently separated stage where appearances were hard to guage, even if they were not so systematically rigged or, indeed, camouflaged as had been anticipated by the anti-Bolshevik commentators who warned of Potemkin villages.

I I

Fact-Finding with Limousines

As in Petrograd, the drive was just like a moving picture.
George Lansbury[1]

The dishes as they appeared were like things we have seen in dreams
Clare Sheridan[2]

At some point during the visit, a member of the British Labour Delegation noticed that many Russian girls and women were wearing socks, and enquired whether this was 'the latest fashion' among Moscow women. '"No," came the brisk reply, "it is not the latest fashion but the last economy. Socks use up less wool than stockings. It is considered good fortune to have either socks or stockings. Most people have neither."'[3] The British delegates were fully capable of putting their feet in their mouths without assistance from the Bolsheviks. Yet the hostile commentators who had warned of Potemkin villages were right to suggest that they also risked a more systematic kind of derangement.

By 1920, when Ethel Snowden found it wrapped around Russia, the 'iron curtain' was being remade as a cordon sanitaire composed of a band of reshaped countries. However, it remained a 'psychological' phenomenon too: a barrage of contrary propagandas in which, thanks to the cancellation of more reliable information, fact, fantasy, and ideological allegation had become extravagantly confused. There could be no question of getting 'behind' a division such as this merely by stepping across an increasingly armoured frontier. The iron curtain went with the delegates as they travelled through Red Russia: constraining their view, polarizing their impressions, mixing repulsion with enchantment, and casting its own deceptive glare over the realities they had come to investigate. It created a confusion of perspectives which, from the early days of Soviet Russia, prompted Western visitors to remember Lewis Carroll's *Through the Looking-Glass*.

The iron curtain hovered over the delegation in its internal arguments, dividing those who were for Bolshevism from those espousing a more liberal approach to socialism. It loomed ominously when three members of the delegation, including Ethel Snowden, were getting into a car to visit Count Vladimir Tchertkoff, a Christian pacifist who had also been a friend and follower of the late Leo Tolstoy: as they drove off in this officially disapproved direction, Mme Balabanova, who was preparing to take the rest of the delegation to a large 'propaganda' meeting, waved at Tchertkoff and called out, 'We are going to life. They are going to death.'[4]

It would keep clattering up and down during the course of the delegation's encounter with Lenin in the Kremlin. Convinced of the importance of impressing foreign visitors,[5] the Bolshevik leader asked the chairman, Ben Turner, for his impressions of Bolshevik Russia so far. A stickler for the ballot box, Turner was certainly not inclined to gaze into Lenin's eyes, as George Lansbury had done two months earlier, and feel ashamed of 'the stupendous crimes of the Allies against Russia and her people'.[6] Instead, he announced that Russia reminded him of a patient convalescing after a serious illness—to which Lenin quickly countered that he would do better to describe the Bolshevik coup as an 'operation'.[7] When Lenin suggested that Bolshevik means were justified by their revolutionary ends, Chairman Turner replied, 'your methods are not those of Englishmen'.

The division could find expression in a characteristically British haughtiness too, as in Mrs Snowden's account of the delegation's meeting with the Commissar for Foreign Affairs, Georgi Vasilyevich Chicherin. This leading Bolshevik was now 'master of the foreign policy of a country the size of Europe' and yet to the British visitors 'he looked as if all the woes of the world had been laid by force upon his frail and inadequate shoulders. His clothes appeared to be many sizes too big for him. He looked over his collar like a frightened owl over a hedge fence.' For Mrs Snowden Chicherin was still the pitiful figure she had seen fidgeting nervously on the edge of a chair in London during the Great War. She remembered him pleading, in a strained and high-pitched voice, that the executive committee of the National Council for Civil Liberties (founded in 1916) should take steps to help Russian prisoners in Britain: 'His manner was shrinking. He lacked the usual voluble earnestness of the Socialist exile. He suggested the gentle and refined artist, the man of taste and leisure. He was full of a timid courtesy. His diffidence was a temptation to the coarse and undiscerning to be rough and contemptuous of the suppliant.'[8]

Chicherin had himself later been imprisoned in London at the same time as Bertrand Russell and Clifford Allen. Judging by the tone of Mrs Snowden's description, however, his real offence was only just becoming apparent. Like the other Bolshevik leaders, Chicherin had failed to grasp that, with Germany now defeated, Britain was the historically sanctioned home of socialism. The red flag surely belonged there, where it had long since been pitched as a sign of more or less Christian fellowship among the leafy and organic visions of John Ruskin and William Morris. From Mrs Snowden's perspective, it was destined to be carried forward into the twentieth century not by the Bolsheviks and their upstart Communist International, but by the British members of the reformist Fabian Society, the Independent Labour Party, and the more revolutionary Social Democratic Federation, all three of which had come together in 1900 to form the Labour Representation Committee, relaunched as the Labour Party in 1906.

Delusions of a Promised Future

These conflicts within international socialism remained powerfully influential, but it was not owing to them alone that the risk of misrecognition lay all around the British delegates. Dr Haden Young wrote that one of the 'grave evils' of the Allied blockade of Bolshevik Russia was 'the making of that country into a mystery land inhabited either by angels or by devils'.[9] He rejected both alternatives, declaring that 'The marvellous "Red" legend of a country on which the sun of Communism is rising is as untrue as the "White" legend of a country in which civilization is drowned in blood and horror.' The truth may have been more 'humdrum', as Haden Young insisted, but it would prove hard, even for the most determinedly 'independent' investigator, to establish in the distorting mirror that Bolshevik Russia turned out to be.

After visiting in September 1920, H. G. Wells, who was far from enthusiastic about doctrinaire socialism, described Russia as 'a vast irreparable breakdown'. Having toured Petrograd and Moscow, he also declared 'the fact of Revolution' to be 'altogether dwarfed by the fact of this downfall'.[10] It was, after all, capitalism not communism that had built 'impossible' cities such as St Petersburg (then known as Petrograd). The war had been the work of European imperialism not the Bolsheviks; and the continuation of the misery was the fault of the 'atrocious blockade' backed by 'the vindictive French creditor, the journalistic British oaf'.[11]

Be that as it may, Wells was surely right to insist that the Bolshevik revolution remained largely unachieved in 1920. However fierce the scarlet slogans draped across the Kremlin and other historical buildings, it could not reasonably be identified, either by its enemies or by its ardent proponents, with the general reality of post-war Russia. In April 1918, Lenin himself had announced that 'the problem of management' and 'practical organisation' was now both the most difficult and the most promising challenge facing the Communist Party as it set about building a socialist future.[12]

That drive for new forms of organization and discipline would come to be mixed with techniques of stage management as the Bolshevik authorities tried to create a prefigurative impression of the better world-to-come. Communism was presented as a yet-to-be-realized promise set off against the chaotic and all too persistent 'heritage' of tsarism, civil war, and blockade. Its exhibits included a series of future-orientated projects: still partly hypothetical initiatives designed to indicate what 'New Russia' might look like in different domains—family life, schools, industry, health care, and the military. Built for internal as well as external show, these projects were like experimental probes reversed into the present from the promised future. In many instances, the display was still dressed in the idealism—the 'revolutionary dreams'[13] as Richard Stites has called them—of the first months of Bolshevik power: a time when Soviet educationalists had talked of the ideas of John Dewey and Maria Montessori as well as of Tolstoy and Kropotkin; when Bukharin recommended the playing of chess in schools;[14] and when Lunacharsky, speaking as 'Commissar of Enlightenment' at the 'First All-Russian Congress on Education' in 1917, had proclaimed that 'The basic task of man is to make himself and everything around him beautiful.'[15]

In more stable societies the reality confronting a visitor might seem largely continuous with both the past and the anticipated future, but the travellers who entered Bolshevik Russia had to reckon with a confusing, and often highly antagonistic, polarization between the two. Bolshevik Russia was, wrote Bertrand Russell shortly after returning to England, a strange and troubling world of 'dying beauty and harsh life'.[16] He was worried about the 'heritage of civilisation' espoused by Conservatives and so fiercely mocked as a reactionary totem by the Bolsheviks (another version, perhaps, of Vernon

Lee's 'tinselled wax doll', this invocation of 'heritage' was easily dismissed as a decadent glorification of tsarist Russia's notorious 'backwardness'). Yet he also immunized himself against nostalgia for the 'dying beauty' of the old regime by remembering the brutality of the tsars' rule: the revolutionaries who had been tormented in the fortress of Peter and Paul, the 'poverty, drunkenness, prostitution in which life and health were uselessly wasted'. As he declared, 'By hatred of the old, I become tolerant of the new, but I cannot love the new on its own account.'

Other Western visitors tried to overcome the difficulties of travelling between ideologically opposed worlds by idealizing this Communism of the future, and then adhering to it come what may. 'Material discomfort' was everywhere, as one visiting British Communist and shop steward would admit, and yet the 'spiritual values' of Communism commanded overriding loyalty as 'guarantors of the future'.[17] This was how Robert Williams and A. A Purcell proceeded through Russia—striding past scenes of the starkest misery and chaos but seeing 'an entirely new civilisation' (Williams) in the making. George Lansbury had pioneered this approach before the British Labour Delegation arrived. Having invested his best hopes in the Bolshevik revolution, he defended his faith against the contrary evidence of his senses by robustly blaming all evils on the 'other' side (tsarism, imperial war, continued Allied hostility, etc.). Alexander Berkman had seen Lansbury's technique in action in February 1920. Sent as a translator to accompany Lansbury and a colleague from the *Daily Herald* as they travelled by train from Petrograd to Moscow, he remembers how they arrived at the frozen railway station in Moscow to find themselves surrounded by desperate women and children, begging and some of them barefoot in the snow. '"How starved they look, and how poorly clad," I remarked. "No worse than you see at the London stations," Lansbury replied curtly. "You're hypercritical, Berkman."'[18]

A correspondent to *The Times* would later write of 'a strange hypnotism' when describing this 'refusal to be undeceived in the face of incontrovertible evidence',[19] but it was actually the iron curtain internalized: not just a Potemkinist delusion but a carefully balanced machinery of equivocation without which the vision of the New Jerusalem would be overwhelmed by the horrors of the war-mangled world in which it was expected to unfold. With the help of this mental device, adherents such as George Lansbury and Robert Williams could walk through hell and see only paradise coming. Indeed, for those who followed this redemptive logic, the worse things were, the greater the promise of the coming transformation had to be.

Lansbury may provide an early example of the adherent's habit of rationalizing human suffering as the inevitable 'cost' of the revolution. Yet he also espoused the Christian view that redemption would enter the world through the miserable and oppressed, and he was by no means alone among visiting Western socialists in being compelled by the thought of a promised future. Whatever their view of Bolshevism, the members of the British Labour Delegation were predisposed, by the history of their own movement, to envision socialism as a reality that was still to come. They too believed in what Edward Carpenter had called 'that great twentieth century bridge which will in its due time lead us into another world',[20] and they gazed across it to the anticipated day when an electoral majority would bring their young and untested Labour Party into power for the first time. Yet nothing, including the hope of a better world to come, is quite as it seems when reality is divided by an iron curtain, and the British investigators found their perceptions complicated, and their convictions sometimes quite undermined, by sudden oscillations of meaning.

The delegation included pacifists, anti-war protestors, and guild socialists whose idea of social revolution was certainly not about armed legions marching to the rhythm of the militarized state. They may soon have got used to hearing the Internationale, first composed as the song of the Paris Commune just after its bloody suppression by the French military in 1871, converted into a Bolshevik anthem and bashed out by Red Army bands. But selected delegates also found themselves visiting tank and aeroplane factories, and they were all expected to stand for hours at huge military and naval parades. As a Fabian hygienist, Dr Haden Young could at least spend the time reviewing the fitness of the passing troops (categorizing them variously as B, A, and A4—which was to say 'boys undeveloped'[21]). Other delegates, however, were frankly dismayed. At one point, while surveying the same vast demonstration in Petrograd's Uritski Square, Mrs Snowden objected 'What a display of military!'—provoking Emma Goldman to point out frostily, 'Madame, remember that the big Russian army is largely the making of your own country. Had England not helped to finance the invasion into Russia, the latter could put its soldiers to useful labour.'[22]

Thus did the 'reality' of Bolshevik Russia keep dissolving into its opposite. If Russia's militarism was the fault of the Allied intervention, then who could be certain that the starved condition of the people was not the fault of the Allied blockade nor, as Clifford Allen put it, the legacy of tsarist brutality?[23] As for the 'exercise of frightfulness'[24] under the Red Terror and the 8,500 executions admitted by Felix Dzerzhinsky's Extraordinary Commission (the 'Cheka' or OGPU, as the secret police would later become known), perhaps even these developments, so the delegates were firmly told, should be understood in the light of 'the sinister part played by our own Foreign Office, and particularly by Mr. Winston Churchill'.[25]

Entertainments, Rallies, and Statistics

As they tried to resolve these awkwardly doubled (and then redoubled) impressions, the more 'impartial' members of the British Labour Delegation found themselves fighting illusions projected from both sides of the division. The notorious 'techniques of hospitality',[26] with which the Soviet authorities would later manipulate so many credulous Western 'pilgrims', were by no means fully in place. Yet the Bolsheviks certainly brought pressure to bear on the delegation.

Angelica Balabanova, who was responsible for receiving the British visitors in Petrograd, describes arguing with the leaders of the Third International—both Chicherin and Karl Radek—who had insisted on the 'absolute necessity' of creating 'extraordinary privileged conditions' for the visitors, and even of providing them with the wines and liquors that were forbidden in Russia at that time. Why, Balabanova asked, should the English visitors not 'live a few weeks as our people have lived for years? What have we to conceal?'[27] According to Berkman, she was convinced that the best policy would have been to show the delegation 'the whole truth concerning Russia, and to enlist their friendship and cooperation in the work of upbuilding the country by their adequate understanding of its needs, rather than by the lack of it'.[28] This, however, was not the opinion that prevailed. In the disillusioned words of Emma Goldman, 'luxury was heaped upon them while the people slaved and went hungry'.[29]

If the British visitors were indulged gastronomically, steps were also taken to ensure that they travelled through the best exhibition that could be made of Russia. They may never have been shown the 'sky full of diamonds' and other 'wondrous things' that the Soviet war correspondent Isaac Babel would imagine offering tormented Jews as he followed the Red Cavalry in their assault against Poland later that summer.[30] But there were visits to the opera, ballet, and theatre, as well as to huge rallies and trade union receptions. The delegation travelled in specially decorated tramcars as well as in the late tsar's automobiles and their trains arrived at orderly stations, previously swept clean of the usual bedraggled workers and beggars. Its members visited factories, food stores, schools, and other institutions, many of which had been carefully 'prepared' for their arrival. On first arriving in Moscow, they were fed sandwiches by white-frocked servants on the third floor of a hotel in which 'that floor alone had been prepared' in anticipation of their visit.[31]

Those without any 'industrial' experience only had the word of A. A. Purcell, when this seasoned 'wood worker' declared that Russia's aeroplane factories compared favourably with anything in Britain.[32] However, the Bolshevik authorities ensured that they were also plied with statistics—be they about industrial output, food prices, or the number of 'enemies of the revolution' executed by Felix Dzerzhinsky's 'Extraordinary Commission' — which they could only suspect were exaggerated or diminished as the case may be. They gazed out over apparently joyful crowds of welcoming workers, who could hardly let it be known, as one exhausted woman would tell Emma Goldman at a rally somewhat later in the year, that she had been up since five in the morning and, like everyone else at her factory, been dragooned into attendance by a threatened withdrawal of bread rations.[33] The presentations persisted with this 'mask of pretence'. At the final banquet given for the delegation before they left Petrograd for Moscow, the chairman of the Petrograd Soviet of Labour Unions, Antselovich, went so far as to announce that 'full individual liberty is established in Russia', a ludicrous claim that Alexander Berkman recognized as 'an insult to the intelligence of the Mission' and left out of his translation.[34]

The Russia seen by the delegation may have smelt of fresh paint and disinfectant, wiped over the floors of the Kremlin to prevent typhus reaching the leaders of Churchill's 'Bolshevik Plague'.[35] Its rulers may have tried, as Dr Haden Guest would claim, to screen the 'crude and naked verities' of their struggle for power behind a 'camouflage of socialist and communist wording'. They may also have struck an 'attitude of uncompromising heroism',[36] which appealed 'especially to the dramatic instinct' and left Bertrand Russell convinced that nothing useful could be done except with 'slower and less showy methods'.[37] Yet it was by no means an entirely manipulated Potemkin village. One member complained about the 'prison atmosphere'[38] in which the delegation was kept but it was not just the ardently pro-Bolshevik Robert Williams who would counter such impressions by insisting 'We went where we liked; we interviewed whom we pleased.'[39] Russell said much the same and so too did Dr Haden Guest, claiming that, while the Bolsheviks had indeed shown the delegates 'the better instead of the worse places', this would equally have happened in New York or London, and also that they were able 'unofficially' to see as much as they had energy or wit to 'see for themselves'.[40]

Chairman Turner recalls that, on their first day in Petrograd, he and Buxton had been free to hire a droshky and to travel about delivering letters from people in England who had relatives living in the area: 'It has been said that we were piloted around, watched and spied upon by the Soviet emissaries. This is not true, for nobody but our antique driver was with us, and he did not go into the houses with us.'[41] Later, while some of the delegates were sailing down the Volga on the steamboat *Belinski*, Buxton was able to grab his bag and slip down the gangplank at Samara, leaving his host and minder, A. Losovsky of the All Russian Council of Trade Unions, frantically yelling orders from the boat as it was carried off by the current. He then found a carriage and a helpful companion (to whom he would later give the pseudonym 'Telegraphist Petrov'), and set off across the steppe in a spirit of friendly curiosity to conduct his own week-long investigation of conditions in and around the remote village of Ozero.[42] During the course of this excursion, he explored a neighbouring settlement, identified only as 'K', which was still influenced by a priest 'of the most unbending and dogmatic type'. Leading villagers here appeared to speak freely and without fear of reprisals: '"We are living under a Government of brutes [*zoyerini*]. It is like Catherine the Great's time. We are slaves."'[43]

The Committee of Welcome may have tried to keep their visitors on a tight schedule of official receptions, visits, and concerts, but some delegates got into the habit of going for walks, with or without interpreters, and then turning up unannounced at churches, schools, or apartment buildings that could not have been prepared for their appearance. They also encountered discontented Westerners who were appalled to find themselves on the wrong side of the divide. A Frenchwoman spoke to Tom Shaw when he and other delegates visited a state-controlled stud-farm outside Moscow: a governess before the revolution, she spat in contempt when asked about her present employment raising Angora rabbits for their fur.[44] Visiting the Russian American tool shop, established by seventy of those who had been deported from America on the 'Red Ark' alongside Goldman and Berkman, they encountered a man who—despite the censure of his still loyal comrades—yearned to get back to the USA, being 'disappointed and disillusioned because he had to work just as hard here as in America, and had far fewer of the amenities of life'.[45]

Some delegates also managed to arrange meetings with various private citizens and opposition figures. They had conversations with Tolstoyans and anarchists, including the elderly Prince Kropotkin. Through Buxton, who had acquired his address before leaving London, they also made contact with the Menshevik leader Fedor Il'ich Dan.[46] Most memorably, three of their number—Purcell, Skinner, and Wallhead—were present at a mass meeting of the Moscow Printers' Union, called by the Mensheviks in a defiant attempt to break through the Bolsheviks' presentation and convince the British visitors of the true state of political opinion among Moscow workers. Well over three thousand gathered in the Moscow Conservatory, and various opposition socialists made what were effectively their last public statements against Bolshevism. Wearing a long beard and, in one account, dark glasses, the Social Revolutionary leader Victor Chernov mounted the platform and spoke at some length, comparing the teachings of socialism to the teachings of the early Christians, and likening the Bolsheviks to the degenerated Pauline church. According to Dan, his speech was far too abstract and literary to move the crowd, but it was an electrifying appearance nonetheless. Chernov was in hiding at the time, and the Bolsheviks at the meeting were enraged by his appearance in front of the British visitors, and even more so when Chernov, who had also warned the British delegates not to be duped by the 'Potemkin villages' prepared for them,[47] managed to escape back into the crowd before the secret police could arrest him.

The defining moment of this meeting, as recorded in the Labour delegation's *Report*, was attributed to Mark Kefali, a prominent member of the Russian Socialist Democratic Labour Party who was also leader of the Printers' Union. This speaker, whose speech may actually have become somewhat confused in the British record with that of the Menshevik Fedor Il'ich Dan (who describes saying remarkably similar things at the same gathering), chided the English delegates for their naïvely enthusiastic remarks, and reminded 'Comrade Wallhead', who had praised the revolution, that the Bolshevik regime had left the Moscow printers, the founding figures of Russian trade unionism, with 'no right to vote, no right to assemble, no right to print' anything except 'calumnies against themselves'. He insisted, momentously, that the international working-class movement faced a great divide and would have to choose between two ways of arriving at socialism:

One way is the way of democracy of working men; the way of raising the level of production; of voluntary self-reliant activity, self-discipline of the masses. This is, in our opinion, the only way that can lead—and will inevitably lead— to the triumph of Socialism; while the other ruinous way is the way of the deprivation of the working masses themselves of every right and liberty, the way of transforming the working masses into a scattered human herd, submitted to benevolent dictators, benevolent specialists of socialism, who drive men in this paradise by means of a stick.[48]

Enraged by this meeting, the Bolsheviks organized a demonstration immediately afterwards. According to Dan, this only made matters worse, since little more than one hundred people joined the march, thereby showing 'the real sentiments of the Moscow proletariat'. News of the Bolsheviks' 'vicious' response to the Printers' meeting (military occupation of the Moscow Printers Union office, arrest of the Administrative Council, and starvation of the printers who went on strike in protest) was handed to Buxton, together with various appeals made by the strikers to the international labour movement, when he, the last delegate to leave Russia, passed through Moscow at the end of June. They were later edited by Haden Guest and printed in the Labour delegation's report.

The Atrocity Show

If troubles rarely came singly for those who crossed the iron curtain between Bolshevik Russia and the West, this was because they found themselves performing on two irreconcilable stages at once. While the more liberal-minded members of the British Labour Delegation had to cut through the Bolsheviks' still far from fully organized attempts to control their impressions, they also had to withstand the onslaughts of the Western anti-Bolshevik press, which was scouring the Soviet media for evidence of the delegation's concessions to the enemy.

Suspicions were confirmed easily enough thanks to Russian wireless broadcasts relaying comments that had, so Sylvia Pankhurst found out when visiting Russia not long afterwards, been 'deliberately incited' out of delegates at banquets.[49] At the reception welcoming the delegation to Moscow on 16 May, 'Comrade Turner' was reported to have promised that the English proletariat 'would do all in its power to enable the Russian proletariat to accomplish in quietness their mighty undertaking'.[50] An equally enthusiastic

A. A. Purcell announced that British trade unionists were looking forward to welcoming a delegation of Russian comrades in the near future. And none of the delegates were reported to have demurred when Kamenev spoke of the fast approaching day when the English workers would rise up: all would then be well in Russia and 'the Red flag would wave over England' too. Intended to serve the Bolshevik cause, these reports were also a gift to British papers, including *The Times*, which was pleased to repeat the pronouncements of Robert Williams especially. In Petrograd, this leader of the British transport workers' union declared that the delegation had come 'to learn a lesson from the Russians, who had taught the entire world that the working class could be victorious'.[51] In Samara, he announced that 'the British workers were pleased at every Soviet victory over the counter-revolutionaries and every victory over the Poles on the Western front'.

William Meakin, who travelled with the delegation for the Liberal *Daily News,* tried to counter this hostile commentary in his despatches, insisting that the recent reports in the English press were 'fantastically contrary to the facts', and that 'No obstacle is placed by the authorities in the way of the fullest enquiry by the delegation. The suggestion that show places would be carefully selected are simply nonsense.'[52] The socialist *Daily Herald* offered similar reassurances, promising that 'the short comings have been as easy to see as the fine things'.[53]

Yet Western hostility to Bolshevism was far too agitated to be calmed by such denials. By 1920, and thanks not least to the dearth of genuine information created by the iron curtain, the Russian Revolution was being interpreted as the catastrophic outcome of a deeply rooted Jewish conspiracy. This anti-Semitic version of events was being propagated by future British fascists, including Mrs Nesta Webster and Captain George Henry Lane-Fox Pitt Rivers, and approved by Winston Churchill, who backed Zionism as the acceptable alternative to an imagined worldwide Jewish 'conspiracy for the overthrow of civilisation'.[54]

According to one pro-Soviet analysis, the burgeoning 'campaign of slander'[55] against Bolshevism had commenced before the October Revolution and in Russia itself. In the spring of 1917, the Provisional Government and the general staff of the formerly tsarist army spread various calumnies about the 'sealed railway carriage' in which Lenin and other leading Bolsheviks had been conveyed from Switzerland to Russia, alleging that the returning Bolshevik leaders were actually German agents whose revolutionary exhortations were intended to pull Russia out of the Allied war effort. The allegations about 'German advisers' had continued after the Bolshevik revolution: indeed, few opportunities were lost in the Allied world to portray Soviet Russia as 'a midnight assassin, with a blood-stained knife clenched between his teeth'.[56] When this rapidly overworked 'bogey' lost its powers of compulsion, a new approach had been adopted, often entailing documents forged in 'lie factories' run by White Russians and other enemies of the revolution.[57]

White propaganda and anti-Semitic conspiracy theories were perhaps easy to deny as fantastic. But there was other testimony to consider too. The pro-Bolshevik adherents on the Labour delegation might sing the Internationale as heartily as they liked and the more liberal-minded members could equivocate. Neither tendency, however, were in any position to silence the chorus of denunciation emerging from steamers such as the *Tagus*, which had sailed into Southampton a few weeks earlier (in April 1920), carrying 260 refugees from Russia, some of whom were said to have been changed out of all recognition by their recent experiences. Respectable British women told of being forced to dig graves and trenches, or to shovel snow in order to secure even a grossly inadequate ration of food. They brought news of Mr Metcalf, the former steward at the British Club at Moscow, who had been thrown into a 'Bolshevist charnel-house' where he starved to death aged 70. A wealthy young Irishwoman, Mrs Kathleen ffrench, alleged that no less a monster than Madame Trotsky herself was now tussling with the official Bolshevik body to gain possession of her stolen diamonds.[58]

Six weeks later, on 22 May, the *Dongola* had reached Southampton with 300 British and French refugees in charge of the Revd. F.W. North, the long-serving Anglican chaplain at the British Church in Moscow. He disembarked as spokesman for the British colony in Moscow and Petrograd, which had been attacked by the Bolsheviks in August 1918: its embassy overrun (despite the resistance of the naval attaché, Captain Cromie, who was gunned down after killing two of his assailants on the steps) and its members assaulted and imprisoned—some of them packed into cells already jammed with starving Russian prisoners in Petrograd's Fortress of Peter and Paul. Stepping down the gangplank to relay 'the cold, unvarnished truth' about Bolshevik Russia, North described how his refugees had been stripped at the border and the women searched in 'a most unseemly manner'. He confirmed that the Russia shown to the Bolsheviks' 'dangerously idealistic' Western guests was indeed a series of theatrically constructed Potemkin villages.[59] He had seen 'disreputable schools of starving children ... metamorphosed into orderly institutions' for a day, and 'plant carried from a dozen disused factories to make complete one factory, in order to deceive the paternal, benevolent eyes' of some British dreamer. He also spoke out against George Lansbury, who had come to see him during his recent pilgrimage to Soviet Russia: 'every time he was cornered in the course of conversation' this ardent Christian socialist had blithely swept aside all criticism of the Bolsheviks with the excuse '"It is a revolution." That statement covered a multitude of sins.'

These accounts of mistreatment added to the 'Bolshevik atrocity' stories already circulated by the British government in a White Paper entitled *A Collection of Reports on Bolshevism in Russia* and issued in April 1919.[60] This collection of diplomatic communications and unattributed eyewitness accounts had been published without any attempt at authentification: an omission justified on the grounds that the documents 'speak for themselves in the picture which they present of the principles and methods of Bolshevik rule'.[61] Its appearance had been eagerly anticipated by Winston Churchill, who, as Secretary of State for War, had been having trouble motivating British volunteers to serve alongside the White Russian forces in Archangel and Murmansk.[62] Among its stories of murder, torture, and unjustified imprisonment, it included a report by a chaplain to the Forces, the Revd. B. S. Lombard, who claimed that, by the time he left Russia in October 1918, 'the nationalisation of women' was considered 'an accomplished fact'—although, he conceded that, 'with the exception of at Saratoff', he could not prove any actual proclamations to this effect had been issued.[63]

A favourite trope of anti-Bolshevik polemics (and sometimes combined with the claim that the Bolshevik's anti-religious education polices amounted to a 'nationalisation of children'), this persistent allegation still circulates among journalists and historians, some of whom have yet to catch up with Ethel Snowden's insistence that 'There is not one atom of truth in the story, and those who repeat it cover themselves in discredit.'[64] Having visited Saratov during the delegation's excursion down the Volga, Snowden announced that the allegation had actually originated in the pronouncements of a tiny anarchist sect that dreamed of 'a state of society in which men and women would dispense with marriage in their relationships with one another'.[65] It was, she rightly said, 'unscrupulous propaganda' to confuse this utopian recipe—or the dubious 'decrees' in which it was said to be embodied—with Bolshevik policy.[66]

All the delegates, including those whom Lenin would condemn as 'petit-bourgeois renegades', understood that to be 'independent and impartial' investigators entailed opposing the anti-Bolshevik 'atrocity' stories circulating in the British press. The alleged destruction of religion was countered by the insistence that they had seen many icons both in schools and in the Putilov steelworks (they did not, apparently, entertain the suspicion that the fourteen icons that Chairman Ben Turner counted in this crucible of Bolshevik revolution in Petrograd might have been placed there for their benefit).[67] Buxton acknowledged the severe hardship suffered by children in Soviet Russia, but repudiated 'the stories about "no children under two left alive in Petrograd"' as 'childish nonsense'.[68] He indicated the untrustworthiness of the British newspapers by referring to the *Morning Post*'s special correspondent in Reval (Tallinn), a man who would report every violent or abusive act of the Bolsheviks, but could not find a word to say about death sentences passed on strikers in Estonia.[69]

It was both necessary and possible to maintain a sceptical view of 'atrocity' stories in the British press, but Buxton felt 'humiliated' by his own lack of knowledge as he tried to establish the facts of the situation in Russia itself. Faced with layer after layer of legends, rumours, propaganda, and unverifiable data, he reluctantly concluded, in a sentence that would be omitted from the articles that appeared in George Lansbury's *Daily Herald,* that 'our desire for really accurate information was alien to the Russian mind'.[70] It was a difficulty that, over the years to come, would leave many Western visitors trying to evaluate Communist Russia with little more than a repertoire of superficial and often crazily inadequate transnational comparisons.

Buxton hunted up his own British analogy as he tried to answer those in the capitalist world who argued that Communism had brought only 'ruin and desolation' to Russia.[71] Noting that the luxury shops had been closed and boarded up on famous shopping streets such as Petrograd's Nevsky Prospect or the Tvertskaya in Moscow, he conceded that 'Something has been destroyed in Moscow and Petrograd which made a part of all our lives in the Western States of Europe—a part of the rich man's life because he enjoyed it; a part of the poor man's life because he looked on and snobbishly admired it. We might call this something "Regent Street".'

War and revolution had combined to cancel 'the glow and glitter, the shouting advertisements, the ingenious display, the subtle response to every kind of taste and whim'. Gone was the 'unending carnival' of Nikolai Gogol, who had described the 'all-powerful Nevsky Prospect',[72] as a place of glassy surfaces, where 'everything, not only the street lamp, exudes deceit'.[73] The luxurious stores of tsarist times were being replaced by unglamorous institutions bearing names such as 'No. 25 Supply Shop of the Moscow Soviet of Workers and Red Army Delegates'. People who had once enjoyed such places lamented the change as if 'civilisation itself' had been destroyed. Bolsheviks, on the other hand, were more inclined to gloat, in the manner employed by the British Communist Harry Pollitt in 1921. Visiting Petrograd for a meeting of the Communist International, he peered into some large shop windows on Gorki Street, and found them empty of goods except for a collection of 'Morton Christmas Puddings' dated 1913: time-expired British imports that remained quite unwanted, so Comrade Pollitt was pleased to report, even though the people of the city were going hungry.[74]

Though less inclined to smirk, Buxton persisted with his own question: 'Is Regent Street civilisation?' To abolish London's famous street, with its stucco-fronted and, in the eye of its critics, therefore also 'sham' Georgian buildings designed by John Nash,[75] would be to create a 'terrifically painful upheaval'. Yet, 'when all is said and done, Regent Street is not a thing to be admired. It is the symbol of the dominance of a class'. It betrayed a 'lack of proportion' to treat the fate of Russia's most luxurious streets as a measure of the revolution. Aware that the thought of those roughly reduced shops supported anti-Bolshevik prejudice, Buxton insisted that there was 'another side to the picture altogether'. A short detour behind these once opulent façades would reveal former slum dwellers rehoused in flats that had previously been the exclusive domain of the middle class. Even those who lamented the fate of Russia's large country houses might, so Buxton thought optimistically, be less scandalized if they could see them now in use as children's homes, hospitals, rest-centres for workers. These arguments would do little to persuade the enemies of Bolshevism, but they were neither insincere nor hypocritical. Buxton and his wife Dorothy had both been raised in English country houses, but they had long since adopted a deliberately 'simplified' way of life, living for ten years in Kennington Terrace, South London, and then moving, in 1914, to a villa in Golders Green.

For Mrs Snowden, these difficulties of interpretation across the iron curtain came to be focused on the question of drunkenness and its contribution, or otherwise, to the revolution. The British government's collection of *Reports on Bolshevism in Russia* portrayed Lenin's Red Guards as intoxicated thugs whose even more drunken Lettish and Chinese auxiliaries enjoyed carving noses off White Russian faces and sawing captured officers into pieces. Other eyewitness confirmed this impression of the revolution as a frightful upsurge of drunken barbarism.[76] Mrs Snowden was familiar with 'the Drink Question' as a long-standing concern of the British Non-conformist Church and suffragist movement, and also as a humanitarian preoccupation of many socialist parties within the pre-war Second Inter-national—committed as they had been to the sober decision of a widely enfranchised electorate. For decades, she had shared the cause of temper-ance with her husband Philip Snowden who, writing for the Independent Labour Party in 1908, had devoted an entire book to this 'evil', insisting that it was 'but one phase of the Social Problem; that it cannot be completely solved apart from the treatment of the whole problem of the economic and social condition of the people'.[77] Yet she was reluctant to lay the charge of drunkenness at the Bolsheviks' door. She had indeed seen some drunkenness in Russia, but she was more inclined to record the hypocrisy of the fellow delegate, almost certainly Robert Williams, who was quite happy to toast the Bolsheviks with vodka and then pronounce that 'the coming revolution in Great Britain' would surely also require total prohibition of strong drink.[78] Predisposed by her background, she associated the revolution with sobriety rather than drunkenness and praised the Bolsheviks for maintaining the tsar's wartime ban on alcohol. In her opposition to the British government's anti-Bolshevik propaganda, she went so far as to insist that 'the absence of drinking-shops and of public drinking, and consequently of men and women the worse for liquor is a commendable feature of social life in Russia, and accounts for many good things, probably for the Revolution itself, almost certainly for the almost unvaried success of the Red Army'.[79]

Red Against Pink

Ethel Snowden would be roundly mocked for interpreting the Russian Revolution as the product of a morally improving spell of state-imposed sobriety. She may indeed have succumbed to her own obsessions as she opposed the anti-Soviet myths propagated on the British side, yet she was certainly not going to be bounced into the pro-Bolshevik camp. Her refusal of this course brought Snowden into 'hourly conflict'[80] with those members of the British Labour Delegation who were prepared to toler-ate the cruelty of Bolshevism on the Leninist grounds that this was 'war communism' and all its excesses the fault of the Allied blockade.

Taking a last look at the Red Flag from the train that carried her back across the frontier from Russia to Estonia, Ethel Snowden was dismayed to think of what Bolshevism had done to Russia's 'great experiment'. A similarly unimpressed delegate travelling with her responded to the sight by suggesting a new verse for that anthem of an older British socialism, 'The Red Flag':

> The people's flag is palest pink,
> It's not so red as you might think;
> We've been to see, and now we know
> They've been and changed its colour so.[81]

Although apparently never in doubt that true socialism belonged in Britain rather than Russia, this 'disillusioned observer' had, in Mrs Snowden's view, come to Russia without the slightest bias against the revolution, which he saw as 'a very big thing'. He left convinced that 'there is practically no Socialism in Russia worthy of the name. And the people are utterly wretched.'

The point was reiterated by Snowden and Dr Leslie Haden Guest, who was almost certainly Snowden's 'disillusioned observer' (he later wrote that 'The Red flag is being overlaid with gold embroidery and military inscriptions'[82]) as they passed through Stockholm on their way home via Germany. Declaring that much of what they had said in their addresses had 'not been to the liking of the Soviet authorities', they also voiced their suspicion that potential witnesses had been prevented from approaching the delegation by fear of punishment. When *The Times*'s correspondent ventured that this did not say much for Bolshevist liberty, 'Dr. Guest's only reply was a burst of laughter, which implied much.' Ethel Snowden was more explicit: 'I return home with the absolute conviction that we have nothing to learn or gain from Bolshevism. England is a very conservative country, but Socialism has a better chance there than ever in Russia through Bolshevism.'[83]

By that time, the British Labour Party was coming to the same conclusion at its twentieth congress in Scarborough: guided in its deliberations by Ben Turner and also Tom Shaw MP ('I do not like Bolshevism'[84]), delegation members who had returned from Russia early—partly for 'internal digestive reasons' as the portly Ben Turner confessed ('that black bread broke me down at the finish'),[85] and partly in order to inform the conference that the Bolsheviks had promised to imprison opposition socialists and even to hang them from lamp-posts.[86]

The conference was also influenced by a report, apparently originating from Dr Haden Guest in Tallinn, that the Labour delegation's other secretary Charles Roden Buxton, who was still in Russia at the time of the Labour Party Congress, had been arrested in Samara. Buxton had indeed been

ordered back to that town on the Volga, having set off, against the explicit
(but conveniently unread) orders of the Samara Soviet, on his unofficial
fact-finding expedition into the surrounding countryside. This admittedly
'peremptory' order would be cancelled and replaced with profuse apologies
once it emerged that Buxton's 'arrest and imprisonment' had become yet
another 'Bolshevik atrocity' story in the British press.[87]

Instructed by Chicherin, Buxton telegrammed his wife on 25 June, dismissing the rumour as 'ridiculous'. He then boarded a train for the frontier at Estonia, where he would sit in a richly provisioned 'Refreshment
Room', eyeing the 'gigantic' veal cutlets and penning a further despatch
about 'the great human experience'[88] he had passed through in Soviet Russia
(see Appendix II). In this, he railed once more against the Allied policy of
Intervention and Blockade ('We have forced them to employ many odious
means to maintain their footing—and then abused them for employing these
means'). In the same article, Buxton also took his distance from the idea of
impartial social investigation: 'I feel that I cannot isolate the machine of the
Revolution from the human elements that play around it and make, mar, or
modify it. I think of the nervous suspicions generated by months of internal
conspiracy. I think of the heroic patience and endurance of the Russian town
populations. I cannot examine this people as if they were beetles or butterflies.' By that time, however, the story of his 'arrest' had already caused a 'most
serious impression' at the Labour Party conference. On 26 June, *The Times*
reported that the motion, proposed by members of the affiliated British
Socialist Party, that the Labour Party should leave the Second International
and join the Third had been defeated by 2,950,000 votes to 225,000.

The 'constitutionalists' on the British Labour Delegation will have been
satisfied both with this outcome, and also with the similar conclusion reached
by the Independent Labour Party. The ILP's chairman, R. C. Wallhead, may
have been scolded for giving too much credit to the revolution at the famous
printers' meeting in Moscow, but he too had come home unpersuaded. In his
report to the National Administrative Council, he declared that, while the
motives of the Bolshevik leaders could not, in his opinion, be impugned,
'the exercise of absolute power, unhampered by effective criticism through
the agency of a free Press and a free platform, cannot possibly result in
the best form of Socialism, which can be introduced really only as the
outcome of self-action of the working class'.[89] Advised by Wallhead and
Clifford Allen, the ILP resolved to leave the Second International, generally
viewed as moribund. However, its members also voted by a large majority
not to join the Third.

Having visited the Communist International's office in Moscow, Wallhead and Allen concluded that this ostensibly 'International' organization was both administratively incompetent and impossibly 'nationalistic' in its politics: determined to use Lenin's twenty-one conditions of membership to ensure that the world communist movement was firmly under the Kremlin's thumb. Objecting to the 'pontifical attitude'[90] displayed by Radek, Bukharin, and other Comintern leaders, Allen argued that the time had come to form a new, inclusive international in which both Bolshevik and democratic socialists could work together to resolve their differences. This must be based on neutral ground outside Russia, since it would be impossible 'to get the Russians to face the facts as reported by other countries ... so long as Conferences are held in their own country, where they are hosts, where they are the Government, where the arrangements are in their hands, and where they spend their time in displaying their achievements to the representatives of other countries'.[91]

Robert Williams was certainly not of that opinion. At the Trades Union Congress, held in Portsmouth in September 1920, he would declare the Bolshevik revolution to be 'the most magnificent experiment to establish the rule of the people'.[92] The leader of the British Furniture Workers, A. A. Purcell, drew similar conclusions. At the end of July, Purcell attended a meeting at the Cannon Street Hotel in London and, having described the personally communicated expectations of the Russian leadership, pressed the case for a merger of the British Socialist Party with other marginal groups, including Sylvia Pankhurst's Workers' Socialist Federation, to produce the Communist Party of Great Britain. In Britain as elsewhere, the left would be split, and its loyalties divided between the rival internationals. As attempts at cooperation failed, the 'iron curtain' found a new theatre of operations. It went into service as the prophylactic device with which the majority democratic socialist parties sought to protect themselves against infiltration by the revolutionary Communists to their left.

Not Just the Bright Side

Ethel Snowden would be little thanked for her efforts as a member of the British Labour Delegation to Russia. Her 'impartial' demeanour had not impressed her Bolshevik minder in Petrograd, Angelica Balabanova, who disliked her worrying about the fate of the evicted Princess Naryshkin, and suspected her of feeling more sympathy for the old aristocracy than for the struggling proletariat. Snowden had met but failed to establish any useful contact with Alexandra Kollontai, a member of the already formed Workers' Opposition who was also striving to advance women's interests in the Soviet regime. Nor did she impress the American anarchist deportees who served the delegation as interpreters. Alexander Berkman portrays her sitting on that luxurious train to Moscow, expressing reservations and 'preserving the well-bred dignity of high society',[93] as if she had been a duchess rather than the daughter of a Harrogate building contractor. Having studied Mrs Snowden's behaviour at the delegation's farewell banquet, Emma Goldman recorded that she refused to offer a word in reply to a speech made on behalf of Russian women proletarians, but became uncommonly enlivened once the formalities were over and 'she got busy collecting autographs'.[94]

In his 'Letter to the British Workers', carried back to England and presented to British Communists by the delegation's chairman, Ben Turner, Lenin refrained from naming Ethel Snowden alongside Dr Haden Guest and Tom Shaw as class enemies who should be swept aside by a properly violent working class revolution in Britain. Yet her description of the delegation's visit, *Through Bolshevik Russia,* would certainly not get off scot-free. In his introduction to the Russian edition of Buxton's book about his fact-finding mission to the countryside around Ozero, the Bolshevik Theodore Rothstein, who had lived for many years in London before 1917, declared Snowden guilty of 'seeking out and underlining our mistakes and failures, and making them into a bouquet to present to the English working class for its edification, and to the English bourgeoisie for its satisfaction'.[95]

Her book would be derided in Britain too, and not just for its peculiar suggestion that the Russian Revolution may have been a fit of social-mindedness induced by the tsar's enlightened ban on alcohol.[96] The scepticism of the more anti-Bolshevik delegates—Snowden, Turner, Shaw, Haden Guest, etc.—provided a foil for the ardent George Lansbury, who mocked the very idea of a disengaged fact-finding mission when he wrote up his own slightly earlier visit to Bolshevik Russia. Far from travelling as 'a cold-blooded investigator seeking to discover what there was of evil', the editor of the *Daily Herald* now claimed to have gone as a loyal adherent: 'I went as a Socialist, to see what a socialist revolution looks like at close quarters'.[97]

Attacked from the left, Ethel Snowden could only have waited in vain for the commendations of the Conservative journalists who had anticipated that she and the other delegates would be deceived by the 'Potemkin villages' erected for their benefit by the Bolshevik government. For the *Morning Post,* the British Labour Delegation was hardly to be credited for the criticisms of Bolshevik Russia pronounced in its interim reports. Having persistently condemned the delegation as a party of deluded 'Innocents Abroad', it would only revise its position very reluctantly. A leading article declared: 'We have no doubt that every effort was made by the hosts of the Delegation to show them as much of the bright side of things and as little of ugly realities as was by any means possible, but the real state of things in Russia has gone beyond concealment for anyone but a Lansbury.'[98] It then turned to denounce Bolshevist fantasies from the other side, addressing itself to the deluded state in which the members of Leonid Krasin's Russian trade delegation could be imagined to have arrived in London. One obviously confected article, printed in riposte to Lenin's 'letter to the British Workers', offered the report of a nameless 'correspondent' who claimed to have found a member of Krasin's staff standing on the pavement in Piccadilly Circus and gazing, as if 'spellbound', at the traffic.[99] Recognizing this enraptured Russian, the correspondent takes him off to a little teashop, where the foreigner explains his curious fascination with London's busy stream of buses, trams, and taxis. Primed by the Bolshevik press, he had arrived expecting to find England immobilized by strikes and insurrection: there were, he explained, 'innocent fools in Russia who think that England is on the verge of a revolution'.

Leaving aside the drink question and her concessions to the *Morning Post's* treatment of Bolshevism as a Jewish conspiracy, Ethel Snowden had actually held her own against many proffered illusions. Her minder, Angelica Balabanova, testifies that she was so suspicious of being taken to 'show places' that she even declined the chauffeured car offered when she expressed the desire to go to church one Sunday, explaining, implausibly, that she 'hadn't had enough exercise in Russia' and preferred to walk on her own.[100]

Balabanova also confirmed Snowden's realization that some of the most telling 'optical illusions' produced on the Russian side of the iron curtain were not designed only, or even primarily, to impress car-borne Western visitors or to delude them about the nature of Bolshevism and its achievements. Instead, they incorporated the delegation into an exhibition aimed at Russian audiences. With its cancellation of free or accurate exchange of information, the blockade helped the Bolshevik leaders to persuade the Russian people that Britain, like other European countries, teetered on the brink of a proletarian uprising that would soon come to the aid of Soviet Russia.

As Balabanova would later confirm, the British Labour Delegation was enlisted as a visual aid in this exposition:

> The receptions, parades, demonstrations, theatrical performances, etc., staged for the English delegation as long as they were in Russia, were as much intended to impress the Russian workers with the significance of this visitation 'from the representatives of the British Worker' as they were to impress the delegation itself. Every effort was made to use the English delegation for propaganda purposes, to make the Russians feel that the Commission represented the sympathy, approval, and solidarity with Bolshevism of the English working class.[101]

No wonder Mrs Snowden felt 'displayed' when the delegation was put in the tsar's box at the opera in both Moscow and Petrograd.[102] The chairman, Ben Turner, may also have felt uncomfortably exposed. He was, by his own admission, 'a plump kind of cove'[103] and Berkman records how undernourished workers at a reception in Petrograd had eyed up his ample and electrically illuminated figure: '"There, look at him!" a worker behind me exclaimed, 'you can tell he's from abroad. Our people are not so fat.'"

The Bolshevik vision of imminent world revolution was fed by the optimistic prognostications of diverse Western pilgrims, including those members of the British Labour Delegation who had, in Snowden's words, proved 'unable to resist' the atmosphere at such meetings. Moved by rousing speeches, toasts, and great crowds of workers who appeared to be demanding their solidarity, these men had started, just like their predecessors on the French and British delegations of March 1917, to speak 'on true Bolshevist lines'.[104] In this, they appeared to confirm Bukharin's prophecy, made on behalf of the Comintern at a huge reception in Moscow's Bolshoi Theatre, that 'the English Soviet republic'[105] was only just around the corner.

Robert Williams plainly belonged to the 'part of the delegation' that would, so Bukharin confidently predicted, soon join the Third International. Whilst in Russia, he was awarded Soviet Russia's Military Medal, which he was proud to receive from the acting chairman of the Russian Revolutionary Military Council. According to Dan, he was also favoured with special banners placed around him to leave Russian audiences in no doubt of his superior status as he sat on various platforms with less respected members of the British delegation. The revolutionary trade unionist Albert A. Purcell was an equally full-blooded supporter of the Bolsheviks, declaring that 'the libels of the yellow bourgeois press' were spread with the aim of killing the revolutionary movement growing among the English working classes: 'When we return to England we shall tell the workers what is taking place in Russia, and how the Russian proletariat are building up their life so that they may strive to attain the same idea which the Russian proletariat is struggling for.'

Both Williams and Purcell were adherents, who gave their support to the Bolshevik idea of establishing a Moscow-centred Red International of Trade Unions to rival the International Federation of Trade Unions, which had recently established its offices in Amsterdam.[106] Yet even the delegation's roundly sceptical chairman, Ben Turner, is reported to have told the Moscow meeting that 'On arriving here, we found a land being reborn, and a wonderful enthusiasm and love for labour.'

Others were more reticent. Buxton may have impressed Russell as 'pro-Bolsh' when he returned from staying at the dacha of Lev Kamenev, Central Committee member and president of the Moscow Soviet.[107] Yet he had refused to reinforce the illusions of the mixed collection of Russians who gathered around him on the ship's deck as he sailed up the Volga on the way back to Moscow after his visit to the countryside around Ozero. They wanted to talk about the future, and the big question on their minds was 'Is the World Revolution coming?' Many seemed to believe that this redeeming event was indeed just around the corner—as repeatedly promised by Lenin, Trotsky, and Bukharin—and that it would soon bring all Soviet Russia's problems to an end at a stroke. Buxton describes them eagerly awaiting his positive response, and then slowly dispersing in disappointed silence after he deflated their expectations as gently as he could, saying 'I do not think so myself'.[108]

Ethel Snowden also disappointed the Soviet leaders by announcing that Bolshevism had 'not the slightest chance of being implanted in England'.[109] Her claim to this effect is confirmed by a report quoted from *Pravda* that the 'rapprochement' between the Bolsheviks and the British Labour Delegation 'could not be a complete one, that there was something left unsaid'. It could hardly admit that the Soviet management of foreign delegations would be overhauled and tightened after the embarrassing fiasco of the Moscow printers' meeting. However, a much more agreeable level of conformity was expected from the Italian delegation, which arrived in Petrograd on 7 June, almost as soon as the British had left: 'The character of the visit of the Italian delegation is totally different. It is of a definitely political nature. They have come to us as friends.'[110]

Having served as an 'unofficial' interpreter at the request of the British delegation, Alexander Berkman was downbeat about the prospects:

> The Italian Socialist Mission, headed by Serrati, is in the city, and the occasion is celebrated with the usual military parades, demonstrations and meetings. But the show has lost interest for me. I have looked back of the curtain. The performances lack sincerity; political intrigue is the mainspring of the spectacles. The workers have no part in them except for mechanical obedience to orders; hypocrisy conducts the delegates through the factories; false information deceives them regarding the actual state of affairs; surveillance prevents their getting in touch with the people and learning the truth of the situation. The delegates are dined, fêted and influenced to bring their organizations into the fold of the Third International, under the leadership of Moscow.
>
> How far it all is from my conception of revolutionary probity and purpose![111]

Some members of the delegation sent by Italy's General Confederation of Labour may indeed have entered Russia with sympathetic interest in the Bolshevik revolution. They may also have been indulged and guided through 'the traditional Potemkin villages',[112] as alleged by Emma Goldman. Once again, however, the majority saw through these illusions quite effectively. Welcomed by the London *Times* as 'an inexorable criticism of the Bolshevist regime', their report, which was eventually published in October 1920, called on the West to 'help this people in the name of civilization and humanity to emerge from such a miserable situation, and recognize the fallacy of their conception of life'.[113] Angelica Balabanova had long known and respected the mission's leader, Giacinto Menotti Serrati. He was among those who had held the Italian Socialist Party together through the war, retaining its internationalist perspective and withstanding the 'patriotic' desertions of Mussolini and others; and she was impressed to see this friend of the Russian Revolution now resisting the Bolsheviks' attempt to turn the Italian mission into an instrument of Comintern policy. At a meeting held in the tsar's railway carriage, G. E. Zinoviev, who was by this time himself assuming the manners and demeanour of a tsar, failed to shift Serrati, who insisted that his mission had come without any political mandate 'to learn the truth about Russia'.[114]

The Bolsheviks then proceeded to split the mission in two. Just as they had earlier worked to separate Robert Williams as a true believer from the British Labour Delegation's more sceptical majority, they now concentrated their efforts on two of the Italian mission's weakest and most susceptible members: Nicola Bombacci, who would later become a fascist, and the bid-dable Professor Grasiadei. Balabanova watched as Zinoviev and his minions set out to seduce this pair with flattery and luxury, holding them back after the mission's departure from Russia, and then presenting them to Russian audiences as 'authentic representatives of the Revolution'. Unlike Serrati, who was dismissed as a traitor, these men proved to be compliant creatures: 'their speeches were translated into whatever Zinoviev wished them to say. They became completely inebriated with the ovations of the crowds and the flattery of Zinoviev's satraps'.[115]

A few months after the Italian delegation left, Balabanova saw the Bolsheviks' developing cult of personality take another turn for the worse with the arrival in Moscow of Winston Churchill's cousin, the glamorous sculptress and adventurer Clare Sheridan. This 'travelling salesman of the revolution'[116] had started her hero-worshipping series of Bolshevik busts in August 1920, sculpting Lev Kamenev and Leonid Krasin, both still in London as mem-bers of the Soviet trade mission. At Kamenev's suggestion, she followed him back to Moscow in September 1920, where she worried about the stench of the crowds in the theatres and added Lenin, Trotsky, Zinoviev, and Felix Dzerzhinsky to her collection. Angelica Balabanova, however, proved 'not any too amiable'[117] when approached by the English headhunter. This advo-cate of mass mobilization was plainly appalled by her idea of 'immortalising' the leadership of what appeared increasingly to be a usurping vanguard party, and she advised Sheridan to go off and find 'typical representatives from among the workers and peasants—particularly the working women whose suffering and heroism were expressed so graphically in their faces'.[118] Balabanova herself quit Russia at the end of 1921, moving to Vienna via Stockholm at roughly the same time as Alexander Berkman and Emma Goldman took their leave, using passports provided at the insistent request of German anarchists who, fearful of their prospects in Russia, had invited them to an International Anarchist Congress in Berlin.

An Invitation to British Workers

Winston Churchill, meanwhile, stood firm against all equivocation. He rebuffed his cousin Clare Sheridan, explaining that he had no desire to see her after her adventure with the 'Bolshevik butchers' in Moscow.[119] And there is nothing to indicate that, as Britain's Secretary of State for War, he felt anything but contempt for the British Labour Delegation with its attempt to soften the iron curtain by condemning both the admitted excesses of Bolshevism and the Allied policy of intervention and blockade, and to turn the tables on hostile critics in the manner employed by Ben Turner when he told *The Times*: 'some of [the Bolsheviks'] proposals regarding production and the abolition of the strike would gladden the heart of some employers of labour here, but they do not suit me or some of my colleagues'.[120]

As an unyielding enemy of Bolshevism, Churchill was altogether more at home with Lenin's 'Letter to the British Workers', brought home by Ben Turner and passed on to British Communists as requested. This entirely one-sided document, which called on British workers to waste no more time in precipitating the revolution, prompted him to issue another warrior's blast against the man who had reduced 'the noble and mighty Russian State and nation' to an 'enslaved, infected, starving and verminous Bedlam', and who now looked forward to establishing his murderous regime 'upon the ruins of the British Commonwealth'.[121] Having reissued his condemnation of the Germans for having sent Lenin and his fellow Bolsheviks back to Russia in a sealed train—'as poisoned gas is sent sealed in a cylinder'—he then recommended that Lenin's 'Letter to the British Workers' should be circulated as widely as possible in Britain: 'When the monster lifts his veil, descends from his throne of skulls, and starts writing political squibs to British working men, we get something about which any intelligent elector, man or woman, can form his own opinion.'

Churchill was unmoved by the 'Peace with Russia' demonstrations held around the country on 22 August 1920 (at the central demonstration in Trafalgar Square, George Lansbury hailed Lenin as 'a pure-hearted, noble-souled man').[122] He had nothing conciliatory to offer James H. Baum, the secretary of the Leicester and District Trades Council, who had written to Churchill a few weeks earlier, denouncing him as 'a menace to this country's welfare'[123] and insisting, with the help of evidence leaked from Moscow, that he had secretly agreed to supply troops to serve against Bolshevism alongside the White leader Kolchak in the Russian Civil War. 'All my life I have been opposing the crazy section of the Socialist Party',[124] Churchill told Baum, going on to insist that the Bolsheviks were 'doing their best to light the flames of war in Persia, Afghanistan and, if possible, in India. Their avowed intention is to procure by violence a revolution in every country.'[125] He would carry this lurid anti-Bolshevism straight into the general election of November 1922, in which he and a second National Liberal MP would lose Dundee to Prohibitionist and Labour candidates. The Labour Party's victor was none other than the unsuccessfully smeared E. D. Morel, the founder of the Union of Democratic Control, who had earlier remarked: 'I look upon Churchill as such a personal force for evil that I would take up the fight against him with a whole heart.'[126]

There can be no doubting the constancy of Churchill's position on Bolshevik Russia, which is more than can be said for Lenin's favourite member of the British Labour Delegation. Robert Williams had come home insisting that the British working class, far from being 'mere passive agents in the work of revolution', should 'definitely and finally overthrow those who live on rent, interest and profit'.[127] Yet he lost all credibility as a revolutionary trade union leader in April 1921. Poised to go on strike, the British miners had appealed for solidarity from the National Union of Railway Workers (NUR) and the United Transport Workers' Federation (UTWF), with which they had earlier formed a 'Triple Alliance'. At that moment their leader, Frank Hodges, had raised the possibility of a temporary settlement. He was acting without the authority of his membership but, on a day that would come to be known as 'Black Friday', Robert Williams caved in, together with Ernest Bevin (also of the UTWF) and J. H. Thomas of the NUR, and refused to initiate a strike. Shortly afterwards, Williams was kicked out of the British Communist Party as a class traitor. It was an outcome that satisfied Bertrand Russell, who records that, in his private meeting with Lenin, he had warned the Bolshevik leader of his disciple's unreliability.[128] Russell had passed his own immediate judgement on Bolshevik Russia while staying in Stockholm's Continental Hotel on the way home. 'Bolshevism', so he declared in a letter to Lady Ottoline Morrell, 'is a close tyrannical bureaucracy with a spy system more elaborated and terrible than the Tsar's, and an aristocracy as insolent and unfeeling, composed of Americanized Jews.'[129]

PART
IV

The Broken International
(1921–1927)

The commencement of the Second Congress of the Third
International, finally the unification of all peoples has been
realised, everything is clear: two worlds and a declaration of war.
We will be fighting endlessly. Russia has thrown down a challenge.
We will march to Europe to subjugate the world.

Isaac Babel, 1920 Diary, 8 August, 1920

Internationalism is just a word that sounds fine from a soap-box.
Nobody ever means it; not the Bolshevists either. Stay with your
own tribe.

B. Traven, *The Death Ship* (1926)

'Learn Esperanto,' said a Norwegian dramatist, with a mournful air.

Nikos Kazantzakis, *Toda Raba* (1929)

12

The View from Locarno

In March 1925, a flamboyant Bohemian artist visited Berlin, putting up at the British Embassy as a guest of the ambassador, Lord D'Abernon. Augustus John carried on as usual during his stay. He met the distinguished German-Jewish painter Max Liebermann, and inspected ancient frescoes recently excavated from collapsing caves in the Gobi Desert. He drank in the luxurious Hotel Adlon, just inside the Brandenburg Gate, as well as in a disreputable 'Bodega' where a young woman made off with his watch hidden in her stocking.[1]

Thanks to Lord D'Abernon's influence, John also found himself painting a portrait of 'the leading statesman of the new German Republic'. The Welsh artist would later recall liking Gustav Stresemann, writing that, though 'cast in no heroic mould', Germany's foreign minister and former chancellor 'presented none the less an interesting exterior. That square cranium housed a cultured mind, informed with the old German idealism.'[2] He would also record that, when confronted with his 'not in the least flattering' portrait, Stresemann 'faced it bravely' even though his beloved wife was plainly 'taken aback'.

Lord D'Abernon agreed that John's portrait made the Weimar Republic's great negotiator look 'devilishly sly, but extremely intelligent'.[3] Yet he had other reasons for attending the sittings. Pleased to be able to spend several hours talking with Stresemann, the ambassador was actually engaged in a process he named 'Diplomacy assisted by Art'.[4]

First Demilitarized Zone

Posted to Berlin in 1920, D'Abernon had seen defeated Germany teetering on the brink of collapse—starved, economically ruined, tempted by violent revolution and reaction alike. He had also initiated his own campaign to secure Germany's place in a new balance of power as, in the words of one historian, 'an ex-enemy whom it was desirable to treat with fairness and generosity in order to strengthen the elements making for peace in that country and in Europe generally'.[5]

In January 1923, the industrial areas of the Ruhr had been occupied by France, determined to extract unforthcoming reparations specified in the Treaty of Versailles. This greatly resented encroachment had been met with a policy of passive resistance in Germany, and there was concern about its consequences in France too. On 28 December 1923, Paul Reynaud, of the centre-right Alliance Démocratique, warned the Chamber of Deputies in Paris that, while the abandonment of reparations was plainly an impossibility, there was only danger in insisting that Germany pay, while at the same time 'lowering an iron curtain on the frontiers of unoccupied Germany'.[6] Such an approach would turn the occupied Ruhr into 'a port without a hinterland' and, by aggravating both Germany and Great Britain (which would fear for its markets in Germany), create 'eternal hate' and perhaps even 'a war of revenge'.

Two months later, in February 1924, D'Abernon had outlined his own, far less threatening proposal to Britain's newly elected Labour prime minister, Ramsay MacDonald. Formulated with a view to easing France's eventual withdrawal from the Ruhr, his idea was to reduce tensions by creating a demilitarized zone in the Rhineland. D'Abernon suggested that the area should be left under German administration, but governed by a mutual understanding that it was not to be used for any military purposes. In communication with the British leader, he likened his demilitarized Rhineland to 'an iron curtain between a stage and an auditorium', expressing the hope that while such an arrangement might not render a fire impossible, it would 'considerably reduce the danger'.[7] In September 1924, D'Abernon informed MacDonald that this idea of a 'reciprocal iron curtain'[8] seemed acceptable to Gustav Stresemann, even though the German leader had warned that France was likely to reject any such arrangement as greatly reducing its ability to assist and supply its Polish ally to the east of Germany.

Like his Chancellor of the Exchequer, Philip Snowden (and also other members of his minority government, including Arthur Henderson and Charles Trevelyan), Ramsay MacDonald had opposed the Great War as a member of the Union of Democratic Control. Though he had since distanced himself from the pacifism of that earlier period, in which he had once declared 'There is no halfway abiding-place between absolute peace and absolute militarism',[9] he was still predisposed to favour D'Abernon's idea of turning the iron curtain into a demilitarized zone that might be overseen by the recently founded League of Nations. Lord D'Abernon's proposal surely represented another imaginative recycling of redundant war materials. If tanks could be turned into 'snowcutters' on mountain roads in France,[10] and if adjusted torpedoes could be used to smuggle whisky across the Detroit river between Ontario in Canada and Michigan where prohibition ruled,[11] then the 'iron curtain' too might be converted to peaceable use.

By the end of the year, however, D'Abernon saw history sliding into reverse, and threatening to take his pacified 'iron curtain' with it. Britain's first Labour government had turned out considerably less forceful than the 'Socialist monstrosity'[12] anticipated by Winston Churchill. Indeed, after only eleven shaky months in power, it lost to the Conservatives in October 1924: a result that was influenced by the widely publicized accusations of such Tory anti-Communists as Lord Birkenhead[13] and Churchill (who rejoined the Conservatives in 1924 and won Epping in the October election), and also by the Conservative press's publication, four days before the polls closed, of the infamous 'Zinoviev letter', a forged document in which the chairman of the Communist International, G. E. Zinoviev, appeared to urge British Communists to stir up a revolution in Britain.

Lord D'Abernon may have felt his plans were relatively safe with Stanley Baldwin's speedily appointed Chancellor of the Exchequer. Yet if Winston Churchill thought that France should be left to 'stew in her own juice',[14] the new Foreign Secretary, Austen Chamberlain, seemed to favour the old idea of a pact between Britain and France: 'an anti-German defensive league' that would only perpetuate war animosities and divide Europe into 'two hostile groups'.[15] On 10 December, D'Abernon wrote to the British ambassador to Belgium, Sir George Grahame, declaring himself 'violently opposed' to any such development, and remarking that he was 'driven back therefore to the iron curtain idea which I think we have discussed, i.e. a fringe of territory or an imaginary line which neither side can traverse without becoming an aggressor'.[16] D'Abernon envisioned the iron curtain as a security device capable of calming tensions in preparation for a new balance of power, but Grahame replied that such a concept would only create suspicion. The French, he observed, 'would declare that behind the iron curtain which they were not allowed to traverse, Germany would be preparing a military tornado which when ready would burst upon France'.

This fact might effectively have finished off D'Abernon's vision of a mutually agreed 'iron curtain' between France and Germany, but the ambassador pressed on with a more elaborate proposal. On 29 December 1924, he had a meeting with Carl von Schubert, state secretary of the German Foreign Ministry, in which he urged the German authorities to consider advancing a new scheme based on the idea first advocated by their chancellor Cuno in 1922. This had sought to stabilize the Rhineland by means of a 'bilateral security pact' involving Italy and Britain as well as France and Germany. It was largely thanks to himself, so D'Abernon would claim, that this idea had been revised and put forward again in a memorandum sent to the British government on 20 January 1925.

Augustus John painted his portrait of Gustav Stresemann at a time when the German leader—who had successfully negotiated an easing of reparations under the Dawes Plan of mid-1924—was still affected by the rudely indifferent attitude with which Chamberlain and his civil servants had received this new approach.[17] John spoke no German, so D'Abernon and Stresemann were able to converse in complete confidence. The British ambassador claimed also to have been aided by John's insistence that his model, who was normally both quick to speech and inclined to monologue once started, must maintain 'immobility and comparative silence'. Taking advantage of 'the inhibitive gag of the artist',[18] D'Abernon used the sittings to work his way through Stresemann's reserve and encourage him to persist in his attempt to achieve international conciliation.

In the ambassador's version of these events, Augustus John's visit represented a crucial moment in the negotiations that would eventually lead to the Treaty of Locarno, signed in that Swiss resort at the end of 1925. This agreement, which committed Britain and Italy as guarantors of its settlement between Germany and France, was viewed with considerable optimism in its time. D'Abernon considered himself a primary architect of the agreement, and in this sense also a contributor to the 'Peace' with which Stresemann and the other leaders finally brought the Great War to a close.[19]

The West European Security Pact agreed at Locarno was considerably more elaborate than the simple Franco-German agreement proposed by D'Abernon at the beginning of 1924. However, the British ambassador claimed it as the direct descendant of his scheme. During the course of the negotiations, D'Abernon had noticed that Britain would gain nothing from the proposed pact, even though she, like Italy, would undertake to guarantee both France and Germany against aggression. With this in mind, he noted in his diary that

> so far no-one has brought forward the idea of guaranteeing the inviolability of the English Channel. Under the proposed Pact, England guarantees the security of both France and Germany against aggression, but obtains no increase of security herself. ... I remain convinced that the best protection to both France and Germany is the 'iron certain' idea, i.e. a neutralised zone, the crossing of which would constitute aggression. Could not the Channel be considered an 'iron curtain'?[20]

Nothing came of that particular scheme, but D'Abernon would muster other testimony to establish that his idea was indeed the inspiration behind Locarno. He quotes Carl von Schubert, who obligingly confirmed that the Locarno pact, which placed 'a barrier between France and Germany preventing either power from making war without becoming definitely the aggressor and so incurring the hostility of the civilised world', was indeed the 'same idea' as D'Abernon had proposed in December 1924.[21] He also reports Stresemann generously acknowledging his prescience in February 1926: 'I recollect so well when you spoke to me about the iron curtain idea. It was while I was sitting to Augustus John for my portrait. That gave precision to the negotiations.'[22]

Russia: Wrapped Again

By the mid-1920s, the 'iron curtain' that had descended between Germany and the Allies in August 1914 had softened sufficiently to be reimagined as a bilaterally agreed demilitarized zone: albeit one that offered only a flimsy illusion of security, as would be claimed by Georges Clemenceau and others who still wanted to confine Germany behind an 'impregnable wall'[23] of the kind that would soon enough be built as the heavily armoured Maginot Line.

Many, beside Lord D'Abernon, had welcomed Locarno in the expectation that it would lead to Germany's acceptance into membership of the League of Nations. Others, including some British Conservatives, approved it for pulling Germany into alignment with the Western Powers, thereby contributing to a new system of 'encirclement' that would isolate Soviet Russia (which did indeed react by promptly entering a mutual non-aggression treaty with Turkey in December 1925). The hope that Germany would be admitted into the League of Nations was cancelled when Brazil refused to vote in favour—perhaps prompted by the US government's fear of an anti-American coalition developing in Europe. At that point, in March 1926, Soviet Russia entered a non-aggression treaty with Germany too.

The final collapse of Locarno would not come until 1936, when Hitler repudiated the pact and reoccupied the Rhineland, leaving the British to ignore their guarantees to France. Long before then, however, disappointed internationalists had witnessed an alarming reappearance of the 'iron curtain' that Ethel Snowden had earlier found surrounding Soviet Russia.

The Allied blockade had been lifted in 1920, an Anglo-Russian trade agreement was established in 1921, and Soviet Russia had been formally recognized by Britain and later also by France in 1924. Yet the 'barrier of otherness' would be firmly back in place by the time Charles Roden Buxton made his second visit to Russia in the summer of 1927. Travelling on from Danzig (Gdansk), where they had attended the World Esperanto Congress, the Buxtons and their two grown-up children went at a time of renewed international tension that prompted Buxton to recall 'a phrase of Vernon Lee's about the "monstrous iron curtain" that falls between nations in time of war'.[24] Describing his journey for the Independent Labour Party's *New Leader*, he would regret that a 'similar' barrier had descended once again between Soviet Russia and Britain: 'Something of the same kind happens when diplomatic relations are broken off, when hostility is deliberately fostered by the Press on both sides, when prejudice grows and ignorance deepens in the absence of free intercourse and reciprocal knowledge.'

Buxton was referring to the Conservative government's severance, in May 1927, of Britain's diplomatic relations and trade agreements with Russia. Backed by the Trades Union Congress and followed by the dissolution of the recently formed Anglo-Russian Trade Union Unity Committee, this action reflected tensions that had been building since the demise of the first Labour government, which lost office before its recognition of Soviet Russia—communicated in a note issued on 1 February 1924—had been formally ratified.

Baldwin's Conservative government proved intransigent from the start. In February 1926, Sir Austen Chamberlain had presented the Soviet chargé d'affaires in London with a note complaining about Soviet instigation of attacks on British interests in China and elsewhere. Claiming that the Politburo's continuous onslaughts against the British Empire were in breach of propaganda clauses in the trade agreements of 1921 and 1923, the note cited hostile articles in *Izvestia,* including a 'grossly insulting and mendacious' cartoon in which Chamberlain himself was shown applauding the execution of Lithuanian Communists.[25] Some three months later, the strain was increased by Soviet financial aid (presented as donations from Russian trade unions) for workers involved in Britain's General Strike.

The breach of May 1927 was prompted by a police raid on the Russian trade delegation in Moorgate, London. A three-day search of the building failed to turn up the missing War Office document cited in justification of the raid. However, it did reveal, to the obvious satisfaction of the Home Secretary, Sir William Joynston-Hicks, that the Soviet organization, together with its trading company Arcos (All-Russian Co-operative Societies), was being used—as Churchill had predicted in 1920—as a base for subversive activities extending through the British Empire. Recently released government documents leave no doubt that the Soviet Union was guilty, even if not exactly as charged.[26] At the time, though, many on the left (and not just Communist sympathizers) saw the raid as yet another provocation perpetrated by a Tory government that had come to power by blackguarding the Labour Party in October 1924, and then gone on—sustained by the inflammatory rhetoric of Winston Churchill—to turn its fire on the General Strike of May 1926.

Charles Roden Buxton was among those who refused to countenance the government's accusations against the Russian trade delegation. Being primarily concerned to de-escalate tension between Britain and Russia, he confined his condemnation of the Arcos raid to the anti-Bolshevik propaganda that attended the British action. As he would write, whilst looking back on these events a couple of years later:

> When I think of the fantastic travesty of Russia which is conveyed to the unfortunate British public by men such as Mr. Winston Churchill and Lord Birkenhead, I feel that my humdrum powers of expression fail me. The thing is at once too dreadful, and too comic, for me to handle. I fume in impotence, and end by hoping against hope that another Swift may some day be raised among us, and the lightning shafts of Satire may pierce and dissipate the poisoned mist that surrounds us.[27]

Buxton saw the reinstated iron curtain between Russia and the West as an instrument of barely restrained warfare: by isolating the peoples on both sides, and plunging them into confusion, misunderstanding, and suspicion, it worked as a cause of rising international tensions. On this basis his call for a new Jonathan Swift may have been justified. However, the 'lightning shafts' of this hypothetical satirist would surely soon have strayed far from the stock figures of Churchill and Lord Birkenhead (by now the Tory government's fiercely anti-Bolshevist Secretary of State for India). Indeed, the confusions generated around the relowered iron curtain would ensure that, when fired by the satirists who duly rose to the occasion, their missiles found many appropriate targets in the prognostications of Russia's liberal and socialist visitors: people like the Buxtons themselves.

An Assisted Passage

Trains, planes, telephones ... The 1920s were a time of rapidly improving communication technologies and yet, as Hans Magnus Enzensberger once pointed out, the barriers between Communist Russia and the capitalist world gave new currency to the anachronistic system of the traveller's eyewitness account.[28] For those Westerners who mistrusted both the propaganda of their own governments and the fiercely biased claims of the capitalist press, much would depend on reports brought back from the other side by assorted 'tourists of the revolution'.

Though often grossly ignorant of the USSR and its languages, the wanderers who made up this 'pre-industrial messenger service'[29] in the first, comparatively open years of the decade, were inclined to present themselves as 'detectives' seeking out the 'truth' about a wildly misrepresented new world.[30] Some came back to feed the Western left's insatiable appetite for 'concrete utopias', while others were intent on reassuring more liberal-minded readers that Russia remained a backward and 'semi-Asiatic' country, and that its revolution was consequently not to be feared as a prefiguration of the European (even less the American) future. Convinced anti-Bolsheviks, meanwhile, sought out picturesque illustrations of the evils of the Soviet regime, exemplified by the 'proletarian poodle' glimpsed on the streets of Moscow in the summer of 1921. Once carefully frizzled, shaved, and cosseted by its vanished bourgeois owner, this derelict creature was now on its own: weighed down by filthy and matted black hair but still fit for exhibition as perhaps 'the saddest sight in all Moscow'.[31]

Though impressed by the visionary gleam in George Lansbury's eye, Lenin and the early Bolsheviks had scarcely been inclined to portray Communist Russia as an achieved island utopia. Foreign sympathizers might continue to kiss the soil as they crossed the frontier in that spirit, yet it was actually in a very different sense that Buxton's iron curtain made utopians of Soviet Russia's Western visitors. With its cancellation of 'free intercourse and reciprocal knowledge', it created a situation in which visiting investigators had little on which to base their assessment of Soviet Russia except the fleeting occasions when the script in their heads seemed suddenly to correlate with the appearances passing before their eyes. Whether their minds were filled with a sense of revulsion or with passionate anticipation of the redemption to come, the risk of error was at its highest at precisely such moments of apparent recognition. As for the idea that reality might intrude to contradict or merely moderate the perceptions of the more visionary pilgrims, the record amply confirms Jacques Rancière's observation that 'the spectacle of reality disillusions the missionaries of utopia only very rarely. More often they go back home because they are tired of walking so much.'[32]

The explorers of the mid-1920s found the Soviet frontier reinforced from the Russian side, and much improved in its symbolic aspect too. By the end of 1924, a year that had opened with the death of Lenin on 21 January, sympathizers entering Russia from Latvia had been able to kiss the soil next to a 'specially constructed arch', adorned with red cloth and slogans prophesying international solidarity and the fast-coming day when the Communist economy would eliminate its capitalist rival from the world.[33] Western travellers taking the international train from Poland also approached the frontier station as if it were the gateway to a great Enigma, and the land beyond a mythical prospect that inspired chaotically mixed thoughts of Eldorado, Gomorrah, Paestum with its ancient Greek ruins, and the 'Icarie' of nineteenth-century French socialist utopianism.[34]

What they actually discovered at Negoreloye was a new customs house, built of huge logs and equipped with bright red curtains—a heated and well-lit structure that impressed one French visitor as having the air of a 'provisional exhibition' of the revolution, despite the official who went through his luggage and, without a word of explanation, confiscated two books by Maxim Gorki, who was then still living in Italy.[35] Such was the condition of the trains laid on for international visitors that even a thoroughly convinced anti-Bolshevist, such as the former *Daily Telegraph* correspondent and Tory MP Ellis Ashmead-Bartlett, would concede that the Russian *wagon-lit* was still more comfortable than its narrow-gauge equivalent in the West: perhaps 'the only institution in Russia which has stood every assault of Communism, without changing a single iota'.[36]

By 1927, help was at hand, even for the more sceptical visitor. Soviet Russia was seeking to manage its contact with the West through measures of 'cultural diplomacy' (defined by an early analyst as 'the manipulation of cultural materials and personnel for propaganda purposes').[37] This entailed a considerable projection of revolutionary culture into the West, where much excitement would be generated by Soviet theatre, dance, art, literature, newsreels, and also avant-garde film-making, with directors such as Eisenstein and Pudovkin being feted as they followed their epics on regular visits.[38] Students would gaze at Mayakovsky's revolutionary posters or watch the Odessa steps scene in Eisenstein's *Battleship Potemkin,* and abandon their career plans for the life of the dedicated revolutionary. It looked like 'the beginning of a brilliant new era'[39]—even without Alexandra Kollontai's advocacy of sexual emancipation in the New Russia, in which, to Lenin's dismay, love-making was famously declared as natural as 'drinking a glass of water'.

Besides encouraging the Western travels of Mayakovsky, Ehrenburg, and other cultural ambassadors, the Soviet authorities had formalized the delegation system, through which they hoped to ensure that foreign visitors to Russia were flattered and indulged, and their attention confined, far more effectively than had been achieved with the delegations of 1920, to the painted side of the scenery. Intourist, which provided guided visits for the 'ordinary tourist and minor intellectual', would not emerge from the Travel Bureau of the Soviet Merchant Fleet until 1929.[40] Before then, however, many cultural visitors were invited and chaperoned by the All-Union Society for Cultural Relations with Foreign Countries (VOKS), set up in 1925 with a statement of aims alleged to have been carried over from an abortive attempt to establish a Russian-American Club.[41] Other guests were invited and guided around by the All-Union Central Council of Trade Unions, and the Union of Soviet Writers. Some condemned these reception agencies as worse than useless. However, the Frenchman Henri Béraud found VOKS so efficient in hunting up compliant teachers, Arabists, naturalists, or whoever else their foreign guests declared a wish to meet, that he compared it to the famous London department store (presumably Harrods), which promised immediately to find its customers an elephant, a kingfisher's feather, or any other exotic item they might wish to order.[42]

The Soviet authorities had also been busy with the legacy of Prince Potemkin. As was noted by the French observer Alfred Fabre-Luce, Catherine the Great's lover had been converted into a battleship and then, after the sailors mutinied in 1905, into a celebrated propaganda film by Sergei Eisenstein (1924).[43] Yet for those who hated and opposed the Soviet regime, the 'Potemkin villages' continued to figure largest. Repeatedly warned that his journey could never be anything but a 'Potemkin voyage', Fabre-Luce insisted that the critical spirit was not so easily defeated: even in factories and textile mills chosen to impress foreigners, the outdated foreign machinery and the high levels of absenteeism ensured that the vices of the regime 'exploded' before the onlooker's eyes.[44] His optimism in this regard would not have impressed Mr Ostermeyer, a Hamburg baker who had visited Soviet Russia with a party of German workers, and, in February 1927, protested that this so-called 'second German delegation' had been controlled by Communist members and, despite its requests to the contrary, only allowed to visit approved and prepared sites: 'the delegation was only shown Potemkin Villages'.[45]

The Austrian writer Stefan Zweig might have hesitated too. In 1928, he would spend two weeks in Russia, having been invited to participate in the centenary celebrations of Tolstoy's birth. Though wafted through the country on 'waves of warmth', he was able to resist the 'magic intoxication' that had led so many delegates to applaud the regime, thanks partly to a letter he found secretly slipped into his pocket after a group of students led him back to his hotel.[46] 'Don't believe everything you are told,' it warned: 'Do not forget that with all that they show you there is much that is not shown you. Remember that most of the people who talk to you do not say what they wish to say, but only what they may tell you. We are all watched and you yourself no less.'[47] People were certainly being deceived and, as Zweig came to suspect during a visit to a factory, it wasn't always the Western delegates. A proud worker showed his party an industrial sewing machine and uttered the word 'Electric'. He then stood there and watched Zweig 'in expectation of wonderment and admiration', as if visitors from Europe and America could never have seen such an astonishing thing: as if, indeed, electricity was the transforming power of revolution itself and sewing machines had been invented by 'the little fathers Lenin and Trotsky'.[48]

Some anti-Bolshevik visitors actually maintained a considerable investment in the idea of Soviet Russia as a land of systematically manipulated appearances. It enabled them to display their own critical acumen in seeing through the sham, and also to emphasize how thoroughly more sympathetic Western visitors were duped. A typical example of the latter accusation was provided by the British journalist and former guild socialist C. E. Bechhofer, who had gone to Russia in 1921 to report on the famine and drought then engulfing the countryside. Bechhofer spent much of his time visiting Samara and other straitened places on the Volga, but it was in Moscow that he encountered 'Mr Jock Mills of Dartford', a member of the Labour Party and a *Daily Herald* journalist, who announced, provocatively, 'There is complete liberty in this country.'[49] Having arrived in the city by train earlier that same day, Mills had, so Bechhofer reported, formed his unassailable conviction with the help of a Bolshevik minder who had driven him past the old Anarchist Club and assured him, as the building obligingly slid by, that anti-Bolshevik literature was indeed freely published and sold there.

In 1920, the show institutions had been presented as prefigurative and future-orientated projects designed to provide visitors with a glimpse of the world as it might be once redeemed by Communism.[50] Two or three years later, the Soviet authorities would be found guilty of scene-building of a grander and altogether more manipulative kind. They had, so Professor Charles Sarolea of Edinburgh University judged in 1923, learned to make full use of American propaganda and publicity techniques of the kind pioneered by Walter Lippmann and others convinced of the need for scientific 'mastery' of public opinion,[51] and were now magnifying their displays for the benefit of internal audiences as well as of the foreign visitors who were themselves routinely exhibited to the 'credulous Russian' as if they were all ardent admirers of the Soviet dictatorship.[52]

Hotels remained part of the regime's *mise-en-scène*, filled not just with potted plants, but with workers who were actually secret police spies—including the notorious Mr Fine at the Savoy Hotel in Moscow, who would be likened to a 'Venetian senator' by the French novelist Paul Morand.[53] The opera houses and theatres were also generating impressions as usual: the audiences may no longer have been so filthy as 'the great unwashed' who, in 1920, had 'neutralised' Mrs Clare Sheridan's evening of dramatic pleasure with their 'concentrated aroma',[54] but they remained sufficiently proletarian to leave Ellis Ashmead-Bartlett reaching for the obvious British comparison (it was, he concluded, as if London's great opera houses had been 'invaded by hordes from the East End').[55]

Soviet methods of street-cleansing had also been extended far beyond the controversial measures of 1919/20, which had obliged householders to clear the snow blocking the road outside their properties. Far from being abolished, Russia's notorious drunkenness had been swept out of view—confined to the home or to the ubiquitous beer-houses that foreign tourists never entered. Likewise, the abandoned and orphaned children (*bezprizorny*) who roamed the streets 'like packs of wolves': they were said to have caused such a public scandal that 'a clean sweep was made in Moscow and Leningrad of these young wolf-cubs. God knows what has become of them.'[56]

The parades, meanwhile, had become grander and more spectacular: especially the annual 7 November celebrations of the Bolshevik revolution, which were no longer 'dwarfed' by their surroundings as H. G. Wells had reported in 1920, even though, in Ashmead-Bartlett's words, the glum banner-bearing crowds 'resembled automata' and the whole performance could be unintentionally threatened by a single fashionably dressed English girl. 'Miss B', who happened to be stopping over in Moscow during a train journey to the Far East, accompanied Ashmead-Bartlett as he walked into Red Square to see the celebrations of November 1928. Resplendent in her lynx fur, silk stockings, and brilliant patent leather shoes, this golden-haired 'mannequin from Bond Street' loudly asked 'Who was Lenin?' as she scrutinized the late Bolshevik leader's then still wooden mausoleum. Dressed as if for Cup Day at Ascot, she drew such excited attention from the otherwise expressionless crowds that the visitors were quickly ordered out of the square and obliged to retreat to their rooms in the Savoy Hotel.[57]

As hostile commentators pointed out, the Soviet authorities had started lavishing resources on vast public exhibitions, designed for internal as well as external consumption. One example, which the admittedly 'hypercritical' Professor Sarolea judged 'as wonderful as any Potemkin village', was devoted to the electrification schemes ('electrifictions' as their early critics called them) announced by Lenin in the chaotic conditions of December 1920.[58] Soviet electrification had, for years, oscillated between vast promise and paltry reality. Alexander Wickstead, a British Quaker, recalls a rumour that, in the early days, 'there was in Moscow a large building that bore an enormous sign stating that it was the home of the "Commission for the Electrification of All Russia"; on the door was pinned a small notice "Please knock, as the bell doesn't work"'.[59]

For Professor Sarolea, however, the major attraction in Moscow during the summer of 1923 had been the All-Russian Agricultural Exhibition. The materials may have been commandeered on the old Bolshevist principle, and the unpaid builders threatened with jail if they pushed their complaints too far. However, even sceptics among the specially invited foreign visitors felt obliged to admit that 'the completion of the vast exhibition buildings within a few months was a triumph of rapid and efficient organisation', and the result 'as striking as any Potemkin village under the old régime'.[60] Foreign visitors mixed with hundreds of thousands of children and peasants, sent to Moscow from the hungry countryside at their own villages' expense, and marched along walls covered with the statistics and diagrams that had become so characteristic of the USSR's self-presentation. There was a special 'House of Lenin', in which 'the gospel according to Saint Marx' was expounded, but Sarolea was more disconcerted by the sight of a vast pictorial flowerbed, arranged on a slope with its blossoms forming a 'gigantic portrait' of Lenin: 'They have made Lenin into a flower-bed; they have made Nature herself an accomplice in his glorification.'[61]

13

Snapshots from a Land of Contrasts

Ten years after the revolution, some Western visitors were still reluctant to grant the status of reality to Russia's outward show. Among them was the German cultural theorist Walter Benjamin. He was in Moscow, staying with his Bolshevik lover, Asja Lacis, from December 1926 to February 1927. Writing about the experience, this recent convert to Marxism insisted that visitors would get nowhere by 'observing' events as outsiders: it was necessary, instead, to 'take a position while you are in the midst of them'.[1] Benjamin agonized over his own inability to meet this requirement ('it is not possible for me to get involved'), but he would nevertheless restate the case after returning to Berlin:

> the only real guarantee of a correct understanding is to have chosen your position before you came. In Russia, above all, you can only see if you have already decided. At the turning point in historical events that is indicated, if not constituted, by the fact of 'Soviet Russia', the question at issue is not which reality is better, or which has greater potential. It is only: which reality is inwardly convergent with truth? Which truth is inwardly preparing itself to converge with the real? Only he who clearly answers these questions is 'objective'. Not towards his contemporaries (which is unimportant) but toward events (which is decisive). Only he who, by decision, has made his dialectical peace with the world can grasp the concrete. But someone who wishes to decide 'on the basis of facts' will find no basis in the facts.[2]

Less philosophical travellers would be more simply troubled by the thought that the visible 'facts' of the situation in Russia could not be correlated with a 'truth' that might actually turn out to be no more 'dialectical' than blind faith or, as time went on, the desperate sloganeering with which adherents sought to justify the latest turn of the Communist International's vagrant party line. More than two decades later, Arthur Koestler would write of 'a haze of dialectical mirages which masked the world of reality'.[3] Yet by the mid-1920s, there were already achieved realities as well as future potentialities to be faced.

Playing to Two Galleries

The confusions awaiting those who crossed the iron curtain in this period were well characterized by Ante Ciliga, a Croatian/Yugoslavian Communist who had himself moved to 'the Land of the Disconcerting Lie' in 1926. As this freethinking leftist opponent would point out after spending many years in Stalin's jails, foreign observers were now inclined to see Soviet Russia only in its 'contrast' with the more 'static' capitalist regimes on their own side. Trapped in this theatre of polarized images, they failed to acquire a perspective that would reveal the true dynamics of Soviet society, and their impressions therefore consisted only of superficial 'snapshots'.[4] This charge might have been raised against anti-Bolshevik visitors but Ciliga was actually thinking of people with views closer to his own.

The lockstep Communists of the 1920s liked to measure their own 'hard-boiled' certainty against the sloppy inconstancy of democratic socialists who, lacking a zealous dogma to bring them down firmly on the Russian side, were left swaying about between worlds and in (at least) two minds about the works of the Soviet regime.

Such was the contrast drawn by Freda Utley, a recent graduate of the London School of Economics who visited Russia in the summer of 1927 with a delegation of the University Labour Federation. She recalls how Russians repeatedly asked her: 'Why is it that so many English Labour people come here and say things are going splendidly with us and then go home and say the opposite?'[5] It was a question that had also exercised the Soviet leadership after the departure of the first British Labour Delegation. In September 1920, Trotsky furiously threatened Clare Sheridan with dire consequences if, like so many other foreign 'friends', she started spouting calumnies about Bolshevism as soon as she was back on the other side.[6] Maxim Litvinov would later make the same objection to Ellis Ashmead-Bartlett, declaring his preference for a 'consistent reactionary' over wind-blown foreign visitors who profess to be friends while in Russia but 'go home to say the worst they can about us'.[7] Indeed, Ashmead-Bartlett was not the only such unyielding 'open enemy' of the USSR whom the acting

Commissar for Foreign Affairs preferred to two-faced socialists: 'Why don't Churchill and Birkenhead visit our country? They have nothing to fear. We would give them the time of their lives.'[8]

Freda Utley's assault on vacillating Labour Party tourists was a way of declaring the cadres of the Communist Party of Great Britain, which she had already resolved to join on her return, to be heroically constant: pro-Soviet in all places and despite all challenges. It was also a little English reflection of Stalin's insistence, to be fought out with appalling consequences in Germany and elsewhere, that 'social democracy' rather than fascism was the main enemy of the Communist International.

Whether or not they were spineless opportunists, as their Communist rivals repeatedly charged, there can be little question that socialists with a liberal conscience suffered confusions of their own as they set out to penetrate the reinstated 'iron curtain' while refusing to accept 'reality' as it was configured on either side of the ideological divide. In 1927, these difficulties were exemplified as well by the Buxtons as by anyone else.

As a member of the Labour Party, which had closed its ranks to Communists under Ramsay MacDonald in 1924, Charles Roden Buxton stood at a distance from the fervent members of the Communist International. Yet he and his wife had found Russia in relatively prosperous shape as they travelled through it in the summer of 1927. Manufactured goods were still in short supply, but the private enterprise allowed under the New Economic Policy (introduced by Lenin but vigorously opposed by Trotsky and his fellow left oppositionists in the Soviet Communist Party) had filled the markets with fruit, vegetables, and dairy products. Severe shortages would be reported before the end of the year, but the Buxtons found bread in the shops, and not just black rye bread of the kind that had so effectively devastated the constitutions of the British Labour delegates of 1920.

These may have been comparatively 'easy times'[9] in Soviet Russia. Yet Buxton still found himself surrounded by evidence of the 'horrible warping of opinion which is caused, on both sides, by political controversy'.[10] Visiting a Workers' Club in the suburbs of Moscow, he was mildly amused to come across a shooting gallery in which Britain's Conservative Secretary of State for Foreign Affairs, Sir Austen Chamberlain, was lined up as an open-mouthed target between a tsarist general and a bloated capitalist. He found a more detailed Soviet portrayal of the newly exacerbated division on a Volga steamer. The left-hand side of this prominently displayed poster was red, and represented the heroic achievements of Bolshevik Russia. The right side was yellow, and enumerated the many crimes of the war-fomenting British: the troops landing at Murmansk in 1918; the setting up of a sham government at Archangel; the shooting of Commissars by British troops in Baku in 1919. The first Labour government's recognition of Soviet Russia was acknowledged, but 'English mercenaries' (Buxton added 'sic' by this phrase), were alleged to have been behind the murder of two Soviet ambassadors: Vatslav Vorovsky in Lausanne, 1923; and Pyotr Voikov in Warsaw in June 1927. There was no quarter for the anti-Bolshevist leader of the British Labour Party, Ramsay MacDonald, denounced as 'an extreme opportunist, and a social traitor'.

As this inventory of imperialist evil showed, a 'very vigorous and intensive' anti-British campaign was under way in Soviet Russia in 1927, and Buxton found the illusions it promoted to be every bit as fantastic as those projected by anti-Soviet propaganda in the West. At the heart of the Soviet message was the assertion that Britain was organizing a 'Bloc' against Russia, with a view to leading an imminent anti-Soviet war. Majority and 'Opposition' factions within the Russian Communist Party had disputed whether this vividly imagined prospect was real or a disconnected 'hallucination', as Buxton himself judged it to be. Both knew, however, that 'the fear of external attack, whether well-grounded or not, is a convenient means of rallying the people, as it always does in similar cases, around the Government of the day'.

Buxton was determined not to take up any position on the crazily pivoted see-saw of 'Bolshevism versus anti-Bolshevism'. Having used his improving Russian to talk with newspaper sellers, railway and construction workers, peasants, clerks, teachers, and keepers of those reassuringly ubiquitous little fruit and vegetable stalls, he was pleased to report that the Russian people, like their British counterparts, 'long to penetrate the curtain'. Such was his premiss: 'Owing to the breaking off of diplomatic relations, the two peoples are drifting into deeper and deeper ignorance of one another's concerns.'[11] Diplomatic, economic, and cultural relations must be resumed and further developed if the contrary propagandas were to be overcome and the hostility between the opposed systems was not to escalate further towards war. Freer exchange would enable the peoples on either side of the iron curtain to reach a much better understanding than their polarized governments allowed.

This analysis differs significantly from that developed by Mrs Dorothy Buxton, who came home from the same trip to write about the Russia she had seen from the point of view of Quakerism. Mrs Buxton was a distinguished humanitarian yet, in *The Challenge of Bolshevism*,[12] she demonstrated that

Christian idealism could be a blinding liability. She declared herself most impressed by the 'moral advance' the Communists were trying to establish. They were to be commended for restoring the 'sympathy' that had been destroyed in the capitalist world, and even for having driven Russia and her people back to the bare fact of life itself—a course that impressed Mrs Buxton not as a terrifying reduction of humanity to abject survival under the state, but as a return to the raw material from which 'a new social idea' was being moulded.[13] Other Western visitors might recoil from the 'drabness' of Russian clothing, but Mrs Buxton, who felt a Quaker loathing of extravagance (as well as a feminist hatred of Western women's hats in particular), commended Communism for its abolition of fashion, which she declared 'an absolute tyranny in our Western civilisation'. 'What lady', after all, 'would venture to walk down Regent Street in an overall[?]'[14]

Such imperfections as Dorothy Buxton came across in Russia served to remind her of the blind eye that capitalist regimes turned on their own faults. For her, indeed, to visit Russia in 1927 was not just to be racked by the sense of class guilt and even masochism that would compel so many Western fellow-travellers in the 1930s.[15] It was to become aware of the 'spiritual prison' in which the capitalist states confined their subjects. It was to recognize that 'the Society ... into which one is born inevitably does most of one's thinking for one' and, indeed, to welcome the destruction of one's inherited sense of judgement. Though different from one-eyed Stalinism, this was no closer to the attitude of a truly 'independent spirit' of the kind commended by Romain Rolland in his opposition to the Great War. Nor did it much resemble the outlook of those among the members of the Union of Democratic Control who had insisted, despite their extreme unpopularity at the beginning of the Great War, on doing their thinking for themselves.

Aware that some of her readers were likely to be surprised to find how thoroughly impressed this Quaker humanitarian had been by Soviet Russia, Dorothy Buxton explained that by crossing from the capitalist system to its Communist rival she had broken the ideological chains that 'Society' had placed even in her dissenting and well-travelled mind:

> But why did I need a journey in the USSR to awaken me to such facts? I think it was the psychological result of crossing a frontier which reversed the position of a vast number of received ideas; the commonplaces and dogmas on the familiar side of the frontier had become the heresies of the land beyond; and the ideas scorned and rejected on the familiar side, on the other were found to be controlling life's daily practices.

This disorientating 'reversal' of values, through which what was judged good on one side reappeared as evil on the other, may help to explain some of the more exotically appalling errors made by Westerners who visited Russia in the inter-war years. In setting herself so strongly against the auto-mated thinking that Western society 'does for one', Mrs Buxton put her own judgement on the line at the very moment she plunged herself into a welter of powerfully unfamiliar impressions. Her confusion confirms Ante Ciliga's warning about the danger of building a picture of Soviet Russia through 'contrast' alone.[16]

Like his wife (and, for that matter, many other 'tourists of the revolu-tion'), Charles Roden Buxton projected his own desires and preferences onto the sliding surfaces of Soviet life. As an admirer of Virgil, Dante, and Goethe, he praised the 'intense seriousness' of Russian reading habits, noting that there was 'hardly a trace of light or frivolous literature of any kind'. He recognized that, in their anticipation of an imminent 'World Revolution', the Soviet newspapers presented a picture of the world that was distorted 'to an almost incredible degree'; and yet, as a veteran of the Union of Demo-cratic Control who had struggled for years to free the British public from war chauvinism, he was impressed to find that these same papers expected Soviet citizens to maintain a serious interest in economics and international affairs.

As for the children living wild on the streets, whose presence had sup-ported one of the oldest and most familiar 'distortions on our side', he insisted they had been orphaned by the famine of 1921/2 and not just by the state's premature closure of orphanages. Undoubtedly, abandonment imposed a terrible degradation, especially on the girls among this alarming population. Yet, in his attempt to counter Western representations, Buxton also ventured the apologetic remarks that would be quoted against him by opponents at home. He suggested it was 'a point of honour' with the homeless children to 'wear rags that will only just hold together', that 'many people like to be beggars', and, moreover, that in Russia 'people like to be begged from. It is a simple and easy method of exercising charity.'[17]

Buxton did not join his wife in asserting that Russian Communism was striving towards true democracy rather than the 'sham' version established in the capitalist West. Indeed, he declared the 'theoretic materialism' espoused by the Bolsheviks to be 'a doctrine so fantastically impossible as an explan-ation of the world, that it cannot possibly endure'. He also assured readers of *Labour Magazine* that he had come home no more of a communist after this second visit than he had ever been before. Huge gains had been made since the starvation and famine of 1921/2, but they had been won at 'a terrible price'—ongoing political repression, arbitrary arrests, a lack of free speech and information—that would never be acceptable in Britain.

Yet everything is ghosted by its opposite when reality is divided by an 'iron curtain', and Buxton's bright and optimistic descriptions of Russia and her truth-seeking people were like painted leaves floating on contrary currents of political calculation. While in Russia, he had tried to reduce tension by countering the Bolshevik regime's allegations of imminent British attack. At home in London, where he hoped the Labour Party would encourage an official rapprochement with the USSR, he was careful to avoid saying anything that might feed anti-Bolshevist suspicions. He wrote about his journey as if it had been an ordinary family holiday, giving no indication how he went about securing unusual permissions from the Soviet authorities, and taking care not to advertise the fact that, in Moscow, he and his family were entertained by Maxim Litvinov.[18]

One of Buxton's articles about the visit was published in the *Socialist Review,* but not before a line had been put through the paragraph in which he described the activities of the Soviet secret police, who took advantage of the Buxtons' excursion into the countryside to go through their luggage and scrutinize their notebooks and papers. This deletion was made even though Buxton had dutifully blamed this unjustified interference on continued Western hostility thanks to which, so he had suggested in the excised paragraph, the fight against 'counter-revolution—with all its results in political repression and the absence of free speech—has to continue in full force ten years after the Revolution'.

Buxton's policy of calling down a plague on the propaganda machines of both states entailed treating the governing regimes on both sides as if they were mirror images of one another, equivalent in their sinfulness and in the mendacity of their propaganda machines. This tendency to equalize responsibility while attributing it to states rather than people, may have been inherited from Vernon Lee's Anglo-German 'iron curtain', through which Britain and Germany were indeed constructed as identically guilty warring empires. That equivocation would become altogether more contorted when the curtain fell between democracy and dictatorship, reform and revolution, the rule of law and absolute state power. Under these circumstances, the claim to impartiality did indeed become a front, which made it easier for Buxton to blame the imperfections of the Soviet Union on British aggression, and to advance his primary aim, which was to bring about a restoration from the British side of peaceable relations with the Soviet Union.

There would be no escaping from the polar oppositions of the iron curtain without the help of a third term, a horizontal axis which could provide a standpoint outside the theatre of contrasts and schismatic polemic. Many versions would be tried over the decades of East–West division—Humanitarianism, Democracy, Charity, Human Rights, Justice, Literature, Science, Peace, even Folk Music would be mobilized—and all would become ideological salients as they were claimed and fought over by both sides.

For Charles Roden Buxton, like Vernon Lee before him, the key lay in valuing 'people' as distinct from their bellicose states. The photographs taken by his son, David Roden Buxton, as they wandered through villages around the upper Volga, leave no doubt that the Buxtons experienced vivid and moving encounters. They sat in a horse-drawn 'tarantass' smiling at the curious peasants gathered outside the ancient log buildings of their new 'Kollectiv'. They stood among fascinated children in the same spirit of friendliness, and watched as women winnowed grain and carried water up from the well with wooden yokes and metal pails. In Sokolischchi, they met a picturesque old village carpenter, who showed them the coffin he had made for himself and kept ready in the roofbeams overhead.

These photographs may have been considerably more revealing than 'snapshots' of the merely contrasting kind condemned by Ante Ciliga. Yet, as Charles Roden Buxton expressed it in 1927, his commitment to 'people' on both sides inevitably also involved a retreat into abstraction. At that time, it was only by lifting his 'people' out of history, and gathering them into an undivided and more or less spiritualized idea of humanity, that Buxton could avoid taking sides between the opposed political and economic systems in which they lived.

And taking sides in this manner was something he adamantly refused to do. Rehearsing arguments that he and others had previously made against the exclusive patriotism of the nation state, Buxton argued that it was no longer possible to conduct foreign affairs on the assumption that one country has absolutely no concern in the 'internal affairs of another'.[19] The founding premiss of the Labour and Socialist International (the post-war successor to the Second International and a democratic reformist rival of the Communist International) was that 'the exploited sections of each community have a common interest, and are fighting, up to a certain point, the self-same battle. We see no reason in principle, for example, why the Socialist Party of one country should not assist the Socialist Party of another. The limits to such a policy are limits of practical expediency, not of principle.' Yet this was only part of his point, since it had become abundantly apparent in the era of the iron curtain that the actions of one country could certainly 'affect the internal concerns of another, but not in the crude way that is so often supposed'. It had to be realized that 'in every country, there are two parties at least, and all depends upon the effect of our action upon this delicate "internal" balance. What matters, in other words, is the things which we give to the rulers of the other country to say to their own people—the arguments which we place in their hands.'

As a Quaker, Buxton may have felt bound to insist that expressions of hostility were entirely counterproductive, and yet he was also correct in identifying this particular deadlock. Expressions of hostility might indeed play directly into the hands of the 'enemy' state when relayed across an iron curtain lowered between opposed regimes, both of which use state propaganda to create a 'poison mist' around their own people. During the post-revolutionary period, the Allied blockade of Russia had turned the Bolshevik leaders into the representatives of a Russian patriotism they had previously only despised. And it was the same again ten years later, when the British broke off diplomatic relations and trade agreements with Russia:

> If, for example, the Russian rulers can say, 'England is inevitably hostile—and the proof is that she has broken off relations, and discredits us throughout the world in every way she can', then they are enabled to weaken all those sections of opinion in Russia itself which are moderate in their views of foreign policy. It strengthens the position of all those who wish to maintain the worst features of Bolshevism. These can justify a suspicious attitude abroad and a political tyranny at home, on the ground that 'England is organising a bloc against Soviet Russia, designed to lead an anti-Soviet war.' They can justify propaganda on the ground that it is 'hitting back' for the antagonism shown by us. They can justify armaments, on the ground that Russia has nothing but her own strong arm to rely on.[20]

British Idiocy 1: the Trade Union Delegation of 1924

'There does not exist a single truth which we should smother for tactical reasons'. So the ex-Communist Manès Sperber proclaimed early in 1953, while condemning those members of the Western left who railed against

McCarthyism in the United States but—true to 'the logic of the struggle'—found nothing to say against tyranny behind the Iron Curtain.[21] That was a hard-won lesson of the 1930s, and one with which Buxton himself might have struggled in 1927.

Buxton's attention to the symbolic play of power between the two sides of his 'iron curtain' distinguished him from the Cyclopean partisans of the Comintern. However, it also exposed him to 'tactical' considerations that complicated his attachment to the single 'truth' about Soviet Russia. The world was divided between polarized political systems, and so too were the audiences that Buxton felt obliged to address as he set out to ease tensions. In his endeavour to convince the British Labour Party of the wisdom of re-establishing trade and diplomatic relations with Russia, Buxton would emphasize how much the labour movement had done to build 'reciprocal' understanding between Britain and the USSR. Writing for circulation within the Labour Party, he cited the demonstrations 'held under Labour auspices' in August 1920, when the British government, and Winston Churchill in particular, seemed to threaten Soviet Russia with war in response to the Red Army's soon to be reversed advance on Warsaw. He reminded readers that the Labour Party had campaigned for the introduction of trade agreements, formally recognized Russia while in government in 1924, and also sent various delegations to 'study the Russian situation most carefully'. Naturally, he listed the British Labour Delegation of 1920, but he also cited the 'most elaborate' report of a delegation of Labour MPs and trade union leaders sent to Russia by the British Trades Union Congress in December 1924.

Here Buxton conceded everything to party realpolitik. The 1924 Trades Union Delegation could truthfully be added to a list of Labour Party projects aimed at securing amicable relations with Soviet Russia. But it was also a shabby initiative, which would be identified, decades later, as the first delegation to 'lend itself' to a new Soviet policy of courting and systematically manipulating visiting Western delegations, and using them as 'weapons in the long-term struggle against non-Communist labor leaders'.[22]

Chaired by A. A. Purcell, who had in no way moderated his adoration for Soviet Russia since his initial pilgrimage in 1920, this seven-man deputation had travelled in response to an invitation issued by the Soviet trade union delegation that attended the British Trades Union Congress in September 1924, a month after the general treaty had been signed between Russia and Britain's first Labour government. Published at the end of February 1925, the delegation's report prompted *Labour Magazine* to declare that 'the Trade

Union and Labour Movement has reason to be proud of the work of this Delegation'.[23] Others vehemently disagreed, and not surprisingly since the report repeatedly collapsed into the most abject conformity with the Soviet view of reality.

The contrary view would be supported, most damningly, by the fiercely anti-Bolshevist Joseph Douillet, an aid worker and former Belgian consul to Russia, who returned to the West in 1926, after a period of seven months' imprisonment in which he saw far deeper into the GPU's murderous jails than the anti-Soviet British Conservative Mr Ashmead Bartlett, whose tour of a well-presented jail in Moscow would prompt him to concede:

> The atmosphere of a Soviet prison is entirely different from that in other countries. In all but No. 1 prisons the captives are never locked in their cells, but roam about at large. The warders and prisoners live on terms of equality. The atmosphere is one of good-will and *bonhomie*. But for the loss of liberty, the conditions of life compare most favourable with those of the mass of the population outside. In fact, I saw more smiling faces in prison in half an hour than I had seen during the whole of my stay in Moscow.[24]

In his book *Moscou sans voiles* (1928)—a publication that would inspire Hergé's first Tintin book, *Tintin in the Land of the Soviets* (1929)—Douillet insisted that the delegations of foreign workers being toured around Russia under the auspices of the Communist International were actually being shown 'isolated and artificially prepared "oases" in the hopeless desert of the real state of the country'.[25] In the early 1920s, the Soviet authorities had deliberately established a series of officially designated 'show' factories, prisons, schools, crèches, hospitals, and rest-houses. There were model institutions in all branches of social life, and the 'alluring vistas' they opened in the minds of visiting proletarians were carefully tended by 'Guide-interpreters' specially recruited and trained by the GPU.[26] This systematic 'staging' of new Russia had been remarkably successful: 'very few visitors have succeeded in lifting, ever so little, the fringe of the curtain which hides the real state of affairs in the country'.[27]

The British Trades Union Delegation of 1924 was, Douillet affirms, considered of unusual importance, and 'most careful' preparations had therefore been applied to its route through Russia. As a representative of the Catholic Mission and other famine relief agencies in Rostov-on-Don, Douillet had twice joined the delegation during its tightly scheduled visit to the region. He describes one occasion when the rigging failed. The local authority had mistaken the day of a visit, and the delegation's train was obliged to stop for over an hour at a little station where only a short stay of five minutes had been planned. While it sat there, peasants from the surrounding villages were frantically carting loads of straw to an idle factory (disused since the Civil War) not far up the railway track:

> Only when the straw had been delivered to its destination, wetted and set alight, and the chimney stacks of the works began to emit a thick black smoke, giving the illusion of a virile and active Soviet industry, was the train allowed to proceed with the delegation.

> I do not know what the delegates thought when they saw the numerous peasants' carts returning to the village along the road running by the side of the railway line, but I heard what the peasants said when they saw the train with the delegates. I am at a loss to repeat it, however, on account of the strong adjectives which were addressed to the train and its occupants.[28]

Douillet saw further evidence of scene-shifting when the delegation arrived in Rostov. A grand reception was held at the 'Sovprof' (Council of Trade Unions) building in Rostov, but not before many of the Professional Union's departments had been moved to the back of the building, and confined to a separate entrance. This was done to ensure that the British visitors saw nothing of the arguments that frequently flared between the Sovprof management and its 'oppressed' workers, and were instead impressed by a steady stream of 'pseudo-workmen', who poured into the building with various requests and petitions which were 'satisfied there and then by the "solicitous" representatives of the Professional Union'.[29] The Britons were also guided around a large railway works, but only after several hundred politically unreliable workers at this carefully prepared show institution had been ordered to take a day's leave and, here as elsewhere, their places were taken by 'secret collaborators'[30] provided by the GPU.

Having watched the Bolsheviks 'preparing their rigs', the local population had asked themselves 'Can the foreigners possibly believe all this?' The illusions were maintained with the help of an 'impenetrable wall'[31] of secret police agents, who stood between the British delegates and ordinary Russians who might have challenged their impressions. Even the young man who, while travelling on the same train as the delegation, found a cap misplaced by one delegate in the restaurant car and returned it to him with a few words of English, was arrested, convicted of spying for a foreign power, and, as Douillet happened to find out later when himself incarcerated in Moscow's Butirky prison, sentenced to three years in a concentration camp on Solovetsky Island.[32] If the British trade unionists quite failed to see through this flapping veil of illusions, this was partly because of their fondness for banqueting and drink: the latter being a 'peculiarity' of the English trade unionists that would be much discussed after they had passed through, becoming, as Douillet emphasizes, the subject of anecdotes that continued to circulate for years.[33]

Douillet's damning testimony would not be published in English until 1930, but the British Trades Union Delegation's overproduced report had been shot to ribbons long before that. In a pamphlet entitled *Soviet Eyewash: Socialist Eyewash,* one anonymous but thoroughly disgusted anti-Bolshevist remarked that the delegation had allowed its reason to be 'drowned in a riot of sensations'. According to this writer, one only had to glance at the Soviet newspapers to discover how gleefully pro-Bolshevist delegates such as A. A. Purcell were said to have gone around urging British workers to 'Take the bourgeoisie by the throat!' or 'Act in Russian!' while also praising the Soviets for 'their great achievements' and prophesying, with the usual Comintern-stoked optimism, that 'the great mass of our workers would loudly demand similar changes in England'.[34]

The condemnation of the 1924 British Trades Union Delegation was by no means monopolized by the right. The anarchist Emma Goldman was enraged by the delegation's luxurious report. Visiting England in 1924/5 to speak out against the Bolshevik seizure of the Russian Revolution she was dismayed to find many members of the British Labour Party quite unwilling to hear her message. Even Clifford Allen, whom she had admired as a member of the British Labour Delegation to Russia in 1920, now allowed 'considerations of business' to loom higher than 'human values':[35] he informed Goldman that, as chairman of the Independent Labour Party, he could not be seen to oppose Bolshevism.

So Goldman picked up her pen, convinced that 'until present misunderstandings have been cleared away' it was a waste of breath to hope, as many still did, of combining the democratic and Bolshevist lefts into a 'United Front'.[36] Writing under the auspices of the British Committee for the Defence of Political Prisoners in Russia, she denounced the Trades Union Report as a 'complete whitewash': so complete that, as she demonstrated by detailed quotation, a far truer account of the oppression in Russia could actually be deduced by reading the heavily partisan Soviet press. This aspect of her argument would be weakened by the suggestion that the Soviet newspapers in which the British delegates were quoted making blood-curdling remarks, might actually have been forgeries produced by White Russian 'lie factories' still operating in the West.

Yet Goldman was undoubtedly correct on the basic facts of the case. Seven men, all of them ignorant of Russia and the Russian language, had devoted five weeks to visiting a very large land—so vast that they had spent most of their time, as one of the delegates had publicly admitted, travelling on trains. How, then, had they managed to produce 'a vast encyclopedia of Russia's past history and present conditions'? Goldman raised these questions in public lectures too, saying that, as someone who had 'participated in some of the demonstrations organised for various missions', she knew how thoroughly things were organized in Soviet Russia 'when it was a question of dazzling and overawing foreign visitors'.[37] Since it had been 'physically impossible' for the delegation to 'get at the facts' in the time available to them, their report should be dismissed as 'a replica of material supplied by the Soviet government' and 'a travesty of actual conditions in Russia'.

Not content with reproducing Emma Goldman's views on the subject, *The Times* was pleased to convey the news that the Trades Union Delegation's Report was going down poorly in the Balkan states where Dr Paul Schliemann, editor of *Rigasche Rundschau,* the largest German-language paper in the region, had dismissed it as 'silly and beneath criticism'.[38] It also printed letters in which unidentified Russians claimed to have watched the delegation pulling into Ilovaiskaya station in its train of special railway carriages, and alighting to meet a 'selected' Russian public in the first-class waiting room. They remained quite ignorant of the third-class waiting room where they might have found '300 ragged, barefoot savage miners', who had been 'purged' or 'combed out' of the Christiakovsky mines and who, with winter pressing in, were desperately trying to find their way back to Kharkov. This stream of condemnation disconcerted one member of the delegation, the railway trade unionist and Labour MP for Barrow John Bromley, who urged the public 'not to believe that the delegates were led round like stock lions on chains'.

Lions? Emma Goldman might have scoffed at that suggestion, even if she required no convincing about the chains. Reading the delegations' report, she had been reminded of her own 'first vacation' in the New York State penitentiary on Blackwell's Island. A young reporter had come to interview her. When she refused to see him, he told the warden that 'he could just as well write a story about Emma Goldman by merely looking at the Penitentiary from the New York side of the East River'. The British Trades Union Delegation had proved just the same. 'Hypnotised during their stay', they had 'written a story about the Russian people—their lives, work and aspirations—by merely looking at the penitentiary into which the whole of Russia has been turned. From the vantage point of the favoured, feted and chaperoned official guests, they saw everything in glowing colours.'[39] It was, perhaps, generous of Goldman to attribute the report to the 'extreme naiveté' of the British delegation. The document was an unreliable package of ignorant and ungrounded impressions, lies and official statistics, in which even the Bolshevik regime's prisons were commended as places of 'very great humanity'.[40] As Goldman herself concluded of this glossy, bank-rolled document, 'No amount of whitewash can obliterate the outstanding fact that Russia and her people are State-ridden, State-driven and State-gagged.'[41]

Friedrich Adler and the Case of the
Red-Haired Waiter

The British Trades Union Delegation's report had been vigorously condemned in Europe too. In Paris, Russian exiles, of various political hues, combined to dismiss it as more or less unmixed Bolshevist propaganda, singling out the delegation's praise of the Soviet prison system as especially sickening.[42] But the most penetrating European analysis was provided by one of early twentieth-century socialism's noblest political assassins.

Friedrich Adler was the son of Victor Adler, founder of the Austrian Social Democratic Party. Before August 1914, he had known Trotsky and other leading Bolsheviks during their exile in Switzerland and he stuck to his internationalist principles once the war between nations had broken out (unlike the executive committee of the Austrian Social Democratic Party, which he continued to serve as secretary through the first two years of the war). Adler was not content with repeatedly denouncing the war as 'a crime against the peoples'.[43] On 21 October 1916, in the restaurant of Vienna's Hotel Sacher, he took out a revolver and murdered Count Karl von Stürgkh, the prime minister who had presided over Austria's conversion into a military dictatorship defined by censorship, police harassment of dissenters, and the suspension of both Parliament and trial by jury. In the words of the Socialist Publication Society of New York, Adler's action was 'like the flare of a rocket' that suddenly revealed the benighted condition to which Austria had been reduced.[44]

Though he had loudly commended the Zimmerwald Conference of 1915, when he stood before a 'special tribunal' of six judges in Vienna, Adler was not content to rail against capitalist imperialism in the name of the 'dictatorship of the proletariat' nor to sloganize, along Bolshevik lines, that the war between nations should be converted into a class-based civil war. Defending his action before a military tribunal in May 1917, he cited the 'destruction of legal security' in Austria, declaring that, following Count Stürgkh's 'coup d'état', justice had been 'reduced to a war machine'. In one of the great speeches of twentieth-century socialism (in America the text was published under the title of *J'Accuse*), he argued that 'the fact that such trials as this are possible, alone, justifies every act of violence against the rulers of Austria'.[45] Repudiating his lawyer's desperate suggestion that he had shot Stürgkh in a fit of madness, Adler insisted that he had premeditated his action for well over a year, and welcomed the death sentence he rightly anticipated would be passed. The assassination was a 'symbolic act, a parable' intended to 'give the revolutionary spirit a place in our movement' and also to 'establish the psychological premise for future mass action in Austria'.[46]

Pairing him with his friend Karl Liebnecht as 'one of the most prominent German-speaking Bolsheviks', the *New Statesman* would later report that Adler had told the special tribunal he was unable to discuss politics with men who thought in terms of the bourgeois or moderate socialist parties, asserting that the distance between the two points of view was such that they 'might be held on different planets'.[47] Where Rolland and other internationalists had earlier argued for horizontal as opposed to vertical national allegiances, Adler, who was a doctor of physics as well as a revolutionary socialist, made the same point by comparing opposed cosmologies: the closed pre-Copernican universe based on the conviction that the earth stood at the centre of the universe with the sun and stars moving around it; and the heliocentric conception of Copernicus, who had caused great shock and incredulity by insisting that 'this solid earth moves'.[48]

Adler had told the public prosecutor that the two of them represented exactly such distinct outlooks: logically incompatible, even if both might claim to be logically possible. Like the pre-Copernicans, 'You are accustomed to see upon this earth the trenches of national warfare, but I have fixed all my hopes, so long as I have been able to think politically, upon those fronts of the class struggle that also exist in the world.' Adler's internationalist stance 'comes from an entirely different world. For it makes a great difference, whether you look at the world from the walls that separate the nations from one another, from the walls that the war has built, or whether you see it from the wall that to me has always been the most important, the wall of the classes that separates the exploiters from the exploited'.[49] Just as Copernicus had given natural science 'a basis for its entire development', the horizontal perspective of class struggle was 'a new conception'[50] that pointed to the 'higher development of humanity'—unlike the vertical perspective of 'national warfare' and struggle between competing imperialist powers, which promised only hunger, misery, and, indeed, the destruction of the human race.

It was partly thanks to the enormous popularity of Stürgkh's assassination among the Austrian working class that Adler lived to condemn the British Trades Union Delegation's report. His death sentence had been commuted to eighteen years' imprisonment, and, on 31 October 1918, he was granted an amnesty by the outgoing President Karl and released. Charles Roden Buxton had seen Adler's electrifying reappearance at the first post-war meeting of the Second International in Berne, January 1919. Acclaimed for never betraying his internationalist principles during a war that had caused many socialist parties to collapse into conformity with the national purposes of their states, Adler was by then emerging as an 'Austro-Marxist' and a leading defender of Austrian social democracy against Bolshevism, poised to spread there from Hungary.

Leon Trotsky, who had known Adler in Switzerland before his own return to Russia in 1917, would be particularly disgusted by his former comrade's conversion into an anti-Bolshevist revolutionary socialist. Indeed, in November 1919, he had demanded that Adler should be relieved of his honorary membership of the Russian Soviet Congress.[51] Adler would hardly have objected. His own insistence on linking socialism with democracy, legality, and 'judicial security' of the kind that Count Stürgkh had abolished in Austria, had put him emphatically at odds with the Bolsheviks and their dictatorship of the proletariat.

Despite these fundamental differences, Adler had at first hoped to recover the pre-war unity of the divided socialist movement. In February 1921, he led the founding Congress of the 'Vienna Working Union of Socialist Parties', also known as the Second and a Half International because of its desire to bring parties of the Second and Third Internationals into cooperation, thereby preventing what Adler would later describe as 'the impotence of the split'.[52] (Charles Roden Buxton, who befriended Adler in these years, was among the British delegates.) But the search for common ground would quickly be overtaken by events, and Adler crossed the line to become a joint secretary (the other one was the British Labour MP Tom Shaw) of the Labour and Socialist International, formed to resume the work of the defunct Second International in May 1923.

For a man of Adler's convictions and background, the report of the 1924 British Trades Union Delegation seemed an unusually contemptible document. Writing his condemnation from a declaredly 'socialist point of view',[53] Adler ridiculed the claimed 'objective spirit' of the publication, noting that three out of seven of the delegates (including A. A. Purcell) were members of the pro-Communist Anglo-Russian Parliamentary Committee (itself descended from the earlier 'Hands Off Russia' Committee). He denounced its failure to notice that political disenfranchisement was being turned into a permanent condition in Russia, and its scandalous reassurance that the Soviet system could 'retain its vitality without the usual stimulus of an official opposition'.[54] As for the report's expressed contempt for 'sobstuff' emerging from the regime's prisons, Adler was wholly disgusted by Chairman Purcell's refusal to press for the release of 'such irreconcilables' as the Social Revolutionary leaders they had met in a Moscow jail.[55]

Adler went on to attack the whole idea of 'studious travel', insisting it was 'high time that many comrades realized the difference between serious studies and harmful dilettantism'.[56] Given the extraordinarily high passions aroused by Bolshevism, he ventured that 'an unbiased mind is impossible so far as concerns the fragment of history through which we are at present passing'.[57] Nearly all travellers to Russia had started out from a partisan perspective, and their claims to impartiality were inevitably a pretence. On the evidence of the 1924 report, these delegations actually offered little more than 'an interview with the Soviet authorities',[58] followed by a report, which, though signed by the delegates, was actually written by three accompanying 'advisers' (in this case led by George Young, an unreliable expert who had also accompanied the British Labour Delegation of 1920).[59] Adler surmised that, due to their limited previous connections with the labour movement, these shadowy figures were predisposed to jump 'with one bound into the Bolshevist circle of ideas'.[60] All too familiar with the disreputable methods of the British Foreign Office, they were also adept at peddling the Bolshevist line while at the same time strategically referring to the 'dark sides' of Soviet reality in order to 'anticipate the objection that notorious facts have been concealed'.[61]

Having condemned the report as both 'a masterpiece of Bolshevist arrangement' and 'a burning shame for the Labour Movement',[62] Adler ventured some reasons why British tourists seemed more liable to stupefaction than 'studious travellers' from other countries. In part, he suggested, their gullibility followed from their characteristic British empiricism: 'They are accustomed to approach each problem "without bias," that is, they perceive things unfettered by theoretical prepossessions, which really means unfettered by the experience of other men.'[63]

They were also susceptible to a distinctly British kind of hypocrisy. Their country's imperialist history had accustomed them to the idea that a regime that would be considered wholly unfit for proper Englishmen might be perfectly adequate for colonial peoples. Such, Adler suggested, was the double standard that the British Trades Union Delegation now applied to the Russian people and also, more offensively, to the Georgians, whose struggle for sovereignty had culminated in the viciously suppressed uprising of September 1924.

Though supported by a history of empire and also by a nineteenth-century liberal philosophy that had subscribed to the same division,[64] shoddy hypocrisy was not actually the exclusive possession of the British. As time went on, European and American 'tourists of the revolution' would also try to console themselves with the thought that privations they themselves would never tolerate still represented a commendable improvement for the peoples of the USSR. Yet Adler's point was undeniable:

> It is often most astounding to observe how uncritically and credulously such travellers pronounce upon what they chance to hear or see, and how unsuspectingly and readily they formulate their conclusions. Such travellers' reports always remind one of the old anecdote of the English lord who, visiting the Continent for the first time, arrived in Ostend and sitting at the breakfast table immediately made his first entry in his diary: 'On the Continent the waiters have red hair.'[65]

British Idiocy II: Grinning with the Comintern

The foreigners who attended Soviet Russia in the mid 1920s included journalists, writers and artists, political scientists, architects and hydroelectricity experts, financiers and businessmen drawn by the opportunities presented by a regime that was increasingly desperate for the foreign capital it despised.[66] Yet there were others who did not smile ironically as their Moscow-bound train passed under an arch of branches bearing the slogan 'Welcome to the workers of the West'.[67]

Foreign Communists had been pouring into Russia under the auspices of the Communist International, hardly subdued by its failure to bring about the imminent 'world revolution' prophesied by Lenin in the immediate post-war years, and perhaps still convinced of the Comintern's relative independence from the Russian Communist Party. An International Lenin School had been opened in Moscow in 1926. The 'University of the Peoples of the East' catered for students from China, Japan, Korea, and Malaya, while the 'University of the Peoples of the West' included a department dedicated to the education and development of American communists.

In Leningrad, a huge 'International Club' had been installed in the Uritsky Palace. According to Jan Valtin, a militant sailor from Hamburg (real name 'Richard Krebs') who would attend this institution as a member of the Comintern's maritime section, the basement canteen rang with the sound of many different languages while the universally applicable theory and technique of class warfare were taught at the International Division of the Communist University.

Tightly managed and kept apart from ordinary Russian workers, the Comintern's international visitors were turned, as this former adherent would later recall, into 'the unflinching prisoners of a grandiose make-believe, we who looked upon ourselves as hard-headed materialists'.[68] At night, their contempt for the 'bourgeois ideals of a settled existence' would be expressed in saturnalias in which they entered vodka-drinking competitions and made their own 'juicy satire' of the old Allied propaganda about Bolshevism's alleged 'nationalisation of women'.[69] During the day, as a similarly broken-off Swedish witness would later recall, they would zealously study the activities of the Communist parties in their home countries, surveying the party press and the statements of the leadership for signs of the 'rotten liberalism' loathed by the Comintern as an outpost of bourgeois values implanted in the workers' movement.[70]

The internationalism of the Communist International was certainly remote from the peaceable cosmopolitanism espoused by Romain Rolland, Vernon Lee, and others during the Great War. It was an extended form of class warfare to be waged on illegal as well as legal fronts, and it demanded unquestioning obedience—rather than reason, tolerance, or enlightened dialogue—from its zealots. Since its hasty establishment in March 1919, the Communist International had converted Lenin's Russian battle against the hated Mensheviks and Social Revolutionaries into a global war against the Second International and its successor organizations. The aim was to split the working-class movement in all countries, wrecking and, if possible, taking over socialist parties, expelling 'opportunists' and 'reformists', and then 'moulding' them into ferociously centralized vanguard parties, which would carry out regular purges of their membership and remain tightly leashed to Moscow.

In 1925, Stalin informed the Fourteenth Congress of the Russian Communist Party that visiting 'delegations of workers' formed 'the best, most forceful and active propaganda for the Soviet system against the capitalist system'.[71] So 'foreign proletarians' had joined the cultural luminaries and technical experts who found themselves transported through a world in which 'hospitality' would prove to be the least of their problems.

One group that crossed the reinstated iron curtain in the required spirit of furious adoration was the forty-eight-strong 'British Workers' Delegation' of 1927, made up of activists who journeyed to the Soviet Union with the memory of the defeated general strike of 1926 still blazing in their minds. This band of partisan pilgrims was led by Will Lawther, a miner from the Durham village of Chopwell (known as 'little Moscow' and 'the reddest in all England') who had spent two months in jail rather than paying the 50-shilling fine imposed on him for 'interfering with food distribution' and 'intimidating the police' during the General Strike. Its membership included Harry Pollitt, already prominent in the Communist Party of Great Britain, and Shapurji Saklatvala, a Parsee who was then Communist MP for North Battersea in London. Other delegates were drawn from the grass roots of the labour movement: militants from the trade unions and the Labour Party, members of the Women's Co-operative Guild, and other organizations associated with the working-class movement, including the Workers' Esperanto Club in Manchester. Generally both zealous and unaccustomed to foreign travel, its members assembled at Tower Hill in London on Saturday, 29 October and, after a distinctly beery celebration attended by the veteran Communist and labour leader Tom Mann, set off on one of the Soviet Union's two seagoing steamers, the 2,000-ton cargo ship *Soviet*,[72] which, in defiant reaction to the Tory government's refusal to issue the delegates with visas, had sailed up the Thames to collect them from Free Trade Wharf.[73]

In the delegation's anonymously written report, *Soviet Russia To-Day*, the steamer is commended as 'a fitting introduction to what we were to find in Soviet Russia itself'.[74] The delegates praised the 'high level of political consciousness' noted in every member of the crew, and also the facilities provided for these men: from the rest room to the 'Lenin corner', a secular shrine in which images of Lenin took the place of Christian icons. It was, so their report insisted, 'a remarkably pleasant voyage in every way—but for one day's rough weather to which most of us succumbed'. True to its ideological brief, the report makes no mention of the monumental hangovers suffered by some unaccustomed delegates who, drawn into toasting sessions by the comradely crew, had unknowingly diluted their whisky with carafes containing vodka rather than water.[75] Many years would pass before Ellis Smith, a Mancunian activist who had joined the delegation as a member of the United Patternmakers' Association, would write more candidly about the journey. The beds provided for the delegates were rough affairs, rigged up on a frame of tubular scaffolding, and Smith, being among the younger pilgrims, found himself allocated to the top tier of this inherently nauseating construction.[76] They endured what was actually a 'terrible' journey over the North Sea, and then proceeded into the Baltic through the Kiel Canal (where Shapurji Saklatvala and Margaret McCarthy, a member of the accompanying delegation of Communist youth, took advantage of a delay to scribble revolutionary messages in German and drop them into the boats below).[77] 'Such was the feeling in those days', so Ellis Smith would later note, 'that a man said to my mother, that he hoped the boat went down, and it nearly did in the Baltic Sea.'

Once disembarked in a Petrograd that had been officially renamed Leningrad a few days after Lenin's death in January 1924, the British workers wandered around in a state of rapture. A young weaver from Accrington, Lancashire, Margaret McCarthy was astonished to find herself put up in a grand hotel, complete with stuffed bears and potted plants, and taken to see *The Snow Maiden* at the ballet: 'it was', as she later wrote, 'as if I had been conveyed straight into fairyland'.[78]

The briskly exhibited sights of Leningrad included the Winter Palace, and also the Hermitage where no less than forty-four paintings by Rembrandt waited to be revered in their new status as property of the Soviet state. The visitors were also taken to a large mansion: formerly a private house but now in use as a school where children sat on a polished floor and sang a simple song of revolutionary justice: 'This house used to belong to the rich. And now it belongs to us.'[79] After more such encouraging displays, the delegates were shifted to Moscow, departing at midnight on trains that had to plough their way through heavier snow than Ellis Smith had ever imagined. In notes written for a talk given in 1960, Smith would write, 'We landed at Moscow in the early morning, the conditions were terrible, it was bitter cold, thick with snow, few old trams packed with people, people poorly dressed, hundreds of beggars, wild-looking boys and women, moving through the snow.' Still anxious, more than three decades later, not to create a negative impression of Soviet Russia, Smith recorded haunting memories of 'wild men with boy's eyes' but quickly added 'It must be remembered, that was 33 years ago.'

Those desperate, feral-looking street-children would haunt the memories of many who journeyed to the Soviet Promised Land in the late 1920s. The sight of these *bezprizorny* would 'stagger' visiting Communists, even those who managed to avoid having their pockets picked as they walked to Comintern Congress meetings, or their bags stolen through open train windows when their guided tours came to a halt at railway stations. As one disconcerted British visitor wrote as he remembered walking out onto the Moscow streets from the International Lenin School shortly after arriving in Moscow in 1926, 'My prevailing feeling was that my ideas were being confronted by reality, which was at a lower level.'[80]

Soviet Russia's wild and abandoned children certainly found no accommodation in the Report of the British Workers' Delegation. Instead, *Soviet Russia To-day* emphasized the 'glaring' contrast between the reality the delegates had found and the dire accounts so frequently to be read in British newspapers.[81] The capitalist press went on about derelict buildings and unsanitary streets—but the delegation insisted they had seen 'no traces either of exceptional wear and tear or of any disregard for what is now the property of the workers'. Far from being wrecked, Russia's historical streets and buildings were being saved, restored, and even won back from the 'mutilations' inflicted on them during tsarist times. The Kremlin, with its palaces, churches, and museums, may indeed have been damaged when it became 'the stronghold of the reactionary forces' in the 1917 revolution, but all the harm had since been 'made good'. Indeed, it now constituted a 'wonderful sight' with its 'revolutionary decorations' and its Red Flag illuminated from below by a single shaft of light, which played in the 'waving folds' like inspiring 'tongues of flame.'

The climax of this visit came on 7 November 1927, when the delegates mounted a specially provided stand under the Kremlin wall. They would remain there for at least eight hours, chewing on occasionally provided sandwiches and gazing out over a thronging Red Square as the celebrations of the tenth anniversary of the Bolshevik revolution unfolded. They heard speeches by Voroshilov, Commissar for War, and also Kalinin, chairman of the Communist Party, and, by repute 'the most popular man in Russia'.[82] Bukharin spoke, as did various Western Communists, including Shapurji Saklatvala MP and Willie Gallacher, the Glaswegian militant who had brought himself to the Comintern's heel since 1920, when Lenin judged him guilty of 'Left-Wing Communism; an Infantile Disorder'. The delegates watched as a million Moscow workers filed past Lenin's mausoleum in 'a solid unbroken phalanx forty deep'. These dragooned proletarians came with banners, slogans, and even elaborate moving effigies of the revolution's enemies, including Stanley Baldwin and Austen Chamberlain, the Tory prime minister and Foreign Secretary responsible for Britain's renewed trade embargo against Communist Russia. As night fell the whole scene was illuminated by searchlights and the delegates stood there transfixed as a grand climax was provided by the Red Cossack cavalry, who charged across the square at a terrific pace: their lances and magnificent black horses gleaming in the lights of triumphant revolution.

A special two-day play tracing the events of the previous ten years was broadcast over Soviet Russia at the time of the anniversary celebrations. According to *The Times*'s correspondent in Riga, this fiercely anti-capitalist pageant found its climax in the arrival of British delegates who were 'astounded by the feverish progress everywhere' and, at the opening of a vast rural electricity plant, appealed to the assembled peasants 'in affectedly broken Russian', urging them to appreciate the marvellous things the Soviet regime was doing for them.[83] The British Workers' Delegation would appear to have travelled through Russia in exactly that spirit. No pacifist reservations about the militarism of the anniversary celebrations found expression in their report. This document made no mention of Trotsky, who had just been expelled from the Soviet Communist Party, even though, as Ellis Smith would recount much later, they actually saw him and his demonstrating fellow oppositionists being chased out of Red Square, where they had tried to interrupt the anniversary celebrations. Some members of the British Labour Delegation of 1920 had expressed grave doubts about the Bolshevik course. But there is nothing in this later report to suggest that the enraptured pilgrims of 1927 even noticed that their presence was being used to encourage Russians to believe that the international working class was overwhelmingly on the side of Stalin's Communist Party.

The winter of 1927/8 saw acute food shortages in Soviet towns, but any sign of hardship perceived in the Russian crowd was interpreted as a principled rejection of bourgeois extravagance: 'Everyone looks healthy and well-fed, and their clothing was strong and warm. There were no silk hats in evidence, and there were very few silk stockings, but we all got a very clear impression that however dear clothing may be, the workers and peasants were able to get it.'[84] The children too were 'remarkably healthy in appearance', and 'they *all* had strong boots'. Far from being a godless place governed by annihilating atheists, the USSR was a land of contented workers, who enjoyed the use of crèches (both day and night), communal restaurants, comfortable and smooth-running collectivized trains. Visiting a mine in the Donets coalfield, the delegates noted that Russian miners enjoyed six-hour shifts and hot pit-head showers that would make their English equivalent clench their fists in envy. There were more smiles in a Moscow chocolate factory, the products of which were judged to be every bit 'as good as Terry's'.[85] Bolshevik Russia was a place where women were 'encouraged to enter the industrial life of the country' and could hardly contrast more with the 'pitiful household drudge so often seen in capitalist countries'.

The British Workers' Delegation admitted to seeing 'some holes in the pavements', but nothing that could not 'be paralleled in any town in Britain'. They conceded that the Soviet Union had nothing to match the brilliant electric lighting of Piccadilly or Oxford Street in London, but this lack was seen as an admirable sign of restraint: indeed, Communist Russia's lighting compared favourably with that to be found in Britain's industrial districts. As for international solidarity, 'there can be no doubt that the workers in Soviet Russia are politically conscious and that they feel the identity of their struggle with the struggle of the British workers'. Factory after factory told of the collections that had been made for the British miners in the previous year's General Strike, and promised that the same help would be forthcoming in the event of future strikes. Ellis Smith registered these factories as heavenly places—his own Metropolitan Vickers shifted from Trafford Park and relocated in paradise. He and the other delegates marvelled at the freely provided worker's clothing, the co-operative restaurants and stores full of cheap provisions, the libraries and study circles, and, of course, the housing: 'We even came across one case where some of the workers lived in old houses of the Tsarist period not only rent free, but actually received a special allowance for having to live in the old houses, pending the extension of the new housing scheme!'

Members of the British Workers' Delegation even toured Soviet prisons in order to celebrate the sense of humanity and the high standard of welfare they found inside their walls. They visited jails in Moscow—including the soon-to-be-infamous Lefortovo, where they saw nothing to foreshadow the outsized meat-grinder with which Stalin's secret police would later be rumoured to reduce their murdered victims prior to flushing them into Moscow's drains. Certainly, there were political prisoners here as well as ordinary offenders, but the British Workers' Delegation found Lefortovo to be a generous reformatory, full of education, music, and gentle persuasion: 'The whole atmosphere was most unlike anything one associates with prison life.' So impressed were they by what they found in a prison in Baku, that the delegates signed a statement declaring that 'prison life in Soviet Russia is better than the conditions that many British miners have to endure today'.[86]

It would be misleading to suggest that the British Workers' Delegation refused to allow any criticism of Communist Russia. There were occasions when they felt that the revolutionary endeavour might be improved considerably. When the delegates who worked in the British building trade went to examine the working practices of their Soviet comrades, they had been quick to insist that terms and conditions were far better than those endured by their British counterparts, and to approve the absence of supervision 'of the type that we have here'. While accepting that the 'severities' of the Russian winter made 'double windows' necessary, they worried that the walls in new workers' dwelling-houses were simply too thick, and suggested that 'economy could be effected' by inserting a cavity in these over-engineered walls. The scaffolding they saw on construction sites seemed too good for the requirements of the moment, and surely represented a misuse of energies and materials that might have been better employed elsewhere. As for the trowels used for laying cement, these were frankly inadequate: 'it is like laying bricks with a button hook', as one representative of the Amalgamated Union of Building Trade Workers remarked. This act of fraternal criticism was carefully judged to show respect for the achievements of the ill-equipped Soviet builder, while at the same time blaming all his shortcomings on the British government, which had 'prevented trade between Britain and the "workers' Socialist Republics"'.

Judged by their report alone, the members of the British Workers' Delegation were unanimous and unwavering in their misrepresentation of conditions in Russia. So much so, that it might be thought that they never really reached Russia at all, and only toured their own ardent preconceptions. And yet these British adherents did not exactly leave their critical faculties behind. They brought them along, fitted them even more tightly to the party line, and then used Russia as a vantage point from which to condemn the capitalist system at home. As the defeat of the General Strike of 1926 might have indicated for these fervent tourists, time had already expired on the 'world revolution' that Lenin had imagined coming to the rescue of the Bolsheviks in Russia. Yet its often bloody demise only increased the ardour with which foreign adherents now cleaved to the replacement doctrine of 'Socialism in one country', introduced by Stalin after the death of Lenin in 1924. As the historian of the International, Julius Braunthal, would remark, 'The more difficult it seemed for Communists abroad to capture power in their own countries, the more firmly they were forced to rally to Soviet Russia. In this depressing world situation nothing was more natural than that Soviet Russia should become a fatherland for Communists throughout the world.'[87]

14

Comrade Bukharin's Version

Beyond our love for the country of our flesh, we love Russia; today she is the country of all people who are struggling in behalf of the light. Beyond Russia we love suffering humanity; and beyond humanity we serve a mysterious force which appears sometimes as flame and sometimes as light, which the mind calls truth and the heart love.

Nikos Kazantzakis[1]

The thought behind Braunthal's observation might already have troubled the three friends who, on 14 October 1927, gathered for a farewell dinner at the Casenave restaurant on the rue Boissy d'Anglas in Paris.[2]

The first of these splendidly irregular figures was Christian Rakovsky, a seasoned international Communist of Balkan extraction who, having been among the founders of the Zimmerwald Conference in 1915, had served as leader of the provisional Soviet government of Ukraine, appointed by Lenin in January 1919 when the Russian Civil War was still raging.[3] While in this position Rakovsky had addressed himself to the so-called national question, arguing forcefully that the Ukraine, like Georgia and the other Soviet republics, should be integrated into the USSR through a confederative union that respected the rights of its constituent republics.

At the Soviet Communist Party's Twelfth Congress (1923), he had famously challenged Stalin, then the Commissar of Nationalities, opposing his pursuit of centralized power as altogether too close to traditional Russian imperialism, and demanding a far greater degree of autonomy for the republics. Attuned to this problem by his pre-war experience in the Balkans, Rakovsky had urged the congress to grasp its wider implications: 'If we are to become the centre of the struggle of the oppressed nationalities outside the boundaries of the USSR, we must internally, within the boundaries of the USSR, make a correct decision on the national question.'[4]

Though a leading member of Trotsky's left opposition within the Soviet Communist Party, Rakovsky was also the multilingual and highly educated son of a wealthy Bulgarian family into which he was born in 1873. This cosmopolitan inheritance had equipped him to become Soviet Russia's most accomplished diplomat. While still head of the Ukrainian government, Rakovsky had negotiated Soviet Russia's post-war agreement with Lithuania. In 1922, he had skilfully manoeuvred Germany into signing the Rapallo Treaty with Soviet Russia, an outcome that has been described as 'one of the greatest diplomatic coups of all time'.[5] Having led the delegations that negotiated both Britain's and France's recognition of the Soviet government in 1924, he had since spent two years in Paris as Soviet Russia's ambassador to France, to the satisfaction of Stalin who was pleased to keep him abroad. A week before that dinner in the 8th *arrondissement*, however, and allegedly thanks to a declaration in which he, Lev Kamenev, and other members of the left opposition had urged European workers and soldiers to rise up in defence of Soviet Russia, France's recently elected Conservative government had demanded that Rakovsky be recalled to Moscow.

One of the departing ambassador's guests was Boris Souvarine, a younger militant of working-class Ukrainian origins (he was born as Boris Lifschitz in Kiev, 1895) and a fellow admirer of the late Jean Jaurès, who had been a founder member of the French Communist Party and also its representative on the executive committee of the Comintern in Moscow. Shortly after the death of Lenin, Souvarine had found himself excluded from both these organizations on account of his defence of Trotsky and his association with the left opposition within the Russian Politburo. Rakovsky and Souvarine shared this alignment, but they did not pursue their political discussion that evening, thanks, perhaps, to the presence of Rakovsky's second guest, Panaït Istrati, a Romanian (French-language) writer, whose path had crossed that of Rakovsky during the pre-war years when the latter was the leading socialist in the Balkans, but who represented a different kind of communism altogether.

The son of a Greek smuggler and a Romanian laundress, Istrati was born in 1884 at the port of Braila, on the lower Danube. Having left home at the age of 12, he lived for many years as a vagabond, wandering through Asia Minor and the Middle East. Romain Rolland had harped on this romantic theme, when introducing Istrati to the French reading public in 1923, 'He was burned by the wind and drenched by the rain. He was homeless and hunted by night watchmen, hungry, ill, torn by his passions, and in extremes of poverty. He was Jack-of-all-trades: waiter in a cabaret, pastrycook, locksmith, coppersmith, mechanic, workman, labourer, wharf porter, servant, sandwich man, sign painter, house decorator, journalist, photographer.'[6]

Rolland had rescued Istrati after he tried to cut his own throat when starving and desperate in southern France in 1921. Impressed by a letter addressed to him and sent on having been found in Istrati's pocket, he visited the convalescent Romanian during his long stay in hospital and encouraged him to pull himself together and become a writer. He went on to hail Istrati as the 'new Gorki of the Balkan countries', in the introduction to his first book, *Kyra, My Sister,* published to considerable acclaim in 1923, and soon followed by other popular best-sellers concerned with heroic bandits, tavern-owners and other nostalgically framed Balkan figures. Istrati was, as Souvarine would later explain, a communist of the heart: radicalized by experience rather than by party doctrine or systematic study of Marxism. Though not a party member, life had taught him to hate bourgeois society and placed him instinctively on the side of the exploited and victimized.

Aware that he himself would probably never be able to revisit Russia, Souvarine felt regretful as he heard the two Romanians discussing the journey to Moscow on which they would embark the following day. In his excitement, the loquacious Istrati seemed quite unaware of the dissonance between his enthusiasm and the more circumspect attitude of the 54-year-old Rakovsky, who would be returning to Russia not just penniless but as an all-too-well-known member of the left opposition, and a long-standing friend of its increasingly isolated leader, Leon Trotsky.[7] Indifferent to this political drama and, as he would admit, largely unaware of the existence of an opposition within the Russian Communist Party, Istrati hailed Russia as 'the Mecca of Communism'[8] and spoke euphorically of the 'pilgrimage' he would make through the country as a guest of VOKS.

He and Christian Rakovsky travelled together by train, departing the next day, on 15 October, and going their separate ways shortly after arriving at Moscow station, where, as Istrati certainly did notice, no official limousine awaited the USSR's expelled ambassador to France.[9]

Rakovsky quickly moved on to the Ukraine, where he would help to prepare the left opposition to make a critical stand during the approaching celebrations of the Bolshevik revolution's tenth anniversary. Istrati, however, presents himself as having started out as wide-eyed as any devout Western pilgrim. Delighted to be hailed as an honorary vice-president of France's 'Friends of the USSR', he even announced his intention of abandoning the West and settling permanently in the new Russia. On 7 November, he would stand close to Lenin's tomb in Red Square and, like the enraptured members of the British Workers' Delegation, watch the Bolshevik revolution's tenth anniversary celebrations with tears of joy springing from his eyes. He would later declare that it was only in the last three months of his extended visit that 'the charm broke'. Yet he had surely had enough of parades by the end of his first month; and the guided tours quickly came to bore him too. As he wrote, 'factory after factory; museum after museum; hospital after hospital; school after school; banquet after banquet. And above all, above all, the same dreadful speeches.'[10]

As for the scenes in the hotels occupied by foreign delegations, these too provoked feelings of exasperated rage rather than international comradeship. No country, as Istrati would later admit, invites tourists to inspect its refuse pits, and no doubt he too would have produced 'dithyrambic' articles in praise of the Soviet regime if, like so many other foreign delegates, he had gone home after a stay of only six weeks.[11] Yet, as the weeks turned into months, he had come to loathe these pampered and self-important tourists, calling them 'democratic grasshoppers' who hopped about, 'nibbling' here and there as they were introduced to Soviet Russia's carefully prepared surfaces, and displaying nothing but insensitivity, false enthusiasm, and ingratitude as they went.[12]

Like the Greek writer Nikos Kazantzakis, with whom he shared much of his journeying through Soviet Russia, Israti appears to have been particularly disgusted by the British delegates. Kazantzakis describes a Japanese visitor meeting one such specimen in Bokhara, central Asia. This 'ruddy-faced, gold-toothed Englishman' only looks out from under his colonial helmet to complain about the lack of supplies and to scoff at the suggestion that the British Empire might one day be threatened by the spread of Lenin's revolution in Africa and Asia.[13]

Istrati's attitude was neatly encapsulated by a story emanating from the Hotel Krasnai in Kharkov, where a 'score of cretins'—the entire membership of an Anglo-American delegation—had one morning been found doing an agitated 'Charleston' in their socks. Having left their shoes outside their bedroom doors at night, expecting to recover them cleaned and polished in the morning, this party of 'morons' had woken to find every single pair stolen.[14] It was, Istrati declared, a pleasure to learn that such an inspiring, Rocambol-like thief was operating unapprehended in the most luxurious hotel in the Ukrainian capital, even though his actions were tough on the delegation's unfortunate guide, who had to arrange for many shoemakers to visit the hotel before every disgruntled delegate had accepted satisfactory replacements.

By the time he returned to France a full sixteen months later, Istrati had formulated his own response to the famous slogan greeting foreigners as they entered Russia by train. 'Workers of the World Unite', it proclaimed from a scarlet arcade. Istrati's revised version was less succinct: 'Unite and do not send any more delegations of fools to see nothing and report nothing. Instead go alone, without any guide or leader, and you will see more than all the leaders of the world. Be stupid, like your feet.'[15] As for the idea that the regime's foreign visitors were innocents deceived by Soviet showmanship, Istrati would have none of it: 'even to a deaf-mute, the Truth is accessible, wherever one looks'.[16]

Towards the Other Flame

Unlike the Western visitors whom Kazantzakis condemned as 'slipshod romantics',[17] Istrati had wasted no time following his own feet out of the controlled zone that was the International Hotel in Moscow's Tvertskaya. Shortly after his arrival in Russia and through a contact supplied by Souvarine, he met the Belgian-born Communist Victor Serge in Leningrad. By then a pronounced oppositionist, Serge had seen a lot since 1921, when he dismayed the visiting French anarchist Gaston Leval by observing that conditions in Russia were 'worse than during the war under Tsarism, but we are obliged to lie to save what can be saved of the revolution'.[18] Istrati paired up with Nikos Kazantzakis a little later (the future author of *Zorba the Greek* had previously spent considerable time in Soviet Russia, covering events there for an Athens newspaper). After despatching an adoring letter of explanation to Stalin, the two men made their own mission to Greece, where they gave a public lecture on events in Russia to a large audience in the Alhambra Theatre in Athens and were subsequently assailed as dangerous communists by both press and police. Having returned to the USSR in March 1928, they travelled far and wide, assisted by the considerable royalties paid to Istrati for Russian editions of his books and also a Soviet film of his first novel, *Kyra, My Sister*.[19] According to Eleni Kazantzakis, who shared some of the journey, the two men 'were garbed like a pair of twins from the country, in identical, soft blue suits, too tight because they had been made by a ladies' tailor'.[20] Their travels were facilitated by VOKS and yet, as Boris

Souvarine later confirmed, they would see far more of the Soviet Union than had been available to any other foreign visitor before.

Sometimes Istrati was only affronted in his own prejudices. Unlike Kazantzakis, who would celebrate African and Asian delegates as exotic harbingers of the revolutionary future, Istrati was horrified to see a black African Communist—described as a member of the World Congress of Oppressed Peoples and Races—being displayed like a pet mascot. This fellow was, so Istrati claimed, to be found spouting the appropriate 'idiocies' at all the receptions and parades associated with the tenth anniversary, and he was even, as Istrati declared to his particular disgust, photographed sitting on the throne of the bloody Romanovs.[21] Istrati's sense of racial shock was like that felt by E. D. Morel, Ethel Snowden, and other Western socialists when, in April 1920, the government of France used North African troops in their occupation of the German Ruhr (to the regret of some British feminists, Morel had written of 'The Black Scourge' and the French socialist Jean Longuet described the North African troops' occupation of the house in which Goethe had been born as 'a symbol which has painfully affected the whole of thinking in Europe').[22] Such an assault on the colour-line was evidently not the emancipation Istrati expected of the Bolshevik revolution. Yet this chaotic observer, whose 'incessant fluctuations' are well described in Kazantzakis's *Toda Raba*,[23] felt more honourable moments of alarm too.

Much as he had admired the great anniversary parade on 7 November, Istrati could hardly overlook the brawl that broke out beneath the balcony on which he was standing. The commotion was the work of Leon Trotsky and his fellow oppositionists, who tried to address the crowd in the name of the revolution and, as Trotsky himself would later remember, call it back to the true path with placards and slogans: 'Let us turn our fire to the right—against the kulak, the nepman and the bureaucrat'; 'Let us carry out Lenin's Will'; 'Against opportunism, against a split, and for the unity of Lenin's party'.[24] The placards were ripped out of the demonstrators' hands and torn up, while their bearers were 'mauled by specially organized units' and driven out of the square. Trotsky himself found his car shot at by a policeman, and further assaulted by a drunken fire-brigade official who jumped up onto the running board and smashed the glass. It was, he would later conclude, a rehearsal of the coming Thermidor.

Istrati's sense of unease was increased by the trilingual bulletin produced for the foreign delegates, which launched into the most vituperative attacks on Trotsky and Zinoviev, both of whom would be expelled from the Soviet

Communist Party a few days after the anniversary.[25] Further provocations would follow the Fifteenth Party Congress, held in Moscow over three weeks in December. Here ninety-eight other leading members of the left opposition were cast out, including Christian Rakovsky. Having refused to grovel after the rejection of his initial attempt at conciliation, Rakovsky, who, like Lev Kamenev, had earlier been removed from the Central Committee, was repeatedly interrupted and denounced as he gave a speech claiming that Stalin, with whom, six years previously, he had argued momentously about the rights of the republics then being subordinated to the centralized power of the new Union of Soviet Socialist Republics,[26] was quite deluded in thinking that the British and other foreign working classes were in either mind or condition to come to the rescue of the Soviet revolution.

In an appeal submitted to the congress on 19 December, Kamenev, Zinoviev, and some twenty others who had been expelled from the party the previous day, would recant their earlier heresies, condemn the demonstrations with which they had set out to interrupt the anniversary celebrations of 7 November, and promise to submit to the party line in a pitiful attempt to regain their membership.[27] Ordered to make their submissions later and on an individual basis, these supplicants were rejected in their collective appeal and threatened with a torrent of dire metaphors launched by various members of the Central Committee. Stalin had cited Lenin as he called for 'the lid' to be put on the opposition and described the Party as a cart that was 'dangerous for those who do not sit firmly'.[28] Mikhail Tomsky had warned that, with Kamenev and others now out of the party, an 'open door' faced all opposition sympathizers who remained: they must renounce their Trotskyist 'system of views'[29] completely, or share the fate of Kamenev, whom Alexei Rykov had already advised to 'throw himself into the sea and swim, so that he will either get to the other side or drown'.[30]

Nikolai Bukharin would soon enough be approaching Kamenev to express his own doubts about Stalin. At the fifteenth congress, however, the future leader of the 'right opposition' was still in coalition with the general secretary and emerging dictator. As a prominent defender of Lenin's New Economic Policy against its ardent Trotskyist critics, and the leading theorist of an industrialization that would take a conciliatory approach to the Russian peasantry, he too barked ferociously across the 'unbridgeable chasm'[31] that now lay between the party and the expelled members of the left opposition. Having denounced the 'tentacles'[32] with which Trotskyism had reached into both the Comintern and the Soviet Communist Party, he

resorted to familiar theatrical imagery as he mocked the capitulating renegades who were trying to slide back into the party at the last minute.

As Victor Serge would later recall, Bukharin told them 'the iron curtain of
History was falling, and you got out of its way in the nick of time'.[33] It was
a charming phrase, as Victor Serge notes sardonically, adding that Bukharin's
'iron curtain' had quickly turned out to be a guillotine too—albeit, perhaps, still a 'dry guillotine' of the kind Bukharin had earlier employed
when excluding dissenters from the Communist International.[34] In Serge's
judgement, its descent marked Stalin's abandonment of legality as well as
the beginning of a systematic persecution of the left opposition whose
'liquidation' as 'counter-revolutionary enemies of the people'[35] had been
demanded so loudly.

Istrati would make his own protest against these developments in May
1928, when Serge himself was arrested and imprisoned. In September of that
year, Istrati travelled down the Volga, a scenically congenial journey, which
took him to Astrakhan, among the marshes where the Volga joins the Cas-
pian Sea. It was here that he met up once again—he describes the encounter as if it were merely a coincidental accident—with Christian Rakovsky.
Like Trotsky and several hundred other oppositionists, the Soviet Union's
former ambassador to Paris had been banished by Stalin. Astrakhan may not
have been exactly 300 miles from the nearest railway station, as the *International Herald Tribune* had warned when it announced Rakovsky's impending
exile on 10 January 1928, but the isolation was real enough. It had, as Istrati
knew at first hand, been Rakovsky who, in 1905, had first drawn the world's
attention to the mutiny of the sailors on the Battleship Potemkin, having
greeted them, and also tried to stiffen their revolutionary spirit, when they
sailed their ship into the Romanian port of Constanza. But his long years of
service now served only to incriminate him.

On his return from Paris to Moscow, Rakovsky had been invited to capitu-
late to the Central Committee but, as Serge records, he had replied: 'I am
getting old. Why should I blot my biography?'[36] So here he was, stripped
of all privileges and boxed up with his books and papers in a remote mos-
quito-infested marsh, where he worked as a lowly economist in the local
planning department and, in his own time, continued to analyse and condemn the bureaucratic 'decomposition' of the USSR under Stalin.[37] It was a
disconcerting encounter, even if Istrati cannot have known that Rakovsky's
ordeal would culminate ten years later in his appearance as one of the
accused—incriminated by his own spurious 'confession'—in the show

trial that, in March 1938, led to the execution of Bukharin, Rykov, and others (Rakovsky himself would be imprisoned and eventually shot on Stalin's orders in 1941).

Istrati's worries deepened in December 1928, when a campaign of vilification was launched against Victor Serge's father-in-law. A manual worker of forty years' standing, Alexander Ivanovitch Roussakov had a distinguished history as an independent revolutionary in Marseilles, where he had been interned prior to his departure for Petrograd in 1919. He had, as Istrati recorded, wept for joy as he arrived in Russia and, like so many others, bent down to kiss the soil of the beloved revolution.[38] Now, however, he was threatened with the death penalty and savagely attacked in the press, which had cooked up a grotesque array of lies and distortions in support of 'a Communist virago' who wanted to acquire a room in Roussakov's well-appointed flat at 19 Jeliabov Street in Leningrad.

The case was another disastrous 'microcosm' of life in Stalin's Russia. Far from emancipating the peoples of the Soviet Union, the regime was, so Istrati concluded, driving them with 'scientific management' techniques imported from America and terrorizing them with the constant threat of starvation or imprisonment in political labour camps such as Istrati and Kazantzakis had tried to visit on the Solovki Isles on the White Sea.[39] It was making Russia into a land where 'man is a mechanical brute and where existence is nothing but a way of killing life'.[40] Fearless as well as erratic in outlook, Istrati took his objections to senior officials of the Soviet regime and, as Kazantzakis recalls, also urged various audiences to launch a new revolution that would turn its flame against Stalin's bureaucratizing regime.

This was not exactly how things appeared to Kazantzakis. A Bergsonian 'metacommunist', who dreamed of Ulysses, Christ, and Buddha as well as Lenin, Istrati's Greek comrade remained fascinated by the brutally transformative 'spirit' of the ongoing revolution: a spirit of 'leaping ahead, destroying and creating'.[41] In Toda Raba, his 'confession in the form of a novel', Kazantzakis writes of loving not humanity but the 'inhuman flame that devours them'.[42] He sees much individual suffering and cruelty, but registers it as part of the necessary 'crucifixion' of a present that barely existed except as the tortured 'transition' between a past that must be burned away like Pompeii, and a future still to be realized.[43] Old Mensheviks must shuffle off to die, just as the kulaks and Nepmen, who stand in the way of the new Becoming, have to be smashed ('We've got to beat them to death',[44] as one of Kazantzakis's more ardent 'men of action' exclaims).

Without Tint or Hue

Having fallen out with Kazantzakis, Istrati returned to Paris in February 1929 and rented a large workshop near the street on which Boris Souvarine was then living. The two would meet up more or less every day. Souvarine found Istrati in an agitated and confused state: he describes his friend marching about with arms flailing like the sails of a windmill, and bursting with exclamations and reflections: 'some naive and some highly pertinent'.[45] Souvarine set out to lever his Balkan friend's seething impressions onto a properly established Trotskyist foundation, using his own daily scrutiny of the Soviet press in order to establish that the episodes Istrati had seen in Russia reflected the underlying patterns of the totalitarian regime being developed under Stalin.

Soon Istrati resolved to publish a throughgoing exposé of conditions in the USSR. Exploiting his reputation as a commercially successful writer, he would publish no less than three books under his own name. The trilogy would be entitled *Towards the Other Flame,* but Istrati himself would only write the first volume. Published with the subtitle *After Sixteen Months in the USSR* in October 1929, it contained his own autobiographical 'Confession of a Loser', a diary of his journey through Russia, and also his highly critical account of the scandal he would make known as 'the Roussakov Affair'.[46]

A second volume, published a month later as *Soviets 1929,* consisted of a largely Trotskyist analysis of conditions in Russia, given to Istrati by Victor Serge.[47] This opened (and closed) with a contemptuous swipe at the USSR's foreign visitors and their habit of getting a 300-page book out of a stage-managed three week visit. Anybody could use Russia to confirm their prejudices in this manner, whether their wish was to denigrate the Soviet world, or praise it with the help of official bulletins and the elevated view glimpsed from aeroplanes made available by the bureaucracy.[48] For Serge, however, Russia had to be understood as a reality in which the urge for revolution and the urge for capitalist restoration were still fighting it out in all arenas. He condemned those who found it appropriate to hide the ills of Soviet society on the grounds that it was still struggling to be born and one didn't want to feed the enemy. The duty of the revolutionary observer was neither to affect 'absurd neutrality' nor to pretend that the revolution had already triumphed, but rather to 'awaken his brothers to the dangers he sees'.[49] At a time when Stalin was establishing a bureaucratic apparatus of control in the place where emancipation had once been promised, it would be criminal to ignore the internal threat facing the revolution.

Serge outlined the fate of Trotsky, banished to Alma Ata in Kazakstan, and of hundreds of other oppositionists: silenced, driven from their jobs, and forced into the outer darkness. He described the bureaucratization of Soviet life, and the diversion of funds into buildings and projects that suited the controlling apparatus, but left the real needs of the people unaddressed. Noting that no genuinely new political theorists had emerged in Russia over the previous decade, he condemned the debased version of Marxism that was being parroted in the universities and elsewhere by opportunists who wore 'communist camouflage'[50] but were anything but revolutionary at heart. He described the lamentable condition of the Soviet economy, and denounced the international 'Friends of the USSR' for their willingness to obscure the true situation with lies and falsely optimistic reports.[51]

Merciless in his condemnation of most foreign visitors, Serge was more sympathetic towards 'the tragedy of Maxim Gorki', the hugely popular author who finally responded to pressure to break his Italian exile and returned to Russia for several months in 1928, the year of his sixtieth birthday. From the moment he entered the country, Gorki was feted in the most extravagant manner. He wept, smiled, waved into immense crowds, and embraced an endless succession of leaders, deputations and functionaries. 'Never had a writer returning to his country been received in such a manner.'[52] Unaware that he was effectively the captive of those welcoming him, Gorki started making compliant noises: marvelling at the factories, schools, and workers' clubs, giving speeches about the great achievements of the new society, and even promising to launch a new magazine entitled 'Our Success'. As Serge writes, 'The first harangue of this kind seemed *de rigueur*. The second seemed superfluous. At the thirtieth one asked: "But does he see nothing? Does he not understand that real life is utterly different from what he sees as a grand official visitor?"'[53]

At the moment when Russia was entering a terrible grain shortage, and when its autocratic rulers saw fit to exile the heroes responsible for the initial success of the revolution, Gorki saw only a rose-coloured world in which the sky was always bright blue. Some dismayed opposition Communists remembered the diatribes Gorki had published against Lenin and Trotsky in 1917, and told Serge that Gorki was at least consistent, having never been a truly committed friend of the proletarian revolution. For Serge, however, this ritual unmasking was insufficiently attentive to the genuine difficulties of maintaining a sense of perspective when crossing the division between Communist East and capitalist West. Gorki's inability to see through official appearances reflected an 'interior exhaustion' caused by Western anti-bolshevism, a feeling of repulsion inspired by white Russian emigration and reaction, and the fact that this ageing, homesick writer had been disarmed by massive displays of affection organized with all the resources of the state and of a workers' party that represented 'the most formidable concentration of power known to modern history'.[54]

The USSR Stripped Bare

The third volume of Istrati's collaborative denunciation of Stalin's Russia appeared in December 1929 as *La Russie nue*.[55] It was the work of Boris Souvarine, who had initially been highly reluctant to go along with his Balkan friend's unorthodox publication plans. However, summer was approaching and he was both unemployed and broke. He consented soon enough when Istrati offered to advance him some money and threw in a new suit of light summer clothing as a bonus. Leaving Paris for Provence, Souvarine took up residence in a hotel in Carquerianne and set to work producing an analysis of Stalin's Russia that was more analytically grounded than Istrati's own impassioned flight.[56]

Having himself been denounced repeatedly at the Fifteenth Congress of the Soviet Communist Party, Souvarine was well aware of the 'iron curtain' that Bukharin had helped to lower between Stalin's party and the now isolated left opposition at home and abroad. His target here, however, was 'the masking veil of Red propaganda'[57] between Russian reality and the foreign 'pilgrim tourists' who so persistently failed to see through it.

In Souvarine's analysis, the challenge facing visitors to Russia was similar to that experienced by tourists everywhere:

> The difference existing between the outward aspect of things and their intimate content is not peculiar to Russia. Admirers of ancient ruins in any country stand filled with wonder at their picturesqueness without sparing a moment's thought for the unfortunates condemned to spend their lives in such surroundings. Friends of old Paris protest on archaeological grounds against the proposed demolition of the sordid hovels on the Ile St. Louis, while they themselves live in their new, clean houses at Auteuil. The glorious tints and hues of the countryside, which enrapture visitors, do not … hinder men from living there in filth and squalor.[58]

Yet perceptions of Soviet Russia were greatly aggravated by additional considerations. Souvarine cites the Western visitor's ignorance of Russia and the Russian language, the vigilant attendance of official guides, the sense of indebtedness engendered by Soviet 'hospitality', and the fear of persecution silencing those Russian witnesses who might otherwise puncture the *phantastikon* in which the Soviet reception agencies enclosed their Western guests.

Like Istrati, Souvarine insisted that the truth about Russia stood by itself, 'clear and unmistakable',[59] unmoved by the rival pro- and anti-Soviet currents that tried to pull it this way and that. Yet to reach that truth in a situation so largely defined by ignorance, political polarization, and 'legend', it was necessary to meet certain criteria. To start with, it was not enough merely to go to Russia with a view to authenticating your prejudices, for or against. On the contrary, the analyst must, like Souvarine himself, be sympathetic towards the revolution and aware of the appalling injustices and miseries it had tried to address. It was necessary to know the Russian language (as Souvarine, Serge, and Istrati all did), and to have sufficient knowledge of the country and its past to be able to distinguish what is 'Soviet from what is Russian'. Given the disorientating power of the contrary propagandas, Souvarine also stipulated that all the facts cited as evidence must be of Soviet origin, and therefore immune to the accusation that they might be ideologically motivated fictions put about by the regime's enemies.

Scouring the main party newspapers, publications aimed at specialist readerships, and even comic books for children, Souvarine built up a furious indictment of a regime that was sealing its people into a benighted world of hunger, ignorance and terror. Surveying coverage of the trade unions, the co-operatives, and the Communist Party itself, he found ample indications that all were in the hands of corrupt and debauched opportunists who had turned the USSR into a brutish hell where rape and anti-Semitism went unchecked, where alcoholism was resurgent (the famous ban on alcohol having been lifted shortly after Lenin's death), and where illiteracy remained both pervasive and useful. Schools were devoted to the most abject kind of drilling and rote learning, and certainly not to the 'progressive' child-centred ideas that had impressed Dora Russell, Margaret Bondfield, and other British enthusiasts in 1920. The 'Red corners', set up in factories and other workplaces, were often left locked up, or used as shrines to the all-powerful party line rather than places of genuine political education.[60] Behind the 'model' institutions created to distract foreign visitors, the USSR was becoming a dismal forcing house, where all efforts were concentrated on increasing the powers of the state, rather than lifting the people out of the miserable condition in which they had been left by the tsars.

Souvarine certainly had his own article of faith. True to the already conventional Trotskyist schematization, he was adamant that all had been well with the revolution before Lenin died in 1924. In those early days, so Souvarine insisted, Bolshevism had not depended on deceit. Indeed, Russia's first Bolshevik rulers had been genuinely concerned to know the truth about conditions in their lands, and the misery and suffering of the Russian peoples. 'Far from keeping silent concerning the disorganisation in their country, the decay of its productive powers, and the devastating effect of famine throughout vast districts, they relied upon these revelations to stimulate increased support for the movement.'[61] Lenin's epoch was 'certainly not free from illusions' yet, even with the enormous hopes provoked by war and revolution, 'no Communist would have dreamed of claiming that all was for the best in the best of revolutions'. Lenin himself had freely confessed to making mistakes, and the comparatively few 'pilgrim tourists' of that time had not been suborned by the Soviet state: their reports were, Souvarine suggests, still relatively 'artless' in their optimism, and their 'veracity based on their author's word alone'.

Stalin, meanwhile, had not admitted to a single mistake during his six years in power, and he was assisted in his deformation of the revolution by an organized 'troop of sycophants who, under various designations, endeavour to sing his praises on every hand'.[62] It had become 'an act of high treason against the Revolution to state the truth or to make known the actual facts, even when this was done in a spirit which conformed most strictly to Communist inclinations'.[63] In its first years, the Russian Revolution had been 'harried and villified' by foes intent on destroying it. But after Lenin's death, 'the new leaders, suffering from some amazing form of mental aberration, exposed it to even a greater danger; they eulogised it systematically, approved it fanatically, almost slandered it with their extravagant praise; and the results of this policy have been more definitely harmful and lasting than any that preceded it'.[64]

Such was the debased political climate in which the foreign 'delegate' had become part of the machine—'in reality a functionary nominated by other functionaries who are in their turn dependent upon higher officials at Moscow'.[65] The idiocies of these delegates were many. Souvarine mentions the fool who 'insulted' Lenin's memory by praising the Bolshevik leader for having resisted the suggestion that he should have a pair of boots made for himself out of canvas cut from paintings by Van Gogh.[66] He also takes a swipe at a gullible party who glanced out of their passing 'charabanc' to see throngs of people queuing for food, and were all too easily reassured by their minders that these desperate citizens were actually waiting to subscribe to a generous new government loan.[67]

Far from being innocent dupes systematically misled by their hosts, Souvarine judged the foreign 'delegates' who flocked to Russia in 1927 to be 'incompetent, unscrupulous investigators'. As 'hirelings of the Soviet legend' they were all too inclined to dismiss the miseries generated by the Soviet regime as 'the heritage of the past', to be blamed on the tsars, while genuine inheritances from pre-revolutionary times were used to glorify the USSR.[68] Thus, the abandoned and desperate children living on the streets of Russian cities were described as victims of the 1914 war and not (as Lenin's widow N. Krupskaya had protested at the end of 1925) of present unemployment and the appalling condition to which the peasantry had been reduced.

Reading the books and articles of Western 'tourists' who had visited Russia in 1927, Souvarine was disgusted to see the ancient Kremlin itself being converted into an icon of Communist legitimacy. Likewise, the corps de ballet and chorus at the Grand Theatre, and the art galleries with their progressive modern works by Matisse and Cézanne. Even the scenery in Georgia was praised 'just as if it were a result of Soviet rule'. Souvarine would remember wanting to make the same criticism of Istrati's 'enchanted' description of his descent down the Volga. When writing his memoir of *Panaït Istrati and Communism* more than forty years later, Souvarine longed to tap his erratic and by now long-dead Balkan friend on the shoulder and remind him 'that the majesty of the river and the beauty of the countryside were the work of nature, not of Bolshevism, and that the remarkable comfort of the boat on which he travelled was an inheritance from the old regime'.[69]

Souvarine loathed the 'salaried or benevolent apologists who go about the world extolling the system of government established in Russia since the death of Lenin'.[70] And he was in no doubt that these 'blind, obliging tourists'[71] were guilty on both sides of Buxton's 'iron curtain'. In their own countries, 'the Soviet legend, invented, propagated, and kept alive at the instigation of the Government in Moscow, only succeeds in arousing a superficial and entirely verbal solidarity amongst the most backward elements in the working class, at the same time introducing deceptions which will result in an irreparable alienation of sympathy'.[72] These grinning 'friends of the USSR' served differently on the Soviet side of the great division. Exhibited from the regime's grandstands and written up as admirers of party policy, they became demoralizing tools of Stalin's regime.

By 1929, it was common knowledge that Soviet Russia operated show institutions to deceive Western delegates. Yet, as Souvarine noticed as he continued his virtuoso reading of the Soviet press, deceptions of a more inward orientation were being reported too. One of his examples concerned a commission of inquiry sent to examine conditions in a number of mines in the Donets basin. The report of this investigation was highly critical. Supervision of both technical and hygienic matters was found to be 'extraordinarily weak', and the miner's safety lamps were in 'lamentable' shape. Writing in *Izvestia* on 12 July 1929, a reporter who had accompanied the commission noted that attempts were also made to trick the visiting inspectors with "'villages *à la Potemkin*", or, in other words, to camouflage the realities'.[73]

Here too, Souvarine was prescient. Appearing in the winter of 1929, Istrati's trilogy was published at the same time as Stalin's collectivization drive was unleashed on the Soviet countryside. Driven by ideas that Serge and others would rightly claim had been stolen from the exiled left opposition, this fundamental constituent of Stalin's First Five-Year Plan entailed the brutal expropriation and displacement of uncounted millions of 'kulaks': it produced another round of mass starvation and, as was revealed in the haunted dreams of at least one senior commander who supervised punitive 'dekulakization' raids before turning to a psychoanalyst in Berlin, added greatly to the number of abandoned children living wild on the streets of Russian cities.[74]

By the early 1930s all this, so the historian Sheila Fitzpatrick has suggested, would be hidden behind a vast Potemkin village: an idyllic screen adorned with birch trees and copious apple blossom, smiling mothers and patriotic sons, red tractors and balalaikas, spacious new houses complete with lace curtains and pot plants, and further dressed with thoroughly manipulated production figures. Created for internal consumption, this largely unattainable pastorale described the world 'not as it was but as it was becoming, as Soviet Marxists believed it necessarily *would be* in the future', and it meant considerably 'more in Soviet life than a façade to impress visiting VIPs'.[75]

For Kazantzakis and Istrati it was still possible, more than a decade after the Bolshevik revolution, to believe that Soviet reality 'does not exist', except in 'a state of becoming'.[76] This was not how things were presented internally. Reinforced by socialist realism in art, literature, and film, the idea that Lenin's promised future had actually arrived under Stalin would be projected in the innumerable meetings that Communism brought to the collectivized villages, and confirmed by Stalin's proclamation, delivered in front of an audience of outstanding combine operators in 1935, that 'Life has become better and more cheerful.'[77] The idyll would also feature enraptured foreign visitors, wandering through the pavilions of the All-Union Agricultural Exhibition in Moscow, though perhaps no longer quite so pleased to note, as some liberal-minded French delegates are said to have done in 1927, that two old peasants, Rykov and Kalinin, occupied positions at the head of the Soviet state or, for that matter, that Stalin seemed truly to be the King of the Kulaks thanks to 'the confidence he had inspired with his defence, against Trotsky's opposition, of landed property rights'.[78]

The Man Who Will Adhere to Nothing

Serge, Souvarine, and Istrati did much to expose Stalin's emerging deformation of Soviet Russia, but their books were published to very little effect. The two sequels appeared a little later than Istrati's first and more sensational volume (published by Reidel on 15 October 1929), and Istrati wasn't even in France for their appearance: he had returned to Romania where—perhaps partly in an attempt to insulate himself against the coming onslaught from Moscow—he would take up the cause of oppressed workers (shortly before his return in August twenty-one miners had been massacred in Lupeni) and Communists facing trial in Timisoara.[79]

   In Souvarine's retrospective judgement, their collaborative attempt to turn 'fire and flame' on Stalinism was a complete failure. It would be Istrati himself who got burned. Moscow set out to destroy this Romanian 'vagabond' and 'bandit' with a sustained campaign of lying denigration waged through the French Communist press, including *L'Humanité,* which had been among Souvarine's fiercely assaulted targets in *Russia Unveiled.* What Romain Rolland described as a carefully planned 'public execution'[80] was carried out by Henri Barbusse, author of *Under Fire,* France's most celebrated novel of the Great War. By now a craven Stalinist (he had been roundly attacked as such by Istrati), Barbusse enlisted grotesque lies to condemn Istrati variously as an opportunist who had turned on the Soviet Union because they had failed to pay him, as a secret police agent who had participated in the massacre of striking miners in Romania, and as a member of a fascist militia who had betrayed his old comrades in Braila.[81]

Though denounced as a racist and anti-Semitic fascist who had been welcomed on his return to reactionary Romania, Istrati was in reality kept under close watch by the secret police who judged him an 'extreme danger to the Romanian Bourgeois State', and repeatedly attacked by fascists and nationalist students, who reviled him as a Jew. Gravely ill with tuberculosis, and abandoned by his old friends in France, Istrati tried to rise above the torrent of calumnies, declaiming from a Bucharest sanatorium in March 1933, that all 'organization' only served the organizers, and that those who aimed to turn the people into a herd of beasts were no better than assassins.

Caught between the opposed forces of Communism and Fascism, he struck back with a new motto, 'Long Live the man who will adhere to nothing', explaining that he no longer believed 'in any idea, in any party, in any man', and insisting 'I am the eternal opponent'.[82] But the Stalinists' mud stuck and Istrati would not be remembered for his histrionic resistance to both sides of the political barricade: even less, for his Balkan advocacy, issued as an experienced vagabond, of a 'nomadic' way of life that might enable people to escape capture by the systems of 'organization' on either side of the polarization he could not, in the end, escape. Istrati died in April 1935, prompting *L'Humanité,* the French Communist paper which had done so much to brand him a self-seeking opportunist and traitor, to issue another despicable assault on this 'ex-revolutionary writer' who had 'died in the skin of a fascist'.[83] His political books were effectively buried with him: boycotted by Stalinists, they would also be banned by the authorities in occupied France during the Second World War.

Had they been heeded, the warnings of Istrati, Serge, Souvarine, and also, for that matter, of Emma Goldman, Friedrich Adler, and others, might have made some difference by the early 1930s. But they were not, and the dominant criticism of Soviet Russia did not come from any position on the left. Nobody could expect Conservatives such as Lord Birkenhead or Winston Churchill to be much impressed by the arguments of anarchists, anti-Bolshevik socialists, or left opposition Communists whose response to Stalin's First Five-Year Plan, the adoption of which in 1928 heralded the defeat of Bukharin, Rykov, and other 'right deviationists' in the Russian Communist Party, was to complain that he had stolen his best ideas from them: suppress the bureaucracy and the profiteers of Lenin's sadly mistaken New Economic Policy, declare war against the hated kulaks, and force through collectivization of the land.

There would come a time when apostasy and 'recantation' became quite the thing, and many former communists would line up to offer their account of 'The God that failed'. But the left-wing dissidents of the late 1920s were not like that and their objections were little regarded. In Britain, the lack of response, at least from liberals and democratic socialists, may have been directly related to efforts being made to lift a different 'iron curtain': not the one that Bukharin had seen falling around the left opposition at the Fifteenth Party Congress in December 1927, but the version described by Charles Roden Buxton as having descended again between Soviet Russia and the capitalist West when Britain broke off relations a few months earlier.

In 1929, and against fierce Tory opposition, diplomatic and trade relations between Britain and Russia were restored under Arthur Henderson, Foreign Secretary in Britain's second Labour government. Speaking in favour of recognition at a Labour Party demonstration at Fulham Town Hall, Lord Parmoor, the Lord President of the Council, condemned the attempt to recreate the anti-Soviet clamour that had defeated the first Labour government at the time of the Zinoviev letter: 'It is surely time that prejudice, such as was raised in 1924, should be allayed as unworthy of the democracy of this country.'[84] He was attacking Tory scaremongers, yet he also urged the members of his own party to recognize that this was not the time to dwell on the weaknesses of Soviet Russia. The Labour Party must 'avoid undue criticism during the period of the building up of the international policy', since such criticism 'might lead to misunderstanding outside this country'.

Tactical silence may certainly have eased the way to British recognition of Soviet Russia but it would do much heavier work in the 1930s. As the world faced a stark choice between Communism and Nazism, Western perceptions of Russia would be informed less by unruly leftist critics such as Istrati and Souvarine, than by comparatively liberal-minded 'fellow travellers' who, as Trotsky wrote in *The Revolution Betrayed,* could be found benignly drifting through Russia: 'kowtowing before accomplished fact', exhibiting a partiality for 'sedative generalisations', and then coming home, not to revolt against capitalism in their own countries, but to recite the quietening creed that Trotsky eventually mocked as 'socialism for radical tourists'.[85]

PART
V

Stalin's Ring of Trust
(1927–1939)

Mr. A.B. (of the I.L.P)
He went to Russia
To learn the Truth about Russia
(The regeneration of Russia),
And the sights he selected
Bore out what he expected—
    Great factories rising;
    An Enthusiasm surprising
    For welfare and education;
    A New World in formation
    Much better than the Old—
    Just as he had foretold.

Mr. R.S. (who reads the *Express*)
He also went to Russia
(The approaching collapse of Russia),
And (all contradictions rejected)
He saw what he expected—
    Breakdowns in transportation;
    A growing indignation
    With the Communist oppression;
    A steady retrogression
    To chaos, bloody and red—
    Just as he always said.

And I, who read them both.
Have taken a solemn oath
To believe no 'Truth about Russia'
(Friendly or hostile to Russia)
Which harnesses every fact
To a formula exact;
And proves, in the end, to be
What the writer had wished to see.

MACFLECKNOE, 'The "Truth about Russia"',
New Statesman and Nation, 10 September 1932

15

No End to the Potemkin Complex

A reflection is a compressed, condensed 'spiritual reproduction' of reality. An accurate, true reflection is one that precisely condenses these associations, qualities, properties, relationships, and processes, and does not create illusory ones; that is, ones which do not have a material correlate, or any real correlate existing outside of the subject.

Nikolai Bukharin, writing in the Lubyanka prison, 1937[1]

One blazing hot summer evening in the 1950s, the political prisoners who lay sweltering in their underpants in Cell No. 72 of Moscow's Butyrki Prison were surprised by a burst of highly irregular activity. Fifty of them were led away to other accommodation, and the twenty-five who remained in the no longer grossly overcrowded cell were then marched off too.

Apprehensive about their destination, they found themselves in the prison bathhouse where they were shaved, given haircuts, and invited to wash with specially provided bars of 'Lilac Fairy' bathsoap. Having had their toenails clipped and been served an unprecedented feast of porridge and potatoes, they were informed of the dawn of a new era. Admitting 'grave errors of administration' in the past, a senior major promised that the prisoners would henceforth be recognized as 'decent Soviet citizens' and that 'rest-home conditions' would prevail. New clothes were issued—blue silk underwear, suits of imitation twill, ties and shirts, yellow boots supplied by America under the Lend-Lease scheme—and the men were then escorted back to discover their cell amazingly transformed. They found down pillows and canvas webbing where their bug-infested plank beds had been. Bedside tables had appeared, together with bookcases and, even more miraculous, a packet of 'Kazbek' cigarettes, which lay by an ashtray on the centrally placed table. The bars of their cell were now a cheerful blue, and the normally dingy walls had been painted with 'doves with ribbons in their beaks that bore such inscriptions as "Peace in our time!" and "Peace on earth!"' As for the corner where the stinking slop bucket normally stood, it had been converted into a devotional recess for worshippers of diverse faiths: equipped with Bible, Koran, and Talmud, it also featured an icon of the Virgin and Child, a statue of the Madonna, and a smiling bronze Buddha.

This surreal transformation is evoked in 'The Buddha's Smile', a satirical story first composed in Moscow's Butyrki Prison by two political prisoners, Aleksander Solzhenitsyn and Nikolai Andreyevitch Semyonov, and eventually published as part of Solzhenitsyn's *The First Circle,* in the 1960s.[2] It would not be until the next day that the cause of the extraordinary transformation of Cell No. 72 became apparent to its newly relaxed occupants. Left to sleep until noon, they wake to find leisurely magazines being pushed into their cell, followed by two old but comfortable armchairs. Shortly afterwards a party of visitors arrives. 'Mrs. R', widow of 'the famous politician',[3] was accompanied by 'two respectable ladies, who looked like Quakers'. These Westerners had come to Russia to see that aid supplied through the United Nation's Relief and Rehabilitation Administration was reaching the people for whom it was intended, and also to 'discover whether freedom of conscience was being restricted in the USSR'.[4]

Soon enough Mrs R is sitting in one of those recently imported armchairs, telling the prisoners how delighted she is to find their cell, which she presumes to have been 'selected completely at random and visited on the spur of the moment', so light and newly whitewashed and free from flies. One of the inmates is serving ten years for 'being careless enough to make the acquaintance of an American tourist', yet by the time the interpreter has finished converting him into a Gestapo-collaborating murderer and rapist, Mrs R is wondering why the fellow has not been hanged. The prisoners try to complain about their conditions, but the interpreter deftly converts their utterances into unanimous protests against 'the oppression of Negroes in the USA'. Having watched these famished men demolish every scrap of the freakishly adequate food provided during her visit, Mrs R leaves the cell saying to her escorts, 'What coarse manners they have and how uneducated these miserable creatures are! One can only hope they learn to behave better after ten years in here. You have a splendid prison here!'[5]

The Uses of Confusion

Based on a widely circulated 'camp anecdote'[6] about a prison visit alleged to have been made by Mrs Eleanor Roosevelt, 'The Buddha's Smile' may be counted a delayed response to the spectacular idiocy of so many Western visitors to the USSR. Though a literary work, it stands in the tradition of the apparently unprovoked punch that, in 1932, a passing Red Army soldier landed in the face of the British literary investigator, Archibald Lyall, as he walked opposite the Hotel Metropole in Moscow,[7] and also of the large hunks of road surface hurled, that same year, at a departing train on the line between Rostov and Kiev: the latter assault was mounted by enraged peasants who had disembarked, having been forced to 'volunteer' their seats when the carriage carrying a party of British students caught fire due to a shortage of axle-grease.[8]

The phrase 'iron curtain' seems to have fallen into comparative disuse during the 1930s, and yet it was in this decade that the theatrical deceptions earlier described by Douillet, Souvarine, Istrati, and others, were expanded and put on a more systematic basis. It was the time of what the Russian-born American foreign correspondent Eugene Lyons would call 'the Great Tourist Invasion', in which thousands of Westerners flocked year after year to the Soviet Union, drawn by the thrill of a land where, in the words of an American enthusiast, 'the Bolsheviks are endeavouring to change the core of life itself'.[9]

It was a decade of closely organized tourist itineraries, featuring controlled Intourist hotels and a series of show places that had been vastly augmented since the time of the first delegations. The earlier sights had included the factory crèche and kindergarten, special 'prophylacteries' devoted to the rehabilitation of prostitutes,[10] and the Bolshevo prison near Moscow, established as 'The First Labour Commune of the OGPU' in 1924, and eulogized by its frantically happy inmates as an exemplary reformatory without walls.[11] Now, however, the attractions included gargantuan industrial installations. These 'show giants'[12] of the Five-Year Plan were epitomized by the vast steelworks and new city created on the conquered steppe at Magnitogorsk, or the Dnieperstroi dam and hydroelectricity plant on the river Dnieper—both designed and built with the help of American engineers, but exhibited as monuments to the vast reality Stalin had made of Lenin's once incredible dreams of electrification.

Those responsible for preparing Soviet Russia for foreign visitors exploited the historical separation of the cities—Moscow, Leningrad, and a number of provincial cities—from the great expanse of the USSR, which remained remote, inaccessible and largely unvisited. As a contemporary critic remarked of Soviet tourism in the early 1930s, 'The cultural achievements of the capitals are simply a mirage; they characterize a milieu in which a small circle of the elect lives its own life quite apart from the misery and distress of the population.'[13] It was a 'mirage' that required careful maintenance, as was noted by the increasingly doubtful British Communist Freda Utley. Looking out of her Moscow window one day early in November 1933, she saw the police driving 'some wrecks of humanity down into the cellar of our building'.[14] The anniversary celebrations of the October Revolution were approaching, and it had been decided that 'the foreigners must not see the starving, homeless hordes', who were therefore being rounded up, assembled at collection points such as the one in Utley's building, and then driven 40 or 50 miles out of Moscow, where Utley imagined them 'dumped on the road to die, like abandoned dogs or cats'.

There was, to be sure, a Potemkinist aspect to the images offered to the West in the early 1930s. However, the stage on which Russia displayed itself to Foreign visitors was by no means the only, or even the principal, venue of Stalinist theatricality. As various historians have recently argued, the USSR was by this time characterized by a 'way of life'[15] in which reality was constituted by various forms of performance. The Stalinist 'theatre state'[16] directed many shows at the people of the USSR: anniversary parades with foreign delegations attached; a revolving exhibition of the different nationalities and republics exhibited in their participation in the Soviet state; socialist realism, with its pretence that the promised future, once conceived as a shining prospect at the end of the Bolsheviks' path, had at last been realized. Stalin himself would be projected as the smiling hero of a cult of personality. Yet for millions of soviet citizens everyday life also became a theatre of 'impersonation' demanding a systematic 'reinvention of the self'.[17] As Sheila Fitzpatrick has argued, in terms similar to those others have applied to the French Revolution, people learned to 'edit' their life histories in order to establish a correctly 'proletarian' class identity, and in doing so they expose themselves to the ever present danger of being 'unmasked' and denounced as an 'imposter'.[18]

That drama of 'unmasking' would be incorporated into the Stalinist show trials—starting with the Shakhty Trial of 1928 and developing through the Industrial Party Trial (1931), which saw various Soviet scientists and engineers convicted as 'saboteurs', the Metro-Vickers Trial (1933), in which a number of British technicians faced similar charges, to the major political trials of the later 1930s. This particular form of drama culminated in the three spectacular performances of August 1936 (in which Kamenev, Zinoviev, and other leading Bolsheviks were executed and imprisoned), January 1937 (Radek, Pyatakov, et al.), and March 1938, in which Bukharin, Rakovsky, Rykov, and eighteen others were falsely condemned as Trotskyist traitors.

The show trials appealed to a wide range of emotions and employed a crude but colourful vocabulary (germs, slugs, and abscesses figured largely) to engage their audience of proletarians in a simply polarized story of good and evil. They have been described as dramas of 'poetic justice'[19] in which the secret enemies of Communism were dramatically unmasked and, after delivering their contrite and thoroughly rehearsed confessions of guilt, condemned as embodiments of allegorical types of villainy: saboteur, wrecker, Trotskyist, etc.

Played out before international as well as carefully marshalled domestic audiences, these hearings were influenced by the mock trials that had commonly been staged alongside other revolutionary festivities in the twenties, and by the early Bolshevik revolutionary courts (themselves staged in memory of the theatrically conceived popular tribunals of the French Revolution). Above all, however, they were deliberately produced as melodramas. Though akin to the 'twopence coloured' variety that Winston Churchill had once known in the Victorian toy theatre, and perhaps also to the propagandized patriotic versions that Vernon Lee had played in her satirical 'theatre of varieties' during the Great War, Soviet melodrama had its own lineage. In the 1920s it had been strongly promoted in Soviet theatre and film by the Commissar of Enlightenment, Lunacharsky, who, as has recently been suggested, owed his inspiration to Romain Rolland's essay *The People's Theatre* (1903), in which melodrama was commended as the genre that would best reconnect theatre with the masses.[20]

Fooling the Vice-President

There may have been rather less call for externally directed Potemkinist manoeuvres in the late 1930s, when Western travel to the USSR was curtailed by the Great Terror. However, Stalin's riggers would be back at work after the USSR joined the Allies in the Grand Alliance of 1941. One of the most spectacular cases from this period—as grotesque as anything in Solzhenitsyn's prison fiction—would be witnessed by a Dutch woman, Elinor Lipper, and described in a memoir entitled *Eleven Years in Soviet Prison Camps*.[21] Raised in a middle-class family in Holland, Lipper had gone to Berlin to study medicine in 1931. Seeing 'the Nazi monster' already on the rise, she joined a 'Red Student Group' and, in 1937, moved to the USSR, where she quickly came to regret the 'boundless naiveté' that had enabled her to imagine that 'the Soviet Union was the realization of my ideals'.[22] Arrested as a 'counterrevolutionary' only two months after she started work in a Moscow publishing house, she would spend eight of her eleven years in Stalin's gulag at Kolyma in Siberia. It was there that she would come across her version of the visiting Western idiot.

The man in question was Roosevelt's vice-president, Henry Wallace, who passed through Kolyma while on a mission to Soviet Asia in 1944, together with his expert adviser, Professor Owen Lattimore of Johns Hopkins University. Wallace, who was sympathetic to the Soviet Union, had served as minister of agriculture during the pre-war years of the New Deal, and Roosevelt now despatched him to review the ways of life of the tribes who, for centuries, had wandered across the Soviet–Chinese border, and to recommend ways in which the likelihood of conflict might be reduced. Not long after returning to America, Wallace published *Soviet Asia Mission,* a coauthored volume which he presented as 'a simple narrative of what I saw'.[23] For Lipper, this book proved that, for all his lofty words about increasing 'world security on the basis of broader understanding', Wallace had seen absolutely nothing. She condemned his book as 'typical of the superficial and unprincipled reports made by foreign visitors who, after a brief stay, think they are equipped to tell the truth about the Soviet Union'. Her evidence is certainly persuasive; and not just on account of the confidence with which Wallace offers such remarks as 'I do not find the people of Soviet Asia difficult to understand'; or his willingness to inform his hosts that 'Soviet Asia, in American terms, may be called the wild West of Russia'.[24]

Arriving at the new port of Magadan, Wallace and his party were welcomed by Ivan Nikishov, director of the Far Northern Construction Trust, a vast mining operation that Wallace, in the by now conventional delegate's haste to find familiar, and often fatuous, Western comparisons, likened to the Hudson's Bay Company.[25] Wallace parroted Nikishov's remark that 'Twelve years ago the first settlers arrived and put up eight prefabricated houses.

Today Magadan has 40,000 inhabitants and all are well housed.' He did not mention that the entire town had been built 'solely by prisoners working under inhuman conditions'.[26] He admired the new 'all-weather 350-mile highway'[27] running north over the mountains from Magadan, without betraying any understanding that tens of thousands of prisoners had died during its construction, or, indeed, that thousands were still required to keep it open amid 'the continual snowstorms'.

Having inspected the gold mines of Kolyma, Wallace recorded that 'the enterprise displayed here was impressive' and the ongoing development 'much more energetic than at Fairbanks' in Alaska. Quoting the data with which he had been supplied, he noted that there were now more than 1,000 mines in the area and 'about 300,000 persons in the community', without registering that the great majority of the members of this 'community' was made up of starving political prisoners, millions of whom had already died under a brutal regime of forced labour. In his eyes, the Kolyma goldminers appeared as voluntary migrants: 'big, husky young men, who came out to the Far East from European Russia'. The American visitors attended a ballet, and were surprised by the remarkable quality of the 'strictly local' orchestra. They went for a walk in the forest where, as Wallace recalled, Nikishov 'gamboled about, enjoying the wonderful air immensely'.[28] That last remark was particularly galling for Lipper, who replied: 'It is too bad that Wallace never saw him "gambolling about" on one of his drunken rages around the prison camps, raining filthy savage language upon the heads of the exhausted, starving prisoners, having them locked up in solitary confinement for no offence whatsoever, and sending them into the gold mines to work fourteen and sixteen hours a day, at no matter what human cost.'[29]

If Wallace was blithely unaware of the 'grotesque irony of his words', so too was his academic adviser, Owen Lattimore. Writing in the *National Geographic Magazine* in December 1944, Lattimore would assert that, thanks to the political oppression under the tsars, Siberia had been colonized by exiled professors, doctors, scientists, and intellectuals.[30] Unaware that, in Lipper's words, 'the entire population is made up of victims of political oppression', Lattimore commended the fact that the scientists working in the area were no longer 'lonely exiles', but had 'the organized support of the government'.[31] Lipper was no more forgiving about Lattimore's approval of Mr and Mrs Nikishov for their aesthetic sensitivity and their 'deep sense of civic responsibility'.[32] 'What', she wondered, 'would Dr. Lattimore think of a man who, having visited the Nazi camps of Dachau and Auschwitz, afterwards reported only that the SS commandant of the camp had "a sensitive interest in art and music?"[33]

The Elephant and the Flea

Lipper held these senior Americans in undisguised contempt, yet her argument against them was not the same as that of Senator McCarthy, who, in March 1950, would denounce Lattimore as a Communist, possibly the Soviet Union's top spy in the United States. Wallace and Lattimore may have been culpably naïve, but Lipper also conceded that they had been systematically deceived, and that their visit to a theatrically adjusted Kolyma had been in 'the tradition of the Potemkin villages'. All trace of the wooden watch towers lining the access roads to Magadan had been removed before the Americans' arrival, and prisoners had been confined to their camps and even granted a programme of movies shown over the three days of the vice-president's visit. Shop windows had been packed with Russian merchandise that was never normally available (rationing was strict, and Magadan was actually reliant on American goods supplied under the Lend-Lease arrangement). Comely office girls were drafted in to replace starved swineherds at a model farm, and inventive 'interpreters' were brought in to ensure that Wallace, who actually knew a thing or two about agriculture, didn't notice their ignorance when he asked them a question about pigs. Wallace and Lattimore had no sooner left, than the watchtowers went back up, the prisoners went to work again, 'and in the empty shop windows were to be seen nothing but a few dusty mournful boxes of matches'. The deception had been carried off with 'flying colours'.[34]

There can be no doubt, then, that the Stalinist authorities practised showmanship and stage management as they presented the 'bright future'[35] to gullible foreigners. Yet the process of 'duping' Westerners was rarely an entirely one-sided matter of stage management. In 1934, the Hungarian writer Gyula Illyés described 'the Potemkin-complex' contracted by Western visitors as they crossed the frontier into Soviet Russia. 'Its prime symptom', he wrote, 'is that at times the eye becomes a magnifying lens making an elephant out of a flea, while at other times it turns a cow into a mole.'[36] In Illyés's explanation, sufferers from this 'complex' found Soviet reality ghosted by illusions that were themselves divided between anti- and pro-Communist orientations:

In the beginning one stares with dilated pupils at the most unremarkable shack and keeps looking until two of them emerge simultaneously: one is tidy and neat, the other dilapidated and about to collapse. The miracle may be transferred into reality and the photograph of the shack may be one kind or the other depending on whether it is published in the Sunday supplement of an anti-communist or communist newspaper.

Illyés was not alone in judging the success of Stalinist scene-shifting to be dependent on the compliant eye of the foreign onlooker. Panaït Istrati and Boris Souvarine had insisted on this fact, and the French former Communist Louis Rougier would also suggest that, by the 1930s, successful deception owed less to the quality of the presentation than to the determined 'stupidity' of the tourists. By this account, Soviet stage management only had to feed the visitors' optimism, reinforcing the conviction that Communism was the only alternative to Nazism and appealing to their wish to believe that, despite the evident costs and difficulties of the journey, the USSR was at least striving for a better world.

In Rougier's judgement, the intellectuals were the easiest to dupe. They, more than trade union bosses and ordinary visitors, were victims of their own need to believe; and, in the years when Soviet policy was committed to the Popular Front against Fascism (1935-9), they visited the USSR not to 'inform themselves' or to investigate conditions, as at least some of their predecessors had done, but to express their solidarity and 'commune with the masses'.[37] The deceptions carried out on the Russian side were certainly backed by a deliberate suspension of disbelief on the part of such international visitors. However, to grasp how the most disastrous of Soviet realities remained so largely hidden from Western view in the early 1930s, it is necessary to consider other layers of the increasingly institutionalized barrier that Buxton and others had earlier identified as the 'iron curtain'.

16

Friends against Famine

On the evening of 1 September 1931, unexpected difficulties arose at the Komödienhaus in Berlin. The theatre was packed for the opening night of a popular comedy entitled *Konto X* but the audience and actors were to be frustrated in their hopes of seeing one another. Having descended in accordance with the fire regulations before the performance, the safety curtain then 'elected to remain down and successfully resisted all efforts to raise it'.[1] Hands were wrung, money was refunded, and, within a couple of days, readers of the London *Times* were able to smile at the news that Germany's 'iron curtain' was confined to the theatre again, having shrunk back into its pre-war existence as a more or less effective anti-fire device.

No such immediate response awaited Andrew Cairns, a Canadian agricultural expert who witnessed a very different kind of comic theatre some ten months later, having ventured far behind the 'iron curtain' dividing Stalin's USSR from the West. Visiting a small street market in the Ukrainian city of Kiev, Cairns noted the impossibly high prices and that most of the trading was being done in wild strawberries and green vegetables that had obviously been lifted much too early. He also found himself followed through the stalls by a chorus of distressed women. He could scarcely make out what they were saying, since they spoke all at once in both Russian and Ukrainian, and some also paused to weep between each sentence. 'But what first class actresses they were! Despite the tragedy of it all, I could not keep from laughing at the expressions on their faces as they drew their finger like a knife across their throat, pulled in their cheeks and held their hands on their stomachs while they pretended to vomit, and while they bent their backs and hobbled about.'[2] Singling out one of these desperate women for interview, Cairns learned that there was practically no bread in the city because 'the Government had collected so much grain and exported it to England and Italy'.

That same evening, on 17 June 1932, Cairns decided to go out for a walk. Climbing a steep hill in order to look out over the river Dnieper, he came across two women picking what he imagined to be dandelions or leeks. On closer inspection, he realized that they were actually harvesting leaves of grass: their intention being, so they told him, to 'make soup'.[3] He pointed to the river, and said that it was beautiful. They agreed but, in the manner of those who know that a kettle can't be boiled on beauty, quickly returned to the fact that they were hungry. Walking on, Cairns passed several huge churches, all in 'a terrible state of dilapidation' having been variously used as a prison and a workers' club. He saw old priests begging and groups of ragged women and children 'taking turns at killing the lice in one another's hair before retiring for the night on the damp grass'. Strolling back to his hotel, he confronted 'a horrible sight—a man dying in the street. He was apparently insane as he was going through all the motions of eating and rubbing his stomach with apparent satisfaction. A crowd gathered around and some, thinking he was begging, dropped a few kopeks, but he was quite unconscious and soon stopped moving.'

Cairns's report from the Ukraine was obviously of infinitely greater significance than a fleeting anecdote from the Berlin Komödienhaus. His was an early, and quite unambiguous, sighting of the 'Great Famine' created by Stalin's collectivization of agriculture: a deliberately provoked disaster in which uncounted millions starved, and many millions more were driven into forced labour. Yet it was not until over half a century later, in the late 1980s, that this buried document would be exhumed from the British Public Record Office and published by a group of Canadian-Ukrainian researchers.

The Ring of Trust

Diplomatic and trade relations between Britain and the USSR had been restored in 1929/30, yet it would soon become apparent that the barriers surrounding Soviet Russia had been adjusted rather than removed. On their own side the Soviet government may have fused the iron curtain with their own systems of censorship and frontier control, but they had also re-engineered its outer layers, projecting them into the West as a web of 'friendliness'—albeit of a different variety than that espoused by the Western

Quakers who had been ordered out of Russia having carried out so much relief work, not least in the famine of 1921/2.

By the early 1930s, the Soviet authorities were promoting not just world revolution through the Third International, but a more feathery internationalist cause that went by the name of 'Peace' and depended on 'cultural relations which draw the nations nearer together'.[4] Tailored to the diplomatic requirements of Stalin's policy of 'socialism in one country', the rhetoric of 'friendliness' served the ongoing attempt to reach an accommodation with the capitalist nations, to gain diplomatic recognition from the United States of America (finally granted under Roosevelt in 1933), and to bring the USSR into membership of the League of Nations (which followed in 1934). It was also shaped by events in Manchuria, which had been occupied by Japanese forces in 1931 and was then held, while onlookers feared further advances into both Soviet Siberia and China, in defiance of the impotent League of Nations. With this threat building in the Far East, the USSR was inclined to be less bellicose in its relations with the West. Non-aggression pacts were agreed with Finland, Estonia, and Poland, and the USSR participated in both the international Disarmament Conference, which opened in Geneva in February 1932, and the World Economic Conference held in London in June 1933 with a view to establishing an international basis for overcoming economic depression.

The Soviet 'All-Union Society for Cultural Relations with Foreign Countries' (VOKS) was one of the primary generators of 'friendliness'. Through its Liaison Bureau, VOKS had already created a network of supporters overseas. Friendship societies had been established in many countries and augmented by a network of national societies for cultural relations with the USSR, which were also much involved in the recruitment of delegations to visit Russia. As part of this drive, VOKS publications announced that the 'Russia of the Shadows' described by H. G. Wells after his visit in 1920 had long since become a thing of the past and that the USSR was no longer 'separated from the rest of the world by clouds and mist'.[5] Addressing a delegation of Czech students in 1931, the vice-president of VOKS spoke of overcoming 'the barrier of calumny and slander'.[6] In words that would be quoted in the *Soviet Culture Review* of 25 October 1931, E. Lerner announced that the friendship societies overseas 'must organize their work so as to attract such representatives of the working intelligentsia who, in times of great trial, could stand in defence of the USSR. These societies must create a ring of trust, sympathy and friendship around the USSR, through which all plans of intervention will be unable to penetrate.'[7]

There were democratic socialists in the West who wholly mistrusted this appeal to 'friendliness'. To the unillusioned eye of the Austrian radical Friedrich Adler, Stalin's 'ring of trust' could only appear as another circle of deception: a development of the scheming with which the Bolsheviks had wrecked his own attempt to form a 'united front' combining Communists and democratic socialists in Vienna during the years immediately after the Great War. Then still committed to the idea of world revolution, the Communists had joined the United Front not as a way of broadening proletarian democracy but as a 'deliberate manoeuvre or cloak to deceive the workers and to make use of sections of the proletariat for Communist purposes'.[8]

Adler traced this 'double-dealing' tactic back to G. E. Zinoviev, who had confirmed it at the Fourth Congress of the Communist International in 1922. He had seen the same method being brought to bear on both trade union organizations and humanitarian agencies working to relieve hardship in Russia: 'Under the cloak of humanity they appeal to all kind-hearted people, and are always successful with this method.' Adler was especially scathing about 'The Workers' International Relief', an appeal that he denounced as 'a deliberate Communist manoeuvre under the cover of the United Front'. Its president, Clara Zetkin, was a Communist, as was its secretary, Willi Munzenberg, who was then engaged in the Comintern's policy of setting up malleable 'Innocents' Clubs' in the West. Indeed, he was impatient to go further: 'We must penetrate every conceivable milieu, get hold of artists and professors, make use of theatres and cinemas, and spread abroad the doctrine that Russia is prepared to sacrifice everything to keep the world at peace. We must join these clubs ourselves.'

It was partly thanks to a determined extension of this appeal to 'friendliness' that the 1930s would become the decade of the 'fellow-traveller', a creature who was distinct from the fully committed adherents of the Third International. Appealing to scientists, teachers, and doctors as well as Munzenberg's artists and professors, VOKS announced that 'all persons of genuine culture must mobilise all their energies for common work to combat the war danger'.[9] It no longer seemed to matter if their profession of 'friendship' and 'peace' fell considerably short of full-blooded endorsement of the Communist system.

In Britain, the cultural relations movement courted prominent liberals, such as the economist John Maynard Keynes, but senior Fabian socialists were also to be counted among its bearded figureheads. The most prominent of these was George Bernard Shaw, who was now in his seventies and inclined to view history as the world's way of applauding his own prophetic genius. By the early 1930s, indeed, even Shaw's long-standing admirers struggled to defend the great vegetarian anti-war campaigner from the disfiguring consequences of his own vanity. As the pacifist novelist Douglas Goldring wrote in 1932: 'Only very superficial people are prevented from appreciating the real greatness of Shaw by the fact that (in an agony of embarrassment) he is continually harping upon it himself.'[10]

Examples of the harping, at least, are easily found. In a wholly unembarrassed radio talk broadcast to America on 11 October 1931, Shaw recalled how, at the beginning of the 1914–18 war, he had proclaimed—presumably in his essay 'Common Sense about the War'—that the soldiers of the belligerent nations should go home and sort out their difficulties there. Nobody had taken any notice at the time, 'but in 1917 an astonishing thing happened. The Russian soldiers took my advice. They said "We have had enough of this" and came straight home. They formed bodies of workmen and soldiers called Soviets.'[11]

With history now trotting obediently at his heel, Shaw impressed himself further during a brief visit to the USSR—made as a British 'Friend of the Soviet Union' in the summer of 1931. Travelling in the company of Lord Lothian and his immensely wealthy friends Lord and Lady Astor of Cliveden, he went by train from Warsaw and entered the USSR at Negoreloye, where he started as he would carry on. Like Friedrich Adler's English lord who deduced, from his first encounter, that all waiters on the Continent had red hair, Shaw walked into the station restaurant to find two waitresses intimately acquainted with his works.[12] Such a discovery might have aroused suspicion in some minds, but it only prompted Shaw to conclude that waitresses in England were not nearly so well read as their Soviet-Russian counterparts. Later in the visit, when his anti-Communist travelling companion, Lady Astor, objected to the lack of freedom, he replied that the Soviet Russians were at least 'free from the illusion of democracy'.[13] At the Electrozavod factory in Moscow, he followed Lady Astor in addressing the workers from a truck. Astor had caused some concern by introducing herself 'as an aristocrat and a capitalist', and declaring Russian workers to be 'dreadfully meek' in the face of state authority by comparison with their British equivalents. Shaw is said to have added to the workers' sense of dismay by saying, 'The more I see of the proletarians the more I thank God I am not one.'[14]

Speaking at a vast reception held in the old Nobles' Hall to honour his seventy-fifth birthday, he surprised the assembled workers and intellectuals by describing how, in order to demonstrate his rejection of Western propaganda alleging food shortages in Russia, he had thrown his food reserves out of the window as his train approached the frontier from Poland. The next day, over lunch at the Hotel Metropole, the *Christian Science Monitor*'s correspondent, W. H. Chamberlin, tried to convince Shaw that the workers and intellectuals in his audience really were going hungry and, indeed, must have been very sorry that he hadn't waited until he was in Russia before jettisoning his tins of food. In response, Shaw is said to have looked around the hotel restaurant and asked "'Where do you see any food shortage?'"[15] When Mrs Chamberlin informed him that children in Russia were going without milk, he came up with the proposal, modest or not, that Soviet mothers should follow the example of the Eskimos who, so Shaw alleged, suckled their children until they were a good 20 years of age.

Shaw and Lady Astor horrified the Moscow-based foreign correspondent Eugene Lyons, who concluded that Shaw was more interested in 'being seen than in seeing' and that he had only come to Russia 'to make faces at the decaying bourgeois world through Soviet windows'.[16] The erratic posturing of these visiting exhibitionists was also pondered by Soviet audiences. Shaw was not among the despised Western visitors who got shouted at or assaulted in the street. Yet the editors of Russia's comic magazine *Crocodile* are said to have raised the question of Shaw's sanity, while tactfully suggesting that it was only on the far side of the division between the USSR and the West that it might be doubted. Then preparing a special tenth anniversary issue, they included a joke in which Shaw was said to have visited leading brain specialists and had himself certified sane before he left home for Russia, knowing that people would be saying he was barking mad as soon as he returned to England.[17]

In the event, Shaw came home with some provocative epigrams for the eagerly awaiting press. He was quoted as saying 'After you have seen Bolshevism on the spot, there can be no doubt that Capitalism is doomed.' Or again: 'To describe [Stalin] as a great man is to use too mild a term. There is nobody like him in Western Europe.'[18] He presented enraptured accounts of his visit at both the Fabian Summer School[19] and the Independent Labour Party's summer school at Digwell Park near Welwyn. At the latter, he pronounced that the socialism under construction in Russia 'was a Fabian socialism' and insisted on the moral and intellectual superiority of the Soviet leaders.[20]

He stuck to his convictions when he sat down to write about his Soviet tour while staying in South Africa in 1932. He praised the earlier Bolsheviks—both Lenin and Trotsky—describing them not as the blood-spattered axe murderers of Churchillian legend but as revolutionaries of the trained and 'professional' variety made possible by the emergence of modern political science, as pioneered by old Fabians such as himself and, of course, Sidney and Beatrice Webb at the London School of Economics.[21] As for smashing capitalism, this demanded the destruction not just of the system's openly 'predatory and oppressive organs' but also of its liberal trimmings: 'the defensive, humanitarian, palliative and popular brakes and checks and safeguards and franchises and "liberties" with which it has tried to buy off rebellion'.[22]

Refusing to reproach the Bolsheviks for 'frankly shooting anarchists and syndicalists who in the old unkind days were their comrades and helpers and fellow sufferers',[23] Shaw insisted that the larger class enemy had to be liquidated too. Citing the wealthy upper-middle characters in *The Forsyte Saga*, the sequence of socially revealing novels that, in November 1932, would win their British author, John Galsworthy, the Nobel Prize for Literature, he argued that the maintenance of the Soviet 'earthly paradise' was based, 'finally and fundamentally, on the new institution of forsyte shooting, which takes the place of pheasant shooting in England except that it is always in season'.[24] Shaw was not only joking. The 'forsyte' was an exploiter who 'not only robs us but corrupts our morals, stultifies our intellects, and damns our souls. From the Communist point of view there is no arguing with that sort of thing. There is nothing for it but Bang.'[25]

Not surprisingly, perhaps, Shaw never completed this account—whether Swiftian or, as seems more likely, just abject—of his visit to the USSR. Nor did he publish a full description of his audience with Stalin, whom he revered as an enlightened state-builder who had surely demonstrated his espousal of the gradual approach to social transformation in 1927–8, when he broke with Trotsky and the left opposition.

Veiled in Hope

Crazy or not, Shaw was far from alone in his admiration for Soviet Russia. On 2 March 1933, the *Manchester Guardian* printed a letter under the title 'Social conditions in Russia; Recent Visitors' Tribute'. Citing their own tours of the USSR the signatories claimed to have passed through 'the great part' of the Soviet Union's 'civilised territory', and they used their authority as eyewitnesses to dismiss the suggestion that the Russian countryside was experiencing economic slavery, privation or any worse alleged evil. Shaw's signature placed him at the head of a column of twenty-one 'Friends of the Soviet Union.' The politician and lawyer D. N. Pritt was there, together with the architect Clough Williams Ellis and his Communist wife, the writer and children's historian Amabel Williams Ellis. The Anglo-Jewish novelist Louis Golding had been hoisted aboard this ship of fools, as had Margaret Cole, the well-known Fabian (and anti-war activist of 1914–18), together with her brother Raymond W. Postgate, a pacifist and founder member of the British Communist Party who would eventually tire of singing for his Soviet suppers and go on to become, in 1951, the founding editor of Britain's *Good Food Guide*.

Blithely, if not cynically, unaware that millions were starving as they wrote, these 'Friends of the USSR' declaimed, 'We would regard it as a calamity if the present lie campaign were to be allowed to make headway without contradiction.' All this and more was expressed with the confident certainty of 'We, the undersigned ...'. 'No lie is too fantastic, no slander too stale, no invention too absurdly contrary', they declaimed of the critical stories emerging from Russia. Sadly, they added, the truth about Soviet Russia was less sensational than this growing chorus of alarms and, thanks to the slanted capitalist press, 'had no news value in our own countries'.

These 'friends' were actually objecting to the first indications of the Great Famine that had engulfed the grain-bearing regions of the southern USSR. Introduced in 1928, Stalin's First Five-Year Plan entailed a 'collectivization' of agriculture that was also a war against the 'kulaks', a notably slippery word, which, in the worried estimate of one generally pro-Soviet British teacher at the University of Moscow, could be used 'to make out a plausible case for calling almost anyone a Kulak', while also making it 'excessively difficult, once you have been accused, to prove that you are not a Kulak'.[26] Accompanied by an ongoing 'cultural revolution'[27] driven with particular ardour by members of the Communist Youth League (Komsomol), collectivization was imposed through a programme of peasant denunciations, punitive raids, and summary executions: it meant the dispossession, deportation into forced labour, and starvation of many millions, while those who remained were organized into collective farms serviced by new tractor stations. As many desperate people abandoned the land for towns and cities, a system of internal passports had been introduced in 1932, followed by additional legislation—identified as a 'Second Serfdom' since it revived hated tsarist measures—forbidding peasants from leaving their newly collectivized farms. The Great Famine of 1932/4 is rightly judged far worse than that of 1921/2, not just on account of its casualties, which rose to many millions, but because it was the result of deliberate policies imposed with particular viciousness in areas most inclined towards national autonomy, including the famously fertile lands of the North Caucasus and the Ukraine.

Condemnations come easily in hindsight. Yet by the time those British 'Friends of the USSR' made their smiling visits, there were others who had already pressed through the obscuring veils of 'friendliness' sufficiently to suspect the worst about Stalin's method of 'tackling the peasant'.[28]

The likelihood of catastrophe had been reported by Paul Scheffer, a German writer and editor who had lived in Russia for seven years in the 1920s as correspondent for the *Berliner Tageblatt*. He had seen the Soviet censorship increase greatly in 1927, when the Arcos affair revived Soviet fear of attack from the encircling West and 'made it necessary to thicken the fog that was lying between the Red Experiment and the West'.[29] Scheffer had reported bread riots in the Don region, the Ukraine, and along the Volga in 1928 and, in the following year, found himself barred from re-entry to Soviet Russia on the grounds that his articles had been insufficiently friendly over the previous three years.

In a long piece printed in the London *Observer* at the end of 1929, he declared that 'Events in the Soviet Union are steadily moving towards a crisis. Gradually that fact has come to the surface and is plain to the eye. The decisive symptom is the increasing shortage of food supplies.'[30] Scheffer accepted that 'drastic measures' had been necessary to overcome the chaos of a countryside in which individual peasant holdings had actually greatly increased since 1917. But the collectivization had been 'far too fast' and it was 'very possible that millions of peasants in certain provinces will suffer from real famine between now and next year's harvest'. '"We have strong nerves!"' said the men in the Kremlin. Yet, as Scheffer warned, they had wholly misjudged peasant nature: 'They did not anticipate that their Social-ist policy would react so disastrously upon individual cultivation. They never dreamed that the task they took on would rise so high over their heads.' Scheffer's analysis was largely correct, even though the really disastrous fam-ine was not to come for a couple of years.

The delegates sent to Russia by the New Fabian Research Bureau in the summer of 1932 were largely blinkered by their belief, later admitted by Margaret Cole, that Soviet Russia was 'the hope of the world'.[31] According to

Archibald Lyall, a 'non-political' (i.e. supercilious and anti-Bolshevik) British writer who boarded the same Soviet steamer at Hays Wharf in London and observed the delegation's conduct as they crossed the Baltic, the Fabians exhibited 'the simple and credulous mentality of the complete believer', and were inclined to substitute 'sneers for argument'.[32] As Cole herself would later recall, they viewed the secret police who attended their visit as 'kindly souls who came to our rescue and found us seats on crowded trains'.

Thanks to their agricultural expert, John Morgan, she could also insist—with a palpable sense of relief—that they had done rather better when it came to taking stock of the harvest. They were guided around preselected agricultural plants and stations, and further limited in their investigations by the fact that 'rural "Red" Russia has no roads'. Yet Morgan was concerned about the human consequences of collectivization and the frenzied 'Bolshevik tempo' of its implementation. Surveying the land through the train window (the usual vantage point of the Western delegate), he was concerned to see scarcely a tractor at work anywhere, and far too many fields where cereals had been 'ousted' by weeds.[33] The USSR was, he concluded, 'a hungry country. And run by socialists.' Seeking to account for this depressing state of affairs, he blamed the drought and bad harvest of the previous year; the intractable nature of the peasants, who had both failed to seed their land and slaughtered their livestock rather than surrendering it to the Soviet state; the drop in world prices for commodities exported by Russia, which threatened the First Five-Year Plan and increased pressure on the Soviet government to export scarce wheat. Anything, in short, but Stalin's collectivization itself.

The Fabian tourists were only in Russia for six weeks, but that was not the only sense in which Morgan saw much less of the collectivization than Andrew Cairns, the Canadian who, in the same summer of 1932, was sent by the British Empire Marketing Board to review the agricultural situation in southern USSR. Cairns conducted his investigations shortly before the Ottawa Conference at which the countries of the Depression-struck British Empire agreed to introduce tariffs against food and other imports from outside. In May and early June, he visited western Siberia, Kazakstan, and regions around the Volga. Over a period of six weeks from mid-June, he continued his enquiries in the Ukraine, the Crimea, and the North Caucasus. For much of his journey, Cairns was accompanied by Dr Otto Schiller, a linguistically able agricultural attaché at the German embassy in Moscow, and the two investigators found themselves travelling through lands beset by obvious agricultural disaster. Cairns reported abandoned and derelict villages, spring crops that were untended and full of weeds, vast areas of fertile land that, though harvested in 1931, had not even been planted for 1932. Wherever the two investigators went, starving people with 'black bread pot bellies',[34] would gather around them, kneeling and sometimes stretching themselves out on the ground to beg. To Dr Schiller's often expressed surprise, these people were fearless in their complaints. Beyond the usual sense of caution, they poured out news of their sufferings, and begged the two foreign investigators to tell America of their plight so that the humanitarian relief effort, remembered from the famine of 1920/1, might be renewed.

Unlike more 'friendly' visitors, Cairns was alert to the contrast between reality and the rhetoric of official Soviet Russia. Peering through the wooden fence surrounding a prison in the Siberian city of Novosibirsk, he had seen many faces gazing back through the bars in every window and remembered the praise of Soviet prison life ('holidays, freedom, etc.') he had heard from 'friendly' types speaking at 'The Royal Institute of International Affairs', at Chatham House in London.[35] He and Dr Schiller were also fully aware of the Soviet authorities' attempt to hold the line between the 'show' Russia that was to be seen by foreign visitors guided along the carefully prepared tourist itinerary, and the larger reality that was to be kept hidden as much as possible. Cairns noted the attempts to confine him to preordained sites, and the manoeuvres of the translators who tried to counter the charges of desperate peasants by identifying the complainants as 'kulaks'. He records being shown a film about the claimed 'liquidation' and rehabilitation of the notorious homeless children of Soviet Russia, and then stepping out of the theatre to be accosted by three evidently unrehabilitated children begging for money to buy bread. In order to confirm his suspicions, he played his own games as he went round the Intourist hotels: in one he ordered the same food as was being served to a delegation of American tourists, only to find, as he had suspected, that it wasn't available to anyone else.[36] His was a sceptical attitude that might have benefited the Fabian delegation, whose members prided themselves on not being fools, 'nor entirely untrained in looking below the surface'.[37] They visited Kiev that same summer but, to judge by Margaret Cole's retrospective account, saw nothing more troubling than the Lavro Monastery, a view (also taken from high ground) of massive logs floating down the river Dnieper, and 'a wild performance of gipsy dancing'.[38]

Truth and Diplomacy

It might be imagined that Cairns's reports to the Empire Marketing Board were sufficient to dispel 'friendly' illusions about Stalin's Soviet Union. They provided detailed confirmation of a truth that had already penetrated the British and German embassies in Moscow, spelt out in letters from national subjects stranded in the afflicted regions and also from Soviet citizens who were prepared to risk everything to inform the world that despair, death, and even cannibalism stalked Stalin's paradise. With an eye to the approaching Ottawa Conference, Cairns himself hoped that his reports might 'do a great deal to prick the bubble of propaganda about the terrible competitive menace of Bolshevik agriculture'.[39]

He declined an invitation to write for the London *Times,* partly because he thought the anti-Soviet bias of that paper so pronounced that many would automatically discount any arguments presented there. Instead, he hoped the Empire Marketing Board would soon publish a full report that would counter the impressions created by newspapers—Canadian as well as British and American—that were giving all too much credence to exaggerated Soviet claims about wheat production, in order to raise the fear of Russia 'dumping' vast quantities of cheap wheat into Western markets. He also expressed the wish that his reports would be sent both to the premiers of Canada's grain-producing western provinces and also to delegates attending the Ottawa Conference, who might be less inclined to demand the introduction of tariffs if they knew that the Soviet harvest was not at all as the propaganda suggested.[40]

Cairns' reports were well received by the British ambassador in Moscow. An appointee of the second Labour government, Sir Esmond Ovey had arrived in Russia with a genuine interest in establishing the facts of the situation. A year previously, he had informed the British Foreign Secretary, Arthur Henderson, that the truth about conditions in Russia was clouded by the polarized accounts of adherents: 'The unsympathetically disposed observer perceives nothing but privation and inefficiency wherever he goes, while the "Red" sympathiser sees in the broad plains of Russia the asphodel meadows of earthly paradise.'[41]

Together with ongoing attempts at Potemkinist camouflage, the illusions created on either side of the division certainly played their part in impeding understanding of the situation in the famine-struck regions. Yet the truth would also be obscured by manoeuvres of power, international diplomacy, and realpolitik, which could hardly be blamed on Stalin alone. Ambassador Ovey forwarded the Canadian's reports to the Foreign Office in London, where an official noted, 'The pity of it is that this account cannot be broadcast to the world at large as an antidote to Soviet propaganda in general and to the obiter dicta of such temporary visitors as Mr. Bernard Shaw, Lord Marley and others.'[42] The reasoning behind this reluctance was spelt out in June 1934 by the Foreign Office mandarin Sir Laurence Collier. While preparing a ministerial reply to a question raised in the House of Commons, he wrote:

> The truth of the matter is, of course, that we have a certain amount of information about famine conditions in the south of Russia, similar to what has appeared in the press, and that there is no obligation on us not to make it public. We do not want to make it public, however, because the Soviet Government would resent it and our relations with them would be prejudiced.[43]

So Cairn's revelations were regretfully consigned to the vaults in the interests of Anglo-Soviet trade, American recognition, and the USSR's entry to the League of Nations. His travelling companion, Dr Otto Schiller, fared little better in Germany. The polarization between Fascism and Communism was already such that his claims, the publication of which was denounced as an 'unfriendly act' by the Soviet government, could also be conveniently dismissed as so much pro-Nazi propaganda.[44]

Killing the News

'We are face to face with a "going concern" ', so Sir Esmond Ovey had written to Arthur Henderson from Moscow in June 1930: 'One cannot destroy the cake of Bolshevism and still have the cake of trade with Russia.'[45]

Pragmatic considerations of a different kind weighed on Western newspaper correspondents based in Soviet Russia. While officials considered their quandary over Andrew Cairns's reports, hints of the hunger ravaging huge tracts of the USSR had made their way through the veils of obfuscation and appeared in the British press. This was due partly to a delegation of visiting British journalists who had travelled around the USSR as guests of the government, having shipped out of London at the end of July 1932 and sailed to Leningrad on the *Alexei Rykov*, a Soviet steamer that would break up and sink in the Baltic later that summer, but which they successfully shared with the smaller delegation sent by the New Fabian Research Bureau.

The Canadian Andrew Cairns met this party of commentators shortly after dining with a few English tourists in a park restaurant in Stalingrad. Though the restaurant had been carefully prepared for their arrival, the visiting diners had been upset by a hungry man who pushed his way in begging for bread, only to be repulsed by a woman waiter and three men who quickly came to her aid when the trespasser turned as if to hit her. Shortly after leaving the restaurant, Cairns and his English acquaintances happened upon the British journalists, who were in Stalingrad while awaiting their (delayed) train to Rostov. One of the tourists approached Kingsley Martin, the editor of the *New Statesman and Nation,* and suggested that 'he had a lot of nerve dining on caviar and other luxuries when a starving man had just been kicked out, but Martin was sure he must have been an ordinary beggar'.[46]

This was far from promising. And yet, as Cairns soon discovered, the journalists had not been entirely lulled into acquiescence by their escorts. He learned that they had been maddened by bed bugs in their hotel in Nizhni-Novgorod.[47] They had seen terrible brawls as starving people fought 'like wild animals' to gain a place on a river boat.[48] As for their own four day fact-finding trip along the Volga, this had been ruined not by Potemkinist staging of illuminated sights along the river bank, but by an altogether more desperate manoeuvre in which the lights had been turned out altogether: their vessel had developed the curious habit of arriving at all the interesting places at midnight.

One of the visiting journalists, a London stockbroker named McGuire who represented the *Financial News,* was steaming about 'the gigantic fraud' Stalin's 'swine' had cooked up to bamboozle the people of the USSR. When they finally arrived at Stalingrad's crowded railway station for their departure, Jules Menken, editor of *The Economist* and also a professor at the London School of Economics, had told Cairns: 'I can't get over the infernal cheek of these people wanting us to adopt their system. Look at these thousands of hungry people sitting in worse than oriental filth and squalor.' Cairns concluded that their trip had turned out to be 'one more communist experiment gone wrong due to lack of adequate control … I'll be surprised if at least some of the guests don't fairly roast their hosts when they get home.'

'Roasting' may be too strong a word, but these journalists had certainly not just issued formulaic hymns of praise to Stalin's Russia. Through September 1932, they published various articles expressing reservations and anticipating acute food shortages in the future. Sir Walter Layton and Jules Menken would be berated by the Soviet ambassador in London, who objected to articles printed in *The Economist* in September 1932. The ambassador's worries can hardly have been reduced by an editorial printed in Kingsley Martin's *New Statesman and Nation* on 17 September 1932. This condemned the 'insincere and prejudiced nonsense' that made it so difficult for the British newspaper reader to know 'what to believe or what to reject' but then went on to insist that 'the serious nature of the food situation is no secret and no invention'.[49] The Soviet authorities were declared right to identify the 'kulaks' as the chief enemies of socialism, and also in collectivizing the land. However, they had proceeded far too quickly, and lost the cooperation of farmers. Collectivization had produced 'not efficiency but chaos' and, as a consequence, Russia 'has a very hard year in front of her'.

The denial of this unwelcome fact was not left only to George Bernard Shaw and other craven 'friends of the USSR', already inclined to dismiss every criticism as a deviation to the right if not yet an outright concession to Nazism. Western foreign correspondents stationed in Moscow also knew much more than they would communicate about the catastrophe engulfing the Soviet Union's southern areas. As the Russian–American correspondent Eugene Lyons would later declare, they had seen photographs taken by German consular officials in the Ukraine, and they had sat in the bar of the Hotel Metropole, listening to witnesses who had just returned from the famine-struck areas: including Jack Calder, who returned from Kazakstan to describe 'roads lined with stiff corpses like so many logs'. Like Panaït Istrati before him, Lyons reckoned 'a deaf-and-dumb reporter hermetically sealed in a hotel room could not have escaped knowledge of the essential facts'.[50] And yet these same foreign correspondents went out of their way to obscure the true situation and also to denigrate the lesser freelancers who eventually broke news of the famine in the West.

The most prominent among these Moscow-based correspondents was Walter Duranty, the British-born reporter for the *New York Times*. After the worst of the famine was over, he would breezily inform William Strang, counsellor at the British Embassy in Moscow, that perhaps as many as 10 million people had died as a result of food shortages over the previous year.[51] Yet Duranty, who in 1932 had been awarded a Pulitzer Prize for his coverage of Russia, had not passed that news on to his readers in America. He and his fellow correspondents in Moscow had become creatures of the Soviet censors.

For much of the 1920s, censorship had been the responsibility of Theodore Rothstein, appointed chief of the Soviet Press Department in 1923. The pressure had been much milder in those days—so much so that, at a tea party held for foreign correspondents in 1926, Maxim Litvinov had denied there was any censorship at all and there had only been laughter when Walter Duranty suggested he turn to his right where 'the gentleman in question' was sitting. Recalling the passing of this more relaxed era, Paul Scheffer suggested that conditions had changed for foreign correspondents in 1927, a year that saw Stalin's struggle with the left opposition, increasing tension between the country and the city, and a renewed fear of war with the West provoked partly by the Arcos affair in London.

It was at this time that the foreign correspondents were obliged to master 'the art of telling three-quarters, a half, still smaller fractions, of the truth; the art of telling the whole truth up to the point where its negative or positive significance would become apparent'.[52] The censors would suggest acceptable phrases, cast doubts on the accuracy of information, and play one competitive foreign correspondent off against another as they insisted on what they called 'loyal statements'. It was a demoralizing business, as Scheffer concluded: 'it lies in the nature of such police supervision that a reporter's debit-sheet automatically grows to over-reach his credit account, unless he takes heroic measures to preserve his favourable balance'.

And 'heroic measures' could be costly for correspondents who only had to remember the example already made of Scheffer, denied re-entry to the USSR in 1929. Sir Walter Layton and Jules Menken had been free to smile when their articles about Russia were criticized by the Soviet ambassador in London. The pressure was much greater for Walter Duranty in Moscow. Two months later, in November 1932, he was chastised for his unfriendliness and warned of 'serious' consequences, after he published a series of articles about Soviet food shortages in the New York Times.[53] As recent critics of 'Stalin's Apologist' have pointed out, Duranty would have risked his flat, his car, his connections with the regime, and his ability to continue holding court before visiting Westerners in Moscow's Hotel Metropole. The fact that he had a Russian wife and a young son are likely to have increased his sense of caution.

Some of the foreign correspondents in Moscow had been working for some time to snuff out rumours of famine as they appeared in the Western press. Thus, on 28 November 1930, the *Daily Telegraph* carried an interview with a British consulting engineer named Frank Easton Woodhead,[54] part of which also appeared that same day in the *New York Times*. Woodhead was introduced as having taught on an occasional basis at the Lomonosovsky Institute of Engineering in Moscow and visited various places to demonstrate how modern tractors might be used to increase the productivity of Soviet agriculture. He claimed to have witnessed foot riots, and battles between OGPU forces and mutinous Red Army soldiers in central Moscow: 'it is commonly stated that over a thousand men perished in the affair. This was the estimate that was whispered all over the city.'

Woodhead spoke of widespread hunger and a 'growing revolt' against the new system of collective farming. Peasants in some districts had refused to deliver their crops to the government, and had suffered 'disastrous results' when they resisted the cavalry squadrons sent to enforce the demand. There had, claimed Woodhead, been fighting in barracks in Moscow, and further trouble in the nearby villages of Bratovchina and Puskina, which he had previously visited to demonstrate how ploughing could be improved with the help of tractors. Earlier in November, peasants and local militia had combined to demonstrate against the killing of twenty or thirty political prisoners, who had been shot for refusing to work. Artillery regiments who happened to be travelling from the Caucasus to Moscow were detrained to quell the outbreak, which they accomplished leaving an estimated 400–500 casualties. A similar fate met some soldiers at Munish, where there was a camp at which dogs were trained to draw mounted machine guns. Moved by the plight of the starving peasants in the area, they had handed over some meal and meat intended for the dogs. Woodhead asserted that a cavalry force had been sent from Moscow and that, by the time they had finished their bloody reprisal against those soldiers, many bodies could be seen from trains passing on the local line between Moscow and Jaroslav.

Woodhead's article was printed together with an official denial from the Soviet Embassy in London, stating that there was 'no truth in the reports' and that 'There is a sufficiency of all essential foods'. But this was not enough for Louis Fischer, an American correspondent in Moscow, who, the following year, would ridicule Woodhead's 'tissue of lies' in the pages of the *New Republic*.[55] Having been asked to respond to Woodhead's allegations by the British *Daily Herald,* of which he was then Russian correspondent, Fischer claimed to have visited the British Embassy where everyone 'rocked with laughter' over the allegations: he claimed to have heard one British official dismiss Woodhead as 'the greatest liar on God's earth'.

Fischer would place Woodhead's revelations in the tradition of the anti-Bolshevik propaganda pumped out by White Russian 'lie factories' around the world: for him they were part of a malignant and recently intensified campaign, designed to discredit the Soviet Union and counter the triumphs of its industrializing Five-Year Plan. Earlier in the year, in June, Donald Day, the Riga-based correspondent of the *Chicago Tribune* had claimed that 'starving people were collapsing daily in the streets of Moscow, Leningrad and other cities', yet none of this, so Fischer claimed, had been visible to the American correspondent Eugene Lyons. He was in Moscow at the time, along with many tourists and engineers, 'yet, strangely enough, only Mr. Day, ensconced in Riga, was privy to the alarming news that hunger stalked the streets of Russian cities'.[56]

Such had been the spate of alleged revelations at this time, that the Moscow correspondents had faced urgent enquiries from their editors in the West, who wondered why they hadn't been previously informed of atrocities in central Moscow, the Red Army's mutinous assaults on the Kremlin, or the alleged mutiny of the Red fleet at Kronstadt. The reports caused 'mental chaos' but they also served their promoters by damaging both diplomatic relations and the credit terms available for the Soviet government: 'A fortnight's lies may have cost Moscow $1,000,000 in cold cash.' Fischer regretted that even papers that maintained their own correspondents in Moscow succumbed to publishing this sort of low-grade muck in the interests of balance, and of giving 'the other side', which Fischer dismissed as 'the untrue side'. He strongly resented the claim 'frequently made by editors that they must have "Russian" correspondents outside Russia in order to avoid the consequences of news censorship'. Indeed, he dismissed the alleged censorship as little more than a helpful fact-checking service that would 'not prevent a correspondent from sending news unfavourable to the government if his facts are accurate' and, indeed, was positively helpful to the correspondent given that Moscow was such 'a hotbed of rumour'. Because these anti-Bolshevik 'inventions' were sensational, and made 'a stronger impression than a dozen, carefully impartial analyses or a score of denials, hidden away in remote corners, Russia is often seen by the general public and occasionally by statesmen through a smoke-screen of falsehoods and exaggerations which conduce to mistaken policies and to the sort of public prejudice that have in the past made for international hate and war'.

Fischer completed his counter-attack by claiming that, his suspicion aroused by these claims, he had gone to the police headquarters in Moscow, where all foreigners had to be registered, and discovered that Woodhead had arrived in Moscow on 17 April and left by crossing into Poland on 7 May, and that he had not returned since then. Apparently quite unembarrassed about his contact with the Soviet police, Fischer announced that Woodhead could not, therefore, have been in Moscow when the riots he 'saw' were said to have taken place. In the course of making this claim, he misquoted the *Daily Telegraph,* claiming it had introduced Woodhead as a British engineer, 'who has just returned from Russia after a visit lasting several months'. What the *Telegraph* actually claimed, in words that do indeed seem to have been carefully chosen, was that Woodhead had 'left this country in April on his last visit to Russia, and reached home this week'.

The pressure on Western foreign correspondents in Moscow was considerably increased in March 1933 when six British engineers working in Russia with Metro-Vickers were arrested and charged with sabotage, leading to the show trial (12–19 April) in which Vyshinsky stepped into the international limelight as Stalin's public prosecutor. Calculated or not, this crisis coincided with the worst of the famine, and it confronted the foreign correspondents with what Lyons remembered as 'a compelling professional necessity'[57] to stay on terms with the censors.

The Metro-Vickers trial was not the only reason why foreign correspondents eager to stay in Russia, might have been inclined to remain silent about the famine. With America preparing to recognize the USSR under Roosevelt (inaugurated as president in March 1933), the foreign correspondents in Moscow were, perhaps, less valued for their independent judgement than for the immediacy with which they communicated the views of Stalin and his government. Their status was dependent on their access to the horse's mouth, and some came to see it as their job to 'interpret' events from the Soviet point of view. Duranty would write that 'Truth is never so distorted as when it is divided. Part of the truth can be as deceiving as the worst of lies.'[58] The two sides were, he asserted, as blinkered as one another in their portrayals of Russia.

Duranty saw this as an opportunity to correct the balance: less, however, by seeking out the truth than by trading in bias: he would ride the see-saw, rather than encourage his readers to avoid it altogether. There was, as he explained in a magazine interview, a considerable 'barrier' to the sympathetic interpretation of Soviet news, and his job was to make up for this by providing the Soviet version of events. His rewards would include an interview with Stalin himself. Eugene Lyons had been awarded one such interview a few years earlier, but Duranty's was conducted on Christmas Day, 1933. As an acting counsellor at the British Embassy summarized the situation nine months later, 'Duranty is rather persona grata at the Kremlin, which is another way of saying that he has been more favourable to Russia than most of the foreign correspondents.'[59]

There were hints and suggestions, and the employment of censor-approved words such as 'malnutrition' in place of 'starvation', but the unambiguous news that the anticipated famine had arrived was not carried into the West in the reports of the foreign correspondents. For readers of the *Manchester Guardian*, the story was broken in a series of articles published at the end of March 1933. Entitled 'The Soviet and the Peasantry; An Observer's Notes', these unattributed reports were written by Malcolm Muggeridge, then a stringer for the paper who had travelled through the Caucasus, the Ukraine, and the Volga regions. Starting in the South Caucasus, he described a village teeming with well-fed soldiers where 'the civilian population was obviously starving. I mean starving in its absolute sense; not undernourished as, for instance, most Oriental peasants are undernourished and some unemployed workers in Europe.'[60]

There had been, Muggeridge was informed, no bread for three months. 'We have nothing, absolutely nothing,' as one man told him: 'They have taken everything away.' Muggeridge insisted that 'the famine is an organized one', and the starving peasants knew that some of the food taken from them by the Soviet state was still being exported to foreign countries. It was the same story in the Ukraine. Some of the starved were prepared to speak out, even though Muggeridge, like Cairns, found the haggard reality glossed over with stage-managed denials. At Rostov, he happened upon a column of peasants lined up at a cold railway platform: 'Showmanship—most characteristic product of the age—worked its magic. "Have you got bread here in Rostov?" I asked weakly. "Bread, of course we've got bread; as much as we can eat." It was not true; but they had a certain amount of bread. One might go all over Russia like this, I thought—on a wave of showmanship.'[61]

Returning to Moscow, Muggeridge heard that Stalin, not content with coining a slogan for the collectivization drive ('To make every collective farm worker well-to-do'), had recently decreed that 20 million peasants had so far been 'saved from poverty': 'This is a great achievement, comrades.

This is such an achievement as the world has never yet known.' Such was the background against which Muggeridge reiterated that

> To say that there is famine in some of the most fertile parts of Russia is to say much less than the truth; there is not only famine but—in the case of the North Caucasus at least, a state of war, a military occupation. ... The fields are neglected and full of weeds; no cattle are to be seen anywhere; and few horses; only the military and the G.P.U. are well fed, the rest of the population, obviously starving, obviously terrorised.[62]

The Lost Question Mark

This made unpleasant reading for British friends of the Soviet Union, including the senior Fabians Sidney and Beatrice Webb, who were among those who found themselves choking over their copies of the *Manchester Guardian*. Throughout that month, the paper had been full of horrifying reports from Germany, where the newly empowered Nazis had quickly tired of pasting sheets of blank paper over Socialist and Communist election posters. Indeed, they had moved on to rounding up and incarcerating Communists, while Goering ranted about 'eradicating' their movement 'root, stock, and branch' and Brownshirt thugs used their rubber truncheons and steel whips to murder Jews.[63] And now here was the alternative vision of Soviet Communism—the remaining hope of the world—being portrayed as something quite other than state-building of the benign Fabian variety.

The Webbs were well into their seventies by 1933 and using their retirement to write their study *Soviet Communism: A New Civilisation?* Beatrice was disappointed by Muggeridge's revelations and all the more so since she knew the reporter as the intelligent young husband of her niece. Writing in her diary on 29 March 1933, she noted Muggeridge's 'curiously hysterical denunciations', and also his lack of 'any evidence except hearsay for his assertions'.[64] Yet she also found herself disconcertingly short of facts: 'What makes me uncomfortable is that we have no evidence to the contrary.'

The Webbs had by no means always been cheer leaders for Stalinist Communism. Indeed, in 1921, Beatrice had been horrified by the suggestion, made by an admiring British witness of the Russian Revolution, that the Bolsheviks had done nothing new by insisting on 'a strong centralised bureaucracy and on a period of State Capitalism in industry' and, indeed, that this course 'had something in common with the English Fabians'. Her repudiation of this assertion had been quite unambiguous in submitting the Russian peoples to a very different system:

> Our conclusion is that probably Lenin's revolution was the only revolution which could be successful in Russia. Dictatorship was a *sine qua non* for the Russian people. Through the Revolution, Russia exchanged a Dictatorship for the benefit of the rich for one which at any rate aims at being a Dictatorship in favour of the Poor. But it seems hardly worth while for Western democracies to go through a similar experience of famine, disease, civil war and the rapid decay of urban life in order to come out at what Mr. Price, somewhat unkindly believes to be the programme of the Fabian Society. However highly Fabians may value the efficiency brought about by scientific expertness and reasonable discipline, they value even more highly the consciousness of consent dependent on a free democracy, political and industrial. We are left supremely sceptical as to the rightness or even the expedience of the use of physical force to back up moral conviction.[65]

Beatrice Webb had remained critical of Soviet Communism in 1928, when she regretted the 'fanatical fervour' of both the Soviet government and the Communist International, which had 'fomented and subsidized' revolutionary unrest and civil war in most countries of the world.[66] Not content with describing the 'drastic oppression' of individual 'dissentients' in the USSR as 'repugnant' to both Western Christianity and Western democracy, she had also noted that the Soviet government's 'amazing ruthlessness' in its pursuit of 'social services' formed a 'stop in the mind' of Western friends of Soviet Russia, and that this 'stop' was not satisfactorily ignored or dismissed in the usual Communist manner as so much 'Bourgeois ideology'.

In the early 1930s, however, and perhaps assisted by their friend and fellow founder of the Fabian Society, George Bernard Shaw, the Webbs underwent an embarrassing conversion. They had spent two months in Russia in the summer of 1932, following the familiar 'tourist' itinerary some two months after the New Fabian Research Department delegation had passed through: '"We seem to be a new type of Royalty"' as Sidney muttered of their reception in Leningrad.[67] Yet they came home convinced, and were further persuaded when they talked with Ivan Maisky, the former Menshevik who had then recently arrived as the new Soviet ambassador in London. Over lunch at the London School of Economics, Maisky played the by-now well-thumbed 'future' card, remarking that the Soviet Union was still 'in the making' and that the 'fanatical metaphysics and repression of today are temporary, brought about by past horrors and the low level of culture out of which the revolution started'.[68] The idea that Stalin was deliberately starving millions and creating a lasting dictatorship over needs apparently remained unthinkable.

On 30 March 1933, Beatrice Webb picked up the *Manchester Guardian* to find a further account of famine in Russia, 'which certainly bears out Malcolm's reports': it was, she admitted, 'a melancholy atmosphere in which to write a book on Soviet Communism'.[69] Conditions would not get any easier as the year advanced. A day later, after visiting George Bernard Shaw and his wife, Webb wrote that 'The tension between those who accept and those who denounce the USSR increases day by day.'[70] Mrs Charlotte Shaw reported that even her solicitor had 'foamed at the mouth' and refused to obey her instructions when she instructed him to invest £1,000 in the Soviet 15-per-cent loan. The distinguished Liberal William Beveridge had muttered 'a country of wild beasts' when the Webbs lunched with him at the London School of Economics. Their old friend Leonard Woolf also loathed Bolshevism, and was certainly not to be convinced by their vision of Soviet Communism as an improving 'New Civilisation'.

Assailed by doubts, and also their feelings of advancing age, the Webbs wrote on with the help of various assistants: 'We are of course getting a good deal of help in our work which would not be open to other authors, either arranged and paid for by us from non-Bolshevik Russians resident in England or gratuitously from the USSR authorities. What we contribute is our long experience in scheming the investigation and devising the scope and form of the product.'[71] Such was the extent of the assistance accorded to the Webbs by the Soviet authorities that, in September 1934, the elderly Sidney sailed to the USSR, taking with him the draft of *Soviet Communism*, so that Soviet officials could review and revise it. One of his companions on the visit would recall that, throughout the tour, Sidney would whisper, 'with the relish of a scientist whose theoretical proposition has stood the test of practical experiment, "See, see, it works, it works"'.[72] Now convinced that Stalin's Five-Year Plans vindicated many of their own Fabian ideas of centralized state planning, the Webbs would eventually adjust the title of their study, *Soviet Communism: A New Civilisation?* The work was first published in 1935, but the question mark in its title was gone by the time the second edition came out in 1941. In some later accounts, that adjustment would be all that remained of the Webbs' life and work, placing them among the most culpable and 'idiotic' fellow-travellers of all time.

Gareth Jones's Breakthrough

Malcolm Muggeridge was not alone in seeing Stalin's Russia through less misted eyes. The *Manchester Guardian* article that increased Beatrice Webb's sense of irritation was written by a young Welshman and Liberal freelancer named Gareth Jones. An apparently incorruptible figure from a firmly Nonconformist background, Jones was a talented linguist who had been much inspired by the internationalism that once seemed embodied by the League of Nations. Leaving Cambridge University in 1929 with a first-class degree in Russian, French, and German, he embarked on what one of his teachers would later characterize as 'a life of independent activity'[73] by becoming a foreign affairs adviser to David Lloyd George.[74] He had made his first visit to Soviet Russia in 1930, where he saw many signs of increased repression and looming starvation, and developed a thoroughgoing contempt for ignorant foreign visitors who 'go there and come back, after having been led round by the nose and had enough to eat, and say that Russia is a paradise'.[75]

Shortly afterwards, Jones had moved to New York as an adviser to Dr Ivy Lee, vice-president of the American League of Nations Union. Through that connection he embarked on his second visit to Soviet Russia, this time as a guide to Jack Heinz, son and heir of the fifty-seven varieties. In August 1931, the two men boarded a Soviet steamer at London Bridge and sailed for Leningrad, with Heinz clasping a suitcase bulging with cans of baked beans.[76] They shared the voyage with a delegation sent by English Co-operative Stores. This included a number of British Communists who were full of hideous zeal: one of these comrades insisted that the British trade unions must be 'drenched in blood' rather than words, and they all scowled at the comparatively moderate Labour MP who announced that Communism would remain a minority sect because it ran 'contrary to the fundamentals of the British character'.

In Moscow, they conversed with the *New York Times*'s correspondent Walter Duranty, met Radek and other leading officials, and also less exalted Communists who, in the absence of true information, still awaited the revolution that would surely break out any day in America, and firmly believed that thousands of workers were dying of starvation in England and

America.[77] As they travelled about, they also talked with the peasants, hearing stories of Communists being murdered, of reprisal raids and of ordinary peasants being harassed and 'sent away' as 'kulaks'—a fate that, for one group Jones heard about, meant not forced labour but being deported to Tashkent, where they were dumped on the town square and left to starve.[78]

Jones made his third and most decisive trip in March 1933, after a period in which he worked with Lloyd George, researching for the Liberal leader's *War Memoirs* and his articles on the situation in Germany. Proposing to write a book on 'Russia and the League of Nations',[79] he visited Germany, where he met leading Nazis and even flew in Hitler's plane. He then shifted himself to the Hotel Metropole in Moscow. Here he talked with Muggeridge, Duranty (once again), and other foreign correspondents in the city, and also with discouraging staff at the British Embassy, who warned him that, if he insisted on travelling to the Ukraine, he would find himself among peasants who were starving, and likely to steal anything they could lay hands on. Undeterred by that warning, or by the ban forbidding journalists to leave Moscow (imposed on 23 February 1933), Jones filled his rucksack with white bread, cheese, meat, and chocolate and other foods bought at the special foreign currency stores, and set off for Kharkov. Like Muggeridge before him, he avoided the express trains used to ensure that foreign delegations received 'only an impression' of Russia, and travelled 'hard class' with the Russian people, who provided him with an array of characteristic attitudes: ranging from the unyielding communists who insisted that every communist in England was locked up and starving in the Tower of London to the misery of those who moaned 'there is no bread', and then leapt for the spittoon to gobble up Jones's discarded fragment of orange peel.

At Kharkov, Jones stepped off the train and walked up the railway track into the starving countryside. His letters home were full of pleasantries and expressions of gratitude designed for the censor. But when he arrived in Germany on 29 March, Jones gave an interview to H. R. Knickerbocker, German correspondent for the *New York Evening Post*. Within hours his story as 'the first foreigner to visit the Russian countryside since the ban' was being syndicated around the world. Jones, who appears to have been in some competition with Muggeridge, reported 'famine on a colossal scale, impending death of millions from hunger, murderous terror and the beginnings of serious unemployment in a land that had hitherto prided itself on the fact that every man had a job'.[80] Taking another swipe at the delegates who denied the existence of these conditions, he announced that 'After

Stalin, the most hated man in Russia is Bernard Shaw among those who read his glowing descriptions of plentiful food in their starving land.'[81]

On 30 March, the day the *Manchester Guardian* published his article confirming Muggeridge's claims, Jones was in London making the same points in a speech on 'Soviet Russia' at the Royal Institute of International Affairs (Chatham House). Here he described how 'the noose' was tightening around the neck of the Russian peasants, and expressed his disgust at the 'cowardly and hypocritical' attitude of the Liberal press, and the *Manchester Guardian* in particular. Though quick to denounce Nazi atrocities, the latter had found remarkably little to say when 'a hundred million peasants are condemned to hunger and serfdom'. He singled out the *Guardian's* publication of the letter by Shaw, D. N. Pritt, and other friends of the Soviet Union. He had read the Russian version of this 'farcical' document when it appeared in *Izvestia*: 'Viewed from Moscow it was a mixture of hypocrisy, of gullibility and of such crass ignorance of the situation that the signatories should be ashamed of venturing to express an opinion about something which they know so little.'[82] And so Jones continued, producing more than twenty press articles in a few days.

Other voices were raised in denial. Indeed, if Jones was especially enraged by the *Manchester Guardian*, this may well have been on account of the way it treated his article of 30 March. This was published, to be sure, but it can hardly have been by accident that it was immediately followed by an article of equal length calling into question the veracity of 'foreign correspondents' on Russia.

The piece in question reported on a talk given by P. A. Sloan at the Workers' Education Association in Pendleton, Lancashire. Introduced only as a 'late lecturer' at the University of Bangor who had just returned from eighteen months teaching in Russia, Pat Sloan was a Cambridge economics graduate and an orthodox communist. He insisted that the foreign correspondents in Russia were 'isolated' from the workers and the peasants, and far too inclined to fraternise with members of 'the old ruling class', who shared their dislike of Communism and were able to speak Western languages.[83] They were also guilty of viewing conditions in Russia in direct comparison with those prevailing in England, and not in 'the perspective of Russian history'—as was apparent in their negative response to collectivization. 'This "starvation," said Mr. Sloan, was not the result of a breakdown in the system; it was a condition which returned periodically and had existed with far greater severity in pre-revolutionary days. Because the peasants looked—and no doubt were—hungry the foreign correspondent became appalled by this picture of "starvation".' Sloan went on to claim that the peasants were only inclined to moan because their conditions had actually been improved under Communism: 'The existing difficulties were not to be compared with the great famines of the past. Peasants now complained of conditions which before the revolution they would have accepted without a murmur, said Mr. Sloan, the reason being that their standard of living had been raised.'

Pat Sloan was a loyal Stalinist, who would go on to write many pamphlets for the cause. However, his was by no means the most damaging criticism to be levelled against Jones. In the *New York Times,* the attack was led by Walter Duranty, the governing star of the American press corps in Moscow and, in the dedicatory words of an English Quaker who lived and taught in the city, 'the doyen of Moscow correspondents at whose feet we all sit in matters Sovietic'.[84] And this embedded bruiser now came down on Jones with the hauteur of a senior foreign correspondent faced with a pitiful freelancer who, as he made clear, he had met and advised while in Moscow. Jones, who had been in Russia for a mere three weeks, was guilty of producing 'a big scare story', and his walking tour had been short and inadequate to support his generalizations.[85] Duranty admitted some 'deplorable results' had followed the attempt to convert 'stock-raising nomads of the type and the period of Abraham and Isaac into 1933 collective grain farmers'. Conditions were undeniably bad, and the Bolsheviks no more caring about the peasants than the generals of the Great War had been about the men they ordered into slaughter. Yet, as Duranty insisted, 'there is no famine'. In a sentence that would become famous as an example of censored reportage, he announced: 'There is no actual starvation or deaths from starvation, but there is widespread mortality from diseases due to malnutrition.'[86] Conceding that collectivization had been accompanied by some suffering, Duranty nevertheless fell back on a well-known proverb, 'But—to put it brutally—you can't make an omelette without breaking eggs.' It was indeed a brutal usage, and one that was never more effectively answered than by the Romanian writer Panaït Istrati, who is remembered for having said: 'All right. I can see the broken eggs. Where's this omelette of yours?'

Jones, also, came back effectively. In his reply to the *New York Times,* he made clear, if only implicitly, that Duranty was effectively Stalin's stooge. He thanked the American for his help in Moscow, profusely, but in a manner that also indicated how important Duranty's briefings were to the reception of hundreds of American and British visitors to Moscow. He could not give names of the twenty or thirty consular staff he had talked with, since these people were not in any position to give their views to the press. Journalists, on the other hand, were 'allowed to write, but the censorship has turned them into masters of euphemism and understatement. Hence they give "famine" the polite name of "food shortage" and "starving to death" is softened down to read as "widespread mortality from diseases due to malnutrition".' As Muggeridge would later say of Duranty, 'he just writes what they tell him'.[87] Jones, who preceded George Orwell in this diagnosis of language deformed by totalitarianism, had concluded his reply to Duranty with the same point: 'May I in conclusion congratulate the Soviet Foreign Office on its skill in concealing the true situation in the USSR?'

Duranty's lying assault on Jones was part of a concerted campaign by the US Press corps to discredit the British freelancers who had somehow stolen their best story. Louis Fischer, who had left Moscow in December 1932, used a lecture tour in the USA to dismiss claims of starvation. Yet, as Eugene Lyons would later admit, the campaign against Jones (this 'earnest and meticulous little man') was cooked up in Moscow. It was organized at a meeting convened by a senior correspondent, almost certainly Duranty, who brought a number of American foreign correspondents together with the head of the Soviet Press Office, Constantine Oumansky, who seemed unusually affable and relaxed about the situation, not least because he knew he had the advantage over the correspondents thanks to the Metro-Vickers affair.

Lyons was haughtily irritated by Jones, describing him, even after his own recantation, as if he were some sort of cub reporter who had stumbled into the world of journalistic giants. He remembered Jones as 'the sort who carries a note-book and unashamedly records your words as you talk'. Indeed, the statement Jones issued on emerging from Russia was 'little more than a summary' of what he had been told by diplomats and foreign correspondents such as Lyons himself—although the Welshman had tried to protect his sources by emphasizing his 'Ukrainian foray'. As for the Moscow correspondents' demolition of Jones's arguments, Lyons admitted that

> throwing down Jones was as unpleasant a chore as fell to any of us in years of juggling facts to please dictatorial regimes—but throw him down we did, unanimously and in almost identical formulas of equivocation. Poor Gareth Jones must have been the most surprised human being alive when the facts he so painstakingly garnered from our mouths were snowed under by our denials.

Jones would not live to read that confession, or the recantation of Louis Fischer, who eventually conceded the reality of the famine in *The God that Failed*, admitting that 'the price of Bolshevik haste and dogmatism was enormous'.[88] He was to die a year or so after exposing the famine: murdered, under still clouded circumstances, while travelling on a fact-finding mission in Mongolia. He was said at the time to have been kidnapped and killed by Chinese bandits, yet a different explanation is suggested by the recently disclosed connections of those with whom he was travelling. The car was owned by a company now known to have been a trading front for the Soviet secret police and Dr Herbert Mueller, who was 'kidnapped' together with Jones but later released unharmed, is said to have been a representative of the Comintern in China.[89]

17

Steeled Minds and the God
that Failed

Everything was new and steeled: a steel sun, steel trees, steel people

Yevgeny Zamyatin, *We* (1920–1)[1]

Though Potemkinist illusion was by no means the most essential layer of the curtain that prevented news of its existence reaching the West, there can be no doubt that the Great Famine of 1932/4 found its eminent visiting dupe.

The candidate this time was M. Édouard Herriot, the socialist mayor of Lyons who had been prime minister in 1924 when France, having come to terms with Christian Rakovsky's Bolshevik delegation, formally recognized Soviet Russia. On 26 August 1933, Herriot went to Russia as the guest of the Soviet government. He was invited as chairman of the French Chamber of Deputies' foreign affairs committee, and the timing of his visit had been carefully judged. The tour coincided with the new harvest, which was considerably better than the previous year's and would be exhibited as proof that collectivization had worked and that the famine, which had never been admitted, was a thing of the past.

The Soviet authorities had lifted the ban restricting foreign correspondents to Moscow, enabling Walter Duranty to write, that same September: 'I have just completed a 200-mile auto trip through the heart of the Ukraine and can say positively that the harvest is splendid and all talk of famine now is ridiculous.'[2] Rarely has such heavy work been expected of that little word 'now', here used to cart millions of corpses behind those 'splendid' scenes.

Two weeks later Herriot himself returned to the West, insisting categorically that there was no famine in Russia. Indeed, he described the Ukraine as a 'burgeoning garden'[3] and, in the equivocation that would become so characteristic of that era, dismissed all claims to the contrary as Nazi propaganda.[4]

A detailed condemnation of Herriot's visit to the Ukraine would be produced by Dr Ewalde Ammende, a relief worker and political entrepreneur of Estonian German descent, who attacked the Frenchman's tour as an example of 'the methods by which Moscow succeeds in keeping a veil over the real position in Russia'.[5] Ammende had long been concerned with the fate of nationalities dispersed through the system of states established by the Treaty of Versailles. Since the end of the Great War, he had been campaigning for full recognition of minority groups, including Jewish as well as German populations, in Russia and the new Baltic countries.[6] His thinking had been a considerable influence on Estonia's 'cultural autonomy law', enacted in February 1925. He was also a founder, and later secretary general, of the European Nationalities Congress under which he hoped to see the dispersed nations achieve a new form of representation to go alongside that achieved for the post-war system of states through the League of Nations.

Writing about Herriot's tour in his book on the famine in the USSR, Ammende declared it astonishing that, 'in this age of wireless, aviation and speed records of every kind', it was still possible for 'millions to die of hunger in the richest agricultural districts of Europe', while the rest of the world remained unaware, and even foreign travellers failed to observe the least indication of disaster.[7] In explanation, Ammende pointed out that, long before the revolution, it had been possible for foreigners to 'admire the cream of Russian culture and art in Moscow and St. Petersburg', while remaining 'wholly ignorant' of everyday life in the remote and largely inaccessible provinces. Under Stalin, this 'peculiar nature of Russian geography and of Russian communications' had formed 'the foundation of the propaganda exerted to influence foreign public opinion'[8] during the famine of 1932–4.

Guided by one of the Soviet secret police's most influential officials, Herriot spent five days in the south, where the famine had been at its worst, devoting much of his time to the usual banquets and receptions. Accompanied by French journalists, the French ambassador, and a party of Soviet officials, he passed through a world that had been 'prepared in every respect'—right down to the bed in his Rostov hotel, which actually belonged to the local police chief and had, so Ammende insists, been brought in to replace the hotel's insufficiently comfortable model.[9] Herriot soon gave in to the rigging. In Odessa he enjoyed the 'smart, comfortable, ultra-modern Hotel London', the amazing 'cleanliness' of the state bakery he visited, and the positively idyllic appearance of the collective farm he saw at Belyaevka.[10] He visited the German settlements on the Black Sea, where tens of thousands had died, but here too, he registered nothing: 'Nowhere did I find a sign of distress, not even in the German villages, which had been described as suffering from famine.' In Kiev he and his considerable retinue attended the Ukrainian Academy of Sciences, where they were instructed on the great care being devoted to Ukrainian culture and science.[11]

No recognition there for the fact that Ukrainian cultural individuality was then being systematically 'exterminated', or for the apprehensions of the old Ukrainian Bolshevik Nikolai Skrypnik, a friend of Lenin and co-founder of the Soviet state, who had shot himself a few days earlier. No signs of starvation, either past or ongoing, were visible from the steamer *Kalinin*, which took the visitors on a pleasure cruise on the Dnieper, the very river along which Prince Potemkin is said to have organized his original 'villages' for Catherine the Great. As Ammende noted, 'Ukrainian cooking has a good reputation, and it may be assumed that during his fortnight in Russia M. Herriot was one of the best-fed people in the country. No unpleasant interludes marred the feast, and none of the guests was reminded that during the summer thousands of innocent people had perished in that ancient metropolis.'[12]

By coincidence, another Westerner, Harry Lang, an American syndicalist who wrote for the left-wing *Jewish Daily Forward,* was visiting southern Russia at the same time in order to investigate the condition of Jews in the region. He and his wife were in Kiev to see 'the camouflage'[13] being applied to the city in anticipation of the Herriot delegation's visit. In a lecture given at the Sholom Aleichim Club in Paris, Lang would later describe how, at 2 a.m. on the day of Herriot's arrival, the entire populace had been mobilized to clean the streets, decorate the houses, and give the city a more prosperous 'European' appearance. Food distribution centres and co-operative shops were closed and all queues banned for the day. Hordes of starving beggars and street children were swept off the streets, and mounted soldiers were stationed at road crossings, with white ribbons in the manes of their carefully groomed horses: 'a sight never before and never again witnessed in Kiev'.[14]

Having nodded their heads appreciatively in Kiev, Herriot and his delegation were moved on to Kharkov, where they visited another museum, a tractor factory, and a flower-dressed children's settlement named after the founder of the Cheka, Felix Dzerzhinsky. Once again, the day ended with a banquet, at which Herriot proclaimed that 'only the Communist revolution could provide a favourable solution' to the problems facing the Russian peasantry. And so the tour continued, through schools, tractor stations and factories, and the much larger 'show giants' epitomized by the Dnieperstroy dam. The French visitors passed through Odessa, Kiev, Kharkov, and Rostov, and yet they never touched the ground anywhere: 'it was as if a film were shown to Mr. Herriot and his companions'.[15] After returning to France, Herriot would boast of having studied the situation 'with the unbiased eye of a trained administrator' but Ammende would have none of it: 'the result was produced on M. Herriot as on Catherine II. He saw only what his hosts intended him to see, and remained completely ignorant of what was going on a few miles away.'[16]

The 'deceptions à la Potemkin' had continued to the end. In Moscow, Herriot was put up at the Hotel National, where the secret police contrived to fill the 'ordinarily deserted bar' with 'well-dressed "representatives of the population"'. During his last hours in Soviet Russia, Herriot was taken to a 'milk centre', where the president of the Central Committee of the Communist Party, Kalinin, managed to persuade him that the acute milk shortages affecting so many towns were actually just proof of Soviet plenitude. As Herriot pronounced when home in France: 'Actually milk production has very considerably increased in Russia; but at the same time the social services have increased so much that the consumption of milk tends to exceed the production, with the result that regulations had to be made with regard to distribution.'[17] It was another version of the Stalinist trope recited by the Cambridge Marxist Pat Sloan in March 1933: far from starving, the peoples of the USSR only complained of shortages because conditions were actually getting better all the time.

In his younger days Herriot had been leader of the radical-socialist party that had opposed the French Communist Party after the split of December 1920. Yet he emerged from his 1933 tour of Russia as if he was already auditioning for a part in George Orwell's forthcoming satire *Animal Farm*. Like this former prime minister of France, Orwell's Mr Whymper would be led through a carefully rigged Animal Farm at a time when it was being 'put about that all the animals were dying of famine and disease, and that they were continually fighting among themselves and had resorted to cannibalism and infanticide'. Having glimpsed the store-shed, where the empty food bins had been filled with sand and then superficially covered with grain or meal, he reported, as emphatically as Herriot, that 'there was no food shortage on Animal Farm'.[18]

By September 1933, however, Stalin's famine could not be convincingly denied by such strategies. It may have been predictable that, as Ammende records, the right-wing *Action française* (a long-standing enemy of Herriot's) should have reminded its readers that Herriot was mayor of Lyons, a city where many industrial and commercial businesses were heavily committed to Soviet Russia on account of their frozen Russian credits. Yet a wider range of papers in France and French-speaking Switzerland also refused to believe his accounts. *Le Matin* referred to Potemkin and his well-known villages, while the *Journal des débats* condemned Herriot for merely 'shrugging his shoulders' when confronted with inconvenient facts.[19]

If the truth was to be compromised yet again, this was partly thanks to the confusions introduced by Ammende himself. He may have assembled a damning case against Herriot, but it was not just ideological reflex that enabled Stalin's defenders to invalidate his every word as thinly disguised Nazi propaganda. Ammende's opposition to Bolshevism was obvious enough. Yet by the time he wrote *Human Life in Russia,* he was indeed moving in the orbit of Hitler's Nazism, and his once largely benign idea of cultural autonomy for national minorities in Estonia, Latvia, and Russia had been overshadowed by the Pan-Germanist ideas motivating Nazi ambitions for recolonization in the East.[20] By 1933, Ammende was honorary secretary of the 'Interconfessional and International Relief Committee for the Russian Famine areas' set up by Cardinal Innitzer of Vienna, a churchman who would go on to support the Fascist government of Dollfuss and also to commend the Anschluss in which Austria was annexed to Nazi Germany in 1938.

Ammende himself had questioned Nazi anti-Semitism, but he failed to condemn it emphatically enough to prevent Jewish members withdrawing from his Congress of European Nationalities. He had also come to terms with Alfred Rosenberg, the Estonian-born Nazi ideologist whose racial theories had earlier conflicted with Ammende's cultural understanding of national identity. Indeed, *Human Life in Russia,* the book in which he condemned Herriot, was researched and written with financial assistance from Rosenberg's office. Ammende had died by the time the English edition appeared in 1935, but it would not be long before its photographs were being challenged as fraudulent: some of them turned out to be recycled from the older famine of 1921/2. It was an argument that would flare again in the nineteen eighties, when the memory of the Great Famine was recovered and Ammende's testimony, supported by the same dodgy photographs, would be reasserted from the perspective of right-wing Ukrainian nationalism.

A Blade in the Mind

By the early 1930s, the charge of Potemkinism had proved sufficiently justified to incline many who approached the Soviet regime in a spirit of 'friendliness' to acknowledge or even to make their own pre-emptive use of the familiar accusation.

MacFlecknoe's satirical poem 'The "Truth about Russia"',[21] published in the *New Statesman* in 1932, was quoted as a defensive talisman by the medical investigators Sir Arthur Newsholme and John Adams Kingsbury, who used it in the introduction to their study of *Red Medicine* to indicate the opposed biases they themselves claimed not to share.[22] Its warning was acknowledged by Alexander Wicksteed, who had arrived in Russia as a Quaker relief worker in the early 1920s and stayed for ten years teaching English at the University of Moscow. He admitted the existence of Soviet 'window-dressing', but not before opening the door to further confusion by insisting on 'the most valuable lesson that all but the stupidest learn in the Soviet Union'—namely the importance of 'questioning your assumptions'.[23]

By the summer of 1933, Kingsley Martin, the editor of the *New Statesman,* was also coming out strongly against the utopian dreamers who crossed the Baltic in a spirit similar to that in which William Wordsworth had remembered crossing the English Channel to visit the French Revolution ('bliss was it that dawn to be alive'). It was, he decreed, 'only by saving Russia from such friends that one can hope to create any real understanding of the Soviet Regime'.[24] A case, perhaps, of 'friends' against 'friends'.

While Western Liberals and democratic socialists agonized, prevaricated, and yielded sometimes reluctantly measured patches of ground to Stalin's critics, their 'hard-boiled' Communist rivals fell back on their own internalized version of the 'iron curtain', using it to guillotine the encroaching doubts that would otherwise undermine their ability to remain, in one German comrade's phrase, 'as loyal as phonographs'.[25]

As they cleaved to Stalin's wandering and opportunistic party line ('When Stalin turns we all turn'),[26] reasoning was replaced by a wholly prejudged process of comparison, in which every charge against Soviet Communism was immediately countered with an equivalent crime from the West. Thus, for example, criticism of Stalin's system of show trials would be seen off with reference to American injustices—a favourite being the mistreatment of the Italian anarchists Sacco and Vanzetti, condemned and executed in August 1927. This equivocating dynamic is demonstrated repeatedly in the memoirs of George Hardy, an English-born Canadian, who would serve the Comintern on five continents. In order to measure up the savagery with which the US authorities had turned against the International Workers of the World in September 1917—a time, shortly after America entered the war against Germany, when he and other 'Wobblie' organizers had been arrested and locked up in Chicago's Cook County Jail—Hardy only had to compare his experience in that capitalist institution with a Soviet show prison he had later visited in the company of Wal Hannington, leader of Britain's unemployed workers:

> I can still feel the pain of those Chicago nights of thirty-five years ago. But as I think back another picture comes to me. I see another jail, the jail in Leningrad which Wal Hannington and I visited in the early thirties, where a sign in bright gilt letters informs all who enter: 'This is not a prison. It is a home of correction.' We saw class and recreation rooms, library, theatre and dining hall, spotlessly clean. We saw the inmates at work in a tailoring factory. All work was paid for. We spoke to several of them. I asked a tall, blond, smart-looking Russian why he was there. He was a sailor who had been sentenced to five years for the offence, very serious in those days, of selling a revolver. He himself told us it was a 'terrible crime' and, when we asked why, he said: 'It could have been used by a counter-revolutionary.' Education and humane treatment had brought him to see the error of his ways ...
>
> Two pictures—two worlds. On the one hand this Soviet, humane institution, and on the other the barbarous Cook County Jail of U.S. monopoly capitalism.[27]

This polarized way of thinking, in which any lingering idea of objective truth became a toy of overriding class-consciousness, would inflict considerable moral injury on its exponents as they proceeded through the 1930s. It left them to meet the dreadful realities of that decade with little more than a ferociously reductive cry of 'Which side are you on?' No nuances, no complexity, no elaboration—but lots of counter-accusation, tactical silence, and also lies in defence of the chosen future. It was a defiantly crude way of thinking: guarded against any logic but its own and justified by reference to the imperialism of the capitalist states, their inability to run their own economies and societies, their reluctance to stem the rise of fascism or even to support Spain's democratically elected socialist government against the military assault (1936) that led to General Franco's dictatorship.

Earlier in the twentieth century, the Viennese satirist Karl Kraus had famously suggested that when invited to choose the lesser of two evils, it was advisable to choose neither. Kraus's proposition would not have hindered many who became 'friends' of the Soviet Union in the 1930s. For them, everything pivoted on a future-orientated choice between Hitler and Stalin, and it was this ruthlessly simplified opposition that underlay many of the examples of 'useful idiocy' that would be exhibited as monuments to the folly of the fellow-travelling Western left. David Caute once declared that, for the novelists who committed themselves to the Communist cause, 'The inevitable stumbling block was the Party line, that narrow prism of virtue through which no writer has ever attempted to pass without emerging mauled beyond recognition.'[28] Yet it was surely not just loyalty to the party line or, indeed, the intellectual's deluded self-importance, that inclined the French writer André Malraux to hail the USSR as 'the country of Liberty' in 1934,[29] or that enabled the French Communist poet Louis Aragon to applaud the sentences passed at the Industrial Party Trial of 1931, calling out 'Death to the saboteurs of the Five-Year Plan'. The party line was held in place by the iron curtain, a 'psychological deadlock', as Vernon Lee had described it, which isolated the Soviet Union at the same time as setting it up in the minds of its Western defenders as the only effective alternative to the undeniably real threat of Nazism. Though reinforced by this pressing historical circumstance, it was a bipolar disorder in which nothing existed, except as it was projected in opposition to its antagonist on the other side.

The internal diplomacy practised by these fellow-travellers has often been singled out as proof of a particular weakness of liberal and left-wing thought. Yet it is hardly excused by the fact that 'idiocies' were also uttered by those on the opposite side of the ideological division: people who followed the *Daily Mail* in its anti-Communist appreciation of Nazism, or who forgot that G. K. Chesterton was actually attacking 'Modernism' when, in

1933, he described Hitler as 'the last pink promising bud upon the flowering tree of progress'.[30]

Many of the most flagrant and widely exhibited examples of fellow-travelling 'stupidity' were concentrated on a domain in which truth was most fundamentally at stake, namely the Soviet system of justice. In a classic case of iron curtain double-think, the American writer Waldo Frank hailed the Soviet courts for the absence of any signs of bourgeois legality. No black robed judges, bald clerks, or 'sleek' litigants, he noted of an ordinary non-political hearing:'it came to me that this was the first court of human justice I had known'.[31]

Yet, as the Hungarian-American historian Paul Hollander has indicated, this was by no means the worst Western response to the show trials of Stalin's purges. André Malraux, insisted that, just as the Inquisition had not affected the fundamental dignity of Christianity, 'so the Moscow trials had not diminished the fundamental dignity of communism'. The American novelist Upton Sinclair confidently dismissed the suggestion that Stalin's victims could ever be forced into making false confessions. The German dramatist Bertolt Brecht insisted that the purge trials had proved the existence of conspiracies, adding that 'All the scum, domestic and foreign, all the vermin, the professional criminals and informers, found lodging there.' Harold Laski, the British academic and socialist politician, praised Stalin's prosecutor, Andrei Vyshinsksy, as a great reformer of the law. Owen Lattimore of Johns Hopkins University thought the trials showed the power of the ordinary citizen to denounce even 'top officials', adding 'this sounds like democracy to me'. And they were all trumped by the American ambassador, Joseph Davis, who commended the purges for 'cleansing' the country, and then crept up to Stalin as he gazed out from the posters of his own personality cult:'His brown eye is exceedingly wise and gentle. A child would like to sit on his lap and a dog would sidle up to him.'[32]

These prize examples of 'useful idiocy' would be gleefully exhibited by right-wing opponents of Stalinism, but they were also roundly condemned by other voices on the contemporary Western left: by Trotskyists, certainly, but also by the many socialist and labour parties that opposed the system of show trials throughout. The secretary of the Labour and Socialist International, Friedrich Adler, was among the representatives of Western socialism who responded to the so-called 'Menshevik' trial of March 1931, exposing the faked evidence used to support the charge that the Labour and Socialist

International and its affiliated parties in the West were engaged in 'sabotage activity' designed to help the capitalist powers prepare for military intervention against Russia. He noted the lies and inaccuracies in both the indictment and the verdict, and also that those of the accused who confessed to 'sabotage' did so in obviously prepared speeches that caused the prosecutor to smile with the contentment of 'a successful circus tamer'.[33] In 1936, the 'witchcraft' trial of Kamenev, Zinoviev, and fourteen others provoked Adler to 'protest with all my energy against the judicial atrocities in the country which claims the honourable name of "Socialist"'.[34] Once again he set about exposing the false testimony, and pointing to the corrupted staging of the confessions, obviously forced on defendants in the unseen 'preliminary hearings'. He also engaged directly with Stalin's Western apologists, especially the English observers who allowed themselves to become the puppets of the ever more corrupted Communist International.

Among these 'dumb curs or mendacious whitewashers',[35] Adler gave pride of place to the eminent British socialist barrister and Labour MP D. N. Pritt. In 1933 Pritt had distinguished himself in his involvement in the 'counter-trial' held in London and Paris to expose the corruptions of the Nazi Reichstag fire trial. But he went on to prove that, thanks to hypocrisy of the kind earlier exhibited by the British Trades Union Delegation of 1924, an obviously stage-managed Stalinist show trial could satisfy a biased British legal expert. As Adler wrote, 'he drew all his conclusions solely from what the spectator sees in court and did not make the slightest reference to the fact that there might also be problems which lie behind the scenes—in the preliminary investigation'.[36]

Sixteen men had been shot without appeal, having 'voluntarily' renounced their defence counsel, and, as agreed in the preliminary investigation, spouted 'confessions' of Trotskyist plotting that simply could not have been true. And yet Pritt, who had been in Moscow at the time, acclaimed the trial as a great step towards establishing the Soviet judiciary's reputation 'among the legal systems of the modern world'.[37] He praised the 'courteousness' of the court president and even of Stalin's bullying prosecutor Andrei Vyshinsky, saying he 'looked like a very intelligent and rather mild-mannered English businessman'.[38] Only a little surprised to hear the public audience actually applauding Vyshinsky's speeches as if they were in a theatre, Pritt claimed that the absence of any right of appeal was quite reconcilable with political justice, since the accused had the good fortune of coming before the highest court at once. And this, as Adler objected, of a court that consisted only of a

'Collegium of three military judges'. It was, he judged, another example of the British habit of applying double standards to other parts of the world—also pointed out by George Orwell (who later described the Communism of the 1930s English intellectual as 'the patriotism of the deracinated' and condemned Pritt as Stalin's 'hired liar'[39]). Pritt may have been little worse in this regard than many others, including the elderly Sidney and Beatrice Webb, but Adler had no interest in ranking the offenders: 'We shall not discuss this "argument" until Pritt suggests introducing this advantage of the single court, in the case of offences involving the death penalty, for defendants in England as well.'

Margaret McCarthy's Dream

The events of the 1930s would ensure that the Western volunteers who formed that 'ring of trust' around Stalin's Soviet Union had an increasingly demanding job. Those who stayed the course would claim their moment of vindication during the Second World War, after the Soviet Union joined the Grand Alliance against Hitler. Long before then, however, events in the USSR had tested and exposed their illusions. Western Communists and fellow-travelling anti-Fascists were stalked by a growing host of challenging facts, rumours, and suspicions about the direction taken by the Communist International under Stalin.

These included the torments of the Communist Party in Germany, which, from the late 1920s, had found itself fighting not the rising Nazi party but the Social Democratic socialists whom Stalin had declared to be both the class enemy and indistinguishable from fascism. In Prussia, in the summer of 1931, the German Communists went so far as to form a common front with the Nazis in the hope of demolishing Otto Braun's Social Democrat government.[40] In spring 1932, they set out to sabotage the 'Iron Front' formed by democratic parties in a last ditch attempt to halt the Nazis' advance.[41] Further alarms were raised by the Reichstag fire trial of 1933. The German Communist 'Jan Valtin' would claim to have seen Comintern papers proving that Georgi Dimitrov, chief of the Comintern's Western Secretariat, only behaved so courageously in court because he knew that the outcome of this trial had been prearranged as part of a secret collaboration and exchange of prisoners agreed between the Nazis and the Stalinist authorities in Russia.[42] There would be further outrages during the Spanish

Civil War, which Stalin's Communists used as an opportunity to wage their own war against anarchists and non-Stalinist leftists. Some international Communists and fellow-travellers may have managed to maintain a rictal grin as the corpses piled up around them, but the final humiliation came on 23 August 1939, when Molotov and Ribbentrop met in Moscow to sign the Nazi–Soviet non-aggression pact.

Some who remained true to the cause throughout this decade may have been blinded by doctrinaire Marxist certainty, and others by a misapplied idea of Christian or Jewish redemption. Many of them crossed the line as pragmatists rather than seekers after the absolute truth that George Lansbury had espoused: driven less by a sense of revolution than by a reckoning of the usefulness of their stance in a world of brutally simplified options. Yet in the end George Orwell was surely right to conclude that 'in their hearts they felt that to cast any doubt on the wisdom of Stalin was a kind of blasphemy'.[43]

A few of Stalin's British adherents held on into the 1980s: still inclined to dismiss democracy as 'bourgeois ideology', and still turning up at public meetings to wag crotchety fingers at East European dissidents, reminding them that 'it is not easy to change the world'. Yet this was the rump of what had always been a tiny faction within the British labour movement, and one that, by the mid-1930s, was already distinguished by the manner in which people left it.

Some, like the British Communist Harry Wicks, had turned left into the Trotskyist opposition. Yet the characteristically polarized mentality of the Communist adherent would also prove susceptible to the varieties of disillusionment expressed by Koestler, Spender, Gide, and others in *The God that Failed* (1950). Some would be assisted in this conversion by their memory of the benign ideas of emancipation that had led them to espouse socialism in the first place. The famous American 'turncoat' Louis Budenz remembered his youthful interest in 'guild socialism' associated with British thinkers such as G. D. H. Cole and A. R. Orage, editor of the *New Age,* who advocated workers' control and an associative form of socialism very distinct from Stalin's state dictatorship.[44] The Swedish Communist journalist Björn Hallström returned to the spurned religious beliefs of his Protestant childhood—in particular, the social message of the Sermon on the Mount. His rejection of Communism, which he likened to stepping out of a strait-jacket,[45] would also reshape his memory of his first pilgrimage to Moscow. As he would only now admit, reality had quite failed to support the utopian illusions he had entertained as he travelled by train through Finland to Systerback, the last station before the Russian frontier. He had entered Russia filled with the desire to embrace the first Red Army soldier he saw. But the official who first came into view had actually been a secret police-man, and so filthy that Hallström shrank back as he produced his passport for inspection. At the gates of the promised new Jerusalem, he had found a series of little cubicles in which his fellow passengers were made to strip naked and stand about as their underpants were inspected for contraband and their bags rifled for Trotskyist literature.

Some apostates gave up on the cause without escaping the polarized logic of the iron curtain. Love became hate as they leapt from one side to the other: the one-eyed Communist transmogrifying into a one-eyed anti-Communist and, in some cases, including that of Freda Utley, going on to adopt a zealously McCarthyist perspective in the 1950s. But there were others who managed to remove the iron curtain from their thinking altogether. Perhaps the most sympathetic British record of this recovery of mind was provided by Margaret McCarthy. Having travelled through Russia with the Young Communists attached to the British Workers' Delegation of 1927, McCarthy had resumed her labours in the Lancashire weaving sheds, dreaming of what she had seen and felt in Russia and imagining that the straps driving the deafening looms were 'pouring forth the magnificent strains of the "Peer Gynt" suite as I had heard it at the Leningrad ballet'.[46] She started speaking for the British Communist Party, launching her plat-form career in Accrington marketplace in December 1927, and going on to tour Lancashire with the 'Messianic Mission of bringing the truth about the Soviet Promised Land to the Lancashire cotton operatives'.

In 1931 she had returned to Moscow to work and study for a year as a 'practicant' with the Red International of Trade Unions. Though she resisted it at the time, her disenchantment began in Russia. As an ordinary and unpampered foreigner, rather than a visiting delegate, she had seen and also shared the terrible conditions of the Russian workers: sacrificed to the First Five-Year Plan, while the party bureaucrats enjoyed special shops, capacious flats, and dachas—the latter ornamented by luridly 'made-up' wives and serviced by exploited servant girls from the country. She had seen the van-ity and sexual opportunism of the Comintern's visiting stars, including the odious Bill Rust, whom she had known as the Comintern-backed secretary of the British Young Communist League.[47] She had been dismayed to dis-cover that the typists employed by the Red International of Trade Unions did not benefit from trade union conditions, and she had watched the gathering persecution of old Bolsheviks including Zinoviev, Bukharin, Rykov, and Tomsky, whose heresies were already being denounced in lectures she attended at the Lenin University in 1931. She noted the disappearance of Russian comrades, and saw through the lies of the British *Daily Worker,* which had obediently denied the existence of the prison—Solovetsky—in which they were probably held. Perhaps, like another British Communist who gradually came to his senses while studying at the Comintern's International Lenin School in the late 1920s, she visited the Museum of the Revolution and realized from the 'gaps in the display' that history was being rewritten there too.[48] Her dissatisfaction was increased by the utter indifference shown by Harry Pollitt, by then the obedient chief of the Communist Party of Great Britain, as members of Communist parties of China, Bulgaria, Greece, Germany, and America were denounced as renegades. Many of these accused leaders were effectively already prisoners of Stalin, having found refuge in Russia and, in some cases, being under sentence of death in their countries of origin.

Together with a rising sympathy for the arguments of the now beaten and dispersed left opposition, these doubts had failed to break through her resistances by 1932, when McCarthy returned to Britain. However, she found herself being loudly condemned by British Communists when, in the course of speaking at meetings, she mentioned some of the difficulties faced by the citizens of Stalin's Russia. Finding herself increasingly out of favour with a party that refused to countenance the thought that anything could be less than perfect in their promised land, she repressed her worries partly out of loyalty to the international friends with whom she had shared the cause in Moscow.

So strong was her habit of denial, that she only realized she had finally broken with Communism when a doctor in Clitheroe helped her understand the significance of a recurrent dream in which she found herself back on the Soviet side of the division. She was standing on a sea-coast like the one she had enjoyed when sent for a month's convalescence at a party rest home at Gagri on the Black Sea. Yet the mood of the place had changed— the air was heavy, the sea torpid, and she felt 'an all-pervading atmosphere of fearful, hopeless despondency'.[49] She stood silently on the beach, aware of a 'deathly silence' and yet not feeling alone thanks to 'a sort of presence, a melancholy, gloomy spirit' that emanated from 'a smoothly red, massive

25. The Kremlin from Moskva River, 1927 (photo: David Roden Buxton).

26. Street market and secularized church, Arbat Square, Moscow, 1927 (photo: David Roden Buxton).

27. Homeless boys (*bezprizorny*), Russia 1927 (photo: David Roden Buxton).

28. Jurievets, upper Volga, Russia 1927 (photo: David Roden Buxton).

29. Dorothy and Charles Roden Buxton arriving at a *kollectiv* en route to Sokolis-chchi, Russia 1927 (photo: David Roden Buxton).

30. The Buxtons resting beside an alleged 'main road', Lopatishchi, Russia 1927 (photo: David Roden Buxton).

31. Sokolishchi and Lavrovka, Dorothy Buxton far right, Russia 1927 (photo: David Roden Buxton).

32. Carpenter at Sokolishchi, Russia 1927. The elderly man showed the Buxtons
a coffin he had made for himself and stored in the rafters of his workshop (photo:
David Roden Buxton).

33. Armed workers and soldiers mark the tenth anniversary of the Bolshevik revolution, Red Square, Moscow, 7/8 November 1927.

34. Parade in Red Square, Moscow, celebrations on the tenth anniversary of the Bolshevik revolution, 7/8 November 1927.

ПОЛИТИКУ
ТВЕРДОЛОБЫХ

НАШ
твует

ЧУДОВОЙ

ДЕТСКИЕ САДЫ И ПЛОЩАДКИ — ВОТ РОСТКИ
КОММУНИЗМА, ВОТ ПРОСТЫЕ БУДНИЧНЫЕ
СРЕДСТВА НА ДЕЛЕ РАСКРЕПОЩАЮЩИЕ
РАБОТНИЦУ [ЛЕНИН]

35. Children with flags at the tenth anniversary celebrations, 7/8 November 1927.

36. Panaït Istrati and Nikos Kazantzakis (seated) in Russia, 1928.

37. Collectivized farm workers going to work, Moscow region, 27 May 1931.

38. Food queues during famine, Ukraine, 1932.

39. Dead on street during famine, Ukraine, 1932.

40. George Bernard Shaw talking to peasants at the Lenin Farming Cooperative, August 1931.

41. Left to right (front): Karl Radek, Anatole Lunacharsky, Lady Astor, George Bernard Shaw, and Artashes Khalatov, Russia, Summer 1931.

42. George Bernard Shaw visiting the Kremlin, Moscow, 21 July 1931.

44. Nikolai Bukharin, *c.* 1936.

43. Christian Rakovsky, *c.* 1930–2.

45. Andrei Vyshinsky, chief prosecutor, summing up at the trial of Bukharin ('that damnable cross of a fox and a swine') and others, 1938.

46. 1930s show trial proceedings in the Hall of Columns, House of Trade Unions, Moscow.

For dear Jane,
gratefully — — — —
Clare Sheridan
I.L.P.
(Hastings Branch!)
1945.

47. Clare Sheridan as member of the Independent Labour Party, 1945.

48. Mikhail Gorbachev speaking on 'The River of Time and the Imperative of Action', Fulton, Missouri, 6 May 1992.

obelisk of rock which jutted upwards from among the mountains dominating the bay'.

Suddenly, and without any warning, 'the great obelisk fell forward with an overwhelming crash across the bay, plunging from its stupendous height to lie broken on the beach'. When silence returned to the shaken scene, McCarthy was assailed by a sense of 'sudden nothingness' and 'unexpected loneliness'.

> The bay was dead; it had been haunted and dark, and suddenly it was dead, the spirit finished, the darkness empty. It would have been less terrifying if there had been sounds, alarms, screams, but there was no other sound—just the brooding stillness, the sharp rending crash, and then a black void. Every fear and horror were more endurable than the nothingness which at once, implacably and utterly, descended.

In Margaret McCarthy's dream, nothing would improve after the obelisk fell. The sea would congeal, and hordes of menacing crab-like creatures came crawling out of its greasy depths. Margaret McCarthy had lost her world, her perspective, the struggle she had shared with many friends. But she had also freed herself from the excruciating rigs of her time: the unending equivocation, the self-imposed censorship, the lie of so much redemptive politics, the habitual use of a promised future to excuse and obscure monstrosities in the present. The polarizing deadlock that earlier investigators had named the 'iron curtain' no longer dominated her mind.

PART VI

Succession and Afterlife

From the days of the silent movies, there is a recurring scene, in which the backdrops—the horizons—placed on rollers, are moved towards the actors. The space the actors occupy contracts. Aware of a change, the viewer cannot make out the reason for it and feels something disturbing is going on.

Alexander Kluge (*The Devil's Blind Spot,* 2004)

18

Sliding Back to Churchill

It was, to be sure, only a comparatively minor fault of Stalinism that it conspired with Hitler to darken the last years of the group of internationalists and pacifists who had seen the iron curtain descend between Britain and Germany in 1914, and then opposed its reorganization around Bolshevik Russia.

Vernon Lee died aged 78 at her home near Florence on 13 February 1935. She passed away not long after the publication of *Music and Its Lovers* (1932), the long-delayed study (started before 1914) in which this advocate of Bach's polyphony had repeated her condemnation of the 'stupid megaphoned reiteration' with which men of words had reduced Europe to a 'battlefield'.[1] Her obituarists were left to argue over her cosmopolitanism. Had 'nationality and patriotism' been quite outside her understanding, as one suggested? Or, as her friend and literary executor Irene Cooper Willis objected in reply, did *Satan the Waster* prove that she had actually grasped 'better than most people how appeals to patriotism and nationality in war time can completely distort the general understanding of the real issues involved'?[2]

There can be little doubt that Romain Rolland, the French writer and internationalist who had so famously insisted on staying 'above the battle' in 1914, owed his descent to words rather than music. At the end of the Great War, in 1919, he had called for a 'Congress of Humanity', and also a 'Declaration of the Independence of the Spirit'.[3] He had managed to maintain his lofty cosmopolitanism through much of the 1920s, extending it beyond Europe to embrace the India of Gandhi and Rabindranath Tagore. He was still floating 'above the battle' in 1925, when he opposed both Red and White terrors, as they had brutalized Poland, Bulgaria, and Romania, insisting that both sides were dishonoured by their violence and that he himself took the side of 'all the oppressed against all the oppressors'.[4]

By April 1927, when Britain broke off relations with Russia after the Arcos raid, Rolland was firmly on the side of the revolution, which he commended as the greatest and most promising social effort to have been made in modern Europe.[5] He feared the worst when, later that year, Stalin excluded Trotsky and Zinoviev from the Communist Party. Yet he would insist that he was defending not a party or a state regime but the people of Russia, who had so heroically torn down their own version of the Bastille in 1917 and who now found themselves confronting the hostile governments of Europe and America.[6]

Well aware that the situation in Russia worsened dramatically as Stalin tightened his grip, Rolland nevertheless came down, quite unmistakably, on the Great Benefactor's side of the division. Critics might condemn him as a fellow-traveller, yet that was precisely how he would come to define himself: not a member of the Communist Party but a 'companion of the road' who recognized the many faults of the regime while remaining convinced that Russia was constructing a new world and represented, especially in the period of the Popular Front, the main opponent of Fascism and Nazism. Rolland's once superior moral stance would be shredded by the iron curtain. He might have descended into that confusion voluntarily but it was an assisted passage too. His wife, Marie Koudachef, was a half-Russian Communist sympathizer: effectively a Stalinist agent who had initially become his secretary in 1929, having sought him out as part of a 'special mission' ordered by Moscow.[7]

It was in May of that year, that Rolland's former protégé, the Romanian writer Panaït Istrati, had sent Rolland the text of two scathingly critical letters he had written to the secretary of the Soviet secret police while still in Russia. These drew attention to the dictatorial nature of the regime and condemned both the attack on left opposition figures, and the uncritical nature of the support offered by Western supporters such as Henri Barbusse. Rolland replied to his former protégé: 'These pages are sacred. They must be preserved in the archives of the Eternal Revolution, in its golden book. We love you all the more and venerate you because you have written this.' However, he also urged 'But don't publish it. You must not publish it at this time.'[8] Rolland's advice to Istrati would be remembered as a shoddy act of betrayal, and not just of Istrati himself. As the former Communist Manès Sperber would later conclude, 'The French writer, the man who had raised his voice, the voice of conscience, in World War I, acted as one of the moral initiators of the conspiracy of silence that was intended to guard the Soviet Union against any criticism.'[9]

Rolland's 'odious and lamentable' advice to Istrati also became a defining moment for Boris Souvarine. Rolland, as he would write many years later, was effectively saying 'it is not good to speak the truth, the public must be lied to. You must make a religion for the people, and "stuff the heads" of the proletariat.'[10] Rolland may partly have been won over by the Communist agent who became his wife ('nothing would be spared to gain Rolland for Stalinism') but Souvarine reckoned that his susceptibility to Stalinism was also increased by a previously revealed tendency towards anti-Semitism.

A few years later, when the Comintern launched its ferocious campaign of denigration against Istrati, Rolland would not yield to the Romanian's plea, made in a highly pitched open letter printed by *Les Nouvelles Littéraires* in September 1933, that the famous French internationalist (whom Istrati addressed as an exemplar of the idea of justice he had once placed 'Above the Battle') should speak out publicly on his behalf.[11] Rolland replied instead with a private letter, describing Istrati as a 'sincere' man, who was nonetheless guilty of passionate egotism, and too much inclined to identify himself with 'the Beautiful, the Just and the True'.[12] In correspondence with the writer and journalist Jean Guéhenno, Rolland would express his 'disgust and contempt'[13] for the Communist paper *L'Humanité* and its willingness to serve the Comintern by promoting Henri Barbusse and corruptly unmasking Istrati as a fascist, racist, and spy. Yet he also informed Istrati that, while not a member of the Communist Party, he would, in the case of any attack, defend the Soviet Union with all his strength as 'the only bastion' that defended the world against centuries of abject and increasing reaction.[14] Rolland also deplored Istrati's decision to publish the work of Serge and Souvarine under his own name—condemning it as a betrayal of authorship, and an indulgence of highly partial 'anti-Moscow revolutionary anarchists' whose views were not to be trusted.[15]

Rolland was at his best in his opposition to Nazism. He fiercely condemned Neville Chamberlain's policy of appeasing Hitler: 'The Munich "Peace" is a Degrading Capitulation'[16] as his article in *L'Humanité* was headlined. He believed that this position demanded public support for the USSR as fascism's only effective opponent. In 1935, he finally accepted Maxim Gorki's long-standing invitation and visited the Soviet Union, taking his wife as interpreter (she also had a son in the USSR). He was put up as an honoured guest in Gorki's house, enjoying a string of welcoming letters and deputations. He may be imagined standing next to Nikolai Bukharin and drinking champagne at receptions, buried under bouquets of flowers and perhaps also royalty payments from the large Soviet editions of his books.[17]

On 28 June, he was granted an audience with Stalin himself, at which he praised Soviet Russia for creating a new 'proletarian humanism'. In accordance with his belief that the 'fellow-traveller' should nevertheless retain a critical perspective, he also raised a number of the issues that were making it so very difficult for the international friends of the USSR to justify their stance. Rather than confronting Stalin with his perversion of the socialist idea and his outright offences against humanity, Rolland raised his chosen issues as if they were no more than misunderstandings and largely the fault of poor communications and the deliberate distortions of the capitalist press. Indeed, he recommended that the Soviet Union should establish an 'office of intellectual understanding'[18] in the West: a kind of rapid rebuttal unit that could be used to contest malicious anti-Communist rumours before they went into wide circulation. As examples of the 'calumnies' that had been allowed to spread unchecked, he cited the Soviet Union's failure to communicate the reasons, which Rolland was inclined to presume must exist, why Victor Serge had been exiled for the last three years, and its failure to clarify a recently passed law that appeared to expose children as young as 12 years old to the death penalty.

As the 1930s went on, Rolland's position became more untenable, and the division between his private and public utterances all the more extreme. He savaged his old rival Andre Gide, when he came back from being feted in Russia to publish his highly critical *Return from the USSR* in November 1936.[19] He proclaimed the virtues of the Soviet Union during the Spanish Civil War, calling it 'the great country of Socialism' even as it was encouraging the slaughter of anarchists and non-Stalinist Communists, and, as would later become known, charging exorbitant prices for military equipment. He failed, despite the urgent requests of his friends, to condemn Stalin's show trials, chosing rather to parade Soviet arguments about the 'conspiracy' of the accused. He continued to write in the Communist press, and dutifully accused the Trotskyist opposition of being in collusion with the Nazis.

He was effectively silenced on 23 August 1939, when the Nazi–Soviet non-aggression pact was signed in Moscow—a 'double-blow', which betrayed both the Western states and the Soviet Union's supporters in the West.[20] Convinced that every utterance would henceforth be 'exploited by different points of view', he resigned from the Association for the Friends of the Soviet Union, and agreed that *Europe,* a journal with which he was closely associated, had no choice but to suspend publication. He spent his last years at his house in Vézelay, in the Burgundy region of central France. Suffering from ill health, closely monitored and sometimes harassed by the Vichy police, he returned to his musical preoccupations. He died at the end of December 1944, shortly after completing his multi-volume biography of Ludwig van Beethoven, and, as it happened, not long after writing to Elisabeth, the musical queen of the Belgians, to thank her for the gift of some honey.[21]

Approaching the Nazi Embassy

Charles Roden and Dorothy Buxton avoided the 'Great Tourist Invasion' of the 1930s. Indeed, they made no further visits to the Soviet Union after 1927, and did not join Rolland in becoming self-censoring apologists for Stalinism. It was reported to be 'almost certain', when diplomatic relations between Britain and Russia were restored in November 1929, that Ramsay MacDonald would appoint Charles as Britain's new ambassador to Soviet Russia.[22] Yet, despite the second Labour government's desire to break decisively with the old traditions of diplomacy, it opted for a more professionally qualified candidate: so it had been Sir Esmond Ovey who made the journey to Moscow. Earlier that year, Buxton had been returned to the House of Commons, having won the Elland division of Leeds for the Labour Party, but he was also passed over for the post of Colonial Secretary, effectively putting an end to his prospect of serving in senior office. Though described, by a fellow veteran of the anti-war movement, as belonging to 'the "mad-hatter" school of politicians'[23] who quite lacked the popular touch, Buxton continued to campaign through the Labour Party: first as a backbencher, and then, after losing his seat in 1931, as a private Member who refused to believe that a person in that position 'can do nothing'.[24]

One of his two primary concerns after 1927 was colonial reform, and he worked hard to raise its profile on the agenda of a British labour movement that often seemed regardless of its imperial responsibilities. He visited both West and East Africa and is said to have held constant lunches and teas at hotels near Westminster, 'mostly with foreigners, including many Africans'. Both in his writing and at meetings around the country, he emphasized the moral obligation of the colonial power to take steps to prepare colonized peoples for self-government. He proposed an extension of the 'mandate' system developing under the League of Nations: a non-exploitative form of government that, as he saw it, was an outgrowth of the idea of 'trusteeship' that had first been introduced by the Inter-Allied Labour Conference of February 1918 and was later taken up by President Wilson.[25] Buxton would have liked the League of Nations to undertake the 'supervision' of all colonial empires—'those of the Allies, as well as those wrested from the enemy'. This, he was convinced, would ameliorate the economic drive dominating present policy and safeguard the interests of 'all colonies of primitive culture'.

The British Empire, in particular, should be turned into an instrument of benevolent democratic development. Buxton used the old barrier-breaking metaphors of early twentieth-century internationalism to describe the goal: 'the only system which would ensure to the world's consumers a fair share of the world's products is not the existing "vertical" division of the world into political entities, but a "horizontal" division into a series of services or functions'.[26] Pursuing this vision as an adviser on colonial matters to the Labour Party, he maintained an office close to the House of Commons and drafted innumerable questions on colonial affairs for the use of backbench Labour MPs, including Arthur Creech Jones, who would go on to become the decolonizing Colonial Secretary in Attlee's post-1945 Labour government.

While colonial reform was one of their causes, the Buxtons also remained closely attentive to events in Germany. They visited the country repeatedly, persisting in the reparative spirit they had demonstrated in January 1921, when, determined 'not to see Germany as the correspondents see it', they went and lived for a short time with a working miner's family in Essen to learn what conditions were really like behind the Allied blockade ('People do not fall dead in the streets. They are very neat, and keep up a fair outward show').[27]

In 1923, Charles had stood up in the House of Commons and called for a 'fundamental revision' of the Treaty of Versailles,[28] predicting that 'if we do not help Germany all Europe is going to ruin, and we with it'.[29] Like many other veterans of the anti-war movement of 1914–18, the Buxtons continued to deplore the settlement as a grotesquely one-sided measure which had forced Germany 'either to starve, or to borrow on ruinous conditions'[30] and was responsible, to a considerable extent, for the rise and popularity of Hitler.

Unlike some of the 'appeasers' with whom they would later be linked, the Buxtons were fully aware of the evils of Nazism. Charles Roden Buxton was in Berlin to observe the Reichstag elections of 1933, which brought Hitler to power. They both campaigned against Nazi persecution of Protestant pastors and urged the British government to assist those fleeing Nazi Germany, by opening the frontiers of the British Empire to Jewish and other 'non-Aryan refugees'. Dorothy Buxton also used her connections with the Save the Children Fund to secure a meeting with Goering in March 1935. It was a spectacularly unsuccessful encounter. She was in a state of nervous exhaustion at the time, and had fainted shortly before the meeting. Yet she still managed to enrage Goering when she tried to warn him that Nazi persecutions, and even the denial that such persecutions existed, might lead to war.[31] It is said that she emerged from the encounter so shattered that she could scarcely remember the details of their conversation.

As the 1930s progressed, Charles Roden Buxton brought together his two primary interests—Germany and colonial reform—over the territorial claims being used to justify belligerent policies in the three countries he described as the Treaty of Versailles's 'dissatisfied powers'. Frustrated in its aspirations for both trade and migration, Japan was forcing itself on Manchuria and China.[32] Italy had invaded Abyssinia in October 1935, claiming 'the right to colonise and the duty to civilise'.[33] As for Germany, Buxton remained vehemently critical of the idea that the German people should be 'compelled to accept the colonial status quo established at Versailles in 1919, and excluded for all time, or even a long time, from the colonial field'.

To think thus, as he declared in a letter to *The Times* in March 1939, was 'a lamentable example of the danger of being dominated by the emotions of the moment, to the exclusion of long-range considerations and of the lessons of history'.[34] Buxton deplored the persecution of German Jews, but he could not see this outrage as reason to drop the question of 'colonial readjustment'. Faced with the threats posed by Germany and the other 'dissatisfied powers', his answer was to avert war by recognizing the at least partial legitimacy of their claims and making appropriate concessions. Against those determined never to yield a single inch to the demands of the Nazi government, he condemned their willingness to 'draw upon the inexhaustible sources of vituperation to be found in the anti-German oratory of 1914–18'. It was time, Buxton suggested, to offer Hitler a new settlement, which would undertake a 'redistribution of territory in West Central

Africa', while also providing 'complete equality of economic opportunity' throughout the area, together with protection for 'the rights of native races'.

With this belief in mind, Buxton applied his efforts to the avoidance of a new war with Germany, keeping the possibility of a settlement open in his mind until long after the moment that Churchill and others recognized as the last minute. At the end of May 1939, he wrote to the *Manchester Guardian,* asserting that Hitler's speeches did not actually reflect the assumption that another war was inevitable. Germany, he said, was beset with a fear of 'encirclement', a lack of *Lebensraum,* and an acute shortage of natural resources. With his mind's eye still governed by the iron curtain he had opposed so vehemently in the 1920s, he saw these problems as the fault of post-war Allied policy and the Treaty of Versailles, which had left Germany reduced and highly dependent on a surrounding world that was actually closed to it owing to economic nationalism and the policy of boycott.[35] No alleviation or concession had been allowed in the early years, and it was hardly surprising that Hitler did not believe that Germany's problems could be reconciled by international negotiation.

Though strongly criticized for his views, Buxton pressed on, declaring that Hitler's critics were guilty of 'reckless misrepresentation' of what the Nazi leader had actually written in *Mein Kampf*—suggesting, just as he had done in the Great War, that this sort of propagandizing 'not only poisons the wells of truth but damages the relations between our two peoples'.[36]

Buxton is said to have visited Germany three times in 1939, finally leaving in August on what was practically the last train out before the invasion of Poland.[37] Hindsight would place him in a retrospectively unified gallery of 'appeasers', standing alongside Neville Chamberlain and Lord Halifax in the Conservative Party; Nancy Astor and her so-called 'Cliveden Set'; Sir Arthur Salter, Norman Angell, Harold Nicolson, and other members of the Foreign Affairs Group at All Souls College, Oxford; and also the outright fascist sympathizers of the far right.

Buxton's version of 'appeasement' actually had little in common with that expressed by Lord Halifax who, in November 1937, had met Hitler and commended him for the 'great services' he had rendered in the rebuilding of Germany and further declared that 'by destroying Communism in his country, he had barred its road to Western Europe, and that Germany therefore could rightly be regarded as a bulwark of the West against communism'.[38] Buxton was not so enchanted by Nazism. Indeed, he would have hated this revived theory of the 'bulwark' as yet another part of the ruinous legacy of Versailles. Yet, in the words of Clifford Allen, who was now Lord Allen of Hurtwood and a member of the All Souls Foreign Affairs Group, he was convinced that one should 'never reject a chance of talking peace with the devil himself'.[39]

On 29 July 1939, Buxton made a private visit to the German Embassy in London, as would be revealed in 1948 when the Soviet government published secret documents from the captured archives of the German Ministry of Foreign Affairs in Berlin. He talked with chargé Theodore Kordt, who, in his note of the discussion, reminded his superiors in Berlin that the Buxtons had become known in Germany thanks to their 'courageous defence of the German civilian population during the French occupation of Upper Silesia and the Ruhr'.[40] Buxton, who regretted the policy (approved by the British Labour Party) of sanctions and 'encirclement' raised against Nazi Germany, made it clear that he was not an official emissary either of Neville Chamberlain's Conservative government or of the Labour Party, in which, so Kordt estimated, his position might be compared with that of 'a leading General Staff officer in the Operations Department'.[41] He then went on to make a proposal that betrayed every principle he had once espoused as a member of the Union of Democratic Control.

Buxton had strongly condemned secret diplomacy during the Great War. He had even published the translated texts of tsarist Russia's secret agreements when the Bolsheviks pulled them out of the files after seizing control of the revolution in October 1917.[42] Yet he now informed Counsellor Kordt that attempts to preserve the peace between Britain and Nazi Germany could not be pursued through public discussion. 'The nations were at such a pitch', he suggested, the peoples so 'excited', and the atmosphere so 'overcharged',[43] that it was necessary to 'revert to a sort of secret diplomacy'. Citing the secret treaties Britain had made with France and Russia in 1904 and 1907, he recommended that Germany and Britain should now take similar steps to 'eliminate' antagonism by agreeing distinct 'spheres of influence'.[44]

In this scheme, Germany would undertake not to interfere in the affairs of the British Empire and also to enter a bilateral arms reduction programme. In return, Britain would agree to respect German interests in eastern and south-eastern Europe (Germany's ambassador Dirksen was left in no doubt that this meant Britain would renounce guarantees previously given to some states in the proposed German sphere).[45] Britain would also take steps to influence France in the same direction, and give up its 'present negotiations'[46] intended to establish an anti-fascist pact with Russia.[47] Buxton had professed to be acting without mandate and on no one's behalf. Yet Kordt, who claimed to have sounded him out carefully, concluded that his proposed scheme was probably 'a feeler' extended on behalf of the prime minister, Neville Chamberlain, and his adviser, Sir Horace Wilson.[48] It was a desperate proposition, to be sure; and to the extent that intelligence about this sort of secret scheming reached Moscow, it can only have inclined Stalin further towards the Nazi–Soviet non-aggression pact, signed in Moscow one month later.

The coming of the Second World War mortified Buxton: his wife Dorothy would recall how it struck as 'a sword in his heart'.[49] He resigned from his position as parliamentary adviser to the Labour Party, informing the leader, Clement Attlee, that he did so because he could not agree with the party's policy of not pursuing peace terms. He then began making the case for an early 'non-vindictive' peace and writing pamphlets in which he suggested that, if the war wasn't stopped soon, 'something very like Nazism will establish itself in this country'.[50] He wrote letters, pressing his views on Lord Halifax, Neville Chamberlain, David Lloyd George, and no doubt others too.[51] Unwell and assailed by a sense of failure, he is said to have been struck dumb as much-loved churches by Sir Christopher Wren were destroyed during the London Blitz.[52]

Among the thirteen Wren churches lost to incendiary bombs in the night of 29 December 1940, was St Mary the Virgin, Aldermanbury, which, two decades later, would be acquired by Westminster College, and reassembled as a monument to Churchill's 'iron curtain' speech in Fulton, Missouri. Later casualties would include the partly twelfth-century Temple church, restored by Wren after the Great Fire of 1666. This 'holy place of the Knights Templar' was reduced to 'a charred shell' in the night of 10 May 1941.[53] Eight of its nine thirteenth-century stone effigies of knights were burned and covered with molten lead: some, indeed, were reported 'pounded to dust' by falling girders and other debris. Also utterly destroyed was the seventeenth-century organ, built by the German organ-builder Father Smith, and played by the composer Henry Purcell long before Christmas Eve 1914, when it had torn through 'the veil of silent prayer' with 'the first rasping notes' of Bach's Christmas music, and prompted Vernon Lee to lament the 'monstrous iron curtain' that had so suddenly descended between Germany and Britain.

During the course of 1940, Buxton had also recovered his interest in the art of political oratory, first developed in the opening decade of the twentieth century, when he had been involved with the Workers' Education Association and also honorary principal of Morley College (1902–10) in south London. In those distant times his inspiration had been provided by such eighteenth-century politicians as Charles James Fox, Richard Brinsley Sheridan, and Edmund Burke. He now found himself deeply moved by the great speeches of Winston Churchill who, having replaced Chamberlain as prime minister on 10 May 1940, had gone on to rally the nation in its year of looming defeat. Buxton was by no means the only elderly socialist who was glued to a wireless during those alarming months. Now in her eighties, Beatrice Webb described Churchill's 'This was their Finest hour' speech, broadcast on 18 June 1940, as 'admirably conceived and perfectly expressed: he is wise and eloquent, a great wielder of words'.[54] Buxton was equally impressed. In the words of his sister, 'He was almost carried away by the heroic speeches of 1940–41.'[55]

During the 1930s, Churchill had won new respect by standing against Chamberlain and the national government's appeasing foreign policies. Writing in 1939, Douglas Goldring, a pacifist writer who had fiercely opposed Churchill in the early 1920s, praised him as a 'patriot and a realist' who had 'constantly warned the country of Hitler's aims' and was now 'the non-political Englishman's chief champion'.[56] This new enthusiasm represented a sharp break with habit for the Buxtons too. Over the years, they had kept an eye on Churchill, and treated him as one of their most abiding reference points. They had noted his more promising remarks: his condemnation of the starving effects of the Allied blockade in Austria and Germany, for example; or his statement, made at a meeting of empire representatives on 21 June 1921, that, when it came to migration within the British Empire, there should be no 'barrier of race, colour or creed' that would 'prevent any man by merit from reaching any station if he is fitted for it'.[57]

Yet their more characteristic reference to Churchill had been a note of appalled disagreement. This was the spirit in which they had judged his sabre-rattling about armaments, his ferocious anti-Bolshevism, his refusal to recognize any fundamental difference between Lenin's Communism and the democratic and more Christian socialism of the British Labour Party. They had disagreed with Churchill over the future of the British Empire too. In November 1936 Charles Roden Buxton had, in his own cautious phrase, 'taken the liberty' of sending Churchill a copy of his book *The Alternative to War: A Programme for Statesmen*. In his accompanying letter, he acknowledged that Churchill would probably not agree with his arguments, but thought he might nevertheless be interested in the chapter on 'The Contribution of the British Empire', in which he might find 'ideas ... which have not been presented in any other book, and yet which are of importance'.[58]

Here Churchill might well have found stuff to chew over and plenty to spit out in disgust too. A note on the surviving copy of that letter reveals that Churchill 'thanked' Buxton a month or so after receiving his book. It is impossible to establish whether he found the time to engage with Buxton's arguments, or, indeed, whether he read far enough into the book to find himself described as a man 'who may be trusted to find picturesque phrases to express the typical John Bull reactions of the moment'.[59]

Buxton died of lung cancer (perhaps aggravated by the Turkish assailant's bullet, which had remained in his lung since 1914) aged 67, on 16 December 1942. He 'passed on',[60] in Dorothy's preferred phrase, just over three years before Winston Churchill drove through Fulton, raising his hat to the Missourians who were counselled by President Hoover to understand that this particular 'John Bull' was now a 'world citizen', and then lowering the 'iron curtain' into the nuclear theatre of the new Cold War.

Held at St Mark's church at Peaslake in Surrey, Buxton's funeral combined Anglican ceremony with Quaker silence and African friends reading from the Bible. The occasion belonged to his family and, since travel was difficult at this time, a small handful of friends. Some of the mourners represented Protestant churches: the Society of Friends, the Church of England, and the German Lutherans too. Some attended in the name of campaigning organizations associated with Buxton's chosen causes: the Labour Party, the League of Coloured Peoples, the National Peace Council, the Save the Children Fund, the Anti-Slavery and Aborigines Protection Society ...[61] More than two hundred others wrote to Dorothy, commending their late friend's altruism, his 'great gentleness' (Lady Clifford Allen), his perfection of spirit (F. M. Cornford), his 'devotion to humanity' (Clement Attlee), his 'pure souled' nature (G. M. Trevelyan), his personal modesty (many), and the courage with which he had stood out against 'the prevailing spirit by which most people are accepting the present terrible situation' (Lord Ponsonby). He is not much remembered in the Labour Party today.

Inheriting a Picturesque Phrase

As for the expression 'iron curtain', the memory of its earlier usages would also be buried in the years to come, despite the fact that Winston Churchill had been acquainted with some of their exponents. He knew both Charles Roden Buxton and Ethel Snowden if not Vernon Lee, and he had met Elisabeth, queen of the Belgians, at Antwerp during the Belgian retreat in 1914. His work also brought him into contact with Lord D'Abernon, the British ambassador in Berlin during the early 1920s. Indeed, in *My Early Life* (1930), Churchill had thanked D'Abernon for his memoirs, albeit not on account of the final volume, in which the former British ambassador to Germany described his attempt to establish a demilitarized 'iron curtain' between Germany and France. Instead, he cited a description, contained in the earlier second volume, of his mother as D'Abernon had known her at the viceregal lodge in Dublin during her 'panther'-like youth.[62]

Churchill must surely have encountered it in the 1920s yet, by 1946, the 'iron curtain' had a different currency. Though it is plainly not the case that it was 'originated' in 1942 by Hitler's finance minister, Count Schwering von Krosigk,[63] the phrase was definitely employed in Germany during the last months of the Second World War, when the Nazis saw ruinous defeat pressing in from the east. In July 1944, *The Times* had noted that the German Press was publishing highly coloured accounts of the fighting on the eastern front. It was said that the war was so pitiless and unending that the retreating German soldiers had abandoned the singing and reading with which they had earlier filled their time: 'Before all these pleasures an iron curtain fell. Every soldier lost his individuality, all melted into uniformity in one great pot between Byelgorod and Jassy, caring nothing for Michael Angelo, Beethoven, Schopenhauer and Homer, but talking mostly of dirt, dust and heat.'[64]

By the last months of the war, and as Soviet forces continued their advance on Berlin, the 'iron curtain' was also being used by the Nazi leadership. Writing in his diary on 13 March 1945, Goebbels noted that the *Manchester Guardian* had joined the chorus of criticism directed at the Soviet Union for cutting off Romania after invading it. He described these as 'the old Kremlin tactics'—'as soon as the Soviets have occupied a country, they let fall an iron curtain so that they can carry on their fearful bloody work behind it'.[65]

On 25 February of that year, with the Soviet forces already at the banks of the river Oder, Goebbels had published a supposedly prophetic article entitled 'The Year 2000' in *Das Reich*. Given the Yalta agreement between Churchill, Roosevelt, and Stalin, he insisted that 'If the German people lay down their arms ... the Soviets would immediately occupy all of East and Southeastern Europe, including a large part of the Reich. An iron curtain would immediately fall on this huge territory, together with the vastness of the Soviet Union, and nations would be slaughtered behind it.'[66]

On 2 May 1945, the day after Hitler's death was announced, the usage was repeated by Count Schwerin von Krosigk, just appointed foreign minister by Hitler's designated successor, Admiral Dönetz. Broadcasting to the German nation in its 'most tragic hour', he revived what *The Times* named 'the Bolshevist bogy', declaring that 'in the streets of still unoccupied Germany a great stream of desperate and famished people is rolling westwards, pursued by fighter-bombers, in flight from indescribable terror. In the east the iron curtain behind which, unseen by the eyes of the world, the work of destruction goes on is moving steadily forward.'[67]

It is at this point that Churchill's adoption of the phrase comes—shortly after Goebbels and von Krosigk, but before the future director of the CIA, Allen W. Dulles, who indirectly confirmed the accuracy of Goebbels's prediction, remarking on 3 December 1945, of the inhabitants of formerly German lands being handed over to Poland: 'an iron curtain has descended over the fate of the people and very likely conditions are truly terrible'.[68]

As he would later assert, Churchill made his first use of the phrase in two secret telegrams to President Harry S. Truman. In the first, despatched on 12 May 1945, he declared that 'An iron curtain is drawn down upon their front. We do not know what is going on behind. There seems little doubt that the whole of the regions east of the line Lübeck-Trieste-Corfu will soon be completely in their hands.'[69] He repeated the phrase in a second telegram of 4 June 1945, this time warning Truman that American withdrawal from Europe would have the effect of 'bringing Soviet power into the heart of Western Europe and the descent of an iron curtain between us and everything eastward'.

Churchill also employed the phrase publicly in the House of Commons, at the opening of the 1945 session on 16 August 1945. It was a major speech, in which Churchill, now leader of the opposition, reviewed the challenges of the moment. He mentioned the atomic bomb and recalled, perhaps with some regret for his days of power, how he and Truman had made the decision to use it against Japan while at Potsdam in July. He then went on to talk of the need to 'remould the relationships of all men, wherever they dwell, in all the nations'. He was alarmed to hear of the expulsion and exodus of Germans who had found themselves incorporated into the new Poland. The lives of 8 or 9 million German people were at stake—'enormous numbers' of whom were 'utterly unaccounted for'.[70] 'It is not impossible that tragedy on a prodigious scale is unfolding itself behind the iron curtain which at the moment divides Europe in twain. I should welcome any statement which the Prime Minister can make which would relieve or at least inform us upon this very anxious and grievous matter.' For Churchill, then, the Iron Curtain was not just the originating coinage of the Cold War, as it would be celebrated in Fulton and fervently denounced in thousands of Eastern bloc schoolrooms. It also marked the resumption of an older pattern of hostility, which had been complicated by the Popular Front against Fascism, and disrupted more decisively in 1941 when Stalin's Russia joined the West in alliance against Hitler.

There were some Communist apologists, including Hewlett Johnson, the spectacularly deluded 'Red Dean of Canterbury', who would derive idiotic satisfaction from the thought that Churchill had got the 'iron curtain' from Goebbels.[71] Yet that was certainly not the only lineage recognized at the time. Among those prompted to pick up their pen after hearing Churchill's Commons speech was Lord Noel Buxton, brother of the late Charles Roden Buxton and his fellow campaigner since the founding of the Balkans Committee in 1902. In a letter to *The Times,* Buxton quoted the passage about the 'iron curtain' and hoped that Churchill's words might have some good effect. He also noted Churchill's observation that one quarter of Germany's arable land was now Polish: 'a startling fact' at a time when the allies were trying to 'organise the self-support of Germany'.[72] He recognized 'the terrible record of German deeds' but, in words that were entirely consistent with the arguments he and his brother had advanced at the end of the Great War, he also urged that 'the interests of the allies, their tradition of humanity, and the cause of peace in the future' should be remembered. His was a voice from a now violently displaced era, and it would hardly prevail through the Cold War to come.

19

After the Crossing

'Did you get over or under it?' So one British socialist remembers being asked more than once when his delegation returned to England from the other side of the Iron Curtain in 1954.[1] That joke would surely have been lost on Antoni Klimowicz, the Polish stowaway who had nearly died in his attempt to reach London on the MS *Jaroslaw Dabrowski* earlier that year.

For Love of Freedom

Klimowicz had no sooner been rescued by the British police than he found he could earn money from his momentary fame—enough, certainly, for him to donate £150 to the Federation of Free Poles, which had looked after him during his first days in London.[2] His story was acquired by the North American Newspaper Alliance (then part-owned by the writer Ian Fleming and closely involved with Western intelligence services) and published in the *New York Times* over two days in late August.[3]

Entitled 'A Sailor's Story' Klimowicz's testimony was printed alongside 'A Composer's Story' by Andrzej Panufnik, who had recently escaped by outwitting Polish diplomats in Zurich. It was a passionately sincere narrative that served to confirm anti-Communist thinking in the West.

Klimowicz began by remembering the Communist lecturers who had never tired of reciting the litany that post-war Poland was 'a state of workers and peasants, created to deliver them from the ages of exploitation by the aristocrats and capitalists'. 'Well,' as he replied, 'I am from a working family. My father is a worker, my two brothers who are married and away from home are workers, and my only sister married a workingman. Seeing their everyday struggle for existence, I had come to the conclusion that the Communists lie.'

Introduced as a catalogue of 'Scarcity and Woes', the article went on to describe a land of grinding austerity, run by Communist apparatchiks who themselves enjoyed luxury goods provided by 'special stores'. Poland was a land of 'production drives' in which demoralized workers, forced to meet 'work norms' and 'socialist competition', produced coats with one arm several inches longer than the other, and saucepans 'from which handles fall off at the slightest touch'. Family life was under attack from a regime that encouraged women to work so that the state would have greater opportunities to indoctrinate their children. Alcoholism had become so pervasive that even the authorities had been obliged to recognize it as a danger, if only to 'production targets'.

Religious faith was also strongly discouraged. The Communists were trying to liquidate the traditional children's feast of St Nicholas, and replace it with 'a new invention that they call Father Frost'. The previous January, Klimowicz had even seen a brutally secularized Christmas tree decorated with political caricatures of Eisenhower, Churchill, and General Anders. Religious observance had been banned in both schools and the army, and the youth, who had lost their faith in God and 'fallen under the influence of Communism', had taken to 'drinking, rioting, and making love as if they were animals not human beings'. Yet many working people kept up their observances. 'You should have seen the Corpus Christi procession in Gdynia a few weeks before I left home.' Having failed to discourage it by other means, the police had eventually guided this devout column not along its customary route through town, but out from its suburban starting point into fields and uninhabited roads: 'tens of thousands of people followed the procession into the wilderness'.

Klimowicz drew much of his material for his article from his experiences as a conscript in the pontoon service of the Third Warsaw Detachment of Engineers. While cleaning some pontoons shortly after joining, he found that they bore the inscription 'Made in the USA', a discovery that contradicted the ardent company leader's insistence that all their equipment was of Soviet manufacture. Rashly, he had mentioned his finding in the political indoctrination classes, venturing that the pontoons must have been sent to the Soviet Union during the war when Russia and America were allied against Hitler. He was promptly denounced as 'a fascist and likely U.S. Agent'. That error had put paid to his place at NCO training school, bringing him instead two 'very, very hard years' as a private in an ordinary detachment—building Bayley bridges with English equipment, and noting the superiority of American Studebakers when compared with Soviet trucks.

Everyone in Klimowicz's Poland looked west. Indeed, he could say, without any hesitation, that 'For the Polish people, all hope is in the West—which they see as the source of future freedom.' In the evenings, the Poles drew their curtains and listened to the Voice of America, Radio Free Europe, and the BBC. Yet these prisoners of Yalta were also inclined to despair at the fact that 'nothing comes from the west but words, and nothing is done practically to bring help and relief to the people behind the Iron Curtain'.

The view to the east of Poland was contrastingly hideous—a picture of the hell to come if the West remained supine. Some indication of conditions in Russia had been provided by the Soviet seamen who could sometimes be encountered in Gdynia. The officers had a habit of buying everything they could, using roubles at the manipulated and highly advantageous exchange rate, and dragging the spoils back to their ships in heavy suitcases. Having neither money nor contact with the Polish people, the ordinary seamen spent most of their time playing chess. Their ships were always in an 'indescribable state. They undoubtedly are the dirtiest in the world, and are permeated by a stink of half-rotten fish which seems to be the main food of the crews.' Klimowicz recalled the words of an American correspondent who had once travelled on his ship. At Kiel, they had passed one of these demoralized Soviet vessels: 'A great hulk with paint peeling off in places, with some unoccupied sailors lolling around in negligent poses on a messy deck.' The American stared out at this disreputable vessel, and then, looking back at the 'orderly bustle of activities around him' on the Polish ship, remarked in German 'There seem to exist two iron curtains, really.'

As a sailor, Klimowicz had been well placed to 'look behind' that second curtain dividing the 'enslaved people of Europe' from the USSR. He had worked on the Polish ship *Narvik,* which operated on the line to Murmansk, the Barents Sea port built by the Allies during the 1918–20 intervention against Bolshevik Russia. Everything in that benighted place was deplorable: from the primitive dock with its single crane (which turned out to be of American manufacture) to the condition of the people who were 'like beggars in rags which in Poland the poorest man would be ashamed to wear'. The shops were almost empty of provisions, their windows displaying empty cartons and dummies of fruit and meat:

> I can hardly describe our feelings. We all in the crew were shaken to our very depths at out first encounter with reality in the wonderful Soviet land. … Incessantly, our propaganda repeats the same tale about the happiness and achievements of the Soviet Union, and wonderful talents of the Russian people.

But we all know that the truth is as that American had said—a second iron curtain separates us from them. Having seized hold of us, of our fertile lands and industrial resources, they try to grab everything they can find.

The same point was made by the composer Andrzej Panufnik. Referring to musical visits, he noted that the best Russian composers were sent to the West, while only the second-rank came to Poland. There was, Panufnik's article confirmed, 'a curtain within the Iron Curtain'.

Though he had expressed the wish in his first press conference in London, Klimowicz never did find employment as a sailor into the British merchant navy. After a short time in London (he is rumoured to have stayed briefly with a lord), he went north to live with family friends in Cleator Moor in Cumbria. Mrs Genowefa Kwiecinska remembers him being useful in the garden, helping with the shopping and her two young daughters. In the evenings, when Mr Kwiecinska got home from work, the two men often went fishing at Whitehaven.

Yet Klimowicz's English sojourn would only be a short interlude. He soon migrated to the USA, where he stayed with Mr Kwiecinska's parents in Clifton, New Jersey. To begin with, he travelled around, visiting Chicago, Philadelphia, and perhaps also other cities, to speak at gatherings of Polish Americans. He was feted as an exemplary refugee from Communism—an ordinary man, who had courageously risked his life for freedom. There was the possibility of a book deal and even a film, but Klimowicz's moment of fame actually passed quickly. Speaking on the phone from Chicago, Mrs Irene Mizera remembers him as 'just a plain person … very private. Didn't share nothing with nobody.'[4]

It is conceivable, at least, that Klimowicz was held back by fear. He had relatives to worry about back in Poland, and he had been aware of attempts to intimidate him before leaving London in 1954. Towards the end of August that year, a threatening letter had been received by the chairman of a group from the International Commission of Jurists concerned with 'the protection of right against systematic injustice'.[5] This letter had warned Klimowicz not to attend the meeting in which the jurists planned to review his case, and particularly its use of the Habeas Corpus Act, for its possible bearing on other cases involving fugitives from dictatorship.

Yet those who knew Klimowicz in America do not necessarily emphasize such considerations. Instead, they insist upon his ordinariness. He was 'the guy at the back that nobody paid any attention to'.[6] Klimowicz may have come across as a man of burning lucidity in the articles printed under his name in the *New York Times,* but he actually lacked the linguistic skills, the intellectual perspective, and perhaps also the desire to sustain a career as an anti-Communist figurehead. He knew, nevertheless, how to differentiate personal freedom from the fleeting glamour of Cold War fame. Having out-shone the dog and the pigeon that 'busted' the Iron Curtain in the summer of 1954, he withdrew into the modest life of a working man in New Jersey. He found employment in a perfume factory, went to church, played cards, and was so retiring that even his landlord didn't know when he was away. He stayed single and in due course acquired a home of his own. 'Ordinary man,' repeats Mrs Mizera, 'running to freedom.'

Science Divided

Meanwhile Dr Joseph H. Cort who, together with his wife Ruth, had boarded the *Jaroslaw Dabrowski* to take up political asylum in Czechoslovakia, would remain on the eastern side of the Iron Curtain for more than twenty years.

In early October 1954, some two months after he and his wife Ruth had arrived in Prague, Cort received a call from a young British anatomist from University College London. Derrick James was passing through Prague on the way to China with a cultural delegation. Meeting up at the Palace Hotel, he and Cort drank coffee and brandy and talked for several hours.[7]

In his diary, James noted that the American seemed happy in Czechoslovakia. Asked how medical research was funded under the Communist system, Cort explained that each research team would propose its desired programme of activities to its institute, which could then choose to include it in a wider submission to the ministry, which 'makes the relevant capital grants for work-ers and equipment'. To a British scientist accustomed to reaching around in pursuit of funding, this way of administering research may have sounded commendably straightforward. Cort seemed less clear, however, when it came to differentiating Communist science from the version practised on the western side of the Iron Curtain.

A few weeks previously Cort had offended the *New York Times* by pre-suming to 'score' American science low, but Derrick James did not find him signing up for the Soviet version of 'proletarian' science. 'I didn't get Pavlov straight,' he noted: 'Cort says the Czechs regard the Russians as a bit nuts about Pavlov.' Wandering further along this ideological faultline, the two scientists discussed the theories of Olga Borisovna Lepeshinskaya, an elderly former Bolshevik who, in the last years of the nineteenth century, had shared Siberian banishment with Lenin and his wife. More recently Lepeshinskaya had devoted herself to bringing about a revolution in the biological sciences. Dismissing the generally accepted theory that cells were produced by the division of other cells, she conducted some experiments on egg yolk and then claimed to have observed cells being formed out of unorganized 'live matter' or 'Vital Substance'.

Lepeshinskaya's theory represented an ideologically driven return to pre-modern thinking, and her experimental techniques were risible. In a memoir written in 1975, the Russian scientist Jakov Rapoport recalled seeing Lepeshinskaya's daughter pounding beetroot seeds in a mortar prior to an experiment intended to prove that, with the 'Vital Substance' present, any section of a plant ovule could germinate, and not just the part containing the embryo.[8] Yakov Rapoport describes how he left Lepeshinskaya's primitively equipped laboratory 'with the impression that I had been looking into the pots of a medieval alchemist, only to learn some time later that I had been granted the honour of being admitted to Olympus'.[9]

Lepeshinskaya had presented her findings in a book entitled *Formation of Cells from Live Matter,* published in 1945. Her claims seemed ludicrous to many Soviet biologists, but they soon stopped sneering when Stalin harnessed Lepeshinskaya's theories to his drive against 'obsequiousness to the west'.[10] On his orders, the central committee of the Soviet Academy of Sciences had organized a 'Conference on the Vital Substance and the Development of Cells', which was held on 22–4 May 1950. Presided over by the distinguished Soviet biochemist Alexander Oparin, internationally respected for his theories of the origin of life, the event was also attended by Trofim Lysenko, the notoriously bogus geneticist, who had claimed to be able to raise rye and barley from wheat. Lysenko hailed Lepeshinskaya, declaring that her demonstration that 'cells need not be formed from other cells' should be taken as the basis for a new, and eminently engineerable, theory of 'species formation'. Lepeshinskaya was awarded the Stalin Prize and made a member of the Soviet Academy of Medical Sciences. Soviet textbooks hailed her as a genius who had made the greatest discovery in the history of biology, and Russian medical scientists were obliged to praise her discoveries in their lectures. Lepeshinskaya precipitated a rush in sales of baking soda when she announced, quite wrongly, that soda baths would rejuvenate the elderly and enable the young to retain their youth.[11] For a time, it was hoped that she might even find a way of prolonging Comrade Stalin's life.

Derrick James's scientific colleagues at University College London were never in any doubt that the great Soviet Academician must have strained her unusually active egg yolks through a very dirty sock.[12] It was considerably harder for scientists in the Soviet sphere to laugh off Lepeshinskaya. Jakov Rapoport spoke for many humiliated Russian scientists when he declared: 'Not only have they made candy of this shit, but they keep pushing it into our mouths and demanding that we express our delight at the taste.'[13]

In 1951 Lepeshinskaya had informed Rapoport that no less than four Czechoslovak laboratories had confirmed her revolutionary claims.[14] This was not what Derrick James heard from Joe Cort. The recently arrived American was able to reassure him that the scientists with whom he was now working in Prague saw Lepeshinskaya as 'a great joke'. Yet he still left James wondering: 'He said, as is quite true, that English science is meticulously quantitative, but I didn't really understand what he wanted to put in its place. Philosophic integration of science & society is OK, but just how you make science different, and still science, I don't know.'

Making Out in the Camp of Peace

The early American newspaper reports on the Corts' new life were not concerned with science as it was now divided by the Iron Curtain. Instead, they grouped the Corts with other Americans who had moved to Prague. This largely reviled company included Herbert Ward, a musician who had joined a Czechoslovak jazz orchestra, and also the gifted Vienna-trained African-American baritone Aubrey Pankey, who would soon take up permanent residence in the German Democratic Republic, where he would remain (a singer of Schubert who found his niche in the Soviet bloc as a performer of spirituals in the tradition of Paul Robeson) until his death in a traffic accident in 1971.

George Shaw Wheeler was also featured in this gallery of fugitives: the New York Times described him as an economist who had moved to Prague with his wife and four children in 1947, after losing his job with the US military government in Germany on account of his alleged membership of organizations now placed on the Attorney General's list of 'subversive' agencies. Wheeler, however, had earlier offered a very different view of his

relocation. In the immediate post-war years he had been in charge of the
de-Nazification of labour institutions in the American zone of Germany.
He claimed that his endeavours had been thwarted by senior American
officials and representatives of 'international cartels and trusts', who ordered
that certain out-and-out Nazis be retained in key positions, where they
would prove helpful to those trying to bring about a 'remilitarization' of
Germany and organize bases for espionage against the Soviet Union.[15]

Having moved to Prague before the Stalinist coup of 1948, Wheeler and
his wife had eventually asked for political asylum in Czechoslovakia in
April 1950. They made their request in protest against the rough treatment
received by fifty-eight Czechoslovak passengers who had arrived in Munich
airport after eight air staff coordinated the hijack of three airliners, but failed
to ask for political asylum in the West as the American officials expected. As
Wheeler announced, 'I want to have nothing in common with the Gestapo
methods of the executors of American policy … I place myself proudly in
the camp of peace and progress.'[16] His wife Eleanor was of the same mind,
insisting that Communist Czechoslovakia was providing a better education for their four children than the American school in Berlin, which had
'a rowdy Coca-Cola, chewing gum and comics culture' and raised its pupils
in a 'super-race' atmosphere.

A year or so after his arrival in Czechoslovakia, the *New York Times* tracked
Cort down in Prague, and reported that, like George Shaw Wheeler, he was
by now willing to return to the United States if he could find appropriate
work.[17] Cort knew, however, that as a former Communist, he would not
be allowed to work in the army; and he understood from friends in the
United States, that medical researchers with political pasts like his own were
reduced to 'earning a living ghosting other people's scientific papers'. As
for his parents in Brookline, Boston: 'Our folks think we are just a couple
of crazy kids, but we are quite satisfied here to be able to do work that we
want.' So there he was, living in 'a two-and-a-half room flat in a new apartment building', with a 4-month-old baby, born in Prague. Looking forward
optimistically, Cort anticipated 'In a few years the publicity will die down
and maybe the situation will change.'

Thanks to the ongoing Cold War, Cort's bid to return to the USA would
prove an inordinately long-running affair. By 1959 he was satisfied that the
McCarthy era was over and, in the words of the *New York Times,* that 'the
national psychology finally had restored the prospect of a fair trial in this
country'.[18] So, in April that year, he took his long-expired passport to the

American Embassy in Prague and applied for a renewal. His request was denied on the grounds that he had forfeited his right to American citizenship by repeatedly refusing to return to face the doctors' draft. The decision of the passport office was later affirmed by the State Department's Board of Review and Cort was left 'expatriated'.

In 1963, Cort sued the American government with the help of Leonard B. Boudin, a lawyer well known for his defence of radical figures. By this time it was being said of Cort that 'for years he has been trying to get an American passport, return here and pay the criminal penalty for his acts, if any'.[19] He won the case in the Supreme Court, which struck down the Federal statutes that had been used against him—provoking one Democratic representative to condemn the decision as an insult to 'every American who bore arms in the defence of his country'.[20] In reality, the Supreme Court's action made little difference to Cort for many years. The 1960 ruling was upheld through the presidencies of Lyndon Johnson and Richard Nixon, and it was not until 1975 that the indictment was dismissed and Cort was enabled to apply for a new passport.

The fact that Cort did not return to America empty-handed can largely be attributed to the Czechoslovakian Academy of Sciences, where he worked for many of his twenty-two years in Prague. Established in 1952 on the model of the Soviet Academy, this institution was run by its founding president, František Šorm, a man of strong Communist convictions and also a gifted scientist who used his good standing with Novotny's autocratic government to build a research establishment which owed nothing to Soviet pseudo-science of the kind represented by Lysenko and Lepeshinskaya.[21] Šorm was responsible for appointing Cort, but the American fugitive also worked with Josef Rudinger, whose brilliantly productive Peptide Laboratory was part of the Academy's Institute of Organic Chemistry and Biochemistry, which Šorm had established through a departmental merger in 1953.[22]

The American chemist Vincent du Vigneaud, who won the Nobel Prize for chemistry in 1955, was the first to synthesize a biologically active peptide hormone, oxytocin, in 1953. But Rudinger, who was already working along similar lines in Prague, produced an alternative synthesis of oxytocin three years later—one that made it possible to generate a whole series of modified analogues to the naturally existing hormone. As they pursued this line of research over the following years, Rudinger and his researchers formulated many of the classic problems that had to be resolved by scientists exploring the molecular mechanisms by which peptide hormones work in the human body. In the judgement of the distinguished present-day American peptide chemist Garland R. Marshall, Rudinger was 'the first peptide medicinal chemist—a superb synthetic chemist, who also understood about receptors, pharmacology etc.'.[23]

At a time when the Iron Curtain was at its thickest and most unyielding, Rudinger pursued his science as an international endeavour. He had spent much of the Second World War in England, where he completed his first degree in chemistry at King's College, Newcastle, before returning to Prague in 1949, inspired by the Communists who had seized power the year before. Fluent in several languages, he corresponded with many scientists in the west, including Vincent du Vigneaud, and edited the journals that took news of the Prague Academy's work to researchers around the world. In 1958, the year after the first 'Pugwash' conference (a regular meeting of international scientists, inspired by the suggestion of Bertrand Russell, in which Šorm would be much involved), Rudinger used his contacts to organize the first of the still ongoing series of European Peptide Symposia. It was a time of considerable international tension when visas were hard to come by, and when Western travellers going through the Iron Curtain seemed to step through wire into an unknown and alarmingly unpredictable world.

The chemical structure of peptide hormones had only recently been identified, but Rudinger placed the work of the Prague Institute of Organic Chemistry and Biochemistry in the long tradition of research concerned with clarifying the relations between chemical structure and biological activity.[24] Cort would later take a more dramatic view, describing the aim of Rudinger's peptide laboratory as being to 'improve upon God'.[25]

In order to remove the side effects that would follow from clinical use of natural oxytocin and vasopressin, Rudinger's researchers set out to 'change the molecule' and to produce adjusted analogues that would be more effective as drugs. By modifying the molecule at various positions, they established that positive effects could be enhanced, and undesirable side effects diminished or removed altogether. Cort played some part in the research that, in 1965, yielded DDAVP, a vasopressin analogue, modified at position 8 to produce high and also very specific antidiuretic activity. Synthesized with an eye to the problems of people suffering from diabetes insipidus, the Prague scientists tested it on rats, dogs, and then on human patients. It was found capable of controlling bleeding during surgery, helping people suffering from nocturnal bed-wetting, and also of reducing the drinking capacity of beer alcoholics.

Besides his laboratory work, Cort also participated in the international conferences through which Šorm and Rudinger strove to develop and propagate their research—performing as a discussant, an English-speaking go-between, and an editor of published proceedings. He would be encountered in this capacity at international events held in Prague, and he also became 'something of a scientific celebrity'[26] at conferences and symposia in Western Europe. His books—edited, co-authored, or written by him alone—were published in America as well as in Czechoslovakia and East Germany. By the late 1960s, the peptide analogues synthesized in Rudinger's Prague laboratory were being put through physiological and clinical trials in Russia, Britain, and the USA. Indeed, by 1968, Cort had acquired an extra base in Winnipeg, Canada: as professor of Pharmacology and Therapeutics at the University of Manitoba, he was using funds from the Canadian Medical Research Council to conduct trials on peptides synthesized in Prague.[27]

In 1956, when the American scientist and future inventor of the birth control pill Carl Djerrassi gave a series of lectures at the Academy of Sciences in Prague, František Šorm was still using the party line to justify the Soviet invasion of Hungary.[28] Not so, however, when Soviet forces entered Czechoslovakia in August 1968, and set about extinguishing the Prague Spring. Šorm protested against the 'occupation' to the president of the Soviet Academy of Sciences and voted against its legalization in the Czechoslovak Parliament. Abruptly stripped of the presidency of the Academy of Sciences, he became a 'non-person',[29] officially disregarded until his death in 1980.

Josef Rudinger's peptide laboratory was broken up shortly after the Soviet invasion. Rudinger himself left for the West more or less as soon as the Russians arrived to impose their crushing 'restoration of order'.[30] Previously granted a year's leave of absence by the Academy of Sciences (which would itself be cleared at gunpoint), he drove to Yugoslavia, where his wife and daughter were on holiday, and then proceeded to Zurich, where he would work in the Swiss Federal Institute of Technology until his early death in 1975.

Dr Joseph H. Cort, meanwhile, survived the repressions of 1968, emerging as one of the few scientists associated with the restructured Czechoslovak Academy of Sciences who was still able to operate on the western side of the now reinforced Iron Curtain. In 1972, he visited Scheveningen in the Netherlands, where he presented a paper on the anti-diuretic effects of DDAVP, as indicated by tests on healthy volunteers, at the annual scientific meeting of the European Society for Clinical Investigation. His talk was a revelation to the Scottish blood physiologist J. D. Cash. While using vasopressin in his research into blood-clotting, Cash had encountered such severe gastrointestinal side effects that his experiments had ground to a halt. In a recently published article, he recalls having listened to 'a Joe Cort from Prague' with 'mounting excitement. This man had synthesized a peptide with powerful ADH properties but … devoid of the unpleasant side-effects.'[31]

Cash recalls how he 'waylaid Joe as he left the rostrum'. That same day, Cort introduced him to Dr Jan Mülder, the chief executive officer of Ferring AB, the Swedish company that was manufacturing the peptides developed by 'Cort's group' in Prague. Within no time Mülder and Cort were visiting Cash in Edinburgh: Cash remembers Mülder handing over five vials of DDAVP during dinner at the Caledonian Hotel. Within a few weeks Cash had carried out assays which established that DDAVP was indeed capable of stimulating a major release of factor VIII in healthy volunteers. This confirmed a new application for the drug as a blood-clotting agent that might prove invaluable for mild haemophiliacs. Cash could not convince the Edinburgh Haemophilia Centre to allow experimental infusions of DDAVP into one or two patients with Haemophilia A. With Cort's assistance, however, further research was pursued in Malmö and Milan, where Pierro Mannucci and other haemotologists were already seeking a 'pharmacological' treatment for haemophilia.[32] Experiments carried out in September 1973 revealed that DDAVP was increasing factor VIII by a factor of three or four. In the USA, the drug was not evaluated in humans until 1982 (it was eventually licensed for clinical use in 1984). In Italy, however, it was being used on a large scale from the late 1970s. Indeed, it is thanks to DDAVP that many Italians with Haemophilia A escaped the HIV infection that so direly affected those suffering from Haemophilia B, who were still reliant on concentrated blood factors.

Vladimir Gut, who was Josef Rudinger's last Ph.D. student in Prague and who still works at the Czech Academy of Sciences, is not thinking of politics when he remarks that Cort had a difficult life in Prague. By the time Gut knew Cort, his wife Ruth had fallen ill and Cort was effectively bringing up his two children alone, helped by a technician in his laboratory, who would eventually become his second wife, Jitka. Cort may briefly have joined the Communist Party in America, but the man Gut came to know in the 1960s had a benign and pragmatic outlook. A 'nice man', as he murmurs regretfully of his late friend. Yet it is with good reason that Dr Milan Zaoral, who was among the scientists who synthesized and tested DDAVP, describes Cort as very clever, even if not, as subsequent events would suggest, at all 'safe'.

When the day eventually came on 13 February 1977, Cort returned to America as a respected scientist, with plans for the commercial development of work initiated in Prague. He had, so the *New York Times* announced, acquired the patent to the vasopressin analogue DDAVP, and was already a vice-president of Ferring Pharmaceutical Company, licensed to manufacture the drug in Sweden. He also had a job waiting for him as adjunct professor of physiology at the Center for Polypeptide and Membrane research at the City University of New York's Mount Sinai School of Medicine. His champion at Mount Sinai was Dr Irving L. Schwartz, head of the CPMR and also dean of the graduate faculty of the Mount Sinai Medical and Graduate Schools. Schwartz had himself long been involved in researching and developing analogues to pituitary hormones. Indeed, he and Cort had known each other since at least 1963, when Schwartz had travelled to Prague from the University of Cincinnati, to attend the Second International Pharmacological Meeting in August 1963.[33] Schwartz was among the Western scientists who, in the 1960s, had conducted physiological experiments with samples of peptides synthesized by Rudinger's laboratory: he reported the results of one such survey in a co-authored paper presented at an international symposium on natriuretic hormone held by the Czech Academy of Science at Smolenice Castle near Bratislava in June 1969.[34] He and Cort had continued their discussions at a conference in Belgium in 1971. At these meetings, so Schwartz would tell the *New York Times* in 1977, the two scientists had 'talked of one day joining forces'.[35]

Seven weeks after his return, the *New York Times* profiled Cort as an unmistakably heroic figure: no longer a Communist 'draft dodger', but a gifted scientist who had done what was necessary to protect and continue his research through difficult times. Found gazing out over Harlem from his 'antiseptically white' office at Mount Sinai Medical School, the busy Dr Cort was still dressed in heavy twill Czech trousers and 'a shirt far bluer than the waters of the Danube'.[36] 'I haven't had time to buy any new clothes,' he told the reporter. He was already about to make his first return trip to Prague, where he would spend a week sorting out some business connected to one of his patents. Once notorious as the man who 'fled to Communist Czechoslovakia rather than face a draft board at home', liberal America's prodigal son was now coming to terms with a new set of journalistic clichés. With 'faint traces of Middle Europe' audible in his voice, he was portrayed as a dissident of both worlds: East European in his 'rumpled' garb and perhaps also his habit of 'chain-smoking cigarettes', but fully American in his personal triumph over adversity. 'It is', so the reporter ventured, 'possible to see in that life a parable of our time, an analogue—so to speak—of American history.' 'In a sense,' as Cort's lawyer Mr Boudin helpfully added, 'Dr. Cort and his case personify a quarter of a century of American political life that began with the Korean War and ended with the Ford Administration.'

Cort refused to talk about his 'personal life in Czechoslovakia', so there could be no more than a mention of his children, who remained in Prague with his ailing and, it would seem, abandoned first wife, Ruth. He admitted his 'Communist' past—recalling that he had attended 'occasional meetings at which we sat around and discussed Marxist philosophy'. Though he still favoured 'pure socialism of the Swedish variety', he claimed his politics now were 'more or less nil'. As for America during the McCarthy era, he did not regret having escaped 'the most hysterical part of the political climate in this country'. Dr Irving L. Schwartz suggested that his friend and colleague had suffered 'a dirty deal' from the US authorities but Cort rejected the suggestion that he was a 'victim' who might reasonably sue the US government for damages: 'they changed my life but they didn't damage it'.

Cort was commended for ending his long exile 'without bitterness and with the possibility, at least, of scientific accolade and wealth'. As the man who had brought him to Mount Sinai, Dr Schwartz was confident that Cort's research was 'of Nobel Prize level', although he was also well aware that 'the best dreams don't necessarily pan out'. It seemed rather 'less of a longshot' that Cort would be making a lot of money in the near future. According to the *New York Times* journalist, Cort was the author of eight different patents for analogues for pituitary hormones—including DDAVP. Another of his patents appeared to have 'even more momentous potential'. In Europe a vasopressin analogue known as 'glypressin' had been used to treat internal haemorrhages since 1972, and Ferring's researchers in Sweden were now said to be exploring its possible application as the 'long-sought post-conception birth-control drug'. Schwartz reassured the *New York Times* that his friend and colleague's involvement with Ferring AB did not create any conflict of interest: 'he works for Mount Sinai on a half-time basis and ... Mount Sinai will also benefit from any patents he develops'.

For a time, then, Cort was perceived as a brilliant American scientist who had emerged from behind the Iron Curtain with his name attached to some truly remarkable discoveries. This view will not have damaged Mount Sinai Medical School, nor its prospects of raising funds for Cort's research, but it was not well founded in reality. Cort is not necessarily to be blamed for the eminence with which he had erroneously loomed in J. D. Cash's mind as the creator of DDAVP. It would also be wrong to assume immediately that he was responsible for the errors in the *New York Times* article: a reporter who apparently thought that Prague was on the river Danube, may not have needed much help in concluding that Cort personally owned the patent for DDAVP, and that he had played the leading role in its synthesis and development as a clinical drug. There can be little doubt, however, that the man who had once crossed the Iron Curtain to avoid being recalled to McCarthyist America, now allowed that same isolating structure to preserve these inflated ideas of his accomplishments during the years he spent in the late Josef Rudinger's cancelled research institute.

Certainly, there were people in Prague who might quickly have set the record straight. In September 2004, one of the scientists who had first synthesized DDAVP, Dr Milan Zaoral, came to the Prague Congress Center to address a session devoted to commemorating the work of Josef Rudinger at the Twenty-Eighth European Peptide Symposium. Together with Rudinger and Jan Honzl, Zaoral had received the Clement Gottwald State Prize for the oxytocin synthesis of 1956. This once-prestigious award may no longer have been worth mentioning, but Zaoral was determined to remind his younger post-Communist audience that 'DDAVP was discovered, developed and introduced into social practice at the Institute of Organic Chemistry and Biochemistry of the Czechoslovak Academy of Science, in this city and in this country.'[37]

One could sense pride as well as disappointment in his voice as he insisted on what had been possible in the denigrated Communist era. At a time when Russian scientists were still being humiliated by the grotesque 'proletarian' science favoured by Stalin, Czechoslovakia's biochemical researchers had embarked on a course that would break genuinely new ground. For a time, as Zaoral pointed out before offering a roll-call of the various scientists, clinicians, and academics who had assisted in its successful development (a list that did not include Cort), DDAVP had been ranked as one of the fifteen most important drugs in the world.

The *New York Times*'s description of Cort as the patent-holder for DDAVP failed to impress Dr Milan Zaoral when I mentioned it to him after his presentation. 'That is impossible,' he remarked briskly, adding that such a situation would have been 'duplication'. As he had explained in his lecture, a patent application had been submitted by Zaoral, Dr A Machová, and Šorm in 1966, and, after a period in which more detailed pharmacology was carried out along with clinical tests, the patent was granted in 1969. DDAVP was introduced into medical practice in Czechoslovakia in 1972, more than a decade before it was approved for use in the USA. It was put into production at the Léciva plant in Prague in 1976 and, from 1978, marketed under the name Adiuretin-SD. By then DDAVP had already been licensed to the Swedish pharmaceutical company Ferring AB, which produced the drug in Malmö from 1973 and sold it under the name of Minirin from 1975. Even here, however, Zaoral thought it was another Prague scientist, Vladimir Pliska, and not Cort who had first taken the drug to Ferring AB in Sweden.

Truth and Lies in America

Having landed so stylishly in Mount Sinai Medical School in New York, Joe Cort pressed on as an ambitious scientist would. With DDAVP set to make fortunes for Ferring AB once it was cleared for use in the USA, he initiated research that would build on the achievements of the late Josef Rudinger's team in Prague, and justify a whole series of new patent applications. He busied himself setting up experimental trials, seeking funds from foundations and pharmaceutical companies, and writing research papers that were likely to be all the more respected for being coauthored by colleagues at Mount Sinai Medical College, including his old collaborator, Dr Irving L. Schwartz.

Yet something was missing, and Cort was to prove quite incapable of repeating the achievements of the scientists with whom he had worked at the Czechoslovak Academy of Sciences.

The *New York Times* had pictured the newly returned researcher experimenting on a white rat in his laboratory high up in that tower at Mount Sinai, but the project that brought him crashing down entailed a series of perfusion trials carried out on the unique colony of haemophiliac dogs maintained by Dr W. Jean Dodds, a respected veterinary researcher at the New York State Department of Health's laboratories in Albany. On the basis of these tests, Cort claimed to have established beyond doubt that his latest analogue of the arginine-vasopressin molecule would indeed prove invaluable in the treatment of haemophilia.[38]

In December 1979, Cort took news of this alleged breakthrough to the Annual Meeting of the American Society of Haematology. Thanks partly to the reputation of Dr Dodds, who was listed as a co-author in the abstracts of the forthcoming presentation,[39] he was invited to speak at the prestigious plenary session rather than in one of various specialized strands. Far from being a moment of crowning glory, however, the event was to prove his undoing. Dr Dodds remembers becoming suspicious when she read the printed abstracts before the conference, and her doubts were confirmed when she saw a typescript of Cort's paper after the presentation. Reviewing his report of her tests, she noticed that the standard deviation was far too tight—all the points seemed to fall right on the line, which, as she says, just doesn't happen in true research. She also noticed that Cort had claimed considerably more assays than her laboratory had actually conducted on his behalf.

Dodds was unable to prevent herself being listed among Cort's co-authors at the head of an article submitted to the *International Journal of Peptide and Protein Research* in July 1980.[40] She also found it extraordinarily difficult to register her doubts at Mount Sinai Medical School. She phoned to raise the issue, but the dean with whom she spoke was unappreciative and apparently did nothing. Eventually she would be asked to attend an internal inquiry at Mount Sinai, but it was an unsatisfactory encounter. She was not helped by her employer, the New York Department of Health, which was averse to trouble and insisted that she be accompanied by a young attorney, who quickly proved quite out of his depth. Though Dodds will accuse no one who was then at Mount Sinai of direct complicity in Cort's deceptions, she observes that it is possible to remain 'conveniently' ignorant even when the facts are staring you in the face.

Though strongly resisted at first, Dodds's objections proved beyond dispute. Her laboratory records left no doubt as to precisely how many assays she had carried out on Cort's behalf, and since her population of haemophiliac dogs was unique and the only possible source of the necessary reagents, Cort simply could not have conducted additional tests elsewhere. It may have taken far too long, but Mount Sinai eventually came round.

So too did the American Society of Haemotology—although it would be three years before the editors of *Blood* consented to the printing of a single sentence in an 'Errata' section acknowledging that Dodds had asked for her name to be withdrawn from the list of authors on Cort's 1979 abstracts.[41]

Joe Cort's fall is also vividly remembered by Dr Leon Barstow, who was then president of Vega Biotechnologies in Tucson, Arizona. Vega made peptide synthesizers, and, before becoming involved with Cort, had sold two such devices to Mount Sinai Medical School. At some point, Barstow met Dr Irving Schwartz, who said he wanted to go into the pharmaceutical business, with the help of his wife's enormously wealthy uncle, Jacob Merrill Kaplan. After a series of meetings, Kaplan bought Vega: ownership was split 60 per cent to Kaplan, 10 per cent to Irving Schwartz, 10 per cent to Cort, and 20 per cent remaining with Barstow. On Schwartz's recommendation, the company went on to draw up a development plan based on Cort's patent applications.

Since the vasopressin analogues being developed by Vega in Tucson were of very similar molecular structure to DDAVP, which he understood Cort had already licensed to Ferring in Sweden, Barstow insisted that the relationship between Cort and the two companies should be formally clarified. Ferring agreed that a written statement should be drawn up but when Cort eventually produced the agreement Barstow found that he had forged the signature of one of Kaplan's employees. His suspicions aroused, Barstow pulled Cort out of Mount Sinai Medical School, where his troubles were already brewing, and, in December 1980, had him move to Tucson where he could keep an eye on him.

At Vega, Cort continued to work on the development of the modified vasopressin analogue. The company set out to raise $10 million to fund his research and began to prepare for the commercial production of the promising new drug. With this in mind Dr Barstow set up a meeting with Baxter, a company in the blood factor business. The scientific case was prepared by Cort, and Barstow asked a qualified friend to review it before the meeting. He remembers this expert coming back appalled, saying that it had only taken him twenty minutes to realize that Cort's data didn't stack up at all. When confronted by Barstow in December 1981, Cort just rolled over and admitted he had falsified much of the data used to support his patent claims. As Barstow later told the *New York Times*, 'I was flabbergasted. I knew immediately it was disastrous.' He sacked Cort, ordering him to leave the company's premises immediately, while he figured out what to do.

After a couple of days, Barstow called the dean at Mount Sinai, cancelling the licences involving Cort's work, and announcing that Vega would not be paying royalties or milestone payments as expected. The conversation was very short, and the dean did not seem surprised: 'it was like he already knew'. That, he thought, would surely be the end of the matter.

Barstow remembers Cort as a pathalogical 'scam artist' and liar, who would 'exploit anything, anybody'. Yet, he also raises another question. Cort may well have been a 'trickster', in Milan Zaoral's word, but what about Mount Sinai School of Medicine? Barstow has long suspected that Cort was only put through a public unmasking because the people at Mount Sinai eventually realized that they had to take visible steps to cover their own rears. Senior figures there had employed Cort, praised his research to the skies, and allowed themselves to be named as co-authors of his articles. Significant amounts of funding had been obtained, or at least applied for, to support Cort's researches and, as news of the deception leaked out, the various donors would surely be asking questions. Cort's colleagues at Mount Sinai were under pressure, and their 'disproportionate' response was enacted to ensure that all guilt was properly transferred to Cort.

By early 1981, they had launched their long-avoided investigation into Cort's research and patent claims. Two committees were set up: the internal enquiry attended by Dr W. Jean Dodds and others, and also an external review panel of two trustees and two outside scientists. Their findings were indeed damning. It was concluded that 'Dr. Cort had done only one-third of the work that he reported in his successful patent application'. It was judged that one of the five analogues for which Cort had reported results relating to the treatment of haemophilia had never been synthesized: 'It didn't exist,' admitted Dr Thomas C. Chalmers, president of Mount Sinai School of Medicine. Neither, it appeared, did the patented analogue intended for use as a contraceptive.

The investigation was completed in December 1982, and Mount Sinai then launched a considerable campaign of damage limitation—writing disclaiming letters to journals, and notifying funding agencies, including the National Institutes for Health. They even went to the United States Patent Office to explain that Cort had based his applications on false claims. The manner of their approach, which was plainly intended to heap all of the blame on Cort, was 'quite unnecessary', so Barstow remembers Vega's patent expert remarking. This was one of various attempts by Mount Sinai to publicly humiliate Cort and to ensure that, as one furious member of the group promised Barstow, 'he will never see another job in the US'.

At the end of December 1982, the committee's findings were also reported in the *New York Times*. Barstow, who had lost a lot of time and money thanks to the deceptions of a man who had been recommended to Vega by Mount Sinai's Dr Irving Schwartz, remembers reading the article with a sense of amazement and disgust. Five years previously, senior Mount Sinai officials had been happy to appear in the *New York Times*, basking in Cort's reflected glory, but by 1982, things were very different. The article was written by M. A. Farber, who was reputed to be a well-respected investigative journalist. As Barstow recalls, however, it made the Mount Sinai 'fact-finding' inquiry seem like a principled search for truth, rather than a reluctantly convened attempt at damage-limitation. And it enabled those who should have known a lot better, to be seen publicly throwing up their hands in innocent horror. 'It hit us like a ton of bricks,' so the chairman of Mount Sinai's board of trustees, Alfred R. Stern, was quoted as saying. 'I've always had the attitude that it couldn't happen here,' observed Dr Thomas C. Chalmers, president of the Mount Sinai School of Medicine. 'I took him at his word,' said Dr Irving Schwartz: 'What Cort did was professional suicide. He would have been better off robbing a bank.' The long ignored protestations of Dr W. Jean Dodds were left unmentioned.

No longer portrayed as a rumpled but free-spirited dissident who had triumphed over injustice and adversity, the man who had fled behind the Iron Curtain in 1954 was exposed as a disreputable cheat.

This time Cort was guilty as charged, but he had one more act to perform before withdrawing to West Germany, where he would spend the last years of his life. Recognizing the element of public show necessary to his unmasking, he stared into the lights and assisted in his own conversion into a scapegoat. As he was reported to have told the *New York Times*, 'Nobody told me to fake it. It was stupid to do. But I was under a lot of pressure and things got a bit confused. I had to earn the money for research, or die.'

In 1954, when 'scoring' American science for a Czech publication shortly after arriving in Prague, Cort had condemned the pressures weighing on scientific researchers in America. He now returned to this newly convenient theme, blaming his demise on the 'intense commercial pressures' experienced by 'scientists under contract to industry to get results to back up patent applications'.[42]

In this buck-passing exercise, at least, Cort may have been modestly successful. His story would be remembered as proof of the extent to which corporate and funding pressures can corrupt a lonely researcher. Cort went down, less as a victim of McCarthyism who lost his bearings while trying to climb back through the Iron Curtain, than as an example of the 'false prophet' America's competitive system could make of a hard-pressed scientist.[43]

Afterword: Gone with the Berlin Wall?

> Instead of the reality of the world we have an ideal, a concept, a corporal's baton without the army, which is transformed into a shadow.
>
> Nikolai Bukharin, writing in the Lubyanka, 1937[1]

There had been many 'iron curtains' before Churchill went to Fulton in 1946. Yet a new era was also opening and his 'Iron Curtain' soon hardened into a formidable sequel to the versions that the Buxtons, Vernon Lee, Ethel Snowden, and others had opposed earlier in the century.

This model would find its own history within a Cold War defined by the threat of nuclear weapons and the inclusion of the newly dubbed 'Third World' into its theatre of operations. In Africa and other formerly colonized lands, it might remain a flexible screen through which Communist-trained guerrillas, technical advisers, and guns continued to pass. In Asia, it would be transmogrified into the Bamboo curtain, established around Communist China after the 'Liberation' of 1949, just as, in the 1960s, it would descend between warring India and Pakistan, defining this regional conflict as another theatre in which the two blocs squared off against one another. In European and American perceptions, however, the Iron Curtain would remain closely identified with the armed and fortified frontier between East and West Europe, as it had been since long before August 1961, when its most powerful symbol began to emerge as the Berlin Wall.

The theatrical origins of the Iron Curtain would largely be forgotten in the Cold War decades, yet many of the characteristic attitudes of the new division were directly inherited from its predecessor. Both were shaped by the same opposition between capitalism and communism, with its opposed constructions of 'Otherness' and its primary geopolitical front extending from the Baltic to the Adriatic. They reflected similarly polarized systems of state propaganda and continuous, if not identical, techniques of 'containment' and 'cold' warfare: the Allied blockade of 1918–20 being answered by the Berlin blockade imposed by Stalin in 1948, and the later diplomacy of détente being similarly informed by manoeuvres of the earlier period.

Both versions divided opposed political and economic systems while also defining the large areas of common ground over which they would compete for dominance.[2] The Cold War shaped by Churchill's Iron Curtain would inherit both the competitive claims to science, economic rationality, cultural and sporting prowess, and also the compensatory rhetoric of internationalism. The United Nations had replaced the disintegrated League of Nations, but its activities would be attended by similarly lofty appeals to the horizontal interests of humankind, expressed through an inherited imagery of children, motherhood, and doves (the latter having been famously reworked by Picasso).

Like its predecessors, the post-1946 Iron Curtain had pronounced cultural manifestations. In its descent, it would rearrange works of literature, including George Orwell's *Nineteen Eighty-Four* (1949), which drew much of its material from British life but quickly became established as a portrait of Soviet totalitarianism.[3] It sanctioned bipolar bloc-thinking and distorted journalism of the kind that was, once again, felt to be justified by adherents on both sides. Sven Lindqvist, the independent-minded Swedish writer who lived in China in 1961–2, records arguing with a student who defended the lies and selective slant of Chinese reportage about America, insisting on the priority of 'class consciousness' and dismissing the idea of 'objective truth' as a weapon in imperialist America's arsenal.[4]

The new barrier relicensed familiar conventions of literary espionage, with reporters going 'behind' the post-1946 Iron Curtain in the same manner that earlier explorers had once ventured into Bolshevik Russia or 'behind' the Allied blockade. While prompting Hollywood to produce a steady supply of formulaic spy dramas, commencing with William A. Wellman's *Iron Curtain*, a film about the 1946 Canadian atomic spy plot that was released in 1948, it also constituted a new challenge for any writer seriously wanting to articulate the 'truth' of the division. As the German novelist Uwe Johnson wrote of a divided but still unwalled Berlin in 1961, 'a border in this spot creates a new literary form'. For him, as for Vernon Lee in an earlier age, the splitting of reality defied any simple-minded idea of the omniscience of the author: for any writer determined to grasp the truth

David Low, *Evening Standard*, 25 September 1945

Leslie Gilbert Illingworth, *Daily Mail*, 6 March 1946

Leslie Gilbert Illingworth, *Daily Mail*, 28 May 1946

Leslie Gilbert Illingworth, *Daily Mail*, 10 December 1947

David Low, *Manchester Guardian*, 8 June 1955

rather than succumb to one-sided interpretations of the kind that can only 'damage reality', it demanded that 'its subject must be checked against two contradictory tendencies of truth-finding'.[5] Thanks to widespread nuclear anxiety, it was not just close to the frontier that the Iron Curtain loomed menacingly in the 1950s imagination. While dividing Europe from Arctic to Adriatic, it also descended in less obvious venues, including the British bathtub in which the future writer Marina Warner remembers letting her hair fall over her face, and declaiming dramatically about the impenetrable 'Iron Curtain' that now separated her from her infant sister.[6]

The theatrics of the Potemkin village would also be carried over from the earlier period. In the Communist bloc, these techniques re-emerged in architectural form with Stalin's post-war restoration of Warsaw's Old Town and his attempt to rival the Manhattan skyline by planting the Eastern bloc with monumental skyscrapers of his preferred neoclassical variety. They also persisted in the carefully prepared realities that would be shown to credulous Western visitors, whether in Mao's China or in the German Democratic Republic where visible areas of East Berlin, tasked with facing down the glittering prosperity of the West, and also some villages that could be seen from across the wire, were maintained in unusually good condition.[7] Soviet citizens, especially those in the show city of Moscow, experienced a life in which a 'monochrome, rusty, half-broken' reality was hidden behind 'the official shining facades of ideological pretence'.[8] In accordance with the tradition that began with the Bolsheviks' employment of the tsar's automobiles to impress the first foreign investigators, limousines would transport visitors along preselected streets on which buildings were freshly painted, where shop windows were stuffed with desirable goods, and drunks and derelicts had been swept away in early morning raids.

As late as 1988, i.e. well into the time of Gorbachev and *glasnost,* Soviet hospitality was still serving to shape the perceptions of foreign visitors. According to one resident foreign correspondent who kept a sceptical eye on the Western moguls and writers who poured into Russia to meet the architects of perestroika, 'their optimism or pessimism ... depended less on the enormous number of interviews they conducted than [on] the state of their accommodation'.[9] More recently, Potemkinist techniques have been used to create the systems of 'virtual democracy' practised by various actually far from democratic regimes in the post-Soviet world.[10]

Pigeon Lofts to Air Conditioning

Sixty years after the event, it seems all but universally accepted that Churchill's Iron Curtain has been lifted: its disappearance having been televised as the fall of the Berlin Wall. All but the scantest traces of the closed frontier have indeed vanished from the landscape of a reunifying Europe. The hated Fence ('Die Grenze') was ploughed up with such enthusiasm that remarkably few watchtowers, even those overlooking spectacular bends in rivers such as the Elbe, remained to be turned into summer homes or ornithological hides a few years later.[11] In Berlin, the wall that had become the primary symbol of the division did indeed come 'tumbling down', as one chronicler has put it.[12] Indeed, it was so thoroughly demolished that, here as in Fulton, a section has subsequently been reinstated in the combined service of memory and tourism.

Elsewhere, the legacy is more enduring. A tense and massively armed demilitarized zone still divides North and South Korea, and the Taiwan Straits remain vigilantly watched even though the huge loudspeakers that once fired propaganda across the waters have fallen silent. The continuing American embargo has helped to keep Cuba impoverished but, like previous blockades, it has also turned the land of Castro's revolution into something else: not just a stagnant 'rock pool'[13] left behind by the vanishing Soviet tide, but a continuing inspiration in Latin America and, perhaps especially for Europeans, an exotic tourist destination where Cold War 'Otherness' is now romanticized as resistant human authenticity—to be appreciated at least as much as the music and the impressive cocktails. This process is unlikely to be diminished by the warnings of the Cuban poet and former revolutionary Paul Rivero, who on the occasion of Castro's eightieth birthday declared from exile in Spain that Cuba had degenerated into 'a theatrical society whose script is written every day by the official press'.[14]

Many of the 'distorted pictures' (Vernon Lee) that helped to maintain the Iron Curtain in people's minds since 1946 have evaporated in the years following 1989. No Polish visitors landing in New York today would feel as disorientated as did the colonel and spy Pawel Monat, after arriving at Idlewild Airport with his wife and family in September 1955. He was shocked to discover that the traffic jams were real, and not just Potemkinist illusions rigged up to convince people in the Soviet bloc that American workers owned cars; and it took him a while to accept that the boxes protruding from the windows of Manhattan apartment buildings really were air-conditioning units rather than dovecotes, as he had at first told his enquiring wife.[15] Similarly, and despite the persistence of the demilitarized zone, there can be few children in South Korea who now grow up believing, as some of the earlier generations did, that the people in North Korea literally have red faces.

In the West, however, triumphalist legends still thrive on the memory of the Cold War, interpreting it as a simple fable in which the 'Good Guys' vanquished 'the Bad Guys' to create 'a fireside fairytale with a happy ending', as David Caute has written.[16] More specifically, George W. Bush's policy towards Iraq has been closely shaped by the memory of the Iron Curtain. This may have informed the idea of 'containment' applied to that 'rogue state' in the years before the invasion of 2003 but it also fired the hawkish Neoconservatives, who imagined American foreign policy at last bridging the inherited schism between detached idealism and base diplomatic pragmatism by means of a forceful projection of 'democracy' into foreign lands. It was there in the ignorant expectation of those same Neo-conservative advisers, who now confess to having believed that democracy was the 'default condition'[17] and that the peoples of Iraq would welcome their liberation as if they were East Berliners watching the wall come crashing down. The same legacy could be felt in the haste with which some liberal and repentant formerly Marxist commentators leapt to support the war: another clutch of 'useful idiots',[18] so Tony Judt has suggested, brandishing the works of George Orwell as their justification for applying their polarizing habit of thought to a new enemy named 'Islamo-fascism'.

Remembering Vernon Lee's conception of the iron curtain as a theatrically driven 'psychological deadlock', it is also worth questioning the extent to which the widespread belief that the Iron Curtain vanished with the Berlin Wall may itself be mixed with illusion. Momentous events took place in 1989 and Europe is indeed undergoing reunification. Yet leaders and commentators persist in using 'barriers of otherness' (Lee) to impose polarized enclosures on the world, interpreting them as monolithically good, evil, or abject and, as Irene Cooper Willis described, attributing a distinct 'mental condition' to each. More than a decade after the Fall of the Wall, influential voices on the American right would be using these tried and tested techniques to squeeze 'liberalism' onto the satanic plinth formerly occupied by Soviet Communism and to insist, as US Secretary of State Condoleezza Rice has recently done, that American values are 'universal' while also likening Islamist contempt for nationality to the aggressive horizontalism of the old Communist International.[19] Similarly, political adventurers and 'solidarity journalists' on the left would be found overriding established facts and their own sometimes considerable ignorance, in the course of elevating Hugo Chávez's edict-governed and oil-buoyed Venezuela as the central power of an emerging 'axis of hope'.[20]

By the time of the invasion of Iraq in 2003, it seemed that Potemkinism had found a new venue in America's arsenal. With the help of digital satellite mapping technology, it had become possible to create a simulated terrain and then load it into your invading war-machines as a virtual theatre of operations that made knowledge of old-fashioned reality seem strangely beside the point. Thus equipped, politicians and their advisers could imagine landing their forces in an alien and unknown land, confident that they would have 'total situational awareness'[21] and, without having to fall back on any sensor so primitive as the naked eye, know the 'target-rich' environment better than the natives.

It would prove possible to secure spectacular military successes in Donald Rumsfeld's high-tech shooting gallery, and to topple statues of the vile tyrant too. Yet it would also emerge that the victors had enormous difficulties grasping what was going on behind the scenes of their own deceptively precise sighting systems. As the initial sense of triumph dissolved and 'otherness' reasserted itself, the imaging technology of digitized warfare provided no way of telling a citizen from an insurgent or suicide bomber, or of commanding the will of people for whom liberation and the 'promotion of democracy' had quickly become confused with utter disaster.

Yet it is not only through the virtual reality of the contemporary Western arsenal that Potemkinism has found new applications in the country that was being encouraged to recognize itself as the world's only remaining superpower. Thanks to the 'it's a flat world' horizontalism of the globalizing media, the Iron Curtain that once divided the planet has given way, in Russell Jacoby's words, to a 'curtain of images' that 'surrounds us from morning to night and from childhood to old age'.[22] It is in the exploitation of this media curtain—which critics of George W. Bush's Iraq war have described variously as 'an ideological canopy'[23] and an 'eternal present' in which the state also becomes 'entrapped by its own apparatus of clichés' and 'policy-motifs'[24] — that the theatrical manipulation of public understanding continues.

Rulers may always have benefited from theatrical forms of presentation. Yet, as the playwright Arthur Miller argued in his essay 'On Politics and the Art of Acting',[25] the rise of television has made politics newly reliant on dramatic methods of performance. Acting, of the kind in which President Ronald Reagan excelled, may remain central to this applied form of electric theatre, but the art of scene-rigging has also proved decisive. In 1971–2, when American officials went to China to prepare for President Nixon's controversial forthcoming visit, they showed as much concern with television camera angles as with the content of the approaching discussions. At Beijing airport they carefully marked up the runway to ensure that the president's plane came to a halt in exactly the most photogenic position, having landed as planned at 11.30 a.m., which coincided with prime time in all three of America's time zones. It was, in the words of Bob Haldeman, to be 'the key picture in the whole trip'.[26]

Such techniques of presentation were much used during the Cold War, and they have hardly fallen away since 1989. In April 2003, Donald Rumsfeld remarked, with reference to the televised toppling of a statue of Saddam Hussein in Baghdad's Firdos Square, that, 'one cannot help but think of the fall of the Berlin Wall and the collapse of the Iron Curtain'.[27] In truth, however, this carefully framed performance actually testified to the fact that news manipulation of the kind that had indeed formerly been the very stuff of the Iron Curtain was now defining the American presentation of events in Iraq. A few days earlier, the same mixture of false official briefing and media compliance had produced the myth of Jessica Lynch, the wounded 19 year old supply unit clerk who was rescued from an Iraqi hospital, having been spuriously converted into a female 'Rambo', falsely said to have kept firing until her ammunition ran out. But this faked-up mirage would be trumped on 1 May 2003, when George W. Bush visited the homebound nuclear aircraft carrier USS *Abraham Lincoln* as it approached California. Rejecting his conventional helicopter for a more virile-looking jet inscribed 'Navy One', he made an allegedly 'perfect' tailhook landing, and then stepped out to embrace the heroes who had toppled Saddam Hussein. Here was Bush displaying himself as the commander-in-chief, an experienced military pilot who had, as he let it be known, taken the plane's controls during the journey. Standing before a banner reading 'Mission Accomplished' and with both ship and camera strategically positioned to place open sea rather than San Diego in the background, he announced 'One victory' and an 'end of major combat operations'. The Democrat Senator for West Virginia, Robert Byrd, triggered a deluge of hostile press misrepresentation a few days later, when he expressed concern that Bush might have 'exploited the trappings of war' and used the military 'as stage props to embellish a presidential speech'.[28]

Fulton's Backside

A sense of unfinished business lingers on even in Fulton, the little Missouri town where the story of the iron curtain both did and did not begin. One morning in the Loganberry Inn, I came downstairs to be greeted by a genial Southern couple, whose son was a student at Westminster College. Taking me for an envoy of Tony Blair's, they thanked me profusely for the fact that Britain had not left America to invade Iraq alone.

Immediately after this encounter with the rekindled 'special relationship', I went for a walk, curious to glance behind the scenes that, nearly sixty years earlier, had been brushed up to form the background of Churchill's visit. Heading north past Christopher Wren's spectacularly mounted church of St Mary, where a seventeenth-century English pulpit (donated by the Diocese of London and thought to have been designed by Christopher Wren), would soon be installed as a memorial to the victims of 11 September 2001, I found Fulton's African American community only a few hundred yards along the road. Looking at the houses here, I might have felt cautioned by Gyula Illyés's warnings about the 'Potemkin-complex' and the curious way it could induce an 'unremarkable shack' to extrude contrastingly fine and derelict versions of itself, depending on the bias of the observing visitor. Some of these modest structures nevertheless impressed me as being far closer to shacks than to the 'cottage homes' in which Churchill had placed his imagined 'common people' when addressing the world from Fulton in March 1946.

I was in no position to establish whether these streets had been the home of Ulysses Threlkeld, the young African American who cooked Churchill's beef in 1946. It was a plain if not uniformly hard-pressed settlement, which seemed worlds apart from the classical grandeur of the Churchill Memorial and, for that matter, from the liberal humanism of Westminster College, where, by student request, Ralph Nader would follow Churchill, giving the fifty-second 'Green Lecture' in a day or two's time.

People cling to the memory of a distinguished visitor in this neighbour-hood too, but the name attached to park and street hereabouts is that of

George Washington Carver. Born to slave parents in Missouri in the 1860s, Carver went on to become a distinguished agricultural chemist and educator at the Tuskegee Institute in Alabama. An advocate of crop-rotation in the cotton fields, he developed scores of new uses for alternative crops such as peanuts, pecans, soybeans, and sweet potatoes.

Carver visited Fulton in 1937. He is alleged to have proved the hedge apple to be edible during the course of his stay, but his primary purpose was to open a new elementary school for the children of Fulton's black community. The gesture was characteristic of a man who believed that education should be 'made common' and brought closer to the needs and interests of its intended beneficiaries. Unlike the gleaming Churchill Memorial with its appended section of the Berlin Wall, the red brick George Washington Carver Grade School was empty and dilapidated.

A local committee had drawn up plans to convert the redundant building into a museum dedicated to Carver and commemorating the history and achievements of Fulton's black community. Yet the project had been frustrated by lack of funds, and the once segregated school has languished for years on a list, maintained by the Missouri Alliance for Historic Preservation, of the state's ten most endangered historical buildings.

Its future may still be unsecured, but the George Washington Carver Grade School remains to insist that the Iron Curtain was never the only show even in this town. Eloquent in its blighted condition, the school testifies to the endurance of a different division identified by W. E. B. Du Bois in 1903. In that distant time, when the iron curtain was still confined to its original role as a safety device for theatres, he wrote that 'The problem of the Twentieth Century is the problem of the color-line'.[29]

Appendix I

Bach's Christmas Music in England and in Germany by Vernon Lee

I was at the Temple on Christmas Eve for Bach's music. The shimmering double church was full of old and elderly men, of women of all ages, with a sprinkling of soldier-lads, brought along, on what may be their last Christmas in this world, by their mothers and sisters and sweethearts. Everyone—but it was perhaps that my own eyes and heart were opened—everyone seemed so altered from other perfunctory times, grave, sincere, aware of all it meant.

With the first rasping notes of the organ, tearing the veil of silent prayer, there came before my mind, as when a cloud-rent suddenly shows depths of solemn moonlit sky, the fact that *There* also, *There* beyond the sea and the war chasm, in hundreds of churches of Bach's own country (I can see the Thomas-Kirche at Leipzig, where he was Cantor, and the church of his birthplace, Eisenach), *There,* at this very moment, were crowds like this one at the Temple, listening to this self-same Christmas Music. *There* also elderly men, stay-behinds, and many, many women, old and young, and a sprinkling of soldier-lads brought for that, maybe, last Christmas at home and on Earth. Praying like these silently kneeling around me, and praying for the same mercies: Give us, O God, strength to live through these evil times, or, if so be, die to some purpose; suffer not, O Lord, who seest our hearts, that we be crushed in this war not of our making: teach us to forgive the cruel folk who hate us; give us such peace as will never be broken. Forgive us, deliver us; remember, O Father, the peace and good-will which were promised with Thy Son.

Something like that, articulate or not, is welling up with unshed tears and silent sobs in those kneeling crowds, behind those screening hands, both on this side and on yonder, of the shallow seas and the unfathomable ocean of horror and hatred. They are united, these English and those German crowds, in the same hopes and fears and prayers, even as, unsuspecting, they are united in the same sequences of melody, the same woofs of harmonies wherewith, across two hundred years, that long dead but undying organist of Leipzig enmeshes, draws together, nooses and nets our souls to lift them, clarified, close embraced, nay consubstantial, into the presence of the new born, the eternally reborn, Hope of the World.

They are thinking and feeling the same, those German and these English crowds. They are played into unanimity not only by Bach with his tunes and counterpoints, but by the ruthless hands of our common calamity. The same heroic, or resigned, or despairing modes; saddest of all, perhaps, the brief snatches of would-be cheerfulness, and beneath all individual, all articulate differences, the unanalysable harmonies of collective sorrow.

They have come, those German women like these English ones, to seek rest in this church and this music after their day in hospitals and relief offices and committee rooms. They also have brought along with them their soldiers, their boys or their lovers, home perhaps for the last time; brought them from old peaceful habit, or because one can feel nearer together, without the unnerving fear of words and glances, here in this church, side by side, embracing in the music and in God. And, the service over, they will many of them, German women like English, go back to their homes, light up the Christmas tree, pull the paper caps and the favours out of the crackers, and laugh and play, so that the children at least may forget the war, and remember only that the Christ Child has been born once more. German and English, the same burdens have been brought to the church, been laid down in the prayer and the music; the same burdens have been shouldered again. Never have we and they been closer together, more alike and akin, than at this moment when War's cruelties and recriminations, War's monstrous iron curtain, cut us off so utterly from one another.

United, moreover, in the common feeling of Christmas. For a symbol turns the simple fact we can singly know into the myriad applications we can together feel. And the Child Christ, whom, orthodox or unorthodox, we are all celebrating, was not born once, but is born always, over and again. He lies in every cradle, the incarnate, unblemished hope of every land and every generation. And He is the Redeemer because every new life, like every new day after the winter solstice, like the wheat quickening in the winter furrow, is the redemption of our Present by our Future, the deliverance by our Hope from our Despair. Enmity dies and is forgotten, being accidental, changeable, sterile, and against the grain of life. But peace and goodwill on earth is born for ever anew, because it is born of the undying needs of our common humanity.

This is the message of Bach's Christmas music, his cosmic thunders hushed in pastoral flutings; the message of the long-deceased German organist to us English who listen; the message to us listening English back to Bach's fellow-countrymen united with us in listening and in sorrowing and hoping.

As published in *Jus Suffragi*, 9/4 (1 January 1915), 218.

Appendix II

The Refreshment Room at Narva by Charles Roden Buxton

Reval, Esthonia, July 3rd, 1920

Narva is the first station in Esthonia, as you come from Soviet Russia. I had been already two days and two nights in the train—gradually consuming a very tough sausage of the German type, with some cheese and black bread. I had regretfully watched my sausage diminish to a bare stump.

And here was the first refreshment room I had seen for two months! Nice cold fillets of fish, and slices of ham, and delicious clean brown bowls of sour milk—and if you liked to wait, lovely hot veal cutlets of gigantic size. The whole of my *bourgeois* instincts rose up in rejoicing. Here was the normal type of civilized life.

And now that I am at Reval, I find that all the rest is of a piece with it. The shops are full of a (to me) bewildering variety of wares. All is as it should be. The men drink alcohol; the women wear stays; the horses wear bearing reins. It is the old familiar thing again.

But is it the right thing? How many share in it? A goodly number certainly, who in one way or another, like myself, have got hold of the requisite purchasing power. But what of the countless ones to whom the refreshment room is as remote and inaccessible as it is to the dweller in Soviet Russia—to whom the brilliant shops of capitalist cities are merely a show, and not a thing that they ever expect to enter upon and enjoy? What of the innumerable submerged, packed away out of sight behind the glaring main streets?

Here in Reval yesterday, poking about the back streets, I met a woman, a widow, who earns 23 marks a day in a factory. She pays 12 marks of this for bread, and 8 for milk, each day. Does *she* ever go into the Wiru Ulitza to buy in the shops there? Certainly not—the three remaining marks out of her 23 will not run to that. If the Wiru and all its shops were to disappear to-morrow it would make no difference whatever to her, either for good or ill. She has nothing to do with it.

Reval, though it would strike you in the West as a very one-horse show, seems to me a place of unexampled splendour. And what strikes me most of all is the strangely disproportionate part of the social effort which is devoted, even in a town like this, where most people would say there is no luxury at all, to producing and conveying and selling the comforts of one class—a large class, it is true, but not an all-inclusive class.

Some of us have said that a social transformation was possible. Did we really mean it? The Russian Communists have taken it literally, and engaged in the effort at a moment of history which, by its confusion and collapse, gave them the opportunity, but which at the same time was the worst possible moment for the experiment from the point of view of production. If they have not exalted those of low degree in the sense of giving them more to eat than before, they have certainly put down the mighty from their seat. And this was enough to make the world outside fall upon them with horse, foot and artillery, and fortify their internal enemies by every available device. We have forced them to employ many odious means to maintain their footing—and then abused them for employing these means.

My feeling at the moment, on emerging from the great human experience I have passed through, is that there is something almost impudent about a minute investigation into the errors and crimes that have accompanied the Revolution. We contemplate a man whom we have denounced as an outlaw (without knowing anything about him except from his enemies)—bound in fetters, tortured by prolonged hunger, and compelled to dwell among tombs—and we dissect his faults. He may fairly retort upon us—'In God's name let me alone; take off my chains; let me supply myself with food by my labor; remove your ban upon me until you know something about me; and then see what I can do.'

When I think of the colossal effort that is being made, the tragic conditions of the experiment, the feverish atmosphere of excitement, of elation, of depression, now one and now the other, which has surrounded it, I feel that I cannot isolate the machinery of the Revolution from the human elements that play around it and make, mar, or modify it. I think of the nervous suspicions generated by months of internal conspiracy. I think of the heroic patience and endurance of the Russian town populations. I cannot examine this people as if they were beetles or butterflies.

And there is another side to the matter. Why do we not investigate and criticize *ourselves?* Here is Esthonia, for instance. Evidently it is not everybody who thinks that all is well. Three days ago took place the trial of some 20 or 30 Communists. They were, in fact, members of the Executive of the Trade Unions. Two were sentenced to death; eleven to imprisonment for life, or for long terms. On the day of the trial, a general strike took place, as a protest. Cavalry and infantry paraded the streets, to keep order. No newspapers, except an official sheet, have appeared since. Now there may be nothing to criticize here. The offence may have been great, the trial fair; I have not been able to check the facts. All I know is that I have heard horrifying tales of persecution. But why does nobody investigate the matter? The Communists here are regarded with exactly the same suspicion and vague terror as the counter-revolutionaries in Soviet Russia. If this was in Russia, and the trial was a trial of counter-revolutionaries, the air would be thick with accusations. Correspondents would be describing the arrest of the prisoners, the sufferings of their wives and families, their innocence, their fine behaviour, the procedure of the court, the brutal indifference of the judges, the savagery of the sentences. The 'Morning Post' representative in Reval sends full accounts of what he thinks is going on in Moscow. Why does it never occur to him to ask what is going on in the next street in Reval?

Mind you, I have no evidence that Esthonia is worse than any other country. It is a mere accident that it is the first country I come into on leaving Russia. My point is simply that if any capitalist State were to be subjected to the minute examination which Soviet Russia is now undergoing at the hands of numerous delegations it would certainly be found far from perfect. But it is not thought necessary to examine it at all.

As published in *The Nation*, 31 July 1920, pp. 554–5.

Notes

Unless attributed to other archives, the papers of Charles Roden Buxton here cited remain in the possession of the Buxton family. It is anticipated that they will in due course be added to the holding at the British Library of Political and Economic Science, London School of Economics.

INTRODUCTION: PATHS CROSS ON THE *JAROSLAW DABROWSKI*

1. 'New York Hails Carrier Pigeon Which Crashed the Iron Curtain,' *Boston Daily Globe*, 2 August 1954, 11.
2. 'Dog Busts Iron Curtain', *Boston Evening American*, 2 August 1954, 14.
3. '"Statement" by Dr. John', *The Times*, 24 July 1954, 6. Commentators all over the West were trying to get the measure of the sudden relocation of this distinguished anti-Nazi and former participant in the failed July 1944 plot against Hitler. Had he been drugged and kidnapped by a jazz musician, or did his re-emergence in East Berlin prove that he must have been a Communist all along—one who might have helped Britain's 'missing diplomats', Guy Burgess and Donald Maclean, by smuggling them through the Iron Curtain in 1951? See 'John Linked to Briton Who Fled to Iron Curtain', *Boston Daily Globe*, 30 July 1954, 9.
4. Alexander T. Jordan, 'Habeas Corpus to the Rescue', *The Freeman: Ideas on Liberty*, 6/6 (June 1956). This fiercely anti-Communist journal was published by the Foundation for Economic Education (New York) and is now available online at http://www.fee.org/publications/the-freeman/article.asp?aid=192
5. Ibid.
6. 'Police Search of Polish Vessel', *The Times*, 2 August 1954, 6.
7. 'British Take Stowaway Off Cort Ship', *Boston Sunday Herald*, 1 August 1954, 7.
8. 'Polish "Slanders" Denied', *New York Times*, 6 August 1954.
9. 'Police Search of Polish Vessel', *The Times*, 2 August 1954, 6.
10. 'The Corts Depart for Iron Curtain', *New York Times*, 2 August 1954, 4.
11. *Boston Daily Globe*, 3 August 1954, 14.
12. *New York Times*, 10 August 1954, 10.
13. 'Klimowicz Tells His Story', *The Times*, 9 August 1954, 6.

14. 'Polish Stowaway Tells of Ordeal', *New York Times*, 9 August 1954.

15. 'U.S. Ships to Take 100,000 Refugees', *New York Times*, 9 August 1954.

16. Both Polish pilots were greeted as heroes who had flown 'over the top of the Iron Curtain' by pre-war Poland's remaining ambassador in London. See E. Raczjinski's letter to *The Times*, published under the heading 'Flight from Poland' on 25 May 1953, 7.

17. Wojciech Krzywicki, 'Ucieczki z Peerelu' ('Escapes from the Polish People's Republic'), *Karta*, 16 (1995), 121–2.

18. '7 Poles Seize Ship and Seek Asylum', *New York Times*, 24 September 1954, 8.

19. 'Political Asylum for Poles', *The Times*, 13 May 1954, 6.

20. Jan Cwiklinski, *The Captain Leaves His Ship: The Story of the Captain of the S.S. Batory by Jan Cwiklinski, Formerly Master of the Polish Motorship Batory, as Told to Hawthorne Daniel* (London: Robert Hale, 1955), 198.

21. Ibid.

22. Ibid. 199.

23. 'Corts Board Polish Ship for Czecho-Slovak "Refuge"', *Boston Daily Globe*, 31 July 1954, 1–2.

24. Ibid. 1.

25. 'Protest by Poland', *The Times*, 5 August 1954, 6.

26. 'The Corts Depart for Iron Curtain,' *New York Times*, 2 August 1954, 4.

27. Jordan, 'Habeas Corpus to the Rescue'.

28. 'U.S. Doctor and Wife Ordered to Leave', *The Times*, 12 June 1954, 6.

29. Michael Foot, speaking in the House of Commons, 27 January 1954, quoted in connection with J. H. Cort's situation in 'Refugees and the Home Office,' *New Statesman and Nation*, 3 July 1954, 4. For the full context see Hansard, *Parliamentary Debates*, vol. 522, col. 1908.

30. Cort's exchange of letters with the American embassy was so described in 'London Diary', *New Statesman and Nation*, 26 June 1954, 821.

31. 'Asylum for Lecturer', *The Times*, 14 June 1954, 3.

32. 'Cort Left New England 3 Years Ago', *Boston Daily Globe*, 31 July 1954, 2.

33. *Boston Daily Globe*, 30 July 1954, 9.

34. 'Asylum for U.S. Lecturer', *The Times*, 14 June 1954, 3.

35. 'McCarthy Says Red-Hunting Must Be Rough', *Boston Daily Globe*, 2 August 1954, 10.

36. 'The Case of Dr. Cort', *New Statesman and Nation*, 19 June 1954, 776.

37. 'Refugees and the Home Office', *New Statesman and Nation*, 3 July 1954, 4.

38. Prof. A. V. Hill, FRS, letter to the *New Statesman*, 5 April 1954, quoted in 'Case of Dr. Cort', 776. This assessment of Cort's 'Communist' activities is unwittingly corroborated by Dr Charles Nugent, who was a medical student with Cort at Yale. Nugent associates Cort with nothing more 'Communist' than an Association of Interns and Medical Students (AIMS), set up to advocate American adoption of public health measures similar to those to be found

in Britain's new National Health Service. Telephone conversation, 12 May 2004.

39. 'House of Commons, Thursday, June 24', *The Times*, 25 June 1954, 3.

40. C. H. R. Meredith, letter to the editor, *The Times*, 16 June 1954, 9.

41. 'House of Commons, Thursday July 1', *The Times*, 2 July 1954, 3.

42. House of Commons, 6 July 1954. Hansard, *Parliamentary Debates*, vol. 529, col. 2318.

43. Julius Silverman, Labour MP for Birmingham, Erdington, House of Commons, 30 July 1954. Hansard, *Parliamentary Debates*, vol. 531, col. 951.

44. House of Commons 30 July 1954. Hansard, *Parliamentary Debates*, vol. 531, col. 943.

45. Silverman, House of Commons, 30 July 1954. Hansard, *Parliamentary Debates*, vol. 531, col. 956.

46. 'Refugees and the Home Office', *New Statesman and Nation*, 3 July 1954, 4.

47. House of Commons, 6 July 1954. Hansard, *Parliamentary Debates*, vol. 529, col. 2317.

48. House of Commons 30 July 1954. Hansard, *Parliamentary Debates*, vol. 531, col. 945.

49. For this question and Fyfe's written answer of 1 July 1954, see Hansard, *Parliamentary Debates*, vol. 524, col. 111.

50. 'Case of Dr. Cort', 777.

51. House of Commons, 30 July 1954. Hansard, *Parliamentary Debates*, vol. 531, col. 949.

52. House of Commons, 8 July 1954. Hansard, *Parliamentary Debates*, vol. 527, col. 2316.

53. The American paper quoted Benn as saying that the apparatus of two modern states had been used 'to hound him out of one country after another and have hounded him behind the Iron Curtain'. 'Halt Cort Asylum Vessel', *Boston Evening American*, 31 July 1954, 2.

54. 'Cort Scores U.S. Science', *New York Times*, 28 August 1954.

55. 'Cort Joins Prague Institute', *New York Times*, 21 September 1954, 5.

56. 'Corts Listed in Prague', *New York Times*, 4 October 1954, 3.

CHAPTER 1 BULLET'S BIG DAY

1. 'Churchill calls for Anglo-American Alliance', *Washington Post*, 6 March 1946.

2. 'C-T Day' special issue, *Fulton Daily Sun-Gazette*, 5 March 1946.

3. *Kansas City Star*, 20 January 1946.

4. Reports of contemporary investigations into this letter can be viewed in the Freedom of Information Act section of the FBI's website (file No. 9-13682 at www.fbi.gov).

5. *The CALL Bulletin*, 6 March 1946.

6. George W. Barham (a lawyer from Blythville, Arkansas), letter to Winston Churchill, 14 March 1946. Churchill Papers (Churchill College Archives Centre, Cambridge), CHUR 2/224/67.

7. *Kansas City Times,* 6 March 1946.

8. Walter Locke, 'Churchill in Miami', quoted from Martin Gilbert, *'Never Despair':Winston S. Churchill 1945–1965* (London: Minerva, 1990), 183.

9. George Mills, 'Sleepy Fulton Agog over Winnie's Visit', *Des Moines IA Register,* 4 March 1946.

10. 'C-T Day' special issue, *Fulton Daily Sun-Gazette,* 5 March 1946.

11. 'Fulton Mo. Prepares for Churchill Visit', *St Louis Globe-Democrat,* 28 January 1946.

12. Anne O'Hare McCormick, 'Mr. Churchill's Proposal to the Mid West', *New York Times,* 6 March 1946.

13. Sharon Kinney Hanson, T*he Life of Helen Stephens:The Fulton Flash* (Carbondale: Southern Illinois University Press, 2004).

14. Harman W. Nichols, 'Confederate Kingdom Scrubs up for Churchill', *Austin Texas American,* 4 March 1946.

15. Mills, 'Sleepy Fulton Agog over Winnie's Visit'.

16. Henry Bellamann, *King's Row,* introd. Jay Miles Karr (Fulton: Kingdom House, 2002), 1, 2, 437.

17. Ibid. 356, 445.

18. This slogan appears on the VHS of *King's Row* (1942) issued by the Turner Entertainment Company in 1992.

19. According to Professor Jay Karr, who made enquiries shortly after moving to Fulton in the 1960s to teach English at Westminster College, the film company took only a superficial interest in the town. It was said that they had sent a camera and truck through Fulton, filming some of the older streets in order to give their designers in California some idea of what 'King's Row' might look like (author's interview in Fulton, April 2003).

20. Mills, 'Sleepy Fulton Agog'.

21. *St Louis Post-Despatch,* 5 March 1946.

22. Mills, 'Sleepy Fulton Agog'.

23. *Kansas City Star,* 20 January 1946.

24. *Time,* 11 February 1946, 46.

25. 'What Would You Serve if Churchill and Truman Were Coming to Dinner?', *St Louis Globe-Democrat,* 28 January 1946.

26. 'Ham from the Kingdom of Callaway', *St Louis Globe-Democrat,* 29 January 1946.

27. Recollection of John Davenport, communicated to Martin Gilbert in letter of 7 April 1987. See Gilbert, *'Never Despair',* 213.

28. Aaron C. Butler, 'Churchill's Visit', *Weir KS Spectator,* 21 February 1946.

29. Fraser J. Harbutt, *The Iron Curtain: Churchill, America, and the Origins of the Cold War* (New York and Oxford: Oxford University Press, 1986), 168.

30. George Kennan, *Memoirs 1925–1950* (New York: Little, Brown, 1967), 303.
31. Harbutt, *Iron Curtain*, 156.

CHAPTER 2 IN THE NAME OF THE COMMON PEOPLE

1. The text of Winston Churchill's Fulton oration, 'The Sinews of Peace', appears in James W. Muller (ed.), *Churchill's 'Iron Curtain' Speech Fifty Years Later* (Columbia: University of Missouri Press, 1999), 1–13.
2. Churchill, letter to his daughter, 29 July 1945, cited in Martin Gilbert, *'Never Despair':Winston S. Churchill 1945–1965* (London: Minerva, 1990), 115.
3. Herbert Elliston, 'Churchill, Unique Giant, is Still a Paradox', *Washington Post*, 27 November 1949.
4. Aaron C. Butler, 'Churchill's Visit', *Weir KS Spectator*, 21 February 1946.
5. John Ramsden, 'Mr. Churchill Goes to Fulton', in Muller (ed.), *Churchill's 'Iron Curtain' Speech Fifty Years Later*, 42. Early indication of a toughened American policy was contained in Truman's Navy Day speech on 27 October 1945 (see ibid. 40).
6. Attlee telegram to Churchill, 25 February 1946. See Gilbert, *'Never Despair'*, 195.
7. Churchill's party political broadcast was transmitted on 4 June 1945. Quoted from Gilbert, *'Never Despair'*, 34.
8. Quoted in Fraser J. Harbutt, *The Iron Curtain: Churchill, America, and the Origins of the Cold War* (New York and Oxford: Oxford University Press, 1988), 162.
9. Gilbert, *'Never Despair'*, 61.
10. Agnes Heller and Ferenc Fehér, *Hungary 1956 Revisited:The Message of a Revolution—a Quarter of a Century After* (London: Allen & Unwin, 1983), 8.
11. Agnes Heller and Ferenc Fehér, *From Yalta to Glasnost: The Dismantling of Stalin's Empire* (Oxford: Blackwell, 1990), 8.
12. Heller and Feher, *Hungary 1956 Revisited*, 6.
13. Gilbert, *'Never Despair'*, 63.
14. Ramsden, 'Mr. Churchill Goes to Fulton', 23.
15. Robert H. Pilpel, *Churchill in America 1895–1961* (London: New English Library, 1976), 223.
16. Ramsden, 'Mr. Churchill Goes to Fulton', 39–40.
17. The diary of President Truman's press secretary, Charles Ross, as quoted by Ramsden, ibid. 19.
18. These words appear in a note written by Brig. Gen. Harry H.Vaughan, and handed to Dr John F. B. Carruthers at the White House. Churchill Papers (Churchill College Archives Centre, Cambridge), CHUR 2/227/8.
19. Having read a copy on the train to Jefferson City,Truman told Churchill that his 'admirable' speech 'would do nothing but good, though it would make a stir'. See Gilbert, *'Never Despair'*, 197.
20. *Boston Globe*, reported in *Springfield Leaders Press* (Springfield, Mo.), 6 March 1946.
21. *Chicago Sun*, 6 March 1946. Gilbert, *'Never Despair'*, 204.

22. These examples are quoted from Spencer Warren, 'A Philosophy of International Politics', in Muller (ed.), *Churchill's 'Iron Curtain' Speech Fifty Years Later*, 103–6.
23. 'La Bombe Churchill éclate à Fulton', *L'Aube*, 6 March 1946.
24. 'General Smuts Calls for Patience', *The Times*, 15 March 1946.
25. 'Mr. Churchill Appeals to Special Relationship', *The Times*, 6 March 1946. Quoted in Gilbert, *'Never Despair'*, 204.
26. 'Mr Churchill's Defeatism', *New Statesman*, 9 March 1946.
27. Letter from Mr Rentschler of National City Bank, 15 March 1946, Churchill Papers, CHUR 2/224/84.
28. Churchill Papers, CHUR 2/225/177.
29. Churchill Papers, CHUR 2/224/150.
30. Churchill Papers, CHUR 2/224/94.
31. Churchill Papers, CHUR 2/225/30.
32. These and other quoted letters received by McLuer are held in the archives of the Winston Churchill Memorial and Library in the United States at Westminster College, Fulton, Missouri.
33. This file, along with various collections of press cuttings concerned with Churchill's visit, is in the possession of the Churchill Memorial and Library, Fulton.
34. Anne O'Hare McCormick, *New York Times*, 6 March 1946.
35. This revelation emerged after the defection of Igor Gouzenko, a cipher clerk in the Soviet Embassy in Ottowa. Gouzenko had tried to defect with a collection of incriminating documents in September 1945. King had actually been highly reluctant to accept that Stalin might countenance any such activity. But to the conspiracy theorists responsible for this leaflet, the delay in revealing details of the espionage obviously had an altogether more insidious motivation.

CHAPTER 3 PROPHECY AND HINDSIGHT

1. Randolph Churchill, writing in *Europe Today*, October 1946. Quoted in Martin Gilbert, *'Never Despair': Winston S. Churchill 1945–1965* (London: Minerva, 1990), 289–90.
2. [Bill Nunn], *The Words and the Man* (Fulton: The Winston Churchill Memorial and Library, n.d.).
3. Winston Churchill, letter to President Davidson of Westminster College, 26 November 1962. Quoted in Christian E. Hauer, Jr. and William A. Young, *A Comprehensive History of the London Church and Parish of St. Mary, The Virgin, Aldermanbury: the Phoenix of Aldermanbury*, (Lewiston: Edwin Mellen Press, 1994), 378.
4. Edwina Sandys, *Breakthrough* ('a special publication of Westminster College mailed to alumni, parents and friends of the college') (Fulton: Westminster College, 1990), 7.

5. Entitled 'The River of Time and the Imperative of Action', Gorbachev's speech is here quoted from the commemorative publication, *Full Circle* (Fulton: Westminster College, 1992), 10–18.

6. Fraser J. Harbutt, *The Iron Curtain: Churchill, America, and the Origins of the Cold War* (New York and Oxford: Oxford University Press, 1986), 164.

7. Michael Lind, 'Churchill for Dummies', *The Spectator*, 24 April 2004.

8. Louis Budenz, *Men Without Faces: The Communist Conspiracy in the U.S.A.* (New York: Harper & Brothers, 1950), 77.

9. Katharine Bruce Glasier, 'June Joys and "The Summer that will last"', *Labour's Northern Voice* (July 1948), 8.

10. José Luis Cuevas, 'La Cortina Del Nopal' (1957), trans. as 'The Cactus Curtain: An Open Letter on Conformity in Mexican Art', *Evergreen Review*, 2/7 (Winter 1959), 111–20.

11. Harbutt, *Iron Curtain*, 184.

12. Ibid. 224.

13. Gilbert, *'Never Despair'*, 208–9.

14. *People's Daily World*, 7 March 1946.

15. Harold Laski, 'Churchill's Speech Divides Britain', unidentified cutting at the Churchill Memorial and Library, Fulton.

16. House of Commons, 5 November 1919 Hansard, *Parliamentary Debates*, vol. 134, col. 1629. Quoted from W. P. and Zelda K. Coates, *A History of Anglo-Soviet Relations* (London: Lawrence & Wishart, 1943), 1.

17. 'Comrades in War and Peace; the English-Speaking Nations' Task', *The Times*, 17 January 1919, 10.

18. *The Times,* 24 February 1919, 6.

19. Bernard M. Baruch, *The Public Years* (London: Odhams Press, 1960), 119.

20. Churchill Papers (Churchill College Archives Centre, Cambridge), CHUR 2/224/144–5.

21. Churchill Papers, CHUR 2/225/256.

22. Ted Frothingham, 'Charles Henry Davis: Amazing Millionaire', *Yarmouth Register*, 15 June–17 Sept 1972. See Richard F. Weingraff, 'Good Roads Everywhere', www.fhwa.dot.gov/infrastructure/davis.htm.

23. Churchill Papers, CHUR 2/225/291.

24. V. I. Lenin, 'On the Slogan for a United States of Europe', in *Collected Works* xxi (Moscow: Progress, 1972), 339–43.

25. See e.g. Édouard Herriot, *The United States of Europe*, tr. Reginald J. Dingle (London: Harrap, 1930).

26. Baruch, *Public Years,* 313.

27. See 'The Goal of Peace, Mr. Kellogg's Speech to Pilgrims', *The Times*, 23 November 1929, 14.

28. See *Notes and Queries*, 10 January, 21 February, 21 August 1948.

29. John Ramsden, 'Mr. Churchill Goes to Fulton', in James. W. Muller (ed.), *Churchill's 'Iron Curtain' Speech Fifty Years Later* (Columbia: University of Missouri Press, 1999), 15.

30. See e.g. Donald E. Davis and Eugene I. Trani, *The First Cold War: The Legacy of Woodrow Wilson in U.S. Relations* (Columbia: University of Missouri Press, 2002). Also Ted Morgan, *Reds: McCarthyism in Twentieth-Century America* (New York: Random House, 2003).

31. See David Reynolds, *In Command of History: Churchill Fighting and Writing the Second World War* (London: Allen Lane, 2004).

32. Baruch claims to have introduced the 'Cold War' while addressing the South Carolina legislature in April 1947. He attributes this 'graphic expression, which caught the public imagination', to Herbert Swope who had suggested it a year previously, when Baruch was on the United Nations Atomic Energy Commission. See Baruch, *Public Years*, 355. George Orwell used the same phrase in an article entitled 'You and the Atom Bomb', published on 19 October 1945.

33. Mr Jess Stein, letter to Churchill from Random House, 9 May 1951. Churchill's comment is noted on the letter in shorthand, and also recorded on a typed note. Churchill's private secretary relayed it to 'Mrs. Stein' in a letter dated 17 May 1951. Churchill Papers, CHUR 2/391.

CHAPTER 4 FIRST CALL

1. Michael Kelly, *Reminiscences of Michael Kelly of the King's Theatre, and the Theatre Royal Drury Lane* ... (London: Colburn, 1826), ii. 252–3. I have also drawn on the account of the Drury Lane Theatre fire in Fintan O'Toole, *A Traitor's Kiss: The Life of Richard Brinsley Sheridan* (London: Granta, 1997), 429–35.

2. Hansard, *Parliamentary Debates*, vol. xii, col. 1105.

3. Spencer Perceval, letter to George III, 25 February 1809, in The *Later Correspondence of George III*, ed. A. Aspinall, vol. v (Cambridge: Cambridge University Press, 1961–70), letter 3824, 210.

4. Hansard, *Parliamentary Debates*, vol. xii, col. 1106.

5. Judith Milhouse, 'Lighting at the King's Theatre, Haymarket, 1780–82', *Theatre Research International*, 19/3 (Autumn 1991), 215–36.

6. *Authentic Account of the Fire Which Reduced that Extensive Building of the Theatre-Royal Drury-Lane to a Pile of Ruins on the Evening of the 24th of February, 1809, to which is added a Chronological List of all the Places of Public Amusement, destroyed by Fire in England* (London: W. Glendinning (for T. Broom and others), 1809). This publication reprints modified reports that first appeared in *The Times*.

7. *The Times*, 21 September 1808.

8. William Smyth, *Memoir of Mr. Sheridan* (Leeds: J. Cross, 1840), 38.

9. Richard Brinsley Sheridan's letter 'To Prospective Subscribers to the Rebuilding of Drury Lane Theatre', 5 November 1791. *The Letters of Richard Brinsley Sheridan*, ed. Cecil Price, vol. iii, (Oxford: Clarendon Press, 1966), 317.

10. This text is quoted partly from the version of the epilogue attributed to James Boaden in O'Toole, *Traitor's Kiss* (p. 429) and partly from the version presented in Ann Alexander's anonymously published *Remarks on the Theatre and*

the Late Fire at Richmond, in Virginia (York: Thomas Wilson and Son, 1812). For a contemporary account, in which the verses are attributed to the dramatist George Colman, see Kelly, *Reminiscences*, ii. 57.

11. 'Opening of New Drury', *The Times,* 13 March 1794.

12. Robert Treat Paine, 'Dedicatory Address; spoken by Mr. Hodgkinson, 29 October 1798, At the Opening of the New Federal Theatre, in Boston', from *The Works in Verse and Prose of the Late Robert Treat Paine* (Boston: Belcher, 1812), 201. For details of the previous theatre, built in 1793 and also opened with a dedicatory address by Paine, see Charles Prentiss, 'Sketches of the Life, Character and Writings of the Late Robert Treat Paine, Jun., Esq', ibid., xxxi–li.

13. Anon. [Alexander], *Remarks on the Theatre and the Late Fire at Richmond.* This pamphlet was prompted by the fire that swept through a packed theatre in Richmond, Virginia on 26 December 1811, killing some seventy-five people attending a pantomime performance. Miss Farren's Drury Lane epilogue (here named a 'Prologue') is exhibited on the final page as proof of the folly of trying to place an 'iron curtain' between God and an audience of Sinners.

14. Kelly, *Reminiscences*, ii. 57.

15. *Authentic Account*, 16.

16. Thomas De Quincey, 'On Murder, considered as one of the Fine Arts' (1827), in *De Quincey's Works,* iv. *Murder as one of the Fine Arts, the English Mail Coach and Other Writings* (Edinburgh: Adam and Charles Black, 1863), 59–60.

17. *Authentic Account*, 16.

18. Lord Byron, 'Address, spoken at the opening of the Drury Lane Theatre, Saturday, 10 October 1812', in *The Poetical Works of Lord Byron*, ed. W. M. Rossetti, (London: Moxon, 1870), 586.

19. Thomas Moore, *Memoirs of the Life of the Right Honourable Richard Brinsley Sheridan* (London: Longman et al., 1825), 637.

20. 'Further particulars of the Fire at Drury Lane', *The Times*, 27 February 1809, 3.

21. *Authentic Account*, 7.

22. Steven Connor, 'Steam Radio: On Theatre's Thin Air', *Performance Research*, 10/1 (Apr. 2005), 8.

23. The Drury Lane Theatre's was not the first iron curtain to disappoint. The French architect Soufflot had introduced a similar contraption into a new theatre opened in Lyons in 1756. Consisting of 'a large sheet of iron cranked down from the roof' intended for use only in emergencies, this device was soon discontinued when, despite plentiful oiling, it proved reluctant to operate effectively. See F. W. J. Hemmings, 'Fire and Fire Precautions in the French Theatre', *Theatre Research International*, 19/3 (Autumn 1991), 242.

24. Captain Eyre Massey Shaw, *Fires in Theatres* (London: E. & F. N. Spon, 1876).

25. Ibid. 4.

26. Ibid. 10.

27. Ibid. 9.

28. Ibid. 11.

29. This code is reproduced in Captain Eyre Massey Shaw, *Report to the Right Hon. The Secretary of State for the Home Department concerning the fire which occurred at the Theatre Royal Exeter, on the 5th of September 1887* (London: HMSO, 1887).

30. *The Times*, 13 September 1808, 3.

31. Winston Churchill, *My Early Life: A Roving Commission* (London: Thornton Butterworth, 1930), 16.

32. *The Times*, 4 November 1882, 9.

33. Shaw, *Report ... concerning the fire which occurred at the Theatre Royal Exeter*.

34. Major-General Edward William Bray, letter to *The Times*, 12 September 1887, 13.

35. Clark, Bennett & Co., letter to *The Times*, 12 September 1887, 13.

36. *The Times*, 11 January 1888, 13.

37. 'Terry's Theatre', *The Times*, 18 October 1887.

38. *The Times*, 6 October 1887, 7.

39. Christopher Clark, *Iron Kingdom: The Rise and Downfall of Prussia, 1600–1947* (London: Penguin, 2006), 554–5.

40. Webb's recollections are recorded in A. E. Wilson, *Penny Plain Two Pence Coloured: A History of the Juvenile Drama* (London: Harrap, 1932), 26.

41. Winston Churchill, letter to A. E. Wilson, ibid.

42. George Speaight, *The History of the English Toy Theatre* (1946; London: Studio Vista, 1969), 182.

43. Churchill's actual words were 'We shall fight on the beaches, we shall fight on the landing grounds, we shall fight in the fields and in the streets, we shall fight in the hills; we shall never surrender.' Various versions of *The Miller and his Men* were prepared for the nineteenth-century toy theatre. Speaight's is not the same as that published in Webb's Juvenile Drama series during the late nineteenth century. Here Grindoff answers Count Friberg's demand for his surrender with (slightly) less melodrama, saying 'Never! The brave band within the mill is already double your number.' *The Miller and his Men: A Drama in Two Acts. Written expressly for, and adapted only to Webbs Characters and Scenes* (London: W. Webb, [n.d.]), 17.

CHAPTER 5 DIVIDING EUROPE'S HORIZON

1. Irene Cooper Willis, *England's Holy War: A Study of English Liberal Idealism during the Great War* (New York: Knopf, 1928), 92–3.

2. Vernon Lee, *Satan the Waster: A Philosophic War Trilogy with Notes & Introduction* (London: Bodley Head, 1920), 31.

3. Ibid. 33–4.

4. Vernon Lee, *The Ballet of the Nations: A Present-Day Morality*, with a pictorial commentary by Maxwell Armfield (London: Chatto & Windus, 1915) (unpaginated). For an account of Lee's collaboration with Armfield, see Grace

E. Brockington, 'Performing Pacifism: The Battle between Artist and Author in *The Ballet of the Nations*', in Catherine Maxwell and Patricia Pulham (eds.), *Vernon Lee: Decadents, Ethics, Aesthetics* (London: Palgrave Macmillan, 2006), 143–159.

5. Peter Gunn, *Vernon Lee: Violet Paget, 1856–1935* (London: Oxford University Press, 1964), 13, 27.

6. 'Vernon Lee, 'The Renaissance in Italy', *The Times*, 14 February 1935, 17.

7. George Bernard Shaw, 'A Political Contrast', *The Nation*, 18 September 1920, 758–9.

8. Lee, *Satan the Waster*, vii.

9. See e.g. Burdett Gardner, *Lesbian Imagination, Victorian Style: A Psychological and Critical Study of 'Vernon Lee'* (New York: Garland, 1987). A wider account of Vernon Lee and her writing is emerging from more recent studies. See Gillian Beer, 'The Dissidence of Vernon Lee: Satan the Waster and the Will to Believe', in S. Raitt and T. Tate (eds.), *Women's Fiction and the Great War* (Oxford: Clarendon Press, 1997), 107–31; Christa Zorn, *Vernon Lee: Aesthetics, History, and the Victorian Female Intellectual* (Athens, Ohio: Ohio University Press, 2003); Vinetta Colby, *Vernon Lee: A Literary Biography* (Charlottesville: University of Virginia Press, 2003).

10. See H. C. Peterson, *Propaganda for War: The Campaign Against American Neutrality, 1914–1917* (Norman: University of Oklahoma Press, 1939), 12.

11. Vernon Lee, paragraph entitled 'August Harvest-Fields' in 'Before the War—III Notes on the Genius of Places', *North American Review* (December 1917), 926.

12. Lee, *Satan the Waster*, 50.

13. Vernon Lee, letter, *The Nation*, 22 August 1914, 765–7. A. J. P. Taylor argues that radicals such as Lee were wrong in their assessment of Grey, who was actually keen to develop 'an international system of security in order'. A. J. P. Taylor, *The Trouble Makers: Dissent over Foreign Policy, 1792–1932* (London: Heinemann, 1957), 126–7.

14. Vernon Lee attended the 1904 Bach Festival at the Thomas-Kirche in Leipzig, where she would later recall closing her eyes and being carried back into her memories of churches in Rome, transported by the sound of a 'Palestrina-like chorus by Hassler': 'That wave-like sea of voices, in which parts ebbed up and down, seemed to surround me, to BE me, to be such a great and important part of my past; i.e. the childish and adolescent recollections of Sixtine Chapel performances. The complementary vision of the Roman church satisfied and held me.' Vernon Lee, *Music and Its Lovers: An Empirical Study of Emotion and Imaginative Responses in Music* (London: Allen & Unwin, 1932), 344.

15. Vernon Lee, 'Christkinden', in her *Juvenilia: Being a Second Series of Essays on Sundry Aesthetical Questions*, ii (London: Fisher Unwin, 1887), 180–99. See also Gunn, *Vernon Lee*, 2; and Lee's essay on 'German Fir Trees', in Vernon Lee, *The Enchanted Woods and other Essays on the Genius of Places* (London: Bodley Head, 1905), 121–30.

16. *Daily Mail*, 17 August 1914. Quoted in Hamish Miles, *A War Museum 1914–1918* (Here & Now Pamphlets, no. 2; London: Wishart, 1932), 16.

17. 'Music and the War. Patriotism at the First Promenade Concert', *The Times*, 18 August 1914, 8. Works by Mahler and Webern were removed from the programme.

18. This phrase is quoted from the German Professor Otfried Nippold's study of German chauvinism, as summarized by W. H. Dawson in a letter printed under the heading 'Three Stages of Chauvinism' in *The Times*, 2 January 1915, 6.

19. 'An iron curtain had dropped between him and the outer world.' So Wells writes of his Professor Redwood, a scientist responsible for bringing an alarming 'bigness' into the world. See H. G. Wells, *The Food of the Gods* (1904; London: Collins, 1966), 221. See also Wolfgang Mieder, *The Politics of Proverbs: From Traditional Wisdom to Proverbial Stereotypes* (Madison: University of Wisconsin Press, 1997), 57.

20. Ethel M. Dell, *The Safety-Curtain and Other Stories* (London: T. Fisher Unwin, 1917), 110. The film of *The Safety Curtain* starred Norma Talmadge and was released in 1918. In the early weeks of the war, the phrase 'white heater' was used by more moderate members of the new Union of Democratic Control to disparage those who, like Lee and her young friend Irene Cooper Willis, were ardently and explicitly opposed to the war. See Irene Cooper Willis, letter to Vernon Lee, 5 October 1914, Special Collections, Colby College, Maine.

21. Vernon Lee, 'The Psychological Deadlock of the War; apropos of a "Daily News" article', *UDC* 1/9 (July 1916).

22. Lee, *Satan the Waster*, 197.

23. Ibid. xxvii.

24. Ibid. xvii.

25. Ibid. xxxii.

26. Caroline E. Playne, *Society at War 1914–1916* (London: Allen & Unwin, 1931), 12.

27. Ibid. 18.

28. John Maynard Keynes, *The Economic Consequences of the Peace* (London: Macmillan, 1920), 9–10.

29. Ibid. 15.

30. Benedict Anderson, *Imagined Communities: Reflections on the Origin and Spread of Nationalism* (London: Verso, 1991), 7.

31. Michael Howard, *The Invention of Peace* (London: Profile, 2000), 47.

32. For the significance of this edition of the *Encyclopaedia Britannica*, which 'exulted in the endowments of systematic, professional, organized, disciplined ways of thinking [that] transcended the older forms of religion and moral philosophy', see Ira Katznelson, *Desolation and Enlightenment: Political Knowledge after Total War, Totalitarianism, and the Holocaust* (New York: Columbia University Press, 2003), 8–9.

33. Paul Laity, *The British Peace Movement 1870–1914* (Oxford: Clarendon, 2001), 15 and 13.

34. Édouard Herriot, *The United States of Europe*, tr. Reginald J. Dingle (London: Harrap, 1930).

35. Ibid. 6.

36. I take this phrase from Nicholas Murray Butler, the president of Columbia University, who used it as the title of his opening address at the 1912 Lake Mohonk Conference on International Arbitration. See Nicholas Murray Butler, 'The International Mind', *International Conciliation* (monthly publication of the American Association for International Conciliation), 55 (June 1912). Murray's various addresses to the pre-war annual Lake Mohonk Conferences are repr. in Nicholas Murray Butler, *The International Mind* (1912; New York: Scribner, 1932).

37. W. E. B. Du Bois, 'The Color Line Belts the World', *Colliers Weekly*, 20 October 1906, 30. Here quoted from *Writings by W. E. B. Du Bois in Periodicals Edited by Others*, ed. Henry Aptheker (New York: Kraus-Thomson, 1982), 64.

38. Susanna Ashton, 'Du Bois's Horizon: Documenting Movements of the Color Line', *Melus* (Winter 2001).

39. Paul S. Reinsch, 'American Love of Peace and European Skepticism', *International Conciliation*, 68 (July 1913), 5.

40. Ibid. 5 and 4.

41. Paul S. Reinsch, *Public International Unions: Their Work and Organisation. A Study in International Administrative Law* (Boston: Ginn & Company, 1911), 1.

42. Ibid. 3.

43. Louis P. Lochner, 'The Cosmopolitan Club Movement', *International Conciliation*, 61 (December 1912), 5.

44. Reinsch, 'American Love of Peace and European Skepticism', 11.

45. Ibid. 135.

46. Ibid. 4.

47. 'La Vie internationale et l'effort pour son organisation', *La Vie internationale: Revue mensuelle des idées, des faits et des organismes internationaux*, 1 (1912), 9.

48. Gaston Mach, 'La Monnaie internationale', *La Vie internationale*, 5 (1915), 503–22.

49. M. Carl Bourlet, 'Le Huitième Congrès universal d'Esperanto', *La Vie internationale*, 1 (1912), 567–73.

50. 'Le Tunnel sous la Manche', *La Vie internationale*, 5 (1915), 85–90.

51. For the American Association for International Conciliation's version of this idea, see Daniel Gregory Mason, 'Music as an International Language', *International Conciliation*, 68 (June 1913).

52. In a letter of 9 March 1909, Rolland had written to Lee declaring, 'I too am a cosmopolitan. But there are two cosmopolitanisms: that of vile and egoistic pleasure, and that of the courageous souls in all countries who struggle for an ideal.' Rolland declared himself for the second version against the first (Vernon Lee papers at Somerville College, Oxford). According to Vinetta Colby, it was Lee who first proposed Rolland to the committee that awarded him the Nobel Prize in 1915 (Colby, *Vernon Lee*, 299). Documents in the C. R. Buxton

archive at Rhodes House, Oxford, testify to the fact that the British government proscribed the sending of publications from the UDC and other anti-war organizations, when the Nobel committee asked for examples of anti-war work in London.

53. Romain Rolland, *John Christopher*, ii. *Storm and Stress* (London: Heinemann, 1911), 385.

54. Romain Rolland, *John Christopher*, iv. *Journey's End* (London: Heinemann, 1913), 503.

55. Romain Rolland, letter to Vernon Lee, dated 8 August 1908 (Vernon Lee papers at Somerville College, Oxford). While responding gratefully to Lee's review of *La Foire sur la place*, the fifth volume of *Jean Christophe*, Rolland declares: 'My dream is to create a work of most pure French blood, which will be European. I have a passionate love for our dear Europe of the Occident. I would like to be able to unite in one soul the five powerful souls of her old nations, without sacrificing anything of their individuality.'

56. Rolland, *John Christopher*, iv. 504.

57. Ibid. 522.

58. Romain Rolland, 'An Open Letter to Gerhart Hauptmann' (29 August 1914), in *Above the Battle*, tr. G. K. Ogden (London: Allen & Unwin, 1916), 19.

59. Rolland, 'Our Neighbour the Enemy' (March 1915), in *Above the Battle*, 143.

60. Rolland, 'Inter Arma Caritas' (October 1914), in *Above the Battle*, 75.

61. Rolland, *Above the Battle*, 50.

62. Letter to Louis Ferrière (a Swiss pastor), 4 July 1917 in *Selected Letters of Romain Rolland*, ed. F. Doré and M-L Prévost (Delhi: Indira Gandhi National Centre for the Arts, 1990), 8–9. The same letter appears in Romain Rolland, *Un beau visage à tous sens: Choix de lettres de Romain Rolland (1866–1944)* (Cahier 17; Paris: Michel Albin, 1967), 150.

63. Romain Rolland, *Clerambault: The Story of an Independent Spirit during the War* (New York: Holt, 1921), vi.

64. Ibid. 33.

65. See the letter to Romain Rolland from Ellen Key (16 May 1915) repr. in Romain Rolland, *Journal des années de guerre, 1914–1919* (Paris: Michel Albin, 1952), 368.

66. Evelyn Sharp, 'The Congress and the Press', *Towards Peace and Freedom, The Women's International Congress, Zurich, May 12–17, 1919*, 22–3.

67. Helen Addams, *Newer Ideals of Peace* (London: Macmillan, 1907), 3.

68. Ibid. 4. This phrase may reprise the thought of Bertha von Suttner, the Austrian writer and activist, who, in her Nobel lecture the year previously (18 April 1906), had insisted that the cause of peace was no longer lost in 'the fog of pious theories'.

69. Ibid. 5.

70. George Bernard Shaw, 'A Political Contrast', *The Nation* (18 September 1920), 758–9. Shaw had been under attack as a 'traitor' since the appearance of his 'Common Sense About the War', published as a special supplement of the *New Statesman* on 14 November 1914.

71. Addams, *Newer Ideals*, 13, 17, 8.

72. Ibid. 18.

73. Mrs St Clair Stobart, *War and Women: From Experience in the Balkans and Elsewhere* (London: Bell, 1913), 84–5. Stobart's words are quoted in 'A Letter from Miss Emily Hobhouse, London, England, December 20th, 1914', addressed 'To American Women, Friends of Humanity and Peace' and published by the Women's Peace Party in 1915. A copy of the latter can be found in a box file entitled 'Lilian Silk Holt papers' in the Labadie Collection, University of Michigan Library, Ann Arbor.

74. T. P. Conwell-Evans, *Foreign Policy from a Back Bench 1904–1918: A Study Based on the Papers of Lord Noel-Buxton* (Oxford: Oxford University Press, 1932), 40.

75. Ibid. 37.

76. Vernon Lee, 'The Lines of Anglo-German Agreement', *The Nation*, 10 September 1910 (suppl.).

77. Vernon Lee, 'The Sense of Nationality', *The Nation*, 12 October 1912, 97.

78. Roy Jenkins, *Churchill* (London: Pan, 2002), 97.

79. 'Mr. Churchill at Swansea', *The Times*, 17 August 1908, 7.

80. Churchill, quoted in Jenkins, *Churchill*, 152.

81. J. Jemnitz, *The Danger of War and the Second International (1911)* (Budapest: Akadémiai Kiadó, 1972), 22.

82. Randolph S. Churchill, *Winston S. Churchill, ii. Young Statesman 1901–1914* (London: Heinemann, 1967).

83. Jenkins, *Churchill*, 186, 198–9.

84. George Dangerfield, *The Strange Death of Liberal England* (London: Constable, 1936), 87.

85. Lee, 'Lines of Anglo-German Agreement'. Brentano's arguments were made in the wake of the 'Declaration of London' (1909) which contained the conclusions of a ten-state conference that had met in London in 1908, with the purpose of reviewing the definition of contraband and the legitimacy or otherwise of captures at sea.

86. Charles Callan Tansill, *America Goes to War* (Boston: Little, Brown and Co., 1942), 135.

87. Vernon Lee, 'Germany and the Naval Holiday', *The Nation*, 15 November 1913, 322–3.

88. Keith Robbins, *The Abolition of War: The 'Peace Movement' in Britain, 1914–1919* (Cardiff: University of Wales Press, 1976), 25.

89. Vernon Lee, 'Germany and the Right of Capture' (letter), *The Nation*, 29 November 1913, 394. Lee recalled her earlier supplement on Brentano in 'Germany and the Naval Holiday', 322–3.

90. Norman Angell, *Europe's Optical Illusion* (London: Simpkin, Marshall, Hamilton, Kent & Co., 1909), 112, 43. The expanded edition of this book was entitled *The Great Illusion*. First published in 1910, it went on to sell over 2 million copies in twenty-five languages, and to form the basis of a considerable anti-war movement known as 'Norman Angellism'.

91. Ibid. 43.

92. Ibid. 47.

93. Ibid. 25.

94. Ibid. 117.

95. Ibid. 108.

CHAPTER 6 THE BELGIAN VARIATION

1. Alex Vanneste, 'Le Premier "Rideau de fer"? La Clôture électrisé à la frontière belgo-hollandaise pendant la Première Guerre mondiale', *Bulletin de Dexia Banque*, 54/4 (2000), 39–82.

2. Ibid. 43.

3. H. W. Massingham, 'Why We Came to Help Belgium', *The Nation*, 3 October 1914, 11.

4. Émile Cammaerts, *Through the Iron Bars: Two Years of German occupation in Belgium,* illustrated with cartoons by Louis Raemakers (London: John Lane, 1917), 72.

5. Pierre Loti, *Siam* (London: Laurie, 1913), 177.

6. Pierre Loti, 'Two Poor Little Belgian Fledglings', in *King Albert's Book: A Tribute to the Belgian King and People from Representative Men and Women throughout the World* (London: Hodder & Stoughton (for the *Daily Telegraph*), 1914), 31.

7. Pierre Loti, *War* (Philadelphia and London: Lippincott, 1917), 71, 83.

8. Ibid. 118.

9. Ibid. 125.

10. Ibid. 124.

11. Ibid. 126.

12. Loti, 'Some Words Uttered by Her Majesty, the Queen of the Belgians', in *War,* 127.

13. Ibid. 130.

14. Colonel Repington, *The First World War 1914–1918: Personal Experiences of Lieutenant Colonel C. À Court Repington* (Boston and New York: Houghton Mifflin, 1920), i. 33.

15. *The Memoirs of Raymond Poincaré, 1914,* trans. Sir George Arthur (London: Heinemann, 1929), 227.

16. Loti, *War,* 132–3.

17. Georges-H. Dumont, entry on Elisabeth in *Nouvelle Biographie nationale,* i (Brussels: Académie royale des sciences, des lettres et des beaux-arts de Belgique, 1988), 80.

18. *King Albert's Book,* 136.

19. Ibid. 138.

20. Sidney Cuncliffe-Owen, *Elisabeth, Queen of the Belgians* (London: Herbert Jenkins, 1954), 76–7.

21. H. N. Brailsford, *Across the Blockade: A Record of Travels in Enemy Europe* (London: Allen & Unwin, 1919), 61.

22. *King Albert's Book*, 138.

23. Conversation with M. Klobukowski recorded in *Memoirs of Raymond Poincaré*, trans. Arthur, 124.

24. Loti, *War*, 155.

25. Émile Cammaerts, *Albert of Belgium: Defender of Right* (London: Nicholson and Watson, 1935), 176–7.

26. Loti, *War*, 138.

27. Alison Nicholas, *Elisabeth, Queen of the Belgians: Her Life and Times* (Bognor Regis: New Horizon, 1982), 74–5.

28. Cuncliffe-Owen, *Elisabeth, Queen of the Belgians*, 89.

29. 'Belgian Women's Patriotic Union', *Jus Suffragii*, 1 March 1915, 247.

30. Nicholas, *Elisabeth, Queen of the Belgians*, 256, 264.

31. Romain Rolland, *Above the Battle* (London: Allen & Unwin, 1916), 21.

32. *King Albert's Book*, 107–8.

33. Romain Rolland, letter to his mother, Sunday, 10 January 1915, in Romain Rolland, *Je commence à devenir dangereux: Choix de lettres de Romain Rolland à sa mère (1914–1916)* (Cahiers 20; Paris: Michel Albin, 1971), 71.

34. Maurice des Ombiaux, *La Reine Elisabeth* (Paris: Bloud & Gay, 1915).

35. Ibid. 23–6.

36. Ibid. 39.

37. Ibid. 43–4.

38. Ibid. 59.

39. Marie José, *Albert et Elisabeth de Belgique: Mes parents* (Paris: Plon, 1971), 297.

40. Raymond Poincaré, *Au service de la France: Neuf années de souvenirs*, ix. *L'Année trouble 1917* (Paris: Librairie Plon, 1932), 208.

41. Cuncliffe-Owen, *Elisabeth, Queen of the Belgians*, 88.

CHAPTER 7 IN DEFENCE OF OTHERNESS

1. Douglas Goldring, *Odd Man Out: The Autobiography of a 'Propaganda Novelist'*, (London: Chapman and Hall, 1935), 334.

2. See E. D. Morel, '"What will ye do in the end thereof?"; a speech given at a public meeting in the Friends' Meeting House, Manchester, 17 December 1914'; repr. in E. D. Morel, *Truth and the War* (London: National Labour Press, 1916), 43.

3. Ibid. 169.

4. Ibid. xv.

5. H. M. Swanwick, *Builders of Peace: Being Ten Years' History of the Union of Democratic Control* (London: Swarthmore Press, 1924), 52, 100.

6. See Blanche Wiesen Cook's 'Introduction', in Randolph S. Bourne, *Towards an Enduring Peace: A Symposium of Peace Proposals and Programs 1914–1916* (New York and London: Garland Publishing, 1971), 5.

7. Walter Lippmann, 'The Future of Patriotism' (extract from Lippmann's *States of Diplomacy*), ibid. 217–220.

8. Henry Ford, letter dated 27 November 1915, from Suite 717, Hotel Biltmore, New York. On 11 December, not long after the *Oscar II* sailed from New York, Ford issued a statement apologizing to those of his guests who felt 'steamrollered' by measures he had taken to establish a common platform on which the delegation would act. By early 1916, the 'crusade' had settled in Stockholm, where Ford, having himself speedily returned to America shortly after the ship reached Europe, left his managers to fund and forcefully reform a 'Neutral Conference for Continuous Mediation' that had been established earlier by the Hungarian-born feminist and peace activist Rosika Schwimmer. Relationships were very poor. According to Dr Charles Frederick Aked, a once radical British preacher who had joined the Conference as an American delegate from San Francisco, Schwimmer was an 'evil-minded woman' surrounded by idolizing sycophants, who did everything in her power to wreck Ford's attempts to create a credible and also much smaller organization over which she had no influence. He urged Ford's representative, Mr Frederick Holt of Michigan, to 'Read their speeches—the attacks on you; the sneers about Mr. Ford, the references to American money and American intrigues, their Socialist rant about the evils of capital and the capitalist, etc.' He was in no doubt that the reorganization of the conference, which Ford and his staff wished to limit to one representative member per country, must be dictated as a matter of 'arrangement' not 'election'. In a later memo, of 20 April, Dr Aked described working for the conference as 'a heart-breaking experience … The business has been to prevent the doctrinaires and wild theorists doing something idiotic which would close against us the door of every Foreign Office in Europe and make our work impossible. We have been seriously asked by members to demand of the United States the independence of the Philippines, of Great Britain the independence of India and Egypt, and of Russia the independence of Finland. We have been forced to discuss the affairs of Tonkin, Georgia, Persia, Madagascar, Cochin China. We have been asked to stand for Free Trade over all the earth, Socialism and a universal language. All these matters we have had presented to us in formal Resolution. We have spent whole days in debate upon them before succeeding in voting them down by majorities. And ill feeling has been growing all the time between the doctrinaires who could not get their crack-brain theories exploited by the Conference and those of us who could not restrain our indignation aroused by such follies.' These documents are quoted from the Frederick and Lilian Holt Peace Expedition Papers 1915–17, the Labadie

Collection, Special Collections Library, University of Michigan, Ann Arbor. See also Burnet Hershel, *The Odyssey of Henry Ford and the Great Peace Ship* (New York: Taplinger, 1967).

9. G. Lowes Dickinson, *The War and the Way Out* (2nd edn., London: Chancery Lane Press, n.d. [?1914]), 9.

10. This phrase appears throughout Bourne's unfinished essay 'The State'. See *War and the Intellectuals: Essays by Randolph S. Bourne 1915–1919*, ed. Carl Resek (New York and London: Harper, 1964), 69, 71. Bourne died in the influenza epidemic of 1919, but his description of war as 'the health of the state' was reiterated by John Dos Passos, who quoted it in *Nineteen Nineteen* (1932), the first novel of his trilogy *U.S.A.* (Harmondsworth: Penguin, 1966), 425.

11. E. D. Morel, 'An Appeal to President Wilson' (written in May 1915 and published in the *New York Tribune,* 4 July 1915). Quoted from Morel's *Truth and the War,* 120.

12. E. M. Forster, *Goldsworthy Lowes Dickinson* (London: Arnold, 1934), 163–4.

13. Evelyn Sharp, 'Women Voters and the Red Flag', a leaflet published by the Women's International League, *c.* 1919 (British Library, WP 3968). The younger sister of the folk song collector Cecil Sharp, and a journalist with the *Manchester Guardian,* Evelyn Sharp had twice been jailed as a militant suffragette and member of the Women's Social and Political Union. The secret diplomacy she opposed was represented by various 'assurances' provided by the Liberal Foreign Secretary Sir Edward Grey to the French military and naval staffs from 1906 onwards. These agreements, which included a detailed account of the British expeditionary force to be sent to France in the event of German attack, were unknown to Parliament until the day before war was declared. For an account of Grey's 'assurances' and also of the lies with which their secrecy was maintained by Asquith, Grey, and others, see 'The Tied Hands of Parliament', in T. P. Conwell-Evans, *Foreign Policy from a Back Bench 1904–1918: A Study Based on the Papers of Lord Noel-Buxton* (Oxford: Oxford University Press, 1932), 176–80. Writing in the *Labour Leader,* on 13 August 1914, Ramsay MacDonald described how Germany's bid for British neutrality had been rendered futile by Sir Edward Grey's secret alliances: 'The hard, immovable fact was that Sir Edward Grey had so pledged the country's honour, without the country's knowledge, to fight for France, and Russia, that he was not in a position even to discuss neutrality.' Quoted in Douglas Goldring, *Pacifists in Peace and War* (The Here & Now Pamphlets, no. 1; 1932), London: Wishart, 10.

14. Goldring, *Pacifists in Peace and War,* 33.

15. W. H. Dawson, 'Three Stages of Chauvinism', *The Times,* 2 January 1915, 6.

16. Clifford Allbutt, 'The Type of Self-Culture', *The Times,* 8 January 1915, 9.

17. Charles Roden Buxton, 'Why Not Find Out?', *UDC* 1/1 (November 1915). Buxton was among the funders rather than founders of the UDC, providing

salaries for some of its paid officers with income from his shares in the Truman, Hanbury, and Buxton brewery in Brick Lane, East London.

18. Buxton's experience is implied in the title of his pamphlet, *A Practical, Permanent and Honourable Settlement of the War: Lectures intended to be delivered at Devonshire House, Bishopsgate, London, E.C., on January 3rd 10th, and 17th, 1916* (National Labour Press, 1916). These lectures were also published under the title 'Shouted Down', after an orchestrated campaign of interruption made their conventional delivery impossible. CR Buxton Papers at Rhodes House, Oxford, MSS: Brit. Emp. S 405, Box 4. The pamphlet was prefaced with the following quotation from the *Daily Mail:* 'Pandemonium reigned at the Friends' Meeting House, Bishopsgate, yesterday, when Mr. C. Roden Buxton gave, or rather attempted to give an address on after-war problems. ... Mr Richard Glover of the Anti-German Union, kept up a fire of interruption. ... Mr Glover: You preach pro-Germanism under the cloak of religion. I have heard him speak before, and he ought to be hanged by the neck until he is dead.'

19. Vernon Lee, 'The Democratic Principle and International Relations', in C. R. Buxton (ed.), *Towards a Lasting Settlement* (London: Allen & Unwin, 1915), 203–16. Also Vernon Lee, *Peace with Honour: Controversial Notes on the Settlement* (London: UDC, 6d. series, no. 1; (1915).

20. Frank Swinnerton, quoted in Vinetta Colby, *Vernon Lee: A Literary Biography* (Charlottesville: University of Virginia Press, 2003), 294. In the early weeks of the war, the phrase 'white heater' was used by more moderate members of the new Union of Democratic Control to disparage those who, like Lee and her young friend Irene Cooper Willis, were ardently and explicitly opposed to the war. See Irene Cooper Willis, letter to Vernon Lee, 5 October 1914, Special Collections, Colby College, Maine.

21. Forster, *Goldsworthy Lowes Dickinson*, 159–60.

22. Vernon Lee, *Satan the Waster: A Philosophic War Trilogy with Notes & Introduction* (London: Bodley Head, 1920), 67.

23. Ibid. 103, 96.

24. Ibid. 102.

25. Ibid. 72.

26. Ibid. 298.

27. Writing in *The Nation*, Lee's fellow pacifist George Bernard Shaw hailed this strange and brilliant literary hybrid as 'a trophy of the war for England' and saluted Lee for 'holding her intellectual own' as 'the old guard of Victorian cosmopolitan intellectualism'. See George Bernard Shaw, 'A Political Contrast', *The Nation*, 18 September 1920, 758–9. When reissuing unsold copies ten years later, Lee would claim, in a new preface, that the book was 'boycotted' by other reviewers and sold only in negligible numbers. It would not be until the late 1920s that many British readers were prepared to confront the 'waste' of war, and even then they preferred books by veterans such

as Sassoon, Aldington, and Graves, and also English translations of Jünger, Zweig, and Remarque.

28. Colby, *Vernon Lee*, 305.

29. See Sybil Oldfield's entry on Caroline Elizabeth Playne, *Oxford Dictionary of National Biography*, vol. xliv (Oxford: Oxford University Press, 2004), 571–2.

30. Lee, *Satan the Waster*, ix.

31. Ibid. 298.

32. Ibid. 299.

33. Ibid. xviii.

34. Ibid. 293.

35. Ibid.

36. Ibid. xvii.

37. Ibid. 249. A glance here, perhaps, in the direction of Goldsworthy Lowes Dickinson, whom Lee described as 'wrinkled with scruples', after he had listened in noncommittal silence to her ranting against the Allies' pursuit of the war. Colby, *Vernon Lee*, 294.

38. Lee, *Satan the Waster*, xlviii.

39. Ibid. xxxviii.

40. Ibid. xxxiii.

41. Ibid. xxviii.

42. Ibid. xxxviii.

43. Ibid. xxvii.

44. Ibid. 234.

45. Victoria de Bunsen, *The War and Men's Minds* (London: Bodley Head, 1919), 158.

46. Lee, *Satan the Waster*, 68.

47. Ibid. 45.

48. Ibid. 46.

49. Caroline E. Playne, *Society at War 1914–1916* (London: Allen & Unwin, 1931), 15.

50. Vernon Lee, 'The Sense of Nationalism', *The Nation*, 12 October 1912. Quoted in Colby, *Vernon Lee*, 288.

51. Caroline E. Playne, *Britain Holds On: 1917, 1918* (London: Allen & Unwin, 1933), 8.

52. Caroline E. Playne, *The Pre-War Mind in Britain: An Historical Review* (London: Allen & Unwin, 1928), 21.

53. C. E. Playne, *The Neuroses of the Nations* (London: Allen & Unwin, 1925).

54. Playne, *Pre-War Mind in Britain*, 19.

55. Ibid. 31.

56. Playne, *Neuroses of the Nations*, 35.

57. Ibid. 22.

58. Ibid. 19.

59. Irene Cooper Willis, 'Vernon Lee', *The Times*, 16 February 1935, 17.

60. Irene Cooper Willis, *England's Holy War: A Study of English Liberal Idealism during the Great War* (New York: Knopf, 1928), 136. Irene Cooper Willis first

published her analysis of the war in three separate volumes, *How We Went into the War* and *How We Got On with the War,* issued by the National Labour Press (Manchester) in 1919 and 1920 respectively. *How We Came Out of the War* was published by International Bookshops Ltd in 1921. The combined Knopf edition was dedicated to Vernon Lee, with whom Willis shared many of her concerns, including association with the UDC.

61. *Daily News*, 5 August 1914. Quoted in Willis, *England's Holy War*, 87.

62. *The Nation*, 22 August 1914, 765.

63. Willis, *England's Holy War*, 87.

64. Ibid. 135.

65. Ibid. 86.

66. Ibid. 104.

67. *The Nation*, 8 August 1914. Quoted in Willis, *England's Holy War*, 102.

68. *Daily News*, 8 August 1914. Quoted ibid. 87.

69. For Lee's letter to *The Nation* (17 September 1914), see Colby, *Vernon Lee*, 289–90.

70. H. G. Wells is quoted from 'The Sword of Peace' (*Daily Chronicle*, 7 August 1914) and 'The War to End War (*Daily News*, 14 August 1914). See Willis, *England's Holy War*, 90, 88.

71. H. G. Wells in *The Nation*, 29 August 1914. Quoted in Willis, ibid. 96.

72. Ibid. 100–1.

73. Lee, *Peace with Honour*, 2.

74. Ibid. 162.

75. Lee, *Satan the Waster*, xxvi.

76. Ibid. 96.

77. Lee refers to the fictional sea-coast of Bohemia, invented by Shakespeare in *The Winter's Tale* (Act 3 Scene 3). She also shows statesman in various international council chambers demanding re-establishment of the empires of Ziska and the Queen of Sheba, and the kingdoms of Ladislaus, Borislaus, Mithridates, and Tiridates too. *Satan the Waster*, 102–3.

78. Ibid. 296.

79. Ibid. 212.

80. Vernon Lee, 'A Postscript on Mr Wells, *Albany Review*, 2 (October 1907 – March 1908), 173.

81. Lee, *Satan the Waster*, 215.

82. Ibid. 134.

83. E. D. Morel, 'Denials and Avowals' (*Labour Leader*, 3 December 1914), repr. in Morel's *Truth and the War*, 39.

84. De Bunsen, *The War and Men's Minds*, 166.

85. Lee, *Peace with Honour*, 21.

86. Ibid. 26.

87. Lee, *Satan the Waster*, 136.

88. Ibid. 10.

89. Willis, *England's Holy War*, 132.

90. Lee, *Satan the Waster*, 95.

91. Arthur Ponsonby MP, *Falsehood in War-Time: An Amazing Collection of Carefully Documented Lies Circulated in Great Britain, France, Germany, Italy and America during the Great War* (London: Allen & Unwin, 1928), 14. For a wartime expression of this argument, see Arthur Ponsonby, 'First Class Lies', *UDC* 2 (11 September 1917).

92. Ponsonby, *Falsehood in War-Time*, 167.

93. Ibid. 128.

94. Lee, *Satan the Waster*, 95–6.

95. *Daily Express*, 21 April 1917. This extract stands as item 41 in Hamish Miles, *A War Museum 1914–1918* (Here & Now Pamphlets, no. 2; London, Wishart, 1972), 33–4.

96. In truth about an eighth of the town was badly damaged, but Louvain was certainly not completely and systematically wiped from the map. It later emerged that the famous altarpiece in St Peter's church, a fifteenth-century *Last Supper* by Dirk Bouts, which was said to have been deliberately thrown into the flames of the burning library, had actually been saved by a German officer and handed to the Burgomeister. See Ponsonby, *Falsehood in War-Time*, 83.

97. Ibid. 14.

98. Ibid. 25, 15.

99. Leonard Woolf, *International Government: Two Reports by L. S. Woolf Prepared for the Fabian Research Department, Together with a Project by a Fabian Committee for a Supernational Authority that will Prevent War* (London: Fabian Society, 1916), 28.

100. Ibid. 222.

101. Ibid. 218–19.

102. Ibid. 224.

103. Goldsworthy Lowes Dickinson, 'The Basis of Permanent Peace', in C. R. Buxton (ed.), *Towards a Lasting Settlement*, 22–3.

104. Philip Snowden MP, 'Introduction' to Morel, *Truth and the War*, vii.

105. Playne, *Pre-War Mind in Britain*, 35.

106. Vernon Lee, 'The Sense of Nationality', *The Nation*, 12 October 1912, 97.

107. Vernon Lee, *Satan the Waster*, 243–4.

108. Romain Rolland, *Clerambault: The Story of an Independent Spirit during the War* (New York: Holt, 1921), 206, 56–7.

109. Ibid. 254.

110. Ibid. vi, v, 254.

111. As Ford remarked during the interview in which he made his famous utterance, 'The men who are responsible for the present war in Europe know all about history. Yet they brought on the worst war in the world's history.' See 'Fight to disarm his life's work, says Ford; Pacifist sees Submarines as Powerful Agency to Destroy All Armament', *Chicago Daily Tribune*, 25 May 1916, 10.

112. Vernon Lee, The Narthex of Vézelay', *The Golden Keys* (London: John Lane, 1925), 169.
113. Lee, *Satan the Waster*, 219.
114. Ibid. 220.
115. Ibid. 222.
116. Ibid. 123.
117. Ibid. 222.
118. Lee, *Peace with Honour*, 22.
119. Lee, *Satan the Waster*, 224.
120. Ibid. 252.
121. Ibid. 124.
122. Ibid. 256.
123. Playne, *Pre-War Mind in Britain*, 29.
124. Lee, *Satan the Waster*, 243–4.
125. Ibid. 23.
126. Ibid. 51.
127. Ibid. 49.
128. Ibid. 35.
129. Ibid. 38.
130. Lee, *Peace with Honour*, 58.
131. Lee, *Satan the Waster*, 41.
132. Ibid. 50.
133. Ibid. 57, 62.
134. Ibid. vii.
135. Ibid. 234.
136. Ibid. 127.
137. Vernon Lee, 'Shall Prussia Restore the Tsar?', *UDC* 2/12 (October 1917), 145–6.
138. Lee, *Satan the Waster*, 101–2.
139. Ibid. 234.

CHAPTER 8 FIRST DELEGATION

1. 'The King's Ten Days in France; Visit to Messines and Vimy', *The Times*, 16 July 1917, 7.
2. Ben Turner, *About Myself 1863–1930* (London: Humphrey Toulmin, 1930), 211.
3. 'Mission Starts for Soviet Russia', *Daily Herald,* 28 April 1920. For a useful account of the British Labour Delegation, and a record of other sources, see Stephen White, 'British Labour in Soviet Russia, 1920', *English Historical Review*, 109/432 (June 1994), 621–40.
4. The Bolsheviks had previously refused to accept a delegation from the new League of Nations, considering this international body to be nothing more

than a French and British alliance, and therefore part of the continuing war against Russia. Allied delegations of Social Patriots had visited Russia after the February Revolution brought Lvov to power. They were sent by governments concerned to persuade Russia to step up its efforts in the war against the common German enemy. March/April 1917 brought a French delegation selected from the French socialist party Section Française de l'Internationale Ouvrière (SFIO) and consisting of Marcel Cachin, Marius Moutet, and Ernest Lafont; and also a delegation of three representatives of the majority pro-war position within the British Labour Party, consisting of William Sanders, Will Thorne, and James O'Grady. See Arno J. Mayer, *Political Origins of the New Diplomacy* (New Haven: Yale University Press, 1959), 85–9.

5. Leslie Haden Guest would describe the delegation as 'the first responsible body of men and women to officially break the information blockade of Russia, very little being known of the practice of Bolshevism at that time'. See his *The Struggle for Power in Europe 1917–1921: An Outline Economic and Political Survey of the Central States and Russia* (London: Hodder and Stoughton, 1921), 41.

6. British Labour Delegation to Russia 1920, *Report* (London: Trades Union Congress and Labour Party, 1920), 5.

7. V. I. Lenin, 'Speech at Conference of Workers and Red Army Men in Rogozhsko-Simonovsky District of Moscow, May 13, 1920', in *Collected Works*, (4th English edn., Moscow: Progress Publishers, 1965), xxxi. 136–7.

8. Haden Guest, *Struggle for Power in Europe 1917–1921*, 10. Between 1919 and 1921, Haden Guest would visit Austria, Czecho-Slovakia, Poland, Hungary, Romania, and also Bulgaria, where he would be much impressed by the peasant-centred 'Green Communism' (p. 247) emerging under the soon-to-be-assassinated premier, M. Stamboulisky.

9. Mrs Philip Snowden, *A Political Pilgrim in Europe* (London: Cassell, 1921), xii.

10. Charles Roden Buxton, 'Two Months in Soviet Russia' (typescript, 1920). One of the articles drawn from this typescript appeared as 'Tyranny and Bolshevism', *Daily Herald,* 3 September 1920.

11. See *British Labour and the Russian Revolution: The Leeds Convention: A Report from the Daily Herald* (London: Pelikan Press), June 1917.

12. Mrs Snowden, *Political Pilgrim in Europe*, 130.

13. Ibid. 130–1.

14. 'ILP and Moscow International', *The Times*, 6 April 1920, 14.

15. Robert Williams, *Impressions of Soviet Russia* (Amsterdam: International Transportworkers Federation, 1920) (unpaginated).

16. Martin Gilbert, *Winston S. Churchill*, iv. *1917–1922* (London: Heinemann, 1975), 349.

17. Mrs Snowden, *Political Pilgrim in Europe*, 2–3.

18. Ibid. 19.

19. Evelyn Sharp, *Unfinished Adventure: Selected Reminiscences from an Englishwoman's Life* (London: Bodley Head, 1933), 161.

20. Mrs Snowden, *Political Pilgrim in Europe*, 76.

21. Merle Fainsod, *International Socialism and the World War* (Cambridge, Mass.: Harvard University Press, 1935), 66. See also Angelica Balabanoff [Balabanova], *My Life as a Rebel* (London: Hamish Hamilton, 1938), 155.

22. Ibid. 133.

23. Philip Snowden, speaking in the House of Commons, 16 May 1917. Hansard, 5th ser., *Parliamentary Debates*, vol. 93, col. 1635.

24. Mayer, *Political Origins of the New Diplomacy*, 228.

25. House of Commons, 16 May 1917. Hansard, *Parliamentary Debates*, 5th ser., vol. 93, cols. 1652–3. See also Mayer, *Political Origins of the New Diplomacy*, 199.

26. *Daily Herald*, 3 May 1920.

27. Gilbert, *Churchill*, iv. *1917–1922, 395.*

28. Victor Madeira '"Because I Don't Trust Him, We Are Friends": Signals Intelligence and the Reluctant Anglo-Soviet Embrace, 1917–1924', *Intelligence and National Security*, 19/1 (Spring 2004), 35.

29. 'Meeting of Southend Labour Party', *Southend Standard*, 3 April 1919, 10. In the same address, Lansbury had declared that the lack of socialist newspapers in Britain 'went side by side with a widespread lack of belief in the Bible. Love was a great thing to cultivate'.

30. George Lansbury, *Daily Herald*, 11 February 1920. Quoted in W. P and Zelda K. Coates, *A History of Anglo-Soviet Relations* (London: Lawrence & Wishart, 1943), 18.

31. George Lansbury, *What I Saw in Russia* (London: Leonard Parsons, June 1920), xv.

32. *The Times,* 18 February 1920, 13. Founded in January 1920, the Christian Counter Bolshevist Crusade campaigned against the idea that Bolshevism was in any way an embodiment of Christian values. See 'The Church and Russia', *The Times*, 16 August 1920.

33. *Daily Herald,* 28 April 1920.

34. Lloyd George spoke these words in his famous 'Guildhall Speech' of 8 November 1919. See W. P. and Z. K. Coates, *History of Anglo-Soviet Relations,* 2.

35. Churchill to Lloyd George, 26 August 1920. See Anthony Heywood, *Modernising Lenin's Russia: Economic Reconstruction, Foreign Trade and the Railways* (Cambridge: Cambridge University Press, 1999), 116–17. For the letter itself, see the Churchill Papers (Churchill College Archives Centre, Cambridge), CHAR 2/110/157.

36. *Manchester Guardian*, 1 June 1920. Quoted in W. P and Z. K. Coates, *History of Anglo-Soviet Relations*, 26.

37. 'World-Wide May Day Plot. Sensational Statement by U.S. Minister', *Daily News*, 16 April 1920.

38. 'Murder Plot in USA', *Morning Post*, 1 May 1920.

39. E. B. Osborne, 'Certain American Poets', *Morning Post*, 28 May 1920.

40. 'Communist Orator Stabbed. Judge on Bolshevism', *The Times* 13 May 1920, 11. For a different version, see '"Justice" for Communist', *Daily Herald*, 13 May 1920, 5.

41. 'Labour Delegates for Russia; Faith in the Soviet', *The Times*, 6 May 1920, 15. The 'Herr Ströan' here named as leader of Sweden's independent socialists is likely to be Frederick Strom, who was head of Sweden's left Socialist Party. See Clare Sheridan, *Russian Portraits* (London: Cape, 1921), 37.

42. *The Times*, 19 April 1920.

43. 'Labour Delegates for Russia; Faith in the Soviet', *The Times*, 6 May 1920.

44. N. N. Sukhanov, *The Russian Revolution 1917: A Personal Record* (Oxford: Oxford University Press, 1955), 61.

45. Fainsod, *International Socialism and the World War*, 130. Mayer records that Petrograd Soviet had been forewarned about the British and French delegations in telegrams sent by the British ILP and the French minority socialists (*Political Origins of the New Diplomacy*, 87).

46. Sukhanov, *Russian Revolution 1917*, 263. See also Mayer, *Political Origins of the New Diplomacy*, 88.

47. G. Terrell, speaking in the House of Commons on 11 June 1917. Hansard, *Parliamentary Debate*, 5th ser., vol. 94, col. 700. MacDonald and his ILP comrades did not make the trip to Russia, thanks to the British Seamen's Union, which barred the passage of these anti-war figures.

48. Halford J. Mackinder, in the House of Commons, 11 June 1917. Hansard, *Parliamentary Debates*, vol. 94, col. 727.

49. Ibid., col. 726.

50. Ibid., col. 728.

51. See Frans de Bruyn, *The Literary Genres of Edmund Burke: The Political Uses of Literary Form* (Oxford: Clarendon Press, 1996), 165–6.

52. For an account, and also a repudiation of this legend, which is traced back to the accusations of George von Helbig, a Saxon envoy who was not on Catherine the Great's barge for the 1787 trip along the Dnieper, see Simon Sebag Montefiore, *Prince of Princes: The Life of Potemkin* (London: Weidenfeld & Nicolson, 2000), 379–83.

53. See e.g. Lev Manovich, *The Language of New Media* (Cambridge, Mass.: MIT Press, 2001), 145–8. See also Norman N. Klein, *The Vatican to Vegas: A History of Special Effects* (New York and London: Free Press, 2004), 131.

54. See 'The Crimea and Southern Russia', *The Times*, 28 December 1855, 4. As Prince Anatole de Demidoff had written of Odessa, 'All that part which faces the shore wears an appearance of grandeur and opulence'. M. Anatole de Demidoff, *Travels in Southern Russia and the Crimea* (1839; London: John Mitchell, 1853), 290–1.

55. Stephen F. Cohen, *Bukharin and the Bolshevik Revolution: A Political Biography, 1888–1938* (Oxford: Oxford University Press, 1980), 375.

56. Nikolai Bukharin, *How It All Began* (New York: Columbia University Press, 1998), 276. For a contemporary report of this meeting at Reval see 'The Tsar and the Kaiser', *The Times*, 7 August 1902.

57. Leo Tolstoy, *War and Peace*, tr. Rosemary Edmonds (London: Penguin, 1982), 441–5.

58. Quoted from 'The Overcoat' and 'Nevsky Prospect'. See Nikolai Vasilyevich Gogol, *Petersburg Tales, Marriage, The Government Inspector,* tr. and ed. Christopher English (Oxford: Oxford University Press, 1995), 117, 3, 36.

59. Oswald W. Firkins, 'The Cult of the Passing Hour', *Atlantic Monthly,* May 1914. Quoted from Stuart Ewen, *PR! A Social History of Spin* (New York: Basic Books, 1996), 72.

60. George Abel Schreiner, *The Iron Ration: Three Years in Central Europe* (New York and London: Harper, 1918), 10.

61. Solomon J. Solomon, *Strategic Camouflage* (London: John Murray, 1920), 1. For a more detailed account of Solomon's project see my 'Cubist Slugs', *London Review of Books,* 27/12 (23 June 2005), 16–20.

62. Solomon, *Strategic Camouflage,* 53.

63. Guy Hartcup, *Camouflage: A History of Concealment and Deception in War* (Newton Abbott: David & Charles, 1979), 17.

64. Solomon, *Strategic Camouflage,* 28.

65. Olga Somech Phillips, *Solomon J. Solomon: A Memoir of Peace and War* (London: Herbert Joseph, 1933), 128.

66. Solomon, *Strategic Camouflage,* 9.

67. Ibid. 13.

68. Solomon, 'The Secret of German Camouflage', *World's Work* (April 1920), 455.

69. Ibid. 456.

70. Ibid.

71. Solomon J. Solomon, letter to the editor of the *Times Literary Supplement,* in reply to critical review of *Strategic Camouflage,* quoted in Phillips, *Solomon J. Solomon,* 205–8.

72. 'Strategic Camouflage', *Times Literary Supplement,* 6 May 1920, 279.

73. 'Camouflage. Col. Solomon's "Fantastic Ideas"', *Morning Post,* 28 May 1920, 3.

74. For an English translation of the review from *Das Technische Blatt,* see Philips, *Solomon J. Solomon,* 179–80.

75. Lieutenant-Colonel C. Holmes Wilson, letter to the editor, *Irish Times,* 29 October 1920.

76. H. G. Wells, *Russia in the Shadows* (London: Hodder & Stoughton, 1920), 10.

77. James H. Baum, Secretary of Leicester and District Trades Council, letter to Winston Churchill, 27 August 1920, Churchill Papers, CHAR 2/110/166.

78. Annie Kriegel, *Le Congrès de Tours (1920): Naissance du Parti communiste français* (Archives, No. 7; Paris: Gallimard-Julliard, 1984), 49–50.

79. '"Lord Lansbury"', *Morning Post,* 21 April 1920, 6.

80. George Lansbury, '"Lord Lansbury" in Moscow', *Morning Post,* 22 April 1920, 6.

81. Albert V. Frank, *Morning Post,* 26 April 1920.

82. Albert V. Frank, '"Lord" Lansbury in Moscow', *Morning Post,* 28 April 1920.

83. '"Lord" Lansbury and Moscow', *Morning Post,* 17 May 1920, 6. The debate took place on Saturday 12 June. Both the speakers and the chairman, the Revd.

F. W. North (the recently repatriated vicar of Moscow), assailed Lansbury in his absence, pointing out his 'dependence' while in Moscow, on 'A Jew Commissar named Fineberg', offering highly critical accounts of the Bolsheviks' assault on the church, and describing the hideous conditions in their jails. Their testimony on this latter matter prompted the *Morning Post* to declare 'The facts are too revolting for reproduction' ('Mr. Lansbury Given the "Lie Direct"', *Morning Post*, 14 June 1920, 7).

84. 'British Refugees', *Morning Post*, 28 April 1920.

85. 'The Lansbury Challenge, *Morning Post*, 3 June 1920.

86. 'Mr. Lansbury given the "Lie Direct"', 7.

87. *The Times*, 6 May 1920, 15.

88. Turner's second denial appeared as 'What We Saw in Russia, by Ben Turner' in the *Labour Leader*, 17 June 1920, 1. It is quoted in 'What They Saw in Russia: Mr. Ben Turner on the "Red Terror"', *Morning Post*, 18 June 1920.

89. 'Delegation to Russia: Labour Mission's Departure for Russia', *Daily News*, 28 April 1920, 2.

90. Mrs Philip Snowden, *Through Bolshevik Russia* (London: Cassell, 1920), 23.

91. 'Russian Silence Broken', *Morning Post*, 17 May 1920, 7.

92. Mrs Snowden, *Through Bolshevik Russia*, 25.

93. The reference to Cook's tours had earlier been made in a widely reported speech by the president of the National Democratic and Labour Party, J. A. Seddon. Speaking at the end of May 1920, he had denounced George Lansbury, saying 'Not until the great heart of England was broken would she submit to alien dictation based upon cruel methods, crude economics and destructive aims, even though a few Englishmen were given a sort of Cook's conducted tour and returned with praises of Bolshevism.' See 'Reign of Bedlam', *Morning Post*, 27 May 1920, 6. See also 'Moscow is Hell To-day', *The Times*, 27 May 1920, 9.

94. Mrs Snowden, *Through Bolshevik Russia*, 26.

95. Clifford Allen and Robert Williams, wire from Petrograd, *Daily Herald*, 17 May 1920.

96. Haden Guest, *Struggle for Power in Europe*, 95.

97. Mrs Snowden, *Through Bolshevik Russia*, 30.

98. Allen and Williams, wire from Petrograd, *Daily Herald*, 17 May 1920.

99. Mrs Snowden, *Through Bolshevik Russia*, 30.

100. Haden Guest, *Struggle for Power in Europe*, 96.

101. Bertrand Russell, *Autobiography* (London: Routledge, 2000), 336.

102. Robert Williams and Clifford Allen, wire from Petrograd, *Daily Herald*, 17 May 1920.

103. 'In the course of a desperate struggle, the heritage of civilization is likely to be lost, while hatred, suspicion, and cruelty become normal.' Bertrand Russell, *The Practice and Theory of Bolshevism* (London: Allen & Unwin, 1920), 33.

104. Mrs Snowden, *Through Bolshevik Russia*, 34.

105. Born to a wealthy family in the Ukraine, Balabanova had rebelled and left
Russia in the 1890s, studying socialism at universities in Brussels, Leipzig, Berlin,
and also Rome, where she worked under the Marxist moral philosopher
Antonio Labriola. She had then spent many years as an activist and propagandist, first in Switzerland and later also in Italy, where she became prominent in
the leadership of the Socialist Party. Multilingual and well known across the
European left, she had served as secretary and figurehead of the international
conference of anti-war socialists held at the Swiss town of Zimmerwald in
September 1915. Indeed, when travelling back to Russia from Zurich with
other émigrés in June 1917, she had crossed the Finnish–Russian frontier waving a banner improvised out of a stick and a red scarf embroidered with the
words 'Long live Zimmerwald; Long Live the Russian Revolution.'
   Though she had joined the Bolshevik Party on her return, Balabanova had
also developed growing doubts about the conduct of the Bolshevik government as it pressed on with a revolution that appeared more like a smash and
grab raid on the state than a broad mobilization of the kind espoused by the
pre-war Italian Socialist Party. She had recently been removed from her position as founding secretary of the Third International, thanks partly to growing
ideological differences but also, as she would later suggest, to her refusal to countenance Zinoviev's various attempts to get this internationally well-known but
increasingly unreliable figure out of the way before the arrival of the British
Labour Delegation. Balabanova recalls being suddenly recommended for a
period of recuperation in a remote sanatorium, and then strongly encouraged
to take command of a propaganda train that would be spending six months in
Turkestan. See Balabanoff, *My Life as a Rebel*, 167, 262–3.

106. Mrs Snowden, *Through Bolshevik Russia*, 35–6. It was a worry that would not
leave Mrs Snowden. Bertrand Russell describes how she later exhibited the
same chaotically mixed feelings when the delegates were driven around in the
tsar's motor-car—he speaks of her 'enjoying its luxury and expressing pity for
the "poor Czar"'. See Russell, *Autobiography* (London), 333.

107. Robert Williams, *My Impressions of Soviet Russia* (Amsterdam: International
Transportworkers Federation), 1920.

108. Balabanoff, *My Life as a Rebel*, 284. Emma Goldman reveals that Balabanova was
also troubled by the fate of Princess Naryshkin, who one day actually turned up
at her former home begging to be allowed to take a silver icon that had been in
the family for generations, prompting Balabanova to conclude 'How dreadful is
life! I am no good for it; I must get away' (Emma Goldman, *My Disillusionment
in Russia* (New York: Apollo, 1970), 78). Balabanova herself quit Bolshevik Russia
not long after the visit of the British Labour Delegation.

109. Mrs Snowden, *Through Bolshevik Russia*, 38.

110. Ibid. 32.

111. Douglas Goldring, *The Black Curtain* (London: Chapman Hall, 1920), 109.
Goldring's novel is concerned with the 'scattered army' of Bohemians he had

known in Europe and London before the outbreak of war in 1914. Whether revolutionaries or rebels of a more aesthetic variety, these 'fugitives from life' have been shaken loose from their national affiliations, and were searching for a vaguely conceived 'New Order', which would be internationalist or nothing. When 'the world's new liberator' came, he would 'care nothing for political frontiers, for racial prejudices. His army would be unarmed; and it would be recruited from all the races of the earth' (8–9). The war of 1914–18 was the 'black curtain' that largely extinguish these horizontalist hopes, although Goldring still associated this 'New Order' with the promise of the Bolshevik revolution and saw Lenin as a Christ-like 'man of destiny' (235). In his play 'The Fight For Freedom', he hailed Lenin's revolution as the 'Red Dawn'. See Douglas Goldring, *The Fight for Freedom: Plays for a People's Theatre*, i (London: C. W. Daniel, 1919). For Goldring's later recollection of this period, see his *Odd Man Out: The Autobiography of a 'Propaganda Novelist'* (London: Chapman and Hall, 1935), 207.

112. John Maynard Keynes, 'Dr. Melchior: a Defeated Enemy', in *The Collected Writings of John Maynard Keynes*, x., *Essays in Biography* (London: Macmillan, 1972), 399.

113. Ibid. 413–14.

114. Maynard Keynes, 'Dr Melchior'. These lines, which differ slightly from the version reproduced in the *Collected Writings*, are quoted from the manuscript held at Cambridge University Library.

115. This occurs in 'La Divina Commedia', a passage in Rozanov's *The Apocalypse of Our Time*. See Vasily Rozanov, *Solitaria: With an Abridged Account of the Author's Life, by E. Gollerbach. Other Biographical Material, and Matter from The Apocalypse of our Times*, trans by S. S. Kotelianksy (London: Wishart, 1927), 148.

116. Together with her husband, the Labour politician Philip Snowden, Ethel Snowden had a long-standing association with Charles Roden Buxton and his wife Dorothy. The two couples lived close to one another in Golders Green, north-west London, and had campaigned together against the perpetuation of the Great War. In a letter to *The Times* of 4 October 1918, a certain John C. Van Der Veer paired Buxton with Ethel Snowden and denounced them as 'The Enemy Within' on account of the 'mischievous pacifist propaganda' he had come across in the form of 'Women's Peace Crusade leaflet no. 8', written by Charles Roden Buxton of 6 Erskine Hill, Golders Green and published by Ethel Snowden of 39 Woodstock Rd, Golders Green. (Entitled 'Lost Opportunities', this leaflet lists a number of German, Austrian, Russian, and even papal attempts at conciliation that were 'received either with stony silence or as "Peace Traps"' and concludes 'There is no more terrible crime than to prolong the War without EXPLORING EVERY OPENING THAT OFFERS the prospect of PEACE ON HONOURABLE TERMS.')

117. Charles Roden Buxton, letter to Violet Paget (Vernon Lee), 28 December 1922. Vernon Lee Papers, Somerville College, Oxford.

118. Copies of this private (and undated) edition survive among Buxton family papers and in the Vernon Lee papers at the Miller Library, Colby College, Maine. The earlier leaflet version entitled 'Bach's Christmas Music in England and in Germany: A Christmas Message from the League of Peace and Freedom', was published, as Buxton recalled, by the League of Peace and Freedom (London) in 1917.

CHAPTER 9 NOT JUST A FRONTIER

1. Quoted in Édouard Herriot, *The United States of Europe*, tr. Reginald J. Dingle (London: Harrap, 1930), 35.
2. John Lukacs, *A New History of the Cold War* (New York: Anchor Books, 1966), 25.
3. George F. Kennan, *The Decision to Intervene: Soviet-American Relations, 1917–1920* (London: Faber & Faber, 1958), 469.
4. This is the phrase of Anna Louise Strong, an American Bolshevik sympathizer who, in 1921, entered Russia from Poland in the services of the American Friends' Mission. Writing about that crossing some fifteen years later, Strong insists that 'the line in those days was sharp as a drawn sword'. See Anna Louise Strong, *I Changed Worlds* (New York: Garden City Publishing, 1937), 96.
5. Yevgeny Zamyatin, *We* (1920–1), tr. Natasha Randall (New York: The Modern Library, 2006), 5, 11.
6. Griffin Barry, 'First Exiles from US', *Daily Herald*, 20 January 1920.
7. Alexander Berkman, 'The Russian Revolution', *The Blast*, 2/4 (1 May 1917). Collected in Alexander Berkman (ed.), *The Blast* (Edinburgh and Oakland: AK Press, 2005), 229.
8. Alexander Berkman, *The Bolshevik Myth (Diary 1920–1922)* (London: Hutchinson, 1925), 27–8.
9. For an account of these deportations and the subsequent 'Palmer raids' against Communists in America, see Ted Morgan, *Reds: McCarthyism in Twentieth-Century America* (New York: Random House, 2003), 74–87.
10. Barry Pateman, 'Introduction', in Berkman (ed.), *The Blast*, 7. In the penultimate issue, Berkman had declared 'If this issue of THE BLAST is suppressed in free America, we will move to Petrograd' (2/4 (1 May 1917)). *The Blast* was officially 'excluded from the mails' in June 1917.
11. Emma Goldman, *My Disillusionment in Russia* (New York: Apollo, 1970), 2.
12. Griffin Barry, 'Bondage to Freedom', *Daily Herald*, 22 January 1920.
13. Griffin Barry, 'Dramatic Incident on the Red Ark', *Daily Herald*, 21 January 1920.
14. Barry, 'Bondage to Freedom'.
15. *Bericht über die Verhandlungen des III (8) Parteitages der Kommunistischen Partei Deutschlands*, (Berlin 1923), 268. Quoted in J. Braunthal, *History of the International*, ii. *1914–1943* (London: Nelson, 1967), 268.
16. George Lansbury, *What I Saw in Russia* (London: Leonard Parsons, June 1920), 1–2.

17. Bertrand Russell, *The Practice and Theory of Bolshevism*, (London: Allen & Unwin, 1920), 27.

18. Mrs Philip Snowden, *Through Bolshevik Russia* (London: Cassell, 1920), 30–1.

19. Ben Turner, *About Myself 1863–1930* (London: Humphrey Toulmin, 1930), 215.

20. Morris Gordin, *Utopia in Chains: An American's Experiences in Red Russia* (Boston and New York: Houghton Mifflin, 1926), 40.

21. Ibid. 45.

22. George Lansbury, *What I Saw in Russia* (London: Leonard Parsons, June 1920), xv.

23. *The Times*, 26 April 1920, 13–14.

24. Meriel Buchanan, *Petrograd: The City of Trouble 1914–1918* (London: Collins, 1918), 255.

25. R.D.P. (Rhoda Power), 'A Letter from Russia', *Cambridge Magazine*, 3 November 1917, 80.

26. R.D.P. (Rhoda Power), 'An English Girl in Russia', *Cambridge Magazine*, 9 February 1918, 399. See also Rhoda Power, *Under Cossack & Bolshevik* (London: Methuen, 1919).

27. Paul Dukes, *Red Dusk and the Morrow: Adventures and Investigations in Red Russia* (London: Heinemann, 1922).

28. Ibid. 305–6.

29. Ibid. 115.

30. H.V. Keeling, *Bolshevism: Mr. Keeling's Five Years in Russia* (London: Hodder & Stoughton, 1919), 30.

31. Ibid. 47.

32. *The Times*, 29 July 1920.

33. Emma Cochran Ponafidine, *Russia—My Home: An Intimate Record of Personal Experiences Before, During and After the Bolshevist Revolution* (New York: Blue Ribbon Books, 1931), 307.

CHAPTER 10 RELOCATING THE ALLIED BLOCKADE

1. See Independent Labour Party, *Report of the National Administrative Council to the 29th Annual Conference, Easter 1921* (London: ILP, 1921), 29.

2. Robert Williams, *Impressions of Soviet Russia* (Amsterdam: International Transportworkers Federation, 1920). Elsewhere, Williams offered a longer version of this bracing maxim: 'We started the revolution, comrades. We started it alone. Let us and the British and the other propletarians finish it together.' See 'Williams' Reply', *Daily Herald*, 27 August 1920, 3.

3. Alexander Berkman, *The Bolshevik Myth (Diary 1920–1922)* (London: Hutchinson, 1925), 139.

4. Franz Jung, *Der Weg nach unten* (Neuwied: 1961), 169. Quoted in Hans Magnus Enzensberger, *The Consciousness Industry: On Literature, Politics and the Media* (New York: Seabury Press, 1974), 138.

5. Victor Serge, *Memoirs of a Revolutionary, 1901–1941*, tr. Peter Sedgwick (Oxford: Oxford University Press, 1967), 103.

6. Charles Roden Buxton, letter to Dorothy Frances Buxton, written from 'Soviet House No. 2'. The delegates had indeed been submitted to 'a whole series' of embarrassing 'entertainments and shows' but, as Buxton would later write, this reflected the fact that their visit had assumed a 'symbolic character' as 'the first breach in the terrible wall of isolation behind which the Russian people has felt itself immured for so long' (Charles Roden Buxton, 'A Wanderer in Soviet Russia', *Daily Herald*, 2 August 1920, 4).

7. Charles Roden Buxton, 'Two Months in Soviet Russia', typescript used as a source for *Daily Herald* articles, 1920.

8. Churchill, speaking as chairman at a dinner of the English-Speaking Union, *The Times*, 24 February 1919.

9. Churchill speaking in the Connaught Rooms on 11 April 1919. Martin Gilbert, *Winston S. Churchill*, iv. *1917–1922* (London: Heinemann, 1975), 278.

10. Churchill to Lloyd George, ibid. 292.

11. Ibid. 355–6.

12. Ibid. 375.

13. 'Red Fever' was the title of an article by Churchill in *the Illustrated Sunday Herald*, 25 January 1919. See Gilbert, *Churchill*, iv. *1917–1922*, 374.

14. Maurice Maeterlink, *The Life of the White Ant* (trans. of *La Vie des termites*, 1926) (London: Allen & Unwin, 1927), 70.

15. Aware of demonstrators opposing his Fulton speech, he recommended 'our Communist friends' to study the literature on the white ant, which would 'show them not only a great deal about their past, but will give a very fair indication of their future'. Robert H. Pilpel, *Churchill in America 1895–1961* (New York: Harcourt Brace Jovanovich, 1976), 229.

16. Arthur Ransome, *Six Weeks in Russia in 1919* (London: Independent Labour Party, 1919), 148.

17. Ibid. 148–9.

18. Robert Minor, *World* (New York), 4 February 1919, 'Foreign Opinion: A Weekly Survey of Foreign Opinion', *Cambridge Magazine*, 8/26 (5 April 1919), 556.

19. *Tribune* (New York), 14 February 1919, 'Foreign Opinion', *Cambridge Magazine*, 8/26 (5 April 1919), 557. Robins recalled the same conversation with Lenin on 6 March 1918, when testifying before the American Senate's Overman subcommittee hearing on Bolshevism. A former Chicago labour organizer, Robins had first gone to Russia with a Red Cross Commission in August 1917 and went on to become 'the prototypical fellow traveller'. See Ted Morgan, *Reds: McCarthyism in Twentieth-Century America* (New York: Random House, 2003), 68, 36.

20. 'Red Flag Order for Clemenceau and Mr. Churchill', *Daily News*, 10 April 1920, 1.

21. Quoted from the opening editorial in the *Independent Review*, 1/1 (October 1903). Buxton renamed this journal the *Albany Review*, when he took it over in 1906.

22. Quoted from Churchill's 1908 by-election speeches in Randolph S. Churchill, *Winston S. Churchill*, ii. *Young Statesman 1901–1914* (London: Heinemann, 1967), 281.

23. A. J. P. Taylor, *The Trouble Makers: Dissent over Foreign Policy, 1792–1932* (London: Heinemann, 1957), 73.

24. Noel Buxton and Charles Roden Buxton, *The War and the Balkans* (London: Allen & Unwin, 1915), 10.

25. Charles Roden and Dorothy Frances Buxton, *The World After the War* (London: Allen & Unwin, 1920), 22. In the early years of the century, the Buxton brothers had identified the Turkish frontier as the great division defining Europe. As Noel Buxton once put it, 'The Turkish frontier is always alarming. It is not, like most frontiers, an unreal and shadowy existence. The passage from one world to another is always signalised by the mouldering custom-house and the tattered uniform. Usually as civilization increases the picturesque disappears, but here it is not so. "Where the Turkish foot treads the grass never grows"' (Noel Buxton MP, *Europe and the Turks* (1907; London: Methuen, 1912), 96–7). Noel Buxton later participated in the Balkan war of 1912, also accompanying Mrs St Clair Stobart on her preliminary travels and, as chairman of the 'Balkan War Relief Committee', providing the finance that enabled her to bring the Women's Convoy Corps to Bulgaria. See Mrs St Clair Stobart, *War and Women: From Experience in the Balkans and Elsewhere* (London: Bell, 1913), 47.

26. Winston Churchill, letter to Noel Buxton, 31 August 1914, quoted in Mosa Anderson, *Noel Buxton: A Life* (London: Allen & Unwin, 1952), 62–3. See also Noel Buxton and C. Leonard Leese, *Balkan Problems and European Peace* (London: Allen & Unwin, 1919), 70–2.

27. Reported in *Universul* (Bucharest), 6 October 1914.

28. Noel Buxton, *Travels and Reflections* (London: Allen & Unwin, 1929), 128.

29. *Eastern Daily News*, 10 April 1925. Various papers concerned with the renaming of the Old Boyarna Road remain in the possession of the Buxton family.

30. T. P. Conwell-Evans, *Foreign Policy from a Back Bench 1904–1918: A Study Based on the Papers of Lord Noel-Buxton* (Oxford: Oxford University Press, 1932), 112.

31. Anderson, *Noel Buxton*, 73.

32. Stuart Hodgson, 'What Mr. Lansbury Saw', *Daily News*, 17 June 1920, 4.

33. A.G.G., 'The Real Red Terror', *Daily News*, 19 June 1920, 4.

34. E. Harmsworth used this phrase when questioning Churchill in the Commons on 23 June 1920. See 'House of Commons', *The Times*, 24 June 1920, 9.

35. 'New Wealth. Reclothing the Army', *The Times*, 9 June 1920, 9.

36. Reporting that Churchill's proposal had been 'received throughout the country with dismay, and almost with disgust', Mr Palmer (Independent MP for the Wrekin) told the House of Commons 'We had now put the Army on a business footing, and had ceased to attract men by gewgaws and millinery. The lure of a scarlet uniform had gone for ever.' 'The Wasters. Pink Trousers Postponed', *Daily News,* 24 June 1920, 1.

37. A. J. P. Taylor, *Trouble Makers,* 121. Roy Jenkins describes Churchill's loss as 'surely one of the heaviest swings in the country' (*Churchill* (London: Pan, 2002), 376).

38. Gilbert, *Churchill,* iv. *1917–1922,* 365–6.

39. Charles Roden Buxton, 'The Blockade of the Russian People' (material for speeches on Russia), 1920, with the CRB papers at Rhodes House, Oxford, British Emp. 5.405 Box 1, file 6.

40. Alcide Ebray would insist that the blockade was illegal, pointing out that this was also the American objection in the early stages. He declared that international maritime law allowed for 'conditional contraband' to pass through neutral countries, even though 'absolute contraband' (a category in which arms belonged) could not. Having objected on these grounds in 1915, the Americans joined the blockade when they entered the war in 1917. It was often said that German submarine warfare had brought the Americans into the war, but Ebray insists the reality was the other way round since the Germans offered to drop submarine war if the blockade was lifted (Alcide Ebray, *A Frenchman Looks at the Peace* (London: Paul, Trench, Trubner, 1927), 33). The distinction between conditional and absolute contraband was affirmed by the Declaration of London of 26 February 1909. Though not signed, both sides had said they would abide by this codification of existing maritime law.

41. Irene Cooper Willis, *England's Holy War: A Study of English Liberal Idealism during the Great War* (New York: Knopf, 1928), 197.

42. Hansard, *Parliamentary Debates,* 5th ser. – vol. 61, col. 937.

43. Ibid. col. 938.

44. Charles Callan Tansill, *America Goes to War* (Boston: Little, Brown and Co., 1942) 448–50.

45. George Abel Schreiner, *The Iron Ration: Three Years in Central Europe* (New York and London: Harper, 1918), 1.

46. Rear Admiral M. W. W. P. Consett, *The Triumph of Unarmed Forces (1914–1918)* (London: Williams and Norgate, 1928), 22–41.

47. *Le Temps,* 31 December 1918.

48. H. N. Brailsford, 'The New War on Russia', *Daily Herald,* 5 May 1920.

49. Harold Grenfell (Captain R. N. Retd), 'The Hidden Blockade', *Daily Herald,* 8 September 1920, 4.

50. 'First Interim Report', British Labour Delegation to Russia 1920, *Report* (London: Trades Union Congress and Labour Party, 1920), 29.

51. 'The Blockade of the Russian People', typescript marked as 'material for speeches on Russia' 1920. Charles Roden Buxton papers in Rhodes House, Oxford, MSS: Brit Emp. S.405, Box 1, folder 6.

52. Bertrand Russell, *The Practice and Theory of Bolshevism* (London: Allen & Unwin, 1920), 22.

53. Ibid. 19.

54. Letter to Keynes, from Hubert [*illegible*] of the *New Republic* (January 1920) trying to secure regular contributions from the British economist. In Keynes Papers, King's College, Cambridge.

55. John Maynard Keynes, Preface to the French edition of *The Economic Consequences of the Peace,* in *Collected Works,* ii. *The Economic Consequences of the Peace* (London: Macmillan, 1971), xxi.

56. J. M. Keynes, *The Economic Consequences of the Peace* (London: Macmillan, 1919), 276.

57. Georges Clemenceau, 'Introduction' to André Tardieu, *The Truth about the Treaty* (London: Hodder and Stoughton, 1921). It is in this unpaginated introduction that Clemenceau strikes back at Keynes, repudiating his 'virulent' attacks and describing him as a man with 'some knowledge of economics but neither imagination or character'.

58. J. M. Keynes, *Collected Works,* ii. *Economic Consequences of the Peace*, 20.

59. J. M. Keynes, Review of Winston Churchill's *The World Crisis—Aftermath,* in *Nation and Atheneum,* 9 March 1929, quoted from *The Collected Writings of John Maynard Keynes,* x. *Essays in Biography* (London: Macmillan, 1972), 57.

60. C. R. and D. F. Buxton, *World After the War.* The copy in Cambridge University Library was received on 21 May 1920, the same day Buxton wrote to his wife from his hotel in Moscow. This book has not been widely remembered by historians in the West. Neither it nor the UDC are mentioned in Margaret MacMillan's recent book about the Treaty of Versailles, *Peacemakers* (see n. 97, below). The Buxtons are, however, cited on various central European websites, and their book taken to exemplify an idea of Europe that was defeated at Versailles and merits re-examination now that the Cold War is over.

61. Ibid. 34.

62. Ibid. 28.

63. This remark was made by John C. Winant, while awarding Mackinder the Charles P. Daly Medal for 1943, *Dictionary of National Biography* (1941–50), 556–7.

64. Halford J. Mackinder, *Democratic Ideals and Reality: A Study in the Politics of Reconstruction* (London: Constable, 1919), 154–5.

65. Ibid. 160.

66. Ibid. 178.

67. See John Bellamy Foster, 'The New Geopolitics of Empire', *Monthly Review,* 5/8 (January 2006).

68. Roden and Buxton, *World After the War*, 29.

69. Ibid. 22.

70. Ibid. 28.

71. Katharine Bruce Glasier, 'Signs of a New Springtide', *Labour's Northern Voice*, 11/15 (March 1940), 2.

72. Charles Roden Buxton, 'Other People's Point of View', typescript article on Mrs C. R. Buxton's 'Notes from the Foreign Press' (Buxton papers, Rhodes House, Oxford). Here Buxton writes: 'The reason for their success is that they teach us something about other people's point of view. Our ordinary newspapers make no attempt to do this fairly or impartially. For the most part, they quote the violent and extreme things that are said on the other side, but conceal from us the fact that even in the enemy countries there are large and growing moderate parties which want Peace and which are opposed to all annexation of other people's territory. Mrs. Buxton's notes do a great deal to supplement this one-sided picture. They give the moderate and the extreme statements, but they lay stress on the former because they are almost wholly excluded elsewhere. It is not too much to say that the beginning of wisdom in these times is to disbelieve everything that you read in the papers unless you have some special reason for believing it.' For further information about Dorothy Buxton, see Ben Buxton, 'Dorothy Buxton's Long Crusade for Social Justice', *Cambridge* (journal of the Cambridge Society), 50 (2002), 74–7. Also Grace E. Brockington, 'Translating Peace: Pacifist Publishing and the Transmission of Foreign Texts', in Mary Hammond & Shafquat Towheed (eds), *Publishing in the First World War: Essays in Book History* (London: Palgrave Macmillan, 2007), 46–58.

73. Romain Rolland, letter to Louise Bodin, *Le Populaire* (Paris), 18 December 1918, quoted in 'Foreign Opinion', *Cambridge Magazine*, 8/13 (4 January 1919), 280. Rolland mentions his admiration for the Buxtons, and for the 'freedom of spirit' and 'rich information' of Dorothy's work for the *Cambridge Magazine*, in a letter to Charles Roden Buxton, written from a hotel near Vaud in Switzerland and dated 8 February 1919.

74. *Politiken* (Copenhagen), 18 May 1919, 'Foreign Opinion', *Cambridge Magazine*, 8/36 (14 June 1919), 773. For Vernon Lee's observation about Justice see her *Satan the Waster: A Philosophic War Trilogy with Notes & Introduction* (London: Bodley Head, 1920), 261.

75. *Algemeen Handelsblad* (Holland), 8 May 1919, 'Foreign Opinion', *Cambridge Magazine*, 8/33 (24 May 1919), 703.

76. *Social Demokraten* (Sweden), 9 May 1919, ibid. 704.

77. *Corriere della sera*, 14 May 1918, 'Foreign Opinion', *Cambridge Magazine*, 8/34 (31 May 1919), 727.

78. *Germania*, 20 January 1919, 'Foreign Opinion', *Cambridge Magazine*, 8/18 (8 February 1919), 390.

79. 'Foreign Opinion', *Cambridge Magazine*, 8/15 (18 January 1919), 316.

80. J. M. Keynes, *Collected Works*, ii, *Economic Consequences of the Peace*, 3.

81. J. M. Keynes, 'Dr. Melchior: a Defeated Enemy', in *Collected Writings of John Maynard Keynes*, x. *Essays in Biography* 397.

82. Ibid. 442.

83. Francesca M. Wilson, *Rebel Daughter of a Country House* (London: Allen & Unwin, 1967), 173. The 'Fight the Famine' Council was actually first formed as the 'Wilson Welcome Committee' at a special meeting of the Women's International League, chaired by Lord Parmoor on 11 December 1918. Irene Cooper Willis's minutes of this 'Meeting at Lord Parmoor's, 11 December 1918', can be found appended to the minutes of the 19 December 1918 meeting of the executive committee of the Women's International League, preserved in the WILPF papers at the library of the London School of Economics.

84. Dorothy Buxton, 'Hunger Politics', *UDC* 4/7 (May 1919), 323.

85. Speaking at a Lord Mayor's lunch at the Mansion House in the City of London on 19 February 1919, Churchill had raised easy cheers by asserting 'We are going to make Germany pay.' He had then gone on to argue strongly against the idea that Germany should simply be starved into paying reparations by means of a continued naval blockade. Arguing that 'You could not make a pack horse pay by starving him', he suggested that maintaining the blockade against Germany would 'plunge another great area of the world into Bolshevist anarchy'. Pointing to the interconnection of the economy (with arguments similar to those used by both Keynes and Norman Angell), he remarked that such a course would also impoverish the rest of the world, and Britain above all. The 'strong and manly course' was also the humane and far-seeing one. Britain should keep its army on the Rhine in order to maintain order, and the Allies should provide food and raw materials, without which Germany would hardly be able to make reparations. He opposed a policy of starvation, 'which falls so cruelly on women and children, on the sick and the old, and which in the end would only drive the Germans into the quagmire of utter ruin', *The Times*, 20 February 1919, 6. No doubt Churchill was aware that the conditions in Germany had become a matter of concern to the occupying British army. In April that year, the 'Fight the Famine' Council published a leaflet quoting various British army officers who had seen the consequences of the famine in various parts of Germany and, in reports written that January and February, opposed it on humanitarian as well as political grounds. See Douglas Goldring, *What the Army Thinks of the Blockade* (London: 'Fight the Famine' Council, 1919).

86. *Deutsche Allgemeine Zeitung*, 23 February 1919, 'Foreign Opinion', *Cambridge Magazine*, 8/22 (8 March 1919), 479.

87. 'The Relief of Austria', 'Foreign Opinion', *Cambridge Magazine*, 8/16 (25 January 1919), 338–40. Mrs Philip Snowden, who saw Dorothy Buxton in action in Berne in March 1919, writes of 'Endless delays for no obvious reason; endless calls on dilatory officials; endless pleadings with suspicious legations; endless

regulations to be subscribed to, and finally the probability that [the train] would never arrive at its destination'. See Mrs Philip Snowden, *A Political Pilgrim in Europe* (London: Cassell, 1921), 61.

88. *Politiken* (Copenhagen), 5 December 1918, 'Foreign Opinion', *Cambridge Magazine*, 8/13 (4 January 1919), 279.

89. *Literary Digest* (New York), 1 November 1919, 'Foreign Opinion', *Cambridge Magazine*, 9/8 (29 November 1919), 121.

90. Quoted in *Avanti* (Milan), 17 December 1918, 'Foreign Opinion', *Cambridge Magazine*, 8/15 (18 January 1919), 316.

91. W. Martin, *Journal de Genève*, 11 June 1918, 'Foreign Opinion', *Cambridge Magazine*, 8/15 (18 January 1919), 317–8.

92. Maurice Parmelee, *Blockade and Sea Power: The Blockade, 1914–1919, and Its Significance for a World State* (London: Hutchinson, 1925), 119 and *passim*.

93. *New York World*, 26 January 1919, 'Foreign Opinion', *Cambridge Magazine*, 8/21 (1 March 1919), 456.

94. *Weekly Despatch,* 26 January 1919, 'Foreign Opinion', *Cambridge Magazine*, 8/17 (1 February 1919), 369.

95. Anna Louise Strong, *I Change Worlds: The Remaking of an American* (New York: Holt, 1935), 179–80.

96. Herbert Hoover, 'Marketing American Surplus Food Products', *Farm and Home* (January 1920).

97. Notes of a conversation with Lloyd George (11 December 1919), quoted in Margaret MacMillan, *Peacemakers: The Paris Conference of 1919 and Its Attempt to End War* (London: John Murray, 2002), 81. The policy of the 'barbed-wire ring' was discussed in a *Manchester Guardian* editorial on 3 February 1920. See W. P. and Zelda K. Coates, *A History of Anglo-Soviet Relations* (London: Lawrence & Wishart, 1943), 14.

98. Gilbert, *Winston S. Churchill*, iv. *1917–1922*, 379.

99. See G. E. Slocombe's report from Versailles, 'White Ring in Near East', *Daily Herald,* 27 August 1920, 3.

100. *Le Temps,* 13 December 1919, 'Foreign Opinion', *Cambridge Magazine*, 8/13 (4 January 1919).

101. Henry Noel Brailsford, *Across the Blockade: A Record of Travels in Enemy Europe* (London: George Allen & Unwin, 1919), 92.

102. Not long after the Soviet withdrawal from the Great War after the Bolshevik coup of October 1917, Churchill had declared that 'Every British and French soldier lost last year was really done to death by Lenin and Trotsky, not in a fair way but by the treacherous desertion of an ally without parallel in the history of the world.' See Richard H. Ullman, *Britain and the Russian Civil War November 1918—February 1920* (Princeton: Princeton University Press, 1968), 153.

103. Churchill, quoted from *The Times*, 16 February 1920, in W. P. and Z. Coates, *History of Anglo-Soviet Relations*, 17.

104. Mackinder, *Democratic Ideals and Reality*, 202–3, 204–5, 206, 223, 214, 216, 242, 254.

105. Subheading used in 'Foreign Opinion', *Cambridge Magazine*, 8/18 (8 February 1919), 391.

106. *Frankfurter Zeitung*, 26 March 1919, 'Foreign Opinion', *Cambridge Magazine*, 8/28 (19 April 1919), 593.

107. *Arbeiter Zeitung* (Vienna), 23 March 1919, 'Foreign Opinion', *Cambridge Magazine*, 8/28 (19 April 1919), 593.

108. *Il secolo* (Rome), 3 April 1919, 'Foreign Opinion', *Cambridge Magazine*, 8/28 (19 April 1919), 594.

109. *Le Temps* (Paris), 23 March 1919, 'Foreign Opinion', *Cambridge Magazine*, 8/26 (5 April 1919), 563.

110. *Vossische Zeitung* (Berlin), 24 March 1919, 'Foreign Opinion', *Cambridge Magazine*, 8/28 (19 April 1919), 594.

111. *Leipziger Volkszeitung*, 3 September 1919, 'Foreign Opinion', *Cambridge Magazine*, 8/51 (27 September 1919), 1013.

112. Bara Catulla, chief of the Afghan mission to Soviet Russia, quoted from *Isvestia* in *Leipziger Volkszeitung* (3 September 1919), ibid. 1012.

113. *Le Temps*, 9 April 1919, 'Foreign Opinion', *Cambridge Magazine*, 8/28 (19 April 1919), 592.

114. *Springfield Republican*, 30 March 1919, 'Foreign Opinion', *Cambridge Magazine*, 8/41 (19 July 1919), 852.

115. Section heading in 'Foreign Opinion', *Cambridge Magazine*, 8/13 (4 January 1919), 281.

116. *Neue Zürcher Zeitung* (Swiss), 8 December 1919, 'Foreign Opinion', *Cambridge Magazine*, 3/13 (4 January 1919), 279.

117. Arno Dosch in *World* (New York), 14 March 1919, 'Foreign Opinion', *Cambridge Magazine*, 8/26 (5 April 1919), 562.

118. Theodor Wolff, *Berliner Tageblatt*, 10 March 1919, 'Foreign Opinion', *Cambridge Magazine*, 8/25 (29 March 1919), 545.

119. This phrase is used by Matthias Erzberger, the leader of the Catholic democrats who had also signed the Armistice on Germany's behalf, in *Germania*, 25 March 1919, 'Foreign Opinion', *Cambridge Magazine*, 8/27 (12 April 1919), 571.

120. *Frankfurter Zeitung*, 24 January 1919, 'Foreign Opinion', *Cambridge Magazine*, 8/20 (22 February 1919), 441.

121. *Berliner Tageblatt*, 20 March 1919, 'Foreign Opinion', *Cambridge Magazine*, 8/27 (12 April 1919), 572.

122. Dr Weiskirchner, *Neue Freie Presse*, 18 January 1919, 'Foreign Opinion', *Cambridge Magazine*, 8/20 (22 February 1919), 439.

123. *Vossische Zeitung*, 15 March 1919, 'Foreign Opinion', *Cambridge Magazine*, 8/26 (5 April 1919), 561.

124. Bainville in *Action française*, 17 March 1919, 'Foreign Opinion', *Cambridge Magazine*, 8/25 (29 March 1919), 543.

125. *Le Temps*, 29 March 1919, 'Foreign Opinion', *Cambridge Magazine*, 8/28 (19 April 1919), 594.

126. Herbert Hoover, quoted from US Press, 4 January 1919, 'Foreign Opinion', *Cambridge Magazine*, 8/17 (1 February 1919), 369.

127. *New Republic*, 18 January 1919, 'Foreign Opinion', *Cambridge Magazine*, 8/21 (1 March 1919), 454.

128. *Public Ledger* (Philadelphia), 18 December 1918, 'Foreign Opinion', *Cambridge Magazine*, 8/20 (22 February 1919), 432.

129. Churchill to Violet Asquith, quoted in Gilbert, *Churchill*, iv. *1917–1922*, 278.

130. Ibid. 382.

131. Charles Roden Buxton, 'The Brotherhood of Nations' (read at Stratford-on-Avon, August 1915), C. R. Buxton papers at Rhodes House, Oxford (MSS: Brit. Emp S 405 Box 4).

132. See Arno J. Mayer, *Political Origins of the New Diplomacy, 1917–1919* (New Haven: Yale University Press, 1959).

133. Ethel Snowden was among those who considered the League of Nations to be in the tradition of the Socialist International. As she wrote, 'This idea can be safely trusted to persist and grow in spite of every menace, because it is in the direct line of political and economic evolution. It is the next inevitable step in the march of ordered progress.' Mrs Snowden, *Political Pilgrim in Europe*, 272.

134. Wilson in address to Senate, 22 January 1917 (Mayer, *New Diplomacy*, 159).

135. Mayer, *New Diplomacy*, 73.

136. Ibid. 75.

137. Ibid. 77.

138. This was the view of Francis Steiner, a supporter of the Industrial Workers of the World who had been sentenced to death for refusing to fight in what he described as 'this commercial war' (letter to Aloisa Steiner, 8 July 1920) and, with his sentence commuted to fifteen years, was interned at Fort Douglas, Utah. Writing to his sister Anna on 14 July 1920, he describes how the commander of the post had given them a lecture on the Fourth of July: 'I tried to tell him that I was here for the same cause that this nation was celebrating on that day—the "rebels that fought under the red flag with their rattle snake in its field." I told him that I did believe in government and that's why I voted a socialist ticket, but the capitalist being in power, and also, being their war, it was their fight, as I would surely fight like they, the soldiers of this war, if my class, "the working class", was in power and someone tried to destroy it.' Francis Steiner papers, Labadie Collection of Social Protest Material, University of Michigan Library, Ann Arbor.

139. Mayer, *New Diplomacy*, 373.

140. Ibid. 382.

141. *Gazette de Lausanne*, 18 December 1918, 'Foreign Opinion', *Cambridge Magazine*, 8/14 (11 January 1919), 296.

142. *Vorwärts* (Berlin), 24 August 1918, 'Foreign Opinion', *Cambridge Magazine*, 8/18 (8 February 1919), 394. The British publisher Allen & Unwin, publisher to the UDC and the wider anti-war movement, kept a translation of Kant's *Perpetual Peace* in print through the war and post-war period, advertising it in books by Buxton and others.

143. Brailsford, *Across the Blockade*, 155.

144. A.G.G., 'The Real Red Terror', *Daily News*, 19 June 1920, 4.

145. C. R. and D. F. Buxton, *World After the War*, 24.

146. Ibid. 40.

147. Lee, *Satan the Waster*, 246.

148. *Neue Freie Press*, 7 January 1919, 'Foreign Opinion', *Cambridge Magazine*, 8/18 (8 February 1919), 389.

149. Francesco Nitti, *Peaceless Europe* (London: Cassell, 1922), 27.

CHAPTER II FACT-FINDING WITH LIMOUSINES

1. George Lansbury, *What I Saw in Russia* (London: Leonard Parsons, June 1920), 18.

2. Clare Sheridan, *Russian Portraits* (1921; Cambridge: Lincoln House, 1992), 139.

3. Mrs Philip Snowden, *Through Bolshevik Russia* (London: Cassell, 1920), 22.

4. Ibid. 128–9.

5. Lenin is said to have remarked that he would like to see John Reed's book *Ten Days that Shook the World* published in all languages and distributed in millions of copies around the world. See Frederick C. Bargehoorn, *The Soviet Cultural Offensive: The Role of Cultural Diplomacy in Soviet Foreign Policy* (Princeton: Princeton University Press, 1960), 32.

6. George Lansbury, speaking at the Victoria and Albert Hall, *Daily Herald*, 22 March 1920, 7.

7. Ben Turner, *About Myself 1863–1930* (London: Humphrey Toulmin, 1930), 219.

8. Mrs Philip Snowden, *A Political Pilgrim in Europe* (London: Cassell, 1921), 151.

9. L. Haden Guest, *Struggle for Power in Europe 1917–1921* 38.

10. H. G. Wells, *Russia in the Shadows* (London: Hodder & Stoughton, 1920), 11.

11. Ibid. 28.

12. V. I. Lenin, *The Soviets at Work, a Discussion of the Problems Faced by the Soviet Government of Russia after the Revolution: Programme Address before the Soviets April, 1918* (Glasgow: The Socialist Information and Research Bureau (Scotland), 1919), 11–12.

13. Richard Stites, *Revolutionary Dreams: Utopian Vision and Experimental Life in the Russian Revolution* (Oxford: Oxford University Press, 1989).

14. William G. Rosenberg, *Bolshevik Visions: First Phase of the Cultural Revolution in Soviet Russia*, i. *The Culture of a Revolution* (Ann Arbor: University of Michigan Press, 1990), 43.

15. Rosenberg, *Bolshevik Visions: First Phase of the Cultural Revolution in Soviet Russia,* ii. *Creating Soviet Cultural Forms* (Ann Arbor: University of Michigan Press, 1990), 34.

16. Bertrand Russell, *Autobiography* (London: Routledge, 2000), 337.

17. J. T. Murphy, *New Horizons* (London: John Lane, 1941), 108.

18. A. Berkman, *The Bolshevik Myth* (London: Hutchinson, 1925), 44. Since Lansbury's response is so easily judged in hindsight, it may be worth recording his description of scenes encountered a year or so before his first visit to revolutionary Russia. Addressing a Labour Party meeting at Southend, he explained that, on a recent visit to blockaded Germany, 'He had seen in Cologne three hospitals filled with dying babies, and while in the railway station at Berne saw a trainload of Austrian children come in with starvation in their faces. At such sights he had just boiled over in rage, and he felt that he wanted to cry, because he was a human being.' *Southend Standard,* 3 April 1919, 10.

19. 'Labour and Russia. A Strange Hypnotism', letter to the editor from 'Anglo-Russian', *The Times,* 10 September 1920, 11.

20. Edward Carpenter, *My Days and Dreams* (London: Allen & Unwin, 1916), 221–2.

21. Haden Guest, *Struggle for Power in Europe 1917–1921,* 96–7.

22. Emma Goldman, *My Disillusionment in Russia* (New York: Apollo, 1970), 59.

23. Clifford Allen quoted in Arthur Marwick, *Clifford Allen: The Open Conspirator* (Edinburgh & London: Oliver and Boyd, 1964), 62.

24. Charles Roden Buxton, 'The Bolsheviks' Defence', *Daily Herald,* 10 September 1920, 4.

25. 'Appendix II, The Extraordinary Commission', British Labour Delegation to Russia 1920, *Report* (London: Trades Union Congress & Labour Party, 1920), 56.

26. Paul Hollander, *Political Pilgrims: Travels of Western Intellectuals to the Soviet Union, China, and Cuba* (1981; New York: Harper Colophon, 1983), 347–99.

27. Angelica Balabanoff, *My Life as a Rebel* (London: Hamish Hamilton, 1938), 283.

28. Berkman, *Bolshevik Myth,* 135.

29. Goldman, *My Disillusionment in Russia,* 59.

30. Writing in the shtetl of Verba on 23 July 1920, Isaac Babel describes encountering a Jewish family who, having been viciously mistreated by Polish troops, wonder what the Reds might bring to their war-torn community. 'The husband: Will there be freedom to trade, to buy a few things and then sell them right away, no speculating? I tell him yes, there will, everything will be for the better—my usual system—in Russia wondrous things are happening: express trains, free food for children, theatres, the International. They list with delight and mistrust. I think to myself: a sky full of diamonds will be yours, everything will be turned upside down, everyone will be uprooted yet again, I feel sorry for them.' Isaac Babel, '1920 Diary', in *The Complete Works of Isaac Babel,* ed. Nathalie Babel (London: Picador, 2002), 407–8.

31. This was remembered by the Menshevik Gregor Aronson, who was a member of the trade union party that received the delegation in Moscow. Quoted in Stephen White, 'British Labour in Soviet Russia, 1920', *English Historical Review*, 109/432 (June 1994), 634.

32. Robert Williams, *Impressions of Soviet Russia* (Amsterdam: International Transportworkers Federation, 1920).

33. Goldman, *My Disillusionment in Russia*, 77. Mrs Snowden also heard from trade unionists who attended parades under 'threat of penalties' (*Through Bolshevik Russia*, 65).

34. Berkman, *Bolshevik Myth*, 136.

35. For Churchill's 'Bolshevik plague' see *The Times*, 24 February 1919, 6.

36. Haden Guest, *Struggle for Power in Europe 1917–1921*, 43.

37. Bertrand Russell, *The Practice and Theory of Bolshevism* (London: Allen & Unwin, 1920), 186.

38. Berkman, *Bolshevik Myth*, 140.

39. Williams, *Impressions of Soviet Russia*.

40. Haden Guest, *Struggle for Power in Europe 1917–1921*, 42.

41. Turner, *About Myself*, 215–6.

42. Charles Roden Buxton, *In a Russian Village* (London: Labour Publishing Company, 1922). 'Telegraphist Petrov' turned out to be S. Hajdovski, who later wrote to Buxton from Moscow, where he worked in 'the Russian-Canadian-American Passenger Agency'. Letter dated 10 October 1924 placed in Buxton's personal copy of the Russian translation of *In a Russian Village*.

43. Charles Roden Buxton, 'Report on the Village of Ozero', in British Labour Delegation to Russia 1920, *Report*, 132–3.

44. 'Further Notes from the Diary of Margaret Bondfield', ibid. 108.

45. Ibid. 114.

46. Fedor Il'ich Dan, 'Account of British Workers' Delegation to Moscow, 1920 (trans. Francis King, from Dan's *Dva Goda Skitaniy* [*Two Years of Wandering*], (Berlin, 1922) (available on www.uea.ac.uk/his/webcours/russia/documents/dan-dgs1.shtml).

47. Victor Chernov, *Mes tribulations en Russie sovietique* (Paris, 1922). Quoted in White, 'British Labour in Soviet Russia', 634.

48. 'The Printers' Meeting at Moscow and the Printers' Trade Union: Documents edited by L. Haden Guest', in British Labour Delegation to Russia 1920, *Report*, 65.

49. Sylvia Pankhurst, *Soviet Russia as I Saw It* (London, 1921). Quoted in White, 'British Labour in Soviet Russia', 634.

50. 'British Labour and Soviet. Red Flag for England', *Morning Post*, 19 May 1920.

51. '"Pleased with Soviet Victories." Labour Delegate's Statement', *The Times*, 7 June 1920, 11.

52. Walter Meakin, 'Russia United Against Polish Aggression', *Daily News*, 20 May 1920, 1.

53. 'Petrograd to Moscow', *Daily Herald*, 22 May 1920.

54. Winston Churchill, 'Zionism versus Bolshevism; a Struggle for the Soul of the Jewish People', *Illustrated Sunday Herald*, 8 February 1920. For Nesta Webster's version of this conspiracy theory see her *Causes of World Unrest* (London & New York: Putnam, 1920) and also *World Revolution: The Plot Against Civilisation* (London: Constable, 1921). See also George Lane Fox Pitt Rivers, *The World Significance of the Russian Revolution* (Oxford, 1920).

55. Eden and Cedar Black, *Anti-Soviet Forgeries: A Record of Some of the Forged Documents Used at Various Times Against the Soviet Government* (London: Workers' Publications, 1927), 1.

56. Ibid. 2.

57. Ibid. 2, xi.

58. *The Times*, 5 April 1920.

59. 'Mr North … has seen disreputable schools of starving children … metamorphosed into orderly institutions, to remain such for one day in order to deceive the paternal, benevolent eyes of some dangerously idealistic dreamer from the British Isles. He has seen plant carried from a dozen disused factories to make complete one factory, in order that the same type of visitor might be made to conclude that all factories in Russia are in flourishing condition.' See 'A Ruined Russia', *The Times*, 24 May 1920.

60. A *Collection of Reports on Bolshevism in Russia: Abridged Edition of Parliamentary Paper, Russia No. 1 (1919)* (London: HMSO, 1919).

61. 'Foreword', ibid. vi.

62. Winston Churchill to Lord Curzon, 28 March 1919. See Richard H. Ullman, *Britain and the Russian Civil War November 1918–February 1920* (Princeton: Princeton University Press, 1968), 142 n. 20. Ullman describes the dossier as a 'wildly hysterical piece of propaganda'. Churchill also wrote as follows to Lord Beaverbrook on 23 February 1918: 'I am increasingly convinced that there can be no more valuable propaganda in England at the present time than graphic accounts of the Bolshevik outrages and ferocity, of the treacheries they have committed, and what ruin they have brought upon their country and the harm they have done to us and our fighting men. It seems to me that the papers should be encouraged to give much publicity to all the news which reaches us of the chaos and anarchy in Russia.' Martin Gilbert, *Winston S. Churchill*, iv. *1917–1922* (London: Heinemann, 1975), 229.

63. *Collection of Reports on Bolshevism in Russia*, 68.

64. Mrs Snowden, *Through Bolshevik Russia*, 172. One example of the charge that the Bolsheviks were also engaged in a 'nationalisation of children' is to be found in the protestation of Lieutenant Commander Robson who, in an article headed 'H.M.S. Tilbury and the Bolshevists' and printed in the *Southend Standard* on 1 April 1920, asked 'Would any English mother like to have the infants taken from them and sent to national "nurseries" to be brought up

as scoffers of religion … Would English parents like their daughters to be "nationalised" to be loaned out to prospective husbands on trial?'

65. Mrs Snowden, *Through Bolshevik Russia*, 173.

66. The text of one such 'proclamation' was saved by PO George William Smith who served on HMS *Borodino* during the British North Russian Expeditionary Force of 1918–19. Claiming to be based on the example of the Soviet of Peasants, Soldiers, and Workers' deputies of Kronstadt, this decree was entitled 'Bolshevik Press Message—30th August 1919'. Written in the name of the Association of Anarchists in Saratov, it declares that the existing marriage laws had ensured that 'all the best species of beautiful women have been the property of the bourgeoisie'. Since this had prevented the 'proper continuation of the human race', it was now decreed that women between the ages of 17 and 32 could no longer be held as private property. As the property of the whole nation, they would be made available thrice weekly to men whose papers confirmed their correct working-class status. The 'distribution and management of appropriated women' would be the responsibility of the Saratov Anarchist Club, and those who gave birth to twins would receive a special prize of £20 (www.naval-history.net/WWIz05NorthRussia.htm). Perhaps this is a version of the proclamation that has recently been attributed to the 'provincial welfare department in Saratov' (Orlando Figes, *A People's Tragedy: the Russian Revolution 1891–1924* (London: Cape, 1996), 741). Certainly, the story of Bolshevism's 'nationalisation of women' survived Ethel Snowden's repudiation of 1920. It is said to have re-emerged in the late 1940s, when it inspired primitive peasants in Poland and other East European countries as they looked forward to the pleasures of the new Communist regime (personal communication from Michal Komar). It surfaced again in 2006 when a Russian historian, Ivan Sivoplys, revealed his discovery of a telegram in which Lenin, having been informed that peasants in the Siberian region of Simbirsk (Lenin's own homeland) were enacting this outrageous measure in the name of Bolshevism, replied with the order 'Immediately check in the strictest way if the facts are true. Arrest the guilty. The bastards must be punished severely and quickly, and the local population informed.' In reporting this discovery on 19 April 2006, both the *Daily Mirror* and Scottish *Daily Record* assumed that the repudiated 'edict' ordering the nationalization of women had been originated by Bolshevik committees. Nick Paton Walsh, Moscow correspondent of the *Guardian*, countered that the allegation actually arose as White propaganda during the Russian Civil War. In March 1918, a Saratov café owner of pronounced monarchist and White Russian sympathies, faked the notorious decree, attributing it to the Saratov anarchists and posting it around town. The anarchists responded by murdering the café owner and burning down his premises. The fake order was then adopted by the White Russian generals, and widely reproduced as proof of the barbarism of the Bolsheviks. See Nick Paton Walsh, 'Nationalisation of Wives Made Lenin See Red', *Guardian*, 20 April 2006.

67. Turner, *About Myself*, 216.

68. Charles Roden Buxton, 'Relief of Children in Russia; Report to Save the Children Fund', typescript dated Moscow 29 June 1920.

69. Charles Roden Buxton, typescript entitled 'Two Months in Soviet Russia' (1920).

70. Quoted from a paragraph, cancelled in pencil, from C. R. Buxton's typescript 'Two Months in Russia'. The *Daily Herald* published several articles extracted from this text.

71. Charles Roden Buxton, 'Exit Regent Street', *Daily Herald*, 11 August 1920.

72. 'Nevsky Prospect' in Nikolai Gogol, *Plays and Petersburg Tales* (Oxford: Oxford University Press), 3.

73. Ibid. 36.

74. Harry Pollitt, *Serving My Time: Apprenticeship in Politics* (London: Lawrence & Wishart, 1940), 136.

75. The stucco of Nash's Regent Street buildings was derided as proof of their 'sham' status in the controversy surrounding their demolition in 1924, to be replaced by the present buildings of Portland stone, designed by Sir Reginald Bloomfield. See 'Stucco and Stone', *The Times*, 27 February 1924, 15.

76. As she travelled north by train, Miss Rhoda Power saw drunken Red Guards capering around over Cossack corpses. She also used drink as a measure of the revolution as it developed in Rostov: 'Drunkenness increased, and inert masses of humanity lolled about the streets. A supply of vodka had become available at Novocherkask and women gained money so easily that they gave up their usual work and confined their attention to profiting in vodka, which they bought for five roubles a bottle and sold in Rostov for thirty. One taste of spirit produced an insatiable thirst, and anything alcoholic was imbibed with gusto.' She also recounted the experience of a friend who was in his bedroom when brigands entered. He gave them a bottle of liqueur, which they drank and found too sweet. They then moved on to his hair tonic, saying 'Ah, that's good! It burns' (Rhoda Power, *Under Cossack & Bolshevik* (London: Methuen, 1919), 281).

77. Philip Snowden MP, *Socialism and the Drink Question* (London: ILP, 1908), 3.

78. Mrs. Snowden, *Through Bolshevik Russia*, 26. Snowden does not name this hypocritical delegate as Robert Williams, but there can be little doubt it was he that she has in mind. She remarks that this man—who was 'not a total abstainer'— has since commended the revolutionary government's ban on the drink traffic, and insisted that any future revolution in Western Europe would have to be accompanied by 'the total prohibition of strong drink'. Williams makes this point in his *Impressions of Russia*: 'if we have to pass through a revolutionary crisis prohibition will be absolutely essential during the period of transition'.

79. Mrs Snowden, *Through Bolshevik Russia*, 26.

80. Ibid. 182.

81. Ibid. 180.

82. Leslie Haden Guest later wrote that 'The Red Flag is being overlaid with gold embroidery and military inscriptions, the primitive simplicity of revolutionary

fervour is giving way to the glory of military decorations, insignia of rank, smart belts and all the rest of the familiar paraphernalia. The more we hammer Russia the more her military spirit increases.' See *Struggle for Power in Europe 1917–1921*, 99.

83. 'The Failure of Bolshevism', *The Times*, 24 June 1920.

84. 'Labour MP's estimate of Lenin', *The Times*, 11 June 1920, 18.

85. Turner, *About Myself*, 224, 222.

86. Tom Shaw MP, as reported in *The Times*, 26 June 1920.

87. Buxton, *In a Russian Village*, 62.

88. Charles Roden Buxton, 'The Refreshment Room at Narva. Reval, Esthonia, July 3rd, 1920', *The Nation*, 31 July 1920, 555.

89. A. C. Wallhead, 'Report of the Chairman, Councillor A. C. Wallhead, on his Visit to Russia and Meeting with the Executive of the Third International', in Independent Labour Party, *Report of the National Administrative Council, 1921* (London: ILP, 1921), 36.

90. Ibid. 33.

91. Clifford Allen, 'Letter of Clifford Allen on Visit to Russia and the International, July 21, 1920', ILP, *Report, 1921*, 39.

92. 'Animated Congress', *Daily Herald*, 8 September 1920.

93. Berkman, *Bolshevik Myth*, 137.

94. Goldman, *My Disillusionment in Russia*, 59.

95. Quoted from Theodor Rothstein's 'Introduction' to the Russian translation of Charles Roden Buxton's *In a Russian Village* (Moscow and Petrograd: Gozisdat, 1923), 6. A Lithuanian-born Bolshevik, Rothstein spent many years in voluntary exile from Russia, living in Germany and, from 1891, in Britain. As a writer and activist in Britain, Rothstein campaigned with the Social Democratic Federation and the 'Hands Off Russia' Committee and working as London correspondent to various socialist papers on the Continent. After returning to Russia in 1920, he served as Soviet ambassador in Tehran and was later appointed chief of the Soviet Press Department in 1923. See John Saville, 'Introduction' in Theodore Rothstein, *From Chartism to Labourism* (1929; London: Lawrence & Wishart, 1983), v–xxvi. See also the preface to Paul Scheffer, *Seven Years in Soviet Russia* (London & New York: Putnam, 1931).

96. Ethel Snowden's book would still be attracting derision nearly half a century later, when the socialist historian S. R. Graubard judged that 'the work actually merited slight attention; contradictory and simple, it revealed the operation of an undistinguished mind loosed from its parochial moorings'. Graubard, *British Labour and the Russian Revolution 1917–1924* (Cambridge, Mass.: Harvard University Press, 1956), 218.

97. Lansbury, *What I Saw in Russia*, xiii.

98. 'Pro-Bolsheviks in Straits', *Morning Post*, 12 June 1920, 6.

99. 'As Russia Sees Us. False Ideas Spread by Bolsheviks', *Morning Post*, 21 June 1920, 7.

100. Angelica Balabanoff [Balbanova], *My Life as a Rebel* (London: Hamish Hamilton, 1938), 285.

101. Ibid. 285.

102. Snowden, *Through Bolshevik Russia*, 51.

103. Turner, *About Myself*, 228.

104. Mrs Snowden, *Through Bolshevik Russia*, 59.

105. 'The English Soviet Republic', *The Times*, 20 May 1920, 14.

106. Murphy, *New Horizons*, 161.

107. Entry for 23 May 1920 in 'Journal of Trip to Russia', Bertrand Russell, *Uncertain Paths to Freedom: Russia and China, 1919–1922* (London and New York: Routledge, 2000), 167.

108. Buxton, *In a Russian Village*, 96.

109. *Times,* 24 June 1920, 16.

110. *Times,* 26 June 1920, 15.

111. Berkman, *Bolshevik Myth*, 156. Together with Emma Goldman, Berkman quit Russia after the Bolsheviks' violent suppression of the Kronstadt rebellion in 1922.

112. Goldman, *My Disillusionment in Russia*, 214.

113. 'Russia's Misery. Italian Socialists on Bolshevist Rule', *The Times*, 8 October 1920.

114. Balabanoff, *My Life as a Rebel*, 289.

115. Ibid. 292. Balabanova may have been entirely accurate in her description of the translations. The British Communist J. T. Murphy records that many stories about the Bolshevik treatment of Western delegations circulated among the foreign visitors staying at Moscow's Delavoy Dvor Hotel in the autumn of 1920. Attributed to the American Communist journalist John Reed, the best of these was said to have concerned events that took place at the Baku Conference of Eastern peoples that summer. An English delegate was persuaded to address the conference, in order to demonstrate that there were anti-imperialists even in Britain. The chosen man was reluctant, but he had no sooner started than the floor was taken over by the 'translator', a man named Peter Petrov who launched into his own anti-imperialist flights and raised the audience to a terrific pitch of excitement. As they brandished swords and fired rifles into the air, the English speaker, who found himself hailed as an anti-imperialist hero, started spluttering with objections: 'I'm sure I never said anything like that; I never said anything like that! I demand a proper translation! It isn't my speech! It isn't my speech!' Murphy, *New Horizons*, 121.

116. Goldman, *My Disillusionment in Russia*, 214.

117. Sheridan, *Russian Portraits*, 103.

118. Balabanoff, *My Life as a Rebel*, 318.

119. Winston Churchill, letter to Clare Sheridan, 21 April 1921. Churchill Papers (Churchill College Archives Centre, Cambridge), CHAR 1/138/23.

120. 'A Labour View of Bolshevism. Mr. Ben Turner on the Terror', *The Times*, 10 June 1920, 17.

121. Winston Churchill, 'Russia an Enslaved Bedlam', *Evening News*, 14 June 1920, 1, 5. Churchill's article was reported at length under the heading 'Lenin: Mr. Churchill on the Man of Shame', *Morning Post*, 15 June 1920.

122. 'Peace with Russia', *The Times*, 23 August 1920.

123. James H. Baum, secretary of Leicester and District Trades Council, letter to Winston Churchill, 31 July 1920, Churchill Papers, CHAR 2/110/89.

124. Churchill, undated typescript of reply to Baum, Churchill Papers, CHAR 2/110/141.

125. Winston Churchill, typescript of letter to Baum, 5 August 1920, Churchill Papers, CHAR 2/110.

126. A. J. P. Taylor, *The Trouble Makers: Dissent over Foreign Policy, 1792–1932* (London: Heinemann, 1957), 121. Roy Jenkins describes Churchill's loss as 'surely one of the heaviest swings in the country' (*Churchill* (London: Pan, 2002), 376).

127. 'Williams' reply', *Daily Herald*, 27 August 1920, 3.

128. Russell, *Autobiography*, 333.

129. Quoted in Urmas Sutrop, 'Bertrand Russell in Estonia', *Russell: A Journal of Bertrand Russell Studies*, 26/1 (Summer 2006), 64.

CHAPTER 12 THE VIEW FROM LOCARNO

1. Augustus John, *Autobiography* (London: Cape, 1975), 164.

2. Ibid. 161.

3. Lord D'Abernon, *An Ambassador of Peace, Lord D'Abernon's Diary, iii. The Years of Recovery January 1924– October 1926* (London: Hodder & Stoughton, 1930), 152.

4. Ibid. 153.

5. F. G. Stambrook, '"Das Kind"—Lord D'Abernon and the Origins of the Locarno Pact', *Central European History*, 1/3 (September 1968), 238.

6. 'French Foreign Policy. Chamber Criticism', *The Times*, 29 December 1923, 7.

7. Despatch of 10 February 1924. Quoted by Stambrook, 'Das Kind', 241.

8. D'Abernon, *Ambassador of Peace*, 101.

9. Ramsay MacDonald, *National Defence: A Study in Militarism* (London: Allen & Unwin, 1917), 47.

10. 'Tank as Snowcutter', *Daily Herald*, 10 September 1920.

11. 'New Use for Torpedoes', *Morning Post*, 10 May 1920.

12. Roy Jenkins, *Churchill* (London: Pan, 2002), 386.

13. Having honed his skills as a propagandist while overseeing Britain's press censorship during the 1914–18 war, Lord Birkenhead had wasted no opportunity to associate Ramsay MacDonald's post-war Labour Party with Soviet Bolshevism. C. E. Bechhofer describes Birkenhead as leader of the anti-Russian tendency in the Tory party and declares that 'if ever a man won an

election' it was Lord Birkenhead who won Britain for the Tory party in October 1924. C. E. Bechhofer, *Lord Birkenhead: Being an Account of the Life of F. E. Smith, First Earl of Birkenhead* (London: Mills & Boon, 1926), 159.

14. Jenkins, *Churchill*, 398.

15. D'Abernon, *Ambassador of Peace*, 21–2.

16. Stambrook, 'Das Kind', 246.

17. D'Abernon, *Ambassador of Peace*, 153.

18. Ibid. 16.

19. A. J. P. Taylor, *The Origins of the Second World War* (London: Hamish Hamilton, 1961), 54.

20. Lord, D'Abernon's diary, 20 July 1925, *Ambassador of Peace*, 177.

21. Ibid. 211.

22. Ibid. 222.

23. Bernard M. Baruch remembered how this phrase was used by the French in the discussions at Versailles in 1919. See his *The Making of the Reparation and Economic Sections of the Treaty* (New York and London: Harper & Bros, 1920), 3. The problem of raising the 'iron curtain' separating Germany and France would still be under discussion in British press coverage of the French election of 1928. See, for example, 'French Election Campaign. The Stabilization of the Franc', *The Times*, 6 February 1928, 11.

24. Charles Roden Buxton, 'Behind Russia's Curtain,' *The New Leader*, 21 October 1927, 5.

25. 'The Note to Russia', *The Times*, 24 February 1927, 15.

26. See Jennifer Betteridge, 'The Political Purpose of Surveillance: the Rupture of Diplomatic Relations with Russia', www.leeds.ac.uk/history/e-journal.pdf. Also Harriet Flory, 'The Arcos Raid and the rupture of Anglo-Soviet Relations', *Journal of Contemporary History*, 12 (1977).

27. Charles Roden Buxton, 'Shall We Recognise Russia?', typescript of article written in 1927.

28. See 'Tourists of the Revolution', in Hans Magnus Enzensberger, *The Consciousness Industry: On Literature, Politics and the Media* (New York: Seabury Press, 1974), 129–57.

29. Ibid. 133.

30. Jean-Pierre Gaussen, 'Le Charme discret de la Russie rouge (Paris–Moscou 1927)', *Les Révoltes logiques*, 14/15 (1981), 114–26.

31. C. E. Bechhofer, *Through Starving Russia* (London: Methuen, 1921), 138.

32. Jacques Rancière, *Short Voyages to the Land of the People* (1990; Stanford: Stanford University Press, 2003), 4.

33. *Russia: The Official Report of the British Trades Union Delegation to Russia and Caucasia Nov. and Dec., 1924* (London: Trades Union Congress, 1925), xii.

34. Henri Béraud, *Ce que j'ai vu à Moscou* (Paris: Les Éditions de France, 1925), 14.

35. Albert Fabre-Luce, *Russie 1927* (Paris: Grasset, 1927), 19–20.

36. Ellis Ashmead-Bartlett, CBE, *The Riddle of Russia* (London: Cassell, 1929), 15. A former *Daily Telegraph* war correspondent, Ashmead-Bartlett had broken the news about the disastrous mismanagement of Churchill's Dardanelles campaign in 1915. He had also been Conservative MP for North Hammersmith from 1924 to 1926, when bankruptcy put an end to his parliamentary career.

37. Frederick C. Bargehoorn, *The Soviet Cultural Offensive: The Role of Cultural Diplomacy in Soviet Foreign Policy* (Princeton: Princeton University Press, 1960), 10.

38. David Caute, *The Fellow-Travellers: A Postscript to the Enlightenment* (London: Weidenfeld and Nicolson, 1973), 53–4.

39. Ibid. 53.

40. Sylvia R. Margulies, *The Pilgrimage to Russia: The Soviet Union and the Treatment of Foreigners, 1924–1937* (Madison: University of Wisconsin Press, 1968), 63.

41. Anna Louise Strong, *I Changed Worlds: The Remaking of an American* (New York: Garden City, 1937), 181.

42. Béraud, *Ce que j'ai vu à Moscou*, 81.

43. Fabre-Luce, *Russie 1927*, 83.

44. Ibid. 83.

45. Mr Ostermayer, the delegate of the Hamburg Bakers, made his objection in *Der Socialistische Bote*, 2/3 (5 February 1927), 144–5. He is here quoted from Joseph Douillet, *Moscow Unmasked* (London: The Pilot Press, 1930), 34–5.

46. Stefan Zweig, *The World of Yesterday* (London: Cassell, 1953), 337.

47. Ibid. 338.

48. Ibid. 333. See also Jean-Louis Panné, *Boris Souvarine: Le Premier Désenchanté du communisme* (Paris: Lafont, 1993), 191–4.

49. Bechhofer, *Through Starving Russia*, 31.

50. H. G. Wells, *Russia in the Shadows* (London: Hodder & Stoughton, 1920), 11.

51. For an account of the early twentieth-century emergence of public relations as a reaction against more democratic assertions of public opinion, see Stuart Ewen, *PR!: A Social History of Spin* (New York: Basic Books, 1996).

52. Charles Sarolea, *Impressions of Russia* (London: Nash & Grayson, 1923), 107–8.

53. Béraud, *Ce que j'ai vu à Moscou*, 21.

54. Clare Sheridan, *Russian Portraits* (1921; Cambridge: Faulkner, 1992), 61.

55. Ashmead-Bartlett, *Riddle of Russia*, 191.

56. Ibid. 107.

57. Ibid. 25–27.

58. Sarolea, *Impressions of Russia*, iii, 53–4.

59. Alexander Wicksteed, *Life under the Soviets* (London: Bodley Head, 1928), 163.

60. Sarolea, *Impressions of Russia*, 18.

61. Ibid. 109.

CHAPTER 13 SNAPSHOTS FROM A LAND OF CONTRASTS

1. Walter Benjamin, letter to Jula Radt, Moscow, 26 December 1926. See, *The Correspondence of Walter Benjamin 1910–1940*, ed. Gershom Scholem and Theodor W. Adorno (Chicago: University of Chicago Press, 1994), 311.

2. See 'Moscow' in Walter Benjamin, *One-Way Street and Other Writings* (London: New Left Books, 1979), 177–8.

3. Arthur Koestler, in R. Crossman (ed.), *The God that Failed: Six Studies in Communism* (London: Hamish Hamilton, 1950), 43.

4. Ante Ciliga, *The Russian Enigma* (London: Ink Links, 1979), 27. The quoted passage is from *Au pays du grand mensonge*, first published in France in 1938.

5. Freda Utley, 'The Building of the New Republic', *Socialist Review*, 21 (October 1927), 36.

6. Clare Sheridan, *Russian Portraits* (1921; Cambridge: Faulkner, 1992), 123.

7. E. Ashmead-Bartlett, CBE, *The Riddle of Russia* (London: Cassell and Company, 1929), 42.

8. Ibid. 102.

9. Remembering those well-stocked markets in the more straitened climate of 1932, when he returned to photograph the medieval wooden churches of Russia, the Buxtons' son David would describe the late 1920s as the 'easy times'. David Roden Buxton, 'A Journey in Northern Russia', repr. from *Blackwood's Magazine* (August 1933), 25. DRB returned to Russia in 1928 and 1932, travelling and photographing the architecture of medieval churches.

10. Charles Roden Buxton, 'Russia a Month Ago', *The World Outlook* (a section of the *Friend*), 4 November 1927, 83.

11. Ibid.

12. Dorothy Frances Buxton, *The Challenge of Bolshevism* (London: Allen & Unwin, 1928).

13. A very different account of this sort of 'remoulding' of Soviet humanity was offered by the four anonymous Russian anarchists, whose pamphlet *The Russian Revolution and the Communist Party* was written in June 1921 and published, with a preface by Alexander Berkman, in the Russian Revolution Series, No. 2 (Berlin: Der Syndikalist, 1922). As an example of Bolshevism's 'cynical doctrinairism', they cited Bukharin's declaration that 'Proletarian compulsion in all its forms ... beginning with summary execution and ending with compulsory labor is, however, paradoxical it may sound, a method of reworking the human material of the capitalist epoch into Communist humanity' (11).

14. D.F. Buxton, *Challenge of Bolshevism*, 24–5.

15. David Caute, *The Fellow-Travellers*, (London: Weidenfeld and Nicolson, 1973), 206.

16. Ciliga, *Russian Enigma*, 27. The quoted passage is from *Au pays du grand mensonge*, first published in France in 1938.

17. This is quoted, very selectively, in 'Potted Biographies. – No. 43', an entry about Buxton assembled as part of 'A DICTIONARY OF ANTI-NATIONAL BIOGRAPHY' and first printed in *The Patriot*, 9 August 1928.
18. Victoria de Bunsen, *Charles Roden Buxton: A Memoir* (London: Allen & Unwin, 1948), 47.
19. Charles Roden Buxton MP, 'Shall We Recognise Russia?', typescript of article written in 1927.
20. Ibid.
21. Manès Sperber, *The Achilles Heel* (1959; Port Washington & London: Kennikat Press, 1971), 81.
22. Sylvia R. Margulies, *The Pilgrimage to Russia: The Soviet Union and the Treatment of Foreigners, 1927–1937* (Madison: University of Wisconsin Press, 1968), 20.
23. Friedrich Adler, *The Anglo-Russian Report: A Criticism of the Report of the British Trades Union Delegation to Russia from the Point of View of International Socialism* (London: P. S. King, 1925), 9. This is a British translation of an article first printed in Adler's socialist monthly *Der Kampf* (Vienna).
24. Ashmead-Bartlett, *Riddle of Russia*, 109–10.
25. Joseph Douillet, *Moscow Unmasked: A Record of Nine Years' Work and Observation in Soviet Russia* (London: Pilot Press, 1930), 19.
26. Ibid. 20.
27. Ibid. xiii.
28. Ibid. 23.
29. Ibid. 26.
30. Ibid. 25.
31. Ibid. 26.
32. Ibid. 28.
33. Ibid. 23.
34. *Soviet Eyewash: Socialist Whitewash: An Examination of the Official Report of the British Trades Union Delegation to Russia in November and December, 1924* (Tiptree: the Anchor Press, 1925), 19–20.
35. Emma Goldman, *Living My Life* (London: Duckworth, 1932), ii. 968.
36. Ibid. 3.
37. Emma Goldman, lecture at the South Place Institute, London, reported in 'Trade Union Report on Russia; Miss Goldman's Criticisms', *The Times,* 17 April 1925, 12.
38. 'Trade Unionists and Soviet Delegates; report criticised', *The Times,* 14 April 1925, 10.
39. [Emma Goldman], *Russia and the British Labour Delegation's Report: A Reply* (London: British Committee for the Defence of Political Prisoners in Russia, 1925), 4.
40. *Russia: The Official Report of the British Trades Union Delegation to Russia and Caucasia, Nov. and Dec. 1924* (London: Trades Union Congress, 1925), xvi.
41. Ibid. 31.

42. Michel Federoff, *La Russie sous le régime communiste: Répose au rapport de la Délégation des Trades-Unions britanniques, basée sur la documentation officielle soviétique*, with pref. by Hubert Bourgin (Paris: Nouvelle Librairie national, 1926).

43. Mrs Philip Snowden, *A Political Pilgrim in Europe* (London: Cassell, 1921), 32.

44. 'Introduction' to Friedrich Adler, *J'Accuse: An Address in Court* (New York: Socialist Publication Society, 1917), 3.

45. Ibid. 13, 11, 9.

46. Ibid. 27.

47. 'Russia and the Bolsheviks', *New Statesman*, 17 November 1917.

48. Adler, *J'Accuse*, 20.

49. Ibid. 20.

50. Ibid. 15.

51. Friedrich Adler, *The Witchcraft Trial in Moscow* (New York: Pioneer Publishers, 1937), 7.

52. Friedrich Adler, *Democracy and Revolution* (New York: Rand School Press, 1934), 23.

53. Adler, *Anglo-Russian Report*.

54. Ibid. 29.

55. Ibid. 30.

56. Ibid. 14.

57. Ibid. 15.

58. Ibid.

59. Ben Turner, *About Myself 1863–1930* (London: Humphrey Toulmin, 1930), 211. George Young accompanied the British Labour Delegation of 1920, reporting on their progress through Russia as special correspondent for the *Daily Herald*. His reliability, or otherwise, may be indicated by the fact that he once informed readers, with specious certainty, that the delegation's still unwritten report would declare the institutions of Bolshevik Russia to be 'giving good practical results in all departments investigated'. See his article 'Lenin to English', *Daily Herald*, 29 May 1920.

60. Ibid. 10.

61. Ibid. 15–16.

62. Ibid. 35, 27.

63. Ibid. 12–13.

64. For a revealing consideration of the limited 'universalism' of British liberalism in the age of empire, see Udal Singh Mehta, *Liberalism and Empire: A Study in Nineteenth-Century British Liberal Thought* (Chicago: University of Chicago Press, 1999).

65. Turner, *About Myself*, 13.

66. Sarolea, *Impressions of Russia*, iii.

67. Béraud, *Ce que j'ai vu à Moscou*, 19.

68. 'Jan Valtin' (Richard Krebs), *Out of the Night* (1941; London: Fortress Books, 1988), 127.

69. Ibid. 185.
70. Björn Hallström, *I Believed in Moscow* (London: Lutterworth, 1952), 155.
71. Frederick C. Bargehoorn, *The Soviet Cultural Offensive* (Princeton: Princeton University Press, 1960), 17.
72. Ellis Smith's notes on this journey are held in Salford Local History Library, U294/Z64.
73. Margaret McCarthy, *Generation in Revolt* (London: Heinemann, 1953), 105.
74. *Soviet Russia To-Day: Report of the British Workers' Delegation, 1927* (Labour Research Department, 1927), 81.
75. McCarthy, *Generation in Revolt*, 106.
76. Ellis Smith, Notes for a talk given in *c.*1960, Salford Local History Library, U294/27.
77. McCarthy, *Generation in Revolt*, 106.
78. Ibid. 107.
79. Ellis Smith, notes for a talk given in *c.*1960.
80. Harry Wicks, *Keeping My Head: The Memoirs of a British Bolshevik* (London: Socialist Platform, 1992), 78–9.
81. 'Soviet Russia of Today. As seen by British Co-operators and Trade Unionists', *Millgate Monthly*, 23/270 (March 1928), 327–35.
82. *Soviet Russia Today*, 17–18.
83. 'A Soviet Pageant. Pantomime History', *The Times,* 9 November 1927, 14.
84. *Soviet Russia Today*, 14.
85. Ibid. 30.
86. Ibid. 62.
87. Julius Braunthal, *History of the International 1914–1943* (London: Nelson, 1967), 258.

CHAPTER 14 COMRADE BUKHARIN'S VERSION

1. Nikos Kazantzakis, *Tòda Raba,* tr. Amy Mims (New York: Simon and Schuster, 1964), 117.
2. Boris Souvarine, *Panaït Istrati et le communisme* (Paris: Éditions Champ Libre, 1981), 3.
3. See Gus Fagen, 'Introduction', in Christian Rakovsky, *Selected Writings on Opposition in the USSR 1923–1930* (London and New York: Allison and Busby, 1980), 7–64.
4. 'Speech to the Twelfth Party Congress', ibid. 35.
5. Gus Fagan, 'Introduction', ibid. 37.
6. Romain Rolland, 'Introduction', in Panaït Istrati, *Kyra, My Sister* (1923; London: Toulmin, 1930), 9–10.
7. Souvarine, *Panaït Istrati et le communisme*, 4.
8. Ibid. 3.
9. Panaït Istrati, *Vers l'autre flamme,* 3 vols. (Paris: Reider, 1929), i. *Après seize mois dans L'URSS,* 73.

10. Ibid. 106–7.
11. Ibid. 85, 39.
12. Ibid. 90.
13. Kazantzakis, *Toda Raba*, 58. Shortly after returning to the West after journeying through Russia with Istrati, Kazantzakis withdrew to Czechoslovakia to write about his Soviet experiences. As Eleni Kazantzakis explains, he had intended two volumes of travel sketches, but found himself unable to produce anything but this 'confession in the form of a novel', which would remain unpublished until 1962, when a French edition appeared. The English translation followed in 1964. The character named 'Toda Raba' is a highly exoticized African Negro, who gives up his shamanistic practices to embrace Lenin and makes the pilgrimage to Moscow in time for the tenth anniversary celebrations. According to Eleni Kazantzakis, who shared some of the Soviet journey with her husband, Istrati was taken as the model for a character named 'Azad', a volatile and risk-taking figure, who is inclined to call for a new revolution within the revolution: considered necessary in order to rekindle the flame and shake off the bureaucratization, opportunism and inertia that 'Azad' condemns before all and sundry during the course of his travels. See Eleni Kazantzakis, 'An Afterword', in Kazantzakis, *Toda Raba*, 204–20.
14. Istrati, *Vers l'autre flamme*, i., 91.
15. Ibid. 71–2.
16. Ibid. 51.
17. Kazantzakis, *Toda Raba*, 118.
18. See Fred Kupferman, *Au pays des Soviets: Le Voyage français en Union soviétique 1917–1939* (Paris: Gallimard/Julliard, 1979), 41.
19. Ibid. 108–9.
20. Eleni Kazantzakis, 'Afterword', in Kazantzakis, *Toda Raba*, 209.
21. Ibid. 80.
22. *Coloured Troops in Europe: Report of a Meeting held in the Central Hall, Westminster, on April 17th, 1920* (London: Women's International League, 1920), 9.
23. For Eleni Kazantzakis's, claim that Istrati was the model for the character Azad, see N. Kazantzakis, *Toda Raba*, 212.
24. Leon Trotsky, *My Life: An Attempt at an Autobiography* (Harmondsworth: Pelican, 1973), 566–7.
25. Ibid. 104.
26. Moshe Lewin, *The Soviet Century* (London: Verso, 2005), 24.
27. *Report of the XV Congress of the Communist Party of the Soviet Union: Official Report with Decisions and Discussions* (London: CPGB, 1928), 407–8.
28. Ibid. 162.
29. Ibid. 148.
30. Ibid. 397.
31. Writing on 18 December 1927, *The Times*'s correspondent in Riga quoted this phrase from the resolution expelling Rakovsky, Kamenev, and nearly a

hundred others from the Soviet Communist Party. 'More Expulsions at Moscow. Communist Party Purge', *The Times,* 19 December 1927, 12.

32. Ibid. 328.

33. Victor Serge, *Memoirs of a Revolutionary, 1901–1941,* tr. Peter Sedgwick (Oxford: Oxford University Press, 1967), 232.

34. See Stephen F. Cohen, *Bukharin and the Bolshevik Revolution: A Political Biography, 1888–1938* (Oxford: Oxford University Press, 1980), 268.

35. 'More Expulsions at Moscow. Communist Party Purge', 12.

36. Serge, *Memoirs of a Revolutionary,* 235.

37. See e.g. 'The "Professional Dangers" of Power', Rakovsky's letter to the exiled Trotskyist N. V. Valentinov, written in Astrakhan on 6 August 1928 and collected in Rakovsky, *Selected Writings,* 124–36. Writing in the 1940s, Victor A. Kravchenko recalled an occasion in early 1929, when Rakovsky criticized the party while speaking at a factory in the Ukraine. Workers who expressed sympathy with his views were immediately attended by the GPU, and Rakovsky himself was silenced soon afterwards. See Victor A. Kravchenko, *I Chose Freedom* (New York: Transaction, 1988), 51.

38. Istrati, *Vers l'autre flamme,* i., 211.

39. Ibid. 154.

40. Ibid. 45.

41. Kazantzakis, *Toda Raba,* 120.

42. Ibid. 89.

43. As one of Kazantzakis's characters remarks, 'We are going through a period of transition. … We have almost no present; our mind understands only the past; our hearts aspire to nothing but the future.' Ibid. 33.

44. Ibid. 34.

45. Souvarine, *Panaït Istrati et le communisme,* 17.

46. Istrati, *Vers l'autre flamme,* i.

47. Istrati, *Vers L'autre flamme,* ii. *Soviets 1929.*

48. Ibid. 208.

49. Ibid. 5.

50. Ibid. 174.

51. Ibid. 41, 10.

52. Ibid. 196.

53. Ibid. 199.

54. Ibid. 201.

55. Istrati, *Vers l'autre flamme,* iii. *La Russie nue* For the English translation of Souvarine's volume, see Panaït Istrati, *Russia Unveiled,* tr. R. J. S. Curtis (London: Allen & Unwin, 1931).

56. Ibid. 18–20.

57. Istrati (Souvarine), *Vers L'autre flamme,* iii. *Russia Unveiled,* 11.

58. Ibid. 20.

59. Ibid. 26.

60. Istrati (Souvarine), *Vers L'autre flamme*, iii. *La Russie nue*, 154.
61. Istrati (Souvarine), *Russia Unveiled*, 17.
62. Ibid. 19.
63. Ibid. 18.
64. Ibid. 16.
65. Ibid. 21.
66. Ibid. 23.
67. Ibid. 22.
68. Ibid. 23–4.
69. Ibid. 25.
70. Ibid. 16.
71. Ibid. 175.
72. Ibid. 17.
73. Ibid. 62.
74. The Communist and Adlerian psychologist Manès Sperber describes trying to help 'Robert Plontin', a former commander of punitive raids in the dekulakization campaign, who turned up in Berlin as a Comintern operative haunted by dreams in which his own young son—still in Russia—was converted into a tormented orphan of the kind his raids had created. See Manès Sperber, *The Unheeded Warning 1918–1933* (New York and London: Holmes & Meier, 1991), 127–32.
75. Sheila Fitzpatrick, *Stalin's Peasants: Resistance and Survival in the Russian Village after Collectivisation* (Oxford: Oxford University Press, 1994), 16, 262.
76. Kazantzakis, *Toda Raba*, 63.
77. Fitzpatrick, *Stalin's Peasants*, 277.
78. Jean-Pierre Gaussen, 'Le Charme discret de la Russie rouge', *Les Révoltes logiques*, 14/15 (1981), 126.
79. Jean-Louis Panné, *Boris Souvarine: Le Premier désenchanté du communisme* (Pars: Lafont, 1993), 194. For an informative account of Istrati's return to Romania and also of his demonizaton by Barbusse and others, see Stelia Tomase, 'The Renegade Istrati', *Archipelago: An International Journal of Literature, Arts, Politics, Culture* (www.archipelago.org), 10/1–2 (Summer 2006), 60–98.
80. Rolland used this phrase in his diary, noting his refusal to participate in Barbusse's attack. Quoted in 'Justice pour Panaït Istrati: Radiographie de la campagne mensongère et calomnieuse d'Henri Barbusse', in Istrati, *Vers l'autre flamme* (Paris: Gallimard, 1987), 283.
81. Ibid. 274–95.
82. 'L'homme qui n'adhère à rien', *Les Nouvelles Littéraires*, 8 April 1933. Ibid. 244–9, 282.
83. *L'Humanité*, 17 April 1935. Ibid. 305.
84. Lord Parmoor, speaking at a Labour Party demonstration in Fulham Town Hall, See 'Relations with Russia. Lord Parmoor on "unworthy prejudice"', *The Times*, 19 November 1929, 9.

85. Leon Trotsky, *The Revolution Betrayed: What Is the Soviet Union and Where Is It Going?* (1936; London: New Park, 1973), 2–3.

CHAPTER 15 NO END TO THE POTEMKIN COMPLEX

1. Nikolai Bukharin, *Philosophical Arabesques* (London: Pluto, 2005), 272.
2. See Aleksander Solzhenitsyn, *Invisible Allies* (London: Harvill, 1997), 16.
3. Roosevelt had died on 12 April 1945, and his widow Eleanor Roosevelt was US delegate to the United Nations. She chaired the UN's Commission on Human Rights, founded in 1946, and was a leading campaigner for the UN's adoption of the Universal Declaration of Human Rights in 1948. She visited Moscow in 1957.
4. Aleksander Solzhenitsyn, *The First Circle*, trans. M. Guybon (London: Collins, 1968), 337.
5. Ibid. 339.
6. Michael Scammell, *Solzhenitsyn: A Biography* (London: Paladin, 1986), 375.
7. Archibald Lyall, *Russian Roundabout: A Non-Political Pilgrimage* (London: Harmsworth, 1933), 165.
8. Ibid. 130.
9. Margaret Bourke-White, 'Louis Fischer's Soviet Journey', *The Nation*, 140/3641 (17 April 1935), 460.
10. Pierre Pascal, a recanted French sympathizer, would remember visiting such a place and failing to realize that prostitution had actually disappeared because, like so much else, it had been 'sent to Siberia' (Fred Kupferman, *Au pays des Soviets: Le Voyage Français en Union Soviétique 1917–1939* (Paris: Gallimard/Julliard, 1979), 40).
11. See G. Allen Hutt, 'In the Hands of the O.G.P.U', *British Russian Gazette & Trade Outlook*, 7/8 (May 1931), 186–7.
12. Ewald Ammende, *Human Life in Russia* (London: Allen & Unwin, 1936), 202.
13. Ibid. 197.
14. Freda Utley, *Lost Illusion* (London: Allen & Unwin, 1949), 140.
15. Stephen Kotkin, *Magnetic Mountain: Stalinism as a Civilization* (Berkeley and Los Angeles: University of Californian Press, 1995), 23.
16. Jeffrey Brooks, *Thank You, Comrade Stalin! Soviet Public Culture from Revolution to Cold War* (Princeton: Princeton University Press, 2000), 78.
17. Sheila Fitzpatrick, 'Making a Self for the Times: Impersonation and Imposture in 20th-Century Russia', *Kritika: Explorations in Russian and Eurasian History*, 2/3 (Summer 2001), 469–87.
18. Ibid. 469. See also Sheila Fitzpatrick, *Tear off the Masks! Identity and Imposture in Twentieth-Century Russia* (Princeton: Princeton University Press, 2005). For a discussion of Edmund Burke's denunciation of the comparable performances and 'public rituals and denunciation' demanded during the French Revolution,

see Frans de Bruyn, *The Literary Genres of Edmund Burke: The Political Uses of Literary Forms* (Oxford: Clarendon Press, 1996), 166–7.

19. Julie A. Cassidy, *The Enemy on Trial: Early Soviet Courts on Stage and Screen* (Dekalb: Northern Illinois University Press, 2000), 173.

20. Ibid. 85–7.

21. Elinor Lipper, *Eleven Years in Soviet Prison Camps* (1950; London: Hollis & Carter, 1951).

22. Ibid. 14.

23. Henry A. Wallace with the collaboration of Andrew J. Steiger, *Soviet Asia Mission* (New York: Reynal & Hitchcock, 1946), 18.

24. Wallace, *Soviet Asia Mission*, 15, 20.

25. Ibid. 33.

26. Lipper, *Eleven Years in Soviet Prison Camps*, 111–12.

27. Wallace, *Soviet Asia Mission*, 34.

28. Ibid. 35.

29. Lipper, *Eleven Years in Soviet Prison Camps*, 112.

30. Owen Lattimore, 'New Road to Asia', *National Geographic*, 86/6 (December 1944), 641–76.

31. Lipper, *Eleven Years in Soviet Prison Camps*, 115.

32. Lattimore, 'New Road to Asia', 657.

33. Lipper, *Eleven Years in Soviet Prison Camps*, 116.

34. Ibid. 269.

35. V. M. Berezhkov, who would later become Stalin's translator, uses this phrase in his memoirs, *At Stalin's Side* (New York, 1994). Quoted in Brooks, *Thank You, Comrade Stalin!*, 74.

36. Gyula Illyés, 'Oroszország 1934' ('Russia 1934'), *in Szives Kalauz: Utijegyzetek, Külföld* (The Cordial Guide: Travel Notes from Abroad) (Budapest, 1966), 21–2. I quote this from Paul Hollander, *Political Pilgrims* (1981; New York: Harper Colophon, 1983), 107–8; see also 455 n. 16.

37. Kupferman, *Au pays des Soviets*, 101.

CHAPTER 16 FRIENDS AGAINST FAMINE

1. 'The Iron Curtain', *The Times*, 3 September 1931, 8.

2. Andrew Cairns, report to E. M. H. Lloyd of the Empire Marketing Board, 3 August 1932, in Marco Carynnyk, Lobomyr Y. Luciuk, and Bohdan S. Kordan (eds.), *The Foreign Office and the Famine: British Documents on Ukraine and the Great Famine of 1932–1933* (Kingston, Ontario: Limestone Press, 1988), 106.

3. Ibid. 107.

4. 'The Third Anniversary of V.O.K.S. To the Intellectuals of the World', *VOKS Weekly News Bulletin* (September 1928). Quoted in Ruth Emily McMurry and Muna Lee, *The Cultural Approach: Another Way in International Relations* (1947; Port Washington, NY, and London: Kennikat Press, 1972), 111.

5. 'VOKS on the Threshold of 1929', *VOKS Weekly News Bulletin*, 14 January 1929. Quoted in McMurry and Lee, *Cultural Approach*, 115.

6. Ibid. 117.

7. Ibid. See also Sylvia R. Margulies, *Pilgrimage to Russia* (Madison: University of Wisconsin Press, 1968), 61.

8. Friedrich Adler, 'The United Front, True and False', in *The Anglo-Russian Report* (London: P. S. King, 1925), 44, and 46–7.

9. *VOKS Weekly News Bulletin* (September 1928). Quoted in McMurry and Lee, *Cultural Approach*, 111.

10. Douglas Goldring, *Pacifists in Peace and War* ('The Here and Now Pamphlets', No. 1; London: Wishart, 1932), 11.

11. George Bernard Shaw, *Look you Boob ... What Bernard Shaw told the Americans about Russia!* (London: Friends of the Soviet Union, 1931).

12. *The Rationalization of Russia by Bernard Shaw*, ed. and introd. Harry M. Geduld (Bloomington: University of Indiana Press, 1964), 16.

13. Ibid. 18.

14. Ibid. 21.

15. Eugene Lyons, *Assignment in Utopia* (1937; New Brunswick: Transaction, 1991), 430.

16. Ibid. 428–9.

17. S. Wicksteed, 'Statistics of Humour', *British Russian Gazette and Trade Outlook*, 8/12 (Sept. 1932), 301.

18. The *Western Independent* as quoted in Derek Wilson, *The Astors 1763–1992: Landscape with Millionaires* (London: Weidenfeld and Nicolson, 1993), 237.

19. *Fabian News*, 42/9 (Sept. 1931), 1.

20. 'Mr. Shaw's Comparison', *The Times*, 6 August 1931, 7.

21. *Rationalization of Russia by Shaw*, ed. Geduld, 58.

22. Ibid. 40.

23. Ibid. 71.

24. Ibid. 82.

25. Ibid. 85.

26. Alexander Wicksteed, *Ten Years in Soviet Moscow* (London: Bodley Head, 1933), 101.

27. Sheila Fitzpatrick, *Tear off the Masks!* (Princeton: Princeton University Press, 2005), 38–9.

28. Wicksteed, *Ten Years in Soviet Moscow*, 5.

29. Paul Scheffer, *Seven Years in Russia* (London and New York: Putnam, 1931), ix.

30. Paul Scheffer, 'Full Light on Russia. The Crisis of Fate. Stalin and Gathering Shadows. Ruining Agriculture to force "Socialisation." A Mighty Tyranny and its Nemesis', *Observer*, 8 December 1929, 6.

31. Margaret Cole, *Growing Up into Revolution* (London: Longmans, Green and Co., 1949), 159.

32. Archibald Lyall, *Russian Roundabout: A Non-Political Pilgrimage* (London: Harmsworth, 1933), 15.

33. John Morgan 'Agriculture', in Margaret I. Cole (ed.), *Twelve Studies in Soviet Russia* (London: Gollancz, 1933), 111–12.

34. Description of a Tour in the Volga Region; Report by Andrew Cairns (Moscow), 22 August 1932, in Carynnyk et al. (eds.), *Foreign Office and Famine*, 182.

35. Andrew Cairns, report to E. M. H. Lloyd, 7 June 1932, in Carynnyk et al. (eds.), *Foreign Office and Famine*, 40. In the same report, Cairns records that while he was in Russia in 1932, he read Soviet newspaper reports that George Bernard Shaw had 'told the South African *Cape Times* that never since the days of Napoleon had the world seen such energy as the Russian peasants were now displaying'. He also recalls a Chatham House meeting the previous winter at which an editor of the *New Statesman and Nation*, who was also a professor at the LSE (Harold Laski?) announced that 'the real wages of the Russian people were rapidly rising' (75).

36. Cairns, ibid. 153.

37. Cole, *Growing Up into Revolution*, 159–60.

38. Ibid. 158.

39. Cairns, report to E. M. H. Lloyd, 7 June 1932, 74.

40. Ibid. 75–6.

41. Sir Esmond Over to Arthur Henderson, 3 June 1930. Quoted by Gordon W. Morrell, *Britain Confronts the Stalin Revolution: Anglo-Soviet Relations and the Metro-Vickers Crisis* (Waterloo: Wilfrid Laurier University Press, 1995), 55.

42. C. H. Bateman, minute to Cairns's report to the Empire Marketing Board, 7 June 1932. Carynnyk et al. (eds.), *Foreign Office and Famine*, 76.

43. Sir Laurence Collier, head of Foreign Office Northern Department, in 'Foreign Office Notes for a Reply to Sir Waldron Smithers in the House of Commons, 2 July 1934', in Carynnyk et al. (eds.), *Foreign Office and Famine*, 397.

44. Dr Otto Schiller, *Die Krise der sozialistischen Landwirtschaft in der Sowjetunion*, Reports on Agriculture, 7 (1933). See Ewald Ammende, *Human Life in Russia* (London: Allen & Unwin, 1936), 29–31.

45. Morrell, *Britain Confronts the Stalin Revolution*, 55.

46. Report by Andrew Cairns (Moscow), 22 August 1932, in Carynnyk et al. (eds.), *Foreign Office and Famine*, 185–6.

47. Ibid. 186–7.

48. Two medical investigators, who travelled down the Volga in August 1932, also declared themselves 'amazed and distressed' to see the crowds, often loaded by bundles which 'appeared to contain all their possessions', who jostled desperately to board their already jammed steamer. While not attributing their situation to famine, they were not persuaded by those who cited the hordes to be found at every river and train station 'as evidence of the freedom of the worker'. See Sir Arthur Newsholme and John Adam Kingsbury, *Red Medicine: Socialized Health in Soviet Russia* (London: Heinemann, 1934), 123.

49. Editorial, *New Statesman and Nation*, 17 September 1932, 302.

50. Lyons, *Assignment in Utopia*, 572.

51. William Strang (Moscow) to Sir John Simon, 26 September 1933, in Carynnyk et al. (eds.), *Foreign Office and Famine*, 313.

52. See 'Preface: The Journalist in Soviet Russia', in Scheffer, *Seven Years in Russia*, x.

53. William Strang (Moscow) to Laurence Collier, 6 December 1932, in Carynnyk et al. (eds.), *Foreign Office and Famine*, 209. The first of Duranty's offending articles appeared as 'All Russia Suffers Shortages of Food', *New York Times*, 25 November 1932. Further articles appeared over the following five days.

54. 'Mutiny in the Red Army; Fierce Fighting seen by Englishman', *Daily Telegraph*, 28 November 1930, 11–12.

55. Louis Fischer, 'Lies about Russia', *New Republic*, 10 June 1931, 94–6.

56. Louis Fischer, 'Lies about Russia: II', *New Republic*, 8 July 1931, 199–202.

57. Lyons, *Assignment in Utopia*, 575.

58. Walter Duranty, *Russia Reported* (London: Gollancz, 1934), 366.

59. 'Noel Charles (Moscow) to J. M. K. Vyvyan, 1 September 1934', in Carynnyk et al. (eds.), *Foreign Office and Famine*, 428.

60. [Malcolm Muggeridge] 'The Soviet and the Peasantry. An Observer's Notes; I. Famine in North Caucasus', *Manchester Guardian*, 25 March 1933, 13.

61. [Malcolm Muggeridge] 'The Soviet and the Peasantry. An Observer's Notes; II. Hunger in the Ukraine', *Manchester Guardian*, 27 March 1933, 9.

62. [Malcolm Muggeridge] 'The Soviet and the Peasantry. An Observer's Notes; III. Food Harvest in Prospect', *Manchester Guardian*, 28 March 1933, 9.

63. 'More Arrests in Germany' and 'Berlin under the New Regime', *Manchester Guardian*, 2 March 1933, 9.

64. *The Diaries of Beatrice Webb*, ed. Norman and Jean Mackenzie (London: Virago, 2000), 514.

65. Beatrice Webb, review of M. Phillips Price, *My Reminiscences of the Russian Revolution, Fabian News*, 32/6 (June 1921), 27–8.

66. Beatrice Webb, Introduction to Alexander Wicksteed, *Life under the Soviet* (London: Bodley Head, 1928), vii–viii, xiii.

67. Margaret Cole, *Beatrice Webb* (London: Longmans, Green and Co., 1945), 170.

68. *Diaries of Beatrice Webb*, ed. Mackenzie, 511.

69. Ibid. 514.

70. Ibid. 515.

71. Ibid. 516.

72. Barbara Drake, quoted ibid. 527.

73. Dr H. J. Stewart, *The Times,* 19 August 1935, 15.

74. See Margaret Siriol Colley, *More than a Grain of Truth: the Biography of Gareth Richard Vaughan Jones* (Newark (Notts): Nigel Linsan Colley & Margaret Colley, 2005).

75. Letter to parents, 26 August 1930, quoted in Colley, *More than a Grain of Truth*, 85. Later in 1930, Jones also wrote a series of unattributed articles for *The Times*

in which he declared: 'Visitors to Tsarist Russia often returned to England impressed with the apparent loyalty of the whole population to the Emperor and entirely unaware of the rapidly growing discontent which was seething beneath the surface. Today history is repeating itself. Groups of tourists, biased from the very beginning in favour of the "workers' paradise," are being shown by competent and charming guides the façade of Soviet Russia and leave the country enthusiastic over the success of the Socialistic experiment. Not possessing the slightest knowledge of the language, and meeting few people other than active Communists, they leap to the conclusion that the majority of Soviet citizens are ardent supporters of the present regime. The politeness of Communist officials, and their willingness to spare no trouble in impressing their guests, disarm criticism and leave the foreign delegations blissfully ignorant of the hunger, discontent, opposition, and hatred which in the last few months have been steadily growing in intensity and are spreading through all parts of the Soviet Union and through all sections of the community.' See 'The Two Russias; 1. Rulers and Ruled', *The Times,* 13 October 1930, 13. For these and other documents see also the Colleys' website, www.garethjones.org.

76. Colley, *More than a Grain of Truth,* 120.
77. Ibid. 127.
78. Ibid. 129.
79. Ibid. 197.
80. Ibid. 227.
81. Ibid. 228
82. Ibid. 229.
83. 'Russia To-day. Criticism of Press Correspondents', *Manchester Guardian,* 30 March 1933, 12.
84. See the dedication in Wicksteed, *Ten Years in Soviet Moscow,* v.
85. Walter Duranty, 'Russians Hungry but not Starving', *New York Times,* 31 March 1933, 13.
86. Colley, *More than a Grain of Truth,* 260.
87. Malcolm Muggeridge, letter to Gareth Jones, 29 September 1933, quoted ibid. 267.
88. Louis Fischer, in Arthur Koestler et al., *The God that Failed: Six Studies in Communism* (London: Hamish Hamilton, 1950), 210.
89. See the text of a speech given by Nigel Colley at St Patrick's Cathedral, New York, 19 November 2005. http://www.garethjones.org/st_patrick's_2005.htm

CHAPTER 17 STEELED MINDS AND THE GOD THAT FAILED

1. Yevgeny Zamyatin, *We* (1920–1; New York: The Modern Library, 2006), 43.
2. Article from September 1922, collected in Walter Duranty, *Russia Reported* (London: Gollancz, 1934), 354.
3. Herriot in an interview in *La Nouvelliste,* 14 September 1933.

4. Ewald Ammende, *Human Life in Russia* (London: Allen & Unwin, 1936), 255.

5. Ibid. 21.

6. See Martyn Housden, 'Ambiguous Activists: Estonia's Model of Cultural Autonomy as Interpreted by Two of its Founders, Werner Hasselblatt and Ewald Ammende', *Journal of Baltic Studies*, 35/3 (Fall 2004), 231–53.

7. Ammende, *Human Life in Russia*, 186.

8. Ibid. 187.

9. Ibid. 224–5, 203.

10. Ibid. 225–6.

11. Ibid. 227.

12. Ibid. 229.

13. Ibid. 230.

14. Ibid. 230–1.

15. Ibid. 239.

16. Ibid. 240.

17. Ibid. 242.

18. George Orwell, *Animal Farm: A Fairy Story* (1945; London: Penguin, 2003), 55.

19. Ammende, *Human Life in Russia*, 250.

20. For Ammende's relations with Nazism, see Housden, 'Ambiguous Activists'.

21. MacFlecknoe, 'The "Truth about Russia"', *New Statesman and Nation*, 10 September 1932, 280.

22. Sir Arthur Newsholme and John Adams Kingsbury, *Red Medicine: Socialized Health in Soviet Russia* (London: Heinemann, 1934), 7–8.

23. Alexander Wicksteed, *Ten Years in Soviet Moscow* (London: John Lane, 1933), 17, 20.

24. Kingsley Martin, *New Statesman and Nation*, 8 July 1933, 53.

25. Richard Krebs attributes this phrase to his wife 'Firelei'. See 'Jan Valtin', *Out of the Night* (London: Heineman, 1941), 306.

26. George Orwell cited this as the motto of Stalin's Western supporters in his review of *Warfare* by Ludwig Renn (*Horizon,* February 1940). See *The Complete Works of George Orwell,* xii. *A Patriot After All* (London: Chatto & Windus, 1998), 12.

27. George Hardy, *Those Stormy Years: Memories of the Fight for Freedom on Five Continents* (London: Lawrence & Wishart, 1956), 81.

28. David Caute, *The Fellow-Travellers: A Postscript to the Enlightenment* (London: Weidenfeld and Nicolson, 1973), 233.

29. Fred Kupferman, *Au pays des Soviets: Le Voyage français en Union Soviétique 1917–1939* (Paris: Gallimard/Julliard, 1979), 103.

30. G. K. Chesterton, 'Our Notebook', *Illustrated London News,* 30 September 1933, 488.

31. For these and other examples, see Paul Hollander, *Political Pilgrims: Travels of Western Intellectuals to the Soviet Union, China, and Cuba* (New York: Harper Colophon, 1983), 160–5.

32. Ibid. 171.
33. Friedrich Adler, R. Abramovitch, Léon Blum, and Emile Vandervelde, *The Moscow Trial and the Labour and Socialist International* (London: Labour Party, 1931), 8.
34. Friedrich Adler, *The Witchcraft Trial in Moscow* (New York: Pioneer Publishers, 1936), 29.
35. Ibid. 31.
36. Ibid. 17–18.
37. D. N. Pritt, quoted from *News Chronicle*, 3 September 1936. Adler, *Witchcraft Trial*, 17.
38. Ibid. 20.
39. George Orwell, 'Inside the Whale' and letter to Humphry House, 11 April 1940, in *Complete Works*, xii., 103, 140.
40. Julius Braunthal, *History of the International*, ii. *1914–1943* (London: Nelson, 1967), 370.
41. Jan Valtin (Richard Krebs), *Out of the Night* (London: Heinemann, 1941), 306.
42. Ibid. 427–8.
43. George Orwell, 'George Orwell's Proposed Preface to Animal Farm', *Animal Farm*, 108.
44. Louis Budenz, *This is My Story* (New York: McGraw-Hill, 1947), 39–40.
45. Björn Hallström, *I Believed in Moscow* (London: Lutterworth, 1953), 171.
46. Margaret McCarthy, *Generation in Revolt* (London: Heinemann, 1953), 119.
47. See Andrew Flinn, 'William Rust: The Comintern's Blue Eyed Boy?', in John McIlroy, Kevin Morgan, and Alan Campbell, *Party People Communist Lives: Explorations in Biography* (London: Lawrence & Wishart, 2001), 78–101.
48. Harry Wicks, *Keeping My Head: The Memoirs of a British Bolshevik* (London: Socialist Platform, 1992), 100.
49. McCarthy, *Generation in Revolt*, 227–9.

CHAPTER 18 SLIDING BACK TO CHURCHILL

1. Vernon Lee, *Music and Its Lovers: An Empirical Study of Emotion and Imaginative Responses to Music* (London: Allen & Unwin, 1932), 560–1.
2. See '"Vernon Lee"; the Renaissance in Italy', *The Times*, 14 February 1935; also '"Vernon Lee"', *The Times*, 16 February 1935, 17.
3. Romain Rolland, quoted in Bernard Duchatelet's 'Introduction' to Romain Rolland, *Voyage à Moscou (juin–juillet 1935)* (Cahiers 29; Paris: Michel Albin 1992), 35.
4. Romain Rolland, letter to Madeleine Herr, 25 September 1925, ibid. 42.
5. Ibid. 47–8.
6. Ibid. 51.
7. David James Fisher, *Romain Rolland and the Politics of Intellectual Engagement* (Berkeley and Los Angeles: University of California Press, 1988), 272.

8. Romain Rolland, letter to Panaït Istrati, 29 May 1929, Panaït Istrati, *Vers l'autre flamme: Après seize moins dans l'URSS* (Paris: Gallimard, 1987), 202–3. For Istrati's letters to Guerson of the Soviet secret police, see 197–201.

9. Manès Sperber, *The Unheeded Warning, 1918–1933* (New York and London: Holmes & Meier, 1991), 165.

10. Boris Souvarine, *Panaït Istrati et le communisme* (Paris: Éditions Champ Libre, 1981), 22, 16, 23–4.

11. Istrati, letter to Romain Rolland, *Vers l'autre flamme* (Gallimard, 1987), 250–4.

12. For Istrati's open letter and Rolland's reply see, Istrati, *Vers L'autre Flamme* (Gallimard, 1987), 250–5.

13. Romain Rolland, letter to Jean Guéhenno, 9 October 1929. Quoted in Fisher, *Romain Rolland*, 217.

14. Ibid. 254–5.

15. Ibid. 216.

16. Ibid. 280.

17. For Rolland's diary of the trip, and examples of the rapturous letters and speeches of welcome with which he was greeted, see Rolland, *Voyage à Moscou*.

18. Ibid. 238.

19. Fisher, *Romain Rolland*, 271–4.

20. Ibid. 288.

21. Romain Rolland, letter to Elisabeth (31 October 1944), in *Un beau visage à tous sens: Choix de lettres de Romain Rolland (1886–1944)* (Cahiers 17; Paris: Michel albin, 1967), 378–9.

22. 'Our Man for Moscow; Mr. R. Buxton, MP, Almost Certain', *Sunday Dispatch*, 13 October 1929.

23. Douglas Goldring, *Odd Man Out: The Autobiography of a 'Propaganda Novelist'* (London: Chapman & Hall, 1935), 274. Clifford Allen and Charles Roden Buxton were among those whom Goldring described this way.

24. CRB quoted in Victoria de Bunsen, *Charles Roden Buxton: A Memoir* (London: Allen & Unwin, 1948), 118.

25. Charles Roden Buxton, *The Alternative to War: A Programme for Statesmen* (London: Allen & Unwin, 1936), 117.

26. Ibid. 51–2.

27. Charles Roden and Dorothy Frances Buxton, *In a German Miner's Home* (ILP Pamphlets, NS 41; London: ILP, 1921).

28. CRB made this demand on 15 November 1923. Reported in *The Times*, 16 November 1923, 7.

29. De Bunsen, *Charles Roden Buxton*, 153.

30. C. R. and D. Buxton, *In a German Miner's Home*, 12–13.

31. De Bunsen, *Charles Roden Buxton*, 161. A handwritten note in Dorothy Buxton's own copy of this book, explains that she tried to warn Goering 'that

persecutions might lead to war' as, indeed, might 'even denying that there were persecutions or any threat to peace from Germany'.

32. Charles Roden Buxton, 'Far Eastern Issues at the Yosemite Conference', *Nineteenth Century and After*, 717 (November 1936), 538.

33. [Buxton et al.], *The Demand for Colonial Territories and Equality of Economic Opportunity* (London: Labour Party, 1936), 3.

34. Charles Roden Buxton, 'Germany and the Colonies', *The Times*, 1 March 1939, 12.

35. Charles Roden Buxton, 'Public Opinion in Germany', letter to the *Manchester Guardian*, 30 May 1939.

36. C.R.B., 'Quotations from "Mein Kampf"', *Manchester Guardian*, 16 June 1939.

37. De Bunsen, *Charles Roden Buxton*, 162.

38. 'Record of a conversation between the Führer and Reichskanzsler and Lord Halifax, in the presence of the Reichminister of Foreign Affairs, in Obersalzberg, 19 November 1937', Ministry of Foreign Affairs of the USSR, *Documents and Materials Relating to the Eve of the Second World War* (Moscow: Foreign Languages Publishing House, 1948), i. *November 1937-1938*, 19-20.

39. Lord Allen of Hurtwood letter to Julian Trevelyan, 28 February 1938, S. Aster (ed.), *Appeasement and All Souls 1937-1939* (Camden 5th ser, 24; Cambridge: Cambridge University Press, 2004), 66.

40. 'Report of German Ambassador in London Dirksen to Secretary of State in the German Foreign Office Weizsäcker', Ministry of Foreign Affairs of the USSR, *Documents and Materials Relating to the Eve of the Second World War*, ii. *Dirksen Papers (1938-1939)*, 106.

41. Shortly before his visit to the German embassy, Buxton had written to the abdicated Edward VIII, now the Duke of Windsor, commending him for a speech broadcast from Verdun on 9 May, in which he had urged that 'the use of the terms "encirclement" on the one side, and "aggression" on the other side' should be banned and that statesmen should act 'as good citizens of the world'. Buxton, letter to HRH the Duke of Windsor, 5 June 1939. Together with the Duke of Windsor's appreciative reply (19 June 1939), a copy of this letter survives in CRB's sister Eglantyne Jebb's 'autographs' file, presently in the ownership of the family.

42. *The Secret Agreements: with a Preface by Charles Roden Buxton and Nine Maps* (Manchester: The National Labour Press, February 1918).

43. 'Dirksen's Survey of his Ambassadorship in London', Ministry of Foreign Affairs of the USSR, *Documents and Materials Relating to the Eve of the Second World War*, ii. (New York: International Publishers, 1948), 185.

44. Ibid. 109.

45. Ibid. 186.

46. Ibid. 111.

47. Ibid. 271.

48. Ibid. 185.

49. Dorothy Frances Buxton, letter to David Roden Buxton, 17 December 1942.

50. Charles Roden Buxton, *The Case for an Early Peace* (London: The Friends' Peace Committee, 1 January 1940), 7.

51. The letters saved in Eglantyne Jebb's 'autographs' file include communications from David Lloyd George (who wrote on 24 November 1939 to agree that 'peace talks become increasingly difficult as a war progresses' but also expressing the fear that 'we have allowed the last opportunity to pass'), Neville Chamberlain (who wrote to thank Noel Buxton for sending a copy of his brother CRB's notes of 'possible terms of peace' on 21 October 1939), and Lord Halifax, who, on 1 February 1940, acknowledged a memorandum of points sent by CRB and drawn from an earlier conversation between the two men.

52. De Bunsen, *Charles Roden Buxton*, 130–1.

53. 'Ruins in the Temple', *The Times*, 29 May 1941, 2.

54. *The Diaries of Beatrice Webb*, ed. N. and J. Mackenzie (London: Virago, 2000), 579.

55. De Bunsen, *Charles Roden Buxton*, 131.

56. Douglas Goldring, *Facing the Odds* (London: Cassell, 1940), 171.

57. Ibid. 138. Churchill's declaration that this was the only 'ideal' that could guide the British Empire was made with reference to Indian migration to Kenya and other countries in the empire. See 'Value of Crown Colonies', *The Times*, 23 June 1921, 9.

58. Charles Roden Buxton, letter to Winston Churchill, 28 November 1936, Churchill Papers (Churchill Colleges Archives Centre, Cambridge), CHAR 2/260/171.

59. C. R. Buxton, *Alternative to War*, 34.

60. Dorothy Buxton, letter to David Roden Buxton, 28 December 1942.

61. *The Times,* 22 December 1942, 6.

62. Winston Churchill, *My Early Life: a Roving Commission* (London: Thornton Butterworth, 1930), 18–19. D'Abernon's words about his mother, which actually appear in a a glowing 'personal appreciation' of Churchill himself, are here quoted from Viscount D'Abernon, *An Ambassador of Peace*, ii. *The Years of Crisis, June 1922–December 1923* (London: Hodder and Stoughton, 1929), 36.

63. Robert H. Pilpel, *Churchill in America 1895–1961* (London: New English Library, 1977), 221.

64. 'German Picture of Russian Retreat. Song Knocked Out of Soldiers' hearts', *The Times,* 11 July 1944, 3.

65. *The Goebbels Diaries: The Last Days,* ed. Hugh Trevor-Roper (London: Secker & Warburg, 1978), 22.

66. Joseph Goebbels, 'Das Jahr 2000', *Das Reich*, 25 February 1945, 1–2.

67. 'Krosigk's Cry of Woe. Bolshevist Bogy Revived', *The Times*, 3 May 1945, 4.

68. 'That was Then: Allen W. Dulles on the Occupation of Germany', *Foreign Affairs* (November/December 2003). Dulles was Berne Station Chief of the

Office of Strategic Services, a forerunner of the CIA, and he made this remark on 3 December 1945, at a meeting at the Council on Foreign Relations.

69. Winston Churchill, *The Second World War*, vi, *Triumph and Tragedy* (London: Cassell, 1954), 498–9, 523. These passages are quoted in Wolfgang Mieder, *The Politics of Proverbs: from Traditional Wisdom to Proverbial Stereotypes* (Madison: University of Wisconsin, 1997), 55–6. See also Martin Gilbert, who implies von Krosigk as Churchill's source (*'Never Despair': Winston S. Churchill 1945–1965* (London: Minerva, 1990), 7).

70. Winston Churchill speaking in the House of Commons, 16 August 1945. *Hansard, Parliamentary Debates*, 5th Series, vol. 413, col. 84.

71. Hewlett Johnson, *Searching for Light: An Autobiography* (London: Michael Joseph, 1968), 249.

72. Noel Buxton, 'Polish frontiers', letter to the editor, *The Times*, 31 August 1945, 5.

CHAPTER 19 AFTER THE CROSSING

1. Ellis Smith, Labour MP for Salford, remembers being asked this question after returning from China in the Autumn of 1954. See Ellis Smith papers, Salford Local History Library, V294/Z68.

2. 'Commission to Hear Klimowicz', *The Times*, 21 May 1954, 3.

3. Antoni Klimowicz, 'A Sailor's Story' and Andrzej Panufnik, 'A Composer's Story' appeared under the joint heading '2 Exiles From Red Poland Tell of Scarcity and Woes,' *New York Times*, 23 August 1954, 1–2. The second articles were printed under the heading 'Exiles Say Soviet Drains Poland and Ruins Creative Life', *New York Times*, 24 August, 1954, 12.

4. Irene Mizera, telephone conversation, May 2003.

5. 'Pole's Escape Studied by Legal Group', *New York Times*, 24 August 1954, 12.

6. Lydia Banek, telephone conversation, June 2003.

7. Dr Derrick James, 'Diary of a Trip to China, 1954'. In the possession of Dr Tim James, London.

8. See Yakov Rapoport, 'Olga Lepeshinskaya: The Vital Substance and its Inglorious Demise', in Rapoport, *The Doctors' Plot* (London: Fourth Estate, 1991), 254–72.

9. Ibid. 257.

10. Ibid. 269.

11. Ibid. 260.

12. I owe this information to Dr Elizabeth James, who remembered hearing it from her husband, the late Dr Derrick James.

13. Rapoport, *Doctors' Plot*, 124.

14. Ibid. 268.

15. 'American Couple Ask Czech Haven', *New York Times* (8 April 1950), 1 and 3.
16. Ibid.
17. Jack Raymond, 'Two Expatriates Want to Return', *New York Times*, 30 October 1955, 17.
18. Arthur Krock, 'Close Decision in "Lost Citizenship" Cases', *New York Times*, 21 February 1963.
19. Anthony Lewis, 'Supreme Court Rules Out 2 Expatriation Statutes', *New York Times*, 19 February 1963, 4.
20. Representative Francis E. Walter, of Pennsylvania, quoted in *New York Times*, 21 February 1963, 10.
21. See 'The Restoration of František Šorm', in Eugene Garfield, *Essays of an Information Scientist: Of Nobel Class, Women in Science, Citation Classics, and other Essays*, xv. *1992–1993* (Philadelphia: Institute for Scientific Information), 51–6.
22. See John Jones, 'The Life and Work of Josef Rudinger', *Journal of Peptide Science*, 10 (2004), 393–413.
23. Garland R. Marshall, email to the author, 13 May 2004.
24. J. Rudinger and K. Jost, 'Synthetic Analogues of Oxytocin and Vasopressin: Structural Relations', in Josef Rudinger (ed.), *Oxytocin, Vasopressin and Their Structural Analogues: Proceedings of the Second International Pharmacological Meeting, August 20–23, 1963* (Oxford, London, Edinburgh, New York, Paris, Frankfurt: Pergamon Press, 1964), 3.
25. 'Researcher Faked Data at Mt. Sinai Medical School', *New York Times*, 27 December 1982, B4.
26. 'Scientist Faked Results in Race for Patent', *New Scientist*, 6 January 1983, 3.
27. See I. Vavra, A Machova, B.V. Holocek, J. H. Cort, M. Zaoral, F. Šorm, 'Effect of a Synthetic Analogue of Vasopressin in Animals and in Patients with Diabetes Insipidus', *Lancet*, 1 (4 May 1968), 948–952.
28. Carl Djerassi, *The Pill, Pygmy Chimps, and Degas' Horse* (New York: Basic Books, 1992), 319. Quoted in Garfield, 'Restoration of František Šorm'.
29. Šorm described his situation thus, when he met Carl Djerassi in Sofia in 1969. See Djerassi, *Pill, Pygmy Chimps, and Degas' Horse*, 194.
30. See Milan Simecka, *The Restoration of Order: The Normalisation of Czechoslovakia* (London: Verso, 1984).
31. J. D. Cash, 'DDAVP and Factor VIII: A Tale from Edinburgh', *Journal of Thrombosis and Haemostasis*, 1 (2003), 619–21.
32. P. M. Mannucci, 'Desmopressin (DDAVP) and Factor VIII: The Tale as Viewed from Milan (and Malmö)', *Journal of Thrombosis and Haemostasis*, 1 (2003), 622–4.
33. P. Eggena, I. L. Schwartz, and R. Walter, 'Action of Aldosterone and Hypertonicity on Toad Bladder Permeability to Water,' in Rudinger (ed.), *Oxytocin, Vasopressin and their Structural Analogues*, 182–92.

34. Schwartz's paper describes research into the way hormones affect toad bladder permeability to water—including a sample for which he thanks Josef Rudinger. J. H. Cort and B. Lichardus (eds.), *Regulation of Body Fluid Volumes by the Kidney* (Basel: Karger, 1970).

35. Carey Winfrey, 'Noted Scientist Ends his "Exile" after 25 Years', *New York Times*, 1 April 1977, B14.

36. Ibid. B1, B14.

37. Dr Milan Zaoral, 'DDAVP—A Successful Neurohypophyseal HORMONE Analog: Fate of Research', paper presented at the 3rd International and 28th European Peptide Symposium, Prague, 8 September 2004.

38. The molecule in question was described as one in which 9-D-Ala-NH2 was substituted for 9-Gly-NH2. Informed of this claim, Dr Milan Zaoral immediately refers to an article published in Prague in 1966, in which he, Šorm, and other researchers described how they had prepared 3 vasopressin analogues modified at position 9 in Prague. See M. Zaoral et al., 'Preparation of Three Lysine-Vasopressin Analogs Modified at Position 9; 9-D-Ala-Lysine-Vasopressin, 9-Ala-Lysine-Vasopressin and 9-Ethylenediamine-Lysine-Vasopressin', *Collection Czechoslov. Chem. Commun.* 32 (1967), 843–53. Zaoral, letter to the author, 28 September 2004.

39. J. H. Cort and W. Jean Dodds, 'Evidence for the Existence of a Factor VIII Releasing Factor from the Brain Released by the Action of Vasopressin-Like Cyclic Nonapeptides', *Blood*, 54 (suppl. 1), (1979), 274a. Also J. H. Cort et al., 'Receptor Requirements for the Action of Vasopressin-Like Peptides on Factor VIII Release', *Blood*, 54 (suppl. 1) (1979), 275a. My account of these events also benefits from a telephone conversation with Dr W. Jean Dodds, 6 May 2004.

40. J. H. Cort, A. J. Fishchman, W. Jean Dodds, J. H. Rand, and I. L. Schwartz, 'New Category of Vasopressin Receptor in the Central Nervous System; Evidence that this Receptor Mediates the Release of a Humoral Factor VIII—Mobilizing Principle', *International Journal of Peptide and Protein Research*, 17 (1981), 14–22. This article was submitted and accepted for publication in July 1980.

41. 'Errata', *Blood,* 262/5 (November 1983), 1152.

42. 'Biotechnologist faked results in race for patent,' *New Scientist*, 6 January 1983, 3.

43. Alexander Kohn, *False Prophets* (Oxford: Blackwell, 1986), 115–16.

AFTERWORD: GONE WITH THE BERLIN WALL?

1. Nikolai Bukharin, *Philosophical Arabesques* (London: Pluto, 2005), 246.

2. For this and other aspects of the cultural Cold War see David Caute, *The Dancer Defects: The Struggle for Cultural Supremacy during the Cold War* (Oxford: Oxford University Press, 2003).

3. See Russell Jacoby, *Picture Imperfect: Utopian Thought for an Anti-Utopian Age* (New York: Columbia University Press, 2005), 9–10.

4. Sven Lindqvist, *China in Crisis* (London: Faber, 1965), 98.

5. Uwe Johnson, Berlin, 'Border of the Divided World', *Evergreen Review,* 5/21 (November–December 1961), 18–30.

6. Personal communication, October 2004.

7. Daphne Berdahl, *Where the World Ended: Re-Unification and Identity in the German Borderland* (Berkeley and Los Angeles: University of California Press, 1999), 149–50.

8. Lev Manovich, *The Language of New Media* (Cambridge, Mass.: MIT Press, 2001), 146.

9. Patrick Cockburn, *Getting Russia Wrong: The End of Kremlinology* (London: Verso, 1989), 20.

10. See Andrew Wilson, *Virtual Politics: Faking Democracy in the Post-Soviet World* (New Haven: Yale University Press, 2005).

11. One such converted watchtower is to be found in Rüterberg, a small village—once completely encircled by East German wire—on the eastern bank of the river Elbe.

12. Frederick Taylor, *The Berlin Wall 13 August 1961–9 November 1989* (London: Bloomsbury, 2006), 404.

13. Michael Howard, *The Invention of Peace* (London: Profile, 2000), 90.

14. Paul Rivero, speaking from exile in Spain on the BBC website. See 'Cuba President: "fear is everywhere"', http://news.bbc.co.uk/1/hi/world/americas/4789080.stm. Accessed on 7 August 2006.

15. Pawel Monat (with John Dille), *Spy in the U.S.* (New York: Berkley Medallion, 1963), 16–17.

16. David Caute, review of John Lewis Gaddis, *The Cold War: A New History*, in the *Spectator* (14 January 2006). Quoted from Tony Judt, 'A Story Still to be Told', *New York Review of Books,* 23 March 2006, p.15.

17. Francis Fukuyama, *After the Neocons: America at the Crossroads* (London: Profile Books, 2006), 116.

18. Tony Judt, 'Bush's Useful Idiots', *London Review of Books,* 28/18 (21 September 2006).

19. David Samuels, Grand Illusions, *The Atlantic*, June 2007, 48.

20. See Phil Gunson, 'Bolivarian Myths and Legends', *Open Democracy,* 1 December 2006. See also Alma Guillermoprieto, 'Don't Cry for Me, Venezuela', *New York Review of Books,* 6 October 2005, 26–34. For Tariq Ali's memorable account of touring Venezuela and Bolivia with Richard Gott see 'Diary', *London Review of Books*, 21 July 2007, 35. Chàvez's optimistic admirers might do well to reflect on E.P. Thompson's words of caution, issued in 1968 with reference to an earlier generation of disenchanted romantics: 'There must be some objective reference for social hope, and it is one trick of the mind to

latch on to an unworthy object in order to sustain such hope.' See 'Disenchantment or Default? A Lay Sermon', in E.P. Thompson, *The Romantics: England in a Revolutionary Age* (Woodbridge: Merlin), 69. In this connection, it may also be worth recalling the argument advanced by Agnes Heller and Ferenc Fehér, opposition socialists who arrived in the West having been pressured out of Hungary in the 1970s. In various pamphlets and books published through the 1980s, they argued that, after Stalinism and other deformations of socialism, the intellectuals of the Western left should desist from just sounding off against capitalism, and instead maintain a critical watch over their own emancipatory movements in order to ensure that they did not suffer comparable degeneration. The argument was far from well received, even if its advocates were not invariably rejected as 'agents of American imperialism'.

21. For an account of the virtual terrains of 'digitized' warfare as they existed at the US Army Armor Center (Fort Knox) in 1996, see 'Fort Knox: Cybertanks and the Army after Next', the closing chapter of my *Tank: the Progress of a Monstrous War Machine* (New York: Penguin, 2003), 409–46.

22. Russell Jacoby, *Picture Imperfect*, xvi.

23. Mark Danner, 'IRAQ: The War of Imagination', *New York Review of Books*, 21 December 2006, 83.

24. Retort, *Afflicted Powers: Capital and Spectacle in a New Age of War* (London: Verso, 2006), 23.

25. Arthur Miller, *On Politics and the Art of Acting* (New York: Viking, 2001).

26. Margaret Macmillan, *Seize the Hour: When Nixon Met Mao* (London: John Murray, 2006), 22 & 151.

27. See Frank Rich, *The Greatest Story ever Sold: the Decline and Fall of Truth* (New York: Penguin Press, 2006), 83.

28. Brendan Nyhan, 'The Myth of Robert Byrd and the USS Abraham Lincoln', 8 June 2003, wwwspinsanity.org/columns/20030618.html.

29. W. E. B. Du Bois made this announcement in the opening paragraph of *The Souls of Black Folk* (1903). It is here quoted from Henry Louis Gates Jr. and Nellie Y. MacKay (eds.), *The Norton Anthology of African American Literature* (New York and London: Norton, 1997), 613.

Photographic Credits

Index

Note: page references in *italic* refer to cartoons.

Abraham, Pether 69
Abraham Lincoln, USS (aircraft carrier) 386
Action française, L' 107, 185, 325
Addams, Jane 88, 89
Adler, Friedrich 295, 329–31
on 1924 Trade Union Delegation 252–3
Stürgkh, murder of 249–51
Afghanistan 184, 217
After Sixteen Months in the USSR (Istrati) 271
Aked, Dr Charles Frederick 410 n. 8
Albany Review 166–7
Albert, king of the Belgians 99–102
Alexander I, king of Serbia 169
Alexander, Ann 68
Alexei Rykov (Soviet steamer) 305
Algemeen Handelsblad (Dutch paper) 177
All-Russian Agricultural Exhibition 233
All-Union Central Council of Trade Unions 230
All-Union Society for Cultural Relations (VOKS) 230, 294, 295
Allen, Clifford 133, 196, 347
and British Labour Delegation to Russia (1920) 132, 137
and Communist International 209–10
and ILP 209, 247
America, *see* USA
American Society of Haematology 370–1
Ammende, Ewald 322–6
Andronoffsky Monastery Prison Camp 148
Angell, Norman 94–5, 106, 110, 119
Anglo-American Pilgrims Society 60

Anglo-Russian Parliamentary Committee 252
Anglo-Russian Trade Union Unity Committee 226
Animal Farm (Orwell) 324–5
Anti-German Union 412 n. 18
anti-Semitism 178, 202, 274, 325, 341
Antselovich, Naum Markovitch 198
Antwerp Free Trade Congress 93
Aragon, Louis 328
Arbeiter Zeitung, Vienna 183
Arcos (All-Russian Co-operative Societies) affair 227, 300, 307, 340
Armfield, Maxwell 78
Aronson, Gregor 437 n. 31
Ashmead-Bartlett, Ellis 229, 232, 233, 236, 245
Asia, and Bolshevism 183–4
Association of Anarchists, Saratov 439 n. 66
Association of Interns and Medical Students (AIMS) 394 n. 38
Astley's Amphitheatre, London 66
Astor, Lady 296, 297
atom bombs 31, 32–3, 42, 59, 353
Attlee, Clement 13, 35
Austria 175, 176, 189
blockade of 172, 179–80
and Bolshevism 183, 184
Avanti 180

Babel, Isaac 197, 219
'Bach's Christmas Music in England and in Germany' (Lee) 79, 86, 89, 153, 389–90
Backer, Henry 11–12
Balabanova, Angelica 151, 192, 215
and E. Snowden 210–11, 212
and techniques of hospitality 197, 212–13, 216

Balfour, A. J. 165
Balkan War (1912) 89, 427 n. 25
Balkan War Relief Committee 427 n. 25
Balkans 38, 167–8, 248
Ballet of the Nations, The (Lee) 76–8, 86,
    114, 121, 125–6
    revision of 113, 116, 127
Baltimore Sun 45
Bamboo Curtain 55, 375
Barbusse, Henri 278–9
Barstow, Dr Leon 371–3
Baruch, Bernard M. 31, 50, 58–9,
    61, 444 n. 23
Bataille, Georges 129
Batory, MS (Polish liner) 8–9
Battleship Potemkin (Eisenstein film) 230–1
Baum, James H. 146, 217
Bechhofer, C. E. 231–2, 443 n. 13
Beethoven, Ludwig von 343
Belgian Woman's Patriotic Union 106
Belgium 96–108
    Albert, king of the Belgians 99–102
    Elisabeth, queen of the
        Belgians 100–7, 109, 343
    and Germany 98–100
    iron curtain imagery 105, 107
    and Netherlands 96–7
Bellaman, Henry 24–5
Belsky, Franta 53
Benjamin, Walter 235
Benn, Tony 13, 14, 15
Béraud, Henri 230
Berezhkov, V. M. 454 n. 35
Berkman, Alexander 197, 211, 213,
    216, 446 n. 13
    deportation from America 155–6
    disillusionment of 162, 195, 215
    as interpreter to foreign
        delegations 195, 198
Berlin blockade (1948) 376
Berlin Wall 53, 375, 383
Berliner Tageblatt 168
Bernstein, Ethel 156
Beveridge, William 36, 91, 314
Bevin, Ernest 35, 137, 218
Big Three 38–9, 40; *see also* Churchill;
    Roosevelt; Stalin
Birkenhead, Lord (F. E. Smith) 223
Blast, The 155, 424 n. 10

Blatchford, Robert 91
Bolsheviks and Bolshevism 132–3, 136,
    151, 158, 181, 218
    and Allied blockade 171–2
    and Baltic states 155
    Britain and 137–9, 201–5,
        207–8, 214
    Churchill and 40, 56–8, 134, 138,
        164–6, 182, 217–18
    and foreign delegations 142–3, 146,
        149, 163, 212–13
    Germany and 184–5, 186
    Lansbury and 137–8
    and League of Nations 416 n. 4
    Mensheviks and 200–1
    perceived threats from 139, 183–5,
        186, 217
    and USA 181, 188
    see also Comintern
Bombacci, Nicola 215–16
Bondfield, Margaret 132, 134
Boston Daily Globe 1, 5, 9
Boston Evening American 1, 15
Boston Globe 46
Boston Sunday Herald 4, 5
Bottomley, Horatio 80
Boudin, Leonard B. 362, 367
Bourne, Randolph S. 110, 111
Brailsford, H. N. 103, 110, 167,
    172, 182
    on League of Nations 189
Braunthal, Julius 261
Brecht, Bertolt 329
Brentano, Professor Lujo 93–4, 184
Briand, Aristide 60
Brigode, Jane 106
Britain
    Academic Assistance Council 12
    American loan 23, 30, 31, 50, 59
    and Bolshevism 137–9, 201–5, 214
    communism in 210, 218
    diplomatic and trade relations with
        Russia 280
    entente cordiale 90
    fascism in 202
    General Strike 227, 255
    and Germany 78–80, 89–90, 91,
        92–5, 182
    navy 92–3

1917 delegation to Russia 140–1
1920 delegation to Russia 131–53,
   162–4, 191, 214, 216–17
1924 delegation to Russia 244–9, 252–3
1927 delegation to Russia 226,
   137–43, 244, 255–60
and Poland 137; *see also* Klimowicz
socialism 210
Treaty of Collaboration and Mutual
   Assistance (with Soviet Union) 42
and USA, special relationship with 12,
   41–2, 46, 50, 387
British Empire Marketing Board 301–3
British Seamen's Union 419 n. 47
Bromley, John 248
Brown, Dr 13
Brown, John 59
Browning, Robert 63
Buchanan, Meriel 158
Buck, Pearl 46
'Buddha's Smile, The' (Solzhenitsyn and
   Semyonov) 284, 285
Budenz, Louis 55, 332
Buford, USS 156
Bukharin, Nikolai 194, 268–9, 283,
   375, 446 n. 13
and Potemkinism 142–3
show trial 287
Bulgaria 167–9
Burke, Edmund 141–2
Bush, George, Sr 51
Bush, George W. 384, 385–7
Buxton, Charles Roden 133,
   170, 343–50
and Adler 251
on Allied blockade 209
appeasement 346–8
biographical details 163, 166–7, 168,
   169, 206, 350
on blockade of Russia 172–3, 174,
   175–6
on Bolshevism 132–3
Brotherhood of Nations 187
and Germany 344–8
and Hitler 345–6
on iron curtain 227–8
on League of Nations 189
1920 delegation to Russia 17, 132, 162,
   200, 205, 206, 214

1924 Trade Union Delegation 244
1927 visit to Russia 226, 237–8,
   240–3, 244
and Paris Peace Conference 186–7
Parliamentary career 343–8
'The Refreshment Room at
   Narva' 391–2
in Samara 199, 208–9
and socialism 164
and UDC 112, 117, 153
Buxton, David Roden 17, 446 n. 9
1927 visit to Russia 242–3
Buxton, Dorothy Frances 206, 343,
   348, 349
on Allied blockade 174, 175–6, 178
on Clemenceau's cordon sanitaire 184
food aid 178–9
'Foreign Opinion' 176, 179, 183, 189
Goering, meeting with 345
on League of Nations 189
1927 visit to Russia 237, 238–40
and Paris Peace Conference 186–7
and socialism 164
Buxton, Lord Noel 167–8, 169,
   353, 427 n. 25
Byrd, Robert 386–7
Byrnes, James 31, 32, 50
Byron, George Gordon, Lord 69

Cachin, Marcel 140–1, 146, 417 n. 4
cactus curtain 56
Cadbury, George 110
Cairns, Andrew 292–3, 301–3, 304, 305
Calder, Jack 306
Call Bulletin 34
Cambridge Magazine 159, 176, 180
Cammaerts, Émile 98, 105
Camouflage
   British Labour Delegation and 190
   Cachin on 146
   Ethel Snowden on 149
   Great Famine and 303
   Herriot and 323–4
   Lansbury on 146
   Serge on 272
   Solomon on 143–6
   Souvarine on 277
   Wells on 146
   Western front and 131

Canada
  Permanent Defence Agreement (with
    USA) 42
  Soviet spy ring, Ottawa 31
Canning, George 65
Carnegie Endowment for International
  Peace 93
Carpenter, Edward 106, 196
Carver, George Washington 387–8
Cash, J. D. 365, 368
Catherine the Great 142
Caute, David 328, 384
Chaliapin, Feodor 149
Challenge of Bolshevism, The
  (D. F. Buxton) 238–9
Chalmers, Dr Thomas C. 372, 373
Chamberlain, Austen 223, 226–7, 237
Chamberlain, Joseph 89–90
Chamberlain, Neville 341
Chamberlin, W. H. 297
Channel Tunnel 85
Chávez, Hugo 385
Chernov, Victor 200
Chesterton, G. K. 328–9
Chicago Sun 46
Chicherin, Georgi Vasilyevich 192–3,
  197, 209
China 375
Christensen, S. 49
Christian Counter Bolshevist
  Crusade 138
Christian Science Monitor 181
Churchill, Randolph S. 52, 91
Churchill, Winston 4, 72, 106, 146
  on Allied blockade 171, 178
  army uniforms 170
  and Balkan Committee 168
  Baruch, friendship with 58–9
  and Bolshevism 57–8, 134, 138, 144,
    164–5, 182, 204
  and British Labour Delegation
    (1920) 216–17
  and C. Buxton 166–8, 169, 349–50
  and camouflage 145
  and communism 56–7
  and cordon sanitaire policy 182
  and France 223
  Fulton oration 16, 34–45, 56–7, 61
  Fulton oration, conjectured
    content 29–31

Fulton oration, reaction to 45–50, 55
  on Germany 171, 186
  and internationalism 90–2
  and 'iron curtain' phrase 43–4, 60–1,
    351, 352–3
  and Russia 42–3, 137
  and special relationship with USA 12
  and Stalin 42
  threat against, at Fulton 21–2
  toy theatre 74–5
  and Truman 30
  UN as 'temple of peace' 39, 41, 42, 60
  visit to Westminster College,
    Fulton 16, 21–3, 26–9
  and Welsh miners 90–1, 92
  and Zionism 202
Chuter Ede, James 13
Ciliga, Ante 236, 240
Clarion magazine 91
Clark, Bennett Co. 73
Clemenceau, Georges 107–8, 131–2, 172,
  174, 185–6
  cordon sanitaire policy 181–2, 184
Clerambault (Rolland) 123
Clinton, Bill 51
Cobden, Richard 93
Colby, Vinetta 405 n. 52
Cold War 376
  origins of phrase 61
  presentation techniques 386–7
Cole, G. D. H. 332
Cole, Margaret 299, 300–1, 302
Collection of Reports on Bolshevism in
  Russia, A (White Paper) 204, 206
Collier, Sir Laurence 304
Color-line (Du Bois) 183, 388
Comintern, see Third International
Commission for Relief in
  Belgium 103
Committee for Democratic Control,
  USA 110
communism 46, 194, 210, 218
  Churchill and 42, 43–4, 46, 49–50,
    56–7
  see also Bolsheviks and Bolshevism
Communist International, see Third
  International
Communist Youth League
  (Komsomol) 299
Congo Free State 110

cordon sanitaire policy 181–4
Corriere della sera 177
Cort, Dr Joseph H. 9–16, 358–9, 360, 361–2, 363–9
   research in Prague 363–4
   return to America 361–2, 366–74
   and University of Manitoba 364
Cort, Dr Ruth 9–11, 15–16
Courtenay, William 32–3, 47
Covent Garden Theatre 66
CPUSA (American Communist Party) 11, 50, 55, 61
Crocodile magazine 297
Cromer, Lord 91
Cuba: American embargo 383
Cuevas, José Luis 56
Cwiklinski, Jan 9
Czechoslovakia
   Academy of Sciences, Prague 362, 364, 368
   and blockade 179
   and Bolshevism 183
   Corts in 9–16, 363–4
   Institute of Organic Chemistry and Biochemistry, Prague 363, 368
   Prague Spring 364
   scientific research in 362–9

D'Abernon, Lord 221–5
Daily Express 88, 112
Daily Herald 137, 139, 202, 205
Daily Mail 80, 412 n. 18
Daily Mirror 439 n. 66
Daily News 117, 118, 119, 169–70, 202
Daily Record 439 n. 66
Daily Telegraph 98–9, 106, 310
Daily Worker 13, 334
Dan, Fedor Il'ich 200–1, 213
Dangerfield, George 19, 92–3
Danuser Machine Company 23
Davidson, Robert L. D. 52
Davis, Charles Henry 59
Davis, Jefferson 24
Davis, Joseph 329
Day, Donald 309
DDAVP (vasopressin analogue) 363–6, 367, 368–9
De Bunsen, Victoria 116 (n. 45)
de Quincey, Thomas 69
deception

in Russian fiction 284, 285
in warfare 143–5
see also Potemkinism
Delcassé, Théophile 169
Dell, Ethel M. 80
Demidoff, Prince Anatole de 419 n. 54
Denby, Edwin H. 59–60
Denikin, Anton Ivanovich 175
Depage, Dr Antoine 102
des Ombiaux, Maurice 107
Deutsche Allgemeine Zeitung, Berlin 178
Dimitrov, Georgi 331
Dirksen, Herbert von 347
Disarmament Conference (1932) 294
Djerrassi, Carl 364
Dodds, Dr W. Jean 370–1
Donnay, Maurice 102, 103
Donnelly, Phil M. 21, 29
Dos Passos, John 411 n. 10
Douillet, Joseph 245–7
Du Bois, W. E. B. 83–4, 388
du Vigneaud, Vincent 362
Dukes, Paul 159–60
Dulles, Allen W. 352
Dulles, John Foster 50
Duranty, Walter 306–7, 310–11, 318, 319, 321

Eastman, Max 110
Ebert, Friedrich 151
Ebray, Alcide 428 n. 40
Economics and Reparations Commission 58
Edmunds, H. Spencer 49
Edward VII 93
Egerton, Francis 71–2
Eisenstein, Sergei 230
Eleven Years in Soviet Prison Camps (Lipper) 288
Eliot, T. S. 139
Elisabeth of Bavaria, queen of the Belgians 100–7, 109, 343
   iron curtain imagery 105, 107
   as 'Red Queen' 106
Emden, Walter 73
Encyclopaedia Britannica (11th ed.) 83
Enzensberger, Hans Magnus 228
Erzberger, Matthias 185
Esperanto 85, 213, 226

Europe (journal) 342–3
European Peptide Symposia 363, 368

Fabian Society 122, 132, 193
Fabre-Luce, Alfred 230, 231
famine 17, 175–9, 292–3, 297, 298–312,
	314–319, 321–5
Farber, M. A. 373
Farren, Elizabeth 67
fascism 39, 202, 237, 304, 331
Federal Street Theatre, Boston 67
Federation of Free Poles 6
Fehér, Ferenc 468 n. 20
fellow-travellers 295, 312–15, 328–32
	Rolland and 339–43
Ferring AB (pharmaceutical
	company) 366, 367–8, 369, 371
ffrench, Kathleen 203
Fichte, Johann Gottlieb 189
'Fight the Famine' Council 178, 431 n. 85
Fires in Theatres (E. M. Shaw) 70
First Circle, The (Solzhenitsyn) 284
Fischer, Louis 308–10, 319, 320
Fitzpatrick, Sheila 277, 286
Fleeson, Doris 31
Fleming, Ian 354
Food Control Act (1917), USA 181
Food of the Gods, The (Wells) 80
food supplies
	for Germany 152–3
	USA 171–2
	as weapon 178–81
Foot, Michael 11
Ford, Gerald 51
Ford, Henry 110–11, 123, 135
Foreign Affairs bulletin 112
'Foreign Opinion: a Weekly Survey of
	the Foreign Press' 176, 179, 183, 189
Formation of Cells from Live Matter
	(Lepeshinskaya) 359
Forsyte Saga, The (Galsworthy) 298
Foundation for Economic Education 10
France 223
	Alliance Démocratique 222
	entente cordiale 90
	'Friends of the USSR' 264
	1917 delegation to Russia 140–1
	occupation of Ruhr 222
	and reparations 177–8
Frank, Albert V. 147–8

Frank, Waldo 329
Frankfurter Zeitung 146, 183, 185
Freikorps 151
'Friends of the USSR' 264, 272,
	299, 342
Fulton, Missouri 16, 21–4
	Churchill memorials 16, 51–3
	Churchill's visit to 16, 21–3, 26–9
Fulton Daily Sun-Gazette 21, 33, 45
Fulton oration 16, 34–45, 56–7, 61
	conjectured content 29–31
	reaction to 45–50, 55
Fyfe, Sir David Maxwell 5, 13, 14

Gage, Danny 45
Gallacher, Willie 258
Galsworthy, John 298
Gardiner, A. G. 118, 170, 189
Gazette de Lausanne 187
George V, king of England 104
George Washington Carver Grade
	School, Fulton 388
Germany 43–4, 92, 151, 152, 186
	Allied blockade of 144, 171–2, 175–9,
		181, 184, 189–90
	and Britain 78–80, 89–90, 91,
		92–5, 182
	and Bolshevism 184–5, 186
	camouflage 144–6
	communism in 331, 334
	division of 38, 174–5
	food supplies for 152–3
	iron curtain 96–7
	and League of Nations 225–6
	Loti and 98–100, 103–5, 107
	Nazi-Soviet non-aggression
		pact 332, 342
	reparations 57, 59, 178, 222
	socialists in 151
	starvation in 179, 180, 182
	and Turkey 167, 169
	and United States of Europe 60
Glasier, Katharine Bruce 55–6
Globe, The 88
Glover, Richard 412 n. 18
Glowacki, Captain 3, 4–5
Goebbels, Joseph 351–2
Goering, Hermann 345
Gogol, Nikolai 143, 205
gold curtain 55

Golding, Louis 299
Goldman, Emma 155, 156, 196, 211, 216,
    422 n. 108
  on 1924 Trade Union
    Delegation 247–9
  and techniques of hospitality 197
Goldring, Douglas 109, 152, 296, 349
Gorbachev, Mikhail 54–5
Gordin, Morris 158
Gorki, Maxim 272–3
Gouzenko, Igor 398 n. 35
Grahame, Sir George 223
Grasiadei, Professor 215–16
Greece 168, 169
Green Communism 417 n. 8
Grenfell, Harold 172
Grey, Sir Edward 79, 93, 112,
    167, 169
Gut, Vladimir 365–6

Haden Guest, Dr Leslie 132, 150,
    211, 417 n. 5
  on Allied blockade 193
  and Bolshevism 134
  and British delegation (1920) 196, 198,
    199, 201, 208
Hague Peace Conferences 84, 88
Hajdovski, S. 437 n. 42
Haldeman, Bob 386
Halifax, Lord 37, 346
Hallström, Björn 332–3
'Hands Off Russia' Committee 137, 252,
    441 n. 95
Hanson, Sidney Albert 139
Harbutt, Fraser 32, 55
Hardy, George 327
Harper's Magazine 32
Harriman, Averell 31–2
Harrison, Walter 21
Haymarket opera house, London 66
Heath, Edward 51
Heciak, P. 6
Heinz, Jack 315–16
Helbig, George von 419 n. 52
Heller, Agnes 467 n. 19
Henderson, Arthur 280, 303
Hergé (Georges Remi) 245
Herriot, Édouard 321–5
Hill, Archibald Vivian 12
Hitler, Adolf 226, 328–9, 345–6

Hobhouse, Emily 89
Hobsbawm, Eric 18
Hobson, John A. 110, 116
Hodges, Frank 218
Hollander, Paul 329
Holt, Frederick 410 n. 8
Honzl, Jan 368
Hoover, Herbert 50, 103, 181, 186
Hoover, J. Edgar 156
Horizon; a Journal of the Color Line, The 84
Horreur allemande, L' (Loti) 99
Hortus Vitae (Lee) 114
How It All Began (Bukharin) 142
Hugo, Victor 59–60, 83, 154
Hull-House, Chicago 88
Human Life in Russia (Ammende) 325–6
Humanité, L' 278, 279
Humphrey, Hubert 51
Hungary 179, 180
Hurtwood, Lord Allen of, see Allen,
    Clifford
Hussar, HMS (cruiser) 168
Hyèna enragé (Loti) 99

ICRC, see International Committee of
    the Red Cross
Illingworth, Leslie Gilbert 378, 379, 380
Illyés, Gyula 290–1, 387
Independent Labour Party (ILP) 132,
    135, 193, 209
  and Russia 133, 141
India 375
Industrial Party Trial (1931) 286–7, 328
Ingle, Truman L. 27
Innitzer, Cardinal 325
International Commission of Jurists 357
International Committee of the Red
    Cross (ICRC) 110
International Court of Justice 84
International Federation of Free
    Journalists 4
International Federation of Trade
    Unions 214
International Herald Tribune 269
*International Journal of Peptide and
    Protein Research* 370
International Labour Office, Basel 85, 92
International Labour Party 133
International News Service 31
International Red Cross 84, 85

international socialism 193
International Woman Suffrage
    Alliance 106
International Women's Relief
    Committee 106
International Workers of the World 139
internationalism 84, 95, 219
    Bolshevist 188, 219
    Churchill and 90, 95
    of Communist International 254–5
    and nationalism 122, 126
Internationals
    First 83
    and foreign delegations 253–5
    internationalism of 254–5
    Second 83, 133–4, 135, 209, 255
    Second and a Half 251
    see also Third International
Interpol 85
Intourist 230
Iraq 384, 385–6
Irish Times 146
Iron Curtain 375
    converted watchtowers 383
    as declaration of war 55
    origins of phrase 17–18, 60–1, 105
    in theatres 63, 67, 70, 73–4, 80
    see also iron curtain imagery
Iron Curtain (Wellman film) 376
Iron Curtain crossings
    carrier pigeon 1
    Corts 9–16
    eastward 1–2, 9–15
    Klimowicz 2–6, 16
    police dog 1–2
    westward 1–8
iron curtain imagery 191–2,
    222–5, 226
    Belgium and 96–8, 105, 107
    Churchill and 43–4, 60–1, 80–2, 352–3
    Lee 80–2, 89, 94–5, 109, 114, 115–16,
        118, 119, 120, 124, 127, 171
    Nazism and 351
    Rhineland 222
    E. Snowden 152, 153, 155
    between Soviet Russia and the
        West 154–5, 160–1, 163–4
    Wells and 80
Iron Curtain speech, see Fulton oration

Istrati, Panaït 263–7, 269–70, 277, 291,
    318, 340–1
    and Bolshevik revolution 10th
        anniversary celebrations 264–5, 267
    condemnation by Barbusse 278–9
    return to Romania 278
    Roussakov affair 271
Italian Socialist Mission, to
    Russia 215–16
Italy 169, 215, 224, 345

J'Accuse' (Adler) 250
Jacoby, Russell 385
James, Derrick 358–9, 360
Jaroslaw Dabrowski (Polish freighter) 2–7, 9
Jaxa, Jan 4
Jean-Christophe (Rolland) 86
Jebb, Eglantyne 179
Jenkins, Roy 182, 428 n. 37
jingoism 116
John, Augustus 221, 224
John, Dr Otto 2
John Bull 80
Johnson, Hewlett 353
Johnson, Uwe 376
Jolly George (cargo ship) 137
Jones, Arthur Creech 344
Jones, Gareth 315–20
Jordan, Alexander T. 10
Journal de Genève 180
Journal des débats 325
Jowett, Fred 110
Joynston-Hicks, Sir William 227
Judt, Tony 384
Jung, Franz 162–3
Jus Suffragii 79, 105, 106

Kalinin, Mikhail Ivanovich 324
Kamenev, Lev 138, 202, 216, 287
Kansas City Star 30–1
Kansas City Times 22
Kant, Immanuel 83, 189
Kaplan, Jacob Merrill 371
Karolyi, Count Mihaly 183, 188–9
Karr, Jay 396 n. 19
Kazantzakis, Eleni 266, 450 n. 13
Kazantzakis, Nikos 219, 262, 265, 266–7,
    270, 277
Keeling, H.V. 160

Kefali, Mark 200–1
Kellogg, Frank B. 60
Kelly, Michael 65, 67, 69
Kennan, George F. 31, 154–5
Kennedy, Joseph 50
Kerby, Captain 15
Kerensky, Aleksandr Fyodorovich 159
Keynes, John Maynard 82, 152–3,
    173–4, 177
King, Horace 13
King, Mackenzie 31, 50
King Albert's Book 98–9, 102, 106–7
Kings Row (Bellaman) 24–5
Kings Row (film) 25
Kingsbury, John Adams 326
Klimowicz, Antoni 2–6, 9–10,
    16, 354–6
    in America 357–8
    on Soviet Russia 356–7
Klotz, M. 178, 186
Kluge, Alexander 337
Knickerbocker, H. R. 316
Koestler, Arthur 235–6
Kollontai, Alexandra 211, 230
Kolyma gulag 288–90
Komödienhaus, Berlin 292
Komsomol, see Communist Youth League
Kordt, Dr. Theodor 347, 348
Korea 383, 384
Koudachef, Marie 340
Krasin, Leonid 138
Kraus, Karl 328
Kravchenko, Victor A. 451 n. 37
Krebs, Richard, see Valtin, Jan
Krosigk, Count Schwering von 351, 352
Krupskaya, N. 276
Kun, Bela 183
Kwiecinska family 357
Kyra, My Sister (Istrati) 264, 266

Labour and Socialist International 242–3,
    252
Labour Magazine 244–5
Lacis, Asja 235
Lafont, Ernest 417 n. 4
Lane, Winthrop D. 110
Lang, Harry 323
Lansbury, George 169, 191, 195–6, 211
    and Bolsheviks 137–8, 204

and British delegation to Russia
    (1920) 146–8, 157
    on Lenin 217
Lark, Frank Robert 139
Laski, Harold 56–7, 329
Lattimore, Professor Owen 288, 289,
    290, 329
Law, Andrew Bonar 121
Lawrence, Mr Justice 139
Lawther, Will 255
Layton, Sir Walter 306, 307
League of Nations 39, 111, 119, 180, 182
    Balkan Committee 167, 168
    Bolsheviks and 416 n. 4
    foundation of 109, 187
    Germany and 225–6
    Lee on 189–90
    mandate system 344
    E. Snowden on 434 n. 133
    UDC and 126
    USSR and 294, 304
Leahy, Admiral William D. 21
Leaping Lena (carrier pigeon) 1
Lee, Dr Ivy 315
Lee, Vernon 17–18, 76–80, 88, 153, 339
    on Bolshevism 126–7
    and foreign policy 90, 93, 94
    on history and heritage 123–4
    iron curtain imagery 80–2, 89, 94–5,
        109, 114, 115–16, 118, 119, 120, 124,
        127, 171
    on League of Nations 189–90
    and nationalism 116, 122
    on patriotism 122–4
    and UDC 110, 112–15, 123
    and Wells 118, 120
    on WWI 78–82, 86, 109, 114–15
    see also 'Bach's Christmas Music in
        England and in Germany'; Ballet of
        the Nations; Satan the Waster
Lenin, V. I. 60, 138, 194, 275
    and foreign visitors 132, 165–6, 192
    'Letter to the British Workers' 211, 217
    on nationalization of
        women 439 n. 66
    and New Economic Policy 237
    and Rakovsky 262
    and Wilson's Fourteen Points 188
Lepeshinskaya, Olga Borisovna 359–60

Lerner, E. 294
'Letter to the British Workers'
    (Lenin) 211, 217
Leval, Gaston 266
Liberal Party 166, 167
Liebermann, Max 221
Lifschitz, Boris, *see* Souvarine, Boris
Lindqvist, Sven 376
Lipman, Samuel 156
Lipper, Elinor 288, 289–90
Lippmann, Walter 46, 110, 232
little iron curtain 55
Little Rock Gazette, Arkansas 30
Litvinov, Maxim 132, 236–7, 241, 307
Lloyd George, David 172, 178
    on Bolshevism 185
    and cordon sanitaire policy 182
    Guildhall Speech 138
Locarno, Treaty of 224–6
Lombard, Revd B. S. 204
London: Wren churches 16, 52, 66, 348
London, Declaration of 93–4, 407 n. 85
Longuet, Jean 267
Losovsky, A. 150, 199
Loti, Pierre 98–101, 103–5
Low, David 377, 381
Lowes Dickinson, Goldsworthy 111, 113,
    413 n. 37
Ludendorff, General Erich 145, 186
Lukacs, John 154
Lunacharsky, Anatoly Vasilyevich 194, 287
Lvov, Prince George 133, 159
Lyall, Archibald 285, 300–1
Lynch, Jessica 386
Lyons, Eugene 285, 297, 306, 309, 311, 319
Lysenko, Trofim 359

McCarran Act (1950) 12, 14
McCarthy, Joseph 12, 290
McCarthy, Margaret 256, 333–5
McCarthyism 11–12
McCluer, Dr Franc 'Bullet' 21, 26–8, 47,
    48, 49, 51
McCluer, Mrs 28–9
McCormick, Anne O'Hare 24
MacDonald, Ramsey 238, 343, 411 n. 13
    and Russia, visit to 135, 141
    and Third International 134
    and UDC 110, 222–3

McGuire 305
Machová, Dr A. 369
Mackenzie, Dr A. 146
Mackinder, Halford J. 136, 141, 174–5,
    182–3
Madame Chrysanthème (Loti) 98
Maeterlinck, Maurice 165
Maisky, Ivan 313–14
Malan, Dr Daniel François 46
Malraux, André 328, 329
Manchester Guardian 138–9, 298, 311,
    317, 351
Mann, Tom 255
Mannucci, Pierro 365
Marie José of Belgium 107–8
Marshall, Garland R. 363
Martin, Kingsley 305, 326
Mason, Daniel Gregory 85
Matin, Le 325
Mayer, Arno J. 187
Meakin, William 202
Melchior, Carl 152–3
Menken, Jules 305, 306, 307
Menshevik trial (1931) 329–30
Mensheviks 133, 151, 200
Metric Union 85
Metro-Vickers Trial (1933) 287, 310
Michaelis, Karin 179
Michelet, Jules 83
Middle East 183–4
Miller, Arthur 386
Mills, Jock 232
Milosz, Czeslaw 63
Miners Eight Hours Bill 90–1
Minin (Russian flagship) 142
Minor, Robert 165
'Miss B' 233
Missouri School for the Deaf, Fulton 45
Mizera, Irene 357, 358
Monat, Pawel 383
Morand, Paul 232
Morel, E. D. 120, 121, 267
    on Churchill 170
    and UDC 109–10, 112
Morgan, John 301
Morning Post 139, 145–6, 147, 149,
    205, 212
Moscou sans voiles (Douillet) 245
Mother Earth 155

Mount Sinai School of Medicine, City University of New York 366–8, 369, 370–3
Moutet, Marius 417 n. 4
Mudd, E. J. 49
Mueller, Dr Herbert 320
Muggeridge, Malcolm 311–12, 319
Mülder, Dr Jan 365
Munzenberg, Willi 295
Murphy, J. T. 442 n. 115
Music and its Lovers (Lee) 339

Nagashmia, R. 184
Naryshkin, Princess 151–2, 422 n. 108
Nation, The 78, 93, 94, 117, 118, 120–1, 412 n. 27
National Council for Civil Liberties 12–13, 192
National Council of American-Soviet Friendship 49–50
National Council of Frenchwomen 176
National Democratic and Labour Party 421 n. 93
National Union of Railway Workers (NUR) 218
National Union of Women's Suffrage Societies 135
nationalism 116, 122
Nazism 291, 312, 325, 328
  C. Buxton and 345, 346, 347
  German communists and 331
  iron curtain imagery 351
  Rolland's opposition to 341, 342
  and Versailles, Treaty of 345–7
Neue Freie Press, Vienna 190
Neue Zürcher Zeitung 184
Neutral Conference for Continuous Mediation 410 n. 8
New Fabian Research Bureau 300–1, 305
New Leader 17, 226
New Republic 173
New Statesman 46–7, 250
New Statesman and Nation 11, 12, 14, 281–2, 306
New York Times 32, 360
  on Cort 10, 15, 361, 366–9
  on Fulton 24, 49
  Klimowicz's story in 354–5

New York World 180–1
Newer Ideals of Peace (Addams) 88
Newsholme, Sir Arthur 326
Nicholas, tsar 142
Nikishov, Ivan 288–9
Nineteen Eighty-Four (Orwell) 376
Nippold, Professor Otfried 112
Nitti, Francesco 190
Nobel Prize committee 405 n. 52
Nolte, Ray 49
North American Newspaper Alliance 354
North Korea 383, 384
North, Revd F. W. 148, 203–4, 420 n. 83
Noske, Gustav 151
Notes and Queries 60
'Notes from the Foreign Press' 176
Nott-Bower, Sir John 4
Nugent, Dr Charles 394 n. 38
NUR, *see* National Union of Railway Workers

Obdurate, HMS (British destroyer) 4
Office Central des Associations Internationales, Brussels 85
Ogden, C. K. 176
O'Grady, James 141, 417 n. 4
Ohle, Mrs Ernest L. 48
Old Drury Lane Theatre on Fire, February 24 1809 (Abraham) 69
Omaha Evening World 31
Oparin, Alexander 359
Opéra-Comique, Paris 73
Opera House, Nice 72
Orage, A. R. 332
Orwell, George 324–5, 331, 332, 384, 459 n. 26
Osborn, E. B. 139
Oscar II ('Peace Ship') 110–11, 123, 135
Ostermayer, Mr 231
Ottawa Conference 301, 303
Oumansky, Constantine 319
Ovey, Sir Esmond 303, 304, 343

Paget, Violet, *see* Lee, Vernon
Paine, Robert Treat, Jr 67
Paine, Thomas 141
Pakistan 375
Palmer, Mr (Independent MP) 428 n. 36

Palmer, A. Mitchell (Attorney
    General) 139, 156
Palmer, Sidney 2
Panaït Istrati and Communism
    (Souvarine) 276
Pankey, Aubrey 360
Pankhurst, Sylvia 137, 201
Pantheon, Oxford Street, London 66
Panufnik, Andrzej 354, 357
Paris, Pact of 60
Paris Peace Conference 59, 185, 186–7,
    188–90
    and blockade 172, 173, 181
    see also Versailles, Treaty of
Parmoor, Lord 280
Pascal, Pierre 453 n. 10
Pashich, Nikola 169
Paton Walsh, Nick 439 n. 66
patriotism 87, 121–4
'Peace Ship', see *Oscar II*
'Peace with Russia' demonstrations 217
People's Daily World 56
People's Theatre, The (Rolland) 287
Perceval, Spencer 65
'Perpetual Peace: a Philosophical Sketch'
    (Kant) 83, 189
Persia 184
Petrov, Peter 442 n. 115
Pitt Rivers, George Henry
    Lane-Fox 202
Playne, Caroline E. 116, 117, 122
Pliska, Vladimir 369
Poincaré, Raymond 101, 108
Poland
    alcoholism 355
    and Bolshevism 183
    and Britain 137
    under Communism 355–6
    exodus from 2–8
    religion in 355
    and Soviet Russia 137
    and Ukraine 136
    see also Klimowicz
Polish Ex-Combatants Association 4, 6
Politiken (Danish paper) 177, 179
Pollitt, Harry 137, 206, 255, 334
Ponafidine, Emma Cochran 160
Ponsonby, Arthur 110, 121–2
Poole, DeWitt C. 154–5
Popular Front against Fascism 291

Postgate, Raymond W. 299
Potemkin, Prince 142, 230–1
Potemkinism 203–4, 286, 298–9, 326,
    382–3, 385
    Bukharin on 142–3
    British Labour Delegation (1920) 146,
        211–12, 215–16
    British Labour Delegation
        (1924) 245–7
    Fabre-Luce and 231
    Herriot and 321–4
    Illyés on 290–1, 387
    Lansbury and 146–8
    Lipper on 289–90
    Rougier on 291
    Souvarine on 273–4, 275–7
    Wallace and 288–9
Pound, Ezra 139
Power, Rhoda 158–9, 440 n. 76
Praca (Polish freighter) 8
Pravda 56
Prince of Wales Theatre, London 73
Pritt, D. N. 299, 330–1
Psychology of Jingoism, The
    (Hobson) 116
Public Ledger, Philadelphia 186
Pudovkin, Vsevolod Illarionovich 230
Purcell, Albert A. 134, 195, 198, 201–2,
    210, 213–14, 252
    and 'Hands Off Russia'
        Committee 137
    1924 Trade Union Delegation 244,
        247
Pyatakov, Georgy Leonidovich 287

Quakers 83, 110, 132
Queen Elisabeth International Music
    Competition 106

Radek, Karl 197, 287
Radio Free Europe 1, 6
Rakovsky, Christian 262–3, 264, 268,
    269–70, 287
Rancière, Jacques 229
Ransome, Arthur 165
Rapallo treaty 263
Rapoport, Yakov 359, 360
Reader's Digest 32
Reagan, Ronald 25, 53–4
'Red Ark', see *Buford*, USS

Red International of Trade Unions 214, 333–4
Red Medicine (Newsholme and Kingsbury) 326
Reed, John 442 n. 115
Refreshment Room at Narva, The (C. Buxton) 391–2
Reichstag fire trial 330, 331
Reinsch, Paul S. 84–5
Remarks on the Theatre (Alexander) 68
Revolution Betrayed, The (Trotsky) 280
Reynaud, Paul 222
Reynolds, Sir Joshua 144
Rice, Condoleezza 385
Rigasche Rundschau 248
Riley, Athelstan 138
Ring Theatre, Vienna 72
Rivera, Diego 56
Rivero, Paul 383
Robins, Colonel Raymond 165–6
Robson, Lt. Comm. 438 n. 64
Rolland, Romain 106–7, 176–7, 263–4, 278, 287
    and fellow-travellers 339–43
    and ICRC 110
    on Lee 123
    Nazism, opposition to 341
    Nobel Prize for Literature 87
    on WWI 86–7
Romania 168, 278, 279
Roosevelt, Eleanor 453 n. 3
Roosevelt, Franklin D. 32, 38–9
Rosenberg, Alfred 325
Rothstein, Theodore 211, 307
Rougier, Louis 291
Roussakov, Alexander Ivanovitch 270
Rowntree, Arnold 110
Royal Circus, London 66
Royal Institute of International Affairs 317
Royal Saloon, London 66
Rozanov, Vasily Vasilievich 153
Rudinger, Josef 362–3, 364, 368
Ruhr, occupation of 222
Rumsfeld, Donald 385
Rural Electrification Administration 23
Russell, Bertrand 110, 363, 422 n. 106
    on blockade of Russia 173
    on Bolshevik Russia 194–5, 218

and British Labour Delegation (1920) 132, 133, 150, 157, 198–9
Russia, *see* USSR
Russia Unveiled (Istrati) 278
Russian Civil War 57
Russian Revolution 126, 131
Russian Revolution and the Communist Party, The (anon) 446 n. 13
Russian Trade Delegation (1920) 138–9
Russie nue, La (Souvarine) 273
Rust, Bill 333
Rykov, Alexei 268, 287

'Safety-Curtain, The' (Dell) 80
Saint-Saëns, Camille 107
Saklatvala, Shapurji 255, 256, 258
Sandburg, Carl 139
Sanders, William 417 n. 4
Sandys, Edwina 53
Sarolea, Professor Charles 232, 233, 234
Satan the Waster (Lee) 113–14, 123–6, 177, 339
'Save the Children Fund' 179, 344
Scévola, Guirand de 144
Scheffer, Paul 300, 307
Schiedemann, Philip 151
Schiff, Victor 185
Schiller, Dr Otto 301–2, 304
Schliemann, Dr Paul 248
Schubert, Carl von 224, 225
Schwartz, Dr Irving L. 366, 367–8, 369, 371, 373
Schwimmer, Rosika 135, 410 n. 8
Second International 133–4, 135, 209
secret police
    Romania 279
    USSR 197, 198, 232, 241, 245, 246, 285, 320, 324
Section Française de l'Internationale Ouvrière (SFIO) 417 n. 4
Seddon, J. A. 421 n. 93
Semyonov, Nikolai Andreyevitch 284
Serbia 169
Serge, Victor 163, 266, 269, 271–3, 278
Serrati, Giacinto Menotti 215
SFIO, *see* Section Française de l'Internationale Ouvrière
Shakhty trial (1928) 286
Sharp, Evelyn 411 n. 13
Shaw, Charlotte 314

Shaw, Eyre Massey 70–1, 72
Shaw, George Bernard 46, 295–9, 306, 313, 412 n. 27
  on Lee 77, 88
  1931 visit to USSR 296–7
  views on USSR 297–8
Shaw, Tom 132, 199, 208, 211, 252
Sheridan, Clare 191, 216, 232, 236
Sheridan, Richard Brinsley 65, 66–7, 69, 71
Sime, M. 148
Sinclair, Upton 329
Sivoplys, Ivan 439 n. 66
Skrypnik, Nikolai 323
Sloan, Pat A. 317–18, 324
Smith, Ellis 256, 257, 258, 259–60
Smith, George William 439 n. 66
Snowden, Ethel 132, 196, 211–12, 213
  and Bolshevism 134, 204, 206–8, 214
  and British Labour Delegation (1920) 131, 149, 150–2, 157, 210–11
  on D. F. Buxton's food aid 431 n. 87
  on Chicherin 192–3
  in Christiana (Oslo) 136–7
  iron curtain imagery 152, 153, 155
  on League of Nations 434 n. 133
  opposition to secession from Second International 133–4
  and suffragism 134–5
Snowden, Philip 110, 122, 136, 187, 207
Soames, Lady Mary 52
Social Democratic Federation 193, 441 n. 95
Social Demokraten (Swedish paper) 177
Social Insurance and Allied Services report 36
Social Revolutionaries (Russia) 133, 151
Socialist Review 241
Society for the Promotion of Permanent and Universal Peace 83
Solomon J. Solomon 143–6
Solzhenitsyn, Aleksander 284
Šorm, František 362, 363, 364, 369
Sothern, Edward H. 102
South Korea 383, 384
Souvarine, Boris 266–7, 271, 273–7, 278, 291, 341
  and Trotsky 263, 264
Soviet (cargo ship) 255–6

Soviet Asia Mission (Wallace) 288
Soviet Communism: A New Civilisation? (S. and B. Webb) 312–15
Soviet Culture Review 294
Soviet Eyewash: Socialist Eyewash (anon) 247
Soviet Russia To-Day report 256, 257–8, 261
Soviets 1929 (Serge) 271
Spanish Civil War 331–2
Speaight, George 74–5
Sperber, Manès 243–4, 340, 452 n. 74
Springfield Republican 184
St Joseph Missouri Gazette 30
St Joseph Missouri News-Press 31
St Louis Globe-Democrat 23–4, 26, 29
'ST-25' (Paul Dukes) 159–60
Stahlbehl, L. 48
Stalin, Joseph 31, 32, 38, 271–2, 275, 327
  Berlin blockade 376
  Churchill and 42
  on collectivization 293, 311–12
  Five Year Plans 277, 279, 299
  Fulton oration, reaction to 56
  and iron curtain 43
  and Rakovsky 262, 263, 268
  show trials 286–7
  theatre state 286–7
  Truman and 34
Stamboulisky, M. 417 n. 8
Stein, Jess 61
Steiner, Francis 434 n. 138
Stephens, Helen 24
Stern, Alfred R. 373
Stites, Richard 194
Stobart, Mrs St Clair 89, 427 n. 25
Stockholm conference 135–6
Strategic Camouflage (Solomon) 144–5
Stresemann, Gustav 221, 222, 224, 225
Strom, Frederick 419 n. 41
Strong, Anna Louise 424 n. 4
Sturdee, Nina 47
Stürgkh, Count Karl von 249–51
Sunday Pictorial 88
Suttner, Bertha von 406 n. 68
Swinnerton, Frank 113
Swope, Herbert 400 n. 32

Tagus (steamer) 203

Taiwan Straits 383
Taxim, Hassan 168
Taylor, A. J. P. 403 n. 13
Tchertkoff, Count Vladimir 192
Technische Blatt, Das 146
Teheran conference (1943) 38
Telegraphic Union 85
Temps, Le 182, 186, 188
Terry's Theatre, London 65, 73
Thatcher, Margaret 51, 54
Theatre Royal, Dublin 71–2
Theatre Royal, Exeter 72
Theatre Royal, London
    fires in 65, 66, 67–70
    iron curtain in 67, 70
    rebuilding of 66–7
theatres
    fire hazards and precautions in 66–8,
      70, 72, 73, 401 n. 23
    fires in 71–2
    safety precautions 71, 72
Third International (Comintern) 157,
    237, 255, 422 n. 105
    Fourth Congress 295
    ILP and 133, 135, 209–10
    Italian Socialist Mission and 215–16
    Second Congress 163, 219
    Zimmerwald conference and 135
Third World 375
Thomas, J. H. 218
Thorne, Will 417 n. 4
Threlkeld, Ulysses 28
Through Bolshevik Russia
    (E. Snowden) 152, 211
Time magazine 26
Times, The 10, 46, 80, 112, 131,
    303, 351
    on Bolshevism 172, 202, 215
    on British Labour Delegation to
      Russia (1920) 140, 141
    on fire-fighting measures, Theatre
      Royal 67, 70
    on fire hazards in theatres 72, 73
    on iron curtain 63, 67, 70
    on 1924 Trade Union Delegation 248
    on Theatre Royal fire 68–9, 70
Times Literary Supplement 145
Tintin in the Land of the Soviets
    (Hergé) 245

Toda Raba (N. Kazantzakis) 219, 267, 270
Tolstoy, Leo 143
Tomsky, Mikhail 268
Towards the Other Flame (Istrati) 271
toy theatres 74–5
Toynbee Hall, East London 88
Trades Union Congress (TUC) 131, 133,
    210, 226
Traven, B. 219
Trevelyan, Charles 110
Trigg, Mrs Baker 29
Trotsky, Leon 180, 185, 236, 251, 267–8
    and Bolshevik revolution 10th
      anniversary celebrations 258, 267
    and New Economic Policy 237
    and Souvarine 263, 264
Truman, Harry S. 21, 27, 30, 34, 51, 353
' "Truth About Russia", The'
    (MacFlecknoe) 281–2, 326
TUC, *see* Trades Union Congress
Turkey 167, 168, 169
Turner, Ben 205, 208, 211
    and British Labour Delegation
      (1920) 132, 148–9, 157, 192, 199,
      201, 213, 214

UDC, *see* Union of Democratic Control
Ukraine 136
Ullman, Richard H. 438 n. 62
UN, *see* United Nations
Under Fire (Barbusse) 278
Union of Democratic Control
    (UDC) 110, 111–15, 123, 132
    and League of Nations 126
    and Wilson's Fourteen Points 188
Union of Polish Journalists 3
Union of Russian Workers 156
Union of Soviet Writers 230
United Nations (UN) 38, 56, 57, 376
    as 'temple of peace' 39, 41, 60
United States of Europe vision 59–60
United Transport Workers' Federation
    (UTWF) 218
Universal Postal Union 85
University Labour Federation 236
USA
    and Allied blockade 171
    Communist Party of America 11, 50,
      55, 61

USA (*cont.*)
 J. Cort in 366–74
 and Cuba 383
 House Un-American Activities
  Committee 11
 Klimowicz in 357–8
 loan for Britain 23, 30, 31, 50, 59
 Permanent Defence Agreement (with
  Canada) 42
 special relationship with Britain 12,
  41–2, 46, 50, 387
USSR 42–3
 All-Russian Conference of the Soviet
  of Workers' and Soldiers'
  Deputies 188
 Allied blockade of 163–6, 171, 172–3,
  174, 177, 178, 184, 209
 Allied Intervention 40, 56–7, 134, 138,
  165, 166, 187, 209
 American deportees to 155–6
 anti-British campaign 237–8
 Baltic states, treaties with 155
 Bolshevik revolution 10th anniversary
  celebrations 258, 264–5, 267
 Bolshevo Prison 285
 British Empire Marketing Board visit
  to 301–2
 British journalists' delegation 304–6
 Butyrki Prison 246
 Butyrki Prison (in fiction) 283–4
 censorship 307, 309, 310, 311, 319
 collectivization 277, 293, 299–301, 306,
  308, 311, 318
 Constituent Assembly 133, 151
 cultural diplomacy 230
 diplomatic and trade relations with
  Britain 280
 diplomats, departure of 154–5, 158
 and Disarmament Conference 294
 drunkenness 206–7, 232–3, 274
 electrification 233
 English Co-operative Stores
  delegation 315
 famine 307–8, 322–6
 Fifteenth Party Congress 268, 273
 Five Year Plans 277, 279, 285, 299, 301
 food shortages 237, 259, 272, 276,
  296–7; *see also* USSR: Great Famine
 food supplies 163

 foreign correspondents 317–19
 Fourteenth Party Congress 255
 and friendship societies overseas 294
 German delegation to 231
 Grand Alliance 288
 Great Famine 292–320
 Great Terror 287
 Great Tourist Invasion 285–6
 gulags 288–90
 Herriot's 1933 visit 321–4
 hotels 149, 162–3, 198, 232, 256, 265,
  266–7, 302, 322–3, 324
 iron curtain and 191–2
 and Italian Socialist Mission 215–16
 Klimowicz on 356–7
 and League of Nations 294
 Lefortovo prison 260
 Mensheviks 133
 nationalisation of children 204
 nationalisation of women 204, 254,
  438 n. 64, 439 n. 66
 Nazi-Soviet non-aggression
  pact 332, 342
 'New Diplomacy' 187–8
 New Economic Policy 237, 268
 New Fabian Research Bureau visit
  to 300–1
 1917 delegation to 140–1, 213
 1920 delegation to 131–53, 162–4,
  191–2, 196–200, 214, 216–17
 1924 Trade Union Delegation 244–9,
  252–3
 1927 British Workers' Delegation 226,
  237–43, 244, 255–60
 non-aggression pacts 294
 'Peace' cause 294–5
 perceived threat from 30–2
 perceived threat of deception 146–9
 Peter and Paul Fortress,
  Petrograd 150, 203
 Petrograd Soviet 187–8
 Poland and 137
 Printers' Union 200–1
 prisons 245, 260, 285, 302, 334, 327
 prisons (in fiction) 283–4
 prostitution 285
 Provisional Government 133,
  188, 202
 refugees fleeing 157–8, 159–61, 203

secret police 197, 198, 232, 241, 245, 246, 285, 320, 324
show trials 142, 287, 310, 329–30
Social Revolutionaries 133
Solovetsky prison 334
Soviet Academy of Sciences 359
street children 233, 240, 257, 276, 277, 302
Trade Union Delegation to (1924) 252–3
Treaty of Collaboration and Mutual Assistance (with Britain) 42
travellers' impressions of 228–30
Twelfth Party Congress (1923) 262
University Labour Federation delegation 236
and World Economic Conference 294
see also Bolshevism; British Labour Delegation (1920); Potemkinism
Utley, Freda 236, 237, 286, 333
UTWF, see United Transport Workers' Federation

Valtin, Jan (Richard Krebs) 254, 331
Van Der Veer, John C. 423 n. 116
VanSant, Thomas H. 27
Vaughan, Harry H. 27, 45
Vega Biotechnologies, Tucson, Arizona 371–2
Venezuela 385
Venizelos, Eleutherios 169
Verhaeren, Émile 102–3
Versailles, Treaty of 57, 173, 186–7, 190
and Nazism 345–7
Viaud, Louis-Marie-Julien 98–9
Vie internationale, La 85
Vienna Working Union of Socialist Parties 251
Voikov, Pyotr 238
VOKS, see All-Union Society for Cultural Relations with Foreign Countries
Vorel, Comrade 183
Vorovsky, Vatslav 238
Vorwärts, Berlin 189
Vyshinsky, Andrei 310, 329, 330

Walesa, Lech 51
Wallace, Henry 32, 288–9, 290

Wallhead, R. C. 132, 133, 209–10
War and Peace (Tolstoy) 143
Ward, Herbert 360
Warner, Marina 382
Washington Post 35
Watson, Siddie 28
We (Zamyatin) 129, 155
Webb, Beatrice 312–15, 349
Webb, Sidney 312, 313, 314–15
Webb, W. 74
Webster, Nesta 202
Wedgwood Benn, Anthony, see Benn, Tony
Weir Spectator, Kansas 30, 35
Weiskirchner, Dr 185
Wellman, William A. 376
Wells, H. G. 118, 120, 294
iron curtain imagery 80
1920 visit to Russia 146, 193–4
West European Security Pact 224
Westminster College, Fulton, Missouri 21, 25–6, 47, 387
Churchill memorials 51–3
Churchill's visit to 26–9
Gorbachev's visit 54
Wheeler, Eleanor 361
Wheeler, George Shaw 360–1
Wherry, Kenneth 31
Wicks, Harry 332
Wickstead, Alexander 233, 326
Wierzbianski, Boleslaw 4
Wilhelm, Kaiser 142
William Woods College, Fulton 24, 33
Williams, Robert 133, 210, 214, 218
and British Labour Delegation (1920) 134, 137, 151, 195, 198, 202, 207, 213
Williams, William Carlos 139
Willis, Irene Cooper 76, 117–18, 119, 121, 339, 384
Wilson, Woodrow 57–8, 131–2, 180–1
on Bolshevist threat 186
Fourteen Points 187, 188
at Paris Peace Conference 187, 188–9
'witchcraft' trial 330
Wolff, Theodor 184–5
Woman International Suffrage Alliance 79
Women's Convoy Corps 89, 427 n. 25

Women's International League for Peace
    and Freedom 87–8, 89, 135, 431 n. 83
Women's Peace Crusade 132
Women's Peace Party, USA 89
Woodhead, Frank Easton 308–9, 310
Woolf, Leonard 122, 314
Wordsworth, William 326
Workers' Education Association 166
Workers' International Relief 295
World After the War, The (C. and
    D. Buxton) 174
World Economic Conference (1933) 294
World Government Foundation 59
World's Work 145
Wren, Sir Christopher 348
    St Mary the Virgin Church 16, 52, 66

Yalta conference (1945) 38–9
Young, George 252

Zamenhoff, L. L. 85
Zamyatin, Yevgeny 129, 155, 321
Zaoral, Dr Milan 366, 368–9, 466
    n. 38
Zetkin, Clara 156–7, 295
Zimmerwald Conference 135, 262
Zinoviev, G. E. 223, 267–8, 295
    and Italian Socialist Mission 215, 216
    show trial 287
'Zinoviev letter' 223
Zionism 202
Zweig, Stefan 231

London. Pub. by W.